OUT OF FOCUS
RUSSIA AT THE MARGINS

LEGENDA

LEGENDA is the Modern Humanities Research Association's book imprint for new research in the Humanities. Founded in 1995 by Malcolm Bowie and others within the University of Oxford, Legenda has always been a collaborative publishing enterprise, directly governed by scholars. The Modern Humanities Research Association (MHRA) joined this collaboration in 1998, became half-owner in 2004, in partnership with Maney Publishing and then Routledge, and has since 2016 been sole owner. Titles range from medieval texts to contemporary cinema and form a widely comparative view of the modern humanities, including works on Arabic, Catalan, English, French, German, Greek, Italian, Portuguese, Russian, Spanish, and Yiddish literature. Editorial boards and committees of more than 60 leading academic specialists work in collaboration with bodies such as the Society for French Studies, the British Comparative Literature Association and the Association of Hispanists of Great Britain & Ireland.

The MHRA encourages and promotes advanced study and research in the field of the modern humanities, especially modern European languages and literature, including English, and also cinema. It aims to break down the barriers between scholars working in different disciplines and to maintain the unity of humanistic scholarship. The Association fulfils this purpose through the publication of journals, bibliographies, monographs, critical editions, and the MHRA Style Guide, and by making grants in support of research. Membership is open to all who work in the Humanities, whether independent or in a University post, and the participation of younger colleagues entering the field is especially welcomed.

ALSO PUBLISHED BY THE ASSOCIATION

Critical Texts
Tudor and Stuart Translations • New Translations • European Translations
MHRA Library of Medieval Welsh Literature

MHRA Bibliographies
Publications of the Modern Humanities Research Association

The Annual Bibliography of English Language & Literature
Austrian Studies
Modern Language Review
Portuguese Studies
The Slavonic and East European Review
Working Papers in the Humanities
The Yearbook of English Studies

www.mhra.org.uk
www.legendabooks.com

SELECTED ESSAYS

Each title in *Selected Essays* presents influential, but often scattered, papers by a major scholar in the Humanities. While these essays will, we hope, offer a model of scholarly writing, and chart the development of an important thinker in the field, the aim is not retrospective but to gather a coherent body of work as a tool for future research. Each volume contains a new introduction, framing the debate and reflecting on the methods used.

Selected Essays is curated by Professor Susan Harrow (University of Bristol).

APPEARING IN THIS SERIES

1. *Enlightenment and Religion in German and Austrian Literature*, by Ritchie Robertson
2. *Perpetual Motion: Studies in French Poetry from Surrealism to the Postmodern*, by Michael Sheringham
3. *Putting it About: Popular Views of Social Rights and Wrongs in Spain in the Long Nineteenth Century*, by Alison Sinclair
4. *Perspectives on Culture and Politics in the French Antilles*, by Celia Britton
5. *Italian Rewritings: Subtexts and Reworkings in Italian literature from Dante to Calvino*, by Martin McLaughlin
6. *Dante, Petrarch, Boccaccio: Literature, Doctrine, Reality*, by Zygmunt G. Barański
7. *Creativity under Pressure: Essays on Antisemitism and the Achievements of German-Jewish Refugees*, by Edward Timms
8. *Out of Focus: Russia at the Margins*, by Catriona Kelly
9. *Brute Meaning: Essays in Materialist Criticism from Dickens to Hitchcock*, by David Trotter
10. *For the Love of Art*, by Peter Dayan
11. *Spanish Culture from Romanticism to the Present: Structures of Feeling*, by Jo Labanyi
12. *Contemporary Fictions: Essays on American and Postcolonial Narratives*, by Judie Newman

Managing Editor
Dr Graham Nelson, 41 Wellington Square, Oxford OX1 2JF, UK

www.legendabooks.com

Out of Focus

Russia at the Margins

CATRIONA KELLY

Selected Essays 8
Modern Humanities Research Association
2023

Published by Legenda
an imprint of the Modern Humanities Research Association
Salisbury House, Station Road, Cambridge CB1 2LA

ISBN 978-1-78188-782-0 (HB)
ISBN 978-1-78188-786-8 (PB)

First published 2023

All rights reserved. No part of this publication may be reproduced or disseminated or transmitted in any form or by any means, electronic, mechanical, photocopying, recording or otherwise, or stored in any retrieval system, or otherwise used in any manner whatsoever without written permission of the copyright owner, except in accordance with the provisions of the Copyright, Designs and Patents Act 1988, or under the terms of a licence permitting restricted copying issued in the UK by the Copyright Licensing Agency Ltd, Saffron House, 6–10 Kirby Street, London EC1N 8TS, England, or in the USA by the Copyright Clearance Center, 222 Rosewood Drive, Danvers MA 01923. Application for the written permission of the copyright owner to reproduce any part of this publication must be made by email to legenda@mhra.org.uk.

Disclaimer: Statements of fact and opinion contained in this book are those of the author and not of the editors or the Modern Humanities Research Association. The publisher makes no representation, express or implied, in respect of the accuracy of the material in this book and cannot accept any legal responsibility or liability for any errors or omissions that may be made.

Trademark notice: Product or corporate names may be trademarks or registered trademarks, and are used only for identification and explanation without intent to infringe.

© Modern Humanities Research Association 2023

Copy-Editor: Charlotte Wathey

CONTENTS

Acknowledgements   x
List of Illustrations   xii

Introduction — Out of Focus and Close Up: Russian Subjects, 1760–1990   1

PART I: BORDERS OF PROPRIETY

1   Educating Tatiana: Manners, Motherhood, and Moral Education [1996]   15

2   The Uses of Refinement: Etiquette and Uncertainty at the Russian Court [1997]   41

3   The Education of the Will: Advice Literature, *Zakal*, Manliness, and Modernity [2002]   61

PART II: HUMAN AND NONE TOO HUMAN

4   'Man-Footed Beast' versus 'Beast-Footed Man': Animals as Slaves, Servants, and Companions [2014]   81

5   A Wolf in the Nursery: Freud, Ethnography, and a Border-Crossing Life [2007]   105

6   The Redress of Art: Anna Akhmatova and Boris Anrep [1993]   137

7   At Peace with the Wolf? Prokofiev's 'Official' Soviet Works for Children [2003]   155

PART III: SMALL PEOPLE AND BIG HISTORY

8   Making Memories: Children and the Personal Past in Early Twentieth-Century Russia [2007]   175

9   The End of Empire: Jewish Children in the Age of Revolution [2017]   191

PART IV: 'EVERYTHING FOR THE CHILDREN'

10   'I Want to Be a Tractor Driver!' Gender and Childhood in Early Soviet Russia [2003]   211

11   'Comrade is a Sacred Word': Children and Soviet Friendship [2009]   235

12   Essential Luxuries: Goods for Children in the Last Decades of Soviet Power [2007]   259

PART V: ON THE SOVIET PERIPHERY

13　The Many Lives of Konon Molodyi ('Gordon Lonsdale'): Espionage, Disinformation, and the Moral Universe of the Late Cold War [2021]　283

14　The Black-and-White Poppies of Russian Arthouse: Central Asian Directors at Lenfil'm [2018]　309

Index　335

For my family, with love

ACKNOWLEDGEMENTS

Work collected over nearly three decades leaves far more debts than can be recognised in a few words. The notes to individual articles acknowledge particular individuals, but I also want to offer general and warm thanks to my workmates and former students at the School of Slavonic Studies, University of London (now UCL) and at New College and the Faculty of Medieval and Modern Languages, University of Oxford, and to my current colleagues at Trinity College and the Slavonic Studies Section at the University of Cambridge. I am also deeply indebted to my fellow academics and friends in Russia, the USA, and across Britain and Western Europe, for their companionship, intellectual stimulation, and emotional support, and to my family, who have sometimes missed out on quality time, but have, fortunately, been very ready to complain. Could I dedicate the book to anyone else?

For the suggestion that I compile this collection, and for putting it through the process of publication, I am indebted to everyone at Legenda, particularly Susan Harrow, Graham Nelson, and Charlotte Wathey.

I am grateful to the British Academy for sponsoring, through Small Research Grants in 1994 and 1996, and places on its exchange scheme with the Russian Academy of Sciences in 1997, 1998, and 2000, my research for the three essays in Part 1 ('Borders of Propriety').

My work on children's history was funded by a project grant from the Leverhulme Trust ('Grant F/08736/A: Childhood in Russia: A Social and Cultural History', 2003–06), and by the John Fell Fund, University of Oxford. My thanks to both these bodies. I would also like to thank the project interviewers, in Moscow (Yuliya Rybina, Ekaterina Shumilova, Vitaly Bezrogov), Perm (Svetlana Sirotinina), St Petersburg (Alexandra Piir), Taganrog (Yury Ryzhov, Lyubov' Terekhova), settlement, Leningrad province (2004, Oksana Filicheva, Ekaterina Mel'nikova) and settlement, Novgorod province (2005, Oksana Filicheva, Veronika Makarova), and the late Vitaly Bezrogov and Al'bert Baiburin for help with project coordination (see <www.mod-langs.ox.ac.uk/russian/childhood> [accessed 5 October 2022]).

Finally, I would like to thank the AHRC for funding, through the award of a Fellowship, the larger research project, 'The Soviet Cine-Underground: Lenfil'm (the Leningrad State Film Studio) and the Transformation of Late Soviet Culture, 1956–1991', on which I draw in 'The Many Lives of Konon Molodyi' and 'The Black-and-White Poppies of Russian Arthouse'.

The author and publisher acknowledge the following sources of material reprinted here:

Chapter 1: 'Educating Tatiana: Manners, Motherhood, and Moral Education (Vospitanie), 1760–1840', in *Gender in Russian History and Culture*, ed. by Linda Edmondson (Basingstoke: Macmillan, 2001), pp. 1–28.

Chapter 2: 'The Uses of Refinement: Etiquette and Uncertainty in the Autobiographical Writings of Aleksandra Tyutcheva', *Aspects of Gender and Russian Literature* (= special issue of *Nordlit*, 4 (1998)), 61–98.

Chapter 3: 'The Education of the Will: Advice Literature, *Zakal* and Manliness in Early Twentieth-Century Russia', *Russian Masculinities in History and Culture*, ed. by Barbara Clements, Rebecca Friedman, and Daniel Healey (Basingstoke: Palgrave, 2002), pp. 131–51.

Chapter 4: 'The "Man-Footed Beast" versus the "Beast-Footed Man": Animals as Slaves, Servants, and Companions in Post-Enlightenment European Culture', published in Russian translation as '"Chelovekonogii zver'" protiv "zveronogogo cheloveka": zhivotnogie kak raby, slugi i sputnik cheloveka v evropeiskoi kul'ture epokhi postprosveshcheniya', *Novoe literaturnoe obozrenie*, 5.141 (2016) <https://www.nlobooks.ru/magazines/novoe_literaturnoe_obozrenie/141_nlo_5_2016/article/12189/> [accessed 18 October 2022].

Chapter 5: 'A Wolf in the Nursery? Freud, Ethnography, and the History of Russian Childhood', online publication of the Centre for the Study of the Culture of Childhood, Russian State Humanities University, 2008 <http://childcult.rsuh.ru/article.html?id=67313> [accessed 18 October 2022].

Chapter 6: 'The Redress of Art: Anna Akhmatova and Boris Anrep' (as 'Anna Akhmatova and Boris Anrep: An Afterword'), *Irish Slavonic Studies* no. 16 (1996), pp. 1–29.

Chapter 7: 'At Peace with the Wolf: Prokofiev's "Official" Soviet Works for Children', *Three Oranges*, 12 (2006), 3–9.

Chapter 8: 'Making Memories: Children and the Personal Past in Early Twentieth-Century Russia', published in Russian translation as 'Kak sdelany vospominaniya: deti i lichnoe proshloe v Rossii nachala XX veka', *Istoricheskaya pamyat' i obshchestvo v Rossiiskoi Imperii i SSSR (konets XIX-nachala XX vv.): nauchnye doklady* (St Petersburg: Evropeiskii dom, 2007).

Chapter 10: 'I Want to Be a Tractor Driver', published in Russian translation as 'Khochu byt' traktoristkoi!', *Sotsial'naya istoriya: Ezhegodnik 2003* (Moscow: Rosspen, 2005), pp. 385–410.

Chapter 11: 'Comrade is a Sacred Word': The Regulation of Children's Affective Relationships in Soviet Culture', published in Russian translation as '"V nashem velikom Sovetskom Soyuze tovarishch — svyashchennoe slovo": emotsional'nye otnosheniya mezhdu det'mi v sovetskoi kul'ture', *Detskie chteniya*, 1.3 (2013) <https://detskie-chtenia.ru/index.php/journal/article/view/54> [accessed 18 October 2022].

Chapter 12: 'Essential Luxuries: Goods for Children in the Last Decades of Soviet Power', published in Russian translation as: 'Roskosh' ili pervaya neobkhodimost'? Prodazha i pokupka tovarov dlya detei v poslestalinskuyu epokhu', *Teoriya mody*, 8 (2008), 141–85.

Chapter 13: 'The Many Lives of Konon Molody (Gordon Lonsdale): Espionage, Disinformation, and the Moral Universe of the Late Cold War', includes material originally published in Russian translation as 'Chelovek na vse sezony: apsaikling odnogo shpiona-geroya pri sovetskoi vlasti i pozzhe', *Novoe literaturnoe obozrenie*, 3 (2021), 102–26.

Where not otherwise indicated, all translations are my own.

c.k., Cambridge, December 2022

LIST OF ILLUSTRATIONS

Fig. I.1. Quimper, Brittany, 1948. Photograph Margaret Moncrieff.
Fig. I.2. View from the flat owned by Madame Chopfer in Passy, Paris, 1948. Photograph Margaret Moncrieff.
Fig. 1.1. Lazarevskoe Cemetery, St Petersburg. Photograph Catriona Kelly.
Fig. 4.1. 'Pavlov and his Dogs'. Internet meme. Creative Commons.
Fig. 4.2. 'The Bull Who Didn't Want to Be a Bull'. Russian popular print, 1820s or 1830s. D. A. Rovinsky, *Russkie narodnye kartinki*, Atlas, 5 vols (St Petersburg: tipografiya Imperatorskoi Akademii Nauk, 1881), 1, 176.
Fig. 4.3. Lewis Gompertz, design for a velocipede. 1829. J. T. Goddard, *The Velocipede: Its History, Varieties, and Practice* (New York: Hurd & Houghton, 1869), p. 11.
Fig. 5.1. Sergei Pankeev at Vasilievka, late 1890s. The other young man is probably his cousin Georgy. Library of Congress, Sergius Pankejeff Papers.
Fig. 5.2. Sergei Pankeev as a toddler, wearing a white furry coat. Library of Congress, Sergius Pankejeff Papers.
Fig. 6.1. Boris Anrep, St Anne. Cathedral of Christ the King, Mullingar, Ireland. Photograph Ian Thompson.
Fig. 9.1. Girl spinning. Photograph Solomon Yudovin, for Semyon An-sky's ethnographical project in Galicia, 1912–14. Courtesy Judaica Centre, European University, St Petersburg.
Fig. 9.2. Rabbi's family, Ostroh, Ukraine. Photograph Solomon Yudovkin, for Semyon An-sky's ethnographical project in Galicia, 1912–14. Courtesy Judaica Centre, European University, St Petersburg.
Fig. 9.3. Children at the Jewish National Home in front of their agitational 'wall newspaper'. Courtesy Valery Dymshits.
Fig. 10.1. A page of clothing for small girls from the catalogue of Paul Karlson, Chemisier, St Petersburg, 1900. Author's collection.
Fig. 13.1. Donatas Banionis (right) as Ladeinikov in Kulish's *The Dead Season* (1968). Archive of Lenfil'm Studio.
Fig. 13.2. Konon Molodyi on a postage stamp <https://commons.wikimedia.org/wiki/File:The_Soviet_Union_1990_CPA_6268_stamp_(Soviet_Intelligence_Agents._Konon_Molody).jpg>.
Fig. 13.3. Konon Molodyi clings to the running-boards of his cousin George Jaure's car, probably in Berkeley around 1934. (UK National Archives, KV2-4451)
Fig. 14.1. Image of a veiled woman, from Shamshiev's *The Scarlet Poppies of Issyk-Kul* (Kirgyzfilm Studio, 2971) <https://www.kino-teatr.ru/kino/movie/sov/197/foto/12/158665/>.
Fig. 14.2. Publicity still from Khamraev's *The Black Sands*. Archive of Lenfil'm Studio.
Fig. 14.3. Dinara Asanova on the set of her *Woodpeckers Don't Get Headaches*. 1974. Archive of Lenfil'm Studio.
Fig. 14.4. Image from Orynbasarova's *A Sacrifice for the Emperor* <https://www.kino-teatr.ru/kino/movie/sov/2219/foto/718884/>.

INTRODUCTION

*Out of Focus and Close Up:
Russian Subjects 1760–1990*

Once in my life I have fallen into what Russians call 'Big History'. I was staying with Leningrad friends when we woke up on the morning of 19 August 1991 and heard that a *coup d'état* had taken place. The effect was more like grief or clinical shock than insight. Something was out of kilter, for sure, but there was a strange vacuity. You filled time to avoid the terrifying question of what had happened. After watching grimly immobile newscasters impart the General Emergency Committee's address to the nation, I went to a local shop and bought a decorated Uzbek plate to bring home as a gift. At the next counter, people were panic-buying rusks, a much more logical response. When Ian, my partner, got through later that day, my friends and I knew that the plotters had not digested their Lenin: lesson number one of successful political action is, cut off communications first. Next day, I joined other friends, and crowds on Palace Square, for a huge demonstration, but you could only hear the speeches on someone's transistor. On day three, a friend and I went and steamed in a bathhouse, with news playing on the radio all the while. The promised, or threatened, tanks never arrived in Leningrad. Even when something important happens, it turns out that it hasn't.

Tolstoy was right, in his afterword to *War and Peace*: shape comes after experience has ended. Immediate impressions are desultory. Or perhaps I saw August 1991 like this because I had read Tolstoy? At any rate, sharing Tolstoy's scepticism, I'm inclined to avoid 'events' in the world of imagination or thought. I mostly don't watch films for the plot, and rarely find slow-moving, visually seductive movies tedious (while action thrillers often bore me). I've never much wanted to add to the mountains of books about the Second World War (partly because I spent my childhood hearing about it), or indeed the Russian Revolution, the Great Terror, or the 'collapse of the USSR'. The Russian invasion of Ukraine, which burst on the world just when I was finishing this book, had the same kind of confusion written over it. This was quintessentially not 'an event', even at a distance. It was a tragic, confused surge of violence and destruction, with no moral or narrative sense, driven by one country's determination to inflict on another a fate contrary to possibility as well as reason and justice: political and cultural non-existence.

Yet even at a period of history when 'events' elude our grasp, to abandon writing about them means abandoning the mainstream, at least among Westerners interested in Russia and the former Soviet Union — and particularly so-called 'general readers' and journalists. If you don't write books on what Soviet culture planners termed 'magisterial themes', you can forget widespread newspaper coverage, literary prizes, and deferential copy along the lines 'among the very best of our historians'. Indeed, people will probably doubt your claims to historical knowledge at all.

This is not a complaint. Books have their fates, and so do the people writing them. Almost any kind of reputation is double-edged, and with a book that was relatively celebrated, by my standards, also came accusations from a frenzied author that I had stolen the idea from him.[1] A more rewarding question is why your work ends up 'out of focus' to start with — beyond the customary gaze, among the unconsidered trifles. I think the reasons can be traced back to my childhood, so I'll begin with a word or two about that, before returning to the choice of texts in this book, which gathers together pieces written over twenty years about peripheral, peculiar, or errant types of subjectivity: the out-of-focus experiences and perceptions of, say, women, émigrés, young people, ethnic minorities — though the lives of establishment figures, too, start to blur and acquire a creative oddity if you put them under the same kind of lens.

★ ★ ★ ★ ★

In various ways, my own background was marginal. My parents, both born in Edinburgh, came from nearly as far apart on the social scale as two inhabitants of a small former capital who manage, in the end, to meet each other, could possibly be. My mother, Margaret, grew up in a house with fourteen rooms and five servants, if you include the man who mowed the lawn and the man who wound the clocks. Her father, Alexander Moncrieff, came from an old Perthshire family that went back to a Spanish mercenary rewarded by the position of Keeper of the Wardrobe to Alexander I. After changing sides at least twice in the troubled post-Reformation era, the family went into the professions, first of all the church (one of them, after studying in the Netherlands, founded his own sect of radical Presbyterians), and later the law. In the late eighteenth century, a Moncrieff daughter married John Pattison, a prosperous muslin merchant and anti-slavery campaigner; the convictions lasted longer than the money, which ran out in 1808. Moncrieff waywardness persisted in their children; one was a pioneering professor of anatomy who had to leave Glasgow because of his relationship with a married woman, and who preferred to settle academic disputes by challenging opponents to duels.[2] My grandfather, who lived in less colourful times, made his name as a judge with the 'Paisley Snail' case, which laid the foundations of modern consumer legislation across the Commonwealth. Later, after the 1945 election, he was appointed Lord Justice Clerk and a privy councillor — despite being rather too old for the post,

---

[1] Yuri Druzhnikov after the publication of *Comrade Pavlik: The Rise and Fall of a Soviet Boy Hero*. Druzhnikov also argued that I was a tool of the FSB, and his evidence for plagiarism ran to pointing out that I had used the same *Pravda* articles, hardly an esoteric source. Few took his defamatory stories seriously, though they have always had a certain currency among the kind of Russians who think foreigners steal their ideas.

[2] This was Granville Sharp Pattison (1791–1851), whose first names honoured the author of *A Representation of the Injustice and Dangerous Tendency of Tolerating Slavery* (1769). Pattison ended his life as Professor of Anatomy at New York University.

he was the only candidate of merit who was also politically acceptable to the new Labour government, having never voted Conservative in his life.[3]

My father Alec, on the other hand, was born out of wedlock to Annie Lugton, who was herself a servant: she kept house for an elderly, widowed bank manager who was probably Alec's father. At any rate, she retained her position, while Mr Manford paid for the baby to be placed in a foundling home, and would sometimes, during my father's childhood, hand him a ten-shilling note, then fantastic largesse. Alec was first fostered, and later adopted (Annie wasn't keen, but Alec's foster sisters told her not to be so silly) by Mary Kelly, a diminutive but dynamic miner's wife from the village of Gilmerton. She and her husband James had rural origins — before the First World War he was a ploughman, and Mary kept hens all her life. Miners worked right through the Great Depression, so the family was, by working-class standards, comfortable. In any case, Mary was a force in her own right. After their marriage (went a plausible family legend), James did as his workmates did, and went to the pub. Mary stormed in and dragged him out by the scruff. I don't know when they converted to Plymouth Brothers, but that's what they were all my father's life, though his membership of that strict faith didn't endure beyond childhood, and eventually he joined the rest of us in the Catholic Church (while regularly complaining how awful the sermons were, which was true).

The alliance certainly didn't amount to dirt poor on the one side and filthy rich on the other. But it still caused shock and consternation when Alec and Margaret announced their plans to marry. For my father's side, marrying a Catholic meant bringing the Antichrist across the threshold. In painful symmetry, Margaret's godmother anxiously asked Archbishop (later Cardinal) Gray whether it was appropriate for her spiritual charge to marry a foundling. (He politely replied that a certificate of baptism would suffice.) All the same, my grandmother, Helen, took to my father immediately — even though, three decades before, she'd stopped Margaret playing with a friend who'd 'infected' her with a Scottish accent, and Alec's stayed with him all his life.

Yet Helen's background a century back was not so different. Her father, John Robinson Adams (born in Liverpool, 1833), gave his father's profession on the certificate of his second marriage in 1876 as 'gentleman'. But he was actually the son of a gentleman's gentleman — in other words, a valet — originally from Newport in Essex, over two hundred miles away. It was, I imagine, a generous employer who paid for his apprenticeship to a solicitor at the end of the 1840s, after

---

3 Alexander Moncrieff was the judge in the original case, finding in favour of the plaintiff, Mrs Donohue, who had argued that the mollusc-contaminated ginger pop had caused her material harm. His judgement was eventually upheld in the House of Lords and established the principle of responsibility of manufacturers and suppliers to consumers. It is now a textbook example in tort law. On the 'marginality' theme, I note wryly that often the judges in the House of Lords take all the credit, and also that my mother never mentioned this case either — she did not get on well with her father and was not very interested in his life. So I take the information about the family not from her account alone — *Worlds Apart: Memoirs of Margaret Moncrieff (Helen McClelland)* (London: Bettany Press, 2003) — but also from what Hope Mirrlees (my grandfather's niece) wrote about her mother Emily Lina (my grandfather's elder sister), and from George Seton, *The House of Moncrieff* (Edinburgh: printed for private circulation, 1890) — though Seton does not mention Ramerus de Muncrefe's Spanish origins.

a rough few years for him and his parents (the 1841 census has them in a village on the site of modern Everton, where the father, also John, worked as a labourer). By 1861, advantageously married to a farmer's daughter from Kirby, John Robinson Adams had moved to London, and in the 1890s, he deserted south London (the Loughborough estate in Brixton, and then College Avenue in Dulwich) for a new and luxurious mansion block in Kensington. He ended his life in a substantial Hampstead villa, with one of his daughters married to a lieutenant-colonel from the Anglo-Irish gentry, and another, Frances (Fanny), the wife of Herbert, the son of arts-and-crafts architect Charles Voysey.

To be honest, I had no idea, till I followed its documentary traces, that this impressive social mobility was possible in England at the time. It certainly puts into context my grandmother's concern for social proprieties — though by the time she was born, there was a quite a lot of money around (enough to buy her a top-of-the-range rocking horse and, as a wedding present, a rosewood grand piano of drawing-room size made by the German company Blüthner — a tribute to her love of German culture).[4]

Helen was the daughter of her father's second marriage, and in turn, my mother was from *her* second marriage. Both my grandparents were the youngest children in long families. Last children are usually family favourites, but peripheral too, and particularly when it comes to dividing up possessions. Few of the objects that filled the different houses in Glasgow (Kelvingrove, Mount Blow), London (32 Pembridge Square, 2 Nutley Terrace, Hampstead), Edinburgh (8 Abbotsford Crescent) swam into our ken. Four Scottish Chippendale chairs from two large sets once in Kelvingrove, a Chinese mazarine and gilt export ware vessel ('the Kelvingrove punchbowl'), a beautiful but valueless carriage clock with blue-and-gold peacocks in a battered red leather travelling box (only the repeat now works) — that kind of thing. As for Mary Kelly, once she could afford new furniture in the 1950s, she made a joyful bonfire of her old things, not sparing even a square piano that she'd used as a side table. Her daughter, also Mary, owned an upright, which is how Alec started playing to begin with; he had his first few lessons with Mary, who taught the piano a little, but quickly realised his capacities were beyond her own, and passed him to the professionals.

4   My grandmother in fact studied German at Bedford College in the late 1890s, though she never took a degree (and probably simply audited courses before her first marriage, aged twenty). Her mother, born Helen Boyd McClelland, came from a west Scottish family of the minor gentry that moved to London in the 1870s. A family legend was that Helen senior married late (aged thirty-three) and to a widower because she was 'damaged goods', having tried to run away with an unsuitable man before her brothers caught up with the pair at the station and horsewhipped him. Perhaps this explains the relocation south. Helen died of breast cancer aged thirty-seven, not long after the death of her first child, James, then aged about three. After Helen junior's diagnosis with supposedly fatal heart disease (though she ended up living to eighty-three rather than nine), John Robinson Adams decided he could face no more deaths, and Helen was boarded with Mrs Riley, the widow of a doctor, whose daughter Dorothy, just a year younger, became her closest friend. In another revealing detail, it turned out later that Mrs Riley, despite the impressive set of full mourning (which we later inherited from Dorothy), was in fact a divorcee (the 1891 census records her as sharing a house in New Windsor with one Dr Cunvey, as well as Helen and Dorothy).

My mother had little concern for inherited objects. It was my father who cared when other family members, clearing out 8 Abbotsford Crescent, then resplendently decayed after my grandmother's death, decided that Alec and Margaret couldn't possibly want the surviving eighteenth-century sherry glasses because they weren't a set. Incensed though Alec was by this conventionality, he was also far more concerned about table manners than my mother; she had decided that she'd never make a fuss because her own father used to throw almost daily tantrums about people arriving late to meals. Indeed, we never had a formal dining room, and it's much more difficult to be pompous over a kitchen table that also contains several days' post, uncleared marmalade and Marmite jars, and various donated objects that no-one has the heart to throw away.

The table was set with great-grandmother's wedding silver, but that's because my parents didn't have the money to buy anything else. Cash was short pretty well all the time (at least until the Royal Academy of Music started paying salaries to their professors in 1980) — though there was enough family money on my mother's side to buy a house in south-west London, and sometimes (in the form of gifts from friends and better-off relations) to pay for special holidays. Then the bank manager funded a loan to buy a semi-derelict cottage in the west of Ireland and the repairs to make it habitable ('This is a mad idea, but sometimes one should follow mad ideas' — bless his heart). But a few years later, after a different manager arrived, my father had to change banks to buy another piano, the drawing-room Blüthner not being up to his or his students' professional needs. Apparently, the acquisition of an instrument was considered 'frivolous' (back then, if you said you were a musician, there was a high chance of the reply: 'But what's your real job?'). Few things annoyed my father more than the people down the street who placed their baby grand by a window facing the street — and used the closed lid as a cocktail bar.

Like a lot of Londoners, we didn't belong. My parents were insistent that we were Scots: the earliest family quarrel that I remember was when I tearfully insisted, aged about eight, that I was English, and was told that was *definitely* not the case: 'If a cat has kittens in the oven, they're not buns'. I think this primordialism is typical of migrant families; no-one had spoken Gaelic for several generations, but if they had done, we would surely have learned it. Into the bargain, they gave both me and my sister Alison completely Scottish first names (unlike the ones they had themselves). I encountered only two namesakes during seventeen years of education in the south of England, one of whom used to break into *Für Elise* on the classroom piano in the middle of, say, a German lesson, while the other preferred to be known as Kate.

There must be millions of not-quite-English children who have the experience of being called something unlike what they're called at home: the only person at school who could correctly pronounce my friend Nalini's name was an English teacher who wrote it down in phonetics. 'We've used the *English* pronunciation for everyone else,' an employer told me in the late 1970s — and proceeded to mangle my name for the next six months.

This fostered a lasting sympathy for people who don't fit in. I now realise that most of my friends, and even people I liked in a distant kind of way, at the various schools we went to, came from offbeat backgrounds: half-French, half-Russian, half-American, with a *Kindertransport* father, Indian, Sri Lankan... Our part of London, with its village pond, its villas in which seventeenth- and eighteenth-century celebrities such as Godfrey Kneller and Henry Fielding had summered, and the sea of early twentieth-century brick houses built on what had once been Kneller's orchard, seemed totally 'English' (people's main pastimes, back in the 1960s, were washing their cars and doing their gardens, neither of which ever happened at number 32). But our immediate neighbours were an Armenian couple who had moved to London from Burma, and a family known locally as the 'Beatniks', because their main source of financial support (apart from the legacy of a family laundry in Whitechapel set up by refugees from the Jewish Pale) was a succession of long-haired, guitar-playing, and (so the more strait-laced neighbours across the road said) pot-smoking twenty-somethings, many of them friends of their two grown children, one of whom ended up in Mexico and the other in Denmark.

Actually, even the more 'strait-laced' neighbours were wonderfully mad: one used daily to don her sensibly capacious bra right in front of her bedroom window, while another, in middle age as round as a robin, had won a horse race out in the Raj as a slim eighteen-year-old because the organisers forgot to impose a handicap. The smell of curry was as likely to come from that house as from the Armenians next door. Conventionality or otherwise isn't a question of where you come from or where you live, it's a state of mind, and actually nobody is really 'unconventional' in their own terms, they just jar with someone else's set of rules. Or that's what I concluded from childhood experience.

I've never used the phrase 'people like us' because I have no real idea what it means, though the settled, affluent, provincial (upper) middle class of well-paid professionals and business people is probably one answer. As someone often taken as 'not-English' simply by appearance (to quote a fellow-passenger during a lift to a wedding back in the 1990s, 'Are you at all foreign? Because you're really awfully dark'), I definitely identify more with 'people *not* like us'.[5] It helped that the 1960s, or certainly in south-west London, was an internationalist era: a benevolent time when having Thai, Japanese, Egyptian, and Nigerian children in the class was something to be proud of, an era of public recreation grounds you could walk to without adults, free rose hip syrup at the clinic where you got the polio injections, and infectious diseases as a minor nuisance, rather than a threat to life and limb. The 1970s broke on this as a rude shock, with Enoch Powell's 'rivers of blood', the absurd 'I'm Backing Britain' campaign. The Common Market provided some (now extinguished) hope of an escape from Little England; after the decision came through, we stood and cheered with our cousins as beacons were lit all down the south coast.[6]

5   Winding back a few years, the obsession of 1960s and 1970s popular culture with blondeness reached levels hard to imagine now. My number one wish aged about six was to be blonde, which I didn't manage (unlike my mother) even in early childhood.

6   Our cousins on my mother's side particularly were big presences in our lives. I've not gone into it here because this is not a full-scale memoir, but that side of the family too has an eccentric social place; our half-Dutch and half-Irish uncle by marriage, a high-ranking officer in the Royal Artillery,

Anyway, the oddity of background is perhaps why I ended up studying a language that was considered 'peculiar' — allegedly very difficult, if also 'beautiful', spoken by few people even in my parents' extended circle. It wasn't till I was in my twenties that I realised that my grandparents had a whole collection of Russian bonds, an 'unbeatable investment' in 1913 (ha!), as well as records by Chaliapin and Slobodskaya. This was also the point when I gathered that my mother's first cousin Hope Mirrlees had been an active Russophile and a friend of the Russian émigré critic Dmitry Sviatopolk-Mirsky.[7] My parents loved Russian music, and admired the professional training — way better than what you get in Britain, so they thought. Yet all the same Russian felt, more than anything else, like a chance to go my own way. In other circumstances and eras, it could, I suppose, have been Ancient Greek, or Arabic, or Chinese. The cussedness was turned in the Russian direction by the 1969 BBC Radio 4 adaptation, in twenty instalments, of Tolstoy's *War and Peace*. I was nine at the time, but the novel, read aloud and grippingly acted, is easily in the grasp of fairly young children. Supposedly, I read it not long afterwards, but 'read' is probably a courtesy term: I remember the adaptation much better, and the experiences of being completely caught up in reading are ones that I associate with more obvious pre-teen fare such as Narnia and E. Nesbitt. As an adult, I prefer *Anna Karenina* to *War and Peace*; but one way or another, Tolstoy has gone with me through my entire life.[8]

In terms of the larger world, studying Russian in the 1970s meant (as it still does) working on something that was definitely not 'in focus' (less so, even, than other modern European cultures, such as France, Germany, or Italy, then firmly part of 'the Continent'). Still, at least British people were interested in the USSR, partly because of fears we would all be bombed in our beds. (I never shared these, but

was charged with taking Nazi war prisoners to execution after Nuremburg, and later generations included a specialist in tropical medicine and other doctors, artists, architects, a lawyer working for the EU, a member of the International Commission on English in the Liturgy and so on.

7   This was Hope Mirrlees (1887–1978), author of several novels, including *Lud-in-the-Mist* (1926), D. S. Mirsky's favourite recent English novel, the modernist poem, *Paris* (published by Leonard and Virginia Woolf's Hogarth Press in 1919), and lyric poems, who unfortunately died early in the year that I went up to Oxford, though I well remember her sister, Margot Coker, a character straight out of Saki. Once, she was visited at Bicester House by a retired major recuperating, not very successfully, after a nervous breakdown. He stood up, pointed through the window at the empty lawn, and gibbered: 'What's that yacht doing there?' 'I don't know: people will leave these things lying around', Margot replied majestically. Both she and Hope were very fond of dogs; Margot, in our time, had an overwrought Cavalier King Charles (cue hooting up the stairs: 'Boydikins, boydikins, boydikins, boyd!'). Hope, rather a squat figure in middle age, according to my mother (it was a shock for me to discover she was renowned as a young woman for her beauty and elegance), preferred to salute her pug, 'Tu-whit tu-woo, Mary dog, tu-whit tu-woo, Mary!' Their mother, Lina, was so self-confident a hostess that she was known to go to bed before the start of a dinner she had organised and leave the guests to look after themselves. This sort of zany eccentricity plus impracticality was considered to be diagnostic for the Moncrieff family and its descendants, even if two cousins who would ring for the maid rather than top up the fire with coal themselves were thought to have taken this trait a little too far.

8   In the context of aggressively resurgent Russian imperialism, directly modelled on the Russification of the late Tsarist era, Tolstoy's *Hadji Murat* and *After the Ball* have acquired renewed force. They might get the writer a prison sentence for 'discrediting the army' if written today.

realised from an oral history project in the 2000s that inhabitants of Soviet cities in Cold War days had exactly the same dread, while thinking the rockets would come from the West.) It was a shock to get to Vienna in 1978 and realise that an interest in Russia was a conversation-stopper ('We had enough of them after the War', said one septuagenarian drily). It didn't help that the Viennese were anyway not friendly to foreigners (wearing jeans — Viennese eighteen-year-olds preferred Loden coats and pleated skirts — was enough to get me branded an *Amerikanerin*, another nation guilty of post-war affront). At the time, Vienna was a staging-post for the vast post-1972 Soviet diaspora, which had exacerbated prejudice. The fact that these Russians and Ukrainians were Jewish, and the targets of discrimination in their home country, was immaterial: they were, to Viennese observers, simply, 'Soviet'.

So there was nothing good about Russian, then and there. In fact, I found Vienna such a challenge (despite the kindness of various friends-of-family-friends) that it probably turned me finally in the Russian-not-German direction. That, and the famous fact that when you actually got to know those apparently forbidding 'Soviet' Russians, there weren't any of the same barriers that there were on the Danube. And in a strange way, the culture seemed livelier, too — at any rate, if you compared Moscow's hip Taganka Theatre with the Akademie Theater, where a prominent notice instructed visitors that they should wear 'clothing that conforms with decency'. (I don't think that included jeans.)

Something else that underlined that sense of living on the margins was prolonged contact with rural Ireland. We were summer visitors, for sure, but a cottage up on a mountainside next to smallholdings was not your usual seaside world. I was in my teens before electricity arrived (one of the last surges of the rural electrification scheme: what rural babushkas used to call Lenin's Lamp, only in our case it was Eamon de Valera's). The water main stops well short even now, though we do have a pipe in the stream that feeds actual taps. Back then, every pint of water had to be hauled by bucket. Every so often, our upper neighbour, a stately woman, would sally out from her front door, adjust her skirts, and lift her sizeable rear up the side of the farmhouse. Cows wandered by the door, and drank out of our stream, though donkeys were kept tethered, except when carrying back baskets of turf (usually with the owner perched on the rump) or dragging haystacks round the field.

Someone said recently that Russia must have changed a lot in the years that I've visited. It has — but no more than rural Ireland, or indeed Dublin, with its long vanished Liffeyside warehouses that we passed on the way west after a crane had picked my mother's glamorous but wayward scarlet Triumph Herald off the arriving ferry. (A year later, the first ro-ro, manufactured in Denmark for British and Irish ferries, transformed the entire travel experience: our first and second journeys came from different centuries.)

Immersion in rural Ireland makes it quite comical when people in Russia anxiously apologise because, say, you have to use an earth closet fifty metres from the house, or the only heating is a wood-burning stove. In fact, it was Russian friends who exclaimed over the 'villagey' character of the west of Ireland when they visited as late as 2010 — it completely defied the enduring stereotype of the West as a place of hi-tech sterility. As well as a certain stoicism, I think that I've also absorbed the Irish trait of not considering yourself superior as a nation to others, except perhaps by measure of suffering or enormity of misrule. A financial or bribery scandal is, it sometimes seems, never off page 3 of the *Irish Times* (in England, that page has traditionally served another purpose). Lamentations about the state of the nation are the stuff of life in Ireland, and indeed Russia. The English establishment classes, despite having laid waste large areas of several continents (and sometimes wishing they could do it again) tend to think that, by and large, they have done A Pretty Good Job. The sense of 'affective nationality' was heightened because it was no fun to have an Irish-sounding surname once IRA bombs reached Britain. Sometime in the early 1980s, I innocently called Belfast 'the second biggest city in Ireland' during a conversation in an Oxford college. My intelligent and charming interlocutor went red with fury and started shouting about my 'Sinn Fein ancestors'. When we were going out to Ireland by ferry, Ian (who has a widespread English surname) and I had a game we'd play: every second crossing, we'd register the car under my name and every other time under his. Our record of getting stopped for 'a quick check' was 100 per cent when it was me down as the owner of the car, and 0 per cent when it was him. It wasn't much compared with the prejudice that some other minority groups are exposed to, but it was still a salutary introduction to what prejudice can mean.

That said, marginality is not ethically superior in itself; an intent to visit resentment on others is one possible response to it, and when raised to the level of geopolitics can be devastating, as Russia's determination to 'protect itself' from Ukraine showed in 2022. In any case, my entitlement to a marginal view has strict limits. I've spent my professional life negotiating different sides of the so-called 'Golden Triangle' of English establishment universities, with only the first ten years in precarious temporary positions. And my elective attachments are to places lent allure by peripherality (the west of Ireland, and Russia's 'eccentric [former] capital', St Petersburg). But there was inherited strangeness in the mix. My mother's background might have seemed patrician and stable from the outside, but aged fourteen, she hung out of a classroom window at her convent school, friends clinging to her legs, and wrote TO HELL WITH CORMACK on the wall in unsteady chalk capitals. (John Cormack, founder of the Protestant Action Society, was a flamboyantly demagogic representative of the anti-Catholic feeling that still surfaces even in today's Scotland, and which, at the time, was expressed in serious riots, attacks on public events, and so on.) Two of Margaret's brothers were what was then called 'mentally defective', a terrible social stigma at the time. Her elder half-brother and an aunt on her mother's side were killed in the war (though no particular fuss was ever made about this, and the main story I remember was one of survival: how my first cousin, and later godmother, presciently got under the piano just before a V-1 flying bomb turned most of the house to rubble). In some ways, I think my mother's childhood was less happy than my father's, despite the summers at North Berwick and swimming and golf, the generous living space, and the relative wealth. My father remembered feeling threatened when a sailor looked meaningfully at him once on Princes Street; my mother narrowly escaped rape on the beach, throwing sand in the eyes of the soldier who had tried to push her over. There is some kind of message there — a gender one, to begin with.

* * * * *

I'm not sure that I could point to ways in which this personal history has affected, in any concrete way, the pieces collected here. But in one manner or another, they all reflect a lasting interest in populations beyond the focus of Russian history as conventionally practised. That's partly reflected in absences — of famous people, and by and large (aside walk-on appearances by Catherine II, or Nicholas I, or Soviet General Secretaries such as Stalin and Khrushchev), rulers and political leaders too. Major writers end up in offbeat situations: Pushkin alongside the (often female) authors of the Enlightenment and early nineteenth-century-conservative conduct literature; Tolstoy and Anna Sewell as companions in the fight for animal welfare, yet also advocates, where animals were concerned, of strictly bounded freedoms. And there are unexpected kinds of émigré also: a Russian-Ukrainian patient of Freud's, rather obtusely interpreted by 'the Viennese quack', to use Vladimir Nabokov's dismissive term; mosaic artist Boris Anrep honouring his former lover, Anna Akhmatova, in a provincial Irish cathedral; and the Moscow-born Californian schoolboy-turned-spy Konon Molodyi, living in London as Canadian citizen 'Gordon Lonsdale'.

Several of the essays deal with the lives of children, peripheral where not invisible to much of history, though coming part-way into focus by the early twentieth century. In my front cover image, taken from John Peter Askew's wonderful long-term project with a family in Perm, a child's fierce concentration semantically dominates, but overall, the photograph retains suggestive ambiguity. I love photography and am even a practitioner myself, in a modest kind of way, but am not much interested in high-resolution, high-gloss images (and don't think I ever would have been, even if Instagram had not existed). My mother couldn't bear symmetry and would always, even in temporary refuges such as guest houses, move out of kilter two vases that someone had put in careful relation to each other. I like that sense of rebellion in this photograph of an accidental umbrella in Brittany, 1948, or the snapshot taken by Margaret from her room in the flat owned by her Paris landlady, Madame Chopfer, the partly-American-partly-Alsatian friend of Francis Poulenc, which is alive precisely because it is slightly blurry.[9]

But alongside a preference for the offbeat and the overlooked, 'out of focus' in the title means something else as well: it means, in a contradictory kind of way, a dedication to the sort of concentrated, close-up view that *comes* with focus; to the case study or microhistory, rather than the panorama.

---

9   Poulenc was a terrible snob and Madame Chopfer became bored with being effusively greeted by him at the local metro station in Passy, but cut dead when he was floating round at some reception with, say, the princesse de Polignac. She made her point: 'C'est drôle, Monsieur Poulenc: vous ne me reconnaisez que dans les gares'. After that, he began to recognise her in other places as well.

Fig. I.1. Quimper, Brittany, 1948. Photograph Margaret Moncrieff.

Fig. I.2. View from the flat owned by Madame Chopfer in Passy, Paris, 1948. Photograph Margaret Moncrieff.

Quite a few of my books have been substantial in range and (very much not to the delight of publishers) size. But I wanted this to be a collection of essays in a real sense: sketches and glimpses, rather than magisterial and authoritative statements. I left out most journal articles not just because they are widely accessible in any case, but because I was pushing for a different character and tone. I wanted precisely to end up with the collection of peculiar biographies and wayward investigations that are assembled here. While sometimes inspired by collective discussions to begin with, the different chapters are presented in what resembles (my own limitations aside) the form that I would myself have wanted. They are not tidy, neatly organised articles of the sort that emerge when Reviewer 2 (and sometimes Reviewer 3, 4, 5, 6, and 7) have offered their instructive pontifications. (Sometimes those comments really are instructive: I am not only being ironic here.) The discussions speculate and they sprawl — and the first if not the second is, I think, something essential to intellectual life.

Reviewing material written over more than half a professional lifetime has strange effects. To put it in a shallow way, it's a mixture of, 'If only I could carry that off now,' and 'Did I ever go out in that?' Certainly, you wouldn't want your vintage clothes haphazardly updated. In the same way, I have stopped at a rather minimal level of editorial intervention. Some of the essays (for example, 'Educating Tatiana') appear in abridged form, mainly to trim overlap with texts that have appeared since their original publication.[10] In other cases, I've clarified or amplified a little, or occasionally added a reference to publications by others that have taken the topic further since the original essay was written. I have not altered or improved systematically. Not articles in the ordinary sense, these are, precisely, essays, somewhere at the boundary between academic history and non-fiction, and no doubt, in the end, marginal to both — but, I hope, with their own kind of character precisely because of that.

Catriona Kelly
Oxford, July 2021/Cambridge, April 2022

---

10 Complete avoidance of overlap with texts published later than the original essays, in this case with Chapter 1 of *Refining Russia*, is impossible (the same applies to my essay on Anna Tyutcheva's memoirs, some of which was reprinted in Chapter 2 of that book), but the substance of the discussion is independent.

PART I

Borders of Propriety

FIG. 1.1. Lazarevskoe Cemetery, St Petersburg. Photograph Catriona Kelly.

CHAPTER 1

Educating Tatiana: Manners, Motherhood, and Moral Education

[1996]

The Lazarevskoe Cemetery at Alexander Nevsky Monastery in St Petersburg resembles the teeming town graveyard described by Pushkin in his 1836 poem, 'When, sunk in thought, I wander on the outskirts'.[1] Notabilities from the reigns of Catherine, Paul and Alexander stand as closely packed, in death, as they once did at routs or at balls. Busts and statues stiffly reanimate beribboned jackets and powdered hair; tablets boast of court positions and public offices. But among the routine commemorations of dynastic alliances and the hackwork statues stand some more personal and emotional memorials. One such is the monument erected by the poet and court official Gavrila Derzhavin to his first wife Ekaterina Yakovlevna, née Bastidon, a handsome urn set on a pedestal decorated with a relief of Derzhavina's head, represented as a cameo held by a woman in neo-classical drapes attended by a putto. The inscription commemorates the suffering of 'a sorrowful but grateful husband' in noble verse:

> Где добродетель? Где краса?
> Кто мне следы ея приметит?
> Увы! здесь дверь на небеса...
> Сокрылась в ней — да солнце встретит!²

> [Ah! virtue and beauty, whither fled? | Who can find where her feet now tread? | Alas! heaven's doors have opened wide: | And she slipped through, into the light!]

---

1   A. S. Pushkin, 'Kogda za gorodom zadumchiv ya brozhu', in *Polnoe sobranie sochinenii*, 17 vols (Leningrad: Izdatel'stvo Akademii Nauk SSSR, 1937–59), III, 422 (hereafter in this chapter referenced as *PSS*). The cemetery, reordered in the Soviet period to include graves moved from elsewhere, is now part of the Museum of Sculpture. For its history, see Aleksandr Kobak and Yury Piryutko, *Istoricheskie kladbishcha Sankt-Peterburga* (St Petersburg: Tsentropoligraf, 2011); for the Soviet-era reorganisations, my *Remembering St Petersburg* (Oxford: Triton Press, 2014) <https://www.academia.edu/6847211/REMEMBERING_ST_PETERSBURG> [accessed 22 October 2022].
2   For a selection of such epigraphs, see *Peterburgskii nekropol'*, ed. by V. I. Saitov, 4 vols (St Petersburg: izdal velikii knyaz' Nikolai Mikhailovich, 1912–1913). All English translations in this book are my own, unless stated otherwise.

Less dignified, but more poignant, are the memorials to two other women. Mar'ya Borisovna Yakovleva, 'the wife of a lieutenant-colonel', who died at the age of thirty-one on 20 March 1805, is honoured by the voice of her husband:

> Вот, дети, гроб ея, гроб матери почтенной!
> Крутитеся по ней, а я уж изнемог;
> Источник слез моих среди тоски иссох;
> Подруги нет души, нет сей главы бесценной!
> О чада сирые! Кто вас к груди прижмет?
> Кто в слезном сиротстве у сердца вас согреет?
> Но тот, Кто врановых птенцов хранить умеет,
> Воззвав ее к Себе, ток ваших слез утрет.

[Here, children, is your honoured mother's tomb! | Weep, weep on her behalf, for I am overcome! | The fountain of my tears has dried amidst my anguish; | My soul's dear friend has gone, that precious head is absent! | O orphaned little ones! Who'll press you to her breast? | Who'll warm you tearful orphans at her heart? | But He, Who is the tender fledglings' guide, | Who called Her to Himself, will see your tears are dried.]

Not far away, a substantial sculptural tomb immortalises two members of the Lazarev family who died within days of each other. The draped figure of the mother bends over the cradle of her sleeping infant son; as one hand moves his coverlet in place, another discreetly lifts one corner of her marble veil to her eyes.

The monuments in Lazarevskoe Cemetery were only the most durable tributes to a veritable cult of maternity that developed in Russia during the late eighteenth and early nineteenth centuries. Like the comparable images of maternity in Augustan England, they were products of a 'maternal mythology [...] that at once exploits and denies explicitly maternal agencies and subjectivities, especially as these operate in the public world'.[3] In other words, they represented an understanding of maternity that was highly selective, where social control, as exercised through moral education, was far more important as a feature of ideal maternity than was fertility or emotional nurture.

The ideology of 'pedagogical motherhood', which saw women as the overseers of their children's, and more especially their daughters', moral education (*vospitanie*), was a fundamentally new phenomenon in Russian culture. Certainly, ideal maternity pervaded pre-Petrine religious culture, and mothers were held responsible for providing their daughters with moral guidance. In the *Life of St Yulianiya Lazarevskaya*, for example, we are informed that the saint's grandmother, who fostered her from the age of six, 'raised her in piety and purity' ('vospitayushche vo vsyakom blagoverii i chistote'). But there is no evidence that women — whether saintly or otherwise — were held responsible for their children's intellectual interests. There was no equivalent of the late medieval Western iconographical tradition representing St Anne as educator of the Virgin, and the cult of the Mother of God stressed her part as intercessor between humanity and God (*Zastupnitsa*),

---

3   Toni Bowers, *The Politics of Motherhood: British Writing and Culture, 1670–1760* (Cambridge: Cambridge University Press, 1996), p. 4.

and also as protector of Russia, at least as much as her role as pattern for individual mothers. And, though phrases such as 'caring like a mother' (*aki istovaya mat' pechasesya*) were current in medieval texts, concrete expressions of what such caring signified were scarcely if ever made.[4] To borrow Toni Bowers' distinction: pre-Petrine representations of motherhood illustrate 'what mothers are' (i.e. the symbolic implications of the maternal state) rather than 'what [that] particular culture could (or could not) imagine mothers doing' (that is, the practical duties of a mother).[5] For example, the *Domostroi*, the seminal sixteenth-century manual of house management, provides remarkably little guidance on women's activities as mothers, and certainly no suggestion is made that education should be under their control. In the late eighteenth and early nineteenth centuries, by contrast, 'a mother could not stress too heavily her role as her daughter's educator and guide'.[6] This new pattern of maternity needed to be learned, and the main sources for its transmission included not only visual representations (for instance, the *maternités* painted by Elisabeth Vigée Le Brun during her stay in Russia in the 1790s) and literary texts, but also advice literature, such as conduct books and treatises on education.[7]

Even in the first half of the eighteenth century, some Russians had already acquired a familiarity with Western behaviour books. Notable among them was A. F. Khrushchev, whose library included works by Chétardie (*Instruction pour une jeune princesse*) and Fénelon (*De l'éducation des filles*), and who made translations of these into Russian for private use in the 1730s.[8] By the mid-eighteenth century, books containing advice on behaviour had become one of the most widely marketed types of imported books in Moscow.[9] After 1760, they began to be translated into Russian in ever-larger numbers. Those that seem to have been most widely known (going on the number of different editions) included, apart from Fénelon's work, Anne-Thérèse de Lambert's *Avis d'une mère à sa fille*. But also familiar to Russians were the writings of Sarah Pennington and Pierre Boudier de Villemert;

---

4   'Povest' o Yulianii Lazarevskoi', in *Khrestomatiya po drevnerusskoi literature*, ed. by N. Gudzy (Moscow: Prosveshchenie, 1973), p. 343. On women's education in the pre-Petrine period, see E. Likhacheva, *Materialy dlya istorii zhenskogo obrazovaniya v Rossii (1086–1796)* 3 vols (St Petersburg: tipografiya M. M. Stasyulevicha, 1890), pp. 14–30; Lindsey Hughes, *Sophia, Regent of Russia 1657–1704* (New Haven, CT: Yale University Press, 1990), p. 33. On the image of maternity, see N. Pushkareva, *Zhenshchiny Drevnei Rusi* (Moscow: Mysl', 1989), pp. 95–102. On the cult of St Anne in the West, see Marina Warner, *From the Beast to the Blonde: Fairy Tales and their Tellers* (London: Chatto & Windus, 1994), Chapter 6.
5   Bowers, *The Politics of Motherhood*, p. 24.
6   Jessica Tovrov, *The Russian Noble Family: Structure and Change* (New York: Garland, 1987), p. 192.
7   The *maternités* of Vigée Le Brun, Angelica Kaufmann, and others can be found in Grand Duke Nikolai Mikhailovich, *Russkie portrety XVIII i XIX stoletii*, 5 vols (St Petersburg: Ekspeditsiya zagotovleniya gosudarstvennykh bumag, 1905–09).
8   P. I. Khoteev, 'Frantsuzskaya kniga v Biblioteke Peterburgskoi akademii nauk (1714–1742)', in *Frantsuzskaya kniga v Rossii v XVIII veke: ocherki istorii*, ed. by S. P. Luppov (Leningrad: Nauka, 1986), p. 38.
9   For instance, advice literature was the third most popular category of books sold at the Moscow Academy of Sciences Bookshop, 1749–60: see N. A. Kopanev, 'Rasprostranenie frantsuzskoi knigi v Moskve v seredine XVIII veka', in *Frantsuzskaya kniga v Rossii v XVIII veke*, ed. by Luppov, p. 83, table 6.

large numbers of uncredited tracts and treatises were also published.[10] To judge by library holdings and references in indigenous Russian works such as letters and memoirs, as well as booksellers' catalogues, these books circulated widely and were at least as influential in spreading Enlightenment views on women's education as the prestigious boarding schools, such as Smol'nyi Institute, set up by Catherine II, which themselves were the products of Catherine's interest in educational theory.

Fénelon, probably the most influential writer on girls' education of the eighteenth century, and his successors, were responding directly to the writings of Poullain de la Barre, Marie de Gournay, and other late sixteenth- and early seventeenth-century writers who had argued directly for the absolute intellectual equality of men and women.[11] In contrast, Fénelon proceeds from an assumption of women's 'frailty' in a moral sense, and of the need to place them under the guidance of true Christian belief. This assumption is not contested by his female successors, such as Lambert, who, in her *Avis d'une mère à sa fille* (1728) makes a lucid and elegantly laconic distinction between the moral roles of men and women:

> There are some great virtues which, taken to a certain degree, allow many faults to be pardoned: supreme valour in men, and extreme modesty [*pudeur*] in women. Agrippina, wife of Germanicus, was pardoned everything on account of her chastity.[12]

As *valeur* and *pudeur* are opposed, so too are 'supreme' and 'extreme', with their

---

10 F. Fénelon, *De l'éducation des filles* [1687] appeared as *O vospitanii devits, sochinenie g. Fenelona arkhiepiskopa dyuka Kambriiskago*, trans. by Ivan Tumansky (St Petersburg: pechatano [v tipografii Sukhoputnogo kadetskogo korpusa, 1763) (*Svodnyi katalog russkoi knigi grazhdanskoi pechati XVIII veka, 1725–1800*, 5 vols (Moscow: Kniga, 1962–67), no. 7703 (hereafter referenced as *SK*). This edition was reprinted in 1774 and 1788; a new edition in 1794 included a translation of 'Lettre à une dame de qualité' (*SK*, no. 7705). Other books by Fénelon that circulated in Russia included (apart from the enormously popular *Télémaque*) *Obshchiya pravila zhizni, vzyatyya iz knigi, nazyvaemoi Istinnaya politika blagorodnykh lyudei* (Moscow: Universitetskaya tipografiya, 1779) (*SK*, no. 7706). A.-T. de Lambert, *Avis d'une mère à son fils et à sa fille* [1728]: *Pis'ma gospozhi de Lambert k eya synu o pravednoi chesti i k docheri o dobrodetelyakh prilichnykh zhenskomu polu* (St Petersburg: tipografiya Akademii Nauk, 1761) (*SK*, no. 3425); other translations appeared in 1814, 1834, and 1838. Sarah Pennington, *An Unfortunate Mother's Advice to Her Absent Daughters; in a Letter to Miss Pennington* [1761] appeared (translated from the French!) as *Sovety neshchastnyya materi eya docheryam [...]* (Moscow: Senatskaya tipografiya, 1788) (*SK*, no. 5149). Uncredited manuals include [Anon.], *Opyt o vospitanii blagorodnykh devits, sochinen gospozheyu *** s frantsuzskogo na rossiiskoi yazyk pereveden Mikhailom Semchevskim* (St Petersburg: pechatano pri Artilleriiskom i inzhinernom shlyakhetnom kadetskom korpuse, 1778).
11 See M. de Gournay, *Égalité des hommes et des femmes* [1622], in *Égalité des hommes et des femmes. Grief des dames, suivis du Proumenoir de Monsieur de Montaigne*, ed. by C. Venesoen (Geneva: Droz, 1993). P. de la Barre, *De l'égalité des deux sexes* [1673] (Paris: Fayard, 1984); and *De l'éducation des dames pour la conduite de l'esprit dans les sciences et dans les mœurs*, ed. by B. Magné [1679] (Toulouse: Université de Toulouse-Mirail, 1982); Ian Maclean, *Woman Triumphant: Feminism in French Literature, 1610–1652* (Oxford: Oxford University Press, 1977).
12 A.-T. de Lambert, 'Avis d'une mère à sa fille', in *Œuvres*, ed. by Robert Granderoute (Paris: H. Champion, 1990), p. 100 (this edition hereafter referenced as *Œuvres*.) The dichotomy between valour and shame that Lambert sets up was wholly conventional, in terms of French culture (see Maclean, *Woman Triumphant*, pp. 1–63) but apparently new in Russia: it is striking that the title of the first Russian translation of Lambert drew attention to it by inserting the words *chest'* [honour] and *dobrodetel'* [virtue].

connotations of ascent and sideways movement; in the horizontally determined arena of honour in which women move, the danger of approaching another sort of 'extreme' — that beyond the bounds of decent society — is always present. Accordingly, modesty, self-deprecation, and restraint, though figuring as part of the male aristocratic code, are far less important for men than they are for women.

For all that, though, Fénelon and Lambert are eager to stress that women should not allow men to dictate their behaviour. Madame de Lambert, for example, advises her daughter:

> So far as religion goes, you should submit to the authorities; on every other subject, you should heed no other authority than reason and evidence. If you give too much place to docility, you assault the rights of reason, and do not make use of your own lights, which will accordingly grow dimmer. To confine your ideas to those of others is to allow them too narrow a space. (*Oeuvres*, p. 113)

In her more explicitly feminist *Réflexions nouvelles sur les femmes* (first published, against the author's wishes, in 1727), and *Traité de l'amitié* (1736), Lambert expanded on these ratiocinations, suggesting that 'femmes d'un caractère raisonnable' (rational women) would cultivate platonic love rather than sensuality or flirtation. Both Lambert and Fénelon were concerned that women should be self-reliant, and saw their moral authority as deriving from this. Or, as it was put in *An Essay on the Education of Young Noblewomen*, a treatise translated from the French of an anonymous woman writer which appeared in St Petersburg during 1778:

> When giving your daughter instruction, you should attempt to stamp out in her those fantastical [*mechtatel'nye*] and laughable fancies to which so many women are subject. Here I am speaking not only about the fears and whims that come to them from childhood, but their opinions on dreams, portents of happiness, and all kinds of secret knowledge, which run directly contrary to sound reason [*zdravyi razum*] and which have no other foundation than the superstition of the common people; so too [should you try to stamp out] that extreme instability of feelings [*mezhnost' chuvstv*] which so often causes them unhappiness.[13]

Independence of mind was vital because the writers of conduct books anticipated dynastic marriages in which emotional relations had a minor significance at best. Virtue was essential as a means to independence; it was not primarily an instrument of female subjugation.

The importance of maternity as above all an apotheosis of moral guidance meant that its biological aspects were more or less invisible in eighteenth-century guides for women. Books giving advice on women's health discuss sexual reproduction with remarkable opacity. Take, for instance, this definition of pregnancy published in a guide translated from the German that appeared in Russia in 1793: 'Pregnancy is that state, in which a woman, a few days after her connexion with a man, finds herself in a condition other than the one in which she previously was'.[14] Tasks such

---

13   [Anon.], *Opyt o vospitanii blagorodnykh devits*, p. 37.
14   J. Goulin [as Zh. Gulen] and A. L. B. Jourdin [as A. L. B. Zhurden] , *Damskoi vrach, v 3 chastyakh, soderzhashchikh v sebe nuzhnye predokhraneniya, sluzhashchie k soblyudeniyu zdraviya, s prisovokupleniem*

as breast-feeding, nappy-washing, and other necessities of infant care, remained the concerns of lower-class women (*mamki* and *nyani*), while the upper-class lady busied herself with the spiritual development of her child.

One result of the new ideology of 'pedagogical motherhood' was that elective maternity, the social institution of the *vospitannitsa* (ward or protégée), whereby an aristocratic woman offered motherly guidance and social patronage (aid with the polishing of manners and the facilitation of introductions) to a younger woman who was not necessarily a blood relation, gained great symbolic significance during the late eighteenth and early nineteenth centuries. This arrangement was enthusiastically depicted in Anna Labzina's memoirs (Labzina had been a ward of the poet Elisaveta Kheraskova, herself one of the best-educated Russian women of the eighteenth century).[15] It is strikingly evoked also in two bravura portraits by Karl Bryullov of his mistress, Yuliya Samoilova, *The Countess Samoilova Returning from a Masquerade* (1839) and its pendant, *The Countess Samoilova and Her Ward* (1834). The portraits are representations of idealised maternity in which the link between older and younger woman is no less 'natural' because there is no direct blood relationship.[16]

The fact that Western ideas about maternity soon became familiar did not make them uncontroversial. Emphasis on a mother as moral guide was threatening to traditional Russian perceptions of the family because it could be seen to erode the absolute authority which a husband was supposed to exercise over his wife and children. As the *Domostroi* put it:

> Husbands should instruct their wives lovingly and with due consideration. A wife should ask her husband every day about matters of piety, so she will know how to save her soul, please her husband, and structure her house well. She must obey her husband in everything. Whatever her husband orders, she must accept with love; she must fulfil his every command. Above all, she must fear God and keep her chastity as decreed above.[17]

A wife who had already been given a complete moral education by her mother might well not 'accept whatever her husband ordered with love', and was not

---

VENERINA TUALETA: perevel s frants. M. I. U. Meditsinskogo fakul'teta Student Kodrat Mukovnikov (Moscow: v tipografii A. Reshetnikova, 1793), p. 168. Goulin is equally coy about the sexual act, describing it as 'the moment when two hearts that are strongly bonded and feel the impression of the tenderest love, surrender themselves to pleasure in its most vivid form' (p. 158). On nurses' responsibility for infancy, see *Opyt o vospitanii blagorodnykh devits*, pp. 2–3.

15   A. Labzina, *Vospominaniya 1763–1819*, ed. by B. L. Modzalevsky (Newtonville: Oriental Research Partners, 1974), pp. 47–48. Novels were carefully censored in favour of *lectures solides*, and moral issues assiduously propagandised by the Kheraskovs.

16   I discuss the portraits in more detail in *Refining Russia: Advice Literature, Polite Culture, and Gender from Catherine to Yeltsin* (Oxford: Oxford University Press, 2001). A famous case of this relationship in Britain at the period was Dido Elizabeth Belle (the daughter of an enslaved African, Maria Bell, and her owner, Sir John Lindsay), who was raised by her great-aunt and uncle, Elizabeth and William Murray, the Earl and Countess of Mansfield.

17   *Domostroi*, 'Sil'vesterskaya redaktsiya', Chapter 29: *Domostroi* ed. by V. V. Kolesov and V. V. Rozhdestvenskaya (St Petersburg: Nauka, 1994), p. 104; quotation here from *Domostroi: Rules for Russian Households in the Time of Ivan the Terrible*, ed. and trans. by C. J. Pouncy (Ithaca, NY: Cornell University Press, 1994), p. 124.

necessarily the wife wanted by a conservative member of the Russian nobility. Despite the emphasis of the new books on modesty (a quality essential in terms of Russian, and indeed Byzantine, codes of behaviour for elite women), the space in which they permitted female power to operate was large in terms of Russian normative tradition, and hence the advice that they gave could seem radical.[18]

Inevitably, the clash of old and new led to conflict. An era when tensions lay particularly close to the surface was the 1820s and 1830s, as the literary career of the outstanding writer of the period, Alexander Pushkin, illustrates. But another text of the day, more naive than anything ever written by Pushkin, in its very lack of self-consciousness, its swerves from narrative to moralising, from fact to fairy tale, lays bare the symbolic realities that underlie his far more polished works. This text is a story taken from the memoirs of Sofiya Kapnist-Skalon (1796 or 1797–1861), daughter of the well-known poet and playwright Vasily Kapnist.[19]

The tale told by Kapnist-Skalon occupies only about a dozen of her memoir's hundred or so pages, but merits her own description of it as 'interesting and remarkable' (KS, p. 379). Kapnist-Skalon's cousin, Petr Nikolaevich Kapnist (1796–1865) was an officer of the Guards and a wealthy landowner, the only son of a boorish eccentric notorious for beating his wife in public (at a stage after this had become shocking to the sensibilities of the nobility) and for his exaggerated devotion to his eldest daughter (of five), Sofiya. If Nikolai Vasil'evich's marriage seems a relic of the early eighteenth century, his son's, the object of Kapnist-Skalon's narration, was most definitely a product of the nineteenth. Aged about twenty-seven, he had fallen violently in love with Catherine (Ekaterina), the sixteen-year-old daughter of an aristocratic French émigré, Armand-François d'Allonville (1764–1853), who

18 On representations of virtuous women in the pre-Petrine era, see Pushkareva, *Zhenshchina v Drevnei Rusi*, pp. 101–02; M. Ziolkowski, 'Women in Old Russian Literature', in *Women Writers in Russian Literature*, ed. T. Clyman and D. Greene (Westport, CT: Greenwood, 1994), pp. 1–15, and R. McKenzie, 'Women in Seventeenth-Century Russian Literature', in *Gender in Russian Literature: New Perspectives*, ed. by R. Marsh (Cambridge: Cambridge University Press, 1996), pp. 41–54. On the Byzantine tradition, cf. *The Alexiad of Anna Comnena*, where the writer refers approvingly to her mother's 'extraordinary modesty' (Book 12, iii), p. 375, and her grandmother's piety and virtue (Book 3, viii), p. 120 (all page references to *The Alexiad of Anna Comnena*, trans. by E. R. A. Sewter (Harmondsworth: Penguin, 1969)) Cf. also the earliest Westernised behaviour manual: [Anon.], *Yunosti chestnoe zertsalo, ili pokazanie k zhiteiskomu obkhozhdeniyu. Sobrannoe ot raznykh Avtorov. Napechataetsya poveleniem Tsarskogo Velichestva* (St Petersburg: [n.pub.], 1717) whose second section sets out the twenty 'maidenly virtues': these include, apart from piety in its various manifestations, humility, propriety, gratitude, mercy, cleanliness, restraint, chastity, cheerfulness, generosity, and taciturnity.
19 Sofiya Kapnist-Skalon came from a literary family: her father Vasily Kapnist was a writer with Greek roots brought up on an estate in Mirgorod District, central Ukraine (then 'Little Russia'), while her uncle by marriage was the famous poet Gavrila Derzhavin. She married late, by the standards of the day (in her mid-thirties), to Major-General Vasily Skalon, who was eight years younger than her. The most accessible edition of Kapnist-Skalon's memoirs is in *Zapiski i vospominaniya russkikh zhenshchin XVIII-pervoi poloviny XIX vekov*, ed. by G. N. Moiseeva (Moscow: Sovremennik, 1990) pp. 281–388 (p. 31) (all references to this edition henceforth in text as KS). As Moiseeva points out (p. 34 of this edition), the memoirs, though first published in 1859, were almost certainly composed on the basis of earlier diaries; they are imbued with the spirit of the 1820s and 1830s rather than the 1850s.

had come to Russia in the entourage of the Prince de Condé. Delighted by their engagement, Petr Nikolaevich was eager to show off his bride at a ball; overcoming her reluctance to attend, he presented her with a sumptuous white dress. At the ball, however, she attracted so much attention that he regretted having taken her; directly after the marriage, he took her off to his estate in the Ukraine, where he kept her shut up alone, treating her sternly, Kapnist-Skalon tells us, because he was certain this would increase her fondness for him, but also showering her with presents, to which she displayed almost total indifference. When she expressed a wish to ride, he bought her an expensive saddlehorse and a costly riding-habit, and engaged the best available riding-master for her. On his inviting her into the drawing-room to admire the habit and horse, however, she responded by saying flatly 'Oui, c'est joli, ce n'est pas mal'. After the death of their first child, his feelings for her cooled, and he arranged for them to live abroad, where in due course she fell in love with a young Russian, Bobarykin. Allowed a divorce by Kapnist, Ekaterina remained in friendly contact with him, and to his satisfaction turned out to be as indifferent to Bobarykin's presents as his, greeting each with the words, 'c'est joli, ce n'est pas mal'.

The second marriage turned out to satisfy her as little as the first; she returned to Petr Nikolaevich, who by then had set himself up with an Italian mistress. A year later, after the latter's marriage to a drawing teacher in Khar'kov, Petr Nikolaevich and Ekaterina were left alone; but after the discovery of a packet of letters she had written to the student son of a local aristocrat, Petr Nikolaevich insisted they should again leave the country. Thereafter, Petr and Ekaterina led separate lives in Italy, she (according to Kapnist-Skalon) continuing to engage in scandalous affairs, while he magnanimously arranged the marriage of her two daughters (by Bobarykin), and she attended the wedding of his daughter (by the Italian), and also occupied herself with the education of her son Mikhailo Bobarykin.

At once banal and haunting, the story of Petr and Ekaterina depends on plot figures, such as coincidence, recognition, loss and retrieval, present in medieval romance as well as in folklore (both Russian and Western European). But the central narrative line intertwines two more specific mythic motifs. The first is the subjection of a new wife to moral tests, the excitation of her curiosity by the imposition of prohibitions in order that a didactic message against female curiosity may be propounded (Pandora, Bluebeard, Psyche). The second, more important and, in the 1820s, more topical motif is that of the artificial woman, the companion perfect because she has been manufactured to order. The motif is found both in the Greek legend of Pygmalion and in the modern fiction of the 'Stepford Wives', but was best-known in the early nineteenth century through E. T. A. Hoffmann's story *The Sandman* (1816), in which the hero, Nathaniel, deserts his true love, Klara, for Olimpia, a beauty who turns out to be a mechanical doll, a discovery thrusting Nathaniel into madness.

There is indeed something doll-like in the harmonious figure of Ekaterina Armanovna, 'a charming [*prelestnaya*] blonde, tall, slender, with soft, regular features' (KS, p. 366), as she suffers herself to be dressed and rewarded by successive husbands, mechanically responding 'c'est très joli' as though a string had been pulled in her stomach. Even her attempts to escape seem less acts of will than gestures dictated by some compulsion whose unexplained nature gives it demonic overtones. Indeed, an atmosphere of fatefulness hangs over the relationship from the start, as Kapnist recognises the daughter of the count from whom he is purchasing the estate as the unknown woman whom he had seen earlier at a concert and identified as the embodiment of 'that very ideal of which he had dreamed for so many years and had eventually lost hope of ever encountering' (p. 366). On seeing her for the second time, 'he froze to the spot, and his legs buckled under him; he almost fell, seeing on the wall a portrait of her whom he had seen at the concert, for whom he had so long searched in vain' (p. 367). All but silent throughout the story, and nameless in its first half, Ekaterina seems less, in the end, her husband's toy than the instrument of a vengeful fate, a doll that has become the residence of a malign and indefinable, but certainly not human, force.

It is not, though, the mythic archetypes behind Ekaterina's behaviour (which could also be described as 'somnambulic' or 'mesmeric', according to the occult interests of the early nineteenth century), that finally dominate Kapnist-Skalon's narrative. It is, rather, the anxious and harassed attempt on the part of the narrator herself to apportion blame for marital conflict, while avoiding any explanation of motive. The governing principle is *rien compendre et rien pardonner*. At the same time, the memoirist's task is vexed by her uncertainty about who really is more guilty, the wife or the husband. At first, she seems wholly on Ekaterina's side:

> How delighted I was by this wonderful being [*sushchestvo*], in whose soul the principle of sublimity was ensconced [*imevshee v dushe svoei nachalo vsego prekrasnogo*] and who was prepared to love with her whole soul the one to whom she had entrusted her life. And all could have come into being [*osushchestvit'sya*] if it had not been for the unhappy [*neschastnaya*] system of Petr Nikolaevich, which later brought about the unhappiness [*neschast'e*] of the whole of the rest of their life. Loving his wife passionately, he tried to distance himself from her and to be as brusque as possible with her, assuming this would increase her love for him. But that was where he was mistaken. (*KS*, p. 369)

Kapnist-Skalon's opinion of the unhappy marriage is expressed in her unconscious, and stylistically clumsy, repetition of *sushchestvo* in *osushchestvit'sya* and *neschastnaya* in *neschast'e*. The realisation promised in (if not by) the wife is negated by the unhappy (or ominous, unlucky — the Russian term is ambiguous) ideas of the husband. At the same time, the word *osushchestvit'*, 'to bring into being', introduces the important notion of Ekaterina as an artefact, and hence something beyond blame. As though to emphasise her sexless innocence, Ekaterina is referred to at key points by neuter nouns — 'like a child [*kak ditya*] she felt no particular attraction to him [when she agreed to the engagement]' (*KS*, p. 368); 'I was delighted by this wonderful being [*chudnoe sushchestvo*] (p. 369); 'Sometimes, from afar, in her light toilette, with her bright ringlets flowing on to her shoulders, she seemed like a tender being of the air [*nezhnoe vozdushnoe sushchestvo*]' (ibid.). Ekaterina is also juxtaposed, at one point, to a more ambiguous dark beauty, Baroness Berwick, who spends long evenings playing chess and smoking a pipe with another of Kapnist-Skalon's cousins (pp. 369–70). Though we are told that Baron Berwick preferred his Baroness to wear the short white dresses that had been her uniform in the young ladies' pension where she was educated, the accoutrements of innocence here have a parodic or grotesque resonance. The innocence of Ekaterina, on the other hand, is meant to be taken on trust.

Even the death of Ekaterina's first child in babyhood does not reflect badly on her: 'A child [*rebenok*] herself and an inexperienced mother, she did not know how to look after him' (*KS*, p. 371), while the details given of her husband's behaviour suggest that this went beyond seemly grief — he not only withdraws from his wife emotionally, but also suggests a suicide pact. Their trip abroad seems at first to restore reason to some degree: 'they lived like brother and sister [...] and their feelings towards each other cooled, though they did remain on friendly terms' (ibid.).

However, having narrated this linking section of her tale in neutral tones, Kapnist-Skalon again begins to display bias, this time in favour of Petr Nikolaevich. Describing how Ekaterina, previously wary of male attention, fell in love with Bobarykin and was permitted to marry him (in the Greek Orthodox Church, which recognised such second marriages), the memoirist does not conceal her alliance with Petr Nikolaevich: 'So her fate and that of my unhappy [*neschastnyi*] cousin was sealed' (*KS*, p. 373). Now he, in her description, is transformed from stern prison warder to wise counsellor and confidant, addressed by his wife as 'friend and benefactor', who is always ready to offer friendship and protection. Kapnist-Skalon emphasises his extraordinary complaisance in agreeing, after Ekaterina's return to Russia, to legitimise her daughters by Bobarykin (this was required because a second marriage was not recognised by Russian law), although a condition of granting the divorce had been that she should stay out of the country.

From now on, Kapnist-Skalon's attitude is generally hostile, though with occasional concessions to Ekaterina's position. She notes Ekaterina's 'caustic smile' [*yazvitel'naya ulybka*] when observing Kapnist's Italian mistress, but comments:

> Although I no longer preserved [my former] sincere relations with Ekaterina Armanovna, who had somewhat declined in my opinion, and whom I could not now love as I once had, yet seeing her always sad and pensive, I involuntarily felt pity for her, all the more because in all that had happened I was more inclined to blame my cousin, who, had he not followed his own rather eccentric schemes, might have made what he wanted of her, and then they would both have been happy. (*KS*, p. 376)

Yet only a paragraph later Kapnist-Skalon is describing Ekaterina as 'a thankless and ungrateful woman'. From this point her immorality is emphasised. After being expelled to Italy for her liaison with the student, she 'did not change her dissipated way of life' (*KS*, p. 378). Indeed, she immediately began an affair with the son of her Italian landlord: 'She took full possession of this Italian [*zavladela sovershenno*] [...] who in his turn availed himself of the opportunity to swindle her conclusively' (ibid.). When received back into her husband's house in Venice, 'she behaved so badly, giving herself over to her fatal passions' that the (in the author's perception) long-suffering Kapnist was again forced to eject her. Yet he continued to receive her in his house 'like a distant female acquaintance' (*kak storonnyuyu zhenshchinu*) (p. 379) — a clinching phrase that underlines both her feminine gender and her pariah status.

Though Kapnist-Skalon stated two paragraphs earlier (*KS*, p. 378) 'I do not know what happened to her after that', she in fact draws the threads together tightly, using her cousin's correspondence as authority for describing Ekaterina's fate. 'I can see from his letters to me that they maintain the best relations' (p. 379). This minor contradiction — Kapnist-Skalon alleges that she does not know, then that she does know, the fate of Ekaterina — parallels a much larger contradiction, between Ekaterina as victim and Ekaterina as main instigator of her own and her husband's fate. This supposedly real woman combines in one person the polarities of ingénue and femme fatale, Mariya Volkonskaya and Agrafenya Zakrevskaya (to name two famous beauties of the 1820s, contemporaries of Ekaterina d'Allonville), or their fictional counterparts Tatiana Larina (*Evgeny Onegin*) and Zinaida Vol'skaya ('The guests arrived at the dacha') in Pushkin, Eda (in *Eda*) and Nina (*The Ball*) in Baratynsky, Eleonskaya and Baroness Reichman (in Mariya Zhukova's 'Baron Reichman'), to name only a few examples. From sexless *ditya* Ekaterina becomes *storonnyaya zhenshchina*, the woman whose sexuality makes her both absolutely classifiable and absolutely unclassifiable, something beyond the boundaries of decent society and polite discourse. Thoroughly feminised, even in a grammatical sense, she is at the same time unsexed, as she trades money for sexual favours (with her Italian gigolo, as one might anachronistically name him). Though she may symbolically 'play the role of mother' (the actual phrase used) at her stepdaughter's wedding (*KS*, p. 379), Petr Nikolaevich, in the last part of the story, in fact acts in a manner far more consonant with the role of mother as understood at the time, counselling and nurturing his former wife, daughter, and stepdaughters, and withdrawing from the public and sexually-charged *beau monde* to domestic quietude, alone in Wiesbaden. Forsaking his early role as Bluebeard, the man who acts as his wife's jailor, Petr Nikolaevich has espoused the traditional female recourse of boundless magnanimity towards those who do him wrong.

Finally, Kapnist-Skalon cannot make her mind up whom to blame (her conclusion is strikingly unmoralistic) because both Ekaterina Armanovna and Petr Nikolaevich are double personalities, whose two halves neither determine nor even closely relate to each other. The later Ekaterina cannot be predicted from the earlier, any more than the later Petr's self-sacrificing magnanimity seems in keeping with his original egotistical authoritarianism (his stern regime was instituted, let us remember, to make his wife love him, rather than for her benefit).

But if there is no urgent internal logic in the development of personality here, there is an external causative force that emerges by default, and which becomes clear if Kapnist-Skalon's tale is set in the context of its time. This tale of a motherless girl (Ekaterina's father was a widower) raises the question of who should be responsible for women's moral and sentimental development. Kapnist-Skalon repeatedly suggests that it is the husband — her greatest criticism of Petr Nikolaevich, indeed, is that he failed as an educator ('Had he not followed his own rather eccentric schemes, [he] might have made what he wanted of her, and then they would both have been happy', *KS*, p. 376). Yet Ekaterina's 'ingratitude' is not wholly the product of her husband's aborted plans; a pre-existing and recalcitrant wilfulness emanates from her. A husband-centred concept of wifely education, with the wife as *tabula rasa* for his ten commandments, vies with the idea that Ekaterina, as adult wife, is responsible for her own fate.

The history of Pushkin's notoriously troubled and much mythologised marriage, as it may be reconstructed from the poet's letters to his wife Natalia Nikolaevna, née Goncharova, bears, up to its denouement (which was, of course, the tragedy of a fatal duel rather than the farce of a bungled elopement), a striking resemblance to that of the Kapnist-Allonville alliance. A man of fully formed character, indeed on the verge of middle age (by the standards of the time), marries a much younger woman, a celebrated beauty, whom he tries to shape, morally speaking, according to his tastes, vacillating as he does so between pride and jealousy at her social and sexual success. (As Pushkin's 1831 poem 'No, I do not value stormy pleasures' reveals, educating his wife's sexual responses was an important duty of the husband as tutor.) Unable, or unwilling, to remove his wife from harm's way physically as Kapnist had done (that is, from the town to the country), Pushkin attempted to place a barrier of propriety between her and the moral laissez-faire of aristocratic St Petersburg. The letters that he wrote during his absences from Natalia, and most particularly in 1833–34, are full of anxious attempts to instil in her a sense of prudence and *comme il faut*:

> I don't forbid you coquetry, but I do demand coldness, decency, grandeur from you — not to speak of irreproachable behaviour, by which I don't mean *tone*, but something else, the most significant thing. (8 October 1833).

> Watch out, don't turn into a little girl yourself, don't forget you've already got two children and you miscarried the third, take care of yourself, keep an eye on things: don't dance too much, only take short walks, and above all come down to the country. (19 April 1834).

> Don't let father into the children, he might frighten them or who knows what else. Above all, take care when you've got your periods — don't read filthy books [*skvernye knigi*] from grandfather's library, don't foul your imagination [*ne marai*], wifey. I'll allow you as much coquetry as you want. Don't ride horses that are too wild. (20/22 April 1834)

> You may be young, but you're already the mother of a family, and I'm sure that it won't be harder for you to carry out the duties of a good mother, than it is for you to carry out the duties of an honest and good wife. Dependency and [financial] perturbation are frightful in a family, and no success on vanity's part can reward one with peace and satisfaction. Now there's a moral for you. (26 May 1834).

Leavened as they are by self-parody ('now there's a moral for you'), affection, and humour, these moral lectures are still based on a complete asymmetry of authority between writer and addressee, as is perhaps still clearer when Pushkin is pleased with his wife. 'What a clever little woman you are! what a sweetie! what a long letter! and how full of sense [*del'no*]', he exclaims on 25 September 1832. 'If you're clever, that is, if you keep calm and in good health, then I'll bring you what they call a great big present from the country' [*tovaru na sto rublei, kak govoritsya*], he promises a year later (2 September 1833). As with the Kapnist case, it is childbearing that provokes especially vehement assertions of the need for responsibility: if Ekaterina was taken abroad as a punishment for the neglect of her child, Natalia is constantly reminded of the need to avoid frivolity in the cause of a healthy pregnancy: apart from short walks, the favoured exercise is promenading round the drawing room (10 December 1831). Advice on managing the household is also given — don't spoil the children, don't let the servants get above themselves. Rather than an adult on an equal footing with her husband, Natalia emerges as a charming child in constant need of direction; no wonder that Pushkin is able to tease her by commenting (again in conjunction with advice to be careful in pregnancy): 'Woman, as Galiani says, *est un animal naturellement faible et malade*. What kind of helpers or workers are you? You only work with your little feet at balls and help your husbands squander their money' (14 July 1834).[20]

Natalia's one surviving letter to her husband (a postscript to a missive of her mother's) is bland and anonymous, resembling the impeccably dull letters that Tolstoi's Natasha Rostova sent to Prince Andrei, after getting her mother to correct the grammar and spelling.[21] It is difficult to say whether her half of the correspondence, had it survived, would do much to alter the impression given by Pushkin's letters, of a naive young girl whose husband's epistolary relationship with her is as much parental as conjugal.

To be sure, there was less inequality in the Pushkin-Goncharova match than the Kapnist-Allonville union. Pushkin may have attempted to confine Natalia to her room by long-distance command, but did not actually lock her up, and the occasional brusqueness in his letters emanates from a defensive recognition of his own sexual obsession with his wife, which he displaces on to male society in general: 'You enjoy having men running after you like dogs after a bitch, with their tails in the air and sniffing your arse: a fine thing to enjoy!' (30 October 1833).[22] More often the tone of his letters is affectionate, occasionally chiding, if with an underlying note sometimes of slightly claustrophobic desperation (of the teacher with a stubborn or slow pupil, perhaps). But the differences in nuance do not detract from the fact that in both cases a husband attempts to provide his wife with the education with which, according to certain perceptions, she should have been furnished by her mother.

Kapnist-Skalon and Pushkin both in their very different ways lay bare a con-

---

20   Pushkin, *PSS*, xv, nos. 851, 918, 919, 947, 770, 841; xiv, no. 711; xv, no. 979.
21   N. I. Goncharova and N. N. Pushkina, letter of 14 May 1834, Pushkin, *PSS*, xv, no. 939. A number of Pushkina's letters to her brother, mostly concerning Pushkin's money worries, have survived, and are available in *Vokrug Pushkina: neizvestnye pis'ma N. N. Pushkinoi i ee sester E. N. i A. N. Goncharovykh*, ed. by I. Obodovskaya and M. Dement'ev, 2nd edn (Moscow: Sovetskaya Rossiya, 1975), pp. 117–37. See also Stephanie Sandler's fine study of the Pushkina myth, 'Pushkin's Last Love — Natal'ia Nikolaevna in Russian Culture', in *Gender Restructuring in Russian Culture: Conference Papers — Helsinki, August 1992*, ed. by E. Mantysaari, M. Liljeström, and A. Rosenholm (Tampere: University of Tampere, 1993), pp. 209–21.
22   Pushkin, *PSS*, xv, no. 854.

sensus about the content of women's education, which should instil in its objects a code of self-restraint and self-sacrifice, a sense of women's privileged yet perilous situation as moral arbiters. Kapnist-Skalon's phrase *storonnyaya zhenshchina* accepts the existence of a horizontal arena for women's behaviour such as that sketched out by Lambert. A *sententia* of Pushkin's in a letter of 6 May 1836, 'Modesty is the main ornament of your sex', could come straight from Fénelon or Lambert; so, too, could his torrents of advice in other letters on the treatment of servants (firm but kind), small children (ditto), the avoidance of possibly corrupting books, and the need for judicious social behaviour. But Kapnist-Skalon's strictures on her cousin's manner of re-educating his wife, and Pushkin's obvious irritation at Natalia Nikolaevna's failure to grasp the elementary principles of good conduct, also point to an ambivalence in the writers about whether or not a husband should be concerned with improving his wife's manners and regulating her morals. A similar ambivalence is evident also in the historian Prince M. M. Shcherbatov's pioneering Slavophile polemic, *On the Destruction of Morals in Russia*. Shcherbatov lays the 'destruction of morals' in Russia at the door of women rulers, particularly Catherine II, whose misdemeanours indicate the awful consequences of granting women unnatural authority. Yet he also approves the 'softening of manners' that was brought about by Peter I's introduction of mixed-sex gatherings (*assamblei*) to the Russian court.[23]

The dilemma of these writers was partly traceable to the character of pre-Petrine culture, where women's moral authority was an outlandish concept. But apart from the effects of the historical *longue durée*, other matters also contributed to the doubts and anxieties expressed by Kapnist-Skalon, Pushkin, and others. The first was the telescoping of chronology so often evident in Russian importation of Western ideas. Fénelon and Lambert, with their emphasis on women's need for autonomy within marriage, arrived on Russian soil only slightly earlier than the writings of other Westerners from a significantly later generation, which celebrated a very different kind of marriage, one where women's central duty was to please their husbands. Such writers included Marie Leprince de Beaumont, author of massively popular Socratic dialogues for the schoolroom in which a governess, 'Mrs Morality', instructed her youthful pupils, 'Miss Impetuous' and others, on the rules of good conduct and rational behaviour. Especially popular was *Magasin des enfans*, translated as *Detskoe uchilishche*, which had gone into twelve Russian editions, in print-runs as high as two thousand copies, by 1800. The book also circulated in French: a copy of an edition published in Paris in 1797 was in Pushkin's library.[24]

23 Pushkin, *PSS*, XVI, no. 1190; M. M. Shcherbatov, *On the Corruption of Morals in Russia*, ed. and trans. by A. Lentin (Cambridge: Cambridge University Press, 1969), p. 134.
24 M. Leprince de Beaumont, *Magasin des enfans, ou dialogues d'une sage gouvernante avec ses élèves de la première distinction*, par Madame Leprince de Beaumont (Lyon: J.-B. Reguilliat, 1758); translated into Russian as *Detskoe uchilishche, ili Nravouchitel'nye razgovory mezhdu razumnoyu uchitel'nitseyu i znatnymi raznykh let uchenitsami sochinennye na frantsuzskom yazyke gospozheyu Le Prens' de Bomont*, trans. by P. S. Svistunov, 4 vols (St Petersburg: Tipografiya Sukhoputnogo kadetskogo korpusa, 1761–67; repr. 1776, 1788); another translation appeared in 1792, reprinted 1794, 1800; parts of the book appeared separately in 1763, 1767, 1784, and 1795, and an edition in French was published in Moscow, 1795. (See *SK*, nos. 3623–31, and *Svodnyi katalog knig na inostrannykh yazykakh, napechatannykh v Rossii*

Leprince de Beaumont was, indeed, so well-known in Russia that Louise d'Épinay's *Les Conversations d'Émilie*, a graceful and lively collection of dialogues between a mother and her young daughter, were attributed to Beaumont when first translated into Russian in 1784, and given a title, *The School for Young Girls* [*Uchilishche yunykh devits*], that imitated the titles of the latter's works in Russian.[25]

There was considerable irony in this, given that Épinay, a feminist known for her polemics with Diderot, very much conformed to the older 'Lambertian' model of autonomy within marriage. Where Lambert had stressed the need for women to be independent of their husbands in terms of moral judgement, Leprince went so far, in *Magasin des adolescentes*, as to suggest that even modest attire should be given up if the husband required it. Furthermore, one of the moral tales inserted in Lambert's *Magasin des enfans* was her famous retelling of *La Belle et la Bête*, in which a young woman learns to respect and love an apparently forbidding husband whom she has not chosen for herself. (The woeful tale of Kapnist-Skalon's cousin's marriage can be interpreted as an abortive reconfiguration of this plot, in which Beauty's capriciousness does not allow the magic of the Beast to work.)[26]

By the 1780s, Russians who could read French were also able to absorb the ideas of Madame de Genlis, another advocate of educating girls to suit their husbands. Her treatise-as-epistolary-novel *Adèle et Théodore* (1781), composed as a series of letters written by Adèle and Théodore's mother, set out quite a formidable syllabus of reading for Adèle, ranging from Aquinas to Cervantes, from Corneille to Thomson and Shakespeare, from Ariosto through Petrarch and Molière to Boileau,

---

v XVIII veke, 3 vols (Leningrad: Nauka, 1984–87), no. 1714). *Magasin des adolescentes, ou dialogues entre une sage gouvernante et plusieurs de ses élèves de la première distinction*, par Madame Le Prince [*sic*] de Beaumont, pour servir de suite au Magasin des enfants (London: J. Nourse, 1764); translated into Russian as *Yunosheskoe uchilishche, ili Nravouchitel'nye razgovory mezhdu razumnoyu uchitel'nitseyu i mnogimi znatnymi uchenitsami, sochinennoe na frantsuzskom yazyke g-zheyu le Prens de Bomont, a na rossiiskoi perevedennye v Troitskoi seminarii uchitelem, chto nyne M[oskovskogo] P[okrovskogo] s[obora] i p[rotoerei] Ivanom Kharlamovym*, 4 vols ([Moscow]: Universitetskaya tipografiya, 1774; repr. 1788) (see *SK*, nos. 3462–63). *Instructions pour les jeunes dames qui entrent dans le monde, et se marient. Leurs devoirs dans cet état, et envers leurs enfants. Pour servir de suite au Magasin des adolescentes. Par Mad.* LEPRINCE DE BEAUMONT. *Edition faite sous les yeux de l'Auteur, sur un nouveau Manuscrit plus correct et plus ample que celui de l'édition de* LONDRES, 3 vols (Lyon: J.-B. Reguilliat, 1764); translated into Russian as *Uchilishche devits. Sochineniya g. Bomonta [!]. Perevedeno s frantsuzskogo na rossiiskoi* (Moscow: tipografiya Galchenkova, 1784: first vol. only); *Nastavlenie molodym gospozham, vstupayushchim v svet i brachnye soyuzy, sluzhashchee prodolzheniem Yunoshekomu uchilishchu, gde iz"yasnyayutsya dolzhnosti kak v rassuzhdenii ikh samikh, tak i v rassuzhdenii ikh detei. Sochinenie gzhi le Prens de Bomont, perevel s frantsuzskogo Efim Runich'*, 4 vols (Moscow: Universitetskaya tipografiya, 1788); and as *Pravila dlya obshchezhitiya, ili Nastavlenie devitsam, soderzhashchee svyashchennuyu i svetskuyu istorii i geografiyu, sochinenie g. de Bomont. Perevela s frantsuzskogo M. M. T.*, 5 vols (Moscow: tipografiya Vinkovskogo, 1800–01).

25   L. d'Épinay, *Les Conversations d'Émilie* (Leipzig: Crusius, 1774); 'M. Leprens de Bomont', *Uchilishche yunykh devits, ili Razgovory materi s docher'yu* (Moscow: Vol'naya tipografiya I. Lopukhina, 1784) (*SK*, no. 3641) (the editors state 'Frantsuzskii original ne ustanovlen'). Épinay's book appeared in Russian under its own name in 1798, but was not as popular as Leprince de Beaumont's works (though Karamzin had certainly read Épinay: see W. Mills Todd III, *The Familiar Letter as a Literary Genre in the Age of Pushkin* (Princeton, NJ: Princeton University Press, 1976), p. 96).

26   On Leprince's 'La Belle et la Bête', see Warner's interesting comments in her *From the Beast to the Blonde*, pp. 292–97.

Pope, Locke, and even (after her marriage) Rousseau, and including women writers such as Mary Wortley Montagu and Madame de Lafayette. However, Adèle, as her mother made clear, had been prevented from consuming unduly imaginative works, not because these were likely to corrupt her, but because women were born for 'a dependant and monotonous life', and so 'genius is for them a useless and dangerous gift' ('le génie est pour eux un don inutile et dangereux').[27] Rather than the key to resourcefulness after marriage, education that develops the mind (and does not simply furnish a woman with the means of entertaining her husband) is now seen as a threat to conjugal stability.

The competition between these alternative Western models of marriage was exacerbated after the death of Catherine II. Catherine's male successors, Paul I, Alexander I, and especially Nicholas I, took care to circumscribe the symbolic role of the royal consort, and to emphasise a tsaritsa's status as dependent wife on every possible occasion. Where Catherine and indeed her predecessor Elizabeth, as absolute monarchs, had invoked the stereotype of 'mother of the nation', 'maternity' was now a quality firmly subordinated to the final masculine and militaristic authority of the Tsar himself.[28] Accordingly, when Alexandra Fedorovna was portrayed as an idealised mother, in Zhukovsky's famous ode 'Epistle to the Grand Duchess Alexandra Fedorovna on the Birth of Grand Duke Alexander Nikolaevich' (1818), the representation of royal maternity stressed nurture in the sense of loving watchfulness and protection against harm rather than active intellectual guidance:

> Теперь, едва проснувшийся душой,
> Пред матерью, как будто пред Судьбой,
> Беспечно он играет в колыбели,
> И Радости младые прилетели
> Ее покой прекрасный оживлять;
> Житейское от ней еще далеко...
> Храни ее, заботливая мать;
> Твоя любовь — всевидящее око;
> В твоей любви — святая благодать.[29]

[Now, scarcely awakened with his soul, | Before his mother, as it were before Fate,
He plays in his cradle, free of care, | And the young Joys have flown in | To enliven her beautiful chamber. | Quotidian cares are still far from her... | Guard the cradle, careful mother; | Your love is an all-seeing eye, | And in your love is sacred grace.]

---

27 S. de Genlis, *Adèle et Théodore, ou lettres sur l'éducation, contenant tous les principes relatifs aux trois differens plans d'éducation, des princes, des jeunes personnes, et des hommes*, 3 vols (Maastricht: chez J. E. Dufour & Phil. Roux, 1783), I, 31. Russian translations appeared in 1791, 1792, and 1794 (*SK*, nos. 2209, 2216). Genlis's novel occupies a sort of intermediate genre between the educational treatise and didactic fiction, in which she also specialised. Her works and those of Sophie Cottin (author, inter alia, of *Élisabeth, ou les éxiles de Sibérie* (1806) and *Malvina* (1800) were very popular in Russia).
28 On empress cult, see R. Wortman, *Scenarios of Power: Myth and Ceremony in Russian Monarchy*, 2 vols (Princeton, NJ: Princeton University Press, 1995), I, 250–51.
29 Wortman also analyses this poem: and see his *Scenarios of Power*, too, for a wonderful account of Alexandra Fedorovna as assiduously infantilised by her husband (pp. 260–65).

The phrase 'the all-seeing eye' attributes to mother-love the power of the masculine divinity, but the central image is that of the 'Protection' of the Mother of God: the iconic representation of a guarantee of familial, imperial, and national security that rests on benevolence rather than active intervention. Even during Catherine's reign, an 'ideology of separate spheres' had made itself felt in some areas, as, for example, in the Empress's own reading primer for children, which distinguished carefully between the citizenship duties of men and the domestic responsibilities of women, but under Paul and his successors the ideology became next to all-pervasive.[30]

The 'ideology of separate spheres' combined with the rise of the doctrine that a wife's desires should be absolutely subordinated to her husband's to mean that, under the patronage of Maria Feodorovna and especially Alexandra Feodorovna, Smol'nyi and the other institutes lost their intellectual glitter and increasingly became places that prepared women not so much for being married as for reaching that state. As one former inmate of a conservative inclination, Aleksandra Smirnova, recalled: 'Our late benefactress [Maria Feodorovna] never lost sight of her wards [vospitannitsy]. They could always find support and help when they visited St Petersburg. Those who emerged from her institutes were sincere daughters and good wives and mothers'.[31]

If official, imperial ideology very definitely saw the tsaritsa transformed from matriarch to madonna, and a concomitant emphasis on the family duties (and above all the wifely duties) of the tsaritsa's subjects, an assault on women's cultural authority had also been taking place, since the late eighteenth century, from a quite different direction: among those Russians opposed to autocracy who had been influenced by French libertarian philosophy. One important advocate of education by the husband had been Rousseau, the fifth part of whose Émile had laid out a blueprint for women's education that assaulted institutionalised training, poured scorn on female intellectuals ('I would a hundred times rather have a homely girl, simply and crudely brought up, than a learned lady and a wit who would make a literary circle of my house and instal herself as its president'), and presented Sophie as a properly empty vessel to be filled with Émile's ideas ('Her mind knows nothing, but it is trained to learn; it is well-tilled soil ready for the seed. [...] She will suit him far better than a learned woman [savante]; he will have the pleasure of teaching her everything').[32]

30 Catherine II, *Rossiiskaya azbuka dlya obucheniya yunoshestva chteniyu, Napechatannaya dlya obshchestvennykh shkol po Vysochaishemu poveleneniyu* (St Petersburg: pri Imperatorskoi Akademii Nauk, [1790]), nos. 88, 98 (*SK*, no. 2177).
31 A. O. Smirnova-Rosset, *Vospominaniya* (Moscow: Pravda, 1990) p. 84. On Catherine as educator see I. Betskoi, *Ustav vospitaniya dvukh sot blagorodnykh devits uchrezhdennogo eya velichestvom Gosudaryneyu Ekaterinoyu Votoroyu....* (St Petersburg: [Senatskaya tipografiya], 1764) (*SK*, no. 556). On Smol'nyi, see N. P. Cherepnin, *Imperatorskoe Vospitatel'noe obshchestvo blagorodnykh devits: Istoricheskii ocherk 1764–1914*, 3 vols (St Petersburg: Gosudarstvennaya tipografiya, 1914–15). See also J. L. Black, *Citizens for the Fatherland: Education, Educators and Pedagogical Ideals in Eighteenth-Century Russia* (Boulder, CO: East European Quarterly, 1979), Chapter 7; and, on education and educational theory, Carol S. Nash, 'Educating New Mothers: Women and the Russian Enlightenment', *History of Education Quarterly*, 21.3 (1981), 301–16.
32 J. J. Rousseau, *Émile, ou de l'éducation*, ed. by C. Wirz and P. Burgelin (Paris: Gallimard, 1995),

Naturally, this was deeply uncongenial to Catherine II, who in 1763, shortly after she came to the throne, banned the import or sale of *Émile*. A 1779 edition of Part v (as *Émile and Sophie, or the Well-Bred Lovers*) was heavily cut, omitting the passages above. However, it did still make Sophie's destiny as virtuous wife clear. (Indeed, the Russian text, by substituting *blagopoluchie* (well-being) for 'happiness', places a greater emphasis on duty than the original):

> No one can have a higher ideal of a virtuous woman, and she is not in the least daunted by this; but she would rather think of a virtuous man, a man of true worth; she knows that she is made for such a man, that she is worthy of him, that she can make him as happy as he will make her; she is sure she will know him when she sees him; the only difficulty is to find him.[33]

The suppression of Rousseau's more egregious outbursts of anti-feminism, during Catherine's reign, seems only to have made these the more attractive to young democrats who saw her reign as the epitome of tyrannical female misrule in any case.[34]

There is no uncontestable proof that Pushkin had himself read *Émile*, but if not, he would doubtless have encountered Rousseau's ideas second-hand.[35] Certainly, he was familiar with the anti-feminist writings of Diderot, and also with the biologically determinist opinions of Galiani (quoted in his jibe to Natalia Nikolaevna: 'La femme est un animal naturellement faible et malade').[36]

Galiani, a favourite of Pushkin and the Arzamas circle generally, was a minor Franco-Italian writer and wit whose works were much appreciated throughout Europe in the late eighteenth and early nineteenth centuries. The description of woman as 'naturally weak and sick' comes from a short essay entitled 'Fragment of a Dialogue on Women' ('Croquis d'un dialogue sur les femmes', 1784), which is a direct assault on the argument voiced by Louise d'Épinay, a friend of Galiani, that women's intellectual inferiority was due to the nature of their education. In the 'Fragment', the *Chevalier* remonstrates against this opinion, stating that the natural weakness of women is demonstrated by the relative feebleness of female savages and animals; by the fact that they spend six days a month, i.e. a fifth of their lives, indisposed, before pregnancies are taken into account; that they are capricious and

---

pp. 604, 605–06; *Émile*, trans. by Barbara Foxley (London: Everyman's Library, 1992), pp. 445, 447.
33 Ibid., p. 588; pp. 431–32. Zh. Zh. Russo, *Emil' i Sofiya, ili blagovospitannye lyubovniki* (Moscow: Universitetskaya tipografiya, 1779), p. 18 (*SK*, no. 6234).
34 For the circulation of Rousseau's ideas among select groups of the educated elite, see L. N. Kiseleva, 'S. N. Glinka i kadetskii korpus (iz istorii "sentimental'nogo vospitaniya" v Rossii)', *Uchenye zapiski Tartuskogo gosudarstvennogo universiteta*, 604 (1982), 48–63.
35 A complete Rousseau in Pushkin's library has uncut pages for the *Émile* volumes: B. L. Modzalevsky, *Biblioteka A. S. Pushkina: bibliograficheskoe opisanie* (St Petersburg: tipografiya Imperatorskoi Akademii Nauk, 1910), no. 1332; no references are listed in the index to *PSS*. However, as has been pointed out in other cases, neither of these types of evidence is definitive — Pushkin's edition of Johnson's *Lives of the English Poets* is also uncut, and he does not refer to this in his letters etc., but an acquaintance testified that he had read it (see note to ibid., no. 1032). In the case of *Émile*, the obvious conclusion is that he read the novel well before he acquired the complete works.
36 See above.

irritable, like all invalids. Education cannot be used to demonstrate the contrary, since it follows instinct, rather than leading it. Only religion, for which women have a greater innate propensity [*dose*] — while men enjoy a greater capacity for intellectual evolution — can bring about anything approaching equality (and that, it is implied, in another world).[37]

Pushkin's oblique evocation of all this may, of course, have been a joke, intended to provoke Natalia into an amusingly indignant riposte. However, his citation of Galiani's article reflects the heightened interest in female biology that was beginning to make itself felt in 1830s Russia. In 1837, Verevkin's scurrilous story, *The Woman Writer*, had adduced anatomical reasons why women should stick to domestic duties and not attempt literature.[38] Sentimental treatment of 'natural' motherhood (as in Aleksandra Smirnova's light-hearted reference to a dog of hers that neglected her 'maternal duties') was accompanied by an increasingly coercive emphasis on maternal duties (in Mariya Zhukova's story 'Baron Reichman' (1837) a mother who has engaged in public dalliance with her husband's lieutenant ends up by losing her son), and a decline in the importance of the ideal of intellectual maternity. In the 1830s, the relationship between aristocratic protector and *vospitannitsa* increasingly came to stand for exploitation of the subordinate, rather than symbolising the generosity and maternal tenderness of the protector. Bryullov's portrait of Samoilova can be seen as the last flowering of a tradition that, in literary and artistic circles at least, was close to withering away.[39]

What was more, Pushkin was no straightforward family man, but a creative writer from a generation who had reacted against Sentimentalism's cult of feminine taste and the female 'ideal reader'. In a text written a year before his marriage, 'At the beginning of life I remember a school' (1830), a poem in Dantean terzinas (a form associated in his work with confessional autobiography), he makes a characteristically ambiguous recognition of women's role as guardians of morality and by extension of aesthetics. In the poem, the lyric hero evokes the part played in his early education by a woman:

---

37 *Opere de Ferdinando Galiani*, in *Illuministi italiani. La letteratura italiana. Tomo VI*, ed. by Furio Diaz and Luciano Guerci (Milan & Naples: Ricciardi, 1975), pp. 635–42; The material on d'Épinay comes from the editors' introduction to the text, p. 625.
38 N. N. Verevkin (as 'Rakhmannyi'), 'Zhenshchina-pisatel'nitsa', *Biblioteka dlya chteniya*, 23.1 (1837), 19–134.
39 Among the better-known literary assaults on the institution of the *vospitannitsa* are Pushkin's own *Queen of Spades* (where Liza, after miserable years acting as companion to the self-centred elderly countess, acquires a ward herself, no doubt with the intention of 'abjection displacement') and *A Novel in Letters*, and Tolstoy's *Anna Karenina*, where Anna's neglect of her own daughter Annie, in favour of her adopted English ward Hannah, is used by Tolstoy as an oblique indictment of her artificial and hypocritical life with Vronsky. Portraits by women writers of the *vospitannitsa* (many equally critical) include Mariya Zhukova's *The Locket* (*Medal'on*). On this topic, see also J. Harussi, 'Women's Social Roles as Depicted by Women Writers in Early Nineteenth-Century Russian Fiction', in *Issues in Russian Literature before 1917: Selected Papers of the Third World Congress for Soviet and East European Studies*, ed. by J. D. Clayton (Columbus, OH: Slavica, 1989), pp. 35–48; Joe Andrew, 'Mothers and Daughters in Russian Literature of the First Half of the Nineteenth Century', *Slavonic and East European Review*, 73.1 (1995), 37–60.

> В начале жизни школу помню я;
> Там нас, детей беспечных, было много;
> Неровная и резвая семья.
>
> Смиренная, одетая убого,
> Но видом величавая жена
> Над школою надзор хранила строго.
>
> Толпою нашею окружена,
> Приятным, сладким голосом, бывало,
> С младенцами беседует она.
>
> Ее чела я помню покрывало
> И очи светлые, как небеса,
> Но я вникал в ее беседы мало.
>
> Меня смущала строгая краса
> Ее чела, спокойных уст и взоров,
> И полные святыни словеса.[40]

[At the beginning of life I remember a school, | There were many of us there, children free from care, | A motley and mischievous family. || Humble, and dressed poorly, | But majestic in her appearance, a lady | Kept stern guard over the school. || Surrounded by a crowd of us, | In a pleasant, sweet voice, from time to time | She would speak to us infants. || I remember the veil on her brow, | And her eyes radiant as the heavens, | But I understood little of her conversations. || I was constrained by the stern beauty | Of her brow, her calm lips and gazes | And her words full of holiness.]

This transmutation of the muse into ideal schoolmistress, as well as the source of poetic inspiration, follows the traditions of Russian Sentimentalism, one of whose key texts, Karamzin's 'Epistle to Women' ('Poslanie k zhenshchinam', 1796) had eulogised women in their capacities as ideal readers of and sources of poetry, guides to the philosopher, and educators of the young:

> С любовью матери он мило расцветает,
> Из глаз ее в себе луч кротости впивает,
> И зреет нежною душой.[41]

[With the love of his mother he [the baby] sweetly blossoms, | From her eyes he drinks in the ray of gentleness, | And ripens with his tender soul.]

Karamzin goes on to speak of his own motherless childhood, which has left only 'that sweet, sacred image | imprinted in my breast' ('образ твой священный, милый | в груди моей напечатлен', p. 235).

Though beginning in much the same way as Karamzin's eulogy, Pushkin's poem then takes a turn that is very different from Karamzin's extended celebration of the moral domination of feminine over masculine. It describes a flight from the threatening sternness of the *vospitannitsa*:

---

40 Pushkin, 'V nachale zhizni shkolu pomnyu ya', *PSS*, III, 254.
41 N. Karamzin, 'Poslanie k zhenshchinam', *Aonidy*, I (1796), 234.

> Дичась ее советов и укоров,
> Я про себя превратно толковал
> Понятный смысл правдивых разговоров.
>
> И часто я украдкой убегал
> В великолепный мрак чужого сада,
> Под свод искусственный порфирных скал.

[Shunning her advice and rebukes like a wild creature, | I would pervert in private | The easily comprehensible meaning of her just phrases. || And often I would run off in secret | To the wonderful darkness of another garden | Under the artificial vaults of porphyry cliffs.]

Within the sanctum of this grotto, more congenial, if less morally elevated, company is to be found: 'two demons', one 'the ideal of Delphi' (that is, Apollo, of course), and the other:

> A woman-shaped
> Dubious and false idol
> A magic demon — lying, yet sublime.

This figure is normally glossed by commentators as 'Aphrodite', but is perhaps more likely Hermaphroditos, son of Aphrodite and of Hermes, the patron of liars, a figure about whom Pushkin would have read in Ovid's *Metamorphoses*. Recognising the importance of the tutelary feminine, Pushkin's alter ego at the same time can no longer tolerate a form of aesthetic experience entirely under her guidance.

It may seem a long way from this very abstract perception of women's moral authority to a suspicion of educating mothers, but the link is provided in Karamzin, and at least one text by Pushkin himself draws a parallel between maternal, moral, and literary regulation. In the wickedly ironic dedication to *Ruslan and Lyudmila* (1818), Pushkin sees the mother's supervision of her daughter's reading as an act of censorship, an interference in the proper intercourse (the term seems appropriate) of poet and reader:

> Для вас, души моей царицы,
> Красавицы, для вас одних
> Времен минувших небылицы,
> В часы досугов золотых,
> Под шепот старины болтливой,
> Рукою верной я писал;
> Примите ж вы мой труд игривый!
> Ничьих не требуя похвал,
> Счастлив уж я надеждой сладкой,
> Что дева с трепетом любви
> Посмотрит, может быть украдкой,
> На песни грешные мои.[42]

---

42 Pushkin, *Ruslan i Lyudmila*, *PSS*, IV, 3. In his 'Preface' (*Predislovie*) to the second edition of the poem (1828), Pushkin touched on the same topic, sarcastically twisting Voeikov's suggestion (made in a review in *Syn otechestva*, 43 (1820)) that *Ruslan* should bear the motto 'La mère en défendra le lecture à sa fille' into the distinctly vulgar Russian paraphrase, 'The mother orders her daughter to spit on this tale' ('Mat' docheri velit na etu skazku plyunut') (see *PSS*, IV, 284; gloss given in A. S.

> [For you, enchantresses of my soul, | For you, for you alone, | The fables of past times,
>   In the hours of my golden leisure, | With the whisper of chattering old age in the background, | I have written with a true hand; | Accept my playful work! | Not demanding praise from anyone, | I am happy with the sweet hope | That a maiden, wracked by love's trembling, | May gaze, perhaps secretly, | On my sinful songs.]

Rather than using a claim to female approval as a guarantee of moral elevation, *Ruslan and Lyudmila* trumpets its subversive nature by suggesting that the 'handiwork' on show here appeals to the clandestine tastes of girls reading 'in secret' (that is, away from the vigilant, but fortunately not 'all-seeing', eyes of their mamas, who would undoubtedly — if they were familiar with conduct manuals — forbid the consumption of such a very naughty book).

For the later Pushkin, too, it was not so much a compliment to a work to say that it was liked by ladies, as a compliment to ladies to suggest that they liked a work. The dedications to his *poemy* distinguish firmly between polite compliments to ladies (as in the case of *Poltava*), and more 'literary' addresses to men. And in the unfinished prose fragment 'A Novel in Letters', Liza (a woman who has fled to the country to escape the degradation of the *vospitannitsa* role), observes to her friend: 'It is no wonder that Pushkin and Zhukovskii so love provincial young ladies [*uezdnye baryshni*], since it is they who are the most devoted readers of their work'.[43]

Pushkin's vexed relationship with his wife's upbringing was thus not the symptom of an idiosyncratic misogyny, but part of a cultural complex, a dilemma about moral authority, characteristic of Russian upper-class society of the day on the one hand, and the literary world on the other. Baron Reichman, the main male character in Mariya Zhukova's story of that name, addresses his wife with the ethical impossibility: 'I want you to be free' ('Ya khochu, chtoby ty byla svobodnoi').[44] Pushkin's letters indirectly articulate something of the same contradiction in terms, as he struggles to make Natalia freely accept a view of her behaviour that he has imposed on her.

Though Pushkin was himself unusually well-educated, and his library included at least one very modern book on behaviour, Louis-Aimé Martin's *De l'éducation des mères de famille ou de la civilisation du genre humain par les femmes* (Brussels, 1833), he expressed tastes typical of the conservative Russian gentry when creating his own family life, selecting a wife of little intellectual ambition, and conducting himself, as his sister Ol'ga Pavlishcheva recalled, along the lines of an old-style paterfamilias, not a liberal adherent to Rousseau's principles of 'natural upbringing': 'Aleksandr thrashes his little boy, who's only two, and he beats Masha as well; but on the whole [*vprochem*] he's a tender enough father'.[45]

Pushkin, *Polnoe sobranie sochinenii*, 10 vols (Leningrad: Nauka, 1977), IV, 436).
43   Pushkin, 'Roman v pis'makh' [1829], *PSS*, VI, 46–47.
44   Mariya Zhukova, 'Baron Reikhman', in *Vechera na Karpovke (1837–38)* (Moscow: Sovetskaya Rossiya, 1986), pp. 40–75.
45   See Modzalevsky, *Biblioteka A. S. Pushkina*, no. 1141. Modzalevsky records the pages of this edition as cut, though there are no notes. On Pushkin as paterfamilias, see O. S. Pavlishcheva,

The letters documenting Pushkin's marriage, though they echoed the character of an age when representations of motherhood dominated public discourse, were very definitely private documents whose publication he did not anticipate, and indeed, would have opposed most fiercely.[46] Though this material at least provides an important corrective to the clichéd over-simplification of Pushkin as 'radiant personality' (*svetlaya lichnost*), exploring it at length feels voyeuristic, and it is a relief to turn to those of Pushkin's public, literary writings that examine the dilemma of *vospitanie* with greater detachment and more intellectual freedom than was possible in his agonised private letters. Chief amongst these is *Evgeny Onegin*, Pushkin's most famous literary creation, and far and away his most popular one in Russia.

Initially, Tatiana appears to be yet another representation of moral education by a male partner. The only indications that we have about her upbringing are negative — her mother has *not* taught her to avoid sentimental novels or correspondence with strange men.[47] As a result, Tatiana's first induction into the behaviour of polite society is the scene in which she is taught by Evgenii that young women may not behave in the way that she has done: they may not select their own male partner, and approach him themselves:

« Мечтам и годам нет возврата;
Не обновлю души моей...
Я вас люблю любовью брата,
И, может быть, еще нежней.
Послушайте ж меня без гнева;
Сменит не раз младая дева
Мечтами легкие мечты;
Так деревцо свои листы
Меняет с каждою весною.
Так, видно, небом суждено.
Полюбите вы снова: но...
Учитесь властвовать собою;
Не всякий вас, как я, поймет,
К беде неопытность ведет. »
(*Evgeny Onegin*, Chapter 4, stanza 16)

[There is no turning back dreams and years, | I shall not renew my soul; | I love you with the love of a brother, | And perhaps more tenderly. | Listen to me without anger; | More than once the young maiden | Exchanges dreams for light dreams; | So a little tree its leaves | Changes with every spring. | So, clearly, it is intended by heaven. | You will fall in love again: but... | Learn to control yourself; | Not everyone will understand you as I have, | Inexperience leads to disaster.]

---

letter to N. I. Pavlishchev, 22 November 1835, in *Pis'ma O. S. Pavlishchevoi k muzhu i otsu 1831–1837: Famil'nye bumagi Pushkinykh-Gannibalov* (St Petersburg: Izdatel'stvo Pushkinskogo fonda, 1994), p. 129.

46 On the privacy of Pushkin's letters, see his letter to Natal'ya, 18 May 1834 (*PSS*, xv, no. 942), in which he tells her not to copy his correspondence to her: 'No-one should be received in our bedchamber' ('Nikto ne dolzhen byt' prinyat v nashu spal'nyu').

47 Andrew, 'Mothers and Daughters in Russian Literature of the First Half of the Nineteenth Century', 42–50.

Yet to read *Evgeny Onegin* as a text that advocates conjugal, rather than maternal, education would miss the point. Some commentators (for example, Yury Lotman) have taken at face value the narrator's comment:

> Вы согласитесь, мой читатель
> Что очень мило поступил
> С печальной Таней наш приятель.
> (*Evgeny Onegin*, Chapter 4, stanza 18)

[You will agree, dear reader, that Evgeny treated | Sad Tanya very sweetly.]

But the effect is surely ironic. The next two lines, 'Not for the first time had [Evgeny] revealed | Straightforward nobility of soul' ('Не в первый раз он тут явил | Души прямое благородство') are, to say the least, an odd description of Evgeny's self-centred behaviour so far. An undertow of irony is also evident in the contrast between Evgeny's request to Tatiana not to be 'angry' with him ('Послушайте меня без гнева', Chapter 4, stanza 16), and her actual reaction, 'Not hearing anything through her tears | Hardly breathing, making no objections' ('Сквозь слез не видя ничего/Едва дыша, без возражений', Chapter 4, stanza 17). Because Tatiana's distress is visible as Evgeny speaks, yet he fails to react, his words emerge as a pat speech no doubt recited on many other occasions when a flirtation had, from his point of view, gone too far.

Another irony is that Evgeny is not (now or later) Tatiana's husband or her lover; his quasi-marital reading of morals to Tatiana in fact ensures that he never can be, even at a stage when he has himself come to desire it. Through Evgeny, whose moral sentiments as he enlightens her are impeccably orthodox, both in theme and in expression, Tatiana learns to see through men's motivation (as effectively as Lambert could have wanted); but she also learns to see through the motivation of the man reading the Lambertian lesson, absorbing the tenet of female self-control ('learn to command yourself' ('учитесь властвовать собой', Chapter 4, stanza 17) which was at that lesson's centre.

Accordingly, the famous scene in Chapter 7 in which Tatiana visits Evgeny's library and begins to question whether the figure that she has idolised may be a 'Muscovite in a Childe Harold cloak', is a 'parody' that has its roots in their first confrontation in the garden, in which Evgenii also acts like a parody: but here of the didactic *raisonneur*, not of the Byronic outsider. By finding independence within a marriage that has not been, from her side, a love match, Tatiana learns a lesson that is repeated, almost obsessively, in various other texts that Pushkin wrote during the 1830s (for example, the prose fragment 'Dubrovsky', 1833), and which, his letters suggest, he also wished to teach Natalia.

The pedagogical drive in *Evgenii Onegin* depends, very much in the tradition of Enlightenment conduct manuals, on Tatiana's reading. As in behaviour guides, it is emphasised that reading novels is dangerous. But by learning to read fiction in a properly sceptical manner, and eventually finding her autonomy outside romantic love, Tatiana proves an honourable heiress to the eighteenth-century feminism of Madame de Lambert and her successors. Isolated as she is (according to the classic male myth) from female company and indeed from femininity generally, Tatiana can in an oblique way count as a feminist heroine too, representing, in her final incarnation, the independent woman created by Madame de Lambert and, at the other end of the century, Mary Wollstonecraft. Written at a stage when the eighteenth-century system of education was coming in for increasing ridicule; when the values that had inspired Smol'nyi were in decline; and finished only a decade before a new generation would usher in an assault on the very concept of family-centred education (and indeed woman-centred education generally), *Evgeny Onegin* is at the same time a tribute to the *femme savante*, an ideal that Pushkin assiduously mocked, but with which he had deep, though unacknowledged, affinities.

★ ★ ★ ★ ★

In his influential histories of the development of the family in England, Lawrence Stone observed a transition, during the second half of the eighteenth century, between the old patriarchal family and the new 'companionate marriage', characterised by stronger ties of affect and a higher degree of intimacy between husband and wife, parents and children.[48] In her study of the Russian family, Jessica Tovrov argued for a comparable transition in the second half of the nineteenth century.[49] But a careful consideration of historical sources suggests that this historiological schema may not be sufficiently sophisticated: what is observable more closely resembles a shift in understanding of the patriarchal family. The absolute authority of the husband and father was challenged by a new pattern of family life according to which husband and wife led 'separate but equal' lives, still cemented by a notional subordination of woman to man, but with traditional 'feminine' tasks, such as child-rearing, now given a much higher profile than before.

In Russia, the anxieties raised by the conflict of 'traditional' and 'new' understandings of the patriarchal family were heightened by the presence of a competing ideology representing a form of 'companionate marriage' in which the wife was supposed to devote herself entirely to pleasing her husband. The result was a variety of conflicting interpretations of acceptable family life, so that uncertainty characterised not only the views held in Russian upper-class society generally, but individual appreciations as well. Though normative sources, such as behaviour books, and self-conscious, genre-aware pieces of writing such as letters and memoirs, in no sense offer us a clear window on to lost reality, it would be reasonable to assume that the tensions gripping those who endured that reality were comparable to, or sharper than, those chronicled here.

My thanks to Linda Edmondson, editor of the collection in which this essay originally appeared ('Educating Tatiana: Manners, Motherhood, and Moral Education (Vospitanie), 1760–1840', in *Gender in Russian History and Culture*, ed. by Linda Edmondson (Basingstoke: Palgrave Macmillan, 2001), pp. 1–28), and organiser of the conference at the University of Birmingham, 3–5 July 1996, where the material was first presented, and to the other participants for their useful comments.

48 L. Stone, *The Family, Sex and Marriage in England, 1500–1800* (London: Weidenfeld & Nicholson, 1977); and *The Road to Divorce: England, 1530–1987* (Oxford: Oxford University Press, 1990).
49 Tovrov, *The Russian Noble Family*, Chapter 7.

CHAPTER 2

The Uses of Refinement: Etiquette and Uncertainty at the Russian Court

[1997]

For reasons that may ultimately derive from the traditional use of exemplary narratives in the schoolroom, feminist history has a penchant for rebellious heroines, colourful non-conformists who protest against the roles scripted for them by their culture.[1] Even Marina Warner, whose study of Margaret Thatcher, in *Monuments and Maidens,* emphasises that its subject has 'tapped an enormous source of female power: the right of prohibition', chooses not to dwell on the power of the negative arbitrator. She describes without enthusiasm the substitution, in John Gibson's monument to Queen Victoria, of the new 'womanly' virtue of Clemency for the traditional attribute of Wisdom.[2] Yet it is possible to see the association of women and refinement that was imported to Russia in the second half of the eighteenth century not only as a repressive mechanism (making it more difficult for women than for men to evade behaviour norms, and meaning that they were more virulently condemned, and fiercely punished, when they did), but also as an incentive mechanism, offering women possibilities of power (admittedly of a muted kind), and shaping particular modes of writing at different eras of history.

To put refinement back into history is particularly important, in the Russian context, because women's capacity to arbitrate morality has so often been perceived as innate. Yury Lotman, for example, argues in his essay 'The Woman's World' that 'women and girls of the 1820s were in significant measure responsible for creating the particular moral atmosphere of Russian society', which is reasonable enough. However, he relates this to the fact that 'as wife and mother, woman is to the highest degree connected with transcendental, supra-historical properties'. Lotman's article ignores the role played by new ideologies of wifedom and motherhood in Russian culture during the eighteenth and early nineteenth centuries, some of them articulated by women writers. In particular, he neglects the relationship between

---

[1] An example is Natalie Zemon Davies's triple biography, *Women on the Margins: Three Seventeenth-Century Lives* (Cambridge, MA: Harvard University Press, 1995).
[2] Marina Warner, *Monuments and Maidens: The Allegory of the Female Form* (London: Weidenfeld & Nicholson, 1985; Vintage, 1996), pp. 52, 209.

éducation maternelle or 'pedagogical motherhood' (the notion that women were supposed to be responsible for their children's education, and educated in order to make them fit for this) and issues of women's cultural authority in a wider sense.³

The era that I address here is the mid-nineteenth century; the context, the intermediate stages of the Slavophile movement, accurately described by Andrzej Walicki as a variant of 'conservative Romanticism'.⁴ The democratically-inclined Romantics of the 1810s and early 1820s sought to liberate themselves from what they saw as the stifling pretensions of polite culture. This was directly associated with a rebellion against the Sentimentalist concept of women as ideal readers, and against the supposed tyranny of the salon hostess (which in Russia, given the merely embryonic development of the salon, was always an imagined tyranny in any case). The perceived opposition between an elite, conservative, aristocratic culture, supportive of the autocracy and dominated (behind the scenes) by women, and an innovative, egalitarian masculine culture of political opposition persisted into the 1840s, 1850s, and 1860s as well. Men and women of radical sympathies tried to distance themselves as far as possible from what were seen as the 'medieval Chinese ways' of conventional upper-class society, creating an alternative world that was opposed in every detail to the *bon ton* of St Petersburg polite culture. In his memoirs, the painter Ilya Repin recalled visiting, in the 1860s, a radical 'anti-salon' held in the house of Valentina Serova, woman composer and mother of the famous painter Valentin Serov. The attire of the female guests included short skirts and heavy knee-boots; the hostess was offended when Repin tried to offer her his chair; and some of the young students attending demonstratively smoked and talked the entire way through the chamber music that was provided as entertainment.⁵

Because the Russian radicals were represented in Soviet historiography as 'forward looking' and 'progressive' [*peredovye, progressivnye*], their story has been told many times, and often identified with 'Russian intellectual culture' per se, which is always assumed to be hostile to convention. Much less familiar are the arguments about refinement among thinking individuals whose sympathies were conservative. In what follows, I examine the significance of polite culture for one such individual, a woman associated with the ultimate bastion of aristocratic conservativism, the Russian court, but who also had connections with the anti-aristocratic ideologues of the Aksakov circle of Slavophiles. Anna Tyutcheva (1829–1889), daughter of the poet Fedor Tyutchev and his second wife Eleonore Peterson, and wife of Ivan Sergeevich Aksakov, one of the most prominent Slavophiles of the mid-nineteenth

---

3   Yu. Lotman, 'Zhenskii mir', in *Besedy o russkoi kul'ture: Byt i traditsii russkogo dvoryanstva XVIII-nacha/o XIX veka* (St Petersburg: Iskusstvo-SPb., 1994), pp. 57, 46. Lotman assumes throughout *Besedy* that the two sources for educational ideology were Locke and Rousseau, ignoring the huge influence exercised by Madame de Lambert, Madame Leprince de Beaumont, and Madame de Genlis. See 'Educating Tatiana' in this collection.
4   See Andrzej Walicki, *The Slavophile Controversy: History of a Conservative Utopia in Nineteenth-Century Russian Thought* (Oxford: Clarendon Press, 1975), esp. pp. 8–9.
5   On salons and Romantic 'anti-behaviour', see Chapter 1 of my *Refining Russia*. I. Repin, 'Valentin Aleksandrovich Serov', in *Dalekoe blizkoe* (Leningrad: Khudozhnik RSFSR, 1982), section 1, p. 352. Repin's testimony is striking in that he himself belonged to the radical rather than conservative wing of the Russian intelligentsia.

century, was the author of memoirs describing her time (1853–58) as a lady-in-waiting [*freilina*] to Maria Nikolaevna, wife of the heir to the throne, Grand Duke Alexander Nikolaevich (from 1855, Emperor Alexander II). Later, between 1858 and 1865, Tyutcheva was to be employed as governess to Maria Aleksandrovna, the couple's daughter.[6]

My concern here is with refinement and identity: with Tyutcheva's attempt to construct appropriate autobiographical strategies to express her ambiguous attitude to her position as a courtier. The 'writing self' of the autobiographer is fundamentally if not finally determined by the conceptions of the society for which that 'writing self' is constructed. In Russia, since Westernisation, the understanding of 'selfhood' has been in significant ways distinctive.[7] The term *lichnost'*, personality, overlaps only imperfectly with the Anglophone term 'identity', partly because the etymology of the term (connected with *lichina*, 'mask') can suggest the face that one puts out to the world, rather than any totalising concept of the self. The individualistic traditions of Western philosophy were assimilated problematically and haphazardly, in contestation with Slavophile ideologies that represented Russia's true identity (with whatever historical justice or injustice) as based on communities such as the *mir* (peasant commune) or *sobor* (cathedral synod).[8]

It is hard to imagine any writer in any culture writing an autobiography without any sense of who is likely to read it, or of the relation between first-person narrator and the other characters in the narrative (parents, siblings, friends, enemies). But in Russia autobiographies have often seemed especially crowded, given the importance of autobiography as a vehicle for justifying life choices before the world, and demonstratively associating them with morally empowering patterns of self-fashioning, as well as a certain theatrical flourish. All three dynamics can be seen in one of the most powerful models of autobiographical writing, the seventeenth-century *Life* written by the 'Old Believer' Archpriest Avvakum, in which the autobiographer turns the story of his persecution for refusing to accept the 1640s reforms instituted by Tsar Alexis Mikhailovich and Patriarch Nikon into a first-person hagiography, with many performative asides to the Tsar as antagonist. Another case in point is Dostoevsky's fictional autobiography *Notes from Underground*, where Underground Man's readers are engaged, not only as witnesses to the narrator's many dramatic confrontations, but also as the opponents in his argument to utilitarianism and rational egoism.

6   The best general account of Tyutcheva's biography is A. L. Ospovat and N. V. Kotrelev's article 'A. F. Aksakova' in the authoritative *Russkie pisateli 1800–1917: biograficheskii slovar'*, 6 vols (Moscow: Sovetskaya entsiklopediya, 1987), I, 39–40. She does not appear in *Dictionary of Russian Women Writers*, ed. by M. Ledkovsky, C. Rosenthal, and M. Zirin (Westport, CT: Greenwood, 1994), though coverage of memoirists is generally good.
7   Since this article was written, Irina Savkina has published several important contributions on this topic, e.g. *Pishu sebya: Avtodokumental'nye zhenskie teksty v pervoi polovine XIX veka* (Tampere: University of Tampere, 2001), and '"Pisat' o sebe kosvenno" i dokumental'no-khudozhestvennyi zhanr zapisok', in *Literatura v sisteme kul'tury*, ed. by E. N. Strogonova (Tver': Tverskoi gosudarstvennyi universitet, 2012), pp. 142–53.
8   See Derek Offord, 'Lichnost'', in *Constructing Russian Culture in the Age of Revolution*, ed. by Catriona Kelly and David Shepherd (Oxford: Oxford University Press, 1998), pp. 13–25.

The marginality of Russian autobiography so far as European confessional tradition was concerned may be one reason why Russian women, themselves marginal to the literary process, made so many distinguished contributions to life-writing.[9] However, the idiosyncrasies of Russian tradition also raise important questions about the extent to which it is possible to identify in Russian women's life-writing ideas such supposedly differentiating features of 'feminine' autobiography as the frailty of ego-boundaries, the privileging of the mother-daughter dyad, or the preference of women writers for fragmentary forms.[10] The combative Russian tradition of autobiography as apologetics means that many autobiographers have been precisely concerned with establishing the exceptionality of the first-person hero.[11] Mother-daughter relations have been particularly problematic in this context, since it is often the mother who is seen as the most significant arbiter of convention in the child's world. In 'Maman', by the early twentieth-century feminist, social activist, pamphleteer, and novelist Natalia Nordman, the narrator's realisation that she matters less to her mother than an elegant white-and-pink pot of face powder becomes the central event in the unfolding of childhood identity.[12]

Thus, the mother-child relation is at least as often evoked to reinforce ego boundaries as to suggest their dissolution. (It has been Russian male autobiographers, or fictional autobiographers, such as Tolstoy in his *Childhood*, who have been more concerned to idealise the mother-child relationship as harmonious fusion.)[13] Equally, to see fragmentation as a key feature of women's autobiographical writing is problematic because published memoirs, like other forms of writing in Russia, often acquired their fragmentary character as the result of censorship pressures. For example, the memoirs of Vera Panova, *On My Life, Books and Readers* (*O moei zhizni, knigakh i chitatelyakh*, 1975) were in their published form the result of intervention by

---

9   Another reason for Russian women's notable success in the genre of autobiography may be the fact that it allowed them to give vent to the private considerations that were difficult to express in the Russian novel, which was conventionally perceived as a vehicle for political ideas. On this see B. Heldt, *Terrible Perfection: Women and Russian Literature* (Bloomington: Indiana University Press, 1987), and Catriona Kelly, 'Introduction to the Pandora Edition', in Anna Larina, *This I Cannot Forget* (London: Pandora, 1995). An instance of the importance of theatrical imagery in autobiography is Mikhail Zoshchenko's fictionalised autobiography *Before Sunrise* (*Pered voskhodom solntsa*, 1943). For some brief observations on the genre traditions of Russian autobiography, see Catriona Kelly, 'The First-Person "Other": Sof'ya Soboleva's 1863 Story "Pros and Cons",' *Slavonic and East European Review*, 73.1 (1995), 61–81.
10 See, for example, Estelle C. Jelinek, *Women's Autobiography: Essays in Criticism* (Bloomington: Indiana University Press, 1980), and Celeste Schenk, 'All of a Piece: Women's Poetry and Autobiography', in *Life/Lines: Theorizing Women's Autobiography*, ed. by Celeste Schenk and Bella Brodzski (Ithaca, NY: Cornell University Press, 1988), pp. 281–305.
11 There are, of course, counter-examples: in her excellent 'Introduction' to *The Memoirs of Princess Dashkova*, trans. by K. Fitzlyon (Durham, NC: Duke University Press, 1995), pp. 1–26, Jehanne Gheith addresses the paradox according to which Dashkova 'describes her achievements in a language of self-effacement' (p. 5). But Dashkova came from a generation where modesty was the ideal of behaviour for aristocratic women, an ideal that radical memoirists held in contempt.
12 Natal'ya Nordman, 'Maman', in *Intimnye stranitsy* (St Petersburg: tipografiya M. Stasyulevicha, 1910), pp. 187–92.
13 On Tolstoy's *Childhood* and the tradition that it initiated, see Andrew Wachtel, *The Battle for Childhood: Creation of a Russian Myth* (Stanford, CA: Stanford University Press, 1992).

Soviet editors who forced Panova to excise from her text a description of her second husband's arrest during the Stalin purges, and to insert material about the writer's public role ('books and readers') into what had originally been a private memoir composed for her children.[14]

The fissiparousness of Tyutcheva's writings — a short 'Memoir' in continuous prose that, however, gives only an incomplete account of her early life, and a number of diary entries running from 1853–58, plus a small amount of material from the 1870s and 1880s — also seems partly traceable to censorship. In the 1870s, Tyutcheva began revising her 1853–58 diaries, dealing with the time that she spent as a lady-in-waiting at the Russian court, apparently with a view to publication, and composed the 'Memoir' as a preface, but abandoned the plan to publish because her memoirs totally lacked the adulatory tone that was a *sine qua non* in pre-revolutionary Russia when publishing material dealing with the Imperial Family.[15] The memoirs eventually reached print posthumously, and the version that we now have derives at least in part from editorial decisions made when they first appeared in the 1920s.

That said, the argument that fragmentation is a willed characteristic of Russian women's autobiography does carry some weight. Repetition, restatement, and overlap is typical. The memoirs of Catherine II comprise more than a dozen pieces, from a few pages long up to several hundred. The different autobiographies are associated with a divergent sense of readership. 'Redaction IV', a lengthy account of Catherine's marriage to Peter III, later murdered in order to clear her way to the throne, was intended to legitimate her actions to her descendants, and hence is mostly concerned with Peter's unfitness to rule. 'Redaction I' is a more private and intimate account of Catherine's life before her marriage, containing many details of her childhood and upbringing, which was written for her woman friend Countess Bruce. 'Redaction II', written for a male courtier, Aleksandr Cherkassov, is intermediate between the two extremes.[16] In the second volume of her memoirs, Nadezhda Mandelstam likewise provided an alternative 'redaction' of her life,

---

14 Vera Panova, *O moei zhizni, knigakh i chitatelyakh* (Leningrad: Lenizdat, 1975); on the composition and censorship of the text, see Serafima Yur'eva, *Vera Panova: stranitsy zhizni: k biografii pisatel'nitsy* (Tenafly, NJ: Ermitazh, 1993). The memoirs were published in full only thirty years later: *Moe i tol'ko moe: O moei zhizni, knigakh i chitatelyakh* (St Petersburg: Zvezda, 2005).
15 A. F. Tyutcheva, *Pri dvore dvukh imperatorov: vospominaniya, dnevnik 1853–1855*, ed. by S. Bakhrushin and M. Tsyavlovsky, 2 vols (Moscow: M. i S. Sabashnikovy, 1928–29) (references to this publication hereafter referenced in the main text as 'Tyutcheva' with volume and page numbers). A typical court memoir is Baroness Mariya Frederiks, 'Iz vospominanii', *Istoricheskii vestnik*, 71 (1898), 52–87, 454–84 [part 1]; 72 (1898), 49–79, 396–413 [part 2] (references to this publication hereafter referenced in the main text as 'Frederiks' with part and page numbers). Frederiks (1832–1903 or 1908) was the descendant of a Dutch- or German-speaking entrepreneur who acted as court banker to Catherine II.
16 The fullest edition of Catherine's memoirs is *Sochineniya Imperatritsy Ekateriny Vtoroi na osnovanii podlinnykh rukopisei s ob"yasnitel'nymi primechaniyami A. N. Pypina*, XII: *Avtobiograficheskie zapiski* (St Petersburg: Imperatorskaya Akademiya Nauk, 1907), from which the redaction numbers here are taken. For a discussion of Catherine's different ways of styling the self in her correspondence, see the introduction and commentaries in *Catherine the Great: Selected Letters*, ed. by Kelsey Rubin-Detlef and Andrew Kahn (Oxford: Oxford University Press, 2018).

abandoning the representation of herself as devoted widow curator of her husband's memory that she had espoused in her first book of memoirs, and setting herself up as a defiant critic of her society and her earlier self as representative of that society.[17]

Of the two instances, Mandelstam's seems more relevant to Tyutcheva's case, since Tyutcheva's various autobiographical compositions entirely lack Catherine's sense, coquettish or androgynous or both, of suiting autobiographical self to the assumed reader. Like Mandelstam, her return to an earlier self seems to have been at least partly inspired by a need to critique that self. As she commented in 1880:

> I filled whole notebooks during the first years of my life at court. In these, alongside heaps of sentimentality, fruitless repetitions, and excessively intimate details, may be found a fairly true picture of court life and the events of the era. There are many curious details, which have been preserved with extraordinary freshness and vitality below the surface of sentimentality and naivety, and which are highly characteristic of that antediluvian stage of my first youth.[18]

In the continuous 'Memoir', Tyutcheva makes broad and ambitious judgements on the 1850s in general: St Petersburg, for instance, is described as a culture producing many clever men and women who somehow got no further than the salon (Tyutcheva, I, 72–73). However, any editing of the extant diaries appears, in the event, to have been light, and she certainly made no attempt to 'correct' the earlier self in line with the perceptions of the latter.[19]

In any case, even if the formal characteristics of Tyutcheva's writings do seem to bear some relation to 'women's autobiography' in a broader sense, the persona that emerges is intimately related to the immediate historical context. As Beth Holmgren has argued, work such as Mandelstam's came out of a tradition in which women were perceived as fortunate survivors of the Purges whose continuing existence gave them the opportunity, and the duty, of taking up the pen as chroniclers of their age. This perception of women autobiographers derived from and consolidated an older view, according to which women's memoirs were valued for the supposed

---

17   Nadezhda Mandel'shtam, *Vospominaniya* (New York: Chekhov Publishing Company, 1970), trans. by Max Hayward as *Hope against Hope* (London: Collins & Harvill, 1971); *Vtoraya kniga* (Paris: YMCA Press, 1972), trans. by Max Hayward as *Hope Abandoned* (London: Collins & Harvill, 1974); *Tret'ya kniga* (Paris: YMCA Press, 1987). The composition of 'alternative autobiographies' is far from unknown among Russian men, but seems to have had a rather different significance. For instance, Tolstoy's 'Memoirs' ('Vospominaniya'), a recollection of the writer's childhood written in the 1900s, was intended to repudiate and efface, rather than stand alongside, the fictionalised autobiography composed by Tolstoy in the 1850s, *Detstvo*. See Tolstoy, *Polnoe sobranie sochinenii*, 91 vols (Moscow: Gosudarstvennoe izdatel'stvo Khudozhestvennoi literatury, 1928–64), XXXIV. 343–95.
18   Quoted by S. Bakhrushin in his introduction to Tyutcheva, I, 25.
19   My examination of Tyutcheva's manuscript diaries from 1847–60 and her annotated engagement books from 1856 in the Russian State Archive of Literature and Art (RGALI), fond 10, Aksakovy S. T., K. S., I. S., op. 1, ed. khr. 212–14, suggests that her editing did indeed pare down allusions to family relationships (e.g. on 18 September 1852, ed. khr. 212, l. 147 verso, Tyutcheva remarks that she would rather her sisters had been placed at Court than she), and abridged emotional passages in general (for example, the entry describing the personality of the Grand Duchess Maria Nikolaevna, 21 January 1853, ibid., ll. 171 verso-177 recto, is trimmed to a few sentences), rather than changing the nature of the essential conflict between etiquette and emotion.

accuracy with which they recorded their times.[20] The quotation from Tyutcheva's letter above could be taken to suggest that she too shared the opinion that memoirs were above all valuable as historical records. But, unlike some women chroniclers, who contrived to efface the self almost entirely in the attempt to capture the lives of others, Tyutcheva as autobiographer is involved in an interesting and complex struggle to articulate her own identity.

A good deal of the complexity is traceable to Tyutcheva's political background. Both her father and her husband, the author and essayist Ivan Aksakov (whom she married in 1866, leading to her retirement from court life), were supporters of the Russian autocracy and strong Slavophiles, but also well-educated cosmopolitans with a wide knowledge of Western literature and philosophy. Tyutcheva had similar tastes and intellectual interests: half-German, and largely educated in Germany, fluent in French (in which language she wrote her memoirs) and in German, rather than in Russian, whose grammar and idiom she never fully mastered, she was at the same time Orthodox, a patriot, and a strong believer in Russia's historic destiny. All of this profoundly affected the siting of her autobiographical self.

The preoccupation of Soviet history above all with the Russian radical movement has meant that the life histories of those outside radical circles are relatively unfamiliar. Some excellent work has been done on tracing the characteristic forms of radical self-fashioning: one might mention here Yury Lotman's work on the Decembrists, Irina Paperno's study of the radical thinker and author Nikolai Chernyshevsky, Richard Stites's *The Women's Liberation Movement in Russia*, and Hilde Hoogenboom's reading of the memoirs of the populist Vera Figner.[21] These writers have emphasised breach of etiquette and disruption of convention as crucial elements in the radical discovery of identity. This demonstrative violation of accepted standards of behaviour was an effortless way in which the Russian radical intellectual might act out his or her independence of social constraint, demonstrating identity through a straightforward juxtaposition of accepted norms and individual behaviour. Moreover, Hoogenboom traces a specific pattern for the autobiographies of Russian women radicals, in which both childhood and education, especially the influence of books, play a prominent part; these memoirs trace a trajectory of self-improvement that has marked affinities with that of the saint's life.

For Russian conservatives, however, discarding convention was not so straightforward. Among Russian Slavophiles of the mid-nineteenth century, one possibility was the repudiation of Western manners as 'false', and the espousal of supposedly

---

20 Beth Holmgren, *Women's Works in Stalin's Time: On Lidiya Chukovskaya and Nadezhda Mandelstam* (Bloomington: Indiana University Press, 1993). From the late 1850s, when 'the history of everyday life' (*byt*) became popular in Russia, journals such as *Russkii arkhiv*, *Istoricheskii vestnik*, and *Russkaya starina* regularly published domestic chronicles by women: see, for example, M. F. Kamenskaya, 'Vospominaniya', serialised in *Istoricheskii vestnik* during 1894.

21 Irina Paperno, *Chernyshevsky and the Age of Realism: A Study in the Semiotics of Behavior* (Stanford, CA: Stanford University Press, 1988); Richard Stites, *The Women's Liberation Movement in Russia: Feminism, Nihilism and Bolshevism* (Princeton, NJ: Princeton University Press, 1978), pp. 103–05; Hilde Hoogenboom, 'Vera Figner and Revolutionary Autobiographies: The Influence of Gender on Genre', in *Women in Russia and Ukraine*, ed. by Rosalind Marsh (Cambridge: Cambridge University Press, 1996), pp. 78–93.

more 'sincere' and 'spontaneous' native models. But most of the Slavophiles (unlike their *raznochinets*, déclassé, radical opponents) were members of the *dvoryanstvo* [aristocracy and gentry], to whom status was very important; and this status could only be demonstrated by the adoption of Western behaviour patterns. Hence, as Lyubov' Kiseleva has argued in the case of the Slavophiles' predecessors, the Archaists, there was an explosion of forms of doublethink according to which Western behaviour was attacked in print, but adopted in private. Admiral Shishkov, leading Archaist and patriot, lambasted French culture in his essays, but had Western furniture, wore Western clothes, and employed French tutors to teach his children. In his letters to her before their marriage, Tyutcheva's future husband Ivan Aksakov was later to articulate a description of the predicament of 'ordinary' Russian people, stranded between the new culture and the old; the description fits aristocrats like him just as well as more 'ordinary' citizens. Referring to the distressingly bad condition of churches along the Volga, he comments:

> We have not cut ourselves off from life, we want to live and prosper as everyone else does, but we do not know how to deal with our heritage, we reject it, and now we appear *comme des bâtards* among civilised humanity [...]. One thing is clear: in Russia, modern education is open to the ordinary man only at the cost of his moral decline, i.e. he has to deny in his heart all his spiritual traditions and make his acquiescence in advance with everything that runs contrary to those traditions.[22]

In practice, it was no easier for those who came from less 'ordinary' backgrounds to combine entry into 'civilisation' with a full sense of morality, and 'contradictions' between heritage and Western manners were just as vexed. The tensions were particularly painful for those Slavophiles who, unlike the Aksakov circle, accepted autocratic rule in its contemporary manifestation (the court of Nicholas I) as an appropriate expression of a uniquely Russian national identity.[23]

Anna Tyutcheva was one of these, and hence her memoirs of the Russian court depict an agonised voyage of self-discovery, rather than a triumphant progress to liberation. She was frustrated by the palpable insincerity of court life, but also committed, both by her profession as lady-in-waiting, and her own conservative political beliefs, to the support of autocratic rule and the institutions associated with it. There could be no moment of enlightenment in which she suddenly found herself unshackled from the conditions constraining her behaviour. Her autobiography could not follow the radical 'master-plot', in short. Indeed, in her

---

22 *Ivan Sergeevich Aksakov v ego pis'makh*, 4 vols (St Petersburg: tipografiya M. K. Volchaninova, 1888–96), IV, 107. On Shishkov, see Lyubov Kiseleva, 'The Archaistic Model of Behaviour as a Semiotic Object,' in *Poetics of the Text: Essays to Celebrate Twenty Years of the Neo Formalist Circle*, ed. by J. Andrew (Amsterdam: Rodopi, 1992), pp. 28–34.
23 On the Aksakov view of the Russian court as the haunt of insincerity, see Vera Aksakova, *Dnevnik Very Sergeevnoi Aksakovoi 1854–1855*, ed. by N. V. Golitsyn and P. E. Shchegolev (St Petersburg: Ogni, 1913), p. 33: commenting on an insulting letter sent by her brother to Countess Bludova and refusing her offer of patronage to secure a place at court, Aksakova expresses surprise that Bludova had taken umbrage: 'but court people always remain court people', that is, subject to the prevailing mood around them.

description of the short time that she spent at Smol'nyi Institute for the Daughters of the Nobility, the prestigious boarding-school for aristocratic girls founded by Catherine II, Tyutcheva specifically excluded the possibility of identifying with the Russian radicals. The clinching point that she used to illustrate the perniciousness of the education offered at Smol'nyi was that so many graduates became seduced by nihilism: 'The absence of moral or religious education [at Smol'nyi] flung wide the doors to the propaganda of nihilistic doctrines, which are nowhere so widespread nowadays as in the state educational institutions' (Tyutcheva, I, 62). Rather than a Damascene conversion to radical righteousness, Tyutcheva's diaries depict a process of constant and painful renegotiation of identity in terms of her relationship with court practices and with her employer, Grand Duchess Maria Nikolaevna.

At the same time, Tyutcheva's autobiographical persona has little in common with that adopted by court memoirists in general. The latter sought to efface the self entirely in hagiographical adulation of the royal personages that they served. One of them, Baroness Mariya Frederiks, declared at the outset that the most significant prompting of her autobiography was to defend Nicholas I against the supposed besmirching of his memory by later commentators:

> At the moment (1883), I am sitting before the portrait of our still unforgotten Emperor, Nicholas I, and many thoughts swarm inside my head as I study it. How much injustice and falsehood has been bruited about since the death of this giant of power and glory, who loved Russia with such a great love! (Frederiks, I, 54)

Just as declaratively, Frederiks refers to Alexander II as 'our kind, gentle martyred tsar' (I, 54). In Tyutcheva's memoirs, the members of the royal family are fallible human beings, as grotesquely underlined in the passage where she narrates how Nicholas I had ordered himself embalmed according to the Ganolo system (where an electric charge was run into the corpse's neck). The embalming was duly carried out, but Nicholas's body was neither electrically nor miraculously preserved, and soon began to putrefy noticeably (Tyutcheva, I, 188, 20 and 21 February 1855).

No saint in terms of the after-life (non-corruption of the body is traditionally accepted as a mark of sainthood in Russian Orthodoxy), Nicholas also provoked increasing irony as the memoirs progressed. Appearing in the first entries as a fine figure of a man, he was dismissed in the early months of 1856 as 'a man who was mentally limited and intoxicated by flattery' (Tyutcheva, II, 99, 11 January 1856). There were still less adulatory portraits of some younger royals: the pretty but silly Grand Duchess Alexandra Iosifovna, with her narcissistic efforts to play up her resemblance to Mary Stuart, and her spoilt child's tactlessness and impertinence (I, 165, 8 November 1854), or Grand Duke Constantine, impudently quizzing everyone in sight through an eyeglass (I, 150, 14 July 1854).

There was one point, though, where Tyutcheva's memoirs did observe conventional pieties. She expressed as great a conviction as any other royal memoirist of the necessity of court etiquette. Frederiks had characterised Nicholas I's court as 'imperial, majestic: they understood that prestige was essential to their high status' (Frederiks, I, 76.) A very similar passage was set down by Tyutcheva in 1854, but this time criticising the simplification of court ceremonial that Nicholas had ordered for his own funeral:

> He has directed that the hall where he was to lie in state should not be swathed in black, nor the chapel in Peter and Paul Fortress, and has ordered that his body should be exposed for the people to take their leave only three weeks, instead of the six weeks that had been customary in earlier days, and which allowed those living far away to come and pay their respects to the remains of the dead sovereign. He also ordered that the period of full mourning should last only six weeks.
>
> All this is a terrible mistake. The prestige of authority is to a high extent ensured by the etiquette and ceremonial that surround it, and which have a strong influence on the imagination of the masses. It is dangerous to strip authority of this mystique. (Tyutcheva, I, 188, 20 February 1854)

Even with the wisdom of hindsight, when writing the preface to her diaries, Tyutcheva remained convinced that strict protocol was vital to autocracy. She placed an unfavourable gloss on the changes in court ritual that set in after Nicholas I's death, when the late monarch's obsession with correct time-keeping and punctilious ceremonial was replaced by more permissive attitudes. Alexander II did not subject those late for church to public reprimands:

> I cannot say that this laxity caused life at court to become less tense or more pleasant. Court life is in its essence a conventional form of life and etiquette is essential in order to maintain its prestige. It is not only a barrier dividing the sovereign from his subjects but also a defence of those subjects from the caprice of the sovereign. Etiquette creates an atmosphere of general respect, in which each person purchases dignity at the cost of freedom and comfort. Where etiquette reigns, courtiers are grandees and ladies of society, where it is absent, they are reduced to the level of lackeys and maids, for intimacy without closeness and without equality is always humiliating, both for those who impose it on others and for those who have it imposed upon them. Diderot put it very wittily when speaking of the duc d'Orléans: 'That grandee plays the coquette with me by pretending we are equals, but I distance myself from him with politeness'. (Tyutcheva, I, 101)[24]

Yet, though her later 'Memoir' recognised 'etiquette' and 'intimacy' as opposites, and perceived a court life ruled by impersonality, with courtiers faceless symbols of royal status, as the ideal, both here and in her diary Tyutcheva constantly chafed against the impersonality of court life, attempting to create a dangerous intimacy within its spaces. She vividly evoked how bleak she found the bare quarters allocated to ladies-in-waiting when she first arrived:

> How hastily the poor ladies-in-waiting fled from their lonely rooms, which could never be a home for them [the word 'home' is used in English in Tyutcheva's original text], having neither the comfort of the domestic

---

24 Frederiks uses the identical term, *raspushchennost'* [laxity] in her critique of court manners under Alexander II: 'When, after the death of our wise tsar [Nicholas I], an atmosphere of spinelessness and laxity crept into court life, everyone heaved a sigh of relief and pleasure [...] but what came of all this? The pride of morally crippled degenerates, who set themselves the task of betraying Russia's whole political structure under the mask of fidelity to the fatherland' (Frederiks, I, 55).

hearth, nor the solitude of a monastic cell. Amid the noisy and luxurious life surrounding them, they found only loneliness and a painful sense of abandonment. (Tyutcheva, I, 91)

I cannot conceal that the first time I drank tea in my new quarters, I felt so sad and lonely that I began to weep bitterly. (Tyutcheva, I, 107, 13 January 1853)

Tyutcheva attempted to escape the gloomy, institutional atmosphere of her room not only by taking carriage rides, as the other ladies did, but also by turning her relationship with her royal employer into more than a formal connection. The condition of intimacy between them was constantly examined and found wanting:

Truly, had she not been the Grand Duchess, I would have loved her sincerely, but at present I try to preserve the requisite polite indifference in myself. That is the reason for the falsity in our relations. We live in unnatural intimacy with people far superior to us, we see them constantly and see only them, and quite involuntarily associate our interests with theirs, while they, on the other hand, can only be interested in us so far as we come into contact with them, and they remain, and ought to remain, indifferent towards us and more or less alien to us. This is what makes life at court so empty for anyone who is not plunged completely into frivolity: one searches out emotional or intellectual interest, and finds nothing to satisfy one. (Tyutcheva, I, 120, 12 July 1854; cf. I, 9, 1 March 1854)

Tyutcheva relentlessly delineates the moments of crisis — painful but inconclusive — that beset the relationship. A fit of bad temper on the part of the Empress, for example, produces emotional agony on Tyutcheva's part:

On account of trifles of various kinds she was extremely sharp and spoke more harshly than ever before. I could hardly hold back my tears in her presence, and when I got to my room, I broke down completely. In fact, it tormented me so much that I could not restrain myself from going to the Empress and asking whether she were annoyed with me in some way. She replied that she was seriously preoccupied, and that she was faced with taking a very painful decision, and sent me away. (Tyutcheva, II, 75, 18 October 1855)

Grand Duchess Elena Pavlovna, a highly intelligent salon hostess of liberal inclinations, frankly disliked the Empress, finding her 'intellectually mediocre' and 'inconsistent'.[25] Tyutcheva's devotion to autocracy did not leave her with that recourse. Rather than tracing her unhappiness to the Empress's personal character, she explained it by the division between external observances and internal feelings felt by women of the royal court.

Much the same explanation is offered for Tyutcheva's frustrations with religious worship at the court: condemned on state occasions to the restrained outward observance demanded by etiquette, she laments the impossibility of giving vent to her intense inward religiosity:

The service provoked a feeling of sadness in me. It was all so magnificent, so opulent, so grand. You aren't allowed to kneel down, that would be a breach of etiquette, and you stand before God in full court regalia. I felt like a child who

---

25 See note by S. V. Bakhrushin to Tyutcheva, II, 108–09.

had been commanded to curtsey to her mother rather than kissing her. But in
order to reward myself, I will go to a service tomorrow and pray quietly in a
corner. (Tyutcheva, I, 109–10, 25 January 1854)

Here, Tyutcheva's attitudes again came into conflict with practices at court, which
accorded a purely functionalist role to religious ceremony: services were seen as
part of court ritual generally. Attendance at 'major court ceremonies' ('les grandes
cérémonies') was obligatory; at other occasions, 'les petites fêtes', attendance was an
entitlement rather than an obligation.[26] In other words, presence at the mass was
associated above all with status, rather than with piety, and expressed service to the
royal house rather than devotion to the deity.

More sanguine memoirists than Tyutcheva recall a degree of flexibility in
court etiquette that allowed an expression of personal relations at the interstices of
protocol. The rigid rules might be relaxed, by common consent, during certain
ceremonies. In her history of court etiquette under the French *Ancien Régime*,
Madame de Genlis describes how 'a lady of title' might renounce her right to sit
in the presence of the Queen if she were presenting a lady without title who was
compelled to stand:

> Here, social politeness took precedence over the observation of etiquette: in
> respect for blood relationship or friendship, one refused an honour offered
> to one by a royal personage, and refused it in their very presence, and they
> approved this arrangement.[27]

That personal relations could also impinge on the rules at the Russian court is
indicated by an anecdote of Frederiks, the daughter of a close friend of Empress
Alexandra Feodorovna, who had been more or less brought up with the royal
children. At Frederiks's presentation, the Empress behaved at first with the
dignified impersonality required by the ceremony ('Qui est cette demoiselle?')
before relaxing and allowing everyone to enjoy the joke. 'Though she herself was
frightfully amused by my confusion, she immediately embraced me and comforted
me by treating me as she always did, with never failing kindness' (Frederiks, II, 463–
64). Such choreographed spontaneity was not enough for Tyutcheva: she sought for
an emotional expression that was sincere, yet also illicit.

Tyutcheva's attachment to qualities such as candour often had pietistic overtones,
and, as she put it herself, her early education in a German Catholic convent had
given her 'a saving horror of vanity, frivolity, worldly pleasures, spectacles, fine
clothes, and silly books' (Tyutcheva, I, 62). She was, accordingly, peculiarly ill-
equipped to make a success of her career at the court of Nicholas I.

Though Tyutcheva herself emphasised the fact that court etiquette could
protect courtiers from a sovereign's despotism, other sources suggest that the taste
of individual monarchs was fundamental in setting the tone. The atmosphere of
Catherine's court had been studiedly informal, with its intimate suppers for the
Empress and her chosen circle, sometimes held in a pavilion at Tsarskoe Selo which

---

26 *Almanach de la Cour pour l'année bissextile 1860* (St Petersburg: 1860), p. 135.
27 Stephanie-Félicité de Genlis, *De l'esprit des étiquettes de l'ancienne cour et des usages du monde de ce
temps*, ed. by E. Quesnet (Rennes: Callière, 1885), pp. 16–17.

had been equipped with lifts and a revolving table so that servants did not have to be present. After her death in 1796, all this was driven away by Paul I's 'Prussian' and militaristic taste for elaborate ceremony. Softened during the reign of Alexander I, court ceremonial again became stiffer under Nicholas I; the monarch's sergeant-majorish bearing provoked sarcastic comments from foreign visitors to the court.[28]

The personal preferences of sovereigns also had a marked effect on the role of women at court. Catherine II was herself no feminist, regarding her own tough intellect as 'a man's mind in a woman's body', and seeking the company of men for games of cards, intimate suppers, and other still more private pleasures. Yet she did have a number of close women friends whom she raised to prominent positions, most notably Princess Ekaterina Dashkova, first (and indeed only) woman president of the Russian Academy of Sciences. With the accession of Paul I, on the other hand, came a systematic downgrading of the role of the Empress, whose significance as consort was now underlined in court ceremonial. The firm establishment of a 'separate sphere' for the Empress, a glorification of her significance as the perfect wife and mother also went, predictably enough, with the creation of a marital double standard, according to which the husband's infidelity was taken for granted, but the wife's was subject to total prohibition.[29]

From the reign of Paul, the 'royal mistress' became an institution, and though Nicholas I was not as blatant in his attentions to royal favourites as Paul or indeed Alexander, his attachment to various women, latterly Varvara Nelidova, was very well known among courtiers. The royal women, on the other hand, were subject to a strict code that did not necessarily prevent infidelity, but certainly prohibited its open expression. The prevailing morality was well reflected in the case of Tsaritsa Elizabeth, wife of Alexander I, who had a passionate affair with an officer of the guards in the 1810s, and who was roundly and bitterly condemned by other women of the royal house, such as her sister-in-law, Empress Alexandra Feodorovna, who wrote in her diary on 15 May 1826:

> She even went so far as to write her memoirs, the description of all her wanderings from the path of virtue, which she read out to him complete, barring only a few details that she herself admitted were too stark for any woman to be able to read them aloud. Not only that: she also intended to give these memoirs to Karamzin [i.e. Nikolai Karamzin, the writer and historian], so that he could keep them for her! My God! [...]

And that woman has always been regarded by the whole of Russia and Europe as a pure martyr, a victim! Even now you always hear people say, 'L'ange Elisabeth est allée rejoindre l'autre ange!' Will posterity never judge more justly?[30]

---

28 On Paul's court see S. Kaznakov, 'Pavlovskaya Gatchina', *Starye gody*, 7–8 (1914), 101–88. Nicholas I's bullying behaviour in church is disapprovingly described, for example, in the marquis de Custine's famous denunciation of Nikolaevan Russia, *La Russie en 1839*, 2 vols (Brussels: Societé Belge de Librairie, 1843), I, 184 (letter 11): 'The emperor, before prostrating himself like everyone else, scrutinised the congregation in a rather graceless manner'.
29 See Richard Wortman, *Scenarios of Power: Myth and Ceremony in Russian Monarchy*, 2 vols (Princeton, NJ: Princeton University Press, 1995–2000), I, esp. 250–51.
30 The diary of Empress Alexandra Feodorovna is quoted in S.-N. Iskjul', 'Neopublikovannyi

For Empress Maria Feodorovna, as expressed in her 1820s correspondence with her daughter the Princess of Orange (the former Grand Duchess Anna Pavlovna), the ultimate virtues in women of the court were stoicism and modesty:

> Charlotte Karlovna [Lieven, confidante of Maria Feodorovna], was angry at his tears [i.e. the tears of a Prince de Croquembourg, rejected by the lady-in-waiting he wished to marry]. But the countess expects a perfection from us that is more than men are capable of. We must demand it of women, but men don't follow the same strict rules.

In practice, such moral perfection of course meant surrendering control of areas beyond the purview of refined discourse, such as sexual relations, as the Empress makes clear in her discussion of the health of Grand Duchess Alexandra (the future Empress Alexandra), who was spared the sexual attentions of her husband only when this was ordered by the court doctors:

> The Grand Duchess will need time and medical resources to strengthen her health and her nerves. Nicholas is already distracted at the abstinence he must observe, but all the doctors say that the constitution of the Grand Duchess demands some rest after those close pregnancies. She didn't even have one period between Marie's birth and the pregnancy with the dead baby, and that's why she lost so much blood which has weakened her and caused the poor tone of her skin. She was terribly swollen but thank God that has passed.[31]

Such attitudes had an inevitable impact on the status of women at court more generally. The Empress retained her separate suite of retainers, with its own series of ranks running from unmarried ladies-in-waiting (*freiliny*) at the bottom through married ladies-in-waiting (*shtats-damy*) to 'mistresses of the court' (*gofmeisteriny*) at the top. Yet the decline in the Empress's role curtailed the authority that might be acquired through allegiance with her. The possibility of acquiring real political power (as Ekaterina Dashkova had through her friendship with Catherine when the latter became an autocratic ruler in her own right) had ended. Even the Order of St Catherine, all-female in Catherine's day, acquired male officials in the early nineteenth century.[32] Hence, backstairs manipulation of prominent men (members

---

ocherk Velikogo knyazya Nikolaya Mikhailovicha "Imperatritsa Elisaveta Alekseevna"', *Cahiers du monde russe*, 36.3 (1995), 361–62 (full page spread for publication, pp. 345–76). The irony is that, according to a persistent rumour of the day, the Queen Mother, Maria Feodorovna, here commended for her 'purity', had in fact responded to Paul I's numerous infidelities with a liaison with Maximilian Friedrich Klinger, librarian at the Russian court.

31 *Chère Annette: Letters from Russian 1820–1828: The Correspondence of the Empress Maria Feodorovna of Russia to her Daughter the Grand Duchess Anna Pavlovna, the Princess of Orange*, ed. and trans. by S. W. Jackman (Stroud: Alan Sutton, 1994), pp. 15, 66, 27: cf. pp. 25, 45, 67, 69, 74, 100, 115; on p. 83 the Dowager Empress admires Elena Pavlovna's self-command during the trying and lengthy betrothal ceremony.

32 Compare lists in *Pridvornyi mesyatsoslov na leto at Rodzhdestva Khristova 1774* (St Petersburg: pri Imperatorskoi Akademii Nauk, 1774), and *Pridvornyi mesyatsoslov na leto ot Rozhdestva Khristova 1808* (St Petersburg: pri Imperatorskoi Akademii Nauk, 1808): in the former, the women officials had the same titles as in the male orders, 'Grossmeister' and 'Kavalery'; in the latter, the head of the order, Maria Feodorovna, still bore the 'masculine' title 'Ordenmeister', but the other women officials had been retitled 'Diakonissa' and 'Damy Bol'shogo kresta', and the 'Tseremoniemeister' and 'Sekretar'

of the royal house, powerful courtiers) had become the route to influence. Tyutcheva had herself internalised the double-standard:

> Perhaps because I am a woman, I have always found men much less imposing and frightening than women — they are more benevolent. In relation to women, I feel the difference in my status; in relation to men, only the difference in my sex; and with the Emperor, I feel almost as free as with any man from society. (Tyutcheva, I, 109, 25 January 1854)

Yet she also had a strong grasp of the restrictions that Nicholas I's court placed on women, powerfully evoking the decorative infantilism of Alexandra Feodorovna's life in her prefatory memoir. What is more, she repeatedly rejected the most widespread methods of self-advancement, mysticism and sex.[33] Having first of all been unsettled by the fashion for seances because of the possibility of corruption by demonic forces (Tyutcheva, II, 149, 174), Tyutcheva later dismissed them with dry irony. She relates that, after an encounter with an etiquette-obsessed spirit who communicated through a ouija board that he did not want to be addressed by the familiar second-person singular ('you can only say "tu" to God'), she felt her mind set at rest by the mediocrity of the information purveyed: 'If the devil is involved in all this, you'd think he'd be cleverer' (II, 188). The sexual intrigues of the Russian court are dealt with more obliquely, but the disapproval with which Tyutcheva refers to the 'sinful' behaviour of Nicholas I's mistress, Varvara Nelidova (I, 88), is an eloquent indication of her underlying attitudes.

A more serious threat to Tyutcheva's calm, since it brought into question her whole notion of etiquette as the root of moral relations, emerged when she observed the manipulation of court protocol by, as she saw them, careerists. Alexandra Dolgorukova, another lady-in-waiting to Maria Nikolaevna, and favourite of the Emperor, was able to use Tyutcheva's emotional scenes to her own advantage:

> In such situations, Alexandra is silent. Her current role is to be so overcome by reverential awe that she is no longer able to chatter and joke as before. It is a very skilful performance of respect and timidity; she acts it out with great elegance and delicacy, and I sometimes feel that her ceremonious manner of behaviour is much more appropriate than my tears and meaningless reproaches, or than the insouciant delight that I feel when I spend time [with the Royal Family] and which allows me to forget that they are such elevated persons. I love them as though they were not our rulers at all. (Tyutcheva, II, 15–16, 14 March 1855)

Tyutcheva's dilemma is painfully obvious in her use of the terms 'ceremonious' and 'appropriate', both of which carry positive connotations in her writings. The stereotype of the unimpassioned courtier, like a well-trained servant, was worrying because of its close connection with the crucial role of etiquette in regulating court power. Taking the religious role of royal ceremonial and tsarist authority seriously,

---

were both men, as were the two 'Gerol'dy'.

33 'In this unequal combat [court ladies'] weapons were limited to the meager arsenal of character traits legitimised by their stereotype. Of these the most dynamic — mysticism and sex — could be exploited most effectively to transform their subservient position into a dominant one, though at great cost to the stability of court life' (Alfred Rieber, writing in Tyutcheva, I, iv).

Tyutcheva could not do what most courtiers did — observe the outward forms only.[34] Hence, the moral deficiencies of the court, rather than being the basis for censure of autocracy as such, were the cause of sharp personal pain.

Alfred Rieber has interpreted Tyutcheva's memoirs as a study of how 'education helped free her from the dominant stereotypes at court'.[35] But by contrast with her radically inclined contemporaries, Tyutcheva was not directly concerned with women's liberation, still less with education as a part of this. The primary purpose of education was for her *vospitanie* [moral indoctrination] rather than *obrazovanie* [intellectual training]:

> I believe that sovereigns should be surrounded from their earliest years by an atmosphere of politeness and *bon ton*, by which means respect for themselves and others would be instilled in them, so that it would be possible, in later years, to demand that others respected them in the same way. The Empress is generally in agreement with me, but I have the feeling that she does not pay sufficient attention to the upbringing of her sons, and that they are not being given that polish of cultivation that is more necessary to sovereigns than to anyone else.
> (Tyutcheva, II, 62, 3 October 1855)

Once she had taken over as royal governess, Tyutcheva saw her task as requiring that she should educate her charge, the young Maria Aleksandrovna, into a proper sense of etiquette and rank. In a manuscript treatise dedicated to the Grand Duchess's schooling, Tyutcheva dwelt on the need to educate the child into a sense of her own rank, and of her place at court. On the first page of the treatise, she places this purpose second only to the religious end of education:

> Education has two ends to fulfil.
> The first is to make a person into a good Christian and to prepare him for eternal life.
> The second is to make a person capable of filling the place that God has assigned him in this earthly life.

She then goes on to underline the point: 'The earthly end of education is to teach a person to carry out the duties of the social position to which he has been called in this world'.

In the case of the Grand Duchess, social station dictates, on the one hand, that she be protected from the morally questionable influences of her surroundings ('at court [...] everyone has only one concern, one ambition, one over-riding end in view, and that end is not God or goodness in the sight of God; it is power in all its

---

34 On the private contempt for etiquette expressed by many courtiers, see Custine, *Lettres de la Russie*, p. 17, letter 1: 'Once the Grand Duke has disappeared, they adopt a dégagé tone, confident manners and a haughty air that contrasts, in a not very agreeable manner, with the complete self-abnegation that they were affecting a moment previously'. There is an intriguing resemblance between the way in which Tyutcheva attempts to rationalise her position and the contortions of that ideal female servant and Sentimentalist heroine, Richardson's Pamela: cf. Janet Todd, 'Pamela, or the Bliss of Servitude', in her *Gender, Art and Death* (Cambridge: Polity Press, 1993), pp. 63–80: however, 'passionate intensity' would be a more accurate phrase for Tyutcheva's experience of servitude than 'bliss'.
35 Writing in Tyutcheva, I, iv.

forms, honours, riches, and pleasures'), but also brought to a sense of her unusual social status, and allowed to benefit by this in an intellectual sense:

> A young Grand Duchess, child as she may be, is obliged to converse with large numbers of people who surround her with tokens of esteem and lend to her words an interest rarely given to [what] young children [say]. Let us make use of this in order to put the Grand Duchess in contact with distinguished, intelligent, and cultivated persons of all kinds who can impart taste and familiarity with good conversation to her.

Though Tyutcheva gestures towards a liberal understanding of education, which 'is supposed to develop all an individual's faculties — physical, moral, intellectual — to the maximum possible degree of perfection, and to make him useful to himself and his neighbour', education is for her primarily a means of maintaining the status quo.[36]

Nor was education accredited a liberating role in Tyutcheva's account of her own biography. The move from lady-in-waiting to royal governess is seen in the diary as representing a loss of freedom rather than a moment of unbinding:

> From now on, I shall belong to myself no longer, I shall give up all my life and strength to others, who, let alone giving me anything in return, will probably not even know that I am making any kind of sacrifice. (Tyutcheva, II, 150, 10 August 1858)

If the liberation narratives of radical memoirists, such as Figner, can be related to the 'provincial tale', a narrative of women's liberation depicting how a woman of the country gentry manages to free herself from the stifling constraints of the life conventionally considered appropriate to well-bred young women, Tyutcheva's memoir has strong parallels with the 'society tale', a genre hinging on a clash between the protagonist's inner experience and the possibilities of its representation in the artificial world of high society.[37] Madame de Genlis, herself the author of many society tales, elegantly summarised the starting-point for the genre in her history of court etiquette:

> People of fashion have made a code of love and friendship, whose rules are easy to follow. This code, distinguished by an abundance of artificiality and taste, forbids nothing that is not overt, and condemns nothing but noise [éclat] and scandal; it permits deception and infidelity, so long as these have appropriate [adroites], noble and decent forms.[38]

The opposition between 'deception' and 'scandal' that Genlis draws is fundamental to the society tale, whose stereotypical plot shows how, in high society, an affair

---

36 [Notes on education in French], RGALI f. 10, op. 1, ed. khr. 218, 1. 1 recto, 1. 2 recto, 1. 6 verso, 1. 12 verso.
37 On these genres, see Catriona Kelly, *History of Russian Women's Writing* (Oxford: Oxford University Press, 1994), Chapters 1 and 2.
38 Genlis, *De l'esprit des étiquettes de l'ancienne cour*, p. 118. Given the connection of 'society tales' and some court memoirs, it is an intriguing detail that one of the most famous 'society tales', Julie Krüdener's *Valérie,* was performed at the Russian court theatre in December 1823: see Jackman, *Chère Annette*, p. 83.

that is not based on deception leads to scandal, because concealment of true feeling is impossible, leading to a breach of etiquette's law of silence.

From Empress Alexandra's account, it appears that the memoirs which Empress Elizabeth read aloud to Karamzin were a shaping of a real episode, a genuine love affair, in terms of the classic type of society tale (love taken to the point of scandal), though with the added frisson that the confessional nature of the account breached the convention that the society tale's narrator should only hint at the improprieties threatening the tasteful artificiality of polite society. Tyutcheva's memoirs were, however, also an original and powerful reworking of the 'society tale' because they indicate that friendship, which had been considered by the sentimentalist tradition that shaped the society tale to be a more powerful and reliable emotion than love, could be nearly as 'scandalous' to propriety as romantic love.

Yet, at the same time, the very existence of 'sincerity' depends, in the society tale, on its breaching of the borders of etiquette; the term can only apply to moments that assault generally-accepted rules. Tyutcheva's desire for friendship with Maria Nikolaevna was based, more strongly than anything else, on the sense that they would be close if it were not for the rules (desire is powerful because it is deferred). The conventions of court society might be bewailed, but they were also celebrated by her. Finally, no gesture was possible that was not anticipated by social constraint.

Russian radicals of the 1840s, 1850s, and 1860s regarded women's moral superiority (which they took for granted) as innate, an exemplification of how 'with the most extraordinary ease, [a girl] shakes off the dirt that mires her, overcomes external circumstances by dint of her inner nobility, attains an understanding of life by some process of revelation'.[39] Conservatives such as Tyutcheva, on the other hand, saw women's morality as actively acquired through moral indoctrination (on the part of mothers and governesses), and actively exercised (by observation of morality's dictates). The fact that she viewed etiquette not only as a manifestation of charismatic royal authority, but also as an arena of serious, one might even say professional, endeavour by women, was the reason why straightforward liberation was impossible for Tyutcheva, torn as she was by the conflict between feeling and propriety, morality and *bon ton*. Yet at the same time, she shared the post-Sentimentalist conviction, held also by the radicals, that 'sincerity' depended above all on the open expression of emotion. And this conviction placed her, like the Empress Elizabeth, in direct conflict with the emphasis on stoicism and self-command required from women in the male-dominated courts of Alexander I and Nicholas I.

The sharpness of the dilemma was perhaps the reason why, despite the censoriousness that the later Tyutcheva felt towards her earlier self, her years at the Russian court were by far the most important experience of her life, so far as her writing existence was concerned. After her marriage to Aksakov, she played a prominent role as a hostess and political activist, but the 'autobiographical' element disappeared from her diary. Surviving entries from the 1870s are a dull chronicle

---

39 A. Herzen, *Kto vinovat?*, *Sochineniya*, 9 vols (Moscow: Gosudarstvennoe izdatel'stvo khudozhestvennoi literatury, 1955–58), I, 154.

of events at the Duma and of contacts with fellow Slavophiles, while her published letters, such as those addressed to the woman writer Nadezhda Sokhanskaya, are a heartfelt but banal celebration of domestic bliss: 'How unusually joyful a feeling it is for me to feel myself at home, to feel myself the mistress of a house! [...] We had to unpack everything and organise it all [...] but now everything is tidy and in its place'.[40] Her Russian court diaries, on the other hand, offer fascinating glimpses of a predicament that continues to haunt some royal courts even now; they illuminate the threats to a woman wanting to transgress the boundaries between official and private roles, to be 'queen of hearts' as well as arbiter of the very limited area of social power allocated to her by court convention.[41]

I am grateful to members of the audience at the 'All By Myself' conference on autobiography held at the University of Groningen, November 1996, and at the workshop on Russian literature and gender at the University of Tromsø in June, 1997, for helpful comments on the material presented in this chapter.

40 'Perepiska Aksakovykh s N. S. Sokhanskoi (Kokhanovskoi)', *Russkoe obozrenie*, 10–12 (1897). The quotations here come from 10, p. 410.
41 The phrase 'queen of hearts' was made famous in the interview given by Diana, Princess of Wales, to the BBC television programme *Panorama* in 1995. The text of the interview indicated that the stereotypes of romantic fiction still held their appeal for disaffected women at royal courts, and laid bare the continuing problems of constructing a textual self: in the interview, the princess hardly ever referred to herself as 'I', but often as 'Diana' (when describing other people's reactions to her, e.g. 'Diana's mad'), as 'you' (when generalising from personal experience), and as 'we' (not the 'royal we', but when referring to her problems with bulimia, with 'we' used to mean 'my body and I'). A rather similar experience to Tyutcheva's (and one more comparable in terms of historical setting) was endured by Fanny Burney during her time as lady-in-waiting to Queen Charlotte, wife of George III: see M. A. Doody, *Fanny Burney: The Life in the Works* (Cambridge: Cambridge University Press, 1988), pp. 168–98, and Burney, *Diary and Letters of Madame d'Arblay*, 7 vols (London: Alexander Street Press, 1842–46), II, passim.

CHAPTER 3

The Education of the Will: Advice Literature, *Zakal*, Manliness, and Modernity

[2002]

One of the most salient qualities of the Soviet citizen, or, to adopt the term used in Soviet sources, the 'cultured person' (*kul'turnyi chelovek*), was that of 'steeliness' (*zakalennost'* or *zakal*). The term denoted a combination of physical and mental virtues — fitness, endurance, capacity for boundless qualities of hard work, and resolution — that was the result of a process of 'tempering' (*zakalivanie*). It was meant to be inculcated not only by submission to the military discipline of Party, workplace, and social institutions, and by exposure to the rigours of revolution and Civil War, but also by the performance of exercise programmes (*zariadka*), by other kinds of participation in 'physical culture' (*fizkul'tura*), and by a range of hygiene practices or 'procedures' (*protsedury*), most particularly hydrotherapeutic ones, such as the submission of the body, from early childhood, to douches of cold water and to alternating extremes of temperature.[1] Right up until the end of Soviet power, manuals for nursery-school teachers instructed that children should undergo *zakalivanie* from, at the latest, three years old.[2]

One proclaimed benefit of *zakalivanie* was that the systematic exposure of the body to low temperatures helped prevent the colds and chills that were otherwise believed to be a constant danger from cold draughts (*skvoznyaki*). But this benefit was marginal to the main one: a regimentation and strengthening of the body and an assurance of regularity in physical habits (eating, drinking, urination, and defecation).[3] Brochures for adults propagandised a more rigorous variant of the exercise and bathing routines, with strenuous packages of exercises and passages

---

1   This socialisation by means of institutions is depicted, for example, in Fedor Gladkov's novel *Cement* (*Tsement*, 1925), while *zakalivanie* in the second sense is the subject of Nikolai Ostrovsky's Soviet classic *How the Steel was Tempered* (*Kak zakalyalas' stal'*, 1935).
2   See, for example, *Soviet Preschool Education*, ed. by Henry Chauncey, 2 vols (New York: Holt, Rinehart & Winston, 1969), 1 (Program of Instruction), 52, 77–78, 136–37.
3   Not only teachers, but also parents, were supposed to inculcate this in children. See *Soviet Preschool Education*, ed. by Chauncey, 1, 38, 76–78, 103, and also the model daily schedules for children of various ages (pp. 175–82).

expostulating upon the merits of the cold splash, sea and river bathing, and other challenging exercise.[4]

With physical self-improvement went mental and moral self-improvement. Soviet readers were constantly hectored upon the benefits of 'the hygiene of mental labour' (*gigiena umstvennogo truda*), which required fresh air, frequent breaks, and study that was focused and sensitive of duties to the collective rather than indulged in for its own sake. They were exhorted to maintain punctuality and to streamline work tasks, and sometimes to chart their day minutely in order to ensure that each duty took no more and no less time than it should. The famous 'Gastev system' of work notation was only one of a number of such methods in circulation in the 1920s. *How to be Cultured* (1929), a handily complete guide for the Soviet man in search of ways to temper himself, set out a model chart aimed at the white-collar worker or low-level Party official: 'Wake up 7; bodycare 7–7.16; food preparation and breakfast 7.16–8.03; journey to work 8.03–8.48; discussions with colleagues 8.48–9.52; answering letters 8.48–9.52'.

Once back at home, cultured people were supposed to occupy themselves with reading and a quick meal; the only leisure envisaged was attendance at a film (no doubt of suitably edifying content) between 20.27 and 22.01 precisely.[5] And the final, and perhaps most important, aspect of *zakal* was the cultivation of strong will, 'steeliness' in the moral and mental sense: here again, a host of how-to guides advised on how to inculcate resolve in the self and to suppress shyness and other manifestations of inferior willpower.[6] These qualities were desirable in ordinary citizens, and essential in members of the Party, who were supposed to manifest exceptional capacities for self-discipline and 'political and moral steadfastness'. They were most perfectly manifested, though, in the mythic heroes of Soviet power: the monumental Stakhanovites in official sculptures, rippling their steely muscles, Arctic explorers, test pilots. A particularly striking subject, a pilot killed while flying in the Arctic, is commemorated in an epitaph on a tombstone at the Vagankovo Cemetery, Moscow, as 'a man of iron will and large heart', whose 'bright image is stronger than death'.[7]

Zakalivanie was not intended to be exclusively a masculine programme, or at any rate not in the early Soviet period. However, there was a sense in which 'self-tempering' was seen as an essential in men and a bonus in women. Role models of *Zakalivanie* (for instance, Lenin, or the nineteenth-century radical Nikolai Chernyshevsky) were all men; adventure stories for children (for example, Arkady

---

4 See, for example, L. G. Gol'dfail', *Lechenie vodoi doma, na kurorte i v lechebnom uchrezhdenii* (Moscow & Leningrad: Gosudarstvennoe meditsinskoe izdatel'svo, 1930); V. V. Gorinevskii, *Remont i zakalivanie organizma* (Moscow: Trud i kniga, 1925); A. N. Studitskii, 'Nauchnye osnovy zakalivaniya', *Rabotnitsa*, 6 (1947), 12–13.

5 A. K. Toporkov, *Kak stat' kul'turnym* (Moscow: Rabotnik prosveshcheniya, 1929), p. 83.

6 See, for example, A. L. Mendel'son, *Zastenchivost' i bor'ba s neyu*, 4th edn (Leningrad: Leningradskaya pravda, 1930); P. Razmyslov, 'O vospitanii voli u detei', *Rabotnitsa*, 3 (1948), 13; N. E. Khrisanfov, L. B. Trakhtman, *Pamyatka turista: gigiena i samokontrol'* (Moscow: Profizdat, 1951).

7 'Political and moral steadfastness': see, for example, the character testimonial (*attestatsiya*) for P. N. Sokol'chuk in *Vstrecha s Rossiei*, ed. by V. Zenzinov (New York: [n.pub.], 1944), pp. 584–85; epitaph from grave of V. A. Kolosov (1925–57).

Gaidar's famous *Timur and his Team*, 1940) included a token girl or two, but it was always boys who exercised leadership and authority.[8] And the cult of toughness seems to have had a much larger following among male historical subjects than it had among their female contemporaries, at least to judge by memoirs. The 1930s diarist Leonid Potemkin, who relished 140-mile hiking trips, took part in Universal Military Training, and spent his spare time cultivating an earnest interest in Beethoven and Heine, reveals the association of *zakal* and masculinity in his concept of a suitable Soviet romance:

> With the living image of my brunette constantly on my mind, I [have been] overcome with an even more powerful drive to become a grown man in all senses [so as] to act firmly and confidently for her sake, to be a commander in the broad sense of the word, morally and physically. To speak beautifully and forcefully, not losing my dignity in any situation or conditions. I've become even more enamoured of physical exercise.[9]

The concept of *zakal* was vital to the governing early Soviet myth of a society led by supremely fit and committed citizens, and as a component of the state-sponsored modernisation programme, which promised that in time all Soviet citizens would become 'steely'. However, not only the concept itself, but also its association with manliness and with the health of the nation, can be traced back well before the Revolution. The pre-history of *zakal* in the ideals of male behaviour during the early years of the twentieth century had a direct impact upon the history of *zakal* under Soviet power. The concept of the courageous, resolute, and unflinching male moved from being one of several alternative possibilities for men before the Revolution, to being the preferred ideal of male behaviour in the 1920s, before again becoming marginalised after the Second World War, and the reasons for these shifts in models of masculinity over the years were related to key political and social issues of the day.

Zakal was the Russian term for the quality known in English as 'backbone', 'character', 'moral fibre', or 'strength of will'.[10] The roots of the concept (which has connections with the northern European Romantic celebration of northern barbarism, rather than effeminate southern softness) lay in Western sources as well

---

8   A. Gaidar, *Timur i ego komanda*, in *Sochineniya* (Moscow: Detizdat, 1946), pp. 265–98. For Lenin as a model of *zakal*, see, for example, Mikhail Zoshchenko's 'Stories about Lenin' (1940), and S. Mirev, 'Kogda zhe on spit?', *Rabotnitsa*, 1 (1947), 6; on Chernyshevsky as a glorious example of 'resolute behaviour and capacity to affect one's environment [*sreda*]', see, for example, A. Studentsov, *Chernyshevskii o samoobrazovanii* (Penza: self-published, 1928), pp. 5–6.
9   See *Intimacy and Terror: Soviet Diaries of the 1930s*, ed. by V. Garros, N. Korenevskaia, and T. Lahusen (New York: New Press, 1995), p. 264; and cf. J. Hellbeck, 'Fashioning the Stalinist Soul: The Diary of Stepan Podlubnyi', in *Stalinism: New Directions*, ed. by S. Fitzpatrick (London: Routledge, 2000), p. 100: 'the New Man [...] was a politically inclined individual with a materialistic world-view, who in his character displayed firmness and determination'.
10   The term 'backbone' (*khrebet*) is apparently not used for moral toughness. By the late nineteenth century, *zakal*, which V. I. Dal', *Tolkovyi slovar' zhivogo velikorusskogo yazyka*, 2nd edn, 4 vols (St Petersburg & Moscow: M. O. Vol'f, 1880–82), I, 582, records only in the meanings 'quality' (of steel etc.) and 'a person toughened by severe conditions' had come into use as an abstract noun: Chekhov's story 'Neschast'e' uses the word in this meaning, for instance.

as Russian ones. The ideal of stern manliness was set out not only in literary and philosophical texts (Schopenhauer, Nietzsche, Chernyshevsky, Dostoevsky), but also in mass-market printed books. If 'highbrow' examples of manly resolution (for example, Robert Bage's hero Hermsprong, or Chernyshevsky's Rakhmetov) were usually Romantic natural geniuses of moral fibre, drawing their authority from innate gifts (an idea raised also in Raskol'nikov's theory of the 'two classes' (*razryada*) of human beings, those made to lead and those to follow), popular representations tended to emphasise the imitability of the character types they hymned.[11] Brochures under titles such as *The Education of the Will, Shyness and How to Cure It*, and *The Fight with Idleness*, a genre that began issuing from Russian mass-market presses in the late 1880s, instructed readers on how to become run-of-the-mill supermen, while exercise manuals, such as Jorgen Peter Müller's *My System,* or Joe Edwards's *The Culture of the Body*, laid down the methods by which men could attain *zakal* in the physical sense.[12] Just as after the Revolution, physical and mental control went hand-in-hand. Authors of exercise manuals emphasised that mere muscle-building was not enough, while authors of manuals on 'educating the will' asserted the triumph of mind over matter, even insisting that nocturnal emissions could be controlled through strong-mindedness.[13]

This last detail indicates the explicitness with which strength of will and masculine physiology were identified at this era. To be sure, the Russian intelligentsia's tradition of gender egalitarianism, which went back to the 1860s, sometimes meant that the rigid gender divisions of French, German or English originals were softened in translation. The (female) translator of Payot into Russian, in contrast to her (male) American counterpart, rendered a passage near the beginning of the book in gender-free terms. The English version reads: 'The real obstacle to work lies in a fundamental ever-present state of mind which may be called *effeminacy*, apathy, idleness, or laziness'; the Russian, on the other hand, speaks of '*flabbiness*

---

11   Robert Bage, *Hermsprong, or Man as he is Not*, 2 vols (London: printed for William Lane, at the Minerva Press, 1796); N. Chernyshevskii, *Chto delat'?* [1862], Chapter 3, sections 29–30 (see his *Sobranie sochinenii*, 3 vols (Leningrad: Khudozhestvennaya literatura, 1978), I, 275–319; F. M. Dostoevsky, *Prestuplenie i nakazanie* [1866], in *Polnoe sobranie sochinenii*, 30 vols (Leningrad: Khudozhestvennaya literatura, 1972–90), VI.

12   P. Lévy [as Levi], *Ratsional'noe vospitanie voli: Prakticheskoe rukovodstvo k dukhovnomu samolecheniyu i samovospitaniyu* (St Petersburg: O. Bogdanova, 1912) (from *L'Éducation de la volonté* (Paris: Alcan, 1898); A. L. Dugas [as Dyuga], *Zastenchivost' i ee lechenie* (St Petersburg: V. I. Gubinsky, 1899) (from *La Timidité, étude psychologique et morale* (Paris: Alcan, 1898); L. A. Zolotarev, *Bor'ba s len'yu* (Moscow: tipo-litografiya tovarishchestva I. N. Kushnerov i Ko., 1907); J. P. Müller (as I. P. Miller), *Moya sistema: 15 minut ezhednevnoi raboty dlya zdorov'ya* (St Petersburg: tipografiya F. N. Al'tshullera, 1909) (from the English version of the Danish original, *My System: Fifteen Minutes' Work a Day for Health Sake* (London: Ewart, Seymour, 1905, etc.]); D. Edwards, *Ideal'naya kul'tura tela. Naibolee vernye i deistvitel'no obezpechivayushchie zdorov'e uprazhneniya dlya kazhdogo cheloveka* (St Petersburg: Sotrudnik, [c. 1910]) (I have not managed to locate the original of this book, but Edwards, according to the catalogue of the Russian National Library, was also the author of *Angliiskii boks* [English Boxing] (St Petersburg: Sotrudnik, 1910), which gives him as 'the founder of the Berlin School of Boxing'. For an early twentieth-century photograph of Joe Edwards and his boxing school, see <https://www.alamy.com/boxing-class-in-joe-edwards-school-berlin-image367499263.html> [accessed 20 March 2022].

13   Lévy, *Ratsional'noe vospitanie*, pp. 174–75.

[*vyalost'*], apathy, sloth, or idleness'.[14] But such tentative attempts to preserve gender balance were undermined because translators more often faithfully reproduced many Western manuals' insistence that women had separate and complementary roles. As a translated pamphlet called *The Secrets of Self-Control* put it

> To demand self-control from women would not only be cruel, it would represent a total misunderstanding of their nature and destiny. The activity of a man takes place outside the home; the woman is occupied by domestic matters and the better she copes with this the more calmly she responds to the surrounding world.

In such sources, Russian readers were exposed to an especially rigid variant of the 'ideology of separate spheres', one that not only confined women to the home (as had been traditional for centuries in any case), but which permitted men only the most marginal role in domestic space (something that was rather more novel).[15]

The 'masculine' resonance of 'education of the will' and of *zakalivanie* was enhanced by the existence of a separate tradition of hygiene manuals for women, which stressed above all the need to regulate the female body's potential for pollution and insanitariness.[16] Equally, though texts aimed at women sometimes presented material on the desirability of efficiency (a piquant example was a set of guidelines on 'American behaviour' set out for readers of *Ladies' World* in 1915), such material was scanty compared with the torrents of brochures on 'educating the will' for men.[17]

14 J. Payot, *The Education of the Will: The Theory and Practice of Self-culture*, trans. by S. E. Jeliffe (New York: Funk & Wagnall, 1909), p. 4 (my emphasis); *Vospitanie voli*, trans. by M. Shishmareva, 6th edn (St Petersburg: F. Pavlenkov, 1910), p. 1 (my emphasis). The original French has *mollesse* [softness] (see J. Payot, *L'Education de la volonté* (Paris: Alcan, 1895), p. 3). At least two of the Russian translators of Kipling's poetic celebration of 'backbone', 'If' ('If you can force your heart and nerve and sinew | To serve your turn long after they are gone | And so hold on where there is nothing in you | Except the Will which says to them "Hold on!" | [...] Yours is the earth and everything that's in it | And — which is more — you'll be a Man, my son!) rendered the word 'man' as the gender-neutral *chelovek*. (See the versions by M. Lozinsky and by S. Marshak in R. Kipling, *Stikhotvoreniya* (St Petersburg: Severo-Zapad, 1994), pp. 423–25, 468–69). And women writers (for example, Zinaida Stolitsa in her brochure *Razvitie u detei zhizneradostnosti i bor'ba s pessimizmom* (St Petersburg & Moscow: Tovarishchestvo M. O. Vol'f, 1912)), contributed to the stream of texts pronouncing on the need for backbone (for Stolitsa, too, the children who were to be 'cured' of pessimism included girls as well as boys).
15 Berndt [no first name given], *Sekret samoobladaniya, ili lechenie strastei i dushevnykh stradanii*, trans. by Dm. Kriuchkov (St Petersburg: Kolumbiya, 1910), p. 44. The earliest domestic manuals all over Europe were addressed to men: see, for example, *The Goodman of Paris*, trans. by Eileen Power (London: Routledge, 1928) (the sixteenth-century Russian *Domostroi* accords with this tradition). But later manuals advocated a division of responsibilities within the household, an appreciation that was evident in late eighteenth- and early nineteenth-century translations from French and German into Russian: see, for example, V. Levshin, *Polnaya khozyaistvennaya kniga, otnosyashchayasya do vnutrennego domovodstva kak gorodskikh, tak i derevenskikh zhitelei, khozyaev i khozaek. V desiati chastyakh, s risunkami. Sochinenie Vasil'ya Levshina* (Moscow: v tipografii S. Selivanovskogo, 1813). Nationalist conservatives such as the Slavophile group were later to make the domestic idyll based upon a division of labour a foundation stone of their eulogisation of *russkii byt* [Russian daily life]: for a discussion of this, see Chapter 2 of my *Refining Russia*.
16 On this, see Chapter 2 of *Refining Russia*.
17 See *Kalendar' 'Damskii mir' na 1915 god* (St Petersburg: Damskii mir, 1915), p. 255.

Given that the Russian book market was swift to respond to new interests on the part of its readers (the new craze for motoring, for instance, was humoured almost immediately by the appearance of brochures such as *The Automobilist*), it is reasonable to assume that the arrival of these self-help manuals reflected concerns and anxieties circulating in the public at large, an assumption also supported by the fact that several of them went through repeated editions. Particular popularity was enjoyed by a Russian translation of Jules Payot's *L'Education de la volonté*, reprinted at least nine times by 1917.[18] But what were the implications of 'educating the will', and exactly why did it become so popular in the early twentieth century?

According to their authors, self-help manuals of this kind were aimed at a specifically modern malaise: as summed up in Paul Lévy's *L'Education rationelle de la volonté*, 'The worst illness of our time is weakness of will'.[19] Payot, in similar vein, emphasised to his readers that a slough of sloth always threatened to overwhelm modern man: 'Our passiveness, thoughtfulness and dissipation of energy are only so many names to designate the depths of universal laziness, which is to human nature as gravity is to matter'.[20] As these examples suggest, pseudo-scientific terminology was ubiquitous, and undertones of Social Darwinism often evident. In the words of one author:

> Thanks to the persistent struggle for survival, along with competitiveness and the sense that everyone has an equal right to life's benefits, a mass of inner sufferings and passions has come into being. Happy anyone who has been gifted by nature with a strong character [*sil'nyi dukh*]![21]

Treatises on educating the will showed those not so 'gifted by nature' how to come out winners in the 'struggle for survival', and how to cope with the psychological upheaval and pressure that was held to be a side-effect of modern life. By learning to exercise will, it was proclaimed, readers would learn to take charge of their own lives.[22] The need for optimism was paramount: 'When we get up in the morning, we should always make ourselves believe: "Today is the most wonderful day of the rest of my life"'.[23] (In the 1920s, Pollyanna-ish advice of this kind was to acquire its own mantra, supplied by Dr Émile Coué, whose readers were supposed to recite to themselves daily the formula 'Every day in every way I am getting better and better'. Coué's *Auto-Suggestion* was translated into Russian in 1928.)[24]

18 This information is based on the General Catalogue of the Russian State Library in Moscow, which has the fullest holdings of Russian advice literature anywhere.
19 Lévy, *Ratsional'noe vospitanie*, p. 101.
20 Payot, *The Education of the Will*, trans. by Jeliffe, p. 3; *Vospitanie voli*, trans. by Shishmareva, p. 1.
21 Berndt, *Sekret samoobladaniya*, p. 5.
22 Lévy, *Ratsional'noe vospitanie*, p. 133.
23 T. Mainardt, *Lichnoe vliyanie, ili zakony dukhovnogo prebladaniya. Sila vnutri nas. Rukovodstvo k pribuzhdeniyu i pol'zovaniyu tainstvennymi dushevnymi silami (pyat' chastei prakticheskoi psikhologii dlia sovremennogo delovogo cheloveka)*, 11th edn (Saratov: Nauchno-psikhologicheskoe knigoizdatel'stvo v Moskve. Otdelenie v Saratove, 1910), p. 48.
24 E. Coué [as Kue], *Shkola samoobladaniya putem soznatel'nogo (prednamerennogo) samovnusheniya* (Nizhnii Novgorod: Dom sanitarnogo prosveshcheniya Nizhgubzdrava, 1928). For an enthusiastic Russian reader of the book, see Tamara Talbot Rice, *Tamara: Memoirs of St Petersburg, Paris, Oxford and Byzantium* (London: Murray, 1996).

Admiration for self-assertion had its limits, however. Egotism was as much to be guarded against as pessimism. As their emphasis upon conformity made clear, the guides were aimed not so much at entrepreneurs, as at readers in white-collar employment who needed to learn how to make an impression upon subordinates, superiors, and colleagues in large organisations. In Russia, this advice was especially relevant, since hierarchical relations in private companies lacked the clarity that they had in the Russian civil service, whose notoriously inflexible 'Table of Ranks' ruled out speedy promotion for able social outsiders. The meritocratic egalitarianism of guides to acquiring 'strong will', their emphasis on the need to impose authority by personal qualities rather than by pre-ascribed social rank, made them quite different from the treatises upon appropriate behaviour for men published in Russia in the late eighteenth and early nineteenth centuries. These had also emphasised diligence and efficiency, and the need for self-respect, but had asserted the importance of accepting social station as given, of deferring to superiors and condescending to inferiors.[25]

At one level, then, the cult of 'educating the will' pointed to a sea-change in perceptions of masculine honour (*chest'*), completing the move from a 'feudal' perception of identity, based on birth and family status, to a 'bourgeois', individualist one, emphasising personal qualities, that had begun to be set in train during the Enlightenment. But this was not the only or perhaps even the main significance of the new manliness. As Robert A. Nye points out in his 1998 study, *Masculinity and Male Codes of Honor in Modern France*, 'The corporeal economy became [...] a metaphor for the larger problem of the vitality and prospects of the industrial order'. If the human material on the shop floor could be transformed, then economic success could be ensured. Though this idea was less prominent before the Revolution than it was afterwards (when it was directly expressed in the publications of Aleksei Gastev and other advocates of scientific principles in labour), another obsession of self-help books, 'the education of courage in particular, a quality additionally useful to the nation', was exceedingly important before 1917 as well.[26]

Like France, Germany, and Britain, Russia was, at the beginning of the nineteenth century, a major military power, with ambitions for territorial expansion and for the exercise of further geopolitical authority. In the wake of humiliating defeat for the Russian Army by Japan in 1905, some of Payot's admonitions to his audience of post-Franco-Prussian War Frenchmen must have struck a particular chord:

> A few years ago the power of the French artillery was mediocre, now it is stronger. Why? Because the shell used to explode when it struck the obstacle and would go off without doing any great damage, but now, by the invention

---

25 See, for example, J. Grabiensky, *Conseils d'un ami à un jeune homme qui entre dans le monde* (Berlin: Néaulme & Jasperd, 1760), translated into Russian as *Druzheskie sovety molodomu cheloveku, nachinayushchemu zhit' v svete*, 2nd edn (Moscow: pechatano pri Imperatorskom Moskovskom universitete, 1765).
26 Robert A. Nye, *Masculinity and Male Codes of Honor in Modern France*, 2nd edn (Berkeley: University of California Press, 1998), pp. 222, 224. See also Anson Rabinbach, *The Human Motor: Energy, Fatigue, and the Origins of Modernity* (New York: Basic Books, 1990). A. Gastev, *Trudovye ustanovki* (Moscow & Leningrad: Tsentral'nyi institute truda, 1924).

of a special detonator, the shell, after it has struck, continues to move for a few
seconds, penetrating right into the very heart of the place of attack [...]. In our
practical education we have forgotten to add a detonator to the mind.[27]

However, concern with Russia's military capacity was only part of the complex background to the reception of books on 'backbone', which in several important respects was quite different from that in France (if one credits Nye's description of the latter).

To begin with, the cult of manliness in Russia was more diverse and divided than was the cult of manliness in France. Nye argues for the essential endurance of a code of honour going back to medieval times, which 'survived the destruction of the Old Regime in 1789 by accommodating its practices and usages to the unique sociability and legal arrangements of bourgeois civilization'. This code of honour was remarkably constrictive: 'The men who submitted themselves to the sexual prescriptions and the social rituals of the honour code felt themselves enmeshed in a fatally narrow circle of alternatives'. One result was that duels continued to be taken seriously in France for considerably longer than they did in comparable countries (Britain or America): 'The passion for duelling increased after 1850 when the nation made democratic and libertarian advances that far outpaced other continental countries that conserved the duel'. In a culture which saw the duel as a contribution to the defence of the nation as well as a demonstration of personal valour, and where duels were used against political opponents, as a response to supposed slights by journalists, and even as a way in which French Jews could defend themselves against charges of being unfit for public life, a failure to respond to a challenge was something that only bohemian eccentrics, such as the writer Joséphin Péladan, could afford without cost to their reputation.[28]

In Russia, on the other hand, the practice of duelling had a much more ambiguous status. It was not simply another expression of the same code of 'manliness' that treatises upon 'educating the will' sought to inculcate. To be sure, some commentators on duelling in Russia have argued exactly along Nye's lines, and have asserted that, while the participants in duels may have changed, regard for the custom did not, remaining very high even in the early twentieth century. In the words of Irina Reyfman:

> Duelling did not disappear even when its original proponents, the nobility [i.e. the *dvoryanstvo*], had forfeited the cultural foreground. The duel's high status, established at the beginning of the nineteenth century, survived almost intact until 1917 and, in a certain sense, until the present.[29]

But interpretations of this kind ignore the fact that the duel's persistence into the twentieth century was partly the result of a *revival* of the practice in the late

---

27 Payot, *The Education of the Will*, p. 17; *Vospitanie voli*, p. 7 — note that 'the French artillery' is rendered in the Russian as '*nasha* artilleriya' (my emphasis) [i.e. 'our/the Russian artillery'].
28 Nye, *Masculinity and Male Codes of Honor*, pp. 8, 11, 135.
29 Irina Reyfman, 'The Emergence of the Duel in Russia: Corporal Punishment and the Honor Code', *Russian Review*, 54 (1995), 26. See also the same writer's *Ritualized Violence Russian Style: The Duel in Russian Culture and Literature* (Stanford, CA: Stanford University Press, 1999).

nineteenth and early twentieth centuries. The background to this was the Tsarist administration's attempt to broaden the social base for the recruitment of army officers, while at the same time preserving intact the ethos of the 'officer and gentleman', an attempt that was entirely characteristic of the contradictory commitment to economic modernisation on the one hand, and political conservatism on the other, expressed by the governments of Alexander III and Nicholas II. The egalitarian impact of D. A. Milyutin's reforms in the 1860s, which had emphasised the importance of education and training, was averted by a policy 'promoting norms of officer behavior that were at least theoretically "aristocratic"'.[30] One of these norms was duelling. In 1894 it became incumbent upon officers to fight duels (despite the fact that these were still forbidden by criminal law) in defence of their 'military honour', and tribunals of senior officers (*ofitserskie sobraniya*), later known as courts of honour (*sudy chesti*), were mandated to regulate the practice and to determine when a duel was necessary.[31] Duels were obligatory 'even where the officers concerned did not feel that their honour had been insulted'.[32] Failure to fight a duel when ordered by a court of honour to do so was punishable by dismissal from the service.[33]

This is not to say that duelling was a sort of cultural 'dead letter', a proof of valour recognised in the mind of the Russian military and bureaucratic establishment, but nowhere else. An indication to the contrary is the case of Aleksei Suvorin, the editor of the conservative newspaper *Novoe vremya*, who, in 1911, was incited to

30 W. C. Fuller, Jnr., *Civil-military Conflict in Imperial Russia, 1881–1914* (Princeton, NJ: Princeton University Press, 1985), pp. 22–23.
31 Penalties for participation in duels ranged from three to seven days for issuing a challenge, through three weeks to three months for fighting a duel if no injury took place, up to two to six years for the surviving participant if he killed his opponent. These penalties were significantly lighter than those imposed for murder, which, from 1871, carried a penalty of up to twenty years if premeditated and at least four years whatever the circumstances (see *Entsiklopedicheskii slovar' Brokgauza i Efrona*, 43 vols (St Petersburg: 1902), XXXIV, 400). According to I. A. Mikulin, *Posobie dlya vedeniya del chesti v ofitserskoi srede*, 2 vols (St Petersburg: tipografiya Shtaba voisk gvardii i Peterburgskogo voennogo okruga, 1912), I, 77, after 1868 (when there had been inconclusive discussions about reducing the penalties for duelling) the authorities often avoided imposing the punishments that existed. The process in Germany went exactly the opposite way: a ruling of 1897 discouraged officers from duelling, and from that date courts of honour generally did their best to reconcile antagonists, rather than commanding them to fight (see M. Kitchen, *The German Officer Corps, 1890–1914* (Oxford: Clarendon Press, 1968), p. 55).
32 Paul Robinson, 'Always with Honour: The Code of the White Russian Officers', *Canadian Slavonic Papers*, 41.2 (June 1999), 121–41. My thanks to Dr Robinson for letting me have a copy of this paper in advance of publication.
33 See *Polnoe sobranie zakonov Rossiiskoi Imperii*, no. 10618, 13 May 1894, XIV, 258–59; *Voinskii ustav o nakazaniyakh i Ustav distsiplinarnyi*, 3rd edn (St Petersburg: Voennaya tipografiya, 1906), p. 170, supplement to article 130. The basic brief of the *ofitserskie sobraniya* was to try 'officers who have been found out in unbecoming behaviour, or in acts which, though not forbidden by criminal law, are not in harmony with the concepts of military honour and the personal honour [*doblest'*] of an officer, or which reveal in an officer an absence of respect for the rules of moral and noble behaviour'. See ibid., p. 163, article 130; P. A. Shveikovsky, *Sud chesti i Duel' v voiskakh Rossiiskoi Armii: Deistvuyushchee zakonodatel'stvo so vsemi kommentariyami. Nastol'naya kniga dlia ofitserov vsekh rodov oruzhiya*, ed. by N. P. Vishnyakov, 3rd edn (St Petersburg: V. Berezovsky, 1912), pp. 17–18; Mikulin, *Posobie dlya vedeniya del chesti v ofitserskoi srede*, I, 97.

fury when a general whom he had attempted to call out was decreed not subject to challenge by the General Staff.³⁴ Given that the concept of 'challengeability' (*pravosposobnost'* or *duelesposobnost'*) was now thought by most commentators to be determined by a man's level of 'culturedness' (*kul'turnost'*), rather than by his social status (the estate, *soslovie*, to which he belonged), duelling had a democratic propensity which it had lacked in early nineteenth-century Russia, and still lacked in contemporary Germany.³⁵

However, even officially sponsored duels involving army officers were not particularly common. Between 1894 and 1910, about 20 per year were fought (a total of 322 in sixteen years) — not a significant number given that there were over 35,000 officers on active duty.³⁶ Cases when officers risked dismissal by failing to fight duels, or subverted the process by fighting sham duels, were fairly numerous, and the fact that more than 27 per cent of duels ended in serious injury or death undermined the authorities' pedagogical purpose from a different direction (the imposition of duelling as a corporative responsibility had been meant to produce responsible and comradely officers, not invalids or dead heroes).³⁷

Official sponsorship, all in all, was less than wholly successful in popularising the well-regulated form of duelling (a test of valour rather than a fight to the death) that

---

34 Suvorin had duelled with General Pykhachev of the Border Guards when the latter took exception to a letter in which Suvorin accused Pykhachev's brother officer General Martynov of *korystnye mery* (self-interest, a euphemism for bribery). Both participants were punished, Suvorin by a week in prison for 'intemperate language' (*rezkie vyrazheniya*), Pykhachev by a fine. Unable to bring Martynov to book by other means, Suvorin then challenged him; the two agreed to duel but were prevented when the military command decreed that for generals 'honour was a personal, not a corporative, concept' (see A. A. Suvorin, *Duel'nyi kodeks* (St Petersburg: Novyi chelovek, [1913]), pp. 198–263). Suvorin himself was challenged to a duel around this time by the impeccably liberal politician V. D. Nabokov, who had been enraged by a 'scurrilous piece' in the conservative newspaper *Novoe vremya*, and called out the editor because he considered 'the well-known rascality of the actual author of the article made him "non-duelable" [*neduelesposobnïy*]'. This duel, however, was averted by Suvorin's apology (see Vladimir Nabokov, *Speak, Memory* (Harmondsworth: Penguin, 1969), p. 147: the identity of Suvorin, not given here, is clear from the Russian edition of the text, *Drugie berega*).

35 V. V. Durasov, *Duel'nyi kodeks*, 4th edn (St Petersburg: tipografiya 'Sirius', 1912), p. 13, article 4, stated, 'Duels are only possible between people of equal, which is to say gentle [*blagorodnoe*], birth'. However, Suvorin, *Duel'nyi kodeks*, p. 36, article 138 (1), related 'challengeability' to a man's 'cultural levels': banned from duelling were 'persons who do not have a sufficient level of culturedness, according to the demands of today's society'. And Mikulin, *Sud chesti i duel' v voiskakh Rossiiskoi Imperii*, II, 28, article 100, made a man's 'level of culture' (*uroven' kul'tury*) and his 'position in society' (*polozhenie v obshchestve*) equally important. The appendix of sample decisions for courts of honour included several cases involving an imaginary 'Gentleman B [Dvoryanin B]', who was deemed challengeable in most circumstances, but not, however, if he happened to be in some abject form of employment ('Dvoryanin B, working as a doorman at the Bol'shaya Morskaya Hotel...', p. 135), or still worse, discreditably unemployed ('Dvoryanin B, a street tramp and beggar...', ibid.). On the persistence of rigid notions of *Satisfaktionsfähigkeit* in Germany, see Kitchen, *The German Officer Corps*, p. 54.

36 See Mikulin, *Posobie dlya vedeniya del chesti v ofitserskoi srede*, I, 177–203, appendix, tables 1 and 2. For the size of the officer corps, see Fuller, *Civil-military Conflict*, p. 25.

37 There were fifteen deaths between 1894 and 1910, i.e. nearly 1 in 20 had a fatal outcome: see Mikulin, *Posobie dlya vedeniya del chesti v ofitserskoi srede*, I, 177–203.

the military high command had in mind. The approved procedures — the need to consult courts of honour, to maintain minutes (*protokoly*) of meetings between antagonists, the requirement of agreeing upon precisely which duelling code (*duel'nyi kodeks*) was to be used, and, not least, of being punctual upon all occasions — had a laboriousness that worked against their becoming fully naturalised.[38]

It is reasonable to suppose that the promotion of officers' duels in this bureaucratic form did anything other than enhance the status of the duel among educated civilian Russians opposed to the regime. These were in any case heirs to a tradition of suspicion of, or even contempt for, duelling stretching back to at least the 1840s. The unease with regard to duelling that is evident in Lermontov's *A Hero of Our Time* (in which Pechorin's honour is called into question by the fact that his opponent is so nonentious), had, by the late nineteenth century, been transformed into a widespread conviction that the practice was shameful and preposterous.[39] To be sure, literary figures occasionally indulged in duels (most famously, in the case of Maksimilian Voloshin and Nikolai Gumilev, who fought over the pseudonymous poetess 'Cherubina de Gabriak'); but this was a peculiar and marginal phenomenon, derived from these writers' cult of the Pushkin era, upon whose mores they self-consciously modelled themselves, rather than an expression of intelligentsia passions more generally.[40]

More typical was Kuprin's 1905 story *The Duel*, an excoriation of cynicism, brutality, and corruption in the Russian army, where refusal to fight was represented as more honourable conduct than compliance with the stipulations of the ridiculous 'court of honour'; or a lurid painting by Ilya Repin, showing an injured man tended by friends, and his opponent quivering to his right, while a haughty young blood, clearly the galvanising force behind the encounter, smoked defiantly in the background.[41]

---

38 See the duelling codes on all these. However, A. Vostrikov, *Kniga o russkoi dueli* (St Petersburg: izdatel'stvo Ivana Limbakha, 1998), goes too far in the note to plate 6 (after p. 64), showing Durasov, *Duel'nyi kodeks*, where he comments: 'Let us not forget that those who engaged in duelling did not read these books', since at least some certainly did use them. For instance, Suvorin records (*Duel'nyi kodeks*, p. 207) that he and General Martynov agreed to use the Durasov code for their meeting.

39 Take, for instance, Turgenev's *Fathers and Children*, or Chekhov's story 'The Duel'. It was not only liberal commentators of this kind who rejected duelling. Conservatives such as the Slavophiles considered the practice foreign to Russian culture (cf. Aleksei Khomyakov's comment on Pushkin's duel, 'there was no decent cause for it': letter to N. M. Yazykov, February 1837, quoted in *Pushkin v zhizni*, ed. by V. Veresaev (Moscow: Moskovskii rabochii, 1984), p. 636). Among women conservatives, the employment of the practice as a way of defending women's honour was seen as endorsing female self-indulgence (as in Karolina Pavlova's narrative poem *Quadrille*, 1859).

40 Reyfman, 'The Emergence', p. 26, n. 1, argues that 'the curiously enthusiastic treatment given to it by modern Russian historians' is 'one sign of the duel's lasting prestige'. I would argue that, on the contrary, this 'enthusiasm' is the product of two factors of local significance in Soviet cultural history of the Thaw period, the first of which is the cult of the early nineteenth century that began in the 1960s, initiated by writings such as Okudzhava's novels and the semiotic studies of Yury Lotman, and the second of which is the search for alternative models of masculinity that was provoked by official Soviet propaganda against deviant male behaviour. For a more detailed exposure of these two points, see Chapter 5 of my *Refining Russia*.

41 See A. Kuprin, *Poedinok*, in *Sobranie sochinenii*, 7 vols (Moscow: Khudozhestvennaya literatura, 1964), IV, 5–231; the Repin canvas, *Duel'* (1913), is in the Muzei chastnykh sobranii in Moscow.

Rather than assimilating the new cult of 'backbone' into earlier models of valour, the typical Russian intellectual drew a sharp division between the old and the new. An intriguing illustration of this comes in Chekhov's play *Three Sisters* (1901). One of the opponents in the fatal duel that takes place in Act IV, Solenyi, is a grotesque caricature of the early nineteenth-century *bretteur* (ardent duellist); the other, Baron Tusenbach, is the most spineless, if also the most amiable, of the male characters. The fact that it is precisely the unmanly Tusenbach who has a valorous death thrust upon him calls into question the association between duelling and honour that was essential to the military cult of the practice. For official apologists of the duel, the custom was an external manifestation of internal honour, or 'conscience'.[42] Intelligentsia critics, on the other hand, invoked a distinction between 'honour' in an external sense (status, as preserved by the duel) and 'honour' in an internal sense (conscience) that had been central to Western arguments against duelling since at least the seventeenth century.[43]

Hostility to the duel was exacerbated by early twentieth-century members of the Russian intelligentsia's determination to jettison established practices that were seen as exemplifying the country's 'backwardness'. A distinctive element in the Russian cult of 'steeliness' was the widespread tendency to perceive this quality's negative counter-images — unmasculine flabbiness and pernicious self-indulgence — as national characteristics. For example, L. A. Zolotarev, in his *The Battle with Idleness*, argued that the most 'cultured' nations (Britain, France, Germany, and the Jewish community in Russia) were also those characterised by the highest levels of hard work. This industriousness was incompatible with a penchant for alcohol or illicit sexual activity, to both of which, he implied, Russian readers were sadly prone.[44]

It was frequently argued that qualities such as 'empty dreaming' (*mechtatel'nost'*) or 'passivity' (*passivnost'*) must be jettisoned if society were to be remodelled, as in an essay by Zinaida Stolitsa on the 'fight with pessimism', which singled out the 'characterlessness' and 'instability' of Russian life as factors inhibiting the development of 'joy in life', and contributing to social malaise, as manifested for instance by the high rate of suicide among young people.[45]

Anxieties over Russian social passivity were nothing new in themselves: from the 1840s, they had crystallised in the literary cliché of the superfluous man (*lishnii chelovek*). But this cliché took on a new lease of life and a new resonance during the late nineteenth century. Where earlier generations had seen 'superfluity' as the product of social status (in Ivan Goncharov's famous novel, *Oblomov*, it was an illustration of the indolence fostered in the Russian *dvoryanstvo* by serfdom), by the turn of the century it was usually perceived as a manifestation of a typically 'Russian' propensity for sloth. In the words of D. A. Ovsyaniko-Kulikovsky:

---

42   See Mikulin, *Sud chesti i duel' v voiskakh Rossiiskoi Imperii*, p. 15.
43   See for instance Joachim de La Chetardie, *Instructions pour un jeune seigneur ou l'idée d'un galant homme*, 2 vols (Paris: Girard, 1683) (translated into Russian by Ivan Murav'ev as Trotti de la Shetardi, *Nastavlenie znatnomu cheloveku, ili Voobrazhenie o svetskom cheloveke* (St Petersburg: pechatano pri Artilleriiskom i inzhinernom shlyakhetnom korpuse, 1778]).
44   See Zolotarev, *Bor'ba s len'yu*, esp. pp. 35, 45, 46, 100.
45   See Stolitsa, *Razvitie u detei zhizneradostnosti*, esp. p. 43.

> 'The superfluous man' is created by the interaction of two factors which can be present anywhere and under very different conditions of social life. The first is a person's poor psychic organisation, whether inherited or acquired, and which is expressed in an insufficiency of spiritual energy, flabbiness [*vyalost'*] of feeling and thought, in an incapacity for steady and well-directed work, in an absence of initiative. [...] The second factor is an intellectual and moral disharmony between the individual personality and his environment. [...] Sometimes just one of the above factors is enough to make a man 'superfluous'. But it seems that the interaction of the two is essential if a whole group or type of 'superfluous men' is to come into existence. [...] A man who has large quantities of spiritual energy will find it possible to live an intellectual existence even if he is wholly out of harmony with his environment.[46]

To be sure, the pervasiveness of anxieties about 'poor psychic organisation', and the widespread adulation directed at 'spiritual energy', did not mean that *zakal* was a universally accepted ideal. The British historian Bernard Pares, a frequent visitor to Russia in the 1910s, recorded in his memoirs, with a degree of humorous condescension, that the Russian intellectuals whom he met often felt hostile towards the success ethos, and demonstrated their attachment to 'personal self-respect' everywhere, even on the tennis court:

> Anyone who was successful in so bad a world, nearly all of which was directly or indirectly official, was concluded to be inevitably mean and time-serving. The respect of the public went to those who lived in constant protest. [...] There was an amazing lack of what we regard as the main elements of character: stability, purpose, consistency. Again, mood dominated, and judgement went by whether the mood was 'noble'. One never ceased to hear this word 'noble' (*blagorodno*). Where no public standards were accepted, the individual felt that he must have his personal self-respect. This, no doubt, is simple enough, but it took forms that were at once childlike and absurd. A boy playing tennis served every other ball into the net because a soft service would not be 'blagorodno', but he did not happen to have thought that his was hardly 'blagorodno' to his partner.[47]

'Stability, purpose, consistency' were, then, sometimes considered part of a rather vulgar, success-driven ethos alien to Russian society; the celebration of conformist goal-orientation to be found in depictions of 'willpower' could provoke an assertion of 'personal honour' in the sense of grand gestures of self-sacrifice. The behaviour depicted in Pares's anecdote had a more elevated counterpart in the assertion, among some of the Russian Symbolists, of the same 'empty dreaming' inveighed against by propaganda for backbone.[48]

---

46   D. A. Ovsyaniko-Kulikovsky, *Istoriia russkoi intelligentsii: Sobranie sochinenii*, 9 vols (St Petersburg: izdanie I. L. Ovsianiko-Kulikovskoi, 1914), VII, 91. Contrast, for example, N. Dobrolyubov, 'Chto takoe oblomovshchina?', in *Sobranie sochinenii*, 9 vols (Moscow & Leningrad: Gosizdat, 1961–62), IV, 307–43.
47   Bernard Pares, *My Russian Memoirs* (London: Jonathan Cape, 1931), p. 41.
48   See, for example, Andrei Belyi's journal *Zapiski mechtatelei*, whose first issue (published in 1919) carried an editorial statement asserting that the basis for a new reality would be 'a collective of dreamers'.

Yet whatever their protective feelings towards their own right to passive contemplation and to self-abnegation, adult men were often determined that boys, at least, should be exposed to new behaviour patterns and absorb the virtues of a new kind of manhood. Though a book on the 'education of character' translated into Russian in 1888 argued that a father should take care to be gentle ('It is bad when children fear their father'), it also argued that he should at all costs bear in mind the need to inculcate manliness: 'One must make use of every opportunity in order to teach him [i.e. one's son] genuine virile courage [*istinnoe muzhestvo*]'. Essential were 'exercises in order to temper him like steel [*uprazhneniya v zakalenie*]', whose target was to 'stamp out the natural instinct of cowardice'.[49] An example of a native Russian text adopting this sort of pedagogical attitude is a poem written by the Tsarist schoolmaster and modernist poet Innokenty Annensky to his step-grandson Valery Khmara-Barshchevsky, then aged about twelve:

> Где б ты ни стал на корабле,
> У мачты иль кормила,
> Всегда служи своей земле:
> Она тебя вскормила.
>
> Неровен наш и труден путь —
> В волнах иль по ухабам —
> Будь вынослив, отважен будь,
> Но не кичись над слабым.
>
> Не отступай, коль принял бой,
> Платиться — так за дело, —
> А если петь — так птицей пой
> Свободно, звонко, смело.

[Wherever you stand on the ship, | By the mast or in the bows, | Always serve your motherland well: | She reared and raised you. || Our road is hard, our road is uneven — | Whether we have waves or ruts to cross — | Be patient and be valorous, | But never crow over the weak. || Having begun the fight, do not retreat, | If you must make payment, do so, | And if you have to sing, do so like a bird, | Freely, musically, and bravely.]

There is a striking contrast between the calm didacticism with which Annensky sets out this 'Victorian' code for his schoolboy step-grandson, and his use elsewhere in his verse of a lyric voice characterised by hesitancy and uncertainty, a 'decadent' persona. It is explicable by a polarisation (typical of early twentieth-century Russian social commentators) between a *fin de siècle* despair at the capacities of adults, who were supposedly too exhausted to achieve serious social change, and an optimistic conviction of the promise offered by young people, who were destined to be the salvation of the *nachalo veka* (beginning of the century, but also, dawn of the new age). Whatever their personal distaste for 'backbone', many middle-aged Russians were determined to see it inculcated in the younger generation, and most particularly in male members of that generation.

---

49 See A. Marten, *O vospitanii kharaktera*, trans. by V. Revyakin (Moscow: tipografiya A. A. Kartseva, 1888), p. 398.

After the Revolution, commitment to character-building became still more widespread. Not only was propaganda for *zakal* a central element in prophylactic health literature, and in manuals of self-improvement (see above), but official Soviet novels, such as Anna Karavaeva's *The Saw-Mill* (*Lesozavod*, 1927) often depended on facile polarisations between men of action and weak-willed *intelligenty* of the old 'dreamer' type. And while Mayakovsky's work includes some notably ironic treatments of the 'tough manhood' construct (for example, the opening of *I Love*, which pillories middle-aged man, 'waving his arms like a windmill to Müller's instructions' ('muzhchina po Myulleru mel'nikom mashetsya'), such moments of hesitation or doubt were offset by the poet's vehement expressions of commitment to self-discipline and resolution (a striking example being the finale to his elegy for a fellow poet, 'To Sergei Esenin' ('Sergeyu Eseninu',1925).[50] Now that *zakal* had become an expression of 'Soviet patriotism' and an expression of commitment to utopian collectivism, it was accessible to 'dreamer' intellectuals who would have found *zakal* unacceptable in a context of capitalist self-advancement. Soviet 'revolutionary romanticism', as expressed in say the cult of *turizm* (hiking and mountain-climbing), was a brilliant fusion of the Slavophile myth of Russia as a country of northern asceticism and capacity for endurance, peasant respect for 'hard men', and ideas and techniques drawn from the hygienic and psychological literature on 'educating the will' that had filtered into popular culture before 1917.

There was a defensive colouration to this 'Soviet patriotism' too. The knowledge that the country had emerged from the First World War as a defeated power, and that Soviet rule had with difficulty survived a vicious and divisive civil war, ingrained the association between national self-assertion, military preparedness, and the inculcation of 'courage' and 'will' in the Soviet population.[51] Such a 'survivalist' understanding of *zakal* was characteristic of at least some Russian émigrés as well as Soviet citizens, expressing itself especially in the socialisation of young boys. Illuminating, in this regard, is Nina Berberova's vignette of life in the household of the famous writer Vladimir Nabokov:

> Nabokov took a huge boxing glove and handed it to [his son Dmitri], telling him to show me what he could do. The boy put the glove on and started to hit Nabokov on the face as hard as his childish strength would let him. I could see that Nabokov was in some pain, but he smiled and put up with it. It was physical and moral training [*trenirovka*] — for him and for the boy.[52]

Despite fervently abominating 'the notion that small boys, in order to be delightful, should hate to wash and love to kill', Nabokov remained convinced that some other

---

50 On Mayakovsky and masculinity, see also C. Cavanagh, 'Whitman, Mayakovsky, and the Body Politic', in *Rereading Russian Poetry*, ed. by S. Sandler (New Haven, CT: Yale University Press, 1999), pp. 202–22.
51 One could compare the rise of militaristic, aggressive manliness in 1930s Germany, where, as in Russia, the health and body cult had an ideological centrality that it did not have in Britain or France. In these last two countries, it was institutionalised largely in the construction of open-air swimming pools and other comparatively 'frivolous' sites of physical culture, and was often the preserve of marginal social groups, many of a radical or libertarian coloration.
52 N. Berberova, *Kursiv moi: avtobiografiya* (Moscow: Soglasie, 1996), p. 375.

traditional attributes of masculinity, physical and mental toughness, were crucial goals of a male child's upbringing.[53] This conviction was neither eccentric nor marginal: movements such as 'Sokol', clubs training young men in militaristically coloured gymnastics, and Baden-Powell scouting, had greater proportionate weight in the Russian emigration than they had in Russian-educated society before the Revolution.[54]

The tribulations that Russians endured during the second two decades of the twentieth century were not the only force behind the persistence of belief in *zakal*. During the First World War, all-out industrialised warfare, and the psychological trauma that it brought in its wake, made less of an impact upon the Eastern Front than it did upon the Western Front. Shell-shock was not a 'cultural fact' in Russia in the same way that it was in the West. The ideal of the perfectly resolute male survived because there was not yet a set of circumstances for which that ideal was inadequate.[55] It was only when the Second World War brought 'total war' in the modern sense to Russian soil, and when success proved to emerge from a very different kind of endurance from that propagandised in 'willpower' literature, that *zakalennost'* and the cult of backbone started to lose their dominance in Soviet life. Both during and after the war, mythology emphasised the role of civilians (including women and children) in combatting the enemy: after victory was achieved, the images used to commemorate it were statues of the suffering 'Mother Russia', or burnt-out tanks on pedestals, rather than the heroic male fighters with guns used on revolutionary monuments or memorials to the Civil War. While still seen as a virtue in men, especially young ones, and as an essential of physical health, *zakal* was now allocated a much more constricted niche in Soviet culture generally, its loss of symbolic force both a symptom of, and a contribution towards, the 'de-Sovietisation' of behaviour models that was such a notable feature of the decades after Stalin's death.[56]

---

53   Nabokov, *Speak, Memory*, p. 233. Cf. the writer's horror when a biographer suggested he had told his son to 'spit on the flowers that look like Hitler faces': see letter to Andrew Field, 8 August 1973, in V. Nabokov, *Selected Letters 1940–1977*, ed. by D. Nabokov and M. J. Bruccoli (London: Vintage, 1991), p. 517

54   This argument is advanced by M. Raeff in *Russia Abroad: A Cultural History of the Russian Emigration, 1919–1939* (New York: Oxford University Press, 1990), p. 54; for brief details of these movements and the Vityaz group (in full, The National Organisation of Knights, founded by Nikolai Fedorov in France in 1934 after his succession from the Russian Student Christian Movement), see M. Gorboff, *La Russie fantôme* (Lausanne: L'Âge d'homme, 1995), pp. 114–15.

55   On shellshock in the West and its detrimental effects upon traditional views of masculine identity, see Elaine Showalter, 'Rivers and Sassoon: The Inscription of Male Gender Anxieties', in *Behind the Lines: Gender and the Two World Wars*, ed. by Margaret Higonnet and others (New Haven, CT: Yale University Press, 1987), pp. 61–70; Eric Leed, *No Man's Land: Combat and Identity in World War One* (Cambridge: Cambridge University Press, 1979). On shellshock in Russia, see Catherine Merridale, 'Shell-shock in Twentieth-Century Russia', *Journal of Contemporary History*, 35.1 (2000), 39–55.

56   For instance, a manual for Soviet conscripts, *Poleznye sovety voinu*, 3rd edn (Moscow: Voenizdat 1975), pp. 347–49, has a section on 'self-tempering', and so do men's health books such as S. B. Shenkman, *My — muzhchiny*, 2nd edn (Moscow: Fizkul'tura i sport, 1980). Marginalisation of *zakal* led eventually to an upsurge of anxiety about 'failed masculinity' in the 1960s and 1970s, as

★ ★ ★ ★ ★

In late nineteenth- and early twentieth-century Russia, a cult of 'manly resolve' became pervasive, and with it a model of masculine behaviour that was quite different from the early nineteenth-century ideal of *chest'* (honour or *honnêteté*). There were striking resemblances between Russian models of masculinity and those current in France under the Third Republic, Wilhelmine Germany, or indeed late Victorian and Edwardian Britain. Kipling's poem 'If' had its counterpart (admittedly, a fairly downbeat one) in the poem by Innokenty Annensky addressed to his grandson.[57] Yet if the *content* of masculine behaviour models — notably their emphasis upon 'strong will', 'character', and 'backbone' — was consistent across Europe, there were important differences in terms of the models' location, in terms of broader cultural patterns. In France and Germany, duelling continued to have social weight right up to the First World War; in Britain, it had all but vanished by the mid-nineteenth century; in Russia, official attempts to revive the practice in the late Imperial era were at best partially successful. And in Russia, unlike France, the cult of 'willpower' did not graft itself easily on to an earlier notion of valour, but became associated with a commitment to transforming the 'backwardness' held to characterise traditional Russian culture. If citizens managed to transform themselves, so the reasoning went, Russia would throw off her traditional 'flabbiness' and 'backwardness', and be ready to lead the world. This belief persisted into the Soviet period, at which point the ideal of 'manly resolve' began to be propagandised to a much wider audience, and became directly associated with the authority of the new Party bureaucracy. It was only after the Second World War, most particularly in the post-Stalinist era, when the cult of *zakal* began to retreat from symbolic centrality, a process linked with a downplaying of its moral associations in favour of its hygienic ones.

My thanks to Barbara Clements, Rebecca Friedman, and Daniel Healey, the editors of *Russian Masculinities in History and Culture*, for the invitation that inspired the composition of this essay.

expressed, among other things, in anti-alcohol propaganda, in literature, and in films such as Kira Muratova's *The Asthenic Syndrome* (1989). For a more extensive discussion of this process, and of post-Stalinist behaviour models in general, see my *Refining Russia*, Chapter 5.
57 On 'If', see n. 13 above.

PART II

Human and None Too Human

CHAPTER 4

'Man-Footed Beast' versus 'Beast-Footed Man': Animals as Slaves, Servants, and Companions

[2014]

At the end of February 2014, a meme circulated on social websites with the hashtag #funnyfriday became an instant popular success. In a laboratory stand two dogs; behind them sits a bearded man, intently staring in their direction. The dog closer to the viewer, which is placed on a laboratory bench, and strapped to a wooden frame, with a tin basin in front of it, proves to be a shrewd and ironic observer of the process in train.

FIG. 4.1. 'Pavlov and his Dogs'. Internet meme. Creative Commons.

The meme juxtaposed two kinds of compulsion and two kinds of illusion. Both Pavlov and the dog are trapped by the framework of the experiment, yet both think they are running it. Both are right — and both, of course, are also wrong. This is a neat visual summary of a philosophical tradition that has developed over the last thirty years, and which aims to call into question the extent to which humans actually exercise direct control over their close relationships with animals.[1] It also reflects the sensation of being chivvied and bossed about that would be familiar to many who share domestic space with a 'companion animal'. And the idea of animals directing humans to do things has become increasingly familiar in mass-market culture generally.[2]

At the same time, the idea of the experimental dog as observer was funny because it was unexpected. The familiar situation is still the one where the dogs drool to order, whether we see this as an example of collaboration, or of animals being exploited. The joke is an update of a characteristic scene from the world of late medieval and early modern misrule: the ox flaying the man, or the donkey driving a cart. An early nineteenth-century Russian version (the mild subversion increased by the fact that the layout resembles a hagiographical icon, with a large image surrounded by smaller ones) introduces a whole variety of resurgent animals: the ewe shearing the shepherd, the hare chasing the hunter, the donkey riding in a carriage drawn by two women, the parrot that has put a man in a cage 'to make him speak', and so on. In the centre is the *pièce de résistance*: a bull, dressed in a butcher's apron, is gralloching a human carcass that it has suspended from a meat rack.

At one level, the increased interest in animals' capacity to control interaction with humans reflects the transformation that has come about, over the past two hundred years and more, in the understanding of animals' social role and intellectual and spiritual capacities.[3] Yet the parallel between the internet meme and time-honoured

---

1   See, for example, Mary Midgley, *Animals and Why They Matter* (Athens: University of Georgia Press, 1983); Douglas Candland, *Feral Children and Clever Animals: Reflections on Human Nature* (Oxford: Oxford University Press, 1995).

2   For instance, in 2009, it was reported that the animal behaviourist Karen McComb at the University of Surrey had produced a theory that cats employed a loud and irritating purr when they wished to wake their 'companion humans' up in order to be fed: see Ed Yong, 'Cats Manipulate their Owners with a Cry Embedded in a Purr', 13 July 2009 <http://scienceblogs.com/notrocketscience/2009/07/13/cats-manipulate-their-owners-with-a-cry-embedded-in-a-purr/> [accessed 13 September 2022]. Cats are especially often credited with this manipulative behaviour. The British comedian Eddie Izzard's 2007 sketch 'Pavlov's Cat' contrasts the docile behaviour of the dogs with the experiment Pavlov never reported — which has the cat answering the door, leaving a note to say, 'I've eaten already', stealing the batteries, etc. <https://www.youtube.com/watch?v=lf9Jy9JQgnY> [accessed 18 October 2022]. Of course, all of this rests on a fundamental misunderstanding (translation into folklore) of Pavlov's actual experiments, which were based on a far more complex set of research questions: see Daniel P. Todes, *Ivan Pavlov: A Russian Life in Science* (New York: Oxford University Press, 2014).

3   There is now a huge literature on this. A pioneering work is Keith Thomas, *Man and the Natural World: Changing Attitudes in England, 1500–1800* (London: Allen Lane, 1983). See also James Turner, *Reckoning with the Beast: Animals, Pain, and Humanity in the Victorian Mind* (Baltimore: Johns Hopkins University Press, 1980); Candland, *Feral Children and Clever Animals*; Donna Haraway, *The Companion Species Manifesto: Dogs, People, and Significant Otherness* (Chicago: Prickly Paradigm, 2003).

Fig. 4.2. 'The Bull that Didn't Want to Be a Bull'. Russian popular print, 1820s or 1830s. D. A. Rovinsky, *Russkie narodnye kartinki: Atlas*, 5 vols (St Petersburg: tipografiya Imperatorskoi Akademii Nauk, 1881), 1, 176.

images of animal misrule should give pause for thought. As Mikhail Bakhtin argued long ago, to invert hierarchies is not to subvert these, but rather, to leave the status quo in place.[4] Critique the experimental situation though the dog in the postcard may, and assert its autonomy through humour, it is still strapped to the table. The postcard does nothing to de-normalise the experiment as such.

From the point of view of campaigners for the liberation of animals, the situation represented here would be about as funny as a mother-in-law joke to a radical feminist. Experimentation on animals, along with butchery, is regarded as intolerable on at least two grounds: it inflicts suffering, up to and including the death of the animals concerned, and it is pointless, since research done on animal subjects can be replaced by alternative procedures, in the same way that nut roast can be a substitute for meat loaf.[5]

More broadly, from the point of view of 'animal rights' in this interpretation, the constraints imposed on the dog would be in themselves unacceptable, an assault on his or her autonomy. It is not a question of ameliorating the procedures so that the dog is caused no pain, but of putting an end to practices such as detaining animals in captivity, forcing them into unnatural behaviour such as standing on pieces of furniture, or feeding and watering them by artificial means. For Tom Regan, efforts to alleviate (rather than end) suffering are simply hypocritical. His book *Empty Cages* begins with a horrifying description of a cat being skinned alive and boiled to death by a Chinese cook. Regan concludes the book by deciding that the cook 'treated her [the cat] ruthlessly, heartlessly, without remorse. Of him, however, it can be said: he was an honest man'.[6] The book ends with the vision of liberated animals, which is also represented on the cover: 'All the cages are empty. All the dogs are gone. All the cats (first among them, the fluffy white one) are gone too'.[7]

Peter Singer's *Animal Liberation*, one of the foundational texts of the late twentieth-century animal rights movement, articulates a similar stand:

> Once we give up our claim to 'dominion' over the other species we should stop interfering with them at all. We should leave them alone as much as we possibly can. Having given up the role of tyrant, we should not try to play God either.[8]

According to a radical animal liberationist perspective, 'kind treatment' to subordinate creatures is simple hypocrisy. Not just such obviously 'wrong' activities

---

4   Most famously, in *François Rabelais and His World* (1965). This idea has been extensively developed since: see, for example, Peter Stallybrass and Allon White, *The Politics and Poetics of Transgression* (Ithaca, NY: Cornell University Press, 1985).
5   These arguments are advanced most forcefully by Peter Singer (*Animal Liberation*, first published in 1975; see also the expanded edition (London: Pimlico, 1995), for example pp. 159–60: 'it is impossible to be consistent in one's concern for non-human animals while continuing to eat them [...]. Even if intensive methods are not used, traditional farming involves castration, separation of mother and young, breaking up social groups, branding, transportation to the slaughterhouse, and finally slaughter itself'); and by Tom Regan (see, for example, *Empty Cages: Facing the Challenge of Animal Rights* (Lanham, MD: Rowman & Littlefield, 2004). See also Midgley, *Animals and Why They Matter*.
6   Regan, *Empty Cages*, p. 199.
7   Ibid, p. 200.
8   Singer, *Animal Liberation*, p. 225.

as confining animals to zoos are intolerable, but so is, for example, pet-keeping — which is both unnatural and an assault on the creature's personal dignity. The much more recent concept of 'rewilding' would be unacceptable too, existing as it does in licensed corrals such as the domains of rich landowners.

Such thinking about animal rights emerged from a broader political context. As Singer puts it in the preface to the second edition of his *Animal Liberation*, 'the liberation movements of the Sixties had made Animal Liberation an obvious next step'.[9] The most crucial 'first step' that was invoked in texts of the time was the campaign for racial equality, whose traces everywhere underlie the rhetoric of Singer's texts. Expressing irritation at a British lady who had been foolish enough to assume that he and his wife would be delighted by talk of pets since they must be 'animal lovers', he wrote in the first edition of *Animal Liberation*:

> The assumption that in order to be interested in such matters one must be an 'animal lover' is itself an indication of the absence of the slightest inkling that the moral standards we apply among human beings might apply to other animals. No-one, except a racist commentator concerned to smear his opponents as 'n***** lovers', would suggest that in order to be concerned about equality for mistreated racial minorities you have to love those minorities, or regard them as cute and cuddly.[10]

Singer avoids a direct analogy between slavery and the exploitation of animals. Indeed, at one point he suggests that the latter problem may be more difficult because the exploiters are not capable of even limited empathy:

Almost all of the oppressing group are directly involved in, and see themselves as benefitting from, the oppression. There are few humans indeed who can view the oppression of humans with the detachment possessed, say, by the Northern whites debating the institution of slavery in the Southern states of the Union. People who eat slaughtered non humans every day find it hard to believe that they are doing wrong; and they also find it hard to imagine what else they could eat.[11]

At the same time, there is a clear imputation that the *current* exploitation of animals resembles the *previous* exploitation of humans — which carries also the assumption that, in time, the former will come to seem as disgraceful as the latter now has.[12]

Animal liberation is regularly said to have begun with a passage in the second edition of Jeremy Bentham's *Introduction to the Principles of Morality and Legislation* (1789). Here both the anatomical categorisation of animals as different, and the contention that they lacked reason and language, were ironically assailed:

> The day has been, I grieve to say in many places it is not yet past, in which the greater part of the species, under the denomination of slaves, have been treated by the law exactly upon the same footing as, in England for example, the inferior races of animals are still. The day *may* come, when the rest of

9   Ibid., p. xvii.
10 Ibid., p. x (the n-word edited to suit current conventions).
11 Ibid., p. xiii.
12 Ibid.: 'How many Southern slaveholders were persuaded by the arguments used by the Northern abolitionists, and accepted by nearly all of us today? Some, but not many'.

the animal creation may acquire those rights which never could have been withholden from them but by the hand of tyranny. The French have already discovered that the blackness of the skin is no reason why a human being should be abandoned without redress to the caprice of a tormentor. It may come one day to be recognized, that the number of the legs, the villosity of the skin, or the termination of the *os sacrum*, are reasons equally insufficient for abandoning a sensitive being to the same fate. What else is it that should trace the insuperable line? Is it the faculty of reason, or, perhaps, the faculty of discourse? But a full-grown horse or dog is beyond comparison a more rational, as well as a more conversable animal, than an infant of a day, or a week, or even a month, old. But suppose the case were otherwise, what would it avail? the question is not, Can they *reason*? nor, Can they *talk*? but, Can they *suffer*?[13]

Bentham is represented, by Singer and Regan, for example, as the champion against an earlier strand of thinking in Western philosophy that emphasised the hierarchical superiority of man over animals, and running from Aristotle through Thomas Aquinas through to Descartes.

This progressivist stand towards inherited material carries with it certain problems for anyone who wishes to write about the history of human-animal relations in conditions where 'animal liberation' was not recognised as a desirable, or even a possible, social objective. As an ethical critique of modern society, animal liberationism is extremely effective. It works to expose the tenacity of assumptions about human superiority that, while pretending to scientific authority, rest on a pre-Darwinian understanding of the necessary hierarchy of species. It shows how 'the rationalist tradition did in general, as much as the Christian one, dismiss animals out of hand from the moral scene'.[14] (Anyone familiar with the mechanistic understanding of nature that went with rational materialism in its Soviet incarnation will be able to endorse this interpretation.) Serious discussion of the liberation of animals has also greatly contributed to the imaginative world of the late twentieth century — to an understanding of the fact that, say, birds' navigation may require complex mental processes that are quite beyond the ken of 'superior' species, and that animals' mental efficacy is not to be measured by experiments requiring the performance of complex tasks in a laboratory. As J. M. Coetzee's fictional Elizabeth Costello puts it, the ape forced to retrieve bananas from more and more unlikely places is not displaying 'intelligence': rather, 'At every turn Sultan is driven to think the less interesting thought'. The decline of 'speciesism' should mean not just that such idiotic and degrading routines come to an end, but that human possibilities also expand infinitely: 'Despite Nagel, who is probably a good man, despite Thomas Aquinas and René Descartes, with whom I have more difficulty in sympathizing, here is no limit to the extent to which we can think ourselves into the being of another. There are no bounds to the sympathetic imagination'.[15]

13   Jeremy Bentham, *An Introduction to the Principles of Morals and Legislation* (London: for T. Payne, 1789), p. 122 (Chapter 4; this note does not appear in the 1781 edition). This passage is cited, for instance, by both Singer and Midgley.
14   Midgley, *Animals and Why They Matter*, p. 12.
15   J. M. Coetzee, *The Lives of Animals* (Princeton, NJ: Princeton University Press, 1999), pp. 29, 35.

The difficulty for any historical study comes, as the phrasing of Elizabeth Costello's evocation of her ideal suggests, from the fact that, like other utopian discourses, animal liberation works not just by affirming the present (or, more often, the future), but by denigrating the past. Or at the very least, it means adjudicating beliefs and practices, not to speak of people, from previous eras according to their degree of congruence with present-day values. In this, it resembles, say, first-wave feminism of the 1970s, not to speak of Russian literary history of the Stalin era, with its Manichean division of writers into 'progressive' and 'reactionary' cohorts. The result is that whole areas which might be tricky for the base assumption that minimum impact on animals' lives is the only tolerable position vanish from view. Take, for instance, the failure to discuss whether it is ever acceptable to use animals for work purposes. Perhaps we can look forward to a day when guide dogs for the blind are replaced by robots (though there is some evidence that contact with animals can itself be therapeutically beneficial). But should communities living in places where land is so poor it can only be used for pasture be prevented from, say, keeping sheep for milk and using dogs to herd them?[16] Is it permissible to use mules as pack animals in areas where the terrain is impassable for motorised transport? Until ethical debates can grapple with questions of this kind, animal liberation will remain a 'North Atlantic' discourse that will at most be able to transform the behaviour of some economically and socially advantaged individuals in a geographically restricted location.

The reference to working animals is not meant as a snide attempt to undermine the present force and significance of campaigns for animal liberation. However, it helps explain why, outside the prosperous 'North Atlantic' zone, most people who are sympathetic to animals remain, at best, what Regan calls 'muddlers' with regard to animal rights.[17] They may imagine how they could do without eating animals;

---

16 In 2022, this question has only become more problematic because of carbon reduction objectives. Yet perception of the issue entirely in terms of low-carbon veganism versus high-carbon meat production is simplistic: small-scale food producers do not have the political leverage of oil multinationals, manufacturers of chemicals and artificial fibres, and other economic sectors targeted by proposed reforms.

17 Indeed, it is arguable that even with this prosperous zone, 'muddling' is ubiquitous. Regan himself refers to a category of exceptionally sensitive individuals, whom he calls 'da Vincis', after Leonardo; but the use of animals, whether directly or indirectly, in a range of industries, not just food or pharmaceuticals, is common enough to make guilt by implication widespread. This is surely inevitable. In the same way, one notes that Bentham's principled opposition to enslavement was accompanied by a comment in a letter written from the Russian Empire (Krichyov) on 30 March OS/10 April NS 1786, in which he observed that he had seen, in the house of a local landowner, cabinet-making 'work very neatly executed by a peasant of his own whom he had got instructed for that purpose. These fingering peasants are not uncommon in Russia; I intend to make Sam [Bentham's brother] have one of them before I have done with him' (*The Correspondence of Jeremy Bentham*, 5 vols (London: UCL Press, 2017), III, 464). I have to say that, as someone who since childhood has found the cruel treatment of animals deeply distressing, and been very attached to 'companion animals', I have a 'muddled' position myself, as I do eat and use animal products (while doing the best I can to make sure these are humanely produced, e.g. buying from small farms that allow freedom to roam and use only natural feeds), consider some animal research unavoidable, if only because it also benefits animals and is done in strictly controlled conditions under anaesthetic, and generally adopt a 'welfare' rather than 'liberationist' position, while recognising all the

laboratory testing probably will not cross their horizon; but how they could get by without 'horse power', in the most literal sense of the word (or donkey, mule, or camel) is simply not imaginable. Just as in the case of children's rights, the Western obsession with personal autonomy may strike those who aim to better the lot of animals in modernising societies as wrong-headed; the attack upon paternalism as an incursion upon rights is, after all, only politically powerful where paternalism is an established tradition.[18] Further, in its equation of the enslavement of animals above all with eating, hunting, and experimentation, with peripheral attention given to other 'unnecessary' forms of exploitation, such as the production of fur and leather, or the training of animals to perform in aqua-parks and circuses, the writing on animal liberation over the last half-century seems largely or wholly to have neglected the fact that traditional analogies between animals and slaves rested not just upon arguments about anatomical (dis)similarity and about relative spiritual and mental (in)capacity, but upon the role of those two groups in performing manual work.

Working animals lie, to borrow an image from Mary Midgley, beyond the 'lit circle' of ethical scrutiny that has characterised the history, within animal rights discussions, of thinking about the man/animal division, since examinations of this division have focused upon such attributes as have traditionally be supposed to underpin an absolute division between 'man' and 'beast', such as language and reasoning power.[19] A characteristic that is admitted to be shared by 'man' and 'beast' has not been seen as helpful to the transformation of inter-species perception.

Yet in Aristotle's *Politics*, the performance of manual work was one of the key social discriminators dividing the actual four-footed beast and the 'man-footed beast' (ἀνδράποδον, a customary term for slaves, as opposed to τετράποδον), from fully rational beings, those capable of 'managing' their actions. The treatise's second chapter opened with a homology between slaves and animals:

> Hesiod is right when he says,
> 'First house and wife and an ox for the plough',
> for the ox is the poor man's slave.[20]

Later, this parallel was repeated as an abstraction: 'Indeed, the use made of slaves and of tame animals is not very different; for both with their bodies minister to the

---

contradictions and hypocrisies, from a strictly ethical point of view, in this position.

18   In the case of rights for children also, there has been a historical cleavage between 'rights' in a strict sense, i.e. personal autonomy (as, say, in the 'right' of children to choose their own religion), and 'rights' in the sense of welfare, i.e. access to protection from the 'stronger' members of society (essentially a patronage ethos). For a general discussion, see *Children, Rights, and the Law*, ed. by P. Alston, S. Parker, and J. Seymour (Oxford: Clarendon Press, 1992). In 1920s Russia, there was some campaigning for children's rights in the sense of personal autonomy, but after 1932 the emphasis switched back to protection and welfare (e.g. 'the right to education', as in the 1936 'Stalin Constitution'). See Catriona Kelly *Children's World: Growing up in Russia 1880–1991* (Newhaven, CT: Yale University Press, 2007), Chapters 1 and 2.

19   I have borrowed this image from Midgley, *Animals and Why They Matter*, p. 51, when it is used in the specific context of an argument about how the fixation on contract has excluded entire categories of ethical subjects from consideration in established philosophical tradition.

20   Aristotle, *Politics*, trans. by Benjamin Jowett (Kitchener, 1999), p. 4 (Book I, part II) <http://socserv2.socsci.mcmaster.ca/econ/ugcm/3ll3/aristotle/Politics.pdf> [accessed 13 September 2022].

needs of life'.²¹ It was the performance of work that justified the keeping of slaves: in a famous passage, Aristotle remarked that, 'if every instrument could accomplish its own work', slaves would not be necessary: 'if the shuttle would weave and the plectrum touch the lyre without a hand to guide them, chief workmen would not want servants, nor masters slaves'.²²

Certainly, the performance of work was not the only distinguishing factor of these lower beings (according to Aristotle, 'the slave has no deliberate faculty at all', any more than animals have).²³ But work was an important element in their subordination.²⁴ As Paul Millett has glossed Aristotle, 'The person with foresight is naturally (phusei) ruler and master; the one that can carry out labour is naturally a slave'.²⁵ By extension, it was the 'use' of animals that became the central right of domination — underpinning the social and ecological contract whereby work and the provision of food and other products was rewarded by protection: 'Tame animals have a better nature than wild, and all tame animals are better off when they are ruled by man; for then they are preserved'.²⁶ In this respect, animals could

---

21   Ibid., p. 9 (Book I, part V). Later (ibid., p. 13, part VIII), Aristotle produces a more elaborate distinction between 'man' and 'beasts': 'after the birth of animals, plants exist for their sake, and that the other animals exist for the sake of man, the tame for use and food, the wild, if not all at least the greater part of them, for food, and for the provision of clothing and various instruments', but one notes here too the emphasis on the 'use' of tame animals (presumably including 'the provision of clothing and various instruments' also, but certainly also work).

22   Ibid., p. 7 (Book I, part IV), and cf. p. 11, part VII: 'the master need only know how to order that which the slave must know how to execute'.

23   Ibid., p. 21 (Book I, part XIII). Cf.: 'if life only were the object, slaves and brute animals might form a state, but they cannot, for they have no share in happiness or in a life of free choice' (p. 63, Book 3, part IX), or the disparaging reference to 'that common part of music in which every slave or child and even some animals find pleasure' (p. 189, Book 8, part VI).

24   Cf. the argument that 'the meaner sort of mechanic' stands at a lower ethical level than slaves, since he performs manual labour without the mitigating presence of a master ('for the slave shares in his master's life; the artisan is less closely connected with him, and only attains excellence in proportion as he becomes a slave': Aristotle, *Politics*, p. 22, Book I, part XIII); or that manual labour might injure the status of the master: 'Certainly the goodman and the statesman and the good citizen ought not to learn the crafts of inferiors except for their own occasional use; if they habitually practice them, there will cease to be a distinction between master and slave' (p. 55, Book I, part IV).

25   Paul Millett, 'Aristotle and Slavery in Athens', *Greece and Rome*, 54.2 (2007), 178–209 (p. 180). Cf. P. A. Brunt, 'Aristotle and Slavery', in his *Studies in Greek History and Thought* (Oxford: Clarendon Press, 1993), p. 344–45: 'the philosopher also needed to be free from the incubus of earning his own livelihood', and further, 'Aristotle was therefore convinced that if any men were to lead a good life, they must be able at will to call on the labour of others'; and Peter Garnsey, *Ideas of Slavery from Aristotle to Augustine* (Cambridge: Cambridge University Press, 1996), p. 111: 'in the *Politics* the line between human and animal is usually firmly drawn, but that between slaves and animals is fuzzy'.

26   Aristotle, *Politics*, p. 9 (Book I, part V). On the prevalence of this model of paternalism as legitimating slavery in the ancient world and the antebellum USA (where the exploited English factory worker was usually cited as the counter-case), see Garnsey, *Ideas of Slavery from Aristotle to Augustine*, p. 5. A similar argument is voiced, quite independently, by Pushkin in his essay 'Journey from Moscow to St Petersburg': 'Just read the complaints of English factory workers: your hair stands on end. How many revolting torments, what incomprehensible suffering! What cold barbarity on the one side, fearful poverty on the other! You would think you were reading about the construction of the Pyramids, or the Jewish exiles in Egypt. Not a whit: this is Mr Smith's textile factory or Mr Jackson's needle works. [...] We have nothing like this. The obligations [on Russian serfs] are no burden. The poll tax is paid by the community [*mir*]; the quit-rent [*obrok*] is by

expect at least as good treatment as slaves — better, perhaps, because they do not seem to have excited the same level of mistrust ('the treatment or management of slaves is a troublesome affair; for, if not kept in hand, they are insolent, and think that they are as good as their masters, and, if harshly treated, they hate and conspire against them').[27] Whichever way, both slaves and animals were designed for a life of 'use'.

Thomas Aquinas's writings on animals, as well as underlining the spiritual and intellectual distinctiveness of animals (their possession of 'non-subsistent souls', lack of capacity for language and reason, etc.), reinforced the association of animals and work.[28] His commentaries to the *Politics* expanded on Aristotle's slave/ox analogy: 'For in a poor household the ox takes the place of a servant; man uses an ox, just as he uses a servant, to carry out some work'.[29] An animal, then, was not only a creature of restricted cognitive powers, but also one that was meant to be useful.

Such assumptions proved tenacious; at least at periods later than the Garden of Eden or, more generally, the Golden Age of humanity, sweated labour for some people and almost all tame animals was assumed.[30] Indeed, I recall that in the rural west of Ireland during the late 1960s and early 1970s, non-working animals were simply beyond the ken of local small-holders: a dog was for herding sheep, a cat (if kept at all) for mousing, donkeys were for carrying turf, drawing carts, pulling haystacks around the field, and carrying their owners (who balanced on the rump, behind two full baskets of turf). When animals got beyond work, people simply got rid of them — in the case of dogs, tossed them into the sea with a stone round the neck. (Similar levels of extraction of work from animals were, obviously, the norms implied by the tradition of misrule, as exemplified by the Russian popular print discussed above.) This is not to suggest that deliberate cruelty was the lot of all working animals at all times: they were fed (if only on scraps), watered, and had a

no means ruinous (except in the areas around Moscow and Petersburg, where the variety of forms of industry incites and provokes the self-interest of proprietors). Landowners who exact quit-rent allow the peasant himself to pay what and where he will. The peasant trades where he will and sometimes travels 2000 versts to make his money... There are many abuses everywhere; criminal behaviour is dreadful wherever it occurs' ('Puteshestvie iz Moskvy v Peterburg', in *Polnoe sobranie sochinenii*, 10 vols (Moscow: Nauka, 1977), VI, 395). Pushkin's long apologia for serfdom expresses a characteristically Russian defensiveness of the *tu quoque* kind, where the supposedly better, but in fact worse, alternative is associated with the political and social choices of the so-called civilised West.

27   Aristotle, *Politics*, pp. 40–41 (Book 2, part IX).
28   For the discussion of animals' non-subsistent souls, see Thomas Aquinas, *Summa Theologica*, trans. by Fathers of the English Dominican Province (New York: Benziger, 1947), p. 814, Article 3, question 75 <http://www.ccel.org/ccel/aquinas/summa.toc.html> [accessed 13 September 2022]; on reason, ibid., p. 878, question 78.
29   Thomas Aquinas, *Commentary upon Aristotle's Politics*, trans. by Ernest L. Fortin and Peter D. O'Neill, in *The Complete Works of Thomas Aquinas: Electronic Edition*, p. 304 <https://catholiclibrary.org/library/view?docId=Medieval-EN/XCT.040.html;chunk.id=00000003> [accessed 19 October 2022]. As Brunt points out ('Aristotle and Slavery', p. 355), for Augustine, the discrepancy between toilers and non-toilers was tolerable because the former were regarded as undergoing punishment for sin (*De civitatis Dei*, Part XIX, Chapter 5).
30   R. W. Carlyle, *A History of Mediaeval Political Theory in the West*, 6 vols (Edinburgh: Blackwood, 1970), V, 21 ff. Erwin Panofsky, *Studies in Iconology: Humanistic Themes in the Art of the Renaissance* [1939] (New York: Harper & Row, 1972).

fair degree of freedom of movement, since there were no fences (though both dogs and donkeys were liable to be tethered at least some of the time). They had names, however conventionalised ('Shep', 'Bracken', 'Jacky'), and while we occasionally saw someone kick a dog or donkey, we never witnessed a full-scale beating. But the fundamental relationship remained similar to the one recorded by Aristotle: animals — and notably donkeys and ponies (if not oxen) — remained the 'slaves of the poor'.[31]

The rise of vegetarianism in the second half of the eighteenth century was not necessarily accompanied by a comparable assault on the use of working animals. Following Bentham's contention that 'can they suffer?' should be a primary consideration in human-animal relations, writers of the period dwelled mainly on the iniquities of eating 'brute beasts'. John Oswald's *The Cry of Nature* (1791), for example, criticised the heaviness of the meat diet and praised the superior civilisation of the 'Hindoo', who avoided it. Aesthetic motives for the avoidance of meat carried less weight, however, than ethical ones: 'Are the dying struggles of a lambkin less affecting than the agonies of any animal whatever?'[32] At most, writers might add to their reflections on the sufferings of animals slaughtered for food a sentence or two about the brutal treatment of working animals: Humphrey Primatt's *A Dissertation on the Duty of Mercy and Sin of Cruelty to Brute Animals* (first published in 1776) dwelt in depth upon the sufferings of mothers deprived of their young and stock dispatched to abattoirs, but remarked in passing only:

> A horse may now and then, when provoked, give a man an unlucky kick; but what is this to the blows, and cuts, and spurs, which they receive every day, and every hour, from the brutal rage and unrelenting barbarity of man?[33]

While this assumed the context of a working horse, the point was not made explicit.

The late eighteenth century saw the publication of numerous self-declaredly 'modern' manuals of horse management, often advocating more humane treatment of the animals. John Lawrence's *Philosophical and Practical Treatise on Horses*, first published in the late 1790s, resonantly enquired:

> Can there be one kind of justice for men, and another for brutes? Or is feeling in them a different thing to what it is in ourselves? Is not a beast produced by the same rule, and in the same order of generation with ourselves? Is not his body nourished by the same food, hurt by the same injuries; his mind actuated by the same passions and affections which animate the human breast; and does he not also, at last, mingle his dust with ours, and in like manner, surrender up the vital spark to the aggregate, or fountain of intelligence?[34]

---

31 Paul Millett has pointed out to me that charities arranging sponsorship by Westerners of children in African villages advise against sending photographs of family pets: the attitudes to animals expressed in this relationship seem bizarre to the children concerned.
32 John Oswald, *The Cry of Nature, or an Appeal to Mercy and to Justice, on Behalf of the Persecuted Animals* (Member of the Club Des Jacobines) (London: for J. Johnson, 1791), p. 25.
33 See the second edition as Rev. A. Broome M.A., *The Duty of Humanity to Inferior Creatures, Deduced from Reason and Scripture (Abridged from Dr Primatt): With Notes and Illustrations* (London: for the author, 1831), p. 29.
34 John Lawrence, *A Philosophical and Practical Treatise on Horses, and on the Moral Duties of Man*

But the practical guidance in the book concerned how to treat working horses humanely, rather than how to avoid or even reduce their use. Early legislation, such as the 1822 English statute prohibiting the 'cruel and improper treatment' of farm animals, including 'Horses, Mares, and Geldings' as well as sheep and cattle, also adopted this mitigatory strategy.[35]

A rare exception to the general trend was Lewis Gompertz (1783/4–1861), one of the founders of the Society for the Prevention of Cruelty to Animals, set up in 1824. The Society (the antecedent of the later Royal Society for the Prevention of Cruelty to Animals) was a pioneering institution in the struggle for better treatment of what in the eighteenth century were still known as 'brutes'. Gompertz's *Moral Enquiries on the Situation of Man and of Brutes*, first published in 1824, resolutely argued for the equality of humans and animals in a general sense, contending, for instance, that 'in the playing of two kittens may be discovered many of the chief passions of man'.[36] He was a convinced vegetarian (indeed, a vegan, in that he also decried the use of eggs, milk, and wool — 'I consider it an act of great cruelty to deprive the sheep of their wool, which they require themselves; which they seem keenly to feel the loss of').[37] But unusually, he also presented, in the form of a dialogue between two participants, Y and Z, an argument against the use of horses for work purposes.

According to Z:

> At least in the present state of society, it [forcing horses to work] is unjust. And, considering the unnecessary abuse they suffer from being in the power of man, I think it wrong to abuse them, and to encourage their being placed in his power.

When Y riposted that work, on the contrary, hardly seemed an abuse ('they appear to enjoy their work as well as their masters'), Z argued that this did not make putting horses to work morally acceptable:

> It does not, I understand, perplex you to conceive that it can be wrong to compel slaves to work: and I am at a loss how you can disapprove of the one, and countenance the other, which appears to me to be so similar. Slaves would also at all times prefer working to being kept confined.[38]

When Y asked how he supposed that man could do without horses, Z replied, 'That is his business to find out', before himself supplying an answer in the rise of mechanisation: 'Even now, you see that steam-engines begin to perform in their stead'.

Added to that, there was the issue of necessity, or rather its absence:

> Besides, many of the purposes for which horses are now used, are for things of comparatively trifling importance; or for war; or for the barbarous purposes of hunting, racing, and the like; or for the rich, to show their pomp; or for strong

towards the Brute Creation, 2 vols (London: for T. N. Longman, 1796–98), I, 119–20.
35 On the statute and its background, see Turner, 'Reckoning with the Beast', pp. 33–39.
36 Lewis Gompertz, *Moral Inquiries on the Situation of Man and of Brutes. On the Crime of Committing Cruelty on Brutes* (London: for the author, 1824), p. 25.
37 Ibid., p. 92.
38 Ibid., pp. 99–100.

Fig. 4.3. Lewis Gompertz, design for a velocipede, 1829. J. T. Goddard, *The Velocipede: Its History, Varieties, and Practice* (New York: Hurd & Houghton, 1869), p. 11.

and healthy persons, to encourage sloth and disease; and not very unfrequently, for persons to get their necks and limbs broken. I grant that, without their aid, civilization might have been retarded, but not prevented.

And until the machines appeared, 'we must then, for important commodities, put our own shoulders to the wheel'. To Y's appalled question, 'Then you would have men of rank, and artisans of every kind, occasionally harnessed to a plough or coal-waggon, like so many beasts of burden?', Z calmly replied, 'Yes; and include myself among the number'.[39] A fertile inventor, as well as a homespun philosopher, Gompertz did all he could to foster the new age of machine labour, including among his creations an improved version of the recently-invented bicycle, as well as a design for a carriage that aimed to lighten the load on draft horses.

Gompertz's standpoint was unusual, and his humanitarian ideas, promoted as they were in a self-published pamphlet not reissued until 1992, were less influential than his inventions (for example, an expanding chuck, or, in its day, his 'velocipede').[40] The primary objective continued to be the improvement of the lot of working animals, rather than their release from what Gompertz would have termed slavery.

The lack of attention to working horses is hardly surprising, given the heritage going back to classical times of perceiving the horse as a naturalised slave. A fable traditionally attributed to Aesop (who had, according to the traditional biography, himself been born a slave) saw this as the result of a bad bargain: forming an alliance with man to fight off the challenge of a stag, the horse found himself wearing a bridle for the rest of his existence.[41] There was a note of self-congratulation in this,

39 Ibid., pp. 102–06.
40 For an authoritative account of Gompertz's life, see the article by Lucien Wolf and Ben Marsden in *DNB*. His 'velocipede' and the context of its invention are discussed in David Herlihy, *Bicycle: The History* (New Haven, CT: Yale University Press, 2004), pp. 46–50.
41 'There was once a Horse who used to graze in a meadow which he had all to himself. But one day a Stag came into the meadow, and said he had as good a right to feed there as the Horse,

as one might put it, 'colonial', myth (the horse had let himself be fooled, other fables by Aesop underlined the animal as a symbol of false pride).[42] Yet ambivalence remained, as is clear from the imaginative literature of the eighteenth and early nineteenth centuries, if not from the philosophical literature or from campaigning pamphlets. Swift's superlatively rational Houyhnhnms initiated a tradition that one could call 'beast-footed men': horses that, while retaining their characteristic anatomy, were at the same time more reasonable and articulate than the humans who, in the real world, aimed to dominate them.[43]

By the second half of the nineteenth century, this imaginative trajectory had converged with the rising attention to the welfare of working animals in a practical sense to produce a new kind of writing about such animals, as illustrated by two important equine narratives of the period, Tolstoy's story *Kholstomer* (1885) and Anna Sewell's slightly earlier novel, *Black Beauty* (1877).[44]

Sewell and Tolstoy trace the story of a horse as it comes down in the world, an idea that, like the naturalised slavery of the horse, goes back to Aesop. As 'The Old Horse' (Fable 138) relates, 'An old horse had been sold to a miller to turn the millstone. When he was harnessed to the mill-wheel he groaned and exclaimed:

and moreover chose all the best places for himself. The Horse, wishing to be revenged upon his unwelcome visitor, went to a man and asked if he would help him to turn out the Stag. "Yes," said the man, "I will by all means; but I can only do so if you let me put a bridle in your mouth and mount on your back." The Horse agreed to this, and the two together very soon turned the Stag out of the pasture: but when that was done, the Horse found to his dismay that in the man he had got a master for good' ('The Horse and the Stag', in *Aesop's Fables*, trans. by V. S. Vernon-Jones (London: Heinemann, 1912) <http://www.gutenberg.org/files/11339/11339-h/11339-h.htm#THE_HORSE_AND_THE_STAG> [accessed 13 September 2022]). I am not here so much concerned with the reflection of the ancient Greek world from which these fables emerged (on which see Paul Millett, 'The World of Aesop', in *Ratio et res ipsa: Classical Essays Presented by Former Pupils to James Diggle on his Retirement*, ed. by Paul Millett, S. Oakley, and R. J. E. Thompson (Cambridge: Cambridge Philological Society, 2011), pp. 183–206) as with Aesop's status as one of the canonical texts for teaching in the medieval, early modern, and modern schoolroom — the creation of 'background stereotypes' for writers and teachers, parents, and the guardians of children generally.

42 For instance, in 'The Horse and the Ass', an arrogant carriage-horse kicked an ass in contempt, only to encounter the latter again when he had come down in the world: 'Not long afterwards the Horse became broken-winded, and was sold by his owner to a farmer. One day, as he was drawing a dung-cart, he met the Ass again, who in turn derided him and said, "Aha! you never thought to come to this, did you, you who were so proud! Where are all your gay trappings now?"' (*Aesop's Fables*, trans. by Vernon-Jones).

43 The history of the relationship with horses is of course far more complex than this brief discussion of working horses would suggest. The late Reinhard Koselleck embarked, not long before his death in 2006, upon a historical 'hippology' that attempted to trace the transformation of human culture through the relationship with the horse, as expressed, for instance, in the strategic significance of mounted troops. Ulrich Raulff is now working on a history of the final episode of 'hippological history', the nineteenth century: see his article, 'Das Ende des kentaurischen Pakts', *Frankfurter Allgemeine*, 27 April 2012 <http://www.faz.net/aktuell/feuilleton/pferd-und-mensch-das-ende-des-kentaurischen-pakts-11732601.html?printPagedArticle=true> [accessed 13 September 2022]) (my thanks to Jan Plamper for alerting me to this work). As of 2022, Simon Dixon at University College London is engaged on a large-scale history of the horse in Russian culture.

44 Although Dostoevsky's *Crime and Punishment* includes the famous scene in which Raskol'nikov dreams about the savage beating of a draught horse, both here and in Mayakovsky's 'Kind Treatment of Horses' ('Khoroshee otnoshenie k loshadyam'), the perspective is a human one.

"From the turn of the race course I am reduced to such a turn as this!"[45] But Sewell's and Tolstoy's representations are more substantial than Aesop's comic-strip pun, recording every element of the horse protagonist's descent in the world, and his exhaustion and humiliation in the course of the downward progress.

In many ways, *Kholstomer* and *Black Beauty* are strikingly similar, focusing as they do on a number of crucial points in the horse experience. In both cases, the horse concerned is not just any old nag — rather, his innate nobility points to the incongruity of the later situation:

> You have been well-bred and well-born; your father has a great name in these parts, and your grandfather won the cup two years at the Newmarket races. (*Black Beauty*, Chapter 1)

> I am First Moujik according to my pedigree, and Kholstomer [Yardstick] is my name in common parlance; so the rabble calls me for my long and flamboyant stride, the like of which there has never been in Russia. By descent there is no horse in the world who is of higher blood than me. (*Kholstomer*, Chapter 5)[46]

The first contact with the world of labour imposed by human beings comes as a physical shock to both horses:

> A great piece of cold hard steel as thick as a man's finger to be pushed into one's mouth, between one's teeth, and over one's tongue, with the ends coming out at the corner of your mouth, and held fast there by straps over your head, under your throat, round your nose, and under your chin [...] a stiff heavy collar just on my neck, and a bridle with great side-pieces against my eyes called blinkers, and blinkers indeed they were, for I could not see on either side, but only straight in front of me; next, there was a small saddle with a nasty stiff strap that went right under my tail; that was the crupper. I hated the crupper; to have my long tail doubled up and poked through that strap was almost as bad as the bit. I never felt more like kicking, but of course I could not kick such a good master, and so in time I got used to everything, and could do my work as well as my mother. (*Black Beauty*, Chapter 1)

> I was harnessed for the first time at the age of three. I recall how that first time the head groom, who imagined he owned me, with a rabble of other grooms began to saddle me, imagining that I would be obstreperous or obstructive. They put a twitch on my lip and used ropes to back me into the shafts; they put on my back two broad straps, crossing in the middle, and fixed those to the shafts, so that I could not kick out; but all I wanted was the chance to show my desire to work and my love of labour. (*Kholstomer*, Chapter 6)

As if the harness itself were not enough, both horses then also suffer a breakdown in health. After being worked almost beyond endurance (Black Beauty fetches a doctor to his master's sick wife, while Kholstomer takes *his* master to visit the latter's mistress), they are, fatally, allowed free access to cold water:

---

45   Compare 'The Horse and the Ass' above.
46   The literal meaning of 'Kholstomer' is 'Canvas Measurer', but I have gone for a rendering with a more obvious significance in English. The progression of names is also found in *Black Beauty*: the horse protagonist begins as 'Darkie', before becoming 'Black Beauty', and eventually 'Jack' once he is drawing a cab (some owners do not bother with names).

> Then he gave me a pailful of water to drink; it was cold and very good, and I drank it all; then he gave me some hay and some corn, and thinking he had done right, he went away. Soon I began to shake and tremble, and turned deadly cold; my legs ached, my loins ached, and my chest ached, and I felt sore all over. Oh! how I wished for my warm, thick cloth, as I stood and trembled. (*Black Beauty*, Chapter 18)

> In their service, I lost my best qualities and half my life. They over-watered me and they broke my knees. [...] It was five in the evening and, without ordering me unharnessed, he went to visit [his woman friend]. And, as had never happened before, they whipped me and made me gallop. For the first time in my life, I lost my footing, and I was ashamed and tried to correct myself; but suddenly I heard the Prince crying in a voice not his own, 'Get a move on!' And the whip whistled and cut into me, bruising my leg on the steel apron. After twenty-five versts, we caught up with her. I had got him there, but all night I shook and could not eat even a bite. In the morning, they watered me. After drinking it, I forever ceased to be the horse that I once had been. I was sick and they tormented and cripped me — treated me, as humans call it. My hooves fell off; I became dropsical and my legs bowed, my chest sank, and I was weak and flabby in every way. They sold me to a dealer. (*Kholstomer*, Chapter 8)

Beauty's story is more complicated. He later suffers a second breakdown after he is galloped unmercifully over newly-laid flints on the road by a drunken groom ('my shoeless foot suffered dreadfully; the hoof was broken and split down to the very quick, and the inside was terribly cut by the sharpness of the stones'). His broken knees are treated by the customary method:

> Proud flesh, as they called it, came up in my knees, and was burned out with caustic; and when at last it was healed, they put a blistering fluid over the front of both knees to bring all the hair off; they had some reason for this, and I suppose it was all right. (*Black Beauty*, Chapter 26)

Beauty is then rejected by his master, who 'cannot have broken knees in my stables'. But overwatering and physical breakdown, along with cruel and ignorant veterinary treatment, figure in both texts.

Not only do the same constituents — consciousness of family honour, a drunken groom, a noble horse spoiled by human stupidity, precipitating the horse's decline — come up in both narratives, but in both cases these calamities are narrated by the horse himself, who proves a sharp observer of human folly.[47] Early in his life, Beauty recalls having witnessed gentlemen out hunting a hare in a nearby field:

> As for me, I was so astonished that I did not at first see what was going on by the brook; but when I did look there was a sad sight; two fine horses were down, one was struggling in the stream, and the other was groaning on the grass. One of the riders was getting out of the water covered with mud, the other lay quite still.

---

47 In each case, the drunken groom motif has slightly different effects where the horse is concerned: the drunken groom rides Beauty over the new-made road and fails to notice his shoe is off, while Tolstoy's drunken groom simply fails to feed Kholstomer for a day; but the assumption of culpability is the same, and in both cases, the groom himself suffers as well: Kholstomer's groom gets a flogging for his pains, while Beauty's falls off and is killed.

> 'His neck is broke,' said my mother.
> 'And serve him right, too,' said one of the colts.
> I thought the same, but my mother did not join with us.
> 'Well, no,' she said, 'you must not say that; but though I am an old horse, and have seen and heard a great deal, I never yet could make out why men are so fond of this sport; they often hurt themselves, often spoil good horses, and tear up the fields, and all for a hare or a fox, or a stag, that they could get more easily some other way; but we are only horses, and don't know'. (*Black Beauty*, Chapter 2)

In Kholstomer's case, human rapacity is represented in a more general, abstract way: the horse does not understand how he, or anything else, could be understood to 'belong' to a human being:

> They arrange that so far as one and the same thing is concerned, only one [person] should say: 'It is mine'. And he who, in the course of this game they have arranged is able to say of the most things, 'They are mine' is the accounted the happiest among them. I long supposed this to be a question of some direct advantage; but there, it turned out, I did them an injustice. (*Kholstomer*, Chapter 6)

Notably, many of the later peripeteias in the horse's fate come about after he is sold and falls into the hands of still less considerate 'masters' (the same concept, in Russian *khozyain*, is invoked by both Sewell and Tolstoy). Here, the fate of the horses resembles that of Harriet Beecher Stowe's Uncle Tom, who also passes through the hands of various owners of differing temperament and levels of concern, a factor that was invoked by Stowe at the outset of her novel as demonstrating the central iniquities of the slave's state:

> So long as the law considers all these human beings, with beating hearts and living affections, only as so many *things* belonging to a master, — so long as the failure, or misfortune, or imprudence, or death of the kindest owner, may cause them any day to exchange a life of kind protection and indulgence for one of hopeless misery and toil, — so long it is impossible to make anything beautiful or desirable in the best regulated administration of slavery. (*Uncle Tom's Cabin*, Chapter 1)

The 'horse-slave' analogy is almost irresistible (and Sewell's novel was greeted when it was first published as *Uncle Tom's Cabin* for horses). But both Tolstoy and Sewell stop short of making this analogy explicit or, at any rate, of advocating equine rebellion against subordination. Both Black Beauty and Kholstomer define themselves primarily in terms of loyalty to their master. Indeed, Kholstomer claims that he loved Prince Serpukhovskoi despite the latter's callousness:

> Although he caused my downfall, although he never loved anything or anyone, that was precisely the reason why I loved him, and still do love him. I liked the fact that he was handsome, happy, rich, and on that account loved no-one. You understand these our equine emotions. (*Kholstomer*, Chapter 8)

For his part, Beauty emphasises that he has learned a respect for work and good behaviour from his mother:

> Your grandmother had the sweetest temper of any horse I ever knew, and I think you have never seen me kick or bite. I hope you will grow up gentle and good, and never learn bad ways; do your work with a good will, lift your feet up well when you trot, and never bite or kick even in play. (*Black Beauty*, Chapter 1)[48]

And Black Beauty never loses this, no matter how sorely tried.

The resemblance between the two equine heroes and Uncle Tom is striking. The latter does not attempt escape even when he is sent to Cincinnati alone with five hundred dollars ('Ah master trusted me, and I couldn't'). But Eliza, on the other hand, does make for freedom, and the novel concludes with her safely in Canada. Both *Black Beauty* and *Kholstomer* depend on a contrast between the hero and a giddy young mare, but in neither case does this life-path offer a real alternative: the brown mare in the herd where Kholstomer tells his story, whose expressive neighing completes the panorama of the first chapter, is no more than a nuisance to everyone. The fate of rebellious Ginger is even sadder than that of Black Beauty: she is last glimpsed totally broken-down.

Yet the stories would hardly gain, from a literary point of view, if they were liberation narratives, of the sort characterising Russian feminist prose of this era.[49] Rather, they are powerful precisely because they offset the low outer worth of horses, their insignificance in the human eye, with an angry sense that such exploitation is not just cruel, but an assault on personal autonomy. In both cases, the ingrained assumption that human life is worth more than animal life is explicitly challenged. In *Black Beauty* the horses (and with them the reader) mourn the dead hunter more than the rider who has caused the horse's death, though only the former is the subject of ritualised burial:

> Not many days after we heard the church-bell tolling for a long time, and looking over the gate we saw a long, strange black coach that was covered with black cloth and was drawn by black horses; after that came another and another and another, and all were black, while the bell kept tolling, tolling. They were carrying young Gordon to the churchyard to bury him. He would never ride again. What they did with Rob Roy I never knew; but 'twas all for one little hare. (*Black Beauty*, Chapter 2)

There is an ethical if not stylistic parallel here to the very end of *Kholstomer*, which also juxtaposes the fates of horse and master, with considerably more sympathy expended on the latter:

> A week later, only the big skull and two hip-bones were left lying by the brick shed; the rest had been dragged away. In the summer a peasant bone collector took the hip bones and the skull and put them to use.
>
> The sated and soused dead body of [Prince] Serpukhovsky that had once

---

48 This passage immediately follows the one in which Beauty's mother tells him about his high pedigree. The message is: *noblesse travaille*.

49 For instance, Nadezhda Khvoshchinskaya's *The Boarding-School Girl* (*Pansionerka*, 1860), which represents how a young woman escapes the boredom and constriction of life in the provinces and finds an independent future in St Petersburg. On the 'provincial tale', see my *History of Russian Women's Writing*, Chapter 2.

inhabited the world was cleared into the earth much later. His skin, flesh, and bones were of no use to anyone. (*Kholstomer*, Chapter 10)

Crucial to the eloquence of both texts is that they are not just representations of horses, but equine *autobiographies*. While Black Beauty and Kholstomer may allude at regular intervals to the limitations of their horse understanding, their astute and apt descriptions give the lie to this modesty, not to speak of the traditional idea that animals have no language and no reason. Certainly, this is something a little different from the 'imaginative sympathy' of which Coetzee's Elizabeth Costello spoke, since both stories humanise the animal world. An early draft of Tolstoy's story even had the third-person narrator say that Kholstomer could not avoid feelings of being offended because 'when all's said and done, he was a person' (in later drafts, this became, 'when all's said and done, he was a horse', but the description of the feelings remained the same).[50] In the final version of the story, the horse's stud name was 'Moujik' [Peasant Man] (though he was known to the racing 'rabble' by the name of an inanimate object that worked by purely mechanical means). Under the successive names 'Darkie', 'Black Beauty', and 'Jack', Sewell's horse always retained his human potential, but with his most uncaring masters, lost any name at all.

In these respects, both narratives had something in common not just with *Uncle Tom's Cabin*, but with the most famous slave autobiography of the mid-nineteenth century. Frederick Douglass had described himself at the beginning as being like a horse:

> I have no accurate knowledge of my age, having never seen any authentic record containing it. By far the larger part of the slaves know as little of their ages as horses know of theirs, and it is the wish of most masters within my knowledge to keep their slaves thus ignorant.[51]

And, like Beauty and Kholstomer, he suffered repeated name-changes and inhumane treatment. The difference was that, from an early age, he was, in his own account, conscious that this was deeply unjust. In their representation of the conditions of work as both harsh and inescapable, Kholstomer and Beauty constructed the universe in a different way. They, and perhaps the authors who created them too, could not imagine a world of equality.[52]

---

50 Tolstoy, *Kholstomer*, Chapter 4. For the early variant, see L. D. Opul'skaya, 'Tvorcheskaya istoriya povesti "Kholstomer": Rannyaya redaktsiya (1861–1863)', *Literaturnoe nasledstvo*, 69.1 (1961), 257–76 (p. 273, n. 47). As Opul'skaya points out (ibid., p. 265), in the final redaction, Kholstomer is given more 'appealing' characteristics than before. By this, she evidently means, more human ones, such as reflectiveness, the capacity to meditate on what he sees, etc.
51 *Narrative of the Life of Frederick Douglass, an American Slave, Written by Himself* (Boston: At the Anti-Slavery Office, 1845) <http://www.gutenberg.org/files/23/23-h/23-h.htm> [accessed 13 September 2022].
52 Certainly, to the end of his life, Tolstoy both rode horses and drove them in carriages, though, according to a report quoted by the animal rights activist Henry Salt (who himself disagreed with Gompertz about the use of animals), Tolstoy eschewed some traditional practices of horse handling: 'The representative of an English paper lately had a drive with Count Tolstoi. On his remarking that he had no whip, the Count gave him a glance "almost of scorn", and said: "I talk to my horses: I do not beat them."': Henry S. Salt, *Animals' Rights Considered in Relation to Social Progress* (London: George Bell & Sons, 1892), p. 36.

The resemblance between these two striking representations of the 'horse as slave' (but *willing* slave), written only a few years apart, is probably the result of coincidence, rather than of direct contact. Tolstoy could certainly, hypothetically, have read *Black Beauty* before he embarked on the final version of *Kholstomer*. There is evidence in his diaries and letters from the end of the nineteenth century for a rising interest in animal welfare literature. His *The First Step* (1893), an impassioned sermon in favour of vegetarianism, cited not just the benefits of asceticism to health and morality, but also the appallingly cruel treatment of animals in the abattoir. His trip to witness the slaughter of cattle with his own eyes was, he said, directly prompted by an English-language source: 'Even earlier, long ago, reading the wonderful book, *Ethics of Diet*, I was visited by the inclination to make a trip to an abattoir and see with my own eyes what people are discussing when they talk of vegetarianism'. The book he referred to, by Howard Williams, and published in 1883, was a compendium of quotations in favour of vegetarian practice that closely resembled, in terms of its use of authorities in order to make a moral case by agglutination, Tolstoy's own ethical commonplace-books such as *Krug chteniya* [A Cycle of Reading].[53] Tolstoy had also read work by Henry Salt, one of the foremost late nineteenth-century polemicists in favour of animal rights, and in 1891 corresponded about a possible translation by Vera Zagoskina-Alekseeva of *A Plea for Vegetarianism and Other Essays*.[54] Yet there is nothing in Tolstoy's writings from the late 1870s and 1880s that suggests he had read or heard of Sewell's book. Besides, references in diaries and letters make clear that Tolstoy was working on what he called his 'story about a gelding' as early as 1863, and that this already contained the scene with the drunken groom and the scene set at the races.[55] His motive for turning to the topic again in 1884 was, if her own account is to be believed, the fact that Sof'ya Tolstaya came across the draft in Tolstoy's papers, when preparing a volume of his collected works, and encouraged him to complete the story.[56] A substantial draft of the text, which Tolstoy's editors have confidently dated to 1863, survives, and this contains several of the scenes that parallel those in Sewell's novel.[57]

In any case, there are signal differences between the two stories also, including

---

53 Howard Williams, *The Ethics of Diet: A Catena of Authorities Deprecatory of the Habit of Flesh-Eating* (Manchester: F. Pitman, 1883).

54 See a letter from Tolstoy to V. L. Alekseev (husband of the translator), 10 November 1891, in *Polnoe sobranie sochinenii* (90 vols.; Moscow, 1928–58), LXVI, 82 (hereafter in this chapter referenced as *PSS*). On the same day, Tolstoy wrote to his amanuensis, Vladimir Chertkov, about this project (see editors' note, ibid.), but nothing appears to have come of it.

55 Tolstoy, *Polnoe sobranie sochinenii*, XLVIII, 52. Efforts have been made to argue that Tolstoy began what became *Kholstomer* earlier than 1863. Opul'skaya ('Tvorcheskaya istoriya povesti "Kholstomer"', p. 259) follows a note by Sof'ya Tolstaya dating it to 1861, and the editors of *PSS* assumed that a note in Tolstoy's diary of 1856 (*PSS*, XLVII, 78), 'I want to write the story of a horse', refers to this project (Opul'skaya, p. 272). However, the earliest documented work on 'the story of a gelding' dates from 1863.

56 See Opul'skaya, 'Tvorcheskaya istoriya povesti "Kholstomer"', pp. 257–58.

57 It goes without saying that Sewell cannot have known anything about an unpublished text in a language that she could not read; if one of these narratives prompted the other, it must have been hers that inspired that of Tolstoy.

not just the fact that Kholstomer is explicitly stated to be 'a gelding' (Black Beauty presumably is, yet the point is not made directly), but the fact that his physical decay is crucial to the narrative.[58] Tolstoy also retains an externalised perspective upon the horses, with a third-person 'frame' alongside Kholstomer's inset autobiography, so that the human perspective upon animals (and humans) vies with the animal point of view. Inviting as it would be to trace the inter-resemblance between these two pioneering equine autobiographies published only eight years apart to actual influence, the safe conclusion is that the resemblance between the texts is circumstantial, deriving from contemporary preoccupations with animal welfare and first-hand observation of the pernicious effects of heavy work and ignorant or unthinking treatment upon harness horses.[59] The context for their writing was surely also shaped by the long ambiguity in the cultural perception of horses and donkeys as working animals of a particular sort: at once degraded and ennobled by their role, since they were trusted with the carrying and ferrying of human beings (including, in Gospel tradition, the Saviour). In biblical tradition also, an ass was a rare case of a beast credited with the ability, universal in folklore, to speak a language understood by humans; and Balaam's ass, what is more, presented him with words of truth and admonition. ('What have I done unto thee, that thou has smitten me three times?', Numbers 22:21–38). Horses and donkeys might be

---

58   The fact that only in Tolstoy's text is the process of gelding referred to directly is certainly explained by the difference in gender between the writers. A letter to Tolstoy from Count V. A. Sollogub, undated, but probably written in early 1863, recorded that Tolstoy's sister-in-law Tatiana Behrs was 'right' in her apprehensions about the story 'with her woman's instinct that spurns everything offensive to shame and tender aesthetic emotion' (*PSS*, XLVIII, 381; for the date of 1863, rather than 1865, see Opul'skaya, 'Tvorcheskaya istoriya povesti "Kholstomer"', p. 269). An important change between redactions is that the final version reads, after a description of the horse's imprisonment in a stall and attention from the grooms, 'I became what I am now' (Chapter 6), while an earlier version read, 'I became a gelding' (ibid., p. 280). Thus Tolstoy seems to have 'corrected' the 'impropriety' of his first drafts (Sollogub also advised him to change the title from 'History of a Gelding' to the horse's name, which Tolstoy accordingly did — at first 'Khlystomer' [Whip-Measurer] and later 'Kholstomer').
59   A modern discussion of the situation is Jay Baldwin, 'Welfare Issues with the Carriage Horse', in *Equine Welfare*, ed. by C. Wayne McIlwraith and Bernard E. Rollin (Oxford: Wiley-Blackwell, 2011), pp. 394–407, which points to respiratory problems, rhabdomyolosis (or 'tying up'), colic, skin problems, heat stroke or conversely, hypothermia, as occupational hazards. Some differences between Tolstoy's and Sewell's narratives are attributable to the differences between the traditions of harnessing horses in Russia and in Britain: a particularly impassioned section of *Black Beauty* denounces the 'bearing rein' (American, 'check rein'), a device for inducing horses to keep their heads in the air that vastly increased the stress when they were pulling loads uphill. There was no equivalent of this in Russia. In her *Victorian Fiction and the Cult of the Horse* (Aldershot: Ashgate, 2006), Chapter 3, Gina M. Dorré has argued that Sewell's representation of the bearing rein refracts contemporary arguments about the unhealthiness of the corset in women, but this is certainly not a connection that Sewell herself made explicit, and the link with Uncle Tom seems far more obvious. A further difference is that Tolstoy underlines the herd instincts of horses, including their tendency to stigmatise outsiders, such as Kholstomer himself. This partly derives from the distinctive conditions in which the animals are kept in each case, out on the steppe in the case of Tolstoy's animals, and indoors or in paddocks in the case of those of Sewell. However, some of Tolstoy's horses do have innate 'bad characters' (for instance, Kholstomer's one-time stable-companion Polkan); Sewell shows all such behaviour to be the result of bad treatment (as in the case of Ginger).

functionally similar to oxen, but they were symbolically distinct.[60]

Whatever their origins, Tolstoy's and Sewell's texts remained particularly striking evocations of what the authors saw as the willing slavery (service enforced, yet embraced) of working animals.[61] Unlike recent writers on animal liberation, or indeed Gompertz, both Tolstoy and Sewell emphasised the interdependence of horses and humans. It was precisely the 'love' that Singer disparaged which the stories set out to celebrate. Certainly, in some respects Tolstoy, at least, suggested that the attachment might be deluded; but Black Beauty felt with affection only towards the 'masters' who treated him kindly, and who deserved to be loved, illustrating the basic rationality, in Sewell's eyes, of the emotion.

And here, in the uneasy emphasis on 'love' in conditions where it may often be one-sided, Tolstoy and Sewell return us to an old problem raised also by Aristotle's *Politics*. Can friendship (or more broadly, love) exist in a situation where one side of the attempted emotional dialogue is in relations of dominance over the other?[62] While, as a recent welfare campaigner has pointed out, 'One luxury of living in a modern industrialized nation is the choice of whether or not to employ horses, and other animal companions', the extent to which a friendship based on full equality may, or indeed should, be possible is still an issue with which commentators struggle.[63] Economic development — which, rather than the ethical perfectibility evoked by some narratives of animal liberation, seems to be the real engine of change — has removed certain dilemmas, but created others. As companionship with non-working animals becomes possible, so the anxiety rises that 'pets, like kings' favourites, are usually the recipients of an abundance of sentimental affection but of little real kindness; so much easier is it to give temporary caresses than substantial justice'.[64] It would surely be too depressing a conclusion that *every* type of inter-species relationship with animals was a form of enslavement, but the important 'emotional work' engaged in by animals (the way in which they offer consolation and reassurance to their human companions) has had little recognition in literary

---

60   This is, I think, of more relevance than the eighteenth- and nineteenth-century discussions about the capacity of beasts to communicate (see the interesting discussion in Candland, *Feral Children and Clever Animals*), since these dwelt on relatively primitive cases such as the capacity of horses to count. There is nothing specifically 'equine' in the use of language by Beauty and Kholstomer, but they are, of course, talking to other horses (explicitly, in the case of Kholstomer).

61   For an extensive discussion of *Black Beauty* from this point of view, see Natalie Corrine Hansen, 'Horse Talk: Horses and Human(e) Discourses', in *Speaking for Animals: Animal Autobiographical Writing*, ed. by Margo DeMillo (London: Routledge, 2013), pp. 207–29, which emphasises the sentimentality of Sewell's story and its grounding on 'a humanist model of species difference' (p. 207).

62   As Millett points out ('Aristotle and Slavery', p. 199), Aristotle's treatment of friendship with slaves, as both possible and not possible, is one of the contradictory elements in his discussion; Millett sees this conflict as reconcilable because slaves' ability to at least simulate human characteristics, in Aristotle's view, reflects well on the master's treatment of him — that is, on the superior humanity of the latter (ibid.). See also Brunt, 'Aristotle and Slavery', pp. 367–68.

63   Baldwin, 'Welfare Issues with the Carriage Horse', p. 394. Baldwin is talking particularly about the employment 'for in-profit businesses', but employment in a broader set of economic contexts could also be invoked.

64   Salt, *Animals' Rights Considered in Relation to Social Progress*, p. 42.

texts or in general discussion.⁶⁵ The issues of how to combine affection, and more broadly 'imaginative sympathy', with justice, and how co-operation within a power asymmetry may be possible without exploitation, remain as complicated in the early twenty-first century as they have been for more than two thousand years.⁶⁶

'The beast-footed man' is a reversal of Aristotle's contemptuous description of the slave as 'the man-footed beast'. I would like to thank Irina Prokhorova for the invitation to contribute a paper to the session of the Bannye chteniya, Moscow, 4–5 April 2014, dedicated to the legitimation of slavery, which acted as the stimulus to these reflections. Helpful suggestions about work relating to the history of slavery in the classical world were made by Robin Lane Fox and by Paul Millett. I would particularly like to thank the latter for generously sharing his own work and ideas, and for his support and enthusiasm for the topic. My thanks also to Andrew Kahn, Jonathan Morton, and Ann Jefferson. This paper was first published in Russian, in *Novoe literaturnoe obozrenie*, in 2016.

65   My thanks to Yuri Sorochkin for raising the point about 'emotional work' by pets. This type of activity tends to become a 'cultural fact' only when the animal concerned has an official caring role, as with guide dogs for the blind, 'hearing dogs', etc.
66   For a moving tribute to the possibility of friendship on equal terms with a 'companion animal', see the article by primatologist Barbara Smuts in Coetzee, *The Lives of Animals*. One consideration, it goes without saying, is that societies that have yet to achieve equality for humans are most unlikely to achieve them for animals any time soon — though the history of treating at least some animals rather better than humans might suggest that this is not a final answer either.

CHAPTER 5

A Wolf in the Nursery:
Freud, Ethnography, and a
Border-Crossing Life

[2007]

I dreamed that it is night and I am lying in my bed (the foot of my bed was under the window, and outside the window there was a row of old walnut trees. I know that it was winter in my dream, and night-time). Suddenly the window opens of its own accord and, terrified, I see that there are a number of white wolves sitting in the big walnut tree outside the window. There were six or seven of them. The wolves were white all over and looked more like foxes or sheepdogs because they had big tails like foxes and their ears were pricked up like dogs watching something. Obviously fearful that the wolves were going to gobble me up I screamed and woke up. My nurse hurried to my bedside to see what had happened. It was some time before I could be convinced that it had only been a dream, because the image of the window opening and the wolves sitting in the tree was so clear and lifelike. Eventually I calmed down, feeling as if I had been liberated from danger, and went back to sleep.

The only action in the dream was the opening of the window, for the wolves were sitting quite still in the branches of the tree, to the right and left of the tree trunk, not moving at all, and looking right at me. It looked as if they had turned their full attention on me. — I think that was my first anxiety dream. I was three or four at the time, certainly not more than five. From then on until I was ten or eleven I was always afraid of seeing something terrible in my dreams.[1]

This famous description of an extraordinarily vivid and haunting dream forms the centrepiece of Freud's essay 'From the History of an Infantile Neurosis', better known as 'The Wolf-Man' (originally dating from 1914 and revised in 1918). In Freud's analysis, the dream does not occur as it does here, at the beginning. It is buffered by a long preamble describing the doctor's first encounters with his patient. The narration of the dream comes at a critical point in the 'talking cure', as the patient's resistance begins to break down. And equally, the dream itself is placed by

1   Sigmund Freud, 'From the History of an Infantile Neurosis [The 'Wolfman']', in *The 'Wolfman' and Other Cases,* trans. by L. A. Huish (London: Penguin, 2002), pp. 203–330 (p. 227) (hereafter referenced as *W*; the alternation of italics and roman follows the original text).

Freud at a crucial point in the child's development:

> The period of childhood with which we are particularly concerned can be divided into two phases, a first phase of difficult behaviour and perversity which lasted from his seduction [by his sister] at the age of 3¼ until his fourth birthday, and a longer, subsequent phase dominated by the signs of neurosis. (*W*, p. 226)

Thus, the chronology of the case-study mimics that of the putative childhood to which it refers. The narration of the dream appears at the mid-point of Freud's exegetic narrative, where it acts as the interpretive crux.

Within psychoanalytic tradition, the 'Wolf-Man's' dream is as renowned as Hamlet's encounter with his father's ghost is to readers of English literature, and likewise, the interpretation placed on it by the master. For Freud, the scene constituted an inverted recollection of a time when the Wolf-Man was about eighteen months old. His parents had retired for the afternoon on a hot summer's day, and had placed the child in their room because he was unwell. Assuming he was safely asleep, they started behaving as though he were not present at all, but the child woke up, and 'witnessed "coitus a tergo" repeated three times' (*W*, p. 235). This incident, combined with his father's habit of affectionately threatening to gobble the child up (*W*, p. 230), was (to put Freud's analysis in a walnut shell) at the root of an anal-erotic complex of desire and terror, involving both the wish to have anal intercourse with the father, and the fear of castration should this occur (*W*, pp. 234, 305).

This summary may catch the gist, but it considerably simplifies the narrative organisation of 'The Wolf-Man'. In the case-study itself, the patient's first admission is that he was afraid of wolves generally: he used to 'scream furiously' whenever his sister showed him a picture-book with an illustration of 'a wolf standing on its hind legs and stepping out' (*W*, p. 213). This book was also his own primary association with the dream of the six (or alternatively, five, or seven) white wolves sitting in the tree:

> He always related this dream to the memory that in those childhood years he would express a quite monstrous anxiety at the picture of a wolf that was to be found in his book of fairy tales [...]. Why are the wolves white? That made him think of the sheep which were kept in large flocks quite near the estate. His father sometimes took him to visit the flocks of sheep and he was always very proud and happy when this happened. Later on — inquiries suggest that it could easily have been before this dream took place — an epidemic broke out among the sheep. His father sent for one of Pasteur's disciples, who inoculated the sheep, but after the inoculation they died in ever greater numbers than before.
>
> How did the wolves get up in the tree? A story occurs to him that he had heard his grandfather tell. He cannot remember whether it was before or after the dream, but the content of the story strongly supports the first possibility. The story goes as follows: a tailor is sitting in his room working when the window opens and in leaps a wolf. The tailor hits out at him with his measuring stick — no, he corrects himself, he grabs him by the tail and pulls it off, so that the wolf runs away, terrified. Sometime later the tailor goes into the woods and

suddenly sees a pack of wolves coming towards him, and so he escapes from them by climbing up a tree. At first the wolves do not know what to do, but the maimed one, who is also there and wants his revenge on the tailor, suggests that one should climb on another's back until the last one can reach the tailor. He himself — a powerful old wolf — will form the base of this pyramid. The wolves do as he says, but the tailor recognizes the wolf who visited him, the one he punished, and he calls out suddenly, as he did before, 'Grab the grey fellow by the tail'. The wolf who has lost his tail remembers what happens and runs away, terrified, while the others all tumble down in a heap. (*W*, p. 229)

In later stages of the analysis, the patient remembered — prompted by Freud — that the picture of the wolf that had terrified him was almost certainly an illustration to the tale 'The Wolf and the Seven Little Kids', where the wolf gobbles up six of the seven kids while the last one hides in a clock. In this tale, the wolf disguises himself by getting the baker to white up his paws with flour (*W*, p. 229), thus becoming, for a time and in part, 'a white wolf'.

As usual with his patients' own ratiocinations, Freud regarded the interpretations offered by the 'Wolf-Man' as 'screen-' or 'cover-memories' (*Deckerinnerungen*). So far as deeper, more 'authentic' memories were concerned, these were reconstructed by inference, rather than cited directly from the patient's own discourse. Moving from a thought on the 'Wolf-Man's' part that the opening window in the dream stood for his own opening eyes as he woke up, Freud then proceeded to his interpretation of the dream as a repressed memory of the child, aged about eighteen months, witnessing his parents enjoying sexual intercourse repeatedly on a sultry summer afternoon.

This revelation is presented for maximum shock effect, as a *coup de théâtre*, with Freud anticipating, and thus heightening yet disarming in advance, the resistance of his reader. In the words of the analyst:

> We are now approaching the point at which I must abandon my attempt to draw on the actual course of the analysis. I fear that it will also be the point at which the reader will abandon his faith in what I have to say. (*W*, p. 234)

And faith is indeed expected, because the dream and its interpretation are presented *en face*, as in the juxtaposition of a text and its translation, or as with montage in the cinema. The detailed textual analysis — where Freud argues that the wolves are white because of the white underwear worn by the child's parents, and that they are watching him tensely because the dream reverses the scene actually witnessed (where the boy himself was watching the 'wolves' copulate) is relegated to the margins of discussion — to footnote 13 following the given chapter (*W*, p. 244).

Freud's interpretation of his patient's experience is reductive in several different ways. To begin with, the child's universe is reduced to family psychodrama — the aspect of Freud that receives particularly cogent criticism in Gilles Deleuze and Félix Guattari's *L'Anti-Oedipe* (1972). Certainly, Freud acknowledges that the tree which the child witnessed could also have 'topical' significance, relating to the 'anticipation of Christmas': 'The content of the dream showed him his presents, the gifts that were intended for him[,] hanging on the tree' (*W*, p. 233). But this significance is reduced to the general status of *giving* as part of the anal-erotic complex. Voiding of the bowels and spending in the economic sense (spending money) are understood to be related (*W*, p. 273). It is clear that the gifts on the Christmas tree are also part of the central psychodrama. Indeed every event in the Wolf-Man's remembered childhood, from his fear of butterflies to his relationships with the servants, is drawn into the developmental master-plot.

By extension, all anxiety is reduced down to sexual anxiety. Central is the later episode where the child's terror of the butterfly, which the adult patient remembered as coming from an association between the creature's wings and a woman opening her legs, is cited. Freud comments that the shape also recalled the Roman numeral five (V), the hour at which the child had putatively witnessed his parents having intercourse (*W*, pp. 289, 292). To put the point theoretically, as Freud himself did in his analysis of 'Little Hans' (properly known as 'Phobia in a Five-Year Old Boy'), 'For libido that has been released from the pathogenic material by means of repression is not *converted* — drawn off from the inner sphere and channelled into physical enervation — but allowed to exist freely in the form of anxiety'.[2]

This set of assumptions in turn leads to a particular attitude towards the patient, who, in not acknowledging the primal origins of neurosis — the goal of analysis — is assumed to be concealing or 'covering' (to cite the original term) these behind-, or under-, layers of resistance. By extension, the main purpose of the nurturing culture, in Freud's interpretation, is to provide culturally acceptable forms in which the taboo may be expressed. Folklore, in particular, is a storehouse of symbology that can be used to express the agony (in the Greek sense of 'intellectual conflict', as well as the ordinary one) of an individual subject/patient. For the child, the main narratorial repertoire comprises the images drawn from fantastic tales (*Märchen*: the German word can refer to literary versions of popular tales as well as to the orally-transmitted forms). So, the various other wolf tales to which the 'Wolf-Man' had, according to his memory as represented in the case history, been exposed in childhood, are taken in this interpretive direction too:

> He had been told the story (from *Reineke Fuchs* [*Reynard the Fox*] where the wolf tried to catch fish in winter and used his tail as bait, whereupon his tail froze in the ice and broke off. He learnt the different names used for horses depending on the intactness of their sex. He was thus preoccupied with the thought of castration without believing in it or being frightened by it. Other problems relating to sexuality were posed by the fairy tales with which he became acquainted at this time. In 'Little Red Riding Hood' and 'The Seven Little Kids' children were pulled out of the body of the wolf. Was the wolf female, then, or could men also carry children in their bodies? (*W*, p. 223)

Freud's case history of the Wolf-Man, based on his treatment of Sergei Pankeev, a patient from a Russian-speaking landowning family in the territory of modern Ukraine, was not his only piece addressing the dream of six white wolves. In

---

2   Sigmund Freud, 'Analysis of a Phobia in a Five-Year-Old Boy ['Little Hans']', in *The 'Wolfman' and Other Cases*, pp. 1–122 (p. 95) (hereafter referenced as *H*; the alternation of italics and roman follows the original text).

his essay, 'Material from Folk Tales in Dreams' (1913), written a year earlier than the first version of his case history, he had already set out an interpretation of the dream. Here, the Wolf-Man's primal fantasising is set alongside the dream of a young, newly-married woman, whose vision of a dwarfish, gambolling, Rumpelstiltskin-like manikin with a bald head, and wearing a dark jacket and grey coat (the woman herself saw this as a version of her father-in-law), becomes in Freud's analysis a fantasy of her husband's penis, and of her fear that intercourse might lead her to conceive.³ While this parallel disappeared, the first interpretation of Pankeev's dream was repeated almost word-for-word in the case history of the Wolf-Man itself.

Yet within the wider case history, its effect was less simple. To begin with, the dream stands out generically. Other memories are more fragmentary, and the subject himself was less sure about their likely meanings and associations. The further exemplifications of the Wolf-Man's neurosis serve, therefore, not so much to amplify the sense of primary causality, as to induce a sense of dislocation, a feeling that the dream is a unique case of what Mikhail Bakhtin termed *chuzhoe slovo*, 'the discourse of the other', that stubbornly resists (in the ordinary as well as Freudian sense) the hermeneutic ambitions of the psychoanalyst. One is reminded of Tolstoy's composition of an afterword to *The Kreutzer Sonata* (1887) to explain that he really did endorse the arguments of the story's narrator. Tolstoy's double vision worked in the opposite direction from Freud's — he was trying to simplify what had been presented originally in more elaborate form. Yet in each case, the insistence on the validity of a previous interpretation acts as an unspoken acknowledgement that the material returned to was at some level not amenable to that previous interpretation. An exegesis that is not controversial and troubling does not require reiteration.

It is instructive to compare the narrative mechanisms in 'The Wolf-Man' with those in a later case-history by Freud, 'Little Hans' (1922), whose subject was analysed while he was still a small boy. The child's preoccupation with what the latest English translation calls 'his widdler', and with 'pooing' and 'plopping', and his desperate fear of draught-horses were brought together in a narrative of sibling hatred whose central drive is the subject's association between the (unwelcome) arrival of his younger sister, his desire for his mother, his fear of 'body boxes' (i.e. carriages) bringing new, human, arrivals, and his childish association of defecation with procreation (or, to be more accurate, parturition). The analysis here is much more straightforward, focused as it is upon excerpts from the diary of Hans's father, who understands most (but providentially, for the authority of the psychoanalyst, not all) of his son's metaphorical world. In this smooth, generically homogeneous, document, there is no stretch of the text that has the revelatory quality of the Wolf-Man's dream.

At the same time, it was Hans (rather than the Wolf-Man) who voiced, in a delightfully revealing passage, what might seem — to a sceptical observer — one

---

3   Sigmund Freud, 'Märchenstoffe in Traumen' [1913] translated as 'The Occurrence in Dreams of Material from Fairy Tales'), in *The Standard Edition of the Complete Psychological Works of Sigmund Freud*, ed. by James Strachey and others, 24 vols (London: Hogarth Press, 1953–74), XII, 281–87.

of the main problems with the psychoanalytic narrative: the possible suggestibility of patients:

> I: '*If you'd rather Hanna* [the sister] *had never been born, you can't be very fond of her at all.*'
> Hans: 'Mmm' (agreeing).
> I: '*That was why you thought that if Mummy let go when she was giving her her bath, she might fall in the water...*'
> Hans (finishing the sentence): ' — and drown.'
> I: '*And you would be all alone with Mummy. And a good boy wouldn't want that to happen.*'
> Hans: 'But he's allowed to think it'
> I: '*It's not a good thing, though.*'
> Hans: 'If he does think it, it is a good thing, though, so that we can write and tell the Professor'. (H, p. 57)

The alternation of italics and roman follows the original text. Here Freud's own note adds: 'Bravo, little Hans! I could not hope for a better understanding of psychoanalysis from an adult' (H, p. 82, n. 31).

Equally, one wonders whether part of the Wolf-Man's account might come from desperation to provide the Herr Professor with what he so patently wants — a move from silent resistance to resistance of a kind susceptible to analysis.[4] The former mood is explicitly recorded by Freud:

> The patient I am concerned with here maintained an unassailable position for a long time, entrenched behind an attitude of submissive indifference. He listened and understood but would allow nothing to come anywhere near him. One could not fault his intelligence, but it was as if it had been cut off by those involuntary [*triebhaft*][5] forces that determined his behaviour in the few human relationships left to him. He had to be educated for a long time before he could be persuaded to take an independent interest in our work and when, as a result of our efforts, the first moments of release occurred, he suspended the work immediately to prevent any further possibility of change and to maintain the comfortableness of the former situation. His timidity at the prospect of an independent existence was so great that it outweighed all the hardships of being ill. (W, p. 208)

Freud does not directly confront the possibility of non-cooperation being replaced by invention, or to put it in a less loaded way, collusion, on the patient's part. His aetiology goes back exclusively to direct personal experience — the wolves being sheep that all died in an epidemic. But in fact, the Wolf-Man's tale is saturated with *literariness*. Lermontov appears on at least two occasions:

---

4   It is interesting to note that in an undated typed memoir, 'Der Tod meines Vaters und wieder ein Sanatorium', held in the Library of Congress (henceforth LOC), Sergius Pankejeff Papers, Box 2, Folder 7, Pankeev swithers between psychoanalytical explanations of his motivation (for example, his retreat to Dr Kräplin's sanatorium near Munich after his father's death was likely a reaction to that event, or perhaps it was an excuse to see Therese Keller, later his wife), and a more distanced perspective: 'Those are thoughts that preoccupy me only now, because back then I had no inkling of psychoanalysis and could accordingly have made no such interpretive attempts' (ff. 15–16).
5   Literally, 'driving'.

FIG. 5.1. Sergei Pankeev at Vasilievka, late 1890s. The other young man is probably his cousin Georgy. Library of Congress, Sergius Pankejeff Collection.

> A few months after his sister's death he had himself made a journey to the region where she had died; there he sought out the grave of a great poet whom at that time he idealized, and shed hot tears over the grave [...]. An error in his narrative had given me another indication as to the true meaning of this homage apparently paid to the poet, which I was able to draw his attention to at this point. He had repeatedly told me earlier that his sister had shot herself and then been obliged to correct himself, since she had taken poison. The poet, however, had been shot, in a duel. (W, p. 221)

Less obviously, 'a poor day-labourer' remembered by the Wolf-Man from his childhood, who was unable to speak, 'supposedly because his tongue had been cut out' (W, p. 285), has a literary antecedent: the Malayan servant in Turgenev's lush late story, 'The Song of Triumphant Love'.[6]

---

6   To sketch the plot in more detail: one of the heroine's rival lovers turns up after her marriage to the other accompanied by a mysterious, sad, Malayan servant, whose tongue has been cut out to silence him.

Of course, none of this would invalidate the psychosexual drama that Freud sketches. For any subject who wanted to escape a diagnosis of homosexuality and anal eroticism, Lermontov (the author of some notoriously filthy tributes to cottaging in an all-male boarding school) would be positively the last author who would provide a loophole. Turgenev's Malayan is easy to gloss as a castration fantasy (the 'third unnecessary person' in the love affair, the hapless male left outside the love triangle and beyond the heroine's attention). The fact that the Malayan is placed at one remove, by being placed 'in quotation marks', is neither here nor there. No doubt Freud himself took the same attitude as Karin Obholzer, a journalist who interviewed the Wolf-Man in his old age, and felt that literary chatter was a diversionary tactic: 'He had always made a stiff, almost wooden impression on me and seemed to feel more secure when he could talk in a somewhat superficial way about belletristic matters'.[7]

More important are the hitches in chronology that the Freudian narrative lays bare. For example, the tale of the wolf and the seven little kids is included in Ushinsky's *Native Word* (*Rodnoe slovo*), a standard pre-1917 reading primer.[8] It is possible, therefore, that the Wolf-Man encountered this story much *later* than the primal scene. If dreams can reverse relationships, cannot memory as well? Is it possible that the memories about when the boy was *no longer* afraid of wolves actually refer to a time *before* he was afraid of wolves? Children in the age range five to eight or nine are often much more gleefully macabre than children a few years older. And, when the Wolf-Man was around nine or ten, his family moved to Belorussia, where, as he remembered, 'primeval forests, ponds, lakes large and small, and many bogs impressed one as a remnant of nature still untouched by man. There were wolves in the forests'.[9] Aleksei Konstantinovich Tolstoy's famous poem, 'The Wolves', dating from the 1840s and widely read by Russian children of pre-teen age, portrays a group of seven wolves emerging in the still night to roam into human space, terrifying the life out of anyone who sees them and checking whether the local priest and his family are nursing 'sinful thoughts'. At the back of the group comes a lame wolf; the leader, at the front, is a wolf 'with white fur'.[10] Whichever way, must the Wolf-Man's fear of wolves have derived only from one experience? Is this likely when it comes to a fear that is — in Europe, anyway — a cultural universal?

Freud himself was conscious of the possibility that he had misinterpreted the dream:

> Aspects of personality, a national character which is alien to our own, made it difficult to empathize with him. The contrast between the patient's charming

---

7 Karin Obholzer, *The Wolf-Man: Sixty Years Later*, trans. by Michael Shaw (London: Routledge & Kegan Paul, 1982), p. 247.
8 K. D. Ushinsky, *Rodnoe slovo dlya detei mladshego vozrasta. God pervyi. Pervaya posle azbuki kniga dlya chteniya*, 4th edn (St Petersburg: N. S. Ushinskaya, 1912).
9 *The Wolf-Man and Sigmund Freud*, ed. by Muriel Gardiner (London: Karnac Books, 1972), p. 12.
10 The poem was written in the 1840s. In its final verse, the wolves, shot by bullets filled with goat's hair, turn into nine old women, lying died and smeared with blood, with shape-shifting added to gender fluidity in one eerie image.

and responsive personality, his sharp intelligence and refined way of thinking, and his complete lack of restraint at the level of the drives made it necessary to spend an excessively long time on the work of preparation and education, thus rendering any kind of overview more difficult. (*W*, p. 303)

One might add that the heavy dependence of Freud's method of analysis on linguistic elements, in particular puns, made his conclusions vulnerable when dealing with a patient whose native language was not his own. For instance, an important part of Pankeev's later anxiety complex was his painful encounter with a schoolteacher named 'Wolf'. But in what language was the man called 'Wolf'? Presumably in German, in which case the effect of recognition would be less immediate, more self-conscious, than if he were called, say, *Volkov*. Or was Freud, from multilingual Lemberg-Lwów-Lviv, crediting German with the same hegemony in the 'Little Russian' or Belorussian territory hundreds of kilometres eastwards?

Similar ethnolinguistic problems have been raised in Alexander Etkind's fleeting comments on 'The Wolf-Man' in *Eros of the Impossible*. Etkind takes up the image of the 'walnut trees', and links this to the customary nursery threat to a child, *poluchish' na oreshki!* The phrase can be translated literally as, 'I'll give you the money for nuts!' but in context, it stands for a beating. As Etkind points out, phonetically the phrase is indistinguishable from *poluchish' na oreshke!* (you'll get it on the nut tree) — hence the presence of the tree in the anxiety dream.[11]

Etkind's purpose in citing this detail, though, is not to undermine Freud's analysis, but rather to take it in a different direction — away from the parents and towards the Wolf-Man's nanny, who appears here as an instrument of castration fantasy, and as an asexual force: 'Asexual in the manner of an elderly woman, she lacks the erotic attractiveness of the mother and the libido of the father, which stimulates development and provokes a sense of competitiveness'.[12]

The case history therefore becomes representative of an entire generation, not just because of the Wolf-Man's neurosis, but also because it represents the flight away from sexuality, the avoidance of the conventionally masculine/ machismo in favour not of an eroticised feminine, but of 'grandmotherly asexuality'.[13]

Etkind's is a revision of Freud's text that modifies details of the interpretation, but leaves at the centre both the 'family drama' and the sexual anxiety that formed the crux of the original text. And certainly, one has to recognise that Freud's analysis is unassailable in its own terms, because of its non-dialogic treatment of hypothetical formulations. There is no such thing as a 'fact' that does not fit the central interpretive drive. In this respect, the procedures are provocatively contrary to those of the science, or more broadly, *Wissenschaft* or *nauka*, of the day (and later generations too), where the measure of accuracy or objectivity would be a willingness to modify one's hypothesis as new material presents itself.[14]

11   Aleksandr Etkind, *Eros nevozmozhnogo: Istoriya psikhoanaliza v Rossii* (St Petersburg: 1993), p. 111.
12   Ibid., p. 113.
13   Ibid., p. 114.
14   As, for example, in the famous ethnographer D. K. Zelenin's essay on the ritual of 'warming up the dead' current in parts of rural Russia: 'I began the present study with the idea of discovering in [this ritual] traces of the former custom of consigning corpses to funeral pyres. [...] But my study

Freud was indeed aware that his relationship with the scientific was at best ambiguous. In his 1914 history of the psycho-analytic movement, he had explicitly distinguished the neuro-physiological interpretive line of Breuer, for whom hysteria resulted from non-communication of the working consciousness and other layers of mental activity, and his own, which posited repression as the central organisational drive in hysteria and neurosis generally.[15] He thereby recognised a move away from functional classification, and the study of relationships between fixed domains in consciousness, to a model of consciousness that depends on the interaction of certain key dynamics, not locatable in a materialist or determinist way by relation to contemporary models of neuro-physiology.

Freud's interpretive line is less 'scientific' in the sense of bio-medical than social-scientific or anthropological. His case studies — intimately related to the central modernist project of defamiliarising the known, as in the poetry of Mallarmé or Cubist painting, while conversely literalising the fantastic — went some way towards assailing the mind-body dichotomy of post-Enlightenment Western medicine.[16] And in rhetorical and imaginative terms, they were much richer, more suggestive, than mainstream medical histories of the day. This is brought out vividly by comparison of 'The Wolf-Man' with the narrative of Klavdyia Ba---lina, as printed by the Russian journal *Children's Medicine* in 1901. Kladviya, the case-history related, was suffering from somnambulism:

> At night (or more rarely just after falling asleep), the little girl would get up with eyes open, but cloudy and crazed, and wander round the room, but without stumbling into any of the objects she encountered on her way. She then lay down again, neatly avoiding her godmother, whom she usually shared a bed with, and then sat down and started muttering and whispering something, playing with her hair all the while. She gave no reply to any questions, and apparently paid no attention to her surroundings, 'just like a dead person', in her parents' words, but if she was put back to bed, then she would not resist, and would soon fall asleep. The next day she remembered nothing about the adventures of the previous night. At first, these perambulations occurred not more than once a week, but more recently she was getting up several times a night. Her parents did not observe that her sufferings increased at a certain time of year or in connection with the phases of the moon.[17]

The time-honoured link between phases of the moon and sleep-walking could be empirically disproven, or so it was presumed; the aetiology of Klavdiya's affliction, as explained by *Detskaya meditsina*, lay elsewhere. She had been a normal baby, so

---

adduced nothing to substantiate this idea'. Zelenin's conclusion was that the link of this ritual with the dead was in fact a late incursion into a ritual that had originally been a straight fertility rite, with the figure of the 'house spirit' at its centre. 'Narodnyi obychai "gret' pokoinikov"', in *Izbrannye trudy: Stat'i po dukhovnoi kul'ture, 1901–1913* (Moscow: 'Indrik', 1994), pp. 164–78.

15 Sigmund Freud, 'Die Geschichte der psychoanalytischen Bewegung' [1914], translated as 'The History of the Psycho-Analytic Movement', in *The Standard Edition of the Complete Works of Sigmund Freud*, ed. by Strachey and others, XIV, 11.

16 My thanks to Svetlana Boym for the former point.

17 'Sluchai sonambulizma u devochki 6 let (iz ambulatorii Detskoi bol'nitsy sv. Ol'gi)', *Detskaya meditsina*, 4 (1901), pp. 306–07. My English version, unlike the Russian version, is narrated in the past, rather than the historic present, thus losing some of the suspense of the original.

congenital damage could be ruled out. But there was bad heredity: a nervy mother and a father who had previously drunk to excess. Most important, Klavdiya's diet left much to be desired, and had done even when she was being breast-fed (from birth to seventeen months). The prescribed cure — bromide powders, better diet, and a more effective hygienic regime (no details of this were given) — soon produced what the doctors considered good results: Klavdiya ceased sleep-walking, and after that did no more than sometimes sit bolt upright in bed during the night, before returning to the ordinary sleeping position.[18]

The case history here shows no attempt to understand the individual circumstances of Klavdiya's case, or the nature of her distress (which, one suspects, continued, the bromide having simply masked its most egregious symptoms). Freud, by the 1910s, had, by contrast, come to understand that children, too, could have complex inner lives.[19] He treated his patients, whether children or adults, as ethnographical informants, reaching into their cultural backgrounds in the broadest sense, as well as into their personal backgrounds.[20] The cost of this was that he partook of the flawed universalism of the ethnography and anthropology of his day. On the one hand, he applied a totalising model to child psychology: the mechanisms of neurosis were the same whatever the national context. On the other, he allowed room for ethnic stereotyping of a frankly unreflective kind. In 'The Wolf-Man', Russian culture comes across as anally erotic in the expansive (rather than retentive) sense, as expressed particularly in passive homosexuality, masochism, and financial imprudence.[21] These are traditional traits in Western depictions of Russian culture, and they have a moral overlay that vitiates the pretensions of Freud's representation to analytical neutrality. One is reminded of a point in the 1913 essay about dreams in folk-tales that Freud co-authored with Ernst Oppenheim. Here the authors, having worked through a range of different comic stories in which people wake up after dreaming of themselves shitting to find they actually have soiled the bed, comment, 'One should not be deterred by the often dirty and repulsively indecent nature of this popular material from seeking in it valuable confirmation of psycho-analytic views'.[22] The material presented by 'The Wolf-Man', comparably, is both 'valuable' and abject: like money in the desire system of the anal erotic, it is valuable precisely because it is abject, yet finally to be kept at a distance lest it lay bare the inner fantasies of the observer (desirer) him- or herself.[23]

18 Ibid.
19 In *The Interpretation of Dreams*, on the other hand, Freud saw children's dreams as transparent and not very interesting. He had himself undergone a huge evolution over less than two decades of clinical practice and public discussion.
20 For the general point about Freud as anthropologist, see also the excellent introduction by Ritchie Robertson to *The Interpretation of Dreams*, trans. by J. Crick (Oxford: Oxford University Press, 1999).
21 Cf. also the arguments of Vladimir Medvedev, '"Russkost"' na kushetke. Opyt prikladnoi supervizii sluchaya Cheloveka-Volka', VAPP (Vserossiiskaya assotsiatsiya prikladnogo psikhoanaliza) <http://vapp.ru/projects/imago/2001/08/> [accessed 15 May 2021].
22 S. Freud and E. Oppenheim, 'Träume in Folklore' [1913], translated as 'Dreams in Folklore', in *The Standard Edition of the Complete Works of Sigmund Freud*, ed. by Strachey and others, XIV, 203.
23 I am not here referring to Freud's own likely over-identification with the 'Wolf-Man' in a biographical sense (as argued convincingly by, for example, Medvedev, or James L. Rice, *Freud's*

That 'The Wolf-Man' is also at some level a psychoanalytical study of Russian culture has been widely recognised, and at this level, reaction to the text has been polarised.[24] On the one hand, some orthodox Freudians in Russia and elsewhere have seen 'The Wolf-Man' as an accurate diagnosis, and sometimes also a warning — an identification of Russian culture's need for psychoanalytical treatment and/or of the pervasiveness of faulty procedures in upbringing.[25] On the other hand, the case has been seen as an example of how Freud missed the point, either because his own stereotypes about 'the other' made him draw fantastic conclusions (as Etkind has argued), or because, in Vladimir Medvedev's words, 'the Russianness of wolf-men cannot be cured'.[26] Both Freud's case-study, and more particularly, secondary interpretations of it, were contributions to a rather dubious tradition according to which some so-called oddity in the raising of Russian children — whether this is the tolerance for precocious contact with adult sexual practices, or the habit of swaddling small children — comes to explain the peculiarities of the adult national character.[27]

Such an approach begs two important questions: the relevance, or otherwise, of childhood experience to adult experience; and the extent to which it may be appropriate to extrapolate 'national character' from a single case, one where the informant was not only in a deep state of psychological collapse, but had been transformed into 'a foreigner' by the process of analysis and by his daily life.

Russia: National Identity in the Evolution of Psychoanalysis (New Brunswick, NJ: Transaction, 1993), p. 105, but to his relationship with the material of the case-study in a more abstract sense — its status as a manifestation of an alternative culture.

24   I say 'Russian' because, although Pankeev was brought up in the territory of modern Ukraine, he was a Russian speaker and self-identified as Russian, rather than 'Little Russian' or 'White Russian' (Belorussian), to use the terminology of the era. One could compare the self-perception of another former resident of the Russian Empire and close associate of the psychoanalytical movement, Elizaveta Fen (Lidiya Vitalievna Zhiburtovich, 1899–1983), whose autobiography, *A Girl Grew Up in Russia* (London: Deutsch, 1970) refers to the awful dialect (in fact, the Belarusian language) spoken by the peasants on the family's estate.

25   For a non-judgemental reading of this kind, where Freud is seen as having identified the 'ambivalence' of Russian culture, though not its capacity for 'love/hate', see Rice, *Freud's Russia*, pp. 116–17; for more normative assessments, see, for example, the interview with Nataliya Arkad'evna Kholina, 'Puskat' li detei v spal'nyu roditelei?', Roditel'.ru <http://parent.fio.ru/news.php?n=5860&c=2> [accessed 21 October 2004]; Daniel Rancour-Laferriere, *The Slave Soul of Russia: Moral Masochism and the Cult of Suffering* (New York: New York University Press, 1995), pp. 155–56, where the 'primal scene' is taken as something that any Russian of the day would have been likely to witness in childhood.

26   Etkind, *Eros nevozmozhnogo*, p. 106; Medvedev, ' "Russkost'" na kushetke', p. 13.

27   On swaddling, see for instance the post-war studies of Geoffrey Gorer and Margaret Mead; a question about the practice was also included in the Harvard Project on the Soviet Social System (see 'Manual of A-Schedule Materials', p. 25 <https://iiif.lib.harvard.edu/manifests/view/drs:5646842$153i>[accessed 14 September 2022]). A rather more sophisticated study in ethnic particularism is Herschel and Edith Alt, *The New Soviet Man: His Upbringing and Character Development* ([New York]: Bookman Associates, 1964), which applied the typology of R. F. Peck and others, *The Psychology of Character Development* (New York: Wiley, 1960), in order to suggest that while the goals of Soviet education were the same as in the West ('to achieve a rational-altruistic character'), 'the immediate effort in the Soviet Union [...] is focused on the *conforming* who often becomes the *expedient* character'.

Within psychoanalysis itself, these were non-issues. The acceptance that 'the child is father to the man' was and is a foundation stone of the technique, as is the assumption that people reveal themselves most truly when in a state of mental disintegration. More problematic, even from the point of view of the discipline, would be the way that the issues of 'national character' relate to, and expose, a tension between the imaginary and the real. According to Freud's own appreciations (as set out, say, in *The History of the Psycho-analytical Movement*), it did not matter whether a patient's recollections were invented or based on fact. Yet the evidential procedures of psychoanalysis take for granted the existence of a further authentic reality, as blocked out by 'screen memories' and other repressive mechanisms. The entire therapeutic process is preoccupied with the breakthrough to this reality, and the patient's recovery is taken as proof that such a breakthrough has happened.[28] In other words, subjective and objective truth are distinguished (the routine defence of psychoanalysis is that it deals only in the former), yet also identified (the patient's recovery 'demonstrates' the objective veracity not just of the deductions, but of the local details, that precede the cure). There are serious conceptual problems in using the insights gained by such methods in order to generate further cultural-historical conclusions — to put it simply, to move from the subjective reality of the patient to the objective reality of an entire culture.

We can easily accept that the Wolf-Man need not have witnessed the primal scene in order to have developed anxieties related to it. But it is perhaps more detrimental to Freud's case that the child's whole relationship with his parents, as recollected by Freud's former patient in his old age, seems to have been different from the one projected during analysis. As Pankeev, the real man behind the analysis, recalled in an interview dating from the 1970s, it was his nanny who was the real source of emotion and tenderness in his life, as opposed to his rather distant mother, with whom he exchanged two ritual kisses a day. It was the nanny's room where he slept until he was seven or eight; he could not remember ever being put to sleep in his parent's room.[29]

Pankeev was, by socio-economic criteria, unambiguously 'bourgeois' in a way that many other subjects of the Russian Empire who might have been counselled by Freud would not have been. His father was a civil servant, merchant of the second guild, and the owner of a mansion in Odessa, who had bought, rather than inherited, the family's country estate.[30] However, this was quite a different bourgeoisie from, say, the social layer of the parents of Little Hans, regularly letting the child in their bedroom, and conscientiously recording his feelings about his widdler and doing plops for the august physician.

---

28 In 'The Wolf-Man', this point occurred when the patient's bowel problems started to clear up after Freud had laid bare the connection between defecation and money (*W*, p. 274).

29 Obholzer, *The Wolf-Man*, pp. 36 (sleeping in nanny's room), 73–74 (more on sleeping in nanny's room: she was very tender, his mother undemonstrative).

30 See m-a-d-m-a-x, 'Proekt Ukrains'ki Arkhitekturni Pamyat'ky: Spadshchina', 12 November 2016 <https://m-a-d-m-a-x.livejournal.com/373424.html> [accessed 3 April 2022]. The estate purchased by Konstantin Pankeev, Vasilievka, was a renowned beauty spot, with a large mansion built in 1854 by the previous owners, the Dubetsky family; it was in ruins at the stage when m-a-d-m a x's blogpost was published.

This physical and emotional intimacy was something that Pankeev — like many Russian children from the social elite right up to 1917 — shared with women who were not relations, his nurse and before that his wet-nurse, rather than with his natural mother. Common sense would suggest that these women, and particularly his nanny, who was present in his conscious memory, should have played a far larger role in Freud's analysis than they did. Once again, it is the central psychodrama to which Freud's account relegates the nanny (like the Wolf-Man's sister and her governess): the crucial incident is one in which, rebuked by Nyanya for fiddling with his penis (and warned he'd 'get a wound' there), he became spiteful through his sense of rejection, acquiring a habit of torturing her verbally until she burst into tears (*W*, pp. 222, 224).

But the nanny would also have imposed on Sergei her views of the entire physical and metaphysical world. While the upbringing of a child in an elite household by a peasant nanny was not a 'traditional peasant upbringing' in the full sense, it was certainly not the 'rational upbringing' then being visualised by child-care manuals — and indeed presupposed as the norm by Freud (the great historical leap forward of Freud's work, vis à vis Locke, Rousseau, Froebel, Montessori, and others, being to underline that 'rational upbringing' did not necessarily always guarantee rational results).

My own ambition here is to 're-Russianise' the Wolf-Man in a different, and quite specific sense, from that hitherto attempted: to write him back into historical ethnography.[31] This is not a quest for the 'truth' about Pankeev, an attempt to pin down what his dream 'really' meant about his state when he dreamt it as a child (if he ever had such a dream, which is of course unverifiable to begin with). I am not embarking on a search for the 'Russian national character' in a general sense: ethnic identity, even in small, relatively homogeneous cultures (Ireland, Norway) is fluid over time and diverse at any given era. Nor will I be attempting to recover some mythic 'further truth' in the dream, as Carlo Ginzburg has done in an essay interpreting the Wolf-Man's dream as a phylogenetic memory of shamanistic initiation ritual.[32] It is not ethnography's traditional links with the primal and supernatural on the one hand, or on the other hand, the ethnically particular that attracts me, but rather, the status of the discipline in its post-revisionist manifestation.

---

31 Etkind's reading (*Eros nevozmozhnogo*, pp. 112–14) contains some material on the *nyanya*, but from the point of view of ahistorical speculation: 'the nanny makes every generation begin its search from the starting point — from the zero degree of frozen peasant tradition'.

32 See Carlo Ginzburg, 'Freud, the Wolf-Man, and Werewolves', in *Myths, Emblems, Clues*, trans. by J. and A. C. Tedeschi (London: Hutchinson Radius, 1990), pp. 146–64. Ginzburg extrapolates from common Slavic beliefs about people being born with the caul having the capacity to turn into werewolves to read the dream as a shamanistic vision. However, these beliefs were obscure in Russian folk culture by the late nineteenth and early twentieth century, as is suggested by the usual gloss of *rodit'sya v sorochke* (to be born in a 'shirt', i.e. a caul) to mean simply 'born lucky' (V. Dal', *Tolkovyi slovar' zhivogo velikorusskogo yazyka*, 4 vols (Moscow: M. O. Vol'f, 1880–82), IV, 236). This is not to detract from Ginzburg's contention that 'myths think us up' (i.e. that pre-existing beliefs, sometimes lying unrecognised in a culture, may shape attitudes and behaviour), or equally, the view that Pankeev, who suffered greatly in his own historical context on account of his visions, might have been celebrated for his magical powers in another context.

In recent years, ethnography has turned into perhaps the most self-conscious, studiedly 'dialogic' discipline. Writing about fieldwork is profoundly sensitive to the possibility of scripting informants' responses in advance, to the nuances of performance that take place in interviews or, more generally, encounters, and to the concealed objectives and unrealised promptings of both investigators and those investigated. The ideal form is acknowledged to be a kind of 'palimpsest' of different layers of interpretation, registering the variability of individual responses (including the possibility of different responses from the same person) and the diversity of the different sources from which these are retrieved. A popular genre is the return to the site of former fieldwork carried out by a famous predecessor (Malinowski, Evans-Pritchard), but one can of course never step in the same river twice, and the best that can be achieved will be a questioning of the unitary and classificatory authority of the original description and interpretation.[33] Unlike psychoanalysis (in its classic variants), recent ethnographical practice not only recognises its mistakes (as Freud, to be fair, was also willing to do), it also recognises its own limits, being fundamentally concerned with the autonomy — the capacity to evade — expressed by the subject (the individual, the culture) under study.

I want not only to introduce ethnographical material that might suggest Pankeev's childhood had more to it than Freud suggests, to produce a kind of 'reading in three dimensions', but also to introduce an *ethnographical perspective* to the discussion. Part of this might be described as a project of restitution, a dissolution into the typical of a case that has acquired the status over the years of an exhibit in a psychoanalytical freak-show. If anthropology and ethnography (particularly but not exclusively recently) have been concerned with protecting the anonymity of their subjects, Freud's text did away with disguise from the start. Laying bare the patient's inner self, the case history also provided enough authentic detail about his background to make identification of him easy. By the mid-twentieth century, Pankeev had become post factum public property, a walking historical artefact, as most disgracefully shown by the interviews with Karin Obholzer, who found herself constantly frustrated by Pankeev's inability to 'dish the dirt' quickly enough: 'Although this was difficult for me, I had to adapt to the slowness of an old man and live in perpetual fear that he might die'.[34] Her literature-loving interlocutor might have been reminded of the 'editor' in Lermontov's *Hero of Our Time* who, conversely, rejoices that Pechorin *has* died because now he will be able to publish his private diary.

At the end of his life, Pankeev's status as a psychoanalytical artefact gained

---

33 See, for example, James Clifford, *The Predicament of Culture: Twentieth-Century Ethnography, Literature, and Art* (Cambridge, MA: Harvard University Press, 1988); *Writing Culture: The Poetics and Politics of Ethnography*, ed. by James Clifford and George E. Marcus (Berkeley: University of California Press, 1986); Paul Rabinow, *Essays on the Anthropology of Reason* (Princeton, NJ: Princeton University Press, 1996); Paul Willis, *The Ethnographic Imagination* (Cambridge: Polity, 2000); and the discussion on objectivity and subjectivity in *Antropologicheskii forum*, 2 (2004).
34 Obholzer, *The Wolf-Man*, p. 7. Cf. the commodification of the Wolf-Man's trauma later in his life, when he developed a profitable line in selling paintings of his white-wolf dream to psychoanalysts who wanted a souvenir of this famous patient: *The Wolf-Man and Sigmund Freud*, ed. by Gardiner, p. 353.

tragic proportions. Consigned to the Wilhelmina Hospital in Vienna with what was then diagnosed as 'arterial dementia' accompanied by 'spatial and temporal disorientation', Pankeev, like Gogol's madman, displaced the indignities of his treatment into an alternative world: 'He supposes himself to be on a trip to Odessa with his [long dead] wife, but finds it remarkable that "the people here take so little interest in me"'. The main interest of the case for his doctors was, as a note in his file gushingly puts it, that 'the Pat[ient] is in psychiatric terms a "historical celebrity" — one of Sigmund Freud's first patients!'[35] Even in the professional context, Pankeev's needs as a confused geriatric, an all-at-sea émigré who switched as readily between languages (German, Russian, Italian) as he did between eras, were vastly less important than his star status in the history of medicine.

Where a vulgarised notion of someone's individual personality has been bruited to posterity, according the anonymity that goes with the ethnographical gaze might carry a kind of ethical charge. Less pompously, one might say that (recent Western) ethnography's concern with the surface of things as well as with deep meanings (which meanings it in turn constructs in a very different way from psychoanalysis, or indeed from the ethnography of the 'Golden Bough' kind widely favoured in Russia even in the late twentieth century) is helpful against the background of a historiographical tradition dominated, for the last century, by nuance-effacing 'grand narratives', above all Marxism-Leninism. In particular, the recently-evolved genre of 'auto-ethnography' (i.e. interpreting cultural material according to patterns of association current in a given culture at a given historical moment) does appear to offer a new approach to a text that has traditionally been seen as a key to things about Russian culture that Russians themselves do *not* understand.[36]

Wolves and the Nursery

> Nothing can be of greater value to a young person than a love of nature and understanding of natural sciences, particularly animals. Animals played a large part in my childhood also. In my case they were wolves.[37]

So how might we write about the Wolf-Man in a more contextually sensitive way, one located in a broader perception of late imperial Russian society, and especially of childhood at the time? In order that discussion does not dissipate entirely, I'll concentrate on the issues raised by the dream, and especially on childhood anxiety and the possible meanings and sources of this. I certainly wouldn't want to deny the importance of childhood sexuality in Russia, and particularly not in the era when Pankeev was growing up, a point when experience of this could be relatively explicit. Lower-class Russians with whom children might come into contact could be strikingly direct about physiological matters. The writer Olga Forsh, the daughter of a general, learned when she was seven from her father's batman how to tell female dogs and male dogs apart (as well as about how to polish top-boots to a

---

35 LOC, Sergius Pankejeff Papers, Box 4, Folder 5.
36 Auto-ethnography is espoused by, for example, Katherine Verdery in *What Was Socialism and What Comes Next?* (Princeton, NJ: Princeton University Press, 1993).
37 Sergei Pankeev, quoted by Muriel Gardiner in *The Wolf-Man and Sigmund Freud*, ed. by Gardiner, p. 316.

shine), though relaying this information at a formal dinner meant she was fearfully punished.[38] And there were parents who took their own duties to enlighten children seriously — even if, generally, at a later stage of childhood than the one at which Pankeev was supposedly 'enlightened' by his, and usually with reference to printed texts, rather than to first-hand demonstration.[39]

Yet memoirs and oral history alike would suggest that exposure to sexuality might be exaggerated as a force in Russian childhood experience. There is plenty of evidence that parents, including those from the peasantry, went to considerable lengths to ensure that their children did *not* witness the 'primal scene'. A point sometimes mentioned by peasant women petitioning for separation from violent husbands was the fact that they had been forced into sex in front of their children, which indicates that this was not the norm. By and large, it seems, parents retired to an outbuilding during the daytime in order to engage in conjugal relations (a thoroughly practical way of ensuring privacy when it was customary for each parent to share sleeping accommodation with one or more children of the same sex).[40] During the Soviet period, elaborate precautions were taken by parents sharing rooms in communal flats with their children in order to ensure that sexual relations were concealed, even if the child's bed was not screened off with a partition and a curtain (as became an increasingly common practice in the 1960s). 'They must have waited until we were really soundly asleep', said a lorry-driver's daughter from Leningrad, born in 1969, and both of whose brothers, five and fifteen years younger than her, had been conceived in the single room shared by the family until 1984.[41]

If sexuality has been highlighted in Western accounts of Russian childhood, far less attention has been paid to another side of emotional development: exposure to fear and anxiety. When we interviewed Russian speakers about their childhood in the early 2000s, informants normally answered a question about fears readily and in detail:

> I remember a thing called 'the black crow' [Black Maria, police wagon]. And we'd all [look] with horror... it got passed on to us children, we'd point it out, 'Here's the black crow, there it is, it's coming over here!' We knew there was a court-room on the corner... of Gogol' and Pisemsky streets, and that was where the court was [...]. Prisoners got taken there, arrestees, people being banged up. And sometimes I even heard, 'The black crow'll come and it'll take you away!' [...] But then someone would say, 'But they're enemies of the people!' And everyone would calm down.[42]

---

38   *Sovetskie pisateli: avtobiografii*, ed. by B. Ya. Brainina and E. F. Nikitina, 5 vols (Moscow: Gosudarstvennoe izdatel'stvo khudozhestvennoi literatury, 1959–88), I, 579.
39   On the whole issue, see the published 'mother's diary', 'K voprosu o polovom vospitanii detei', *Svobodnoe vospitanie*, 1 (1910), 51–62 (though, to be sure, the 'enlightenment' offered here was mainly in the form of warnings about disease).
40   See 'Conclusion: The End of Childhood?', in my *Children's World*.
41   See the interview carried out by Alexandra Piir in 2003 for my Leverhulme project, 'Childhood in Russia: A Social and Cultural History', Oxf/Lev SPb-03 PF 15A, p. 38. Further references to the project interviews carry the identifier code Oxf/Lev, a place and date code (here, St Petersburg 2003), and a reference to the tape number and transcript page. See also <http://www.ehrc.ox.ac.uk/lifehistory/archive.htm>.
42   CKQ-Ox-03 PF 6B, pp. 4–5 (woman *b*. 1949, interviewer Catriona Kelly).

> Once my parents — and I believed whatever they told me — told me some dreadful story about a boy, a made-up story, and he went out one day, and someone... Baba Yaga stole him away, and someone came after her too, and when I was about four this just sank right down, I remember it all to this day! [*Laughs*]. I was so afraid of the dark! And even if I had to go to the toilet at nights, I'd wake my mother.[43]

These reminiscences date from the 1950s and from the 1980s respectively; however, fear was just as persistent a motif in early eras as well. The autobiographies of children at village schools in the early 1900s include many that begin with something dreadful happening. A ten-year-old boy, for instance, remembered:

> I started to be conscious of myself [lit., have a memory of myself] at six, when I went for a bathe and nearly drowned, or another time I climbed on top of our hut to see how high up it was and I really plummeted down off it and nearly got all smashed up.[44]

These recollections, to be sure, are affectless: the experiences are *fearful*, but whether those who lived through them were *afraid* is more difficult to state (perhaps the memories constitute a kind of boasting). But other autobiographers were explicit about the fact that unpleasant events generated fear as a reaction:

> I can remember myself from five years old. Once I was sitting on a divan in the kitchen and I wanted a drink of water. The water was in the porch. I jumped off the divan and without paying any attention to what was underfoot went to the door, but before I reached it I saw a viper, which was crawling right up to me. I got really frightened and rushed back.[45]

Both these recollections describe chance occurrences, but traditional Russian upbringing also placed quite a lot of emphasis on *induced* fear. According to material collected in Vladimir Province during the late nineteenth century: 'Beginning from age two, all kinds of bogies are used to scare children: not just the *buka* [bugbear] and the *domovoi* [house spirit], but the doctor and the priest too'.[46] (One might note that both the modern reminiscences cited above evoke situations where the child had been deliberately frightened: 'it got passed on to us children... I even heard people say'; 'once my parents... told me some dreadful story'.) Even before the child reached two, lullabies might evoke scary monsters, conjuring up an image of a ravening beast in order to drive it away:

> Бай-бай, баю-бай,
> Поди, бука, не мешай!
> Поди, бука, на повить,

---

43 CKQ-Ox-03 PF 10B, p. 5 (woman b. 1975, interviewer Catriona Kelly).
44 Russian State Historical Archive (RGIA), f. 803, op. 16, d. 2770, l. 42 (Ivan Lyubomyshchenko, b. 1893, peasant farmer's son).
45 RGIA, f. 803, op. 16, d. 2770, l. 44 (Petr Polyakov, b. 1894, a deacon's son). On these autobiographies, see also Chapter 8 below.
46 B. M. Firsov and I. G. Kiseleva, *Byt velikorusskikh krest'yan-zemlepashtsev: Opisanie materialov etnograficheskogo byuro knyazya V. N. Tenisheva* (St Petersburg: izdatel'stvo Evropeiskogo doma, 1993), p. 266. On corporal punishment and scoldings, see ibid., pp. 216 (begins at around the age of six) and 267 (declines as the child approaches maturity).

> Там кошку дерут,
> Тебе лапку дадут.⁴⁷
>
> [Lullaby, lullaby! | Bugbear, away you fly! | Bugbear, go to the hayloft, | They're tearing a cat apart, | They'll give you a paw.]

Such texts, recited to a child that could not yet speak, were more likely to create an atmosphere of security through intonation than to daunt a child by creating nightmares. But there was an edge of aggression in them, and older children might be intimidated directly. In an eyewitness account dating from around 1903, a boy of about ten recalled how he had been 'cured' of a 'babyish' pleasure:

> When I was little, I used to love rocking in my cradle. Even when I was as old as four, I didn't want to part with it. But then one day when I was outdoors playing, they took the cradle out of the house and hid it in the loft. When I got back and couldn't see my friend (my cradle), I asked my parents where it was and when they said it had been stolen, I started crying inconsolably. Then my parents tried to stop me crying by telling me a frightening story about how, if I didn't stop, some Tatar would turn up, drag me off, and feed me on nothing but straw. Of course, I was really scared and immediately stopped crying, and gradually adjusted to my loss.⁴⁸

Children themselves quickly internalised this 'sadism' (if one wishes so to term it), or — speaking in a less loaded way — preoccupation with the uncanny and unmanageable as a source of retribution. Another early twentieth-century boy memoirist recalled a friend launching into a story:

> 'One day my father was going past the cemetery at night. Suddenly a corpse came running towards him, wearing a white shroud. My father's hair stood on end. He gave his horse a whack with his whip, made the sign of the cross, and fell face-downwards in his sledge.' The boy wanted to go on, but we stopped him. We didn't like that story one bit.⁴⁹

As the story shows, other children, as well as adults, contributed to disseminating fears. Here, certainly, the group stepped in to censor the creepy material that had been put forward, but this was not the only possible reaction. The role of the juvenile community could be (as with teasing) to use fright as an instrument of initiation — those scared by such a tale would then be the objects of mockery.⁵⁰

---

47 *Detskii poeticheskii fol'klor*, ed. by A. N. Martynova (St Petersburg: 'Dmitry Bulanin', 1997), p. 13 (hereafter referenced as *DPF*; citations are to the numbered texts collected in this anthology).
48 RGIA, f. 803, op. 16, d. 2370, l. 130. The practice of scaring children by referring to a 'bogey' from some ethnic minority was widespread. Our interviewing project in Russian villages indicates that this was often a gypsy (*sic, tsygan*), see, for example, the interview by Ekaterina Mel'nikova and Oksana Filicheva, Oxf/Lev V-04 PF17A, p. 5); in parts of Leningrad province, in the post-war years, the scare figures were Finns (Oxf/Lev V-04 PF5B, p. 19).
49 RGIA, f. 803, op. 16, d. 2372, l. 57 rev. For more recent examples of such scary stories, see, for example, *Detskii fol'klor*, ed. by M. Yu. Novitskaya and I. N. Raikova, Biblioteka russkogo fol'klora series (Moscow: Russkaya kniga, 2002); and *Russkii shkol'nyi fol'klor: Ot "vyzyvanii" Pikovoi damy do semeinykh rasskazov*, ed. by A. Belousov (Moscow: Ladomir, 1998).
50 On the other hand, there does not seem to be evidence that scary tales existed as a set genre around 1900, in the way that they did from the mid-twentieth century onwards, when *strashilki* [horror stories] became common on school playgrounds and in other situations of enforced peer-

Children's ambiguous relationship with the uncanny had plenty to feed on. Subject to intimidation from adults, they were also expected (though kept from other primal scenes, such as birth and copulation) to attend funerals.[51] In Tolstoy's pseudo-autobiography *Childhood*, the hero's horror and disgust at his mother's obsequies forms an emotional turning-point in the text. Tolstoy was regularly given to children as suitable reading, so this 'primal scene' was likely to be encountered at second hand, if not at first hand.[52]

Freud's early work was characterised by dissatisfaction with the emphasis placed on anxiety by behaviourists such as Stanley Hall. This in turn led him into a degree of polemical over-statement about other conditioning forces, particularly the libido. But what if anxiety were — as Freud in his later writings, for example 'Das Unbehagen in der Kultur', took aggression to be — an *autonomous* instinctive drive, which attached itself to sexual objects simply because they were an obvious area where a sense of threat and vulnerability might manifest itself? The *primal* fear may well be, as Melanie Klein argues in 'Love, Guilt, and Reparation', 'the anxiety about the death of the loved person', or 'separation anxiety', in the later term, which then generates 'the wish to make reparation', as expressed in various creative activities.[53] But this leaves the possibility that traces of this original fear might be realised differently in different historical or cultural conditions.

Certainly, there was nothing peculiar about childhood fears generally, or a fear of wolves specifically, in late nineteenth- and early twentieth-century Russia. Children who were sent alone into the forest to take cows to pasture, or to check game snares or hives, had no need to stoke up fear artificially, when the thought of marauding bears and wolves, or indeed human predators such as bandits, lay constantly in the back of their minds.[54] Whether wolves were a likely danger in a particular place or not, they were insistently present in folklore directed at

group association, such as the 'dead hour' (*mertvyi chas*) at Pioneer camps, when, instead of taking an afternoon nap, as they were supposed to, children would engage in competitive rounds of such stories. See also below.
51   See, for example, the harrowing description by eleven-year-old Nadezhda Ioganson of seeing her father laid out and the funeral following (1909): RGIA, f. 801, op. 16, d. 2370, l. 69 ob.
52   In the Soviet period, it was common for children to attend, or hear about, or re-enact, funerals as well, including the funerals of other children. 'The Funeral of an Octobrist' is on the activities schedule for a Sverdlovsk province Pioneer troop in 1925: 'Otchet o prodelannoi rabote otryada pionerov No. 1 im. tov. Zinov'eva Tavdinskogo raiona Irbitskogo Okruga s 7go po 20e Maya 25 g.', Central Archive of Public Documents of Sverdlovsk Province (TsADOO SO), f. 1245, op. 1, d. 12, l. 44. Bella Ulanovskaya's story 'Puteshestvie v Kashgar' (1989) provides a fictional account of such a funeral in the early 1950s.
53   See 'Love, Guilt and Reparation' [1937], in Melanie Klein, *Love, Guilt and Reparation and Other Works 1921–1945* (London: Virago, 1988), pp. 306–43 (esp. p. 336). This essay is more useful for historical/ ethnographical purposes than, for example, her 'The Oedipus Complex in the Light of Early Anxieties', in ibid. pp. 370–419, an exercise in neo-Freudian reductionism.
54   See Pavel Starzhinsky, *Vzrosloe detstvo: zapiski syna raskulachennogo* (Moscow: Sovremennik, 1991), p. 90, for example. That said, adults did also use the (in real life possible) presence of wolves as a scare for children: cf. the recollections of a woman born in Pskov province in 1937: '*Int.* And did they try to frighten you, maybe? So you didn't run off there [to the woods]. *Inf.* Well, they used to use wolves to frighten us. So... Don't go off to the woods. Don't go off to the woods. There are wolves there' (Oxf/Lev V-04 PF17A, interview by Oksana Filicheva and Ekaterina Mel'nikova, p. 5).

children. Riddles emphasised the wolf's aggression, especially where directed against children:

> Серовато,
> Зубовато,
> По полю рыщет,
> Телят, ребят рыщет. (*DPF* 1747)

[Greyish, | Toothy, | It searches the fields, | Seeks out calves and children.]

In myths, wolves were represented not just as denizens of the steppe, but as antagonists in the domestic setting. In one riddle, wolves stop farm animals getting home, camped out as they are in the barrier zone of the woods:

> За лесом, пролеском
> Жеребята ржут,
> Домой не идут. (*DPF* 1749)

[Beyond the forest, the copse | The foals whinny, | They don't come home.]

Lullabies also suggested that the wolf was one of the bogies lying in wait in and around the household:

> Баю, баюшки, баю!
> Не ложись на краю:
> Придет серенький волчок,
> Схватит тебя за бочок,
> Он утащит во лесок
> За маленький кусток,
> Там положит на пенек
> И разрубит поперек.
> Придет кошечка играть,
> Будет крепко тосковать,
> Станет Ванюшку искать, —
> Нужно детке крепко спать.[55]

[Lulla, lulla, by! | Don't lie on the side; | A grey wolf will come | And seize you by the tum, | He'll drag you to the woods | And into a bush, | On a stump he'll put you, | And tear you in two, | The cat will come and play | And be sad the whole day; | She'll look for you all night. | Little boys should sleep tight.]

In folk tales, the wolf was often an insatiable aggressor, forever eating other animals, especially small defenceless ones. The seven little kids that Pankeev had read about (in Russian folk versions of this tale, the last of them hides in the stove, not the clock) are one set of victims, but there were others. The wolf could display a strange ability to get hold of prey simply by wheedling for this. In one common folk-tale, for example, he would come and sing to an old man:

> Жил жилец
> На кусочке дворец;

---

[55] A. N. Sobolev, 'Obryady i obychai pri rozhdenii mladentsa i kolybel'nye pesni Vladimirskoi gubernii', *Svedeniya po etnologii Vladimirskoi gubernii: Trudy Vladimirskogo Obshchestva lyubitelei estestvoznaniya*, 3.2 (1912), 41–62 (p. 52).

> У него пять овец,
> Шестой жеребенок,
> Седьмая телка.

[A man did once live, | His palace was on a chip, | He had five sheep, | The sixth was a colt, | The seventh a heifer.]

The wolf would be rewarded for the beauty of this song by being given everything he mentioned, and sometimes the old man's wife into the bargain.[56]

This sense of the uncanny — the wolf as an animal that could get into domestic space — was also underlined in apocryphal tales. The great-grandmother of a friend of mine, born into a Russian gentry family around 1890, had a childhood memory — probably an imaginary one — about riding in a sleigh on a dark night and suddenly seeing the lights of a village close by. Her relief was soon dispelled when the horses started, the coachman said, 'It's wolves', and she realised that what she thought were friendly lights were actually the eyes of the creatures shining as they were caught by the sleigh lantern.

In Russian folklore, as in traditional belief internationally, the wolf was dangerous because of its voracity. It was the key example of how scary beings are, in Marina Warner's words, 'ravenous, and ravenous for the wrong food'.[57] But this was not all. Wolves could dissimulate, as well as confront, and wheedle, as well as attack. They were not so much real animals, as chthonic beings, who could pass as easily into domestic space as they could into the underworld. Indeed, they could cross the divide not just into human territory, but into human identity — as most clearly signalled by the tradition of the werewolf (*volkodlak* or *oboroten'*), a being magically able to slip from one species to the other, often by recourse to the aid of a tree or bush.[58]

While the Wolf-Man was undergoing analysis with Ruth Mack Brunswick, in the 1920s, he had a dream which was highly traditional in terms of these wolf beliefs:

> In a broad street is a wall containing a closed door. To the left of the door is a large, empty wardrobe with straight and crooked drawers. The patient stands before the wardrobe; his wife, a shadowy figure, is beside him. Close to the other end of the wall stands a large, heavy woman, looking as if she wanted to go round and behind the wall. But behind the wall is a pack of grey wolves,

---

56   See 'Volk' in A. F. Afanas'ev, *Narodnye russkie skazki*, 3 vols, (Moscow: Goslitizdat, 1957), I, nos. 49–50.

57   Marina Warner, *No Go the Bogeyman: Scaring, Lulling, and Making Mock* (London: Chatto & Windus, 1998), p. 36. See further (pp. 37–38) on how eating and the bogey are inextricably linked. In Russian folklore, on the other hand, even the wolf's 'teeth' can be primarily glossed in terms of his place in the moral universe: according to one tradition, as a thief had a good hand and a bad hand, so a wolf had a good tooth and a bad tooth — if he ate with the former, the stock would prosper, rather than be devastated.

58   See Dal', *Tolkovyi slovar' zhivogo velikorusskogo yazyka*, I, 233 (*volkodlak*) — a person could turn into a werewolf by sticking a knife into a tree-stump, and pulling the knife out was a way to keep him stuck in that role); II, 611 (*oboroten'*). For the wolf's chthonic associations, see V. V. Ivanov, 'Rekonstruktsiya indoevropeiskikh slov i tekstov, otrazhayushchikh kul't volka', *Izvestiya AN SSSR: Seriya literatury i yazyka*, 34. 5 (1975), 399–408.

crowding toward the door and rushing up and down. Their eyes gleam, and it is obvious they want to rush at the patient, his wife, and the other woman. The patient is terrified, fearing they will succeed in breaking through the wall.[59]

Here, the wolves want to attack the human subjects, and the wall that blocks them is only a temporary obstacle to these creatures, with their greedy, glittering eyes.

The wolves in the original dream, however, have a more ambiguous status. To begin with, they are stationary, fixed on the tree, so that it is simply not clear why they should seem so threatening. The Wolf-Man himself felt compelled to provide a retrospective gloss, 'Obviously fearful that the wolves were going to gobble me up, I screamed and woke up' (W, p. 225). But there is no overt manifestation in the dream that the wolves actually do intend such an act, unlike the picture that so terrified the Wolf-Man when his sister held it up. In this way, the wolves in the dream are unconventional. They fit better with another folk association of the wolf: its capacity to punish wrong-doing. As a proverb recorded by the great folklorist Dmitry Zelenin in Vyatka Province in the early twentieth century put it, 'Wolves ride out to shit on cross-patches'.[60] Moreover, the wolves differ from the usual stereotypes because they are *white*. What could be the significance of this — trying now to reach into folklore, rather than into possible reminiscences by the young Pankeev of his parents' underwear?

If wolves generally are chthonic beings, white wolves, in their unnaturalness, would be likely still more to evoke otherworldly associations, particularly given that white was the established colour of mourning in late imperial Russia. A 1909 memoirist who was a near-contemporary of Pankeev's (he was born in 1884) remembered what a shock his first visit to hospital had been on precisely these grounds:

> They took me into a huge room with big windows. There were seven beds there; six were occupied, and I got the seventh. The room looked really sad, and seeing how sad everything looked, sad thoughts came stealing into my soul. As soon as I went into the room and looked at the beds, with their white blankets, I remembered my father's funeral. The same white blankets, and the people were lying in their beds, worn out by their illnesses, looking like dead people [...]. They started comforting me, and when I had calmed down, they took off my own clothes, and put the hospital clothes on me.[61]

No doubt the effect of whiteness was stronger in peasant households, where the colour was generally avoided in ordinary circumstances. A child from Pankeev's background would have seen sheets, pillowcases, nightshirts, in the course of ordinary routine. But there is still a strong possibility that *white* wolves had funereal associations.

More significant, though, is another possibility of identification. In East Slavonic folk belief, 'white wolves' figured in the roles of power figures. In Smolensk Province, for example, it was believed that the 'Wood Tsar' could take the shape

---

59 *The Wolf-Man and Sigmund Freud*, ed. by Gardiner, pp. 288–89.
60 D. K. Zelenin, *Izbrannye trudy: Ocherki russkoi mifologii* (Moscow: 'Indrik', 1995), p. 56, n. 20.
61 RGIA, f. 803, op. 16, d. 2772, l. 46 rev.–47.

of a white wolf: 'According to the beliefs of the peasants of Krasninsky district [Smolensk province], the wolves are subject to the power of the Honest Forest or the Wood Tsar, who often takes the shape of a white wolf'.[62] These beings, the 'Honest Forest' or the 'Wood Tsar', had the authority to punish those who offended against the moral code of the wolves, both by driving wolves themselves who were in breach of group rules from the herd, and by punishing those who treated wolves cruelly or inconsiderately. Shepherds would sacrifice lambs to them in some places.[63] They were, then, arbiters of morality, their predatory instincts transformed into a punishment drive.

It was, in any case, not just the threatening, aggressive nature of the wolf that was invoked in folklore. Proverbs and sayings also evoked its capacity for dissimulation. The Biblical phrase, 'wolf in sheep's clothing', as suggested by Pankeev's own association of the wolves with sheep, and later a key term in the arsenal of Stalinist political denunciation, was only one of many such sayings. More germane to Pankeev's dream is the dictum 'there is no such thing as a wolf with a fox's tail'.[64] The wolves with foxes' tails in the dream are proverbial impostors: they represent both the terrifying force of the Wood Tsar's gaze *and* the wolves who are to be driven from the herd because they are not wolves at all. Such wolves — not just impostors, but inept impostors — take on another traditional attribute of the wolf in folklore. In traditional tales, particularly, the wolf is often the fall guy, the foil to the ever sharp-witted vixen. In the traditional version of the story about the wolf fishing with his tail that Pankeev knew, it was the vixen who persuaded him to try out this silly version of fishing; in other stories, the vixen gobbled up the wolf (and other animals) after having lured them into a trap.

Sometimes the wolf does get the better of the vixen, but the victory is short-lived. For instance, in a long, involved narrative recorded in Vyatka Province by D. K. Zelenin in the 1910s, the wolf hitches a ride on the vixen's sleigh, and when she worries about the creaking sound, reassures her, 'I'm just chewing nuts'. Eventually the sleigh breaks apart, and while the vixen is fixing it, the wolf eats the guts out of the horse and replaces them with sparrows and straw. When the vixen comes back, and the sparrows fly out, she vows revenge — and here the motif about persuading the wolf to fish with his tail follows.[65] Pankeev's troubled relationship with his

---

62 V. N. Dobrovol'sky, 'Sueveriya otnositel'no volkov', *Etnologicheskoe obozrenie*, 4 (1901), 135–36 (p. 135).

63 Ibid., pp. 135–36.

64 Dal', *Tolkovyi slovar' zhivogo velikorusskogo yazyka*, I, 232. As a matter of fact, foxes' tails and wolves' tails are, both in reality and schematised representations, more or less identical: so this is a saying about *concealed* difference.

65 D. K. Zelenin, *Velikorusskie skazki Vyatskoi gubernii* (Petrograd: tipografiya A. V. Orlova, 1915), pp. 383–85, no. 120. Other stories about wolves recorded here include 'Volk, medved' i lisa', no. 119 (the wolf goes to the fox so he can exact revenge on the bear for having munched him up in a break from hibernating — the bear later belched the wolf up through his mouth); 'Udaloi batrak', no. 34 (the wolf eats a peasant man's horse and ends up dragging the cart himself, then dragging round the barrel the peasant man is trapped inside until it breaks apart — the man uses his tail as a 'rein' and sticks a knife in its backside as a goad). Stories in Afanas'ev's *Narodnye russkie skazki* include 'Ovtsa, lisa i volk', where the wolf tries to persuade the sheep that her coat should be his own, but ends up

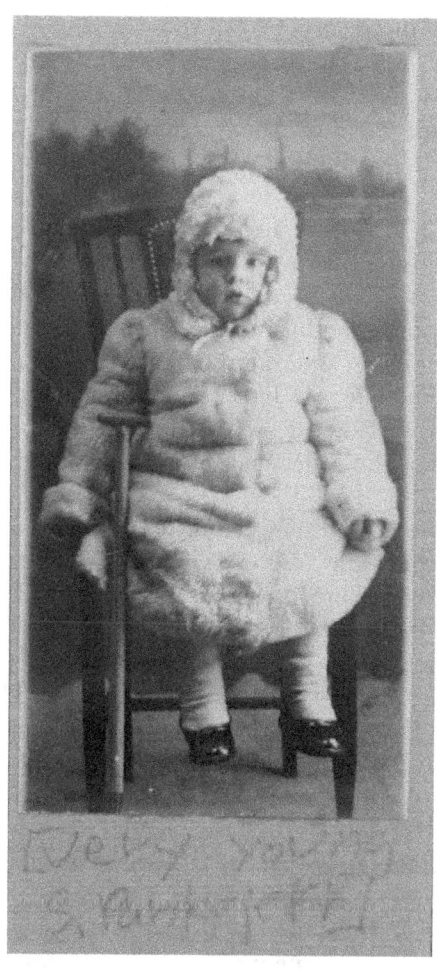

Fig. 5.2. Sergei Pankeev as a toddler, wearing a white furry coat. Library of Congress, Sergius Pankejeff Collection.

sister, who constantly mocked him and yet did her best to stimulate him erotically, 'lead him on', comes to mind.

So far as the wolves in Pankeev's dream are concerned, the wolf's identity as the target and the originator of contempt seems much more important than its role as a voracious aggressor. The wolves in the dream disapprove; they are also the victims of disapproval. The subject, while being looked at by the white wolves, whose number adjusts so that he both is and is not one of them, has himself become a 'white wolf' in one particular meaning of the term: a freak (compare the standard term 'white crow', *belaya vorona*, for a social misfit). (We know from an early childhood photograph that Pankeev was sometimes dressed in a pale furry outfit, see fig. 5.2).

being lured into a trap; 'Volk-duren'', where the wolf is rebuffed by several animals he wants to eat, being told he should wait till they get fatter, and then gets shot by a hunter 'who prepared a couple of nice walnuts for him' ('prigotvoil dlya priyatelya paru khoroshikh orekhov') (*Narodnye russkie skazki*, I, 56).

At the same time, he is subject to disapproving scrutiny from those who have the right to arbitrate whether he belongs or not. The dreamer's own primary association with the dream, we remember, was the story about the wolf who had lost his tail and who, when exposed, made a run, collapsing the entire pyramid that the wolves had built in order to escape danger; in other words, Pankeev himself saw this as a narrative about failure and disgrace.

The aggressive animal reduced to a fool, a victim, is an especially miserable figure. Sometimes in folklore, it was the wolf himself who was the joker: 'At night he'll often run up to a person and topple him over just for a joke, and have a good laugh at how frightened and shocked that person is'.[66] But more often, it was the wolf who was the victim, the target of the punchline, and often the punchbag too. So, the story about the tailor was a version of 'the biter bit' like 'Little Red Riding Hood', but with a different kind of reversal taking place: the socially dominant were transformed into the socially abject, rather than the killer ending up slaughtered himself.

Folklore allowed for the prospect that the wolf might be bought off or averted. It was traditional for shepherds to offer sacrifices to the 'Wood Tsar' as a placatory move. And the boundary-crossing propensity of the creature was not always bad. According to folk tradition, wolves could be placated if they were spoken to directly: 'They'll assure you that if you speak to wolves nicely, they won't touch you — they'll turn off the path and pass by on one side'.[67] As with the *leshii* [wood demon], another dangerous being with whom tracks in the forest might be contested, there was the possibility of a successful challenge to the non-human presence. But the Wolf-Man's dream offers no prospect of escape. The wolves themselves, sitting in the nut tree/ Christmas tree, are the only 'gifts' symbolically present; the dreamer seems (as traditionally in nightmares) to be temporarily speechless, so that he can scream only when waking up. And the wolves remain threateningly silent, their disapproval endless because it is never precisely articulated.

The primary emotion inspired by the dream of the white wolves, then, was fear, and the final effect was mixed fear and shame. Under analysis with Ruth Mack Brunswick, Pankeev was prompted by the shining eyes of the wolves in his adult wolf dream to remember how 'for some time following his dream at four years he could not bear to be looked at. He would fly into a temper, crying, "Why do you look at me like that?"'.[68] Wolves in folklore are capable of provoking both emotions — fear and anger — in extreme degrees: they can also punish both manifestations, eating those who flee (and do not speak to them), defecating on those who are angry.

Of course, the question of how Pankeev might have learned about this is left open. While Pankeev remembered his early contacts with German culture in great detail, he was surprisingly uninformative about the 'Russian' elements in his background. We do know that his nanny came from a peasant background,

---

66 Dobrovol'sky, 'Sueveriya otnositel'no volkov', p. 135.
67 Ibid., pp. 135–36.
68 *The Wolf-Man and Sigmund Freud*, ed. by Gardiner, p. 289.

though whereabouts is not clear; however, she appears to have been a native speaker of Russian, rather than Ukrainian, so may have come from one of the provinces bordering Ukraine — perhaps Rostov or Kursk, or perhaps Smolensk Province, the source of the wolf beliefs recorded by Dobrovol'sky, and lying between Ukraine and Belorussia, where the family settled when Pankeev was nine or ten years old. To be sure, Pankeev's recollections of her in connection with folk tales record only that she was fascinated by the readings of Grimm in the Russian language which his governess Miss Elisabeth (a Russian of Bulgarian origin) would organise in the nursery.[69] But it is hard to believe that a woman who enjoyed folk tales would not have provided fantasy material of her own when entertaining the small Sergei in the nursery, including, no doubt, material about wolves, the standard characters in creepy stories and low farces alike. Later in life, Pankeev remembered that wolves popped up constantly in his own representations: though he loved drawing horses, 'unfortunately they were more like wolves or dogs than real horses'.[70] Wolves, in short, were everywhere.

Frightened Children, Frightened Adults: A Coda

Material from folklore and folk practice during the last part of the nineteenth century would suggest that the scary and haunting character of the Wolf-Man's dream is unlikely to stem from its links with the primal scene. This is not to deny the importance of the physical in children's discourse — elsewhere, the case history of the Wolf-Man himself provides plenty of evidence of this, whether in his fascination with the family maid, or in his early experiments with masturbation. But the development of sexuality, and of a guilt/ shame/ distress/ revulsion complex around it, was only part of the emotional legacy that the Wolf-Man took from his childhood. The question of whether, as a 'basic instinct', fear or sex is more important, cannot be resolved: both are essential in evolutionary terms, guaranteeing the survival of the individual (in the first case), the species (in the second). And it is interesting, and ironic, to note that, *after* his treatment with Freud, the Wolf-Man suffered not just from traumas that could be glossed in terms of sexual neurosis (for instance, an episode where he became convinced that there was something disgusting and morbid about his nose),[71] but also from episodes of paralysing fear, as he remembered the years immediately following the end of the Second World War:

> One day I took my paint-box and canvas and went out into the suburbs of Vienna, to the meadows near the canal. Suddenly the scene reminded me of Russia and my boyhood, and I was quite swept away by nostalgia [...]. I wanted to capture this scene on canvas, and took out my paints and equipment. The first thing that happened was that my painting stool broke — this was the first

69 Ibid., p. 8.
70 See Pankeev, 'Der Tod meines Vaters und wieder ein Sanatorium'.
71 This is another episode with a strong literary colouration: Nikolai Gogol, a famous 'Little Russian' compatriot of Pankeev's, suffered similar delusions at the end of his life, a widely reported episode in his biography with which all educated Russians are familiar.

of several bad omens. But still nothing could stop me, and I began to paint. Clouds came up, the light changed; I painted like one possessed, not noticing anything but the scene and the mood. After a while two figures approached from behind the building; I paid no heed. Then five men approached me; they were Russian soldiers. I could only have been so unaware because I was living not in the present but in the past; but by the time the soldiers had seen me it was too late. And would you believe it, Frau Doktor, although I realized it only much later, this day was the anniversary of my sister's death?

I had wandered into the Russian Zone, the Russians were using this bakery as a military station. The soldiers took me inside, took away my belt and shoelaces and my glasses and began to question me. It was at once clear they suspected me of espionage. In vain I tried to tell them I was just painting for pleasure; they had no understanding of this. The soldiers themselves were mostly simple and decent people, but the terrible thing was that they brought in officers of the secret police, and these men know how to confuse you, torture you, and break your spirit. 'But you have a real Russian name', the officer in charge said to me. 'How is it possible that a real Russian can work against his country?' I felt horribly guilty — a displaced guilt, no doubt, because I had never done any such thing, but they made me feel as though I had betrayed my country. At this moment I understood perfectly how the many victims of the trials in Russia signed confessions of crimes they had never committed. [...] At length [the officer in charge] told me I might go home and return with the paintings. I thought he would ask me to bring them the following day, or at latest in two days. But no! He ordered me to come back in twenty-one days. Can you imagine what that period of waiting was like for me? I think I developed delusions of persecution; I thought people were talking about me or watching me when they certainly were not, though I never had the feeling that anyone was following me. But I simply could not think of anything else. It was like that time with my nose when I went to Dr Brunswick — only then I feared a physical deformity (*Entstellung*) and this time a moral deformity.[72]

Here, emotions not dealt with by Freudian psychology — guilt and loyalty — resurfaced with a vengeance; the conventional psychoanalytic tradition had nothing to offer on this occasion. Notable is also the Wolf-Man's own conviction that this experience was somehow fated — it happened on the anniversary of his sister's death, and he had failed to notice bad omens. He had, then, been 'fooled', had allowed himself to be *seen* (the importance of visual contact is again striking). And once again, the stupid wolf was subjected, in his imagination, to punishment and disapproval, the scorn of the mysterious watching figures: 'I thought people were talking about me or watching me when they certainly were not'.

Freud's interpretation of the Wolf-Man's dream was in many respects a simplification of the subject of the analysis and the culture from which its protagonist came. In particular, as well as displaying zero grasp of the symbology of wolves in Pankeev's cultural world, Freud vastly underestimated the place of fear in the early training of Russian children during the late Imperial era, and the effects that such early training could have on perfectly rational individuals when terror was employed against them. The success of Freud's treatment was in turning a deeply

---

72   *The Wolf-Man and Sigmund Freud*, ed. by Gardiner, pp. 326–27.

unhappy individual into a person who could hold down a modest job for many years, enjoy dabbling as an amateur painter, and have a reasonably happy marriage, albeit one that was eventually interrupted by tragedy.[73] The limitations in the analysis were in providing the Wolf-Man with only some of the resources that he needed to survive. Pankeev was reduced to 'delusions', or close to that point, by his confrontation with the military detachment in the Russian Zone. He was still obsessed with the secret police when Muriel Gardiner encountered him in 1956, five years after the incident.[74] Without her common-sense advice, devotion as a correspondent, and interest in his writing, the Wolf-Man's last decades might not have been as stable as they were.

Like Mikhail Zoshchenko — with whom he shared a pervasive sense of impotence and humiliation — the Wolf-Man was distinguished by his capacity to rationalise and place himself at a distance from the traumatic experiences he had gone through, the positive result of psychoanalysis.[75] But this benefit, in the Wolf-Man's case, came at the price of celebrity not desired or created by him, and resting on a simplified and distorted version of his early life, in whose composition he himself had (unlike Zoshchenko) played the role not of author or of co-author, but of catalyst, inspiration, nothing more than the starting-point. And, if psychoanalysis did much to mitigate his visceral malaises and purely sexual neuroses, it did little to alleviate the potentially crippling fears that persisted from childhood. Throughout his life, the Wolf-Man remained in many ways a frightened child — looking for consolation and counsel to his acquaintances, and deeply ambivalent about relationships with adult women, with the exception of psychoanalysts and the elderly maid, Fräulein Gaby, with whom he, Oblomov-like, seems to have tried to recapture some of the magic and security of youth, safe in the care of a latter-day version of his beloved nanny.[76]

The Wolf-Man's fears when he encountered the Russian soldiers in Vienna were, at one level, perfectly rational. He could have been arrested and repatriated to the Soviet Union, where his fate, as an émigré who had had contact with psychoanalysis, an interpretive method detested and vilified under Stalin, would probably

---

73 Therese, the Wolf-Man's wife, committed suicide in March 1938, in a state of extreme anxiety following the annexation of Austria by the Third Reich (the *Anschluss*). See *The Wolf-Man and Sigmund Freud*, ed. by Gardiner, pp. 116–31. The Wolf-Man himself could not understand the reason for her fears — '"We aren't Jews."' (p. 119). It seems possible, given that Therese's anxiety was heightened when she and her husband were discussing the need to acquire certificates of 'Arian' racial identity (p. 120), that she was in fact partly of Jewish descent, as the Wolf-Man's memoir in fact hints, but never directly states.

74 *The Wolf-Man and Sigmund Freud*, ed. by Gardiner, p. 328.

75 As particularly in *Pered voskhodom solntsa* [Before Sunrise] (1943). On the psychoanalytical resonance of Zoshchenko's biography, see also Alexander Zholkovsky, *Mikhail Zoshchenko: poetika nedoveriya* (Moscow: Shkola 'Yazyki russkoi kul'tury', 1999).

76 See *The Wolf-Man and Sigmund Freud*, ed. by Gardiner, pp. 324–25. Pankeev also remembered (ibid., p. 18), that his nurse became senile in her old age, and treated Pankeev himself as the child he had once been — in other words, she moved into cyclic time from linear time, and hence beyond transience, as Pankeev himself, obsessively harping on his childhood, was also to do in his last years.

have been dreadful (most likely, a 're-educative' spell in a labour camp).[77] Yet the intensity of his anxiety and its aftermath seem, to an external observer at least, out of proportion to the provocation: he was not, after all, a displaced person, but an Austrian resident with many decades of settled life behind him. The disabling effects of his panic require an analysis of childhood experience that goes far beyond the perhaps unlikely assumption that he witnessed the primal scene.

For Freud, the Wolf Man was a national stereotype as well as a person, indeed, more the former than the latter. Obviously, an argument that the primacy of fear becomes some kind of overall heuristic key to the interpretation of Russian twentieth-century subjectivity would repeat the same oversimplification with reference to a different emotional complex. If able to generalise at all, we could only hesitantly arrive at a historically contingent hypothesis. Could the readiness of educated and privileged Russians to believe the charges laid against them during the political purges of the early Soviet era be traceable to the socialisation through fear that they received? We would not be talking here about an explanation for why the purges happened (a considerably more complicated question) but with an explanation for why resistance to them, among the social class of what was described in the 1920s as 'former' people, was so limited. Could the combination of fear and love inspired by the peasant nanny translate into a later view, among the educated 'graduates' of the nanny's care, that the (usually poorly educated and plebeian) representatives of Soviet power, no matter how 'uncultured' they might be, still had an uncontestable force of moral authority in their hands? One might then set up a secondary hypothesis which attempted to construct a correlation between the declining use of fear in the socialisation of small children, and growing confidence among older children and adults in asserting themselves. And it does indeed seem that the late twentieth century saw a move away, at least among educated parents, from the habit of chastening and disciplining through the use of fear and shame that had been so widespread in the late nineteenth century, on the one hand, and a growing unreadiness among children of over nursery age, to respond unquestioningly to authority, on the other.[78] It is commoner to argue for

---

77 The insensitivity of the Wolf-Man's psychoanalytical counsellors, from Freud onwards, to this point is striking, but it was not until 1956, after all, that many Westerners came to realise how pervasive terror had been in the Soviet political system.

78 The importance of not exposing children to fear was already being argued in the early twentieth century. The neurologist and psychologist G. I. Rossolimo, a pioneer of intelligence tests in Russia, argued in 1897 that unresolved childhood fears persisted into adulthood, and listed large numbers of common phenomena that children were afraid of: darkness, death, ghosts, wind, the end of the world, water, bandits, machines, blood, heights, 'themselves' ('soznaniya samogo sebya'), not wolves, though! With charming statistical pedantry, he calculated that girls had on average 3.55 fears each, and boys 2.21. The key ages for fear were seven to fifteen (boys) and four to eighteen (girls). It was important that teachers demonstrate the irrationality of fear and try to overcome it. But it was also essential that those raising children should avoid threats, public humiliations, punishments, and the use of school marks, all of which inculcated the condition (G. I. Rossolimo, *Strakh i vospitanie. Rech', chitannaya v godichnom zasedanii Obshchestva Nevropatologov i Psikhiatrov pri Moskovskom universitete, 22-go oktyabrya 1897 g.* (Kiev: tipo-litografiya tovarishchestva I. N. Kushnerov i Ko., 1898). N. N. Bakhtin's inventory of plays for the children's theatre, *Obzor p'es dlya detskogo i shkol'nogo teatra* (St Petersburg:

a catastrophic loss of faith in Communism (or more broadly, Soviet values), which underwent a fatal shift from religion to routine.[79] But the many members of the educated population who had always been sceptically inclined to the new order were in a different category, and the shift of consciousness among them therefore requires an explanation of an alternative kind. To end on questions and not conclusions may seem unsatisfactory, but uncertainty is, I would say, the most effective response to Freud's tightly constructed narrative, with its authoritative statements, its recognition of alternative perspectives only so that these may be closed off, and its reduction of its subject to an ethnographical curiosity from another time.

My thanks to Ritchie Robertson and Katya Golynkina, and to the audience at the Davis Center, Harvard University, particularly Svetlana Boym and Jurij Striedter, for their helpful comments on an earlier version of this text.

Izdatel'stvo zhurnala "Russkaya shkola", 1912), p. 11, cautions against using frightening fairy tales such as 'Little Red Riding Hood'. In the early Soviet period, calls not to use fear in socialising children were raised loudly. For example, M. Kh. Sventitskaya wrote in the inaugural issue of *Na putyakh k novoi shkole*: 'Fear is the most unpleasant [*tyazheloe*], the saddest feeling, and should not be allowed into children's souls at all' ('Zhizn' doshkol'nikov v detskikh domakh "Detskogo gorodka imeni III Internationala" pri Narkomprose', *Na putyakh k novoi shkole*, 1 (1922), 69. In the Stalin era, when the emphasis on normative sources shifted to the need to inculcate discipline, there was more stress on teaching children to overcome fears than on preventing them from having enduring frights. For instance, a 'class supervisor' in one prestigious Moscow school organised hide-and-seek with her charges outside school as a pedagogical measure (CKQ-Ox-03 PF1B). However, by the late twentieth century, the balance had shifted back again. Interestingly, wolf texts got adapted in line with the sense that it was bad for children to be afraid. In Boris Zakhoder's poem, 'Volchok', *Nedelya*, 9 (1977), 19, the aggressive wolf, with his song of 'Ukhvachu-u-u! | Ukushu-u-u! | Utashchu-u-u! | Udushu-u-u! | I s"em!' [I'll grab 'em tight! | I'll eat 'em up | I'll drag 'em off! | I'll smother 'em! | And eat!] runs round and round in circles until he turns into a harmless little *volchok* ['wolfy', i.e., circular rusk]. (The motif is comparable to the British nursery classic, Helen Bannerman's *Little Black Sambo*, where the fierce tigers run round and round until they turn into ghee.) An earlier example of 'demystification' of this kind is, of course, Prokofiev's *Peter and the Wolf*. Cf. the first-hand account by a worker in a Soviet baby home on how she and the orphanage staff put on a performance of 'Little Red Riding Hood' for the children, but decided that the original plot was too threatening. Instead, the heroine met a bunny on her way to tea with her granny, and arrived to find a whole group of nice animals there, including a wolf, 'but a very kind, good wolf' (Oxf/Lev SPb-04 PF57A, pp. 13–14). On increasingly cynical attitudes to authority, cf. my study of the Russian schoolroom in the post-Stalin era, '"The School Waltz": The Everyday Life of the Post-Stalinist Soviet Classroom', *Forum for Anthropology and Culture*, 1 (2004), 108–58 <https://www.yumpu.com/en/document/read/11815280/the-school-waltz-the-everyday-life-of-the-post-stalinist-soviet-> [accessed 15 September 2022]. On the other hand, one should not over-simplify post-Stalinist culture too, there were other voices: see, for example, N. Berezina, 'Veseloe i grustnoe', where it is argued that it is important to let children have encounters with sad things (i.e. what would in the West be called 'traumatic experiences'): *Nedelya*, 34 (1969), 21.

79   See, for example, Yuri Slezkine, *The House of Government* (Princeton, NJ: Princeton University Press, 2018).

CHAPTER 6

The Redress of Art: Anna Akhmatova and Boris Anrep

[1993]

Throughout her life, but particularly in the 1910s and 1920s, Anna Akhmatova was a favourite subject for artists, some working with graphic means and photography, some with oil on canvas.¹ In most cases, however, the dialogue was one-sided, with Akhmatova merely acting as model (and the artist's engagement extending exclusively to the creation of the image).² But there are some important exceptions. Modigliani's sixteen drawings of Akhmatova were the product of their brief but intense friendship during Akhmatova's visit with her then husband Nikolai Gumilev to Paris in 1911, and at the end of her life, Akhmatova wrote a striking memoir of their encounter.³ A section of *Epic Motifs* (*Epicheskie motivy*, 1913–16) evokes Akhmatova's sittings for Natan Al'tman in his artist's garret above St Catherine's Church on Vasilievsky Island.⁴ But perhaps the most important relationship of all was with the painter, art critic, and mosaicist Boris Anrep (1883–1969).

Akhmatova and Anrep were romantically involved in 1915–16, after meeting through their joint friend (and Akhmatova's former lover) the critic and poet Nikolai Nedobrovo (1884–1919). On Akhmatova's own account, her love for Anrep inspired seventeen poems in *White Flock* (*Belaya staya*) and fourteen in *Plantain Leaf* (*Podorozhnik*). Critics have been generally inclined to suspect that the poet's own estimate may be too low; they have also drawn attention to the important

---

1   See e.g. *Anna Akhmatova v portretakh i fotografiyakh*, 1 (1989). Posthumous images by young artists appear in *L'Image du poète: les images de la poësie. A l'occasion de la centenaire de Anna Akhmatova. Musée de l'art contemporain; Union des peintres de l'URSS* (Moscow: Poligrafekspo, 1989). Of course, the internet has made vast numbers of images, not always meticulously sourced, available at the click of a mouse.
2   So, for example, in the case of the portraits by Ol'ga Della-Vos-Kardovskaya (1914), Yury Annenkov (1921), Zinaida Serebryakova (1922), and Kuz'ma Petrov-Vodkin (1922).
3   Anna Akhmatova, 'Amedeo Modil'yani' (1958–1964)', in *Amedeo Modil'yani v vospominaniyakh docheri i sovremennikov*, ed. by G. F. Kovalenko (Moscow: Buksmart, 2020) <http://www.a-modigliani.ru/library/amedeo-modilyani-v-vospominaniyah-docheri-i-sovremennikov6.html> [accessed 16 September 2022].
4   I have discussed this painting and its poetic traces in 'Painting and Autobiography: Anna Prismanova's *Pesok* and Anna Akhmatova's *Epicheskie motivy*', in *Russian Literature, Modernism, and the Visual Arts*, ed. by Catriona Kelly and Stephen Lovell (Cambridge: Cambridge University Press, 2000), pp. 58–87.

role played by Akhmatova's affair with Anrep as a subtext for *Poema bez geroya*.⁵ As complements to earlier investigations, particularly by Amanda Haight and Wendy Rosslyn, came the posthumous publication in the late 1980s of important memoirs by Anrep and the appearance, or reappearance, of several poems by Anrep dedicated to Akhmatova, most recently the technically insecure, but biographically illuminating, late lyric 'Commemoration' ('Pominanie'), in which Anrep engages in dialogue with the shade of Akhmatova.⁶

If Anrep's impact on Akhmatova has been recorded in every serious account of her early life since the 1960s, 'Akhmatova material' in the medium which Anrep made his own — mosaic art — has attracted much less attention. While Anrep's 1952 portrait of Akhmatova as 'Compassion', part of the mosaic pavement that he executed for the Vestibule of London's National Gallery, has been widely noted, no attempt has been made to analyse the compositional details of the image or their echoes of poems in *White Flock* and *Plantain Leaf*.⁷ As well as making up the deficiency here, I shall also describe what I believe to be a second, previously unidentified and superior, portrait of Akhmatova by Anrep, the mosaic of St Anne in the Cathedral of Christ the King, Mullingar, County Westmeath, in the Irish midlands (completed in 1953–54).⁸

Anrep's two mosaics are excellent examples of the work of a Russian artist of the first rank, whose achievements, much admired in his own lifetime, have faded from view since his death, as with other Russian artists who were not members of the avant-garde.⁹ As tributes to Akhmatova by a visual artist operating in his own

5   On Akhmatova and Anrep, see Amanda Haight, *Anna Akhmatova: A Poetic Pilgrimage* (Oxford: Oxford University Press, 1976), pp. 29–30, 44–51, 191–92; Wendy Rosslyn, 'Boris Anrep and the Poems of Anna Akhmatova', *Modern Language Review*, 74.4 (October 1979), 884–96; Wendy Rosslyn, 'Apropos of Anna Akhmatova: Boris Vasilyevich Anrep (1883–1969)', *New Zealand Slavonic Studies*, 1 (1980), 25–34; G. P. Struve, 'Akhmatova i Boris Anrep', in Akhmatova, *Sochineniya. Tom 3* (Paris: YMCA Press, 1983), pp. 428–38; G. P. Struve, 'Akhmatova i N. V. Nedobrovo', in Akhmatova, *Sochineniya. Tom 3*, pp. 371–427; I. Tlusty, 'Anna Akhmatova and the Composition of her "Poema bez geroya", 1940–1962' (unpublished DPhil thesis, University of Oxford, 1984), pp. 104–14.

6   Boris Anrep, 'O chernom kol'tse', in Akhmatova, *Sochineniya. Tom 3*, pp. 439–53; '["Nikolai Nedobrovo"] and Pominanie"', in 'Iz Akhmatovskikh materialov v arkhive Guverskogo instituta', *Akhmatovskii sbornik I*, ed. by Lazar' Fleishman (Paris: Institut slavyanovedeniya 1989), pp. 165–93. A particularly gruesome example of Anrep's writing (not, however, connected with Akhmatova) is his prose poem, 'Foreword to the Book of Anrep': see below, n. 38.

7   See, for example, Angelina Morhange, *Boris Anrep: The National Gallery Mosaics* (London: National Gallery, 1979), p. 18; Isaiah Berlin, *Personal Impressions* (London: Hogarth Press, 1980), p. 192. The identification of the portrait has been displayed since the 1990s on information boards for visitors placed in the National Gallery's vestibule.

8   'Previously unidentified' applies to the state of things as of 1995, when this article was first published. Since then, my attribution of Anrep's portrait has taken on a life of its own and is now almost universally accepted; a copy of *St Anna* hangs on the wall of the Anna Akhmatova Museum in the Fountain House, St Petersburg. Inevitably, I suppose, my role in discovering this has been forgotten (see, for example, Fintan O'Toole, 'Culture Shock: From Russia with Love Pieced Together in Poetry', *Irish Times*, 29 June 2013 <https://www.irishtimes.com/culture/culture-shock-from-russia-with-love-pieced-together-in-poetry-1.1445227> [accessed 16 September 2022], which gives a summary of my arguments below without credit).

9   John Milner's *A Dictionary of Russian and Soviet Artists* (Woodbridge: Antique Collectors' Club, 1993) includes only a line on Anrep, for instance. Even during the course of his own lifetime, Anrep's

genre, Anrep's mosaics are more memorable and more worthy commemorations of the poet, and more cogent responses to her poetry, than his poems. Where Anrep's verses are, in the words respectively of Struve and Fleishman, 'inarticulate' and 'helpless', his mosaic portraits are works of considerable communicative power and — especially in the case of the Mullingar image — considerable beauty (see fig. 1).

Detailed study of these images contributes to a more balanced appreciation of Anrep's biography than has emerged from work by Akhmatova specialists, where he has been portrayed (following Akhmatova's last, bitter poem to him) as a sensual, self-centred womaniser.[10] There is some truth here: at any rate in his younger years, Anrep definitely was a *bon viveur* whose marital arrangements were of an eye-stretching egocentricity. As Frances Spalding records in her pen-portrait of Helen Maitland, Anrep's second wife (who was to leave Anrep for Roger Fry in 1925):

> Helen had learnt to accept Boris's need for two wives, as she had learned to accept that when he went out socially in Mayfair, both wives were expected to stay at home. According to Romilly John, Boris (who read mainly detective stories) sent the younger woman out to the public library to select books for Helen on the infallible principle that she would select books which Helen would not have chosen for herself [...]. [Anrep] had unusual aptitude and excessive self-confidence; in order to woo the musical Helen he learnt to play the piano, developing the art, he said, in a matter of minutes. He had no intention of marrying Helen, but when in 1918 she bore him a son he immediately made her his wife. Had the child been a daughter their unmarried state would have continued, but Boris disapproved of illegitimate sons. 'There's no sense in marriage,' he once said, 'I prefer collages — associations that everyone knows about'.[11]

Despite his own waywardness and contempt for marriage, Anrep was later to orchestrate jealous scenes when Helen Anrep decided eventually to leave him. Yet this domestic monster was also (in his later years) an excellent cook, a fine conversationalist, and an exceptionally generous, considerate associate who delighted in finding appropriate presents for his many friends and acquaintances. He was affectionately remembered even in the 1990s by inhabitants of Mullingar whom he allowed, as children, to help in fixing his mosaics in place. Besides, he was a hard-working professional whose technical expertise commanded much respect from his artistic peers, and whose relations with clients, as his archive reveals, were a remarkable combination of amiability that sometimes graduated

reputation declined: in a rather tragic slight, the incumbent at the Église de Notre Dame de France, Leicester Square, London, decided in 1960 to have a mosaic altar panel executed by Anrep some years previously covered by a Jean Cocteau fresco, though Anrep had offered to bear half the cost of having his panel moved to a new site in the church. See the correspondence in the National Art Library, London (henceforth NAL), pressmark English MSS: Anrep B.: 88.NN.8. I was told by a custodian at the church when I visited in June 1994 that the panel had, in the event, been left in its original position, but is now obscured by Cocteau's concrete altar frontage.

10   See, for example, Rosslyn, 'A propos of Anna Akhmatova', and Tlusty, 'Anna Akhmatova's *Poema bez geroya*'. A certain latent hostility is perhaps also evident in Henry Lamb's chilly portrait of Anrep (see n. 21 below).

11   F. Spalding, *Roger Fry: Art and Life* (St Albans: Granada, 1980), pp. 248–49. The information following on Anrep's jealous scenes also comes from there.

to friendship, and uncompromising, though always tactful, adherence to his own aesthetic standards.[12] What was more, Anrep, unlike Konstantin Rodzevich, the superficially similar playboy with whom Tsvetaeva was involved in the 1920s, was a creative artist capable of responding to his involvement with a poet on equal terms, albeit belatedly.

Anrep, like Akhmatova, was a St Petersburger, though in his case a native: he was born there in 1883, into the family of Vasily von Anrep, a distinguished physiologist and medical administrator, the holder of numerous professorships and high posts in the civil service. Boris's younger brother, Gleb (1891–1955), was to follow in his father's profession, becoming a cardio-physiologist of international renown, winner of the Sharpey-Schafer and W. Mickle· Prizes, Professor of Physiology at Kasr el Aini, Cairo, and Fellow of the Royal Society from the early age of thirty-seven, among many other honours. For his part, Boris at first looked set for an academic career, though in a different discipline: after an education in Khar'kov and St Petersburg, he graduated from the prestigious College of Jurisprudence (Uchilishche pravovedeniya) in 1905. However, in 1908 he changed course radically, and began to dedicate himself to the visual arts, training in Paris under J.-P. Lauens, and in Edinburgh under F. Morley Fletcher. At this period he also began to move in British artistic circles, making friends with, among others, Henry Lamb, Augustus John and Ottoline Morrell, as well as Roger Fry.

Anrep selected the Russian paintings exhibited at Fry's Second Post-Impressionist Exhibition of 1912, and an exhibition of his own paintings, drawings, and mosaics was held at the Chenil Gallery, London, in 1913. In the following year, he received his first mosaic commission (for the crypt of Westminster Cathedral). At that point, his career was interrupted by military and government service during the First World War, which took him back to Russia (and so afforded him the opportunity for his liaison with Akhmatova). But on his return to England in 1917, he rapidly established himself as a noted mosaic artist. By the time he reached his eighties, when failing strength forced him to abandon mosaic-building, with its need to haul about sacks of cement, glass, and stone, and to climb to the vertiginous heights of church ceilings, he had undertaken many projects in public buildings, including work in the Tate Gallery, the Greek Orthodox Cathedral, Moscow Road, and the Bank of England, as well as the National Gallery and Westminster Cathedral. He had carried out various private commissions as well, including work for Augustus John and Lytton Strachey, and for John Stirling-Maxwell's family chapel at Keir House in Scotland. Anrep was also the author of articles on the visual arts; the brilliance of his lectures was widely admired.[13]

12 On Anrep's better qualities, see e.g. Struve, 'Anna Akhmatova i Boris Anrep', and especially Justin Vulliamy's memoir in *Boris Anrep (1883–1969): A Loan Exhibition* (London: Gallery Edward Harvane, 1973); the reminiscence about the children of Mullingar comes from a letter to me by Father Patrick Moore, then incumbent of the Cathedral of Christ the King, 18 June 1994. A pleasant impression is also given by Anrep's correspondence in NAL (see, for example, nn. 16–17).
13 For more detailed accounts of Anrep's biography, see Rosslyn, 'A propos of Anna Akhmatova'; Tlusty, 'Anna Akhmatova's *Poema bez geroya*'; Struve, 'Anna Akhmatova i Boris Anrep'; and Vulliamy in *Boris Anrep*; see additionally Brockhaus-Efron, *Entsiklopedicheskii slovar'* and *Novyi*

As for the immediate biographical background to the composition of Anrep's two portraits of Akhmatova, he had finally parted from her in February 1917, nearly thirty-five years before he began work on the earlier of the two mosaics, that in the National Gallery. After the parting, neither he nor Akhmatova made any attempt to engage in correspondence. Akhmatova herself always believed, in any case, that her deep attachment to Anrep had not been fully reciprocated: in 1924, for example, she told the photographer and diarist Pavel Luknitsky that Anrep had made his risky final visit to see her, crossing revolutionary Petrograd in his officer's greatcoat with the epaulettes stripped off, simply out of bravado:

> AKHMATOVA   It wasn't because he loved me — he just felt like doing it. He enjoyed going through rifle-fire.
> LUKNITSKY   So he didn't love you?
> AKHMATOVA   He... no, of course not... It wasn't love. [...] But he'd have done anything for me — anything he felt like.[14]

Akhmatova's scepticism had foundation. Anrep was in 1915 still legally married to his first wife Yuniya (née Khitrovo), and had for several years been living in London with Helen Maitland, by whom he already had two children. There is no reason to suppose that his relationship with Akhmatova would necessarily have meant much more to him than other passing affairs at the time. In later years, Anrep was himself categorically to assert that his feeling for Akhmatova had been 'platonic and poetic'. Improbable as this assertion seems, given the sexual mores of pre-revolutionary Russian bohemia and the far from monastic behaviour for which not only Anrep but also Akhmatova were noted at that time, it certainly constitutes an effective denial that the entanglement represented a *grande passion* on Anrep's side.[15] And indeed, his two memoirs imply that his feelings for Akhmatova had four phases, none of them precisely reciprocating the romantic sensibility that she expressed in her poems to him. His original distant and respectful admiration for her grace and her poetic talent was replaced by very brief phase of powerful sexual passion (in 1915–16). After their parting in 1917, any sense of nostalgia soon dulled to a sense of vague regret; then, however, in the last two and a half decades of his life, this in turn gave way to a sharp — indeed, extreme — sense of guilt, an intense feeling that he had betrayed her.[16]

entsiklopedicheskii slovar', 1. My material on Gleb Anrep is taken from J. H. Gaddum, 'Gleb Anrep 1891–1955', in *Biographical Memoirs of Fellows of the Royal Society* (London: Royal Society, 1956), II, 19–31; I am grateful to Ian Thompson for supplying a copy of this article. The name of Anrep's mother (Praskov'ya Zatsepina, 1857–1921), is recorded in documentation held by the Central State Archive, St Petersburg (see the article on Anrep in the Russian version of Wikipedia).
14   Pavel Luknitsky, *Acumiana: Vstrechi s Annoi Akhmatovoi*, 2 vols (Paris: YMCA Press, 1991), I, 41. In the light of the widely-accepted story that Luknitsky was an informer for OGPU, the Soviet secret police — see 'Luknitsky Pavel Nikolaevich', 'Entsiklopedicheskii slovar' "Literary Sankt-Peterburga XX vek"' <https://lavkapisateley.spb.ru/enciklopediya/i-933/luknickij> [accessed 16 September 2022] — these questions about her relationship with a former officer in the Imperial Army who was now in emigration seem less than desultory.
15   Anrep, in 'Iz Akhmatovskikh materialov v arkhive Guverskogo instituta', p. 178.
16   Anrep, 'O chernom kol'tse'; Anrep, in 'Iz Akhmatovskikh materialov v arkhive Guverskogo instituta', passim.

The immediate precipitating factor for Anrep's sense of guilt seems to have been his loss, in the aftermath of a 1944 air-raid on his Hampstead studio, of the 'black ring' — the treasured mourning ring, inherited from her grandmother, that Akhmatova had given to Anrep as a token of love on 13 February 1916 during a tea-party at the Nedobrovos', where Nikolai Nedrobovo was reading aloud from his verse tragedy *Judith* (*Yudif*'). After the air-raid, Anrep, as he relates, was incapacitated for a while by the effects of the explosion, but eventually managed to crawl through the ruins of his studio. However, when he returned the following morning to pick through the rubble, he found plundered the box in which he kept his treasures, and the ring gone:

> I felt rage against the thieves. And shame. I had not taken proper care of this sacred object. Tears of despair filled my eyes. Why had I not given the ring to the bank for safe-keeping? Because I wanted to keep it with me, like a prisoner, so that I could see it whenever I wanted to. But I had gone to Paris without worrying about it. No, it was my fault, there was no more *to* be said! What would I tell A.A., if she asked me about it?[17]

The loss of the ring seems to have brought to the surface a subliminal sense of guilt that Anrep had been feeling with regard to his relationship with Akhmatova as a whole (there is a strongly metaphorical feel to the phrase 'I wanted to keep it with me, like a prisoner, so that I could see it whenever I wanted to'; one has only to feminise the pronoun to grasp the analogy with a mistress abandoned for reasons of personal convenience). Once surfaced, guilt became overwhelming, even obsessional. It wrecked Anrep's last meeting with Akhmatova, in 1965, as Anrep descended into anonymous literary small-talk in the hope of avoiding mention of the ring and its fate. It also caused Anrep, in the last years of his life, to break the command of silence that Akhmatova had — if one is to believe the first stanza of 'Commemoration' — herself laid upon him, and confess the story of the ring in a memoir which he instructed Gleb Struve to publish only after his death.[18] And a decade earlier this sense of guilt underlay the composition of Anrep's mosaic portraits, which were, one may suppose, intended as acts of reparation, as commemorations of his love for Akhmatova that did not require him to breach her confidence, during her lifetime, by exciting the prurience of ignorant outsiders.

The National Gallery mosaic in the North Vestibule, in which Anrep's first portrait of Akhmatova is located, was opened to the public on 25 November 1952. It depicts (to quote Anrep's own description) 'eminent people, portrayed in fantastic settings, personify[ing] ideas important in the artist's opinion'.[19] The central mosaic vignette represents Defiance (Sir Winston Churchill), and round him are grouped a further fourteen smaller images: 'Rest and Be Thankful' ('the signboard of a famous public house'); 'Here I Lie' ('the tomb of the artist'); Delectation (Margot Fonteyn

---

17   Anrep, 'O chernom kol'tse', p. 449.
18   Anrep, 'Pominanie' in 'Iz Akhmatovskikh materialov v arkhive Guverskogo instituta', p. 183; on the posthumous publication of 'O chernom kol'tse', see Struve, 'Akhmatova i Boris Anrep', p. 428.
19   See NAL, 86.NN.11/12 (the quotation comes from a National Gallery duplicated handout dated January 1969).

and Edward Sackville-West); Compromise (Loretta Young); Folly ('a patron of Arts', posthumously revealed as Mrs Maud Russell, Anrep's own friend and sponsor); Pursuit (the astronomer Fred Hoyle); Sixth Sense (Edith Sitwell); Open Mind (Earl Jowitt); Curiosity (Lord Rutherford); Lucidity (Bertrand Russell); Leisure (T. S. Eliot); Humour (with Diana Cooper as Britannia); Wonder (with Augustus John as Neptune); and Compassion (not named in the original artist's description, but since identified as Akhmatova).

The choice of subjects, as with the earlier mosaic floors done by Anrep for the National Gallery, rested with the artist.[20] 'The Awakening of the Muses' (1936), on the Vestibule Landing at the Gallery, illustrates such luminaries as Greta Garbo and the society beauty Christabel, Lady Aberconway (who had herself chosen to be represented as Euterpe); it also, however, contains a more private memento, a portrait (as Urania, the Muse of Geography), of Mariya Volkova, Anrep's sister-in-law (and, from 1917, also his mistress; she was the sister of Gleb Anrep's first wife, Ol'ga Volkova). In the same way, Anrep was able to introduce, among the extremely public and British selection of notabilities in his later allegorical pavement, a portrait of Akhmatova, who was not then widely known among Western literati and glitterati, but who was a figure of immense significance for him personally. As though to emphasise the point, Anrep employs references in his composition that can be decoded only with interior knowledge of his own meetings with Akhmatova, and of her poems of 1915–17.

The mosaic represents Akbmatova lying propped on her elbows, legs extended along the bottom of the image, in a blue scoop-necked dress, bare-headed, and with waving black hair flowing on to her shoulders. To the left stand broken masses of greyish-white masonry; to the right is a black field representing a pit, in which writhe naked and emaciated corpses. To Akhmatova's right hovers an angel, who is making a sign of blessing.

The National Gallery's visitor orientation materials state that Akhmatova is surrounded by 'the horrors of war', but this description requires clarification. Anrep (who had worked as a Russian radio monitor during the Second World War) knew perfectly well that Akhmatova had spent the Leningrad blockade in evacuation. He could not have envisaged her in the role of Ol'ga Berggol'ts, whose readings of her poems about the blockade on the radio sustained millions of Leningraders. The war that is represented must be the First World War; in any case, there are more than martial horrors here. Anrep's own description (see n. 15 above) phrases the situation, with interesting ambiguity, thus: the angel is saving Akhmatova 'from (a *horrible death*) the horrors of war' (Anreps' parenthesis, my emphasis). The clear implication is that the mosaic represents the early days of the Russian Revolution, in the spring of 1917, during which Anrep made his last visit to Akhmatova.

Confirmation of this idea is afforded by Anrep's own references, in his writings, to this meeting. The first comes from the prose memoir, 'The Black Ring':

---

20 I base this assertion on Anrep's correspondence with the National Gallery's management, preserved with other Anrep material in NAL, 86.NN.11.

I could see she was touched that I had come. We went into her room. She half-lay [*prilegla,* that is, lay propped on her elbows] on the sofa. We spoke for a while about the meaning of the revolution that was going on. She was anxious, saying that we had to expect big changes. 'It will be the same as it was in France during the Great Revolution; maybe even worse...' '*Let's* not talk about it.' We were silent. She lowered her head. 'We won't see each other any more. You're leaving.' 'I will come back. See, here's your ring.' I undid the buttons of my tunic and showed her the black ring on a chain round my neck.[21]

The second, and slightly different, account is taken from 'Commemoration':

> Я без погон пришел к тебе.
> У ног молил бежать скорее.
> 'К чему? В гробу лежать теплее
> В отчизне. Я ведь — о себе'.
>
> В ее руке зажаты розы,
> А боль стучит в моей груди,
> И мы одни...
> 'Теперь иди,
> Без страха встречу день угрозы'.[22]

[I visited you without my epaulettes, | And at [your] feet begged you to flee. | 'What for? It's warmer in the grave | In one's fatherland. I mean — for me.' || Her hand grips the roses tightly, | And pain beats in my breast, | And we're alone... | 'Now you must go. | I shall face the day of danger fearlessly'.]

Anrep's prose account introduces two motifs from the mosaic: Akhmatova's 'half-lying' position, and the human horrors brought by the Revolution, to which she gave prophetic expression. The latter point is reiterated in Anrep's poetic recollection, which, however, also introduces another motif: his own attempt to persuade Akhmatova to flee, and her insistence that she would remain in Russia. Akhmatova herself had transformed this scene into art in the famous poem addressed to Anrep, 'A voice came to me. It called with consolation' ('Mne golos byl. On zval uteshno', 1917). Is this motif present in the mosaic, too? It may be, obliquely. 'Angel' was one of the addresses repeatedly used by Akhmatova in her love poems for Anrep, perhaps the most important of which is quoted in his memoir, 'The Black Ring':

> Словно ангел, возмутивший воду,
> Ты взглянул тогда в мое лицо,
> Возвратил и силу и свободу,
> А на память чуда взял кольцо.
> Мой румянец жаркий и недужный
> Стерла богомольная печаль.
> Памятным мне будет месяц вьюжный,
> Северный встревоженный февраль.[23]

---

21 Anrep, 'O chernom kol'tse', p. 167.
22 Anrep, 'Pominanie', p. 183. Anrep's omission of the rose from his mosaic is another sign of how far his talent for art exceeded his talent for poetry.
23 Anna Akhmatova, *Stikhotvoreniya i poemy* (Leningrad: Sovetskii pisatel', 1976), p. 135 (hereafter referenced as *SP*). Among other 'angel' poems are, for example, 'Vybrala sama ya dolyu', Spring 1915, which ends with the lines 'Как от блеска дивной ризы | Стало в горнице светло' [As though

[Like an angel stirring up the water, | You looked then into my face, | You returned strength and freedom to me, | And took [my] ring in memory of the miracle. | My burning and unnecessary flush| Was wiped away by pious sadness. | The month of snows will bring me remembrance, | The northern troubled February.]

'The Black Ring' was written long after the composition of 'Compassion'; it cannot be established for certain that Akhmatova's association directly inspired Anrep at the time. Even if the mosaic angel was intended to symbolise Anrep's own presence, and hence to emphasise the links of 'Compassion' with idealised memories of Akhmatova and Anrep's parting, the conventionally androgynous angel was most certainly not a self-portrait on the part of Anrep (who was a massive, emphatically masculine and, frankly speaking, rather porcine individual).[24] It is, in any case, at least as likely that the angel is a generalised representation of the spiritual side of the sinful, but righteous, world of Russian culture, a dimension which Akhmatova herself had called upon as a token of authority in a poem of 1917 addressed to Anrep:

> Ты — отступник: за остров зеленый
> Отдал, отдал родную страну,
> Наши песни, и наши иконы,
> И над озером тихим сосну. (*SP*, p. 133)

[You are an apostate: for a green island | You surrendered your native land; | Our songs, and our icons, | And the pine above the still lake.]

Whichever of these interpretations one accepts, the strength of 'Compassion' lies in its representation of Akhmatova herself, as she turns from the vision of neo-classical culture in destruction to her right and concentrates her gaze on the human victims of disaster to her left. The gesture may embody private memories of parting, but it also makes Akhmatova a worthy representative of compassion in a broader sense. And, as the bodies on a black field are a standard iconographic motif for Hell, being used in many Byzantine representations of the *Anastasis*, Christ's descent into Limbo, there is a sense in which we may read 'Compassion' as a pictorial representation of one of the most famous and popular manuscript texts of medieval Russia. This is 'The Mother of God's Descent into Hell', itself a feminisation of the more familiar *Anastasis*, in which the Archangel Michael conducts the Mother of God into the presence of the damned:

> И повелѣ архистратигъ явитися ангеломъ отъ полудне , и отверзеся ад, и видѣ во адѣ мучащаяся, и бяше ту множство муж и жен, и вопль мног бяше. И воспроси благодатная архистратига: 'кто сіи суть?' — И рече архистратигъ: 'сіи суть, иже не вѣроваша во отца и сына и святаго духа, но забыша Бога'.[25]

---

from the shine of a wondrous vestment | In the parlour it became light] (*SP*, p. 123); 'Angel, tri goda khranivshii menya', 1922 (*SP*, p. 156).

24 See the portrait of Boris Anrep with his wife Helen and children Igor and Anastasia painted by Anrep's friend Henry Lamb (Tompkins Collection, Museum of Fine Arts, Boston).

25 *Khrestomatiya po drevnerusskoi literature*, ed. by N. Gudzy, 8th edn (Moscow: Prosveshchenie, 1973), p. 93.

[And the Archangel commanded the angels from the south to appear, and the gates of Hell were opened, and She saw those who were tormented in Hell, and there were many men and women there, and there was much wailing. And Our Lady Full of Grace asked the Archangel, 'Who then are these?' And the Archangel said unto Her, 'These are they who believe not in the Father and the Son and the Holy Ghost, but who have forgotten God'.]

The contrast between unbelievers and 'Our Lady Full of Grace' ('grace', *blagodat'*, is also the meaning of the Hebrew noun from which the name Anna is derived) directly replicates that between Akhmatova and the believer, and Anrep the apostate and atheist, in Akhmatova's poetry.

The mosaic's pictorial resonances with Old Russian tradition are muted; although Akhmatova wears the Virgin's canonical blue robe, she lacks her crimson-purple *pokrov* (maphorion), or veil. As Angelina Morhange, the author of a pamphlet on the National Gallery mosaics, has pointed out, the figure of Akhmatova (in expression, position, and the draping of the hair) bears some relation to David's painting 'The Death of Barra' (a representation of Jean-Louis Barra, the adolescent victim of counter-revolutionary murderers during the Vendée uprising).[26] The fact that Akhmatova is lying from left to right, rather than from right to left, as Barra was, may be an attempt on Anrep's part to introduce a semantic reversal into the image, so that a victim of counter-revolution becomes a victim of revolution.

A further possible layer is a reference to Dante's *Inferno* (invoked by Akhmatova herself in 'The Muse' ('Muza', 1924) and 'Dante', 1936), with 'Compassion' meant either as a feminisation of Dante himself or (more probably, given the scarcity of 'compassion' in Dante's perspective) as a representation of Dante's own vision of Beatrice, who appears early in the poem (Canto II) to sustain and encourage him.[27] Taken all in all, Anrep's complex fusion and adaptation of received tradition means that, despite its deep-laid public associations, political and religious, the National Gallery mosaic functions primarily as a cryptic, secular, and personal image; the angel figures as an actor in Akhmatova's (and Anrep's) own religious drama, as understood by an informed reader of her poetry. The contorted figures of the damned represent the actual biographical threat to Akhmatova at the time when Anrep left her — and so touch also on the most important inspiration of Anrep's own sense of guilt towards her.

The Mullingar mosaic, by contrast, is an image whose sacred character, as befits its ecclesiastical function, dominates all other associations. Although, as we shall see, personal matters are not completely absent, there is a lesser sense of personal tragedy and emotional confusion. Set into a wall at the back of the Chapel of St Anne (its border is, unfortunately, to some extent obscured by the altar placed immediately to the fore) the mosaic was commissioned, like its fellow in the Chapel of St Patrick to the south, by John D'Alton, Bishop of Meath (and later Archbishop of Armagh), who had made contact with Anrep though Evie Hone, the well-

26 Morhange, *Boris Anrep*, p. 18, and pls 13 and 14.
27 'Muza', *SP*, p. 183; 'Dante', *SP*, p. 193. For an excellent study of this material, see Pamela Davidson, 'Akhmatova's "Dante"', in *The Speech of Unknown Eyes: Akhmatova's Readers on Her Poetry*, ed. by W. Rosslyn, 2 vols (Nottingham: Astra, 1990), II, 201–24.

THE REDRESS OF ART   147

FIG. 6.1. Boris Anrep, St Anne. Cathedral of Christ the King, Mullingar, Ireland.
Photograph Ian Thompson.

known Irish stained-glass designer, who was a frequent visitor to Paris. A plan for mosaic designs had earlier been submitted to the cathedral authorities by Earley of Dublin, but D'Alton had been 'quite dissatisfied' with it.[28]

Anrep accepted the commission, and completed the first mosaic (of St Patrick lighting the paschal fire on the hill of Slane) in 1949, after some correspondence about the suitability of his design (a pagan idol was at first felt to figure too prominently in the icon).

At the same time, Anrep also made preliminary designs for a mosaic in the Chapel of St Anne, and made a number of investigations about the iconographic traditions and ritual texts associated with the saint, writing to Bishop D'Alton's successor, Bishop John Kyne, to D'Alton himself, and to Father Gervase Mathew, of Blackfriars, Oxford, in order to enquire.[29]

---

28 Letter from John D'Alton to Boris Anrep, 22 October 1945, NAL 86.NN.13/36.
29 Few of Anrep's letters relating to the Mullingar project are preserved; he appears to have kept

Owing to a misunderstanding with the Mullingar ecclesiastical authorities, whom he did not understand to have formally commissioned the second mosaic at the time they agreed to the design for the St Patrick chapel, Anrep did not carry out the St Anne chapel mosaic at the same time as the work on St Patrick.[30] He did not, in fact, begin work on it again until 1953–54, starting work on the project immediately after he had finished the National Gallery mosaic. Despite the nearness in the time of execution, the Mullingar design is strikingly different, at first glance, from 'Compassion'; but the link to the theme of Akhmatova furnishes a hidden bond, as we shall see.

Following Anrep's practice in the case of wall mosaics, in contrast to floor mosaics, the St Anne scene is composed of much smaller tesserae than the National Gallery mosaic, and these are made of Venetian glass rather than marble. They give the work a shimmering, silken appearance, The bright colours of the figures, in silver, light and dark blue, yellow, green, terracotta, and brown, appear to advantage against the geometrical shapes of the background (houses and a cedar to the left; the steps, walls, and golden roofs of the temple to the right), and the field of modulated browns and greys behind the image as a whole.

Compositionally, too, the differences are striking. Rather than a scattering of allegorical motifs, the St Anne mosaic represents a single but dense narrative scene: the Presentation of the Virgin, surmounted by the adult Virgin apotheosised (who, according to time-honoured Catholic tradition, appears crowned, surrounded by angels and supported on a sickle moon). In the central scene itself, the tiny figure of the Virgin is placed in the middle: to her right stand six Byzantine angels, holding tapers, with a geometrically schematised rendering of Jerusalem in the background to their left; in the foreground stands the High Priest, at the gates of the Temple. Although the Virgin's outstanding spiritual role is indicated by the fact that her halo is gold, and not simply marked out with a coloured border, as in the case of the other figures, the composition is dominated by the elongated figure of St Anne herself, who stands beside St Joachim, to the Virgin's right, wearing a long spreading yellow veil over a blue robe. At the bottom of the composition appears an extract from a fifteenth-century hymn to St Anne, recommended to Anrep as a suitable text for the icon by Father Gervase Mathew:

> GAUDE MATER ANNA GAUDE*MATER OMNI DIGNA LAUDE*MATER TANTAE FILIAE* ANNA RECTE NUNUPARIS* QUIA GRATIOSE PARIS*MATREM OMNIS GRATIAE* SALVE MATER MATRIS CHRISTI*QUAE IAM FELIX CONSCENDISTI*IUBILANS IN AETHERA*ITER NOBIS PARA TUTUM*UT IN DOMINI VERTUTUM*COLLOCEMUR DEXTERA.[31]

---

copies only of those concerning financial matters. Neither, apparently, are letters from him preserved in the Mullingar Diocesan Office (information kindly supplied by Father Patrick Moore). However, the fact of Anrep's enquiries is evident from the letters to him by John D'Alton (1 July 1946), John Kyne (29 March 1946), and Gervase Mathew (undated, April-May 1946): NAL 86.NN.13/28, 86.NN.13/34, 86.NN.13/32.

30 See letter from John Kyne to Anrep, 2 November 1948, and from Anrep to D'Alton, 14 November 1948: NAL 86.NN.13/11 and 86.NN.13/10.

31 Boris Anrep and Mairín Allen, *The Mullingar Mosaics* ([Mullingar: Mullingar Cathedral, *c.*

[Rejoice, Mother Anne — Mother worthy of all praise — Mother of so great a child — Anne rightly you are called — for you have brought forth in grace — the Mother of All Grace — Hail, mother of Christ's Mother — who have gone up in bliss to God hymning praise in heaven — prepare for us a way secure — that we may sit among the powers of the Lord — at his right hand.]

In an explanatory text on the mosaic (from which the above translation is taken), Anrep commented in detail upon the character of his representation:

> This mosaic though designed on lines closely parallel to the mosaic in St. Patrick's Chapel has some affinity with the traditional iconographic style as befitting a Biblical subject. It is dedicated to St Anne, whose rightful glory rests on her devotion to the upbringing of the Holy Virgin Mary, the truly momentous event therein being the Presentation of the Virgin. The tall imposing figure of St Anne dominates the scene, standing with her hand outstretched over the head of the Virgin as if protecting her child; the face of St. Anne is full of calm dignity in contrast to the tense expression in the child's face.[32]

But Anrep's interpretation, in the mosaic itself, is not, fortunately, as stilted as this description might suggest. Most of his renderings, certainly, are handsome representations of conventional iconographic types; but the figure of St Anne, which immediately draws the eye, stands out. Unlike her companions, St Anne, with her heavy-lidded eyes, dark brows, prominent cheek-bones, and strikingly aquiline nose, is an individual image: a recognisable portrait, in fact, of Anna Akhmatova. Anrep has even contrived to make her veil (which is folded so as to cover her forehead, rather than following the hairline) suggest the heavy fringe that was Akhmatova's most famous feature. St Anna (to use the Latin form of the name that Anrep himself adopted in his icon), stands commandingly in an enveloping robe. Her manner is very different from the seductively victimised air that 'Compassion' has. This is a representation of Akhmatova's spiritual, incorporeal self, rather than of her sensual, bodily person.

However, for all that, St Anna is still an instantly recognisable recording of the young Akhmatova's face, preserved in Anrep's memory since 1931.[33] The resemblance is pointed, too, by the fact that Anrep has chosen to portray St Anne in blue, a colour with which she is not customarily associated in iconography: this suggests Anne's link both with his own figure of Compassion, and with the Mother of God, to whom the colour is proper both in the Eastern and in the Western Church.[34]

1956]), p. 3. For Gervase Mathews's recommendation of this hymn, see his undated letter of April-May 1946 (n. 27 above).

32 Anrep's reference to 'biblical' traditions is a little misleading; like other subjects from the Life of the Virgin, the Presentation in the Temple appears in the Apocrypha. However, it is a canonical subject in iconography (see also below, n. 33).

33 For a comparable image of the young Akhmatova, see the photograph taken at Slepnyovo in 1916, reproduced in *Anna Akhmatova: stikhi, perepiska, vospominaniya, ikonografiya* (Ann Arbor, MI: Ardis, 1977).

34 It is possible also that the combination of blue robe and yellow veil is meant to echo Natan Al'tman's famous 1914 portrait of Akhmatova wearing a blue robe and a yellow shawl, which Anrep presumably saw on his visits to the poet. It is the painting of this portrait that Akhmatova evokes in

If the resemblance between St Anne and Akhmatova in Anrep's finished image is unquestionable, that of course does not resolve the problem of the extent to which he consciously intended this. Certainly, the association of names, 'St Anna', must have been overwhelming. Anrep was undoubtedly familiar with Akhmatova's autobiographical cycle, 'Epic Motifs' ('Epicheskie motivy'), the first part of which had originally appeared in the first edition of *The Rosary* (*Chetki*, 1914). Here Akhmatova celebrates the saintly connections of her own name, referring to the 'more than twelve festivals' that she enjoys.³² No doubt the fact that some of her poems addressed to Anrep exploited the dual associations of his own first name (Boris as worldly prince and as 'angelic' saint) also played a role in reinforcing name symbolism; evidence, too, that Anrep exercised a high degree of control over the content of his St Anne mosaic. He was prepared to confer with various ecclesiastical authorities about the legends of St Anne, but the final choice of the scene of the Presentation in the Temple seems to have been his. Significantly, this is a canonical subject in Orthodox iconography as well as in Western religious art. Anrep did not utilise the more familiar Western subject of St Anne teaching the Virgin to read, and also silently rejected a suggestion from Gervase Mathew that the most appropriate tribute to St Anne would have been to represent her part in the Virgin's family tree, that is, her role in generating Christ's human self.³⁵ Although he introduced Irish motifs (from medieval high crosses) into the borders of his design (whose speckled background colouring also has a distant and amusing resemblance to tweed cloth), and although he employs the decidedly Western motif of the Assumption, Anrep depicts St Anne herself with no hint of Irishness and with little suggestion of Roman Catholicism as such: the saint's antecedents are primarily Byzantine and Russian.

The degree of Anrep's commitment to the legend of St Anne is indicated by the fact that he apparently reacted with some acerbity to a suggestion by Bishop Kyne that the subject of the mosaic should be changed. On 13 May 1952, Kyne had written to Anrep: 'My Art counsellors have suggested a representation of St. Finian, the Patron of the Diocese, instead of the projected mosaic of St. Anne. If you have not gone too far in your preparations for the St. Anne mosaic I should like you to consider the new project'. On 6 July 1952, however, after receiving from Anrep a

---

'Epic Motifs' (see below).
35   Letter from Gervase Mathew to Anrep (see n. 27, above). Mathew had also nudged Anrep, in this letter, towards Giotto's representation of St Anne and St Joachim at the Golden Gate in the Scrovegni Chapel, Padua, as a possible model. Anrep did not follow this suggestion, nor does his representation of the Presentation bear much relation to Giotto's complex and highly geometrical image. Its obvious precedent is the handling of the subject in Orthodox icons: see, for example, the Greek Baroque icon attributed to Theodore Poulakis, reproduced in Sotheby's catalogue, *Icons, Russian Pictures and Works of Art*, 24 November 1992, p. 90; the cluster of angels, domed temple, and diminutive but precocious figure of the Virgin are all paralleled in Anrep's mosaic. All the same, the indigo and terracotta colouring present in parts of Anrep's mosaic may be an indirect tribute to Giotto (whose frescos are particularly well reproduced in Giuseppe Basile, *Giotto: La Capella delli Scrovegni* (Milan: Electa, 1992), pp. 33–74). Conversely, Mairín Allen has plausibly linked Anrep's representation of Mary in apotheosis with the *orante* figures of Ravenna (see Anrep and Allen, *The Mullingar Mosaics*, p. 11), so we can see a Byzantine connection at this level too.

negative reply to this suggestion, Kyne was to back down:

> Your reasons for not wishing to change to St. Finian are cogent. I have consulted some of my art experts here and also Doctor D'Alton. We are agreed that it is best to continue with the St. Anne design. It was really a few local priests who wished to see St. Finian in the Cathedral, but that design can wait for some other time.[36]

Anrep's possible reluctance to see the effort that he had already spent on designing his St Anne mosaic go for nothing should not, of course, be disregarded. But since he was on the whole inclined to treat with compliance clients' wishes and changes of heart, if these were not totally aesthetically aberrant, the firmness of his resolution on this occasion may be an indication of a particular and personal attachment to the subject of St Anne.[37]

According to the views of the more puritanical branches of Christianity, the representation of St Anne in the guise of a former mistress might be considered inappropriate, or even improper. However, Anrep's action has many precedents (one has only to think of the various Italian Renaissance Madonnas whose features are those of painters' or patrons' mistresses). In any case, Anrep — ironically enough, for an artist many of whose most important commissions were ecclesiastical — was not a religious believer. Late in life, he accepted Akhmatova's poetic description of himself as 'an apostate' and her assertions that he had no understanding of the spiritual life of Russia.[38] For all his unbelief, though, Anrep, like many non-believing Russians, had strong leanings to mysticism. Like many other Russians, too, his quasi-religious mysticism was focused on the cult of art. Undoubtedly sacral in nature, artistic expression was for him also inseparable from sensual, even sexual, feeling. In his memoir of Nedobrovo, Anrep reminisced upon a discussion about art as religion that he saw as a perfect expression of his own credo:

> I, an absolute non-believer, listen to Orthodox church music with reverence and delight, and take joy in the Easter service. I know I share these feelings with many other rational, scholarly people. Enjoyment of the scent of roses has nothing to do with reason either. How do you explain that? [...]
> I can recall almost every word of what Nedobrovo said, and later I was often to remember our conversation. His words would — fill my soul with joy when I was creating my mosaics on religious subjects for churches, and I, a godless man, would form the sacred faces with love and tenderness, and my hands, my soul, stretched out to icons as the most elevated expression of the human soul.[39]

---

36 Letters from John Kyne to Anrep, 13 May and 6 July 1952: NAL 86.NN.13/35 and 86.NN.13/40. On Anrep's co-operation with clients' wishes see, for example, his correspondence with General Stirling (NAL 86.NN.10) and with the National Gallery (NAL 86.NN.11); in the latter case, Anrep accommodated his client's objections even in one instance where his marginal notes indicated that he thought these comical.
37 The question of the precise time at which Anrep's image began to resemble Akhmatova is interesting. According to his correspondence with General Stirling (see previous note), Anrep had his mosaics made up on paper transfers, and would make final adjustments as they were fixed in place; it is possible, therefore, that the St Anne image was reworked at a very late stage.
38 Anrep, 'Pominanie', p. 183.
39 Anrep, in 'Iz Akhmatovskikh materialov v arkhive Guverskogo instituta', p. 179. Cf. Rosslyn,

Central here is the equation of religious feeling with 'enjoyment of the scent of roses', that is, with a sensual response to a physical stimulus transformed into an experience of spirituality. Similarly, Anrep's early prose poem, 'Foreword to the Book of Anrep', describes, in a laughably clumsy imitation of Old Testament language, the mystical vision of a prophet whose spiritual journey includes a bout of lying with the harlots ('Fearlessly they called me to lie with them. Unwisely I fondled the young wenches [...]. The bitches rent the tame rabbit').[40]

For Anrep (as for Akhmatova, in her poems addressed to him) sacred love and profane love were two alternative expressions of the same emotion. One indication of their intertwinedness for Anrep in life was his decision to renew contact with Akhmatova in 1945 by sending her a photograph of a mosaic that he had executed depicting the Sacred Heart.[41] In art, he was to emphasise the connection on many occasions. Two mosaic panels completed for the vestibule landings of the National Gallery show love figuring both among 'The Pleasures of Life' (as 'profane', that is romoiantic, love) and among 'The Duties of Life' (as 'sacred', that is family, love). But it is Anrep's two contrasting portraits of Akhmatova that represent his subtlest and most artistically powerful expression of the closeness of 'sacred' and 'profane'. Here Anrep, himself turned by Akhmatova (in *White Flock* and *Plantain Leaf*) into a metaphor for the duality of love, confected an answering image of Akhmatova.

If Akhmatova's sense of betrayal by Anrep inspired many fine poems in her, the obscure sense of guilt felt by him was the source of equally impressive art. The creation of these mosaics was a movingly direct response to Akhmatova's poetry, as well as to the memory of contact with her in life. If the National Gallery mosaic shows how the poet's image had, in her own words, 'come to the aid of [Anrep's] non-belief', the placing of Akhmatova's portrait in the St Anne chapel in Mullingar was an equally literal realisation of a vision described in the last two stanzas of another poem belonging to the 'Anrep cycle':

> Стал у церкви темной и высокой
> На гранит блестящих ступеней
> И молил о наступленье срока
> Встречи с первой радостью своей.
>
> А над смуглым золотом престола
> Разгорался Божий сад лучей:
> 'Здесь она, здесь свет веселый
> Серых звезд — ее очей'.[42]

[He went to stand by the tall dark church | On the granite of glittering steps, | And prayed that the time should come | For his meeting with his first joy. || And above the dusky gold of the altar | The divine garden of rays blazed up: | 'Here she is, here is the dancing light | Of grey stars — of her eyes!']

'A propos of Anna Akhmatova', p. 32, and Anrep's own article, 'Russian Ikons', *Artworks*, 21 (1930), 40–46, an appreciation both of the aesthetic value of icons as 'artists' visions' and of their ethical value as the product of ascetic self-denial.
40   Anrep, 'Foreword to the Book of Anrep', *Poetry and Drama*, 3 (September 1913), 272–89 (p. 277).
41   Anrep, 'Chernoe kol'tso', p. 449.
42   Akhmatova, 'Dolgo shel cherez polya i sela', *SP*, p. 118.

Anrep's St Anne mosaic, though, exceeds the promise of this charming, but dated, neo-Blokian poem. It has the cultural depth of 'Compassion' without that image's disturbing fretfulness, its elements of inverted self-pity. Rich with association, yet in absolute command of its material and genuinely original, 'St Anna' makes a worthy companion to Akhmatova's own *Poem Without a Hero* (*Poema bez geroya*). The need for expiation and redress that had been the driving-force behind both the National Gallery and the Mullingar portraits had been triumphantly satisfied. Though Anrep himself could never rest easy in life, the wrongs that he believed unappeasable had been transformed, and transcended, in his art.[43]

I would like to thank Father Patrick Moore, Diocesan Archivist, Cathedral of Christ the King, Mullingar, Annabel Anrep, Sir Isaiah Berlin, Dr Wendy Rosslyn, and Dr Ian Thompson for their helpfulness in answering questions during the preparation of this article. Acknowledgements are also due to the National Art Library and Annabel Anrep for permission to quote from the Anrep letters, and to the National Gallery, London, for permission to reproduce the photograph of the mosaic 'Compassion' and for generously waiving the reproduction fee. (The phrase 'Redress of Art' plays on Seamus Heaney's lecture as Professor of Poetry at the University of Oxford, 'The Redress of Poetry').

---

43 Anrep's St Anne mosaic also well illustrates the remarkably high level of many ecclesiastical artefacts in Ireland, a country where standards were set by the excellent work of such native artist-craftsmen as the stained-glass specialists Hany Clarke and Evie Hone: on Clarke, see Paul Larmour, *The Arts and Crafts Movement in Ireland* (Belfast: Friar's Bush, 1992), pp. 183–91; on Hone, *Irish Women Artists from the Eighteenth Century to the Present Day*, exhibition catalogue (Dublin: National Gallery, 1987), pp. 137–38, 168.

CHAPTER 7

At Peace with the Wolf? Prokofiev's 'Official' Soviet Works for Children

[2003]

Western commentators on Russia and the USSR have often concentrated attention on works that attracted the disfavour of state bodies and the establishment: those written for the 'desk drawer', left unperformed, or banned. Yet many writers and artists best-known for their conflicts with the authorities also produced art that could accurately be described as 'official' — in the sense of state-sponsored and greeted with approval by Soviet government and Party bodies. Obvious cases in point are Prokofiev's post-war compositions intended for children, *Winter Bonfire* (*Zimnii koster*, 1949) and *On Guard for Peace* (*Na strazhe mira* 1950). Settings of poems by Samuil Marshak, then the most authoritative and highly regarded Soviet children's poet, the two works were commissioned by Soviet radio, had a prestigious first performance under Samuil Samosud in 1950, and were issued by the state publishers for music, Muzgiz, in the following year. Both at the time of their composition and afterwards, they were warmly praised within the Soviet Union; the award of a Stalin Prize (second class) in 1950 was another token of the establishment's esteem.

Respectful comments continued being made well after the Stalin era too. For instance, Nina Rogozhina in 1964 commended *Winter Bonfire* as displaying Prokofiev's 'inexhaustible imaginative range', and gave a lyrical summary of *On Guard for Peace*, commenting, 'One need hardly say how radiant and spiritually pure is the coloration of this music, portraying children at such a serious and important business'. (The section she had in mind was the one where children learn the alphabet by repeating the phrase 'WE DO NOT NEED WAR'.)[1] Izrail Nest'ev, for his

---

[1] N. Rogozhina, *Vokal'no-simfonicheskie proizvedeniya S. Prokof'eva* (Moscow & Leningrad: Muzyka, 1964), pp. 109, 115; for an enthusiastic response to *Winter Bonfire*, see also V. I. Berkov, 'Syuita "Zimniii koster"' Sergeya Prokof'eva', in his *Izbrannye stat'i i issledovaniya* (Moscow: Sovetskii kompozitor, 1977), pp. 439–72. Cf. Sergei Morozov's life of Prokof'ev in the *Zhizn' zamechatel'nykh lyudei* [Lives of Remarkable People] series of popular biographies, no. 429 (Moscow: Molodaya gvardiya, 1967), p. 256. For a more interesting defence of *Zimnii koster*, for its 'beautiful and noble melodies', see the new *Lives of Remarkable People* (ZML) biography, Igor' Vishnevetsky, *Sergei Prokof'ev* (Moscow: Molodaya gvardiya, 2009), p. 645; *Na strazhe mira*, on the other hand, is described as 'tortured out of' Prokof'ev (ibid., p. 610).

part, termed *Winter Bonfire* 'one of the most brilliant examples of Soviet art intended for the very young'.[2]

Among Western commentators, on the other hand, views of the two works have been equivalently disparaging. Michel Dorigné regarded *Winter Bonfire* as 'an aesthetic débâcle', while *On Guard of Peace* showed Prokofiev 'reaching the ultimate stage of musical compromise', and 'to all intents and purposes putting his talent in leg-irons'.[3] Only slightly less devastatingly, Harlow Robinson considers *Winter Bonfire* 'simplistic', albeit with 'a certain illustrative charm', and *On Guard for Peace* as 'bland, homogeneous', and much inferior to the official music Prokofiev wrote in the 1930s.[4] While rather kinder to *Winter Bonfire* (which he credited with 'plenty of unaffected charm'), Daniel Jaffé lambasted *On Guard for Peace* as 'one of the most overly sentimental works in Prokofiev's archive'.[5]

It might on the face of it seem verging on the blasphemous to consider these two works in the same breath as *Peter and the Wolf*, universally accounted a masterpiece by Western critics as well as by Soviet ones. Yet exactly this connection was made by Shostakovich, who in a eulogy written a year after Prokofiev's death observed, 'Not one Soviet composer has dedicated so many sublime works to children', listing, alongside *Peter and the Children's Songs* of 1936–39, *Winter Bonfire* and 'sections of' *On Guard for Peace*.[6] Generally, however, where the post-war works are held to manifest abject, self-immolatory accommodation with official requirements, *Peter and the Wolf* is understood as a work of outstanding freshness and originality, as — to adapt Nest'ev's sentiments on *Winter Bonfire* — 'one of the most brilliant examples of world art intended for the very young'.[7]

I am not arguing here for a reassessment of *On Guard for Peace* and *Winter Bonfire*, a discovery in them of unsuspected musical sophistication, and/or encoded messages of disaffection with Soviet power. I think one has to take on trust Prokofiev's own connection of these works, in a 1950 essay, to the surge of post-war patriotism and relief at the end of conflict, to the emotional sweep represented by the drive from his dacha into Moscow, a microcosm of the Soviet Union in its combination of woods, tilled fields, and city blocks, and to the conviction that the Soviet artist should be first and foremost a 'citizen':

> What is the content of this humble work [*On Guard for Peace*]? It tells of the difficult days of the Second World War, of the tears of mothers and orphans, of the towns burnt to ashes, the great trials that fell on the shoulders of the

---

2   Israel V. Nestyev [sic], *Prokofiev*, trans. by F. Jonas (Stanford, CA: Stanford University Press, 1960), p. 414.
3   Michel Dorigné, *Serge Prokofiev* (Paris: Fayard, 1994), p. 691.
4   Harlow Robinson, *Sergei Prokofiev: A Biography* (London: Robert Hale, 1987), p. 487.
5   Daniel Jaffé, *Sergey Prokofiev* (London: Phaidon, 1998), p. 208. More recently, in *The People's Artist: Prokofiev's Soviet Years* (New York: Oxford University Press, 2008), Chapter 8, Simon Morrison, while giving a detailed account of both works' genesis, dismisses *Na strazhe mira* and *Zimnii koster* as 'pallid'.
6   See S. S. Prokof'ev, *Materialy, dokumenty, vospominaniya*, ed. by S. I. Shlifshtein, 2nd, expanded, edn (Moscow: Muzgiz, 1961), p. 399.
7   See, among many others, Dorigné, *Serge Prokofiev*, p. 456 ff., Jaffé, *Sergei Prokofiev*, p. 142 ff., Robinson, *Sergei Prokofiev*, p. 319 ff.

people. Later sections are dedicated to Stalingrad, to victory, to the radiant joy of reconstruction, to the happy childhood of our children. I wanted to express in this piece my thoughts on war and peace, my certainty that there would be no more war, that the peoples of the earth would stand up for peace, would save civilisation, children, our future.[8]

For obvious reasons to do with the nature of the leadership as well as the scale of war losses, there was a gulf between the Soviet perception of the Second World War in the late 1940s and early 1950s, and the British or French (to name two other European nations that were on the victorious side in 1945) perception of the Second World War at the same time. Or to be more accurate, there was a gulf between the non-combatant cultural establishment's view of the war in the Soviet Union and in France or Britain. Soviet citizens who had actually fought in the Second World War (for instance, the poets Boris Slutsky and Aleksandr Galich) often had a sober and sombre view of the conflict. But personal experiences that ran contrary to the heroic myth of national suffering transcended had to remain largely unarticulated (at least in public) until the late 1980s.[9]

While celebration of the end of war might be sentimental (and often blot out the particularity of suffering as well), Soviet war losses were so enormous, and the desire to escape a future conflict so great, that the war myth and the slogan 'we don't want war' had a widespread popular resonance. International Children's Day, celebrated for the first time on 1 June 1950 (and evidently the occasion for the commissioning of *On Guard for Peace*), was used within the Soviet Union to underline the state's supremacy in caring for the welfare of children, and to attack the record of the capitalist West. But another theme of International Children's Day, the need to avoid war in order to ensure a proper future for children, was less nationalist in tone, and this association was to gain greater importance in celebrations of the festival during the post-Stalin era.[10] However hypocritical the Soviet peace movement's position was (advocating as it did both world peace and the retention of the state's own 'nuclear defence'), it had widespread resonance with citizens of the motherland.

This means that, at the level of thematics, we are not dealing with a straightforward 'compromise'. Prokofiev's *On Guard for Peace* is no more 'conventional' in the sense of reflecting prevailing sentiments than is Britten's *War Requiem*. If anything, *Winter Bonfire*, with its obvious relevance to the approaching thirtieth anniversary of the Pioneer movement, not to speak of its conscientious evocation of the Soviet 'happy childhood', could be seen as a more 'opportunistic' work. This argument of course does not deal with the accusation of *musical* compromise in *On Guard for Peace*.

8   S. S. Prokof'ev, in *Novosti*, 10 (1950); quoted here from *Materialy, dokumenty, vospominaniya*, p. 255.
9   As discussed, for example, in Nina Tumarkin, *The Living and the Dead: The Rise and Fall of the Cult of World War Two in Russia* (New York: Basic Books, 1994).
10 For the first International Children's Day, see, for example, *Pionerskaya pravda*, 31, 18 April 1950, p. 1 (preparatory materials), and 41, 1 June 1950, pp. 2–3 (materials mostly devoted to the suffering of Western children, though two pieces deal with fathers' defence of children in the army and mothers' protection of them on the home front); and compare *Pionerskaya pravda*, 43, 29 May 1953, p. 1, where the headline item is 'Detyam nuzhen mir!' [Children need peace!].

However, even from a musical point of view, these are not perhaps such simplistic works as they at first seem. Prokofiev's lush, silvery orchestration combines a knowing and sophisticated appropriation of devices that had proved their popularity not only among Hollywood composers of the 1930s and 1940s, but also among their Soviet imitators (for instance, Isaak Dunaevsky, whose scores for film musicals, such as *Volga, Volga!* and *Circus* were among the great popular hits of the day) with specifically 'Prokofievian' elements in what Russian musicologists term 'intonation' (melodic progression).

That said, there probably is too big a gap in taste for present-day Western (or indeed Russian) audiences to find the two 1950s oratorios congenial. In particular, the representation of childhood is, for an audience weaned on *The Turn of the Screw*, disturbingly pious and one-sided: the pure boy soprano, the good children frolicking away joyfully or piping of decidedly abstract war suffering. Especially crass is the finale of *On Guard for Peace*, with its thinly-scored and yet hysterical rising arpeggios wrapped around the name of Stalin: it really does have all the individual appeal of a war memorial copied from a Soviet pattern book.

It's hard to deny that in some ways, these works are aesthetically unrewarding. However, I do not think this emanates purely from a 'compromise' with contemporary cultural Realpolitik. In the martyrology of Soviet artists, Prokofiev's trials ranked fairly low: he was never under nearly such extreme personal threat as Sergei Eisenstein, and yet two of Eisenstein's most impressive films (*Alexander Nevsky* and *Ivan the Terrible*) were made at a period when Eisenstein desperately needed to emphasise his conformity with the Soviet regime.[11] (The same argument can be made about the late 1930s music of Shostakovich.) In any case, *Peter and the Wolf* was, as we shall see, every bit as 'conformist' as the earlier works, if by 'conformist' we mean 'relevant in terms of the mainstream trends of the time'. The history of this work's genesis in relation to the cultural politics of the day is important not because it underwrites a case that Prokofiev surrendered, whether from subservience or external pressure, to political *force majeure*, but because an understanding of the complex relationship between art and politics is an essential requirement for an honest view of Prokofiev as Soviet artist.

11   The background to the composition of *Alexander Nevsky* is discussed by Maiya Turovskaya in 'Mosfil'm — 1937' (see *Sovetskoe bogatstvo: Stat'i o kul'ture, literature i kino: k shestidesyatiletiyu Khansa Gyuntera*, ed. by M. Balina, E. Dobrenko, and Yu. Marshov (St Petersburg: Akademicheskii proekt, 2002), pp. 280–82). Turovskaya shows how Eisenstein's artistic enemies tried to use the case of *Bezhin Lug* in order to get the director into serious trouble (Boris Shumyatsky, then the head of the film censorship body GUK, denounced Eisenstein both in print and in the form of a secret letter to the Politburo on 19 April 1937 proposing that Eisenstein be banned from working as a film director). The Politburo, however, rejected this proposal (and Shumyatsky was to be arrested and shot in the Great Purges), substituting for it the order that Eisenstein be assigned another, more suitable project. *Alexander Nevsky*, based on an idea by Stalin and scripted by the thoroughly *bien pensant* Petr Pavlenko, and awarded a Stalin prize, was genuinely popular in the Soviet Union (it was Eisenstein's biggest distribution success) and is universally acknowledged as a masterpiece. As Turovskaya says, 'Eisenstein's cinematic genius would not change. It was the time that would change, with a new demand for a national myth, meaning that "mythologisation" would cease to be seen as subversion'. For a contrasting interpretation of *Ivan the Terrible*, see Joan Neuberger, *This Thing of Darkness: Eisenstein's Ivan the Terrible in Stalin's Russia* (Ithaca, NY: Cornell University Press, 2019).

The secondary literature on *Peter and the Wolf*, at any rate that accessible to a non-musicologist such as myself, is copious but perfunctory. Again and again, commentary amounts to little more than a paraphrase of the familiar story about how Natalie (really Natalia) Sats, director of the Children's Theatre in Moscow, commissioned the work, followed by some passing observations on the flair for characterisation demonstrated in the finished work, and its deft ability to play on the child's psychology (as though this were something stable and homogeneous).[12] So far as the origins of the text go, almost all commentators on *Peter and the Wolf* have taken on trust Sats's account, written more than twenty years after the event, and emphasising her own centrality to the creation of the work.[13] Prokofiev's own rather terse memoir, however, says more enigmatically, 'The need for children's music could be clearly felt, and in the spring of 1936 I got to work on the symphonic fairy-tale (*skazka*) *Peter and the Wolf*, op. 67, with a libretto written by myself'.[14]

Both Prokofiev and Sats had pressing reasons to emphasise the asymmetrical nature of the collaboration. Prokofiev, writing in the late Stalin era, at a stage when Sats was still in exile after her arrest as an 'enemy of the people' in 1937, would hardly have wanted to implicate himself in what could have looked like an anti-Soviet conspiracy. Conversely, Sats, trying to rebuild her career during the Khrushchev thaw, had every reason to underline her part in the creation of a famous Soviet masterpiece. A more disinterested account of what happened is probably now beyond recall, though two letters from Sats to Prokofiev written in the summer and autumn of 1936 suggest that Sats was the main engine behind the collaboration, if not necessarily the source of the original idea.[15]

Whichever way, *Peter and the Wolf* was understood by Prokofiev (albeit with defensive hindsight) as 'answering a need', that is, relevant to the immediate cultural context. Whatever role Sats took in the creative side of *Peter and the Wolf*, there is no doubt of her involvement in its performance. Sats was not simply a talented, innovative, and extraordinarily energetic young artist (later in life, she seems to have slightly overstated how very young she was when she began running the Children's Theatre shortly after the Revolution, but she was certainly not much more than a teenager). She was also a member of the inner circle of the Stalinist establishment. Married to Izrail Veitser, Commissar of Trade from 1935, she was

---

12 See, for example, V. Blok, *Muzyka Prokof'eva dlya detei* (Moscow: Muzyka, 1969), pp. 22–48. Blok republished the remarks here on at least two further occasions in an abridged, but otherwise unaltered, form: see, for example, *Muzyka — teatr — deti: N. Sats i ee tvorcheskaya deyatel'nost'*, ed. by V. I. Viktorov (Moscow: Sovetskii kompozitor, 1977), pp. 115–32. Even Vishnevetsky, *Sergei Prokof'ev*, includes just a couple of pages (pp. 415–17) on *Petya i volk*, addressing its aims in terms simply of musical education. There is a fuller account, again mainly concentrating on the musical resolution, in Morrison, *The People's Artist*, p. 48.

13 See, for example, Prokofiev, *Materialy, dokumenty, vospominaniya*, pp. 509–13 (the account is repeated in, for example, Natal'ya Sats, *Novelly moei zhizny* (Moscow: Iskusstvo, 1984), pp. 333–42).

14 Prokofiev, *Materialy, dokumenty, vospominaniya*, p. 195.

15 Russian State Archive of Literature and Arts (RGALI), Moscow, f. 1929, op. 1, d. 683, l. 1–2 (for English translations, see the Appendix at the end of this chapter). Both letters date from a stage when work on *Petya i volk* was well under way. As the second letter suggests ('please do ring me sometime'), most business must have been done on the telephone.

also the mistress of Marshal Tukhachevsky (who was in turn a patron of Dmitry Shostakovich). Before her arrest as an 'enemy of the people' in 1937, Sats was one of the best-connected individuals in the cultural world of Moscow, and one of that world's most prominent spokesmen and arbitrators. In 1934, she took part in, and presented a speech at, the First Congress of Soviet Writers; in January 1935, Maxim Gorky recommended her to the literary functionary A. S. Shcherbakov, as a member of the editorial board of a proposed almanac of children's literature. And on 3 February 1936, her Moscow Children's Theatre was transformed by ministerial decree into an institution of pan-Soviet status, the Central Theatre for Children.[16] All this illustrated not only Sats's political clout (and, one suspects, her personal charm — she was a very considerable beauty at this stage of her life), but also the central importance of children's affairs at this particular period, and the huge ideological significance of literature and art for children. The period between the spring of 1936 and the spring of 1937 might even be described as the Stalinist 'year of the child', so marked was the presence of children in propaganda imagery (this was precisely the point when the 'leader with small child' icon began to be a favoured Soviet genre), and so prominent was the coverage of children's affairs in the major metropolitan newspapers.[17]

As a commentator on theatre aimed at children, and on children and the arts generally, Sats had at this point of her life enormous influence, probably only equalled by that of Samuil Marshak and Kornei Chukovsky. Her theatre was a regular point on the itinerary of well-known foreigners visiting the Soviet Union, an indication of its perceived propaganda value.[18] Sats was not so much the mouthpiece of official policy as an official policymaker, or at any rate a translator of abstract policy directives into artistic practice. Her speech at the First Congress of Writers not only celebrated the children's theatre as essentially an invention of the Soviet regime, but also stressed its ideological value. She warned her audience

---

16   For the speech at the First Congress of Soviet Writers, see *Pervyi vsesoyuznyi s"ezd sovetskikh pisatelei 1934: stenograficheskii otchet* (Moscow: Khudozhestvennaya literatura, 1934), pp. 471–73; for Gorky's letter to Shcherbakov, see his *Sobranie sochinenii*, 30 vols (Moscow: Khudozhestvennaya literatura, 1949–63), XXX, 371; for the ministerial decree, see *Muzyka — teatr — deti*, ed. by Viktorov, p. 25. On 18 February 1936, 'Novosti teatr' in *Pravda*, p. 6, reported Sats's appointment as director of the 'Big [Bol'shoi] Children's Theatre' which was to be opened in the annexe of the Moscow Arts Theatre.

17   On the rise of the ruler and child icon, see Catriona Kelly, 'Riding the Magic Carpet: The Stalin Cult for Little Children', *Slavic and East European Journal*, 49.2 (2005), 199–224. Prior to 1935, *Pravda* and *Izvestiya* had contained only occasional child-centred items; during the 'year of the child', coverage was intense. In April 1935 alone, for instance, at least nine prominent items in *Pravda* dealt with children's affairs, from discipline and juvenile delinquency to hobbies and confectionary ('Pervomaiskie syurprizy detyam', 3 April 1935, p. 3) (see my *Children's World*, Chapter 3). Entirely in the governing mood was Sats's article, 'Tsentral'nyi detskii teatr', *Pravda*, 28 February 1936, which, among other things, emphasised that a portrait of 'the one who surrounds their lives with such joy, the leader of the peoples, Stalin' would greet children as they entered the premises, and not just any portrait, but 'one where Stalin is surrounded by children'. On 9 June 1936, a *Pravda* note, 'Khudozhdestvennoe oformlenie detskikh konditerskikh izdelii', reported (p. 2) that among those advising on packaging for children's sweets were Sats and Prokofiev.

18   See, for example, Helen Nichol, 'Theaters for Children', *Soviet Travel*, 1 (1933), 31–33, 43.

that 'Nazi Germany intends to devote deep attention to plays for children', and reminded them of the importance of 'the struggle for youth, the struggle for children'.[19] The repertoire of her theatre in turn reflected the views set out in her public statements. Themes outlined in an English-language publicity brochure of 1934 included class struggle (Robin Hood as a defender of the oppressed), the part played by children in socialist construction, 'equal rights for boys and girls', and internationalism (*The Little Black Boy and the Monkey* (*Negritenok i obez"yana*), for instance, was a story demonstrating 'the senselessness of race prejudice'). In line with this commitment to egalitarianism, the theatre performed, for instance, versions of Pushkin's anti-clerical folk tale, *The Priest and his Worker Balda* (*Skazka o pope i o rabotnike ego Balda*), and Longfellow's *Hiawatha*. Pre-performance activities included sessions of 'Prepared for Defence' (drills with wooden bayonets). Inevitably, pieces about the junior wing of the Komsomol, the Young Pioneers, were also in the repertory, for example an operetta under the title *Pioneers*, which 'deride[d] the sort of education that aims at teaching "good form"', and juxtaposed this to the healthy life of the Pioneer camp, or *We are Strength* [*Ya — malo, my — sila*], which showed 'Pioneers who go abroad to far countries'. Perhaps most significantly in terms of the immediate background to *Peter and the Wolf*, another play, *The Little Communist*, had as its heroine a small girl who argued vehemently with her grandmother, while *The Prankster* (*Buzonada*) showed thirteen-year-old Linka Smekhov ejected from his Pioneer detachment after a row with his Pioneer leader (this second piece involved audience participation, with children invited to voice their views and to take part in a vote about whether Linka should have been expelled).[20]

The core of the Sats repertory was thus made up of pieces with a strong political drift, including work portraying children in successful conflict with adults. At the same time, Sats, like a lot of those pushing forward the cause of artistic education and artistic works directed at children during the 1920s and 1930s, was insistent that the work produced should be child-centred. In her 1934 speech, she lambasted excessive moralising in work for the stage: 'This is not art and it's no use at all'. She emphasised the importance of fantasy (albeit with the classic Soviet sophism, 'Our achievements in life often seem fantastic, yet they remain fully real').[21] 'We know that even physiologically a child is not merely a diminutive grown-up. All the more does this hold true of his inner world, which is peculiar and complicated', she wrote in 1934.[22] What this meant was that work should be vivid and emotionally appealing, without being sentimental (children needed 'nuts to crack with their teeth' and not 'pap').[23]

---

19   *Pervyi vsesoyuznyi s"ezd sovetskikh pisatelei 1934*, p. 473.
20   *The Moscow Theatre for Children* (Moscow: Cooperative Publishing Society of Foreign Workers in the USSR, 1934), pp. 5–9, 19–21, 15, 24–25, 39, 45, 72. I have retained the translations in the brochure even when (as with *We Are Strength*) they are slightly adrift from strict accuracy.
21   *Pervyi vsesoyuznyi s"ezd sovetskikh pisatelei 1934*, p. 472.
22   *The Moscow Theatre for Children*, p. 6. Cf. *Pervyi vsesoyuznyi s"ezd sovetskikh pisatelei 1934*, p. 472, dwelling on the 'age-related specificities' of the child's view of life.
23   *The Moscow Theatre for Children*, p. 8.

Sats was not a lone voice arguing in this way. Rather, her statements reflected what was becoming orthodoxy at this period: children (in the early phases of childhood, anyway), were different from adults, and should not be treated like miniature adults and encouraged to grow up as quickly as possible, but allowed to enjoy their different world-view whilst it lasted.[24] In a speech made at the First Congress of Children's Writers organised by the Komsomol in January 1936, Agniya Barto, a leading official writer for children, expressed her disappointment at meeting a group of bright twelve-year-olds who could talk of nothing but their achievements at school and their visits to the theatre, and who spoke in a disagreeably unchildish, prating, manner. Where, Barto asked, had the 'healthy cheerfulness of childhood' vanished to? Could it be that the practice of training children to 'make formal reports, military style' (*raportovat'*) had led them into this disagreeable practice of spouting officialese?[25] The genre that Barto, Sats, Chukovsky, Marshak, and others, argued was most capable of fusing the two objectives — providing children with material of topical relevance, with a political cutting edge, but doing so in a manner that would be appealing to the child's mind — was the 'Soviet fairy tale' (*sovetskaya skazka*), or in Sats's case, 'the Soviet dramatic fairy tale' (*sovetskaya dramaticheskaya skazka*), a form towards which, she claimed in 1934, her theatre had now begun working.[26]

Sats, like Chukovsky and Marshak, was careful to distinguish the 'Soviet fairy tale' from its pre-revolutionary equivalent. She began her speech at the First Congress of Writers by lambasting the stereotypical 'dream play' in which the heroine saw pass before her eyes 'a parade of little strawberries and raspberries, flower buds, mushrooms, and other sickly nonsense of that kind'.[27] In Marshak's words, the *skazka* did not have to avoid didacticism (after all, 'Little Red Riding Hood' had an unmistakable moral), but it needed to present morals in a particular way. 'Little Red Riding Hood' succeeded because of 'the clarity of the circumstances, the sequentiality and logic of the motivation', so that 'any child can put itself in the place of the heroine of a tale, can play at "being Red Riding Hood"'. The *skazka* was characterised by 'concrete, cleverly and carefully selected details'.[28] In other

---

24 In particular, this meant moving away from celebrations of children's political activism, including the notorious tale of Pavlik Morozov, who had supposedly denounced his father to the authorities: 'My father has betrayed the cause of October!'. See Catriona Kelly, *Comrade Pavlik: The Rise and Fall of a Soviet Boy Hero* (London: Granta, 2005), Chapter 5. It was also the effect of a much greater emphasis on academic values in the teaching of older children, leaving the nursery and younger primary-school ages as the times for fun and play.
25 *Pravda*, 29 January 1936, p. 2. Cf. Nataliya Sats's anecdote of a nine-year-old boy who visited her flat to 'organise an official connection' with her, but got distracted by a parrot in a cage and forgot what he had come for (*Pervyi vsesoyuznyi s"ezd sovetskikh pisatelei 1934*, p. 472).
26 *The Moscow Children's Theatre*, p. 7.
27 *Pervyi vsesoyuznyi s"ezd sovetskikh pisatelei 1934*, p. 471. In the context of traditional Russian orally-transmitted stories, folklorists avoid the term 'fairy tale' because there were no fairies (as opposed to, say, wood and water spirits, and house spirits) in local lore. However, given that 'fairies' is also a genteel euphemism for the formidable spiritual forces known in Celtic lore as *sí*, and that educated Russian parents brought their children up on *The Sleeping Beauty* and *Beauty and the Beast* as well as *Ivan the Fool*, the term 'fairy tale' is an appropriate equivalent for *skazka* in its literary manifestation.
28 *Pervyi vsesoyuznyi s"ezd sovetskikh pisatelei 1934*, p. 28.

words, the *skazka* should have a recognisable and inspiring hero, a simple and easily-followed plot, straightforward character motivation, and entertaining incidentals.

It is important to bear this context in mind when considering the political meaning of *Peter and the Wolf*. Investigating the politics of the piece in the sense of searching for elaborate allegorical meanings — the duck as the timorous bourgeois, the wolf as the ever-threatening saboteur, and so on — would be a fool's errand.[29] Certainly, there is no scarcity of Soviet children's texts that would bear such interpretations, but allegories of this kind, where intended, were hammered home mercilessly to the child viewer. Take Elisaveta Vasilieva and Samuil Marshak's play *The Cat's Home* (*Koshkin dom*, 1922), for example — the resonance of which is now somewhat traduced because the title has become the brand-name for a chain of Russian fast-food restaurants, but which is in fact a kind of Rich Man and Lazarus fable for small children about the fat, smug, bourgeois she-cat who won't help her poor hungry kitten cousins, but eventually finds herself billeted on them when her house burns down and her fair-weather friends won't help out. The moral would probably be obvious even to a Martian.[30] If children were intended to perceive social types behind the characters in *Peter and the Wolf*, one would expect, at the very least, some loaded adjectives in the commentary — the 'smug and overfed' (*sytyi*) cat, perhaps, the 'rapacious' (*khishchnyi*) wolf, or the 'cross, cruel' (*zloi, zhestokii*) grandfather. (An anti-fascist play in the Sats repertoire, according to one foreign visitor generally very admiring of the theatre, was 'bigoted' and 'crudely done propaganda', in which 'fair-haired German children were shown as little monsters, hideously ugly and utterly stupid'.)[31] In any case, by 1936, the year of the Stalinist Constitution, with its emphasis on Soviet unity and social harmony, 'class war' plots of the 'fat bourgeois versus skinny proletarian' were obsolescent if not obsolete. They had become the province of self-educated worker authors in the provinces, not of sophisticated metropolitan artists such as Prokofiev and Sats. Indeed, Marshak had explicitly condemned allegory at the First Congress of Soviet Writers, saying that it made 'details play a secondary, merely decorative role, so the action itself is stripped of concreteness'.[32]

All in all, reading *Peter and the Wolf* as a kind of *skazka à clef* is unjustified. Its political meaning is of a very different and more general kind. The conflict between the boy and his grandfather belongs to an established Soviet tradition showing young pitted against old. For instance, a story by a schoolchild under the

---

29 As in, for example, Victor Seroff, *Sergei Prokofiev: A Soviet Tragedy* (New York: Funk & Wagnalls, 1968), p. 136; or Jaffé, *Sergey Prokofiev*, p. 142, who thinks the hunters might represent 'the state police'. Dorigné, *Serge Prokofiev*, p. 456, understandably cites views of this kind from a position of sardonic scepticism.

30 The play originally appeared in Vasil'eva and Marshak's *Teatr dlya detei: sbornik p'es* (Krasnodar: Kubano-Chernomorskii otdel narodnogo obrazovaniya, 1922; there were further editions in 1923, 1924, and 1927). Marshak republished it (under his own name alone) in 1945 (by then, association with a former 'decadent' poet would have been impolitic, and Vasil'eva had in any case died in 1928).

31 Ethel Mannin, 'Playtime of the Child in Modern Russia', in *Playtime in Russia*, ed. by Hubert Griffith (London: Methuen, 1935), pp. 135–85 (p. 153). The order of the quotations has been altered in my text.

32 *Pervyi vsesoyuznyi s"ezd sovetskikh pisatelei 1934*, p. 28.

title 'They Didn't Cow Me', and published in an anthology of essays and narratives by rural children put out by the magazine *Friendly Kids* (*Druzhnye rebyata*), in 1931, had a boy confronting the disapproval of his elder relations after he joined the Pioneer movement. His parents had seen recruitment as a covert method of conscription: children would be 'fighting for the liberation of workers and peasants from all over the world' in five years' time. His grandfather expressed sardonic contempt about Pioneer ties, which for him were 'like those collars farmers put on calves, they are, they're collars they put on children to make them brave defenders of Soviet power'. No, grandad, the boy insisted: they were Pioneer ties, not collars for children.[33] Indeed, in propaganda texts juvenile interventions often went far beyond this sort of purely reactive expression of staunch Communism. Articles in children's periodicals, such as *Pioneer Pravda* or the magazine *Pioneer*, exhorted children to pester their mothers into attending political meetings, to carry out onslaughts against displays of icons, and to mount campaigns for appropriate hygienic conditions in the home. Questionnaires and essay-writing sessions were organised in schools to encourage pupils to disgorge information about conditions within the family; propaganda articles represented as heroic children who brought into the public domain ideological misdemeanours (a 1930 issue of the journal *The Children's Friend* (*Drug detei*) fulsomely praised some children who had denounced their parents' furtive attempts to provide a substitute Christmas tree by decorating a pot-plant with toys and baubles).[34]

Conflicts of this kind were everywhere in children's literature (and in journalism for children) throughout the 1920s and early 1930s. Robinson is therefore way off course when he suggests *Peter and the Wolf* is 'a subtly subversive tract, encouraging children to rely on their wits and not on the greater experience (and inertia) of their elders'.[35] Equally, one should not overstate the nature of Peter's rebellion, as Jaffé does when he suggests that 'Peter's rebellious, anti-authoritarian stance might appear to chime with the official canonization of Pavlik Morozov (a fourteen year old whose denunciation of his father to the authorities "inspired" the founding of the Pioneers)'.[36] Pavlik Morozov's alleged denunciation of his father to the authorities could not have 'inspired' the founding of the Pioneers, since this had happened nine years earlier, when Pavlik was all of three. Besides, while Jaffé concedes that 'Peter displays considerable loyalty to his animal friends and has an individual ingenuity', he does not observe how different the confrontation between Peter and his grandfather is to the intense, violent conflicts between Pavlik and his older male relatives that were represented in the legends about the boy's life that were published between 1932 and 1936 (which is to say, those that Prokofiev could have read).[37]

33 Kh. Dan'ko, 'Menya ne zapugali', in *Sami pisali: Malen'kie interesnye rasskazy i priklyucheniya: ikh pisali sami chitateli i detkory 'Druzhnykh rebyat'*, 2nd edn (Moscow: Krest'yanskaya gazeta, 1931), p. 13.
34 T. Karpinskaya, 'Kak oboshlis' bez elki', *Drug detei*, 2 (1930), 18.
35 Robinson, *Sergei Prokofiev*, p. 322.
36 Jaffé, *Sergey Prokofiev*, p. 142.
37 There were two book-length lives of Pavlik by 1936: Pavel Solomein, *V kulatskom gnezde* (Sverdlovsk: Uralogiz, 1933); and Aleksandr Yakovlev, *Pioner Pavlik Morozov. Povest'* (Moscow: Detizdat, 1936). There had also been a good deal of coverage about Pavlik in the Pioneer press,

In these, Pavlik was beaten and abused by his father, by his grandfather, and by his cousin Danila, and *still* could not be dissuaded from heroically defending the cause that he, as a Pioneer, knew to be right. In Solomein's brutally naturalistic version of Pavlik's life, the boy even got hot fat tipped over him when trying to avoid his father's pounding fists.[38] And in all the versions of the tale, Pavlik ended up by being 'bestially murdered' (to use the language of the time).[39] In other words, he was a political martyr, a miniature Soviet saint, not a mischievous small boy whose disobedience was of a low-level, everyday kind, and who had nothing more to contend with than a slightly grumpy old grandad. Had Prokofiev known of Pavlik Morozov's existence before he wrote *Peter and the Wolf* (and the first substantial life of the boy to be published in the capital, as opposed to the provinces, came out only in 1936), he would also have realised that Pavlik's life was absolutely not the suitable starting-point for a *skazka* in any circumstances, let alone circumstances that were beginning to be controlled by the neo-classically strict genre conventions of Socialist Realism. Pavlik's life was the stuff of tragedy, not of light comedy: of a brooding tone-poem or a heroic hymn, not a 'symphonic *skazka*'.

Even Peter's status as a Pioneer is, it should be said, rather marginal. Certainly, he is named as 'Pioneer Pete' ('Pioner Petya') in the very first sentence of the libretto, and the references to his behaviour do, in the Russian original, smack of Pioneer cliché here and there. For instance, Petya decides to 'reconnoitre' in the meadow, and the bird tells him 'All's quiet' (but to capture the military undertones, one might render this, 'All quiet on the meadow front'). (Pioneers were being encouraged to help their elders with 'surveillance' during the mid-1930s, as Prokofiev would have known from many of the plays in the repertory of the Children's Theatre.) And, of course, the parade at the end has a slightly 'Pioneerish' flavour (a contemporary listener would probably have imagined Petya in a red tie, and no doubt blowing a bugle or beating a drum as well). But the 'Pioneer' character of the boy really does not go beyond hints: it is not surprising that, in the first draft of *Peter and the Wolf*, the word 'Pioneer' is repeatedly inserted as an afterthought, as though Prokofiev had more or less forgotten that was what the boy was supposed to be. As with the question of 'class war', one has to understand that official children's literature at the time did not usually work by hints: Pioneer identity was, so to speak, shouted from the rooftops. Yet at the same time, *Peter and the Wolf* was written at a time when the character of the Pioneer movement was itself changing to accommodate the new understanding of childhood as a timeless paradise. There was now much more emphasis on play and leisure, and much less emphasis on politics. Accordingly, a politically lukewarm individual such as Prokofiev would have been able to portray a Pioneer without feeling queasy.

All in all, *Peter and the Wolf* could be considered a perfectly orthodox text: the point is simply that the orthodoxy of the mid-1930s was more accommodating

---

particularly during 1932–33. See my *Comrade Pavlik*.
38   Solomein, *V kulatskom gnezde*, p. 12.
39   In fact, as I show in *Comrade Pavlik*, the murder was the one accurate part of the legend, and the event with which Pavlik's cult began.

to imaginative modernist artists, such as Prokofiev and for that matter Sats, than was the orthodoxy of the late 1940s. One should not confuse evaluation — the universally accepted view that *Peter and the Wolf* is an artistic triumph, whereas *On Guard of Peace* and *Winter Bonfire* are works of a secondary order, at best — with ethical judgement or historical analysis.

At the same time, it is also the case that art for children was more important as a refuge for imaginative work at some periods of Soviet history (1932–40, 1960–70) than at others. The requirements were that freedom of expression for adult audiences should be severely curtailed, but that non-traditional methods of representation should be tolerated where their expected audience was children. The only two scenarios out of twenty-six put forward by Mosfil'm in 1937, and accepted by the film censorship board, were the musical *Volga-Volga* and an animation film under the title *The Wolf and The Seven Kids*.[40] Famous cases of artists who took refuge in children's literature during the 1930s include two members of the absurdist Oberiut movement, Daniil Kharms and Aleksandr Vvedensky, or, to give a less dramatic example, the conventional, but intelligent and talented (if personally obnoxious) prose writer Aleksei Tolstoy, the 'Soviet count'. (Tolstoy is believed to have concealed a parody of Blok's famous 1906 love-triangle play *The Little Puppet Booth* (*Balaganchik*) below the surface of his famous children's novel *The Little Golden Key* (*Zolotoi klyuchik*, 1936). Intertextual coat-trailing of this kind would have been risky in the case of an adult novelist, but by presenting his story as an adaptation of Collodi's children's classic *Pinocchio*, Tolstoy was able to suggest that the piece was harmless and to avert interest of the wrong kind.[41] It was probably only in a children's story, too, that Tolstoy could have risked *The Little Golden Key*'s remarkable metafictional ending, in which the heroes, Buratino, Malvina, and Pierrot, stumble on a marvellous mechanical theatre in which they then act out the tale of how they have found this theatre in the first place.[42]

The Little Golden Key is of more than passing relevance to *Peter and the Wolf*: it was premiered in February 1936, as the opening performance of Sats's revamped Children's Theatre, and may well have been one of the performances that Prokofiev saw at that point (if one takes on trust Sats's assertion that he regularly visited her theatre in early 1936). Is there any sense in which *Peter and the Wolf* can be seen as a parallel to Tolstoy's story, that is, a piece where intertextual references that would only be picked up by a well-informed adult are concealed?

Prokofiev certainly tried to decoy any such view himself, remarking, 'I wasn't interested in the tale itself, but in getting children to listen to the music; the tale was just a pretext for the music'.[43] But this is certainly too sweeping. The plot is very simple, but it does have some witty intertextual references too — most obviously, to folk tales, such as *Prince Ivan and the Grey Wolf* (*Tsarevich Ivan i seryi volk*). At the same time, obviously, the hero is not called Ivan or Vanya. The name

40   Turovskaya, 'Mosfil'm — 1937', p. 283.
41   See Miron Petrovsky, 'Chto otpiraet "Zolotoi klyuchik"? Skazka v kontekste literaturnykh otnoshenii', *Voprosy literatury*, 4 (1979), 229–51 (esp. pp. 241–42).
42   A. N. Tolstoy, *Polnoe sobranie sochinenii*, 15 vols (Moscow: Goslitizdat, 1947–51), XII, 130–32.
43   Prokofiev, *Materialy, dokumenty, vospominaniya*, p. 195.

points in another direction: to the traditional puppet hero Petrushka. And there is a strong resemblance between Peter and the version of Petrushka that appeared in adaptations for Soviet children, such as Samuil Marshak's 1927 play *Petrushka the Foreigner* (*Petrushka inostranets*), for instance. Petrushka's naughtiness in this piece is more of a governing characteristic than Peter's — he cheeks his parents, truants from school, gets into trouble in various hiding-places, such as an ice-cream chest (where he melts the contents) and a roundabout (where he doesn't have a ticket), before finally stealing clothes to try and pass himself off as a foreigner — and his disobedience has no good effects whatever. But the scenes between him and adults are much closer in tone to the scenes between Peter and his grandfather than they are to anything in the legends about Pavlik Morozov:

    Родители
    До свиданья, милый Петя,
    Ты один у нас на свете.
    По дороге не зевай
    Да не суйся под трамвай!
    [Уходят]

[Dear little Pete, farewell, | You're all we have in the world. | Pay attention on your way to school | And keep clear of the trams, little fool! | Exeunt.]

    Петрушка
    Ну, теперь я свободная птица
    Буду петь и веселиться.
    Сумку школьную свою
    Я надену на свинью.

[Well, now I'm free as a bird, | I'll sing and I'll chirp. | My schoolbag is much too big | So I'll hang it on a pig.][44]

Feisty heroes, not to speak of wolves, cats, birds, and even hunters, are all the stuff of traditional folklore. The only creature whose precedents are less obvious is the duck. Perhaps Prokofiev was inspired by the animation film. Non-Russian classics of the day included Disney's *The Three Bears* (1933) — which includes, of course, a predatory wolf — and they also, more significantly, included *Donald Duck* (who first appeared in *The Wise Little Hen*, released in 1934). Animation was a major genre of the Soviet cinema too, and articles in film journals during the 1930s and 1940s regularly harped on the need to create a 'Soviet Disney', of equal technical competence, but with very different ideological objectives.

On the other hand, perhaps the duck reference pulls in a different direction — towards the exquisitely sound-orchestrated picture of the goose skidding on the ice that appears in the winter pictures at the end of Chapter 4 of Pushkin's *Evgeny Onegin* (where a pair of wolves also figure):

    Встает заря во мгле холодной;
    На нивах шум работ умолк;

---

[44] S. Marshak, 'Petrushka-inostranets', in *Sobranie sochinenii*, 8 vols (Moscow: Khudozhestvennaya literatura, 1968), II, 240.

С своей волчихою голодной
Выходит на дорогу волк;
Его почуя, конь дорожный
Храпит — и путник осторожный
Несется в гору во весь дух;
На утренней заре пастух
Не гонит уж коров из хлева,
И в час полуденный в кружок
Их не зовет его рожок;
В избушке распевая, дева
Прядет, и, зимних друг ночей,
Трещит лучинка перед ней.

И вот уже трещат морозы
И серебрятся средь полей...
(Читатель ждет уж рифмы розы;
На, вот возьми ее скорей!)
Опрятней модного паркета
Блистает речка, льдом одета.
Мальчишек радостный народ
Коньками звучно режет лед;
На красных лапках гусь тяжелый,
Задумав плыть по лону вод,
Ступает бережно на лед,
Скользит и падает; веселый
Мелькает, вьется первый снег,
Звездами падая на брег.
(*Evgeny Onegin*, Chapter 4, stanzas 41–42)

[The dawn rises in chilly dark, | No work sounds come from the meadow; | With his hungry she-wolf | The wolf walks out on the road. | Scenting him, a passing horse | Snorts — and the anxious traveller | Gallops uphill full-speed; | In the morning light the shepherd | Does not drive his cows from the shed, | And at mid-day his pipe | Does not call them; | Singing in her hut, a maiden | Sits and spins, and the splinter-light, | Friend of winter nights, crackles before her. || And now the frosts are crackling, | And glowing silver in the fields. | (My reader expects the rhyme *roses*: | Well, let's get it out of the way!) | Shinier than fashionable parquet | The river lies, clothed in ice. | The merry tribe of boys | Cuts the ice with their skates; | And on its red feet the heavy goose, | Intending to swim on the bosom of the water | Steps carefully on to the ice, | Slips and falls over; cheerfully | Flashes by, spinning and twisting, the first snow, | Falling like stars on to the banks.]

Evgeny Onegin had been standard reading in Russian schools since the late nineteenth century, and children were made to learn the nature passages in it off by heart; the practice continued into the Soviet period.[45] So perhaps Prokofiev was aiming for a reference an astute child might pick up. Or perhaps more likely (given his limited first-hand experience of Soviet childhood) he may have been thinking

---

45 Indeed, the pre-revolutionary school syllabus was in large measure restored in 1932–36. See *Children's World*, Chapters 3 and 12.

of his own experiences; though fundamentally, *Peter and the Wolf* is less about the childhood that Prokofiev did have than about the childhood he did not have. Even with a relatively down-to-earth and indulgent mother (and not the demanding parents that some child prodigies, for instance Gidon Kremer, have had to put up with), Prokofiev's childhood had been concentrated and serious.

U. C. Knoeplfmacher, in his study of Victorian fairy tales, *Ventures into Childhood*, depicted the typical male creator of the fairy tale as a person traumatised by early expulsion from the nursery. Hence the predilection of such artists for the figure of a pre-pubescent girl, to be understood not as a lust object, but as an alternative self.[46] While this interpretation is more seductive than the banal association of fantasy with paedophile desire, it does not seem to suit the character of the *skazka* as recreated by twentieth-century artists particularly well. There is an edge of danger and brutality in these adventures — albeit of a hypothetical kind (the wolf *might* eat Peter, the puppets in *The Little Golden Key might* end up as slaves of the evil puppet master) that one doesn't find in *Alice in Wonderland* or *At the Back of the North Wind*. In the verse tales of Kornei Chukovsky, similarly, the anti-hero is often a fearful monster (the Giant Cockroach, the Crocodile) who in the course of the tale is routed and tamed (compare the plot of Evgeny Shvarts's '*skazka* for adults' about a fire-breathing reptilian tyrant, *The Dragon* of 1943–44). Equally, the 'parodic deformation of motherhood' that Knoepflmacher sees as central to the Victorian male fantasy is replaced, in Russian literary tales, by a parodic deformation of paternity: maternity is elided altogether.[47]

In narratives of this kind, childhood freedom is gendered as masculine, and comes into conflict with patriarchal authority. The main resemblance to Knoepflmacher's pattern lies in the compensatory status of this vision of childhood rebellion. Prokofiev was a child prodigy who devoted himself to serious study at a young age; Kornei Chukovsky was the illegitimate son of a poor laundress whose childhood was nothing like the joyful world of fantasy that he created for his last child, Murka (on whom he doted). And Sergei Eisenstein, in his autobiography, expressed a similar life-path aphoristically in the image of the mature artist doing the things forbidden to the child — the boy who had never tortured flies turns into the artist whose films were, metaphorically speaking, all about torturing flies.[48]

Prokofiev was less obviously macabre, though there *is* danger in *Peter and the Wolf*, as the fate of the duck indicates. But unlike Eisenstein (in *The Strike*'s abattoir scene, or the Odessa Steps sequence in *Battleship Potemkin*), though like Chukovsky (whose poems 'The Crocodile', 'The Big Cockroach', and 'Barmalei' showed comically terrifying tyrants getting their come-uppance), Prokofiev was, essentially, a sadist only in the universal childish sense — a person prompted not so much aggression as by a curiosity unbounded by identification with the creature that gets hurt. (One might compare Oleg Prokofiev's tale of how one of the boys

---

46 U. C. Knoeplfmacher, *Ventures into Childhood: Victorians, Fairy Tales, and Femininity* (Chicago: University of Chicago Press, 1998), p. 9.
47 Ibid., p. 17.
48 See Sergei Eisenstein, *Memuary*, ed. by Naum Kleiman, 2 vols (Moscow: Muzei kino, 1997), I, 6.

was put in the linen basket, aged about one, so that Prokofiev could watch what would happen; or Oleg's recollection of how his father would pretend not to notice the dog and then sit down on it.)[49]

Robinson's reference to *Peter and the Wolf* as 'a remarkably imaginative form of avoidance behaviour' seems a little sententious, and perhaps also misleading about Prokofiev's need to 'avoid' in 1936 (the early months of 1936 were not, by the exacting standards of early Soviet history, such a particularly 'grim' era).[50] But certainly there is a form of imaginative escape here — though from self as much as anything else. Dorigné's suggestion that Prokofiev may have seen himself as the duck who goes on quacking in the wolf's belly, is a nice one, but I wouldn't see even this as primarily a political vision, a representation of the artist as prisoner of Soviet reality.[51] Rather, I have just the feeling that Prokofiev may have, at some deep level, imagined *his own expectation of himself* (his superego, if we follow Freud) as 'the wolf', and not Soviet power at all. Most creative people, after all, need within themselves, alongside the child who goes heedlessly wandering in the meadow, the grandfather who keeps them out of danger and directed to a larger purpose, even if that disciplinary force is the target of frustration and even hostility, and certainly never of gratitude.

Appendix: Two Letters from Natalia Sats to Sergei Prokofiev about *Peter and the Wolf*

1. 17 June 1936. Typescript. At top right in another hand (Prokofiev's?) is '17 June' with a circle round it. RGALI, f. 1929, op. 1, d. 683, l. 1.

> Dear Serezha,
> My train leaves in just three hours, but I've still managed to dictate the latest version of the *Petya* text. Please check the text yourself, particularly the punctuation, which I didn't have time to deal with.
> I'd be happy if *Petya* could at least reach first proof stage by the time I get back, and I wish it every success in print, and you a good rest and all the best in every way.
> Warm greetings.
> *Nat. Sats* [signed by hand]
> 17 June 1936.

---

49 For the first, see Oleg Prokofiev's sleeve-note for *Peter and the Wolf: A Classic Children's Orchestral Tale. Written by Russia's Great Composer Sergei Prokofiev. First translated into Arabic and Narrated by Nazih Girgis* (1995) (held in the Prokofiev Archive *Peter and the Wolf* file); for the second, Dorigné, *Serge Prokofiev*, p. 455. Prokofiev's abandonment of his first wife Lina and her two sons after he began his liaison with Mira Mendel'son at the end of the 1930s, and refusal to associate with the sons at all after their mother's arrest in 1948 (Vishnevitsky, *Sergei Prokof'ev*, p. 609), also points to a restricted capacity for empathy.

50 Robinson, *Sergei Prokofiev*, p. 319.

51 Dorigné, *Serge Prokofiev*, p. 456.

2. 16 September 1936. Manuscript (dark blue ink and pencil). RGALI, f. 1929, op. 1, d. 683, l. 2.

> Dear Serezha, I send warm greetings, and am sending as a 'memento' two reviews of our concert, which I don't think has had the press attention that it deserves, but on the other hand was a big success on the radio (loads of letters and drawings from children).
> Hurry up with getting Petya into print — there's a demand for him.
> Warm greetings to   1. you
>   2. Lina Ivanovna
>   3. your sons
> Please do ring me sometime. Be sure to [this last sentence added in pencil].
> Nat.   1936 $^{16}/_{\text{IX}}$

This paper was first published as 'At Peace with the Wolf: Prokofiev's "Official" Soviet Works for Children', *Three Oranges*, 12 (2006), 3–9. I am particularly grateful to the late Noëlle Mann for her help when I was researching material in the Sergei Prokofiev Archive at Goldsmiths College, University of London.

PART III

Small People and Big History

CHAPTER 8

Making Memories: Children and the Personal Past in Early Twentieth-Century Russia

[2007]

Recollecting the past is, let us remember, not simply a functional practice. It is an exercise in cultural authority. Those who recall the past have made decisions about what should be preserved, about what merits survival, in a physical or in a symbolic sense. In so-called 'traditional' societies, people themselves become repositories of memory: in this sense, to remember is also to discipline society. One has to be entitled to remember. Perceptions of this link between memory and status are enshrined in the phrases with which memory is evoked: thus, in Russian, *do otsovskikh pamyatei* [before our fathers' memories] means 'a very long time ago', while *devich'ya* or *zhenskaya pamyat'* [girls', womens' memory] signifies a memory that retains very little.[1] The capacity to remember, in normative terms, stretches from (male) elders of society at one end to (female) minors at the other: elders have command of the all-important 'olden time', *starina*, that acts as a moral and aesthetic yardstick for human behaviour.[2]

Certainly, there is another side. Remembering can be seen as an exercise of *vengeful* power: as in the phrase *ya tebe eto popamyatuyu*, 'I won't let you forget it', the opposite of conciliatory expressions such as *budem schitat', chto proekhali i zabyli*, 'let bygones be bygones' (literally, 'we've gone past and forgotten'), where a hurt is deliberately effaced.[3] Excess memory — the burden of recollection weighing on grieving relatives of a dead person, for example — is considered potentially harmful in Russian folk tradition, and there are rituals for keeping it at bay: forgetfulness has healing powers. To 'forget oneself' means not just to lose oneself in a bad sense, but also to find release (to come into contact with an important manifestation of the metaphysics of drunkenness). The word *zabyl'*, which one might suppose meant 'something forgotten' (*zabytoe*), in fact signifies something true, not invented.[4]

1 V. Dal', *Tolkovyi slovar' zhivogo velikorusskogo yazyka*, 4 vols (Moscow: M O. Vol'f, 1880–82), I, 556.
2 Ibid., III, 14. See esp. *pamyatukh/ pamyatukha* and *pamyatchik/ pamyatchitsa*, glossed as 'an oldster who has seen many things and remembers events and the local past'.
3 For the first phrase, see Dal', *Tolkovyi slovar'*, III, 14.
4 Ibid., I, 556.

All the same, to efface the past has been, in the context of Russian society, more often than not a radical act. The rituals of therapeutic forgetting are marginal and insignificant compared with the rituals of remembering: there is no 'day of forgetting', to counterweight the 'remembrance days' of popular Orthodoxy, days traditionally associated with the commemoration, above all, of one's parents. At the level of banal social contact, too, 'memory' is positively valued: the habit of referring to presents as *suveniry* appears to date from the late twentieth century at the earliest, but gestures to evoke happy memories, such as compiling albums, or making donations 'in loving memory', *v dobruyu pamyat'*, were frequent long before then, and the social cliché *Vy nas sovsem zabyli* (we haven't seen you for ages', but literally, 'You've completely forgotten us'), suggested that the act of *not* making contact had a strong emotional resonance.

In this context, the assaults made in the early Soviet period on what were often known as 'accursed traditions' (*proklyatye traditsii*) were shocking not just because they intruded into domains of the sacred: religious practice, family life, domestic existence. The act of forgetting, rather than remembering, signified generational self-assertion as well as contempt for the past; it was an inversion of social authority as well as an expression of iconoclastic morality and aesthetics. In the 1920s, it was not the 'rememberers' of society who held sway, but those who forgot in order to reshape themselves, such as a young worker whose diary was quoted by the pedagogue and specialist in the theory of biography, Nikolai Rybnikov, in 1930:

> I subordinate everything to that — to my own will: feeling, with its passion and its instinct, and self-love and pride, and good and bad habits, and slavish shyness. And all things and everything... and spirit with its weak and strong aspects. I shall assemble everything that is atomised within me, and separate out everything that is useless, and tear it, bleeding and raw though it may be, away, and cast it to oblivion... Let today be the border between the past and the present, let me no longer be as I was from today. Let there be some or many failures; let there be thousands of them. Look elsewhere! Forward, forward! Let me carry this out, find my path, and avoid the path of error.[5]

This young worker's text lies somewhere between a prayer and a spell; it is an expression of desire to purge one's former self, to tear out anything 'useless' (*negodnoe*) like diseased flesh. With stylistic awkwardness, but perfect symbolic logic, the text shifts from therapeutic self-mutilation to another metaphor: the choice of the 'right path', here expressed as 'one's own', rather than the 'false' one. In some texts, though not explicitly here, the metaphor of the path as forward movement was spelled out: for Anna Akhmatova, a poet whose authority depended on commemoration as well as on clairvoyance, 'Lot's Wife' ('Lotova zhena', 1924) was a warning of the dangers of her own position.[6]

---

5   Diary of an anonymous factory worker, 1920s, in N. A. Rybnikov, *Avtobiografii rabochikh i ikh izuchenie: Materialy k istorii avtobiografii kak psikhologicheskogo dokumenta* (Moscow & Leningrad: Gosudarstvennoe izdatel'stvo, 1930), p. 67.
6   See also B. Thompson, *Lot's Wife and the Venus of Milo: Conflicting Attitudes to the Cultural Heritage in Modern Russia* (Cambridge: Cambridge University Press, 1978).

Early Soviet culture did not eschew all commemoration: alongside the famous revolutionary memorials of a three-dimensional kind, and the graves of the heroic fallen, one can place official oral history projects such as the *History of Works and Factories*, initiated with Gorky's blessing, not to speak of the exercise of manufacturing a history for the October Revolution itself.[7] But individual remembrance was often dangerous. The potential for mismatch between personal or family history and the orthodox, mythologised past was always present. What is most often remembered by eyewitnesses of this period (contrary to the clichés about the inalienable differences of private versus public behaviour) is silence about family tradition even in private, an effacement of anything that might make a person stand out, as recollected here by two different historical subjects born in the late 1920s, a woman from Ivanovo and a man from Leningrad:

> They never mentioned our gentry ancestors because my father was afraid. I grew up in the 1930s, and father was afraid to talk about the family that mother came from, and when he was arrested... not arrested, but expelled from the Party and sacked from the factory, sacked, then... um... he started to be afraid of everything, and so everything got burnt, burnt in the stove, all the family documents on both sides.[8]

An implacable taboo lay over my father's fate, and it was only when I finished school and told my mother I was planning to apply for higher education that's he touched on the topic, giving me advice unprompted on how to fill in the bit of the form that asked about my father. She fetched the docket that stated he had been released 'for absence of a corpus delicti', reminded me that he had died of TB, and then she made me learn by heart a text that I have since then always included in application forms. Until 1936, my father served in the army; in that year, he took early retirement on health grounds, and on 30 December 1938, he died of TB in Leningrad. She told me that if I were asked for any other information, I should say my mother hadn't told me anything else.[9]

Here, learning by heart replaces the traditional process of remembering: the historical subject is taught an official record for all circumstances, not just enacting self-censorship in public, but complying with a deep taboo. In a pioneering essay on autobiography in the early Stalin era, Natalia Kozlova spoke of the 'horror of not knowing' that confronted self-transforming individuals from the working class and peasantry.[10] But you could assuage this if you looked to the present and the future,

---

7 On the last issue, see Frederick C. Corney, *Telling October: Memory and the Making of the Bolshevik Revolution* (Ithaca, NY: Cornell University Press, 2004); Svetlana Malysheva, *Sovetskaya prazdnichnaya kul'tura v provintsii: prostranstvo, simvoly, istoricheskie mify (1917–1927)* (Kazan': Ruten, 2005).
8 CKQ-M-04 PF6A, p. 8 (interview in Moscow by Yuliya Rybina; on the Leverhulme Fund project to which I refer here, see Chapter 5 and at <http://www.ehrc.ox.ac.uk/lifehistory/archive.htm> [accessed 23 October 2022].
9 Boris Firsov, '"Orderliness and Efficiency Counted for Every-thing and Self-Expression for Very Little": Was It Always Like That in Soviet Schools?', *Forum for Anthropology and Culture*, 3 (2006), 349–61 (p. 354).
10 Natalia Kozlova, 'The Diary as Initiation and Rebirth: Reading Everyday Documents of the Stalin Era', in *Everyday Life in Early Soviet Russia: Taking the Revolution Inside*, ed. by Christina Kiaer and Eric Naiman (Bloomington: Indiana University Press, 2006), pp. 282–98 (p. 294).

and created an alternative self, rather than asserting your ancestry, your family's place in the past.

Like adults, children had 'file selves' in which family history was limited to the points, 'Social position of parents before and after the Revolution', and 'Is family conflict evident?'.[11] Personal history comprised political sympathies and literacy, academic and school record, acquaintance with 'literature on political questions' and 'proletarian literature', and the possible bad or good influence of the child's 'environment' and 'comrades'.[12] In the context of records of this kind, the crucial term was once more not *memory*, but *forgetting*: the willed suppression or elision of material that was consigned to the 'dustbin of history' by the narratives of transformation that depicted a Soviet subject's path to virtue.[13] *Avtobiografiya* (the preferred official term: people were not asked to compose their *vospominaniya* [memories] or *memuary* [memoirs], but to write a 'life description', without reference to time-frames), became a genre of perpetual reinvention of the self as the given ideological moment might require. In the words of Pavlik Morozov, the key child hero of the Cultural Revolution era, 'He's not my father any more'.[14]

Forgetting the past went hand-in-hand with looking to the future: thus, in the early 1920s and early 1930s, children were encouraged to write essays on topics such as 'School Life in Fifty Years Time'.[15] An ancillary trend was encouraging youngsters to become adult as quickly as possible, to 'put off childish things' — as expressed in Dmitry Moor's poster, 'I am an Atheist!' (*Ya — bezbozhnik*), showing a small boy in his father's army service coat and Budyonnovka cap, which he cannot wait to grow into. The 'adultness' of children (or to be more accurate, of proletarian children, those growing most rapidly to consciousness) was also evoked in the practice of encouraging child activists to make speeches on important occasions, such as the First of May, along with Party and Komsomol representatives. Both trends came together in the work of Anton Makarenko, whose reformatories for young offenders encouraged collective discipline from an early age, on the one hand, and sought to efface the past, on the other. Makarenko and his staff deliberately avoided discussing the case files of their charges, seeking to emphasise that these had entered a new world once they stepped through the orphanage door.[16] Memory was thus a

11   On the term 'file self' in the Soviet context more generally, see Sheila Fitzpatrick, *Tear Off the Masks! Identity and Imposture in Twentieth-Century Russia* (Princeton, NJ: Princeton University Press, 2005).
12   See the pro forma character reference (*kharakteristika*) for graduates of Soviet level two (secondary) schools published in *Russkaya shkola za rubezhom*, 2 (1924), 127. An interesting detail of the pro forma is that *natsional'nost'* [ethnic identity] was *not* included.
13   For a good introduction to the topic of anti-memory, see the recent collection *The Art of Forgetting*, ed. by Adrian Forty and Susanne Küchler (Oxford: Berg, 1999). On transformation narratives, see in particular the work of Igal Halfin, *From Darkness into Light: Class, Consciousness and Salvation in Revolutionary Russia* (Pittsburgh, PA: University of Pittsburgh Press, 2000).
14   See my *Comrade Pavlik*, Chapter 1.
15   See, for example, the material from the Rossiiskaya akademiya obrazovaniya, nauchnyi arkhiv [Russian Academy of Education Scholarly Archive] (hereafter referenced as RAO NA) cited in V. Kozlov and E. Semenova, 'Obydennyi NEP: sochineniya i pis'ma 20-kh godov', *Neizvestnaya Rossiya: XX vek*, 3 (1993), 259–329.
16   As particularly in Makarenko's famous, and much-reprinted (in many editions for the Eastern

faculty with pragmatic functions. It was a repository for information to be ritually regurgitated in the school-room or political meeting, rather than a store-house of experience or personal impressions, which were imponderable and difficult to control.[17]

Yet socialisation of children through remembrance did not always so straightforwardly signify integration into collective values and official politics. Bringing up the young is likely in whatever cultural system, sooner or later, to turn into a commemoration of the past (in the sense that the values imparted to them are those of an earlier generation), and the parents of the 1920s and 1930s had themselves been children at a time when attitudes to memory had been complex and divided. Certainly, the tradition of *anti-memory* had strong antecedents in Russian pre-revolutionary radical culture, particularly of the 1860s, where unstable, non-habituated affective links were championed against the 'loyalty-by-tradition' model of the child-parent relationship or of the monogamous liaison as sanctified in Orthodox Christianity and Tsarist law.[18] However, there was also a strong alternative view, according to which children were encouraged to view the past, and autobiographical reconstructions of this, as an essential aspect of consciousness. The most familiar manifestation of this is the cult of the 'gentry childhood' initiated by Tolstoy's hugely influential 'fictionalised autobiography', *Childhood* (1852).[19] This tradition was of course inimical in the USSR (though widely imitated in Russian émigré writing and subconsciously echoed even in Soviet official autobiography). But while the 'golden childhood' on the country estate (or failing that, dacha) was the most prominent type of self-recollection before 1917, the cultivation of memory also had many other forms. Indeed, the late nineteenth and early twentieth centuries were an era when life-writing both proliferated and became significantly more diverse.

An effect of the rise of child psychology at this era was the emergence of the personal history as a crucial instrument of pedagogical and clinical practice (the key figures in Russia are less Freud than the neurologist G. I. Rossolimo, and N. A. Rybnikov, an educator and pioneer of questionnaires and tests for schoolchildren of the kind that became institutionalised, during the Soviet period, through the efforts of the 'pedological movement').[20] For Rossolimo, the purpose of taking case

European satellite states after 1946 too) *Pedagogical Poem*, 1933–36.
17   One might compare the attack on *impressionizm*, which in practice often meant a lyrical view of the past, in Soviet literary criticism of the early 1930s.
18   There are probably folk antecedents too, given that it was considered appropriate to purge emotions of the kind that might be inspired by nostalgia (fear and anguish, *strakh i toska*): see A. K. Baiburin, 'Toska i strakh v kontekste pokhoronnoi obryadnosti', *Sbornik Etnologicheskogo fakul'teta Evropeiskogo universiteta v Sankt-Peterburge*, 1 (2001), 96–115.
19   Andrew Baruch Wachtel, *The Battle for Childhood: The Creation of a Russian Myth* (Stanford, CA: Stanford University Press, 1990).
20   G. I. Rossolimo, *Plan issledovaniya detskoi dushi (v zdorovom i boleznennom sostoyanii)*, 2nd edn (Moscow: tipo-litografiya tovarishchestva I. N. Kushnerov i Ko., 1909); N. A. Rybnikov, *Derevenskii shkol'nik i ego idealy* (Moscow: Zadruga, 1916). An important discussion published since this article was written is Andy Byford, *Science of the Child in Late Imperial and Soviet Russia* (Oxford: Oxford University Press, 2020).

histories was sometimes to provide information that was of therapeutic value; it was not necessarily the case that articulation of the past was supposed to be a therapeutic benefit in itself (as in the 'talking cure' of psychoanalysis).[21] Rybnikov himself tended to espouse the common-sense view that children and young people were more preoccupied with the future than the past: commenting on the difference between the young person's (*yunosheskii*) and the elderly person's (*starcheskii*) diary, he wrote in 1930: 'The former assesses his behaviour with regard to his future life [...] the old man focuses on the past'.[22] But after 1917, the process of recollection began to be seen as potentially helpful in its own right. Not everyone adopted the *tabula rasa* model celebrated by Makarenko. A specialist in juvenile delinquency wrote in 1925, for example, that children's capacity to forget was less complete than was sometimes supposed:

> A child can forget grief and forget joy. But that does not at all mean that those experiences have no effect on the child's character; on the contrary, that life precisely does make an impact, typically one of feralisation; yet one of the elements of this way of life and this feralisation is the haphazardness and fragmentation of the chronological sequence of events.[23]

In this context (as for psychologists of a Freudian bent), inability to remember was in fact an unhealthy reaction. It signified repression, the burying of the emotional self in 'refuse' (*musor*):

> Children often do not discuss the past, they often even forget emplotment in terms of events, but the memory of the emotions they felt survives. In [their] refusal to talk, in [their] behaviour generally, an emotional reaction to the trials of the past can be clearly seen. In Grisha, though, it was impossible to observe all this. It was as though some layer of refuse covered the customary emotional reactions to be found in children.[24]

In the Russian emigration after the Revolution, the second clinical meaning of 'remembrance as therapy' started to be widely recognised, as witnessed above all in the enormous memoir-writing project for schoolchildren organised by the Zemgor philanthropic movement in 1924–25.[25] And children's fleeting, indeed in some cases nearly non-existent, recollections of the 'motherland' were cultivated in the attempt to ensure national survival, an attempt that became increasingly desperate as émigré activists and writers became convinced of the inevitability of cultural

---

21 I discuss this more extensively in Chapter 5 above.
22 Rybnikov, *Avtobiografii rabochikh i ikh izuchenie*, p. 9.
23 T. E. Segalov, 'Deti-brodyagi: Opyt kharakteristiki', *Pravo i zhizn'*, 7–8 (1925), 84–89 (p. 86). The entire article is this: T. E. Segalov, 'Deti-brodyagi: Opyt kharakteristiki', *Pravo i zhizn'*, 7–8 (1925), 84–89; 9–10 (1925), 89–95.
24 Ibid., p. 87.
25 A selection of the materials was published by the Pedagogical Bureau for Secondary and Primary Education Abroad as *Deti emigratsii: sbornik stat'ei pod redaktsiei V. V. Zen'kovskogo* (Prague: Pedagogicheskoe byuro po delam srednei i nizshei russkoi shkoly za granitsei, 1925): this very scarce edition (held, for instance, in the University of Helsinki Slavonic Library) is also available online at <http://rus-sky.com/history/library/vospominania/#_Toc19331755> [accessed 25 April 2022]. A more recent and fuller edition with a useful historical introduction is *DRE*.

assimilation.²⁶ But 'remembrance as therapy' was also a presence in Soviet practice as well. Makarenko might choose to ignore 'case files', but the composition of such files, accompanied by in-depth interviewing about the past, was a standard procedure at many other children's homes and at 'reception centres', which included educational psychologists on their staffs until the notorious decree of 1936 banning 'pedological perversions'.²⁷

There was thus a place for self-recollection in a formal sense — for the cultivation of autobiography — in pedagogical practice as well as in child psychology (indeed, in a generation when 'pedology' was used to apply both to clinical practice and to work in schools, the line between these two applications of personal memory was often quite hard to draw).

More surprisingly, perhaps, the use of autobiographical testimony as a pedagogical tool was also a widespread feature of the official Tsarist Russian school-rooms of the late nineteenth and early twentieth centuries. In German schools at this period, writing a short autobiography (two-four pages) was a requirement of admission to the school-leaving examinations, and the same requirement was adopted in Russia at the end of the nineteenth century.²⁸ Alongside elite schools, the bulk of whose pupils were drawn from the moneyed classes in urban society, such as the *gimnaziya* (classical high school) and *real'noe uchilishche* (a school offering training in the natural sciences, modelled on the German *Realschule*), more humble educational establishments, such as the parish schools and teacher seminaries run by the Schools Council (Uchilishchnyi sovet) of the Most Holy Synod, also maintained the practice of asking children to write autobiographies. A collection of ninety such autobiographies, by children and young adults ranging in age from eleven or twelve up to their late teens and early twenties, and written in the first years of the twentieth century has been preserved in the holdings relating to the Schools Council in the Russian State Historical Archive (RGIA), St Petersburg.²⁹

26 See, for example, Nadezhda Teffi's story 'Huron' ('Guron') (1928), or V. Rudinsky, 'Emigratsionnaya molodezh'' i denatsionalizatsiya', *Vozrozhdenie*, 65 (1957), 44–50. One major purpose of the 'Days of Russian Culture' held in Paris during the late 1920s and 1930s was to keep alive the attachment of young people to the Russia of the past, a task that was also integrated into the work of youth organisations such as the Russian Student Christian Movement, Sokol, the Russian Scouts, etc.
27 For a pioneering study of child psychology at this era, see Byford, *Science of the Child in Late Imperial and Early Soviet Russia*.
28 I owe the information on the German school system to the late Vitaly Bezrogov, the foremost recent historian of children and education. Autobiographies were also required from pupils sitting the university matriculation examinations (*attestat zrelosti*) as external candidates. For some published examples, see 'Avtobiografii raznykh lits evreiskogo proiskhozhdeniya, prilozhennye k prosheniyam Ekaterinburgskoi muzhskoi gimnazii o razreshenii im sdat' eksternom ekzameny na attestat zrelosti', *Sbornik dokumentov po istorii evreev Urala*, ed. by I. Antonov (Moscow: Drevlekhranilishche, 2004).
29 See RGIA, f. 80, op. 16, d. 2370, d. 2372. The archivist has dated the collection '1909', but this is clearly much too late: for example, the autobiography of Petr Lazeev (b. 1886) (ll. 106–07 ob.) recounts that he had entered school at the age of eight and had then completed three more classes of primary education and taught for a little while in a village school before entering teacher training college. Even assuming that his primary education lasted six years, he cannot have arrived at college later than 1903 or 1904. On the other hand, the relatively full autobiographies left by the younger children suggest that they were surely not less than ten or eleven when these were written (so these

Children writing autobiographies certainly received guidance from their teachers about what to write. Girls seem to have been assigned a particularly rigid format, assigned to write not an *avtobiografiya*, but a text addressing 'My Life as a School Pupil' and 'My Life as a Teacher'. Most pupils faithfully plodded through the required material.[30] Just one, Nadezhda Ioganson, the daughter of a gardener from a small town, and from an unusually fortunate background until her father's death from galloping consumption, produced a full-scale piece of life-writing.[31]

Boys also received detailed guidance. Three headings appearing at the top of an autobiography by a pupil at Tomsk Church School for Teachers (time and place of birth, childhood, and school life), were no doubt copied from the classroom blackboard.[32] Likewise, younger schoolboys uniformly began by relating their earliest memory, which was evidently considered a suitable prompt for the start of the essay. But the directional material was much less restrictive when it came to boys than girls, and the autobiographies themselves did not necessarily have a 'scripted' feel. This first question, for example, provoked quite varied and at times startling answers:

> I remember myself from age six. Once it happened that I was taking the horse to water and it got away and kicked me on the leg and father took me away and my leg hurt for a long time and then once it happened father and I went to Taganrog and we had got halfway and I dropped the reins and tried to pick them up and sat on a sack only the sack fell off the wagon and off I fell too. The horse got scared and started bucking and my father had a job to hold it in and I got real scared. I have spent all my life on our farm [*khutor*] with my family. (Ivan Gurnak, *b.* 1893, Don Cossack Army, St Anastasia's School)

> I started remembering myself from age 7. Once my father and I went to Taganrog and I dropped off to sleep on the cart and fell out and the wheel ran over my hand. Another time I was leading the horse from pasture and fell off and it kicked me on the head, so they had to pour water over me to wake me up. Then once I took the horses to water and almost drowned. (Petr Polyakov, *b.* 1894, Don Cossack Army, St Anastasia's School)[33]

must have been written no *earlier* than 1903 or 1904).

30   See, for example, Ol'ga Tkacheva, *b.* 1893, a pupil at a parish school in the Don Diocese: 'I made efforts to study well, but God had not granted me a good memory and understanding, so I studied badly, even though I always did the homework', or 'My father can read and write and seeing much use in knowing your letters, he took care his children should also. When I had reached 8 years old, he in that same year sent me to school. Having studied for four years, I can see the use of learning' (Kseniya Malenkova, daughter of a peasant from the Taganrog District, parish school, Don Diocese): RGIA, f. 803, op. 16, d. 2370, l. 53, l. 54.

31   Nadezhda Ioganson, *b.* 1888, untitled: RGIA, f. 803, op. 16, d. 2370, ll. 68–70. Ioganson's privilege can be gauged by the fact that her family had a summer residence in the country as well as a farm, and by her literary style.

32   Mikhail Kol'chenko, *b.* 1884, Tomsk Church School for Teachers: RGIA, f. 803, op. 16, d. 2370, l. 123. Unfortunately, after a thorough search in the materials of the Synod's Schools Council, I have been unable to locate any instructions for teachers relating to the autobiographies.

33   RGIA, f. 803, op. 16, d. 2370, ll. 35–35 ob., ll. 44–44 ob. The narrative strategies in post-revolutionary autobiographies are strikingly similar: see, for example, the following text by an eighteen-year-old worker, written in the late 1920s (Rybnikov, *Avtobiografii rabochikh*, p. 45): 'My first memory of childhood coincides with a happening that, I think, I will remember all my life. That

Experiences were not necessarily unpleasant: two children remembered being bought gifts or toys. But they were certainly out of the ordinary. Children were learning, in composing their autobiographies, what was and was not 'worth' remembering.

Pain (especially if overcome) and gifts (especially if gratefully received) are themes that have in themselves a strong didactic resonance. And the subjects of these autobiographies did not omit to give their lives a strong moral teleology in other ways. A leitmotiv is the autobiographer's love of learning, accompanied often by the sense of the schoolroom as a place of intellectual sweetness and light:

> Now I study in that school so as to get a good education and turn out a good person [*vyiti v lyudi khoroshim chelovekom*]. In Russia now there are more and more schools every year and you can get a good education. (Dimitry Bystritsky, b. c. 1895, Form 2, Class 1, Vladimir Diocese, Archangel Two-Year School)

> At first I didn't want to [go to school], I cried and made excuses to stay home [...] [But] In school I came to love my kind and gentle teachers, I came to love them like my parents, and also grew fond of my comrades. (Anonymous pupil at the Church School for Teachers, Voronezh)

> The love of learning and books emerged in me back in the model school. When I left, I would borrow books from the teacher; there was not one book in his library that I did not read. I thirsted to learn, but how could I even dream of that when my brothers could barely feed the family? I was full of radiant hopes, and happily they have been justified: that autumn by intercession of the School Visitor I was accepted in the two-year school. (Petr Lazeev, b. 1886, village in Tambov province, pupil at the Church School for Teachers, Tomsk)[34]

Another standard feature was emphasis on the simple piety of one's parents:

> My mother made me pray, she taught me how to pray, the prayers, that is. She would put me in front of the icon and kneel down beside me, put one arm round me and make me cross myself and repeat the words of the prayers, which I couldn't understand back then. (Pavel Polomoshnov, b. 1889, Church School for Teachers, Tomsk)[35]

It would be hard to predict from any of this material the revolutionary conflicts of 1905, let alone of 1917, or even the widespread atmosphere of aggression in the countryside that some scholars of the Russian peasantry, for example V. P. Danilov, have seen as essential to the development of the younger generation from 1900 onwards.[36] The autobiographies may instructively be contrasted with

---

was when, aged 6, driving out in the sledge, I unexpectedly fell under the horse and broke my arm'.
34 RGIA, f. 803, op. 16, d. 2370, l. 3 ob., l. 107 ob. Here too there are post-revolutionary analogies. See, for example, Rybnikov, *Avtobiografii rabochikh*, p. 36 (boy aged nine, working-class background): 'I now live very well, and not at all badly. I want to take walks outside with my comrades. I love it in school, not home. We study many interesting things at school, and at home nothing at all. I want to learn'. Later, certainly, some 'Soviet' motifs emerge: 'I eat well here, not badly. I went to the shop for paraffin. I keep a diary [indicating this was an assigned task]. I go to school every day. I keep my face clean'.
35 RGIA, f. 803, op. 16, d. 2370, l. 126.
36 V. P. Danilov, 'O vozmozhnostyakh pokolencheskogo analiza v poznanii istoricheskogo

the annihilatingly hostile recollections of religious education set down by the psychologist and educational reformer Nikolai Rybnikov during the Soviet period, or with most of the autobiographies of official Soviet writers who had grown up in village households before 1917.[37]

Yet at the same time, the exercise of memory retrieval was not purely conservative. To begin with, the very practice of writing these alternative self-histories placed the writers at a distance from traditional culture. References to parents were sometimes disparaging. 'Like all peasant children, I was brought up with no supervision and no direction', wrote Spiridon Kozlov, born in Tomsk province, 1884, and a pupil at the Tomsk Church School for Teachers.[38] Striking here is the categorical typification — like *everyone* — as well as the invocation, by inversion, of a didactic, 'non-peasant', model of 'good' upbringing, one dependent on minute regulation of the child.[39]

On the whole, this generation's view of its parents was respectfully distant. One of the most eloquent autobiographers, Petr Lazeev, gave a sympathetic but by no means over-idealised portrait of his father, an unbending man, 'honest and direct', whose efforts to discipline his children never ceased:

> My father started teaching us our letters very early and had no time for idleness; to that end, he sometimes even used physical punishments. Once, having run round all day, I didn't want to get down from the sleeping shelves above the stove for the lesson (my father taught us in the evenings); he thrashed me with a piece of bast and only let me go after I had stammered my way through 'In the Name of the Father'.[40]

The coincidence of prayer and situation would have delighted Freud, but it passes without commentary; for Lazeev, it was simply a detail of the scene.

The pupils writing school autobiographies also depicted themselves as at a tangent from traditional village custom. Particularly interesting here is an extended

---

protsessa v Rossii', in *Otsy i deti: Pokolencheskii analiz sovremennoi Rossii*, ed. by Yu. Levada and T. M. Shanin (Moscow: Novoe literaturnoe obozrenie, 2005), p. 137.

37 For Rybnikov's memories, see *Gorodok v tabakerke: Vzroslye o detakh i deti o sebe. Istoriya detstva v Rossii ot Nikolaya Vtorogo do El'tsina*, ed. by Vitaly Bezrogov and Catriona Kelly, 2 vols (Moscow & Tver': RGGU, 2008). The canonical collection of autobiographies by Soviet writers is *Sovetskie pisateli*, ed. by Brainina and Nikitina. It should be said that more negative memories of school do come up in the RGIA autobiographies: for example, Vladimir Kudryavtsev, born in 1886, a pupil at the Tomsk Church School for Teachers, wrote: 'The first time I was in school, I was specially struck by the large quantity of children who had also come to prayers, and then with great interest I examined the pictures of human skeletons hanging on the classroom walls. I eagerly began studying and could already read quite fluently, only then I started playing up, and our teacher was very strict and also quite nasty. He started punishing me for my mischief: I would get no lunch, or he would put me in the corner, or sometimes hit me with a ruler or pull my hair. That made me afraid of him. Sometimes he would ask me something and I would shake and say nothing, and I lost the will to learn. When my parents found out, they took me out of school, and I spent the rest of the school year at home' (RGIA, f. 803, op. 16, d. 2370, l. 102 ob.)

38 RGIA, f. 803, op. 16, d. 2370, l. 116.

39 There is an amusing contrast in a little tract written by the folklorist Georgy Vinogradov, a populist intellectual, which stresses precisely the *virtues* of peasant upbringing: *Narodnaya pedagogika* (Irkutsk: Vostochno-Sibirskoe otdelenie Geograficheskogo obshchestva, 1926).

40 RGIA, f. 803, op. 16, d. 2370, l. 106 ob.

example of the genre by Dimitry Kuznetsov (b. 1888), a pupil at the Elabuga two-year school, a boy who had grown up in a small village, and whose semi-invalid status (he had been partly paralysed in childhood, perhaps by polio) did not stop him joining in the other children's activities, at least as a spectator. According to his account, many children's pastimes mischievously violated adult proprieties. He recorded not only a session when the boys were telling smutty jokes to each other, only to be interrupted by the local priest, but also rather subtler cases where juvenile and adult aims had come into conflict, for example a meal snatched by the children during the harvest season, when the house was empty:

> On one of those days, we gathered in the house of a comrade. After having rushed around till we were tired, we wanted something to eat. What to do? We didn't want to go back home, and we had no food with us. Our comrade Vanya, the son of the house, solved our indecision. 'Wait, gentlemen!'[41] he said. 'Let me see whether we have anything to eat!' With these words, he opened the oven and began hauling out the pots. It turned out that his mother had left chicken and potatoes cooking before she went to work. She had made huge efforts that day, hoping to have a filling meal when she got back. It was not to be. Our comrade looked into the pot and saw the chicken. He shouted joyfully: 'Efimka, Mit'ka, coom [sic] here, look what Ive [sic] got'. We all rushed over and looked at the boiled chicken. 'Everyone to table!' Vanya ordered. We all sat on the benches down the long table, waiting for our dinner. In a few minutes the chicken and potatoes were on the table and we were tucking in. When we'd eaten our fill, we got up and started jumping round like mountebanks again.
>
> Evening was coming on. Folk were coming back from the fields. Vanya's family arrived too. All of em [sic] were dead tired and dying to eat. Imagine his mother when she looked in the stove and found the empty pots. In a fury she grabbed Vanya and started thrashing him as hard as she could. Poor lad, he certainly paid for treating his guests. When his mother had tanned his hide, she chucked him out of doors, where he spent the entire night.[42]

The striking point in the story is not that the children were punished for their action, but that they embarked on such a 'suicide mission' in the first place. Their action in thieving food was transgressive not only in practical terms (they were depriving the rest of the family, and particularly its working members, of sustenance), but in symbolic terms as well. It was an essential element of meal-time etiquette and eating ritual, preserved well into the post-revolutionary era, that children were served last, after the adults — starting with the *bol'shak*, the senior male — had helped themselves to the tastiest items of food.[43] To be sure, the chicken-stealing incident did not have the character of a coherent rebellion against norms, and its suppression was not recollected in retrospect as unjust. But it does illustrate that

---

41 Not surprisingly, the teacher put an exclamation mark alongside this unlikely phrase.
42 D. Kuznetsov, 'Avtobiografiya', 10 April 1907: RGIA, f. 803, op. 16, d. 2372, ll. 19–20.
43 For a late description of these procedures, see Alex Saranin's memoirs: *Child of the Kulaks* (St Lucia; University of Queensland Press, 1997), p. 5 (the grandmother broke the bread, but grandfather ladled out the soup and other food, and helped himself to the best bits first). Saranin was brought up in a traditional, and originally — till the anti-kulak measures of the 1920s — prosperous household in Rudyanka, south-east of Alapaevsk, to the east of the Urals mountains.

children were capable of identifying, albeit unconsciously, repositories of sacred values in traditional culture, and of targeting their attacks on these.

Kuznetsov also recalled that favoured targets for small boys' attacks in his village were the windows of the bathhouse, and the contents of vegetable gardens.[44] Once again, symbolic as well as practical sensibilities were engaged. Both bathhouse and vegetable garden stood for the autonomy of the particular family, and both were, for different reasons, strictly private.[45] Additionally, in the case of the bathhouse, the traditional use of the building for bringing children into the world made an assault on this building carry the value of an assault on family tradition: the children were engaged in symbolic riot against paternal (maternal) authority.[46]

Memories in these narratives have a double function. At one and the same time they underline a link, inscribed into the past, with tradition and the established order, and at the same time illustrate the subject's distance from the past (as manifested also in the patronising tone that many of the autobiographers espoused when writing about their former selves).[47] The authors were constructing, on the basis of precept, a fundamentally new type of self-consciousness, rooted in the village (and hence, according to the governing paradigms of the Tsarist state, in the ideal past) and yet also shaped by the values of the educational system.[48] Their narratives went beyond this simple duality as well. They were visibly acquiring a new confidence through education that allowed them to form their own decisions not just about village culture, but about the culture that they were imbibing in their parish schools and teacher seminaries. If there is little to suggest direct rebellion against the system that had educated them, there is also little to suggest political loyalty or piety either. It was not customary for the autobiographers to thank God or the Tsar for their good fortune in gaining an education: rather, they remembered relations who paid for them to go to school, and teachers who sparked their enthusiasm or supported their desire to learn.[49] To a large extent, these 'success stories' were individual.

---

44 RGIA, f. 803, op. 16, d. 2372, ll. 13–14.
45 The Russian expression, 'to throw stones in someone's vegetable garden', means 'to cast aspersions on their personal honour', 'spread discreditable rumours about them'.
46 E. A. Pokrovsky, *Fizicheskoe vospitanie detei u raznykh narodov, preimushchestvenno Rossii* (Moscow: tipografiya A. A. Kartseva, 1884). See also Nancy Condee, 'The Second Fantasy Mother, or All Baths Are Women's Baths', in *Russia, Women, Culture*, ed. by Helena Goscilo and Beth Holmgren (Bloomington: University of Indiana Press, 1996).
47 This is a specific variant of the general characteristic of autobiography termed by Mikhail Bakhtin in *Slovo v romane* [Discourse in the Novel] (1941) 'narrative double-voicing'.
48 The need to preserve the past in rural Russia through the socialisation of children was something of an obsession with Tsarist administrators. The explicit function of the 'village refuges', shelters for orphaned peasant children, for example, was to provide a bulwark against the perceived 'decay' of village life by means of an infusion of industrious, well-trained, morally sound, and pious young people, enriched by a sense of God's goodness and of religious principle. *K voprosu ob organizatsii zemledel'cheskikh priyutov dlya sel'skikh sirot* (Petrograd: Gosudarstvennaya tipografiya, 1915), p. 9, pp. 11–12.
49 Cf. a typical story from Ivan Vorontsov, b. 1886, village, Tomsk province, Tomsk Church School for Teachers, 'The religious knowledge teacher used often to tell me: "You, Vorontsov, should study harder so as to turn out a person [= make something of your life], or else you'll end up herding animals somewhere"': RGIA, f. 803, op. 16, d. 2370, l. 111.

Even these autobiographers' ambivalent relationship with 'custom' was a possible source of tension, in terms of the rigid 'estate politics' that characterised the education and welfare regime of Nicholas II. The era was typified by the so-called 'village shelter': a project that placed orphans from peasant families in *style russe* barrack accommodation, provided them with a diet of kasha and cabbage soup, and imposed upon them a demanding regime of agricultural work from early in the morning, in order to feed them back into rural society, once they reached their early teens, as model agricultural workers.[50] Comparably, the training provided for parish school-teachers was supposed to preserve a sense of affiliation with the village and to equip the future educators of the young with the resources to engage in the delicate balancing act of countermanding some customary traditions and reinforcing others. Yet schoolchildren were also learning to think of custom as 'custom', in inverted commas. In depicting their own relationship with it during their early childhood, before they were inured to its purpose, they also acquired a sense that this relationship might be self-conscious. Where traditional rituals made the child the object of social practices performed upon him or her as a means of reinforcing the primacy of the past, the autobiographers depicted ritual as an alien phenomenon with which they had to get to grips.[51] Dimitry Kuznetsov's description of his sister's wedding is a striking example:

> But now the day of the wedding had arrived. The most amazing fuss started in the house from the crack of dawn. The house was packed with people. Everything was ready, the tables were groaning with food to accompany the vodka. The guests were sitting primly in their places. The girls were fussing round the bride, dressing her up for the ceremony. Then suddenly came the sound outside of some loud harness bells and up to the yard gates rode the groom's party. All the horses were wearing their best harness, and had brightly-coloured ribbons woven into their tails and manes. As soon as the group came in through the gates, I was made to sit down at a table and told I should stay there even when the guests came in. Just then, outside the door the voice of the groom (or the best man) said loudly, 'In the name of the Father, the Son, and the Holy Ghost'. 'Amen', everyone inside answered. The door opened, and the guests came in. The best man was walking in front holding a horse-whip. He came straight up to me and shouted to me to get up. To be honest, I had the fright of my life and was on the point of moving, but people all around started making signs that I should stay put. So I did, and when the best man saw that I wasn't going to be intimidated, he flung down twenty kopecks, and I took them and made myself scarce.[52]

---

50 See *Sel'skie detskie priyuty Vedomstva Imperatritsy Marii*, 2 (1915), 94, 97, 80.
51 For example, the cutting off of the umbilical cord, the washing and dressing of the newborn, naming, and so on. Both dressing and naming patterns emphasised the links of a small child with his or her parents and more widely ancestors: a child would usually be dressed in a mother's or father's old shirt (depending on gender), given the name of an older relation, especially a grandparent, etc. See A. K. Baiburin, *Ritual v traditsionnoi kul'ture* (St Petersburg: Nauka, 1993), pp. 40–61; on naming, see also I. A. Razumova, '...I reshili nazvat' Alenoi', and E. A. Belousova, 'Sotsokul'turnye funktsii imyanarecheniya', both in *Rodiny, deti, povitukhi v traditsiyakh narodnoi kul'tury*, ed. by E. A. Belousova (Moscow: Rossiiskii gosudarstvennyi gumanitarnyi universitet, 2001), pp. 266–302.
52 RGIA f. 803 op. 16 d. 2372, ll. 22 rev.-23 rev.

In the accounts of such encounters with 'tradition' and 'custom', one can see the beginnings of individuation, as was brought out also in the essay of Trofim Mekhil'chenkov about local festivals, written in 1907 (he was then in the first division of the second class, and had begun attending school at eleven, so was presumably thirteen or fourteen when he produced it):

> Everyone who has finished the last day of work before a holiday is kind of happy that the day of rest — complete freedom from work — has arrived. As soon as the holiday comes, everyone but the cooks and children, go to church to hear the service. And with everyone else, along go I.[53]

The teacher had made two corrections to this text. He had deleted the phrase, 'complete freedom from work', and substituted for it the phrase 'after many hours of work', no doubt because the word seemed potentially subversive (an action that can only have drawn attention to the associations that he sought to impede).[54] He had also scored out the last sentence of the passage quoted, for, after all, if *everyone* goes to church, it stands to reason that Trofim also would have done. Yet the distinction between 'everyone' and 'me' was, of course, highly significant: Trofim was raising, at least grammatically, the possibility that he might have done something that everyone else was not doing, something on his own. In the later phases of school education, children were confronted with literary texts where using the first person was taken for granted; even in reading primers, though learning patterns might reinforce collective values (lists of moral qualities to be learned, didactic folk tales to be read), individual texts, including, importantly, prayers, could speak with an individual voice.[55]

The autobiographical selves in the writings by pupils from church schools are palpably distinct from those of Tolstoy's many imitators. The only case where the motifs of 'golden childhood' are present is the memoir of Nadezhda Ioganson, whose family background and social origins were very different from those of the peasant boys making up the majority of the autobiographers. A lyrical passage evoking 'entire days, and sometimes nights, spent outside in the garden' ably deploys the standard conventions of Russian nature writing:

> When night fell, I would retreat into a dark avenue, sit down under a tree, and watch the stars light up and hear the nightingale sing; I seemed to forget everything in the world in this magic, wonderful setting. The stars, like angels' eyes, look down from on high, and the moon, wizard of the night, sails across

53 RGIA, f. 803, op. 16, d. 2339, l. 30.
54 On teachers' fear of political censorship by local inspectors, see particularly the diary of N. F. Shubkin, *Povsednevnaya zhizn' staroi russkoi gimnazii: iz dnevnika slovesnika N. F. Shubkina za 1911–1915 gg.* (St Petersburg: izdatel'stvo Russkogo khristianskogo gumanitarnogo instituta, 1998), p. 196. Shubkin describes having to delete references to the political repression of social thought in the 1840s, which he considered factually accurate, but likely to get him into trouble with the school authorities.
55 See, for example, K. D. Ushinsky, *Rodnoe slovo dlya detei mladshego vozrasta. God pervyi. Pervaya posle azbuki kniga dlya chteniya*, 4th edn (St Petersburg: N. S. Ushinskaya, 1912), p. 83: 'Angel of God, My Holy Guardian, granted by God to observe me from the heavens, I zealously pray to you: illuminate me and protect me from all ill, instruct me in the ways of goodness, and put me on the path of salvation. Amen'.

the sky and lights all the paths and trees. Opposite the garden is a park with the white glimmer of a long-forgotten palace, surrounded by fountains and flower-beds; lit by the moon, it seems far more wonderful and magnificent, and from an avenue in the park comes the song of a nightingale.

Equally literary, though the result of direct personal trauma, was Ioganson's description of her father's deathbed: the late-night gathering in his room, the exaction of a promise to visit his grave, the tears of the family, and his groans as he fell into unconsciousness, followed by Nadezhda's own shriek of despair.[56] But convergence with the literary mainstream was exceptional: it was rare for the pupils even to echo in passing the established canons of the childhood recollection.[57]

In acquiring a new identity as parish schoolteachers, destined by the intent of the Synod to be the intellectual (and spiritual) elite of the village, pupils of parish schools and seminaries were also being taught how to remember the past and how to visualise their own relationship with it. Yet not everything about this process was 'conservative'. Remembrance meant distancing oneself from one's former self (or the *self that might have been*, had education not taken place). While the past was not effaced, or examined and exposed as inadequate, there was nevertheless some misfit between this remembered past and the current self; yet such a misfit could also be felt between the remembered past and the past that young people were *supposed to remember* in the exercise of writing an official autobiography. In remembering their own past, young people were thus going through a process that pulled in the opposite direction from the supra-personal memories that they were encouraged to have — the tales of literary and political heroes.[58]

Without access to the later histories of these individuals, which would be difficult to trace, there is no telling what the concrete effects of this process of *re-viewing* may have been, once the autobiographers became fully adult and independent. It is unlikely, one would think, that they had an easy process into Bolshevism's rank and file, since self-conscious, questioning individualism was not a good starting-point. But perhaps some of them identified with the Soviet or socialist mission in a broader sense, and discarded their rather superficial religiosity. Others, though, may well have ended up as conscientious or silent objectors, as Tolstoyans, as supporters of John of Kronstadt, or indeed in any of the other belief permutations so abundantly available at the time. Whichever way, in examining their personal past, and with that past, themselves, these obscure young pupils of the Synodal education

---

56 RGIA, f. 803, op. 16, d. 2370, l. 69.
57 For instance, Ivan Dudkin, b. 1885, of Tomsk Church School for Teachers, inserted into his 1903 essay a close echo of Tolstoy in terms of mood, if not precise phrasing, 'O golden childhood! Where have you gone, where have you fled?': RGIA, f. 803, op. 16, d. 2370, l. 155.
58 For a sense of these, see Rybnikov, *Derevenskii shkol'nik*, which indicates that such heroes included Peter I, Taras Bul'ba, Yury Miloslavsky, Ilya Muromets, Pushkin, Tolstoy, Lomonosov, Suvorov, and Aleksandr II, though also Gulliver, Robinson Crusoe, and Robert Stephenson (the English inventor of the railway engine, about whom such children perhaps knew from Samuel Smiles's *Lives of the Engineers*, translated as *Velikii truzhenik*: see my *Refining Russia*, Chapter 4.). Lomonosov is directly mentioned by one of the autobiographers, Matrena Bespalova, b. 1893, parish school, Taganrog district, 'I really liked Lomonosov and tried to imitate him in every way': RGIA, f. 803, op. 16, d. 2370, l. 56.

system were engaging a trajectory that was no less extraordinary and at the same time typical than that of the proponents of 'Soviet subjectivity' to whom so much historiographical attention has been devoted.

My thanks to Laura Engelstein, Boris Kolonitskii, Nikolai Smirnov, Aleksandr Ivanov, and the other organisers of and participants in the International Colloquium, 'Historical Memory and Society in the Russian Empire and the USSR (Late C19-C20 Centuries)', Institute of History of the Russian Academy of Sciences (St Petersburg), European University, St Petersburg, Carnegie Institution, Yale University, 25–28 June 2007, where this essay first took shape.

CHAPTER 9

The End of Empire: Jewish Children in the Age of Revolution

[2017]

'The world of Russian Jews was anything but traditional and unchanging', wrote ChaeRan Freeze and Jay M. Harris in the introduction to their important anthology of historical documents about pre-revolutionary Russian Jewish experience.¹ Adherents of the Jewish faith were settled across the Russian Empire, from the far west to the east, including communities such as the Bukhara Jews shown in a splendid photograph from the Peter the Great Museum of Anthropology and Ethnography (Kunstkamera), St Petersburg.² Even if one sticks to the more familiar areas of Jewish settlement — the Ashkenazi shtetls in the Pale of Settlement covering parts of modern Belarus', Ukraine, Lithuania, Moldova, Poland, and Western Russia — social and cultural transformation had become, by the 1900s, so unmistakable that calls to preserve 'traditional Jewish life' were widespread.³

At the sharp end of the transformation were the Jewish children who followed their parents into emigration, or moved with them to Russian cities, and who represented family and community hopes for the prospect of a better life. These children were directly affected by the tensions between conservative religious values and the drive to modernise Russian and Jewish society, which could sometimes run right down the centre of the individual household.

In 1899, Chaim Davidovich Grinshtein of Odessa wrote to His Imperial Majesty's Chancery for Receipt of Petitions protesting against the behaviour of his wife, Revekka, who was neglecting the family in pursuit of her medical studies. 'I have been married to Revekka L'vovna Grinshtein for eleven years and have had two children with her — a daughter Raia (seven years old) and a boy Mikhail (three

---

1   *Everyday Jewish Life in Imperial Russia: Select Documents*, ed. by ChaeRan Y. Freeze and Jay M. Harris (Waltham, MA: Brandeis University Press, 2013), p. 45.
2   Accessible on the site of the Museum of Anthropology and Ethnography at <https://www.kunstkamera.ru/museums_structure/research_departments/department_of_central_asia#gallery-14> [accessed 20 October 2022].
3   The preservation of traditional Jewish culture was, for example, a key motive behind An-sky's ethnographical project, discussed below.

years old)', Grinshtein wrote. He concluded:

> Until the past year, our lives passed by happily and quietly, without storms and agitation; however, at the beginning of last year, my wife took it into her head, for no reason at all, to go off to a course in [dental] medicine [...]. In the end, my wife left me and our minor children to the will of fate and devoted everything to the goal of studying dentistry. [...] The tears of the unhappy children calling in vain for their mother are endless; the sight of their tears and bitterness rends my heart. [...] I beg you, All Merciful Sovereign, to look mercifully on my unhappy children.

He pleaded that the Emperor should 'forbid my wife from engaging in the study of dentistry'. Revekka Grinshtein, equally vehement, agreed with the basic facts of her husband's account, but displayed a totally different understanding of their resonance. 'In 1889,' she wrote:

> At the age of eighteen, I was married to the Odessa townsperson [Chaim] Nukhim Abramov Grinshtein with whom I soon had two children. After the passage of a few years, however, I had time to be convinced that my family life had turned out in the saddest way. Apart from the differences in personalities, I was especially oppressed by the disagreement in our moral worldviews, which became manifest with respect to the meaning of the family, the mother's role in it, and concern about the upbringing of the children [...]. I decided to study dentistry to satisfy my thirst for knowledge so far as possible and to support myself and the children with a source of livelihood, being compelled to separate from him.

In the conclusion of her petition, she begged the Emperor, 'Make me happy by your gracious command to issue me a passport [...] I am not attempting to dissolve our marriage but strive only for the possibility of living on my own labor and dedicating myself to the proper upbringing of our children'.[4]

The most obvious way in which to read this contest of narratives relates to the transformation of marital life around the turn of the century. A young Jewish woman, chafing at an arranged marriage, asserts her right to education as a way of escaping a relationship that she herself calls 'oppressive'. In this perception, the couple's children would simply be the rhetorical instruments of the conflict: Nukhim cites his children's tears in order to pillory his undutiful wife, while she emphasises that her desire to study is in order to make a better life for them. But the children themselves can be seen as historical actors too. We do not know how they regarded the breakdown of their parents' marriage, nor how they reacted to the eventually agreed solution. (They were billeted with Rebekka's parents while their mother finished her studies, before being returned to Nukhim's home during weekdays, while their mother was granted 'right of visitation' and allowed to supervise their upbringing.)[5] However, we can at least ask such questions. More broadly, we can ask about how the social and political upheavals of the late nineteenth and early twentieth centuries affected children. The issue is of importance not just in its own

---

4   *Everyday Jewish Life in Imperial Russia*, ed. by Freeze and Harris, pp. 425–26.
5   See the editors' note, *Everyday Jewish Life in Imperial Russia*, ed. by Freeze and Harris, p. 427.

right, but because precisely these individuals reached maturity at the beginning of the Soviet period, making a central contribution both to life in the new society, and in the vast diaspora that departed the former empire after 1917.

Like Jewish adults, children were subject to the imperial policies that placed restrictions on movement and social participation, and which in some respects worsened in the early twentieth century, as the social elite retrenched, fearing its privileges threatened or diluted. But they also enjoyed new freedoms and opportunities. Above all, this was a time when Jewish lives followed a variety of different patterns, even if constricted by the status of what official terminology denominated as *russkie inorodtsy*, non-Christian citizens of the Russian Empire, or 'Russians of other birth', as the literal translation would have it.[6]

★ ★ ★ ★ ★

'I was born in 1904 and lived in St Petersburg, on Mokhovaya Street, at a time when little girls, and also quite big ones, curtsied to their elders and betters', observed Tamara Talbot Rice in her autobiography, first published in 1996.[7] The life that she describes resembles Vladimir Nabokov's recollections in his *Speak, Memory*, except that Tamara's father, the son of a merchant originally from Lithuania, was even richer than Nabokov's mother. The household included a chef and no less than three governesses for the girls, as well as numerous maids, a laundress, a 'majordomo', and several footmen and other manservants. Regular luncheon parties were held for some forty of Tamara's friends, and summers at the family's two estates alternated with trips abroad, during which the family would travel in its own railway carriage. The combination of luxury and leisure exemplifies the good life during the last days of the Russian Empire, before war and revolution destroyed the prosperous elite to which Tamara belonged. But there is also another story to tell.

As Tamara's birth surname, Abel'son, indicates, her father, Boris, was of Jewish descent (his original first name was Izrail). Her mother, Louisa Elizabeth (or Lifa), the daughter of a timber merchant, also from the Baltic, was born into a still more prominent and wealthy clan, the Vilenkins — it was they who owned the estates on which the family holidayed. The certificate of Tamara's birth (as Elena Tamara Abel'son on 19 June 1904) was signed by a rabbi, as was her parents' marriage certificate and the certificate of birth for her brother, Vladimir, in 1897.[8] Tamara's grandfather, Abel' Yankelevich Abel'son, was buried in the Jewish part of St Petersburg's Cemetery of the Transfiguration in 1914.[9] Yet Tamara's memoirs make no mention of the family's inherited confessional background. Rather, she recalls the celebration of Christian holidays, such as her mother's gifts of hundreds

---

6 Non-Orthodox Christian subjects of the Empire were known as *inovertsy* 'those of other beliefs' or *inoslavy*. For a lucid outline of these policies and their contradictory resonance in public life, see Theodore R. Weeks, 'Russification: Word and Practice, 1863–1914', *Proceedings of the American Philosophical Society*, 148.4 (2004), 471–89.
7 Rice, *Tamara*, p. 8.
8 See her daughter Elizabeth's note, 'On the Family', in Rice, *Tamara*, p. 1.
9 See the list of burials posted on the 'Evreiskie korni' site <http://forum.j-roots.info/viewtopic.php?t=139&start=100> [accessed 26 May 2021].

of presents to the household and servants for Christmas, and the amiable absurdity of religious knowledge lessons at school, conducted by a priest whose fumbling explanations 'destroyed my faith in the deity without, however, diminishing my delight in the beauties of the Orthodox Church's ritual'.[10]

Tamara's background represented one end of the continuum of Jewish childhood in the years leading up to the Revolution. Highly educated, multi-lingual, but self-identifying as Russian and indeed Orthodox Christian, she and her brother and many cousins led very different lives from the families in the Pale of Settlement whose experiences might signify 'Jewish childhood' to a casual glance. Yet childhood in the Pale was itself changing at this period, as we can see in the extraordinary album of photographs put together by Solomon Yudovin, who accompanied the writer Semyon An-sky (real name Shloyme Rapoport) on his pioneering ethnographic field trips to shtetls in Galicia from 1912 to 1914.[11]

An-sky had embarked on his folklore-collecting initiative precisely in order to make Jewish children aware of their cultural heritage, and it is not surprising that children were important subjects of the research. At first, An-sky and his companions even offered small sums of money to children in exchange for folklore, until they discovered that the children were making the 'folklore' up, and finding time for their activities as informants by playing truant from their lessons at the heder. An-sky and company, if their questionnaire is anything to go by, depended extensively on leading questions that were intended to prompt their informants into discussions of traditional practices ('Is it a custom to name the first child after the wife's family?'). However, they also recognised contemporary realities: the questions included, 'Do children ever become ill from a teacher's blows?' and indeed 'Have girls become pregnant after pogroms? What do people do in such cases?'[12]

The evidence amassed by the expeditions, and particularly Yudovin's photographs, opens a window into communities that were far from being suspended outside time.[13] Certainly, we can see girls engaged in traditional activities such as spinning, outside wooden houses of indeterminate date. Here, the world looks as it is described in Pokrovsky's ethnographical studies of the 1870s, with children laid in special standing cradles, or ones on rockers, rather than a hanging cradle, and clad in padded jackets over the top of a simple shirt in order to keep them

10 Rice, *Tamara*, p. 11.
11 There is an excellent secondary literature relating to these expeditions. See particularly Gabriella Safran, *Wandering Soul: The Dybbuk's Creator, S. An-sky* (Cambridge, MA: Harvard University Press, 2010), and Nathaniel Deutsch, *The Jewish Dark Continent: Life and Death in the Russian Pale of Settlement* (Cambridge, MA: Harvard University Press, 2011), which includes a complete annotated translation of the elaborate questionnaire used by An-sky and his team.
12 Deutsch, *The Jewish Dark Continent*, pp. 131, 159, 186.
13 For a good discussion of the photographs and their conceptual and ideological background, see *Photographing the Jewish Nation: Pictures from S. An-sky's Ethnographic Expeditions*, ed. by Eugene Avrutin and others (Waltham, MA: Brandeis University Press, 2014), particularly the 'Introduction' by Avrutin and Harriet Murav, and the essays by Alexander Ivanov and Alexander Lvov. Laurence A. Cohen's biography of Anna Spector (1905–1997), from Korsun, Ukraine, *Anna's Shtetl* (Tuscaloosa: University of Alabama Press, 2007), is more focused on Jewish life generally than on childhood, but it is rich in ethnographical detail.

FIG. 9.1. Girl spinning. Photograph Solomon Yudovin, for Semyon An-sky's ethnographical project in Galicia, 1912–14. Courtesy Judaica Centre, European University, St Petersburg.

warm, or, at the other end of the scale, left naked for the first few days, or indeed until circumcision.[14] Other pictures show traditional Talmudic schools in local synagogues, and but for the technology could easily date back to the early nineteenth or indeed late eighteenth centuries.

But in other images again, we can also see a youth coolly smoking a cigarette, or a rabbi's family from the town of Ostrog dressed in clothes indistinguishable from those worn by middle-class Russian or Polish families of the same period.

Memoirs such as those by Mariya Shkol'nik give a different picture — of the hard life on smallholdings under the heel of local landowners and tax officials — but here early Soviet perceptions of shtetl life as 'backward' probably exaggerated how little had changed.[15] Other writers suggest that as state education spread, subjectivity in traditional families altered. The writer Vladimir Bill'-Belotserkovsky, born in 1885, recalled in his 1958 autobiography reading Mayne Reid, Fennimore Cooper, and Jules Verne, trying to body-build under their influence, and vastly preferring

---

14 E. A. Pokrovsky, *Fizicheskoe vospitanie detei u raznykh narodov, preimushchestvenno Rossii* (Moscow: tipografiya A. A. Kartseva, 1884), pp. 187 (cradles), 49 (clothes).
15 See the extract from Shkol'nik's *Zhizn' byvshei terroristki* (1930) in *Everyday Jewish Life in Imperial Russia*, ed. by Freeze and Harris, pp. 477–82.

Fig. 9.2. Rabbi's family, Ostroh, Ukraine. Photograph Solomon Yudovkin, for Semyon An-sky's ethnographical project in Galicia, 1912–14. Courtesy Judaica Centre, European University, St Petersburg.

his state primary school to the heder, since corporal punishment was relatively minimal.[16] An-sky's own life history — his childhood shaped by reading Russian literature, rather than devotional texts — was an indication of shifting allegiances even several decades earlier. Mixed cultural influences were increasingly common: in the 1900s, Samuil Galkin's father, a forester in Belorussia, sang songs to Jewish tunes, but the words were Belorussian.[17] As the 1897 census recorded, the patterns of Jewish settlement were different from those of some other ethnic minorities. Tatar villages were characteristically monocultural, with perhaps only a Tsarist official or two representing an exception. In Kazan' province, only about 15 of over 2000 settlements with a Muslim population had substantial numbers of inhabitants from other religious groups; by contrast, only 11 out of around 2500 settlements in Kiev province had exclusively Jewish populations.[18]

16 *Sovetskie pisateli: avtobiografii*, ed. by B. Ya. Brainina and E. F. Nikitina, 5 vols. (Moscow: Khudozhestvennaya literatura, 1959–1988), I, 154–55.
17 Ibid., I, 279. Galkin was born in 1897 and the memoirs date from 1958.
18 Calculated from the statistics in *Nasalennye mesta Rossiiskoi Imperii v 500 i bolee zhitelei s ukazaniem vsego nalichnogo v nikh naseleniya i chisla zhitelei preobladayushchikh veroispovedanii po dannym Pervoi vseobshchei perepisi naseleniya 1897 g.* (St Petersburg: tipografiya 'Obshchestvennaya pol'za', 1905). The Tatar pattern is comparable with settlement in the rural west of Ireland, as recorded in the 1901 and 1911 censuses there: the only settlements with a substantial Protestant population were those in which

It was an unstable world that Russian Jewish children inhabited, to a greater extent even than for their socially marginal Russian contemporaries. There was, to begin with, the still greater impact of migrancy as a result not just of pogroms, but of increasing financial hardship because the artisanal activities that many Jewish families had relied on became uncompetitive as industry expanded.[19] As conditions in the Pale worsened, the flight to other areas or abroad accelerated, and Jewish migrants were much more likely than Russians to move to big cities with their families. Twenty per cent of Jewish Petersburgers in 1897 were children, as opposed to fourteen per cent of the population generally.[20]

Those children belonged to many different social layers. Some city incomers were Yiddish-speaking artisans concentrated in largely Jewish districts, with the prayer house or synagogue as a community centre.[21] Precarity was the way of life here, with always the possibility of deportation back to the Pale if bribes were not paid or officials decided on a show of force.[22] But the most visible to the Russian intelligentsia and public opinion was the educated, Russifying layer. It is, accordingly, the most historically visible now.

The Abel'sons and Vilenkins were exceptional not just in terms of privilege, but of the degree of their Russification. A hint of apartness remained only in the elaborate (from the point of view of traditional Russian taste) first names of some of the Vilenkin descendants and their spouses — Irma, Amalia, Rosa, James, Jacques, Clarence, and Emma. As in Tatar families, such Westernised names were often a way of treading a middle path between traditional names (Rachel, Itzhak) and names with explicitly Christian connotations, such as Lyubov', Vera, or, more particularly, Maria. But they represented a significant departure from Jewish tradition, as did the fact that not one of Rachel and Abram Vilenkin's children called a child after his or her parents, or, apparently, grandparents.[23]

---

missionary work had taken place, such as Achill Island or parts of Connemara (otherwise Protestants were mainly officials such as policemen and coastguards). The Jewish pattern is more like the small towns of southern, eastern, and central Ireland, where both Catholics and Protestants lived, but distinguished by occupation, settlement, and of course religious practice.

19 See *Everyday Jewish Life in Imperial Russia*, ed. by Freeze and Harris, pp. 31–33.
20 Benjamin Nathans, *Beyond the Pale: The Jewish Encounter with Late Imperial Russia* (Berkeley: University of California Press, 2002), pp. 109–10. While giving little attention to children as such, Nathans's book is an excellent introduction to the Jewish city culture in which they were raised.
21 On settlement patterns, see Nathans, *Beyond the Pale*, pp. 111–20. St Petersburg had just one large synagogue, opened in 1893, but smaller apartment-block synagogues, 'prayer houses', were fairly common (as recorded in documents about their closure after 1917: see, for example, Central State Archive, St Petersburg (TsGA-SPb)., f. 1000, op. 1, d. 282, l. 19, on the closure of two small synagogues on ul. Troitskaya, later Rubinshteina, and Ligovsky prospekt, and a house of prayer on Moskovsky prospekt; and TsGA-SPb., f. 7384, op. 33, d. 60, l. 11, on the closure of two houses of prayer on Vasilievsky Island, 1936).
22 See the petition against deportation in *Everyday Jewish Life in Imperial Russia*, ed. by Freeze and Harris, pp. 483–85 (1890). The editors comment that numerous other such petitions can be seen in the same file.
23 Abram's patronymic was 'Markovich', and there was no Mark among the younger Vilenkins either. On traditional naming patterns, see ChaeRan Freeze, *Jewish Marriage and Divorce in Imperial Russia* (Hanover, NH: University Press of New England, 2002), p. 11.

The Benensons, almost as rich as the Abel'sons, but through oil, eschewed Christmas trees and Easter eggs, and moved in a circle of Jewish friends, but kept only the major Jewish festivals and practically never entered the synagogue.[24] While these two families lived in St Petersburg, there were plutocratic families in other major cities — including Odessa, where over one third of the population were Jewish — that lived in much the same way. For the Pregel' family, it was, once again, only holidays and celebrations (Sofiya, later a prominent poet, remembered her brother's bar mitzvah) that marked a difference from the mainstream population.[25] Other families, while not adopting Orthodox festivals, ignored or avoided Jewish traditions: poet Vera Inber's mother was the headmistress of a Jewish school, but it was hard work and liberal politics that Vera, in retrospect, remembered as the governing values, rather than a specifically religious world-view.[26] Even observant families could be non-traditional, relative to the values of the shtetl, when it came to educational aspirations and the capacity to indulge their offspring, as Muscovite Roza Vinaver (*b.* 1879) recalled.[27]

The term 'assimilation', with its sense of a homogeneous shift to governing cultural patterns, oversimplifies the processes in train. Families Russified to different levels and in ways that reflected the diversity of Russian society itself. The old joke, 'Jews are just like everyone else — except a bit more so', comes to mind. Notably, urbanised Jewish parents warmly shared the characteristic middle-class enthusiasm for 'rational upbringing'. According to ethnographical observers, traditionally Jews did not wash their infants very frequently, or not until after the circumcision had been performed. But educated Jews living in the big cities were among the most passionate proponents of hygienic practices (they were widely represented amongst the pioneers of 'mother and child care' in Russia).[28] The shtetl stereotype of big families notwithstanding, the birth rate was lower among Jews than among any confessional groups bar Protestants by 1899, and by 1910 had even dipped below the birth rate among Protestants.[29] On the other hand, 'modern' counsel in favour of breast-feeding for a generous period by the mother, as put across by advice literature of the period, echoed what had been traditional in Jewish families anyway.[30]

---

24   On the Benensons, see Manya Harari, *Memoirs 1906–1969* (London: Harvill Press, 1972), pp. 17–18. In German-speaking Jewish communities, this kind of loose observance was known as *Fressfrömmigkeit* (roughly, 'piety of the stomach'): see Claudia Roden, *The Book of Jewish Food: An Odyssey from Samarkand and Vilna to the Present Day* (London: Viking, 1997), p. 46.
25   Sofiya Pregel', *Moe detstvo*, 3 vols (Paris: Novosel'e, 1973), I, 59–60 (Jewish festivals), III (brother's bar mitzvah). Isaak Babel' is an example of an Odessa Jew from humbler antecedents brought up in a relatively secular family (though where some of the older generation were observant).
26   *Sovetskie pisateli: avtobiografii*, ed. by Brainina and Nikitina, I, 472–74. There were some conspicuous silences in Inber's recollections, such as the fact that Leo Trotsky (Lev Bronshtein), her cousin, lived with the family for six years while studying at the local Realschule, but Trotsky's own memoirs confirm the picture of a secular upbringing rooted in Russian intelligentsia values.
27   See *Everyday Jewish Life in Imperial Russia*, ed. by Freeze and Harris, pp. 175–79.
28   Pokrovsky, *Fizicheskoe vospitanie detei*, p. 89. Examples of Russian Jews active in the child protection movement included Z. O. Michnik, M. F. Levi, and E. M. Konyus.
29   See *Naselenie Rossii v XX veke: Istoricheskie ocherki*, ed. by Yu. A. Polyakov and V. B. Zhiromskaya, 3 vols in 5 (Moscow: Institut Rossiiskoi istorii Rossiiskoi Akademii nauk, 2000–12), I (1900–39), 45, table 17.
30   David Ransel, 'Mothering, Medicine, and Infant Mortality in Russia: Some Comparisons',

This interest in up-to-the minute child-rearing methods, combined with the new opportunities for social organisation brought by the October Manifesto of 1905, also made some educated Jewish women avid participants in the movement for institutional childcare. By 1913, Kiev had two special nurseries for Jewish children.[31] St Petersburg, for its part, boasted a Jewish kindergarten offering instruction in Hebrew.[32] Already in 1865, a Jewish orphanage was founded in St Petersburg, and from 1881, it occupied a purpose-built block on Vasilievsky Island commissioned by the Ladies' Committee of the St Petersburg Jewish Society. Its purpose was to turn poor orphans from Jewish families that were legally settled in the capital into useful members of society, 'able to carry out artisanal occupations and domestic service'.[33]

Among educated urban Jewish parents, parental attitudes were often far more indulgent than those in traditional shtetl families, as the case of the Abel'sons makes clear. In the shtetl, children were expected to contribute to the family economy early on; well-off families in cities expected the dependent status to continue at least until their offspring married.[34] It would be an exaggeration to suggest that the entire 'happy childhood' ethos later so prominent in Soviet propaganda was invented by Jewish parents. But they were certainly among pioneers of child-centred family relations, not least because the contraction of family size meant that the nurturing drive had fewer objects (as happened to Russian families also later in the twentieth century).[35] Of course, children had always had a central place in the Jewish home anyway: the strict subordination of Russian peasant children to the *bol'shak* (senior male) and adults generally contrasted with the visibility of children,

---

Occasional Paper, Kennan Institute for Advanced Studies, 236 (1990); V. Varshavsky, 'K voprosu o detskoi smertnosti i merakh bor'by s neyu', *Pediatriya*, 4 (1913), 310–14 (p. 311). N. Vigdorchuk, 'Detskaya smertnost' sredi Peterburgskikh rabochikh (po dannym ankety)', *Obshchestvennyy Vrach*, 2 (1914), 212–53 (p. 238), quotes mortality rates of 47.6 per 1000 of population for the 0–5 age group among Orthodox believers, 39.5 per 1000 among Muslims, and 23.9 per 1000 among Jews (the figures date from 1900–04). Similar arguments for a later period are advanced by V. A. Tushnov, 'K kharakteristike byta grudnogo rebenka v tatarskoi sem'e', *Zhurnal po izucheniyu rannego detstva*, 6.2 (1927), 160–65.

31   *Doshkol'noe vospitanie*, 2 (1913), 66. See also *Vystavka 'Detskii trud'* (*Kievskoe obshchestvo Narodnykh detskikh sadov*) (Kiev: tipografiya tovarishchestva I. N. Kushnerov i Ko., 1911), esp. pp. 24–55 (describing the work of individual institutions, some run by the Society and others private). On the rise of civic participation after 1905, see *Everyday Jewish Life in Imperial Russia*, ed. by Freeze and Harris, p. 43.

32   See *Polnoe sobranie zakonov Rossiiskoi Imperii*, 13 (1911), 183, 186.

33   T. E. Mneva, 'Evreiskii sirotskii dom', in *Sankt-Peterburgskaya entsiklopediya* <http://www.encspb.ru/object/%202855755630?lc=ru> [accessed 22 May 2021]. In his fictionalised evocation of the Soviet successor to the Jewish Home for Orphans, the Jewish National Home, *Ten Railway Carriages* (*Desyat' vagonov*, 1931), Doivber Levin quotes inmates to the effect that before 1917, the children had been roughly treated, but I would agree with Valery Dymshits in his introduction to a recent re-edition of the book (*Desyat' vagonov* (Moscow: Knizhniki, 2016), p. 30) that this accusation seems rather implausible, given the amount of money and care expended on the orphans by the Jewish community of the period, and given the hostility to corporal punishment in the child-care literature of the period.

34   On work in shtetls, see Ol'ga Adamova-Sliozberg, *Put'* (Moscow: Vozvrashchenie, 1993), p. 233; Cohen, *Anna's Shtetl*, p. 50, recalls eleven-year-old Anna doing housework such as clearing the kitchen after dinner.

35   See my *Children's World*, especially the discussion of 'serial only children' in Chapter 10.

particularly the eldest son, in Shabbat and holiday rituals.[36]

Added to this, as new members of the social elite, Jewish parents were also keen to 'do the right thing' socially. Hence the provision of all those governesses to give their children a head start, or at the very least, among families of modest income, the engagement of part-time tutors — as in the case of Lidiya Ginzburg, later to be a famous literary historian, who learned German as a girl in Odessa.[37] This emphasis on Western languages was also a contribution to the loss of contact with traditional Jewish life in the shtetls. By the early twentieth century, few families that could afford governesses or tutors seem to have wanted, alongside music, handwriting, deportment, French, German, and English, the Yiddish lessons arranged back in the 1870s for Zinaida Polyakova, daughter of a railway magnate and banker in St Petersburg.[38]

If home schooling for children was widespread in well-off families (just as it was in Russian ones), Jewish parents tended to measure educational success for elder children in terms of achievement at mainstream schools. The anxiety over not doing well enough in entrance tests is a trope in memoirs.[39] Yet Jewish children generally recall being happy and successful once ensconced in the educational establishment, even if other children, whether taking their tone from adults or from the peer group generally, might more or less crudely 'other' their Jewish fellows. The educationalist Nikolai Rybnikov recalled in his autobiography that a 'rather rowdy' schoolfellow ('nemnozhko khuligan') had taunted a girl called Lidiya Shur as a 'she-yid' ('*zhidovka*'), 'even though he wasn't actually a Judeophobe, and he even liked her'. He also recalled, 'For this he got a serious telling-off from his mother', but not every parent would have been so sensitive.[40] Yet it is hard to distinguish this sort of behaviour from the kind of banter aimed at every type of social difference, whether it was age, gender, clothing and appearance, or ethnic background. 'At school, at first I felt oppressed by the other pupils: they pressed round me and laughed at the various things that were wrong with me', Spiridon Kozlov recalled of his first day at school in the mid-1890s.[41] He was a peasant boy

---

36 For child-centered values, see, for example, the rabbinical judgement of 1888 permitting divorce of a wife who had been childless for ten years (*Everyday Jewish Life in Imperial Russia*, ed. by Freeze and Harris, p. 215), and the special prayers for the gift of children (p. 167). For child-centered values in Soviet Jewish families, see Yuri Slezkine, *The Jewish Century* (Princeton, NJ: Princeton University Press, 2004), p. 257: 'More of Hodl's children than just about anybody else's had the proverbial Soviet "happy childhoods"'.

37 See Lidiya Ginzburg, *Zapisnye knizhki. Vospominaniya. Esse* (St Petersburg: Iskusstvo, 2002), p. 383, note of 16 May 1927.

38 See the extract from Polyakova's diaries in *Everyday Jewish Life in Imperial Russia*, ed. by Freeze and Harris, p. 400.

39 For instance, in the autobiography of the future children's writer, Samuil Marshak, *V nachale zhizni: Stranitsy vospominanii* (Moscow: Sovetskii pisatel', 1961), a central place is given to the terror of the classical high school entrance exams, followed by euphoria when all his marks were fives, the highest possible, then despair when the percentage norm meant he did not get a place after all, and finally, relief when another pupil dropped out and he was actually admitted.

40 N. A. Rybnikov, 'Iz roda v rod' (1942), OR RGB, f. 367, karton 8, ed. khr. 2, l. 42; reprinted in *Gorodok v tabakerke*, ed. by Bezrogov and Kelly, 1 (the description relates to the 1880s).

41 Spiridon Kozlov, 'Uchilishchnyi sovet pri Sinode', RGIA, f. 803, op. 16, d. 2370, l. 116.

of Russian descent, and so too was everyone else in the classroom; you did not have to be obviously 'different' to be branded as such. Memoirs suggest that friendship among schoolchildren crossed ethnic divides: Maria Rashkovich, at the Odessa Empress Maria Gymnasium in the 1870s, later remembered that her three closest friends were Roza Yaron, the Belokopytov sisters, and A. V. Baranovskaya, with only Roza coming from her own side of the confessional divide.[42]

Greater anxiety stemmed from the political pressure of the time. No Russian Jew, however privileged, was spared the fears aroused by anti-Semitic violence, fears which were felt especially strongly by children. In a fascinating article about Chagall's unsettling *Dedicated to Christ*, showing a child Jesus crucified, Ziva Amishai-Meisels has traced the image to a subversion by Chagall of the blood libel legend and the imagery of crucified child martyrs popularised by an official Ministry of Popular Enlightenment brochure on saints' lives placed in high school libraries during the late Imperial era.[43] Not all historical subjects could work out trauma so creatively. Manya Benenson, from the family of the oil entrepreneur, and brought up on the Moika, one of the most elegant quarters of St Petersburg, read the newspaper reports of the Beilis trial in 1912, and recalled sixty years later how she was

> haunted by the darkness of the child's fear and pain as described in the newspapers, by the iniquity of the crime [...] by the lie which had given it this dreadful form, and by the ease with which the Russian maids had assumed that the blood guilt was in our blood.[44]

Over Passover that year, the maids mutinously complained, 'This is the anniversary of the death of Christ and the Jews are celebrating', and stones struck the window from outside.[45] This sense of dread multiplied many times in the case of children experiencing an actual pogrom (when even Gentile children, safeguarded by crosses chalked on the doors and icons placed on windowsills to mark the house as 'Christian', cowered in mortal terror as the baying mobs went past).[46]

---

42 See the extract from Rashkovich's memoirs in *Everyday Jewish Life in Imperial Russia*, ed. by Freeze and Harris, p. 402. Rashkovich does not comment on confessional allegiance, but Belokopytova and Baranovskaya are standard Slavonic family names.
43 Ziva Amishai-Meisels, 'Chagall's *Dedicated to Christ*: Sources and Meanings', *Jewish Art*, 21–22 (1995–96), 69–94 (esp. pp. 76–94).
44 For the pervasiveness of fears about 'Jewish crimes' among children also, see the anonymous reply to a questionnaire circulated by the Biographical Institute in the early 1920s (Archive of the Russian Academy of Education [NA RAO], f. 74, op. 1, ed. khr. 23, l. 52 ob.): 'I remember my and my sister's fantasies that no-one else knew about: the man who snatched children and drank their blood (the trigger had been a man we saw on the street drinking red liquid, probably paint, from a bucket). We undoubtedly connected this to stories we'd heard from someone about Jews stealing children'. The respondent brought out this story after a description of the family's moves around, as though suggesting that insecurity were the background to the belief. There is a link here too with the capacity of children to believe horror stories, *strashilki*, at a particular stage of development.
45 Harari, *Memoirs 1906–1969*, p. 20.
46 See, for example Konstantin Paustovsky in his *Dalekie gody* (1946), in *Sobranie sochinenii*, 9 vols (Moscow: Khudozhestvennaya literatura, 1981–86), IV, 119. Some Jewish children were also saved like this: cf. Herschel Alt, in Herschel and Edith Alt, *Russia's Children: A First Report on Child Welfare in the Soviet Union* (Westport, CT: Greenwood Press, 1959), p. 15, remembered 'fear that the

In 1905, outbreaks of violence against Jews escalated out of all proportion as right-wing groups, incited by official anti-Semitism, and tolerated or indeed aided by the Tsarist police, responded to strikes and unrest with a wave of pogroms. Isaak Babel's 'My Dovecote', whose boy narrator has to make his way across town during the height of a pogrom, and arrives to find his uncle murdered (but survives himself), was in fact an understatement of the horrors that took place in some towns. The 285 people killed in the forty-one pogroms that took place in Ekaterinoslav between October 1905 and January 1906 included at least ten children.[47] Yet Jewish children were sometimes themselves seen by the Russian authorities as the root cause of social disintegration.[48] While school teachers and directors usually behaved protectively towards pupils caught up in the protests of 1905, the records of the St Petersburg District Guardian of Schools include the case of Grigory Kramorov, a senior pupil at the Vvedenskaya Classical High School, who was treated very differently. He was summarily expelled 'without the right to enter another educational establishment' for a series of offences, including truancy, rudeness to a concierge, drunkenness, and participation in a demonstration 'demanding closure of trading premises', in the course of which he had allegedly struck a passer-by with a stick. Kramorov had converted to Christianity in 1902 'at his own wish', but for the purposes of the pedagogical council at his school, he still counted as a Jew. There is no comparable case in the files relating to a pupil from the mainstream Orthodox population.[49]

The onset of the First World War brought some respite to Jews in terms of greater flexibility in the residence requirements, but discrimination continued. On the one hand, Jewish refugees from the war zones could more easily move beyond the Pale; on the other, there were cases where they were officially classed as 'aliens' and deported from the front.[50] Jews well beyond the front line also

pogromchiks [sic] would come and destroy us and at the same time warm assurance that, if they did, the Russian family sharing our yard would hang their ikons on their walls and hide my brother and me in their home'.

47 Charters Wynn, *Workers, Strikes, and Pogroms: The Donbass-Dnepr Bend in Late Imperial Russia, 1870–1905* (Princeton, NJ: Princeton University Press, 1992), pp. 214–15; plate 11 shows slaughtered children, though no figures are given. On the background to these pogroms, see Gerald Surh, 'Ekaterinoslav City in 1905: Workers, Jews, and Violence', *International Labor and Working-Class History*, 64 (2003), 139–66. Funk, *Evrei Belarusi*, pp. 60–63, describes the pogroms in that region; *Pogroms: Jewish Violence in Modern Russian History*, ed. by John Klier and Shlomo Lambroza (Cambridge: Cambridge University Press, 1992), is a general study.

48 This was, of course, typical of late Imperial official perceptions; cf. the response to a petition of 1896 by Naum Dashevskii asking to open a Jewish private school in Irkutsk: the opening of a special school in Irkutsk would be undesirable in the highest degree, it would intensify the deep isolation of the Jewish elements and might foster the development of Jewish fanaticism, 'which must be deemed absolutely intolerable' (*Everyday Jewish Life in Imperial Russia*, ed. by Freeze and Harris, p. 398).

49 Central State Historical Archive, St Petersburg (TsGIA-SPb.), f. 139, op. 1, d. 10237 ('Ob uchastii v besporyadkakh, politicheskikh demonstratsiyakh uchenikov i prepodavatelei srednikh uchebnykh zavedenii'), ll. 1–3.

50 On increased freedom of movement, see *Zakonodatel'nye akty, vyzvannye voinoyu 1914–1915 gg.*, ed. by O. I. Averbakh, 4 vols (Petrograd: [no pub.], 1915–16), I, 776 (MVD order, 21 August 1915); III, 259 (order of 4 August 1915). On deportations from the Front, see Yu. V. Funk, *Evrei Belarusi v kontse XIX-nachale XX v.* (Minsk: Belorusskii nauchnyi institut dokumentovedeniya i arkhivnogo dela, 1998), pp. 64–65; Eric Lohr, *Nationalizing the Russian Empire: The Campaign Against Enemy Aliens*

suffered as xenophobia rose. Certainly, this was directed at other ethnic groups as well: Tito Kolliander, from a Swedish-Finnish-English family in St Petersburg, fervently supported the Russian armies in the War, despite his 'alien' status, but had his ardour cooled when he and his siblings were repeatedly bullied at the ice-rink, showered with taunts and pushed over (Tito even cracked a knee-cap in one such incident).[51] However, an official Ministry of Popular Enlightenment file relating to alleged offences by schoolchildren in the war years manifests revealing disproportionality.[52] The file contains a circular of 10 October 1914 banning schools and other educational establishments, both public and private, from admitting as pupils subjects of the Austro-Hungarian Empire, and it records one case of an expulsion of a foreigner, seventeen-year-old Edvard Pedersen of Riga (a Danish subject) for the alleged 'insolent offence to the patriotic feelings of a comrade' at the City Gymnasium where he studied.[53] But of the other twenty-eight cases where school pupils had been expelled from Ministry schools for serious offences in the course of 1914, no fewer than eight involved pupils of, in official Russian parlance, 'the Judaic faith'. Equally revealing was the discrepancy in terms of the nature of the accusations. The nineteen Orthodox Christian (and one Catholic) pupil expelled for misdemeanours stood accused of behaviour running from theft and extortion to assault (*oskorblenie deistviem*), actual bodily harm, and even attempted murder of a teacher. Only one Jewish pupil stood accused of such an offence, and that in company with an Orthodox Christian classmate.[54] The other seven cases related to alleged blasphemy and offensive behaviour:

> 2 April 1914 (*Secret*) Pupil in class 1, Nikopol'skii Higher Elementary School, Ekaterinoslav Province, David Nemtsov, Judaic faith, born September 28, 1900, for a sacrilegious act, expelled from school without right to enter any other educational establishment.
>
> 3 July 1914. Pupils in class 6 at the A. Stepovich Private Boys' Gymnasium [Classical High School] with rights of university entrance, Kiev, Aleksandr Koman (b. 16 April 1897) and Shmar'ya Spektor (b. 12 November 1895) (Judaic faith) 'for a sacrilegious act were expelled from the aforesaid Gymnasium'.
>
> 3 July 1914. Pupil of Class 5, Kerch' Alexander Gymnasium, Bernard Nutis, Judaic faith, 'for an exceptionally crude act toward a teacher'.
>
> 7 August 1914. Pupil of Voznesensk Boys' Gymnasium, David Fel'dman (b. 22 July 1898, Judaic faith), for blasphemy.

During World War I (Cambridge, MA: Harvard University Press, 2003).
51 Tito Kolliander, 'Peterburgskoe detstvo: glavy iz vospominanii', *Nevskii arkhiv*, 2 (1995), 21–22. It is only fair to say that Kolliander and other children at the Swedish school hated and despised Russians long before this: the lavatory was ornamented with a graffito, 'Zdes' russkii dukh: Rossiei pakhnet' [I scent a Russian spirit here: it smells of Russia] (p. 13).
52 TsGIA-SPb., f. 139, op. 1, d. 14261 ('Ob isklyuchennykh uchenikakh po neblagonadezhnosti, za oskorblenie prepodavatelei, bogokhul'stvo, [poruganie] patrioticheskikh chuvsv [*sic*] inogorodnikh srednikh uchebnykh zavedenii i pr.', 23 January-5 December 1914), ll. 1–26.
53 Ibid., l. 26. For the circular, see l. 22.
54 Ibid., l. 9 (30 May 1914: Fedor Goloskov (b. 3 July 1900, Orthodox), and Matvei Chapovsky (b. 15 June 1899, Jewish), expelled from the Novonikolaevskii Realschule 'for extorting money from a local merchant').

>24 September 1914. Pupil of Class I, of the Mrin Lower Trade School, Chernigov Province, Itskhok Logvinsky, Judaic faith, son of a plebeian freeman [*meshchanin*] of the town of Skira, Kiev province, b. 21 February 1899, 'for profaning with foul language in the hearing of pupils of the school the Life-Giving Cross of Our Lord'.
>
>9 December 1914. Pupil of Akkerman [Bilhord-Dmitrovskyy] Gymnasium, Pavel Berkov (b. 2 December 1896, Judaic faith) 'for having passed harsh judgement on the patriotic feelings expressed by his comrades who voiced their wish to volunteer for active service in the army'.[55]

The file points to significant levels of suspicion and hostility among some pupils of their Jewish coevals. At least two of the cases (24 September and 9 December) evidently relied on denunciations by fellow-pupils: cf. the formulae, 'in the hearing of pupils', 'the patriotic feelings expressed by his comrades'. In the Russian intelligentsia, prejudice against Jews was considered unacceptable and, since at least the 1860s, children's writers had been producing didactic narratives that preached the politics of tolerance.[56] The Russian official classes took a very different view, as Vladimir Nabokov recorded in the Russian version of his memoirs.[57] In this context, significant if not surprising was the readiness of the educational authorities to take accusations of blasphemy and unpatriotic thinking by Jews seriously and, by 1914, to collate them as evidence of a threat to national morale. The cases recorded in 1914 related to only a small fraction of the thousands of Jewish pupils receiving education alongside Russians (and in this case, Ukrainians), but their consequences were dire for the accused.[58]

The generalised suspicion of Russian Jews and restrictions on freedom of movement meant that many young people internalised an answering wariness of authority. Samuel Chotzinoff, brought up in Vitebsk during the 1890s, remembered seeing only one official document in the household at any time: his father's 'identification papers as a Jew and a legal resident [...] And I became aware of this sinister paper only because at alarmingly frequent intervals it was held by the local police *not* to be in order'.[59] In Jewish families resident within the Pale of Settlement, it was fairly frequent for parents, during the early nineteenth century, not to bother to register their child's birth because the act was felt to be unnecessary, and because official registration exposed sons to compulsory military service, held anathema by Orthodox Jews.[60] The efforts to get round settlement restrictions outside the

---

55 Ibid., ll. 5, 13, 14, 17, 20, 24, 25.
56 See, for example, the writings of Sof'ya Soboleva.
57 See *Drugie berega* (1954). Writing for an American audience a decade later (*Speak, Memory*, 1966), Nabokov was less frank about this aspect of his background, probably because the Eichmann trials and other recent publicity relating to the Nazi genocide of the Jews had given anti-Semitism a more inflammatory colouration than it had in the immediate post-war years, and certainly for an émigré Russian readership.
58 In 1914, there were 152,110 pupils at boys' classical high schools across the Russian Empire (I. V. Pykhalov, 'Obrazovanie v Rossiiskoi Imperii: fakty I mify', *Obshchestvo. Sreda. Razvitie (Terra Humana)*, 2 (2011), 196–200 (p. 199)), so there would have been around 15,000 Jewish pupils even under the ten per cent quota system.
59 Samuel Chotzinoff, *A Lost Paradise: Early Reminiscences* (London: H. Hamilton, 1956), p. 4.
60 'Ben-Ami', 'Gody gimnazii: vospominaniya', *Vestnik vospitaniya*, 3 (1910), 155–91 (p. 154). For

Pale — registering as an artisan when one was not, bribing officials, staying 'below the radar' — are widely attested.[61] Less frequently observed is the likely impact on impressionable children, who must have grown up with a sense than the Imperial Russian political and social order was not just intrusive, but futile and obtuse.

Suspicion of subversion is a way of creating subversion. The enthusiasm with which many Russian Jews welcomed the demise of the old order in 1917 was a natural response to oppression in Tsarist days. The Civil War represented a further turning-point: Jews suffered anti-Semitic stigmatisation and outright pogroms from forces on all sides of the divide, but violence and abuse were particularly prevalent among the anti-Bolshevik Volunteer Armies and other opponents of Bolshevism.[62] A remarkable source of information here is the collection of autobiographical essays written shortly after the war ended by the pupils of schools across the Russian diaspora.[63] They record not just general assaults on Jews ('There was butchery on the streets, they attacked Jews and robbed the citizenry'), but participation by children and teenagers themselves in the violence.[64] A boy born in 1909 recorded:

> At that point I and other officers' sons started to become increasingly prone to cruelty: we were delighted when they shot a sovdep [representative of Soviet power] at Lopasnaya stanitsa, and when the Cossacks organised a pogrom of Yids on Enakievo stanitsa.[65]

This shamefaced retrospective reaction was not universal: one G. Senyavsky, originally from Yaroslavl, exultantly remembered that he and his fellow-pupils at the local classical high school, having got hold of firearms, went on a violent rampage: 'The very first victim in the school itself was a yid called Ufras, who had spat on the cross. He was killed on the spot by his own pupils'.[66] Those hostile to

---

an actual example of a petition from a couple who had omitted to register one of their children, see *Everyday Jewish Life in Imperial Russia*, ed. by Freeze and Harris, p. 168.

61   Nathans, *Beyond the Pale*, pp. 105, 275–77. See also the issue of the St Petersburg satirical journal, *Novyi Satirikon*, 35 (1915), devoted to bribery, especially O. L. D'Or, 'Kak ya platil', the fictional diary of a Jewish artist.

62   For a first-hand account of the pogroms at this era, see Cohen, *Anna's Shtetl*, pp. 81–88, 128–34. The newspaper of the Odessa Revolutionary Committee (*Izvestiya Odesskogo revolyutsionnogo komiteta*) published a report on 24 February 1921 ('Pervomaisk: kak oni raspravilis', p. 1) about violence in the city of Pervomaisk, about 140 miles north of Odessa. On 1 September, mass rapes had included violation of young girls, and at the end of December, over 500 women and girls in the city had been raped, while murder victims included eight boys ranging in age from one and a half to eighteen.

63   The fullest edition is *DRE*.

64   Young man, b. 20 April 1906, *DRE*, p. 173. Interestingly, this is the only case in the collection where an eyewitness recalls that the violence took place after the Bolsheviks took control (in December 1917).

65   *DRE*, p. 109.

66   *DRE*, p. 250. Senyavsky (b. c. 1905) also recalled that he and his fellow pupils took active part when a pogrom was announced, and that after Yaroslavl was captured by the Volunteer Army, 'I was in the saddle for three whole days, out with the White patrols and hunting for yids and chinks' (ibid., p. 251). Anti-Semitism is depressingly pervasive in these memoirs, even from children who grew up in families sympathetic to revolutionary change: see, for example, the account by A. Sobolev (*DRE*, p. 138) about how he and his brother made donations to the a Provisional Government support fund as children, but in retrospect he regretted the money which was now certainly in the hands of some 'little yid'.

Soviet power often blamed Jews for the disaster they believed had overcome their country ('the Jews rose up, who had nothing to do with the Russian nation', as a boy born in 1907 put it). Sometimes, they even revived the horror imagery of blood libel ('I remember how before my very eyes two yids of some kind and some soldiers knifed a woman and two children, and how the hands of one of the yids were sullied with the blood of innocent babes').[67]

Valery Dymshits has described the violence of the Civil War as 'the forgotten genocide'; up to 100,000 Jews were killed in over 1000 pogroms.[68] A panic-struck flight from affected areas began. Many of the children at the Jewish National Home in Petrograd had been orphaned when their parents were killed by serving military or bandits.[69] In one of the inmates' stories included by Doivber Levin in his *Ten Railway Carriages*, Ienya Malinovsky (modelled on the real-life Iona Malinsky), vividly described the disorientation of arriving in Petrograd speaking only Yiddish, and realising that you could not simply ask any passer-by how to find Aunt Ita. Eventually he found someone who understood the question, but his eventual destination was the GPU (secret police), rather than the aunt: 'And what do you think they did with me? Gave me a roll with sausage, then put me to bed'. After a spell in quarantine, he ended up at the orphanage.[70]

The fact that the new Soviet state in its early years firmly turned its back on the institutionalised anti-Semitism of the past was one reason why, as the Civil War went on, Jewish children and teenagers were increasingly likely to identify with the Red cause, and in some cases, to take an active part in defending it. The fact that the secret police acted as a reception facility for orphaned and abandoned children may have prompted loyalty to this particular institution. A typical biography of the era was that of Mikhail Sheinkman (service name Andreev), born in 1903 in a village in Minsk province, who by July 1920 was already plenipotentiary and deputy chief of the politburo of Mazyr District Cheka. A full forty per cent of senior NKVD post-holders in the late 1930s came from ethnic minority backgrounds, with Jews the largest single ethnic group, considerably above their weight in the population. (Later, these same ethnic minorities were to make up fifty-three per cent of the NKVD staff executed or imprisoned in the Great Terror.)[71]

But Jewish children and young people were not simply forced into combat by revolutionary upheaval. They also enjoyed new freedoms. Equality before the law for all religions and nationalities, declared under the Provisional Government and incorporated into early Soviet policy, was followed by a surge in migration to

---

67 DRE, pp. 144, 464. Against more than fifteen cases where the memoirs record violence against Jews, mainly from a point of view hostile to the victims, can be set just one case where a Jew is evaluated positively: a young man, b. 1900, recalled how he had discussed the situation in 1917 with a Jewish friend, 'a very well-read and all-round knowledgeable' person (p. 407).
68 Dymshits in Levin, *Desyat' vagonov*, p. 23.
69 Ibid., pp. 98–99, 233, 291.
70 Levin, *Desyat' vagonov*, pp. 285–88.
71 The percentages are my calculation from a sampling of 120 service biographies out of the 571 included in *Kto rukovodil NKVD, 1934–1941: spravochnik*, ed. by N. V. Petrov and K. V. Skorkin (Moscow: Memorial, 1999) (see also <http://old.memo.ru/history/nkvd/kto/biogr/index.htm>, accessed 26 May 2021). M. L. Andreev's biography also appears in this publication.

FIG. 9.3. Children at the Jewish National Home in front of their agitational 'wall newspaper'. Courtesy Valery Dymshits.

large cities beyond the Pale (by 1926, the Jewish population of Leningrad stood at 84,000, more than four times the figure recorded in 1900, and by 1941, it had climbed to 180,000).[72] Around fifty per cent of the Jewish population was resident in Moscow and Leningrad, another striking indication of the relative social prestige of this ethnic group. By 1939, Jews were also the ethnic group with the highest proportion of graduates from secondary education (343.7 per thousand, as compared with 158 per thousand in the urban population generally), and by far the highest proportion of graduates from higher education (103.7 per thousand, as opposed to 16.4 per thousand in the urban population generally).[73] From 1917, conditions for Jews living in the former Russian Empire changed out of all recognition. Provided they preferred not to practice their faith, Soviet Jews had every chance of joining the elite of the new nation. Carrying the tenets of 'free education' to younger generations, many of the most prominent and creative authors and illustrators working for the new state's children's publishing houses were of Jewish origins,

72 'Elektronnaya evreiskaya entsiklopediya' <http://www.eleven.co.il/article/12415> [accessed 26 May 2021]. In Moscow, the rise was comparable: from 9300 in 1902 to 28,000 in 1920, and over 250,000 in 1939 (ibid, <http://www.eleven.co.il/article/12853>).
73 *Vsesoyuznaya perepis' naseleniya 1939 goda: Osnovnye itogi* (Moscow: Nauka, 1992), p. 83, table 19 (literacy in the Soviet population); pp. 49–79, table 16 (nationality and residence in cities or countryside); p. 86, table 21 (figures for secondary and higher education relative to nationality).

including world-famous figures such as El Lissitsky, and institution builders such as Samuil Marshak, Natalia Sats, and Agniya Barto, as well as nationally prominent individuals such as the puppeteer Nina Simonovich-Efimova, the painter David Shterenberg, the writers Sofiya Zak and Antonina Saksonskaya (Grushman), and the illustrator Lev Yudin.[74]

Magnates such as the Abel'sons, on the other hand, were turned overnight from social elite to social outsiders, officially stigmatised, along with aristocrats and entrepreneurs from Russian or any other ethnic background, as 'former people' who had lived a parasitic existence at the expense of others. Yet, unlike many Russian exiles, they felt a sense of positive transformation alongside the distress of flight. 'Swallowing my grief, I crossed the little bridge which was to confer on us the inestimable gift of freedom of speech', Tamara Talbot Rice recalled.[75] Tamara, and many other émigrés, were also to discover that an upbringing which had furnished love of European culture as well as competence in foreign languages helped to offset the homesickness that still nagged. For many, including Anna Spector, the land of opportunity lay across the Atlantic in America.[76] If conservative émigrés of Russian background lapsed into bitterness, blaming Jews for their plight, Jews do not seem to have responded (as they might have done) by lamenting the short-sightedness and incompetence of the old establishment. Rather, they made the best of the new life — often, indeed usually, taking advantage of new and freer social circumstances in conditions of relative emancipation, just as they had responded as fully and positively as they could to the 'selective integration' practised in the final days of Imperial Russia.[77]

This essay was originally written for 'Jews In and After the 1917 Russian Revolution' at YIVO, New York, 5–6 November 2017. My thanks to Jonathan Brent, for the invitation to speak, and to the participants and audience, for their lively and engaged queries and suggestions. I am also very grateful to Alla Sokolova and Valery Dymshits for their help, in particular with visual sources.

74   The backgrounds from which these different writers and artists came were very diverse. Saksonskaya (1896–1951) was the daughter of an oil magnate from Baku and his Russian wife, Aleksandra Maklygina; the mother of Nina Simonovich-Efimova (1877–1948), German by birth, was a convert to Lutheranism, and her parents founded the first kindergarten in the Russian Empire (in Tiflis). Sats (1903–1993) was also Jewish on her father's side only, but Lissitsky (1890–1941), Shterenberg (1881–1948), Barto (1901–1981), and Yudin (1903–1941) all came from observant families in the Pale, while Marshak (1887–1964) was the son of a Belorussian artisan who had moved before his birth to Voronezh Province. A gifted child whose patrons were the famous critic Vladimir Stasov and Maxim Gorky, Marshak was also an ardent Zionist in his youth, and wrote a lament for the death of Theodor Herzl in 1904; as a young adult, Shterenberg was a Bundist. For a brief introduction to their work, as well as excellent talks on children's literature in Yiddish, see the YIVO video, 'Jewish Children's Literature in Russian and Yiddish' (June 2021) <https://www.youtube.com/watch?v=SBnGQuKCoS8> [accessed 27 September 2022].
75   Rice, *Tamara*, p. 74 (punctuation edited).
76   Anna Spector (Cohen, *Anna's Shtetl*, p. 170) reached the USA in March 1922; the family settled in Iowa, and Anna, after relocating to St Louis, married in 1925, aged twenty (to another émigré from the former Russian Empire). Her three children included a professor of Chinese at Stanford, an architect, and a professional fund-raiser.
77   The phrase was coined by Nathans, *Beyond the Pale*, p. 78.

PART IV

'Everything for the Children'

CHAPTER 10

'I Want to Be a Tractor Driver!' Gender and Childhood in Early Soviet Russia

[2003]

In 1934, Natalia Sats, director of the Central Children's Theatre, was accorded the honour of presenting an address at the First Congress of Soviet Writers.[1] Sats used the occasion not only to promote her own role as a pioneer of dramatic performances for the under-twelves, and to ruminate on desirable future developments in the Soviet children's theatre, but also to reflect on the representation of children in extant literature and drama. A central problem that she identified was the lack of convincing and properly differentiated portrayals of assertive small girls:

> Where, you wonder, are the girls enjoying equal rights, the women enjoying equal rights, the girl who is engaged in the public life of society [*obshchest-vennitsa*]? And the author's response? There are plenty of boy pioneers around — just change them into girls, and the problem is solved. As though just changing them at the snap of your fingers were completely simple, as though women enjoying equal rights had no specific characteristics![2]

Sats's comments, like most of the remarks made at the First Congress of Soviet Writers, were meant to be incentive, as much as descriptive: to point the way for new endeavours, as much as to assess what had already been achieved. They heralded an era in which activist heroes would start to play a much less significant role in art and literature aimed at children, and when the fairy tale (*skazka*), previously lambasted in Soviet pedagogy, would for a while become the dominant mode of representation in books, plays, pictures, and murals in Pioneer palaces.[3] But

---

1   For more information on the biography of Sats, see Chapter 7 in this book.
2   Natal'ya Sats, in *Pervyi Vsesoyuznyi s"ezd sovetskikh pisatelei 1934: stenograficheskii otchet* (Moscow: Khudozhestvennaya literatura, 1934), p. 472.
3   Krupskaya's notorious attack on Kornei Chukovsky's *skazki* (verse tales) in 1929 (see my *Children's World*, Chapter 2) was only the most prominent of many such assaults: compare *Metodicheskie pis'ma po doshkol'nomu obrazovaniyu*, 10 (1926), 13: 'There is nothing to justify the images of cats dressed up in hats and dogs baking pies; these crude, fairground-style figures add nothing positive either to the child's emotional world or to their understanding of animals'. Conversely, the rehabilitation of the *skazka* from 1934–35 onwards is evident in the leading roles played by Marshak and Chukovsky at the First Congress of Soviet Writers, in Gorky's article 'O skazkakh' (*Pravda*, 30 January 1935;

they were also an at least superficially accurate reflection of the way in which Soviet propaganda texts generally represented girls during the first fifteen or so years of Soviet power. At this period, the ideal child was male, politically active, if possible blonde, and eager to rush through childhood as quickly as possible.[4] In Boris Ignatovich's photograph *The First Tractor* (1927), a small boy sat astride the collective farm's newly-arrived Fordison, triumphantly waving his cap.[5] The same point about accelerated development was made more subtly in Aleksandr Rodchenko's famous trilogy of Pioneer photographs from 1930. All three children were shot from below, rendering their faces monumentally vast, while their eyes were fixed upwards, staring towards the bright future.[6]

It is at first quite hard to grasp that Rodchenko's photograph includes a girl, so effectively is the representation of her assimilated to that of the boys, with short hair and a resolute expression. So far as many propaganda images were concerned, then, Sats's assessment was accurate: the activist Pioneer girl was indeed more or less interchangeable with her activist brother. This point was underlined also by the official uniform of the day, which prescribed trunks (*trusiki*) for girls as well as for boys, as an alternative to skirts.[7] The 1920s and early 1930s cult of hygiene and of 'rational dress' played down differences between the sexes, prescribing straightforward shifts, leggings, and overalls for both boys and girls. A manual published in 1929 shows garments with rudimentary seaming: the models have cropped hair and androgynous features.[8] Clothes were supposed to be lightweight, streamlined, and light coloured. Decorations such as lace or ribbons, particularly hair-ribbons (*bantiki*) were definitely not included: they would have been considered both hygienically and socially dangerous, attracting dirt and manifesting a drift towards 'bourgeois values' (*meshchanstvo*). For its part, traditional peasant clothing

reprinted in *Sobranie sochinenii*, XXVII, 392–401), and in the widespread use of *skazka* themes for the decoration of Pioneer palaces (see, for example, on the Khar'kov Pioneer Palace, Em. Mindlin, 'Lyudi semidesyatykh godov', *Nashi dostizheniya*, 5 (1936), 5–6). On the change in understanding of the child after 1934 to which the rise of the *skazka* was related, see further below. For discussions of the *skazka* from a different perspective (as a governing trope in Stalinist ideology more broadly), see, for example, M. Lipovetsky, 'Skazkovlast': "Tarakanishche" Stalina', *Novoe literaturnoe obozrenie*, 45 (2000), 122–36 (esp. pp. 122–24); V. Papernyi, *Kul'tura "Dva"*, 2nd edn (Moscow: Novoe literaturnoe obozrenie, 1996), esp. sections 12 and 13, 'Realizm — pravda', and 'Delo — chudo', pp. 281–307.

4   The blondeness of propaganda children had, at this stage of Soviet history, nothing to do with ethnic stereotyping. Blondes simply fitted better into the governing trope of 'darkness into light' (on which generally, see Halfin, *From Darkness to Light*, esp. pp. 116–18). This was also the reason why mythic portraits of Pavlik Morozov usually referred to the child as blond (see, for example, the first contribution to the legend in a central metropolitan newspaper, in *Pionerskaya pravda* [hereafter referenced as *PP*], 102 (15 October 1932), p. 4, where Pavlik is described as *svetlovolosyi*). See also my *Comrade Pavlik*.

5   Reproduced in *Sowjetische Fotografen 1917–1940*, ed. by S. Morozov and others (Leipzig: VEB Fotokinoverlag, 1980), p. 103.

6   For the Rodchenko images, see *Aleksandr Rodchenko*, exhibition catalogue (New York: Museum of Modern Art, 1998), plates 277–79.

7   In photographs of Pioneer camps published in *Pioner* and *PP* during the mid-1920s, for instance, girls are often shown wearing shorts, or baggy short skirts that are little different in effect. See, for example, *Pioner*, 4 (1924), 17–18.

8   *Odezhda rebenka-doshkol'nika: Instruktivnoe pis'mo* (Moscow & Leningrad: Gosizdat, 1929).

for girls was considered equally uncultured, as excessively heavy and difficult to clean.⁹

In terms of the child's psychology as well, androgyny, with a bias towards masculinity, was the norm. In Lidiya Seifullina's well-known story *The Young Offenders* (*Pravonarushiteli*, 1922), the girls were conditioned out of 'girlish' behaviour patterns, such as tearfulness and timidity, and took their place in the harmonious and well-disciplined child collective. Anton Makarenko, whose children's commune was the real-life prototype of the orphanage portrayed by Seifullina, was explicit in his preference for a particular sort of inmate: the 'cheeky type' (*nakhal*) and 'Viking' (*varyag*), the assertive male who yet responded well to the military drilling that was used by Makarenko as his central method of 're-education' in his reformatory.¹⁰

Images of children replicated in miniature early Soviet visions of the 'new [wo]man' as militant crusader for social and cultural revolution. In the words of Elizabeth Wood: 'The [female] world presented here [in Soviet propaganda] is dichotomous — either that of the baba, superstitious, apolitical, associated with the "old way of life", or that of the citizen-comrade' (and, one could add, the frivolous bourgeoise, obsessed with her own appearance and with pleasure, as well).¹¹ In the same way, girls were divided into scaled-down miniature comrades, scaled-down babas, or scaled-down bourgeoises, obsessed with their appearance, and with frivolous pursuits such as attending the cinema. Articles in *Pioneer Pravda* provided plenty of examples of girl comrades — for instance, the bobbed 'Coevals of October' celebrated in November 1928. But the paper also lambasted less ideologically fervent types, such as the gossipy and chattering girl who dropped the baby she was minding in a crèche when she became distracted, or the two girls who missed Pioneer meetings because they were promenading round an art gallery.¹² While boys came in for some criticism as well — the Pioneer press of the late 1920s and early 1930s was full of denunciations of fighting and gambling, allegedly the main pastimes of children in all city courtyards in Russia — the emphasis in propaganda upon 'energy' and 'resolution' endorsed potentially disruptive behaviour by boys,

---

9   *Odezhda rebenka-doshkol'nika* advises against silk (expensive, and less practical than wool, p. 11), and heavy woollen petticoats for girls (pp. 23–24).
10 Anton Makarenko, *Pedagogicheskaya poema* (1933–36): in the edition published in Moscow, 1944, this reference is found on p. 409.
11 E. Wood, *The Baba and the Comrade: Gender and Politics in Revolutionary Russia* (Bloomington: Indiana University Press, 1997), p. 225. On condemnation of female frivolity, see, for example, Anne Gorsuch, *Youth in Revolutionary Russia: Enthusiasts, Bohemians, Delinquents* (Bloomington: Indiana University Press, 2000). Eisenstein's 'revolutionary trilogy' — *Strike* (1924), *Battleship Potemkin* (1925), and *October* (1928) — provides an exemplary range of all these female types, from babas (the wives in *Strike* trying to persuade their husbands to go back to work), to *bourgeoises* (the over-made-up women of easy virtue who consort with the bosses in *Strike*, or the members of the Women's Battalion whom *October* shows in their lacy underwear), to the comrades (a female agitator on the Odessa quayside in *Battleship Potemkin*).
12 The 'Coevals of October' ('Odnoletki Oktyabrya') appear in *PP*, 94 (1928), p. 3; the neglectful young nanny is mocked in a cartoon in *PP*, 7 (1925), p. 4 (she is evidently working in one of the temporary creches organised by Pioneers in the countryside so that mothers could attend political meetings); the two enthusiasts for art are also denounced (as 'samye glavnye comple' in their *otryad*) in *PP*, 7 (1925), p. 4.

even as regulations and normative texts sought to curb what were seen as the negative facets of that behaviour.[13] It was characteristic that a child-care guide published in the late 1920s should have asserted, 'quiet, obedient, silent children are, in essence simply abnormal'.[14] While some experts expressed anxieties about traditional boys' toys such as model weapons, which allegedly were likely to cause the child to grow up 'cruel, impervious, and egotistical', more frequent criticism was directed at girls' toys such as baby dolls, which were associated with bourgeois family instincts, and with the development of personal vanity in those who played with them.[15]

One should not, however, assume that evaluative gender stereotyping of this kind was evident everywhere in Soviet society at this time. A significant body of commentators understood childhood in gender-neutral terms. Lev Vygotsky, for example, took little or no interest in the child's development of gender awareness (in contrast to the commentaries on child psychology produced in the Soviet Union in the 1970s).[16] The 'crises' which Vygotsky catalogued in his writings on early childhood were intellectual and emotional in character, and common to both sexes: none of them included anything resembling a 'crisis of gender awareness'. Indeed, Vygotsky expressly set out to play down the value of purely biological explications of developmental thresholds.[17] However, Vygotsky's writings represent a more esoteric level of public discourse than the brochures and pamphlets through which ordinary Soviet readers were most likely to get their information about childcare and health issues in general.

A more important cause for caution is that gender historians' well-founded assertions of the Soviet system's preference for the 'masculine universal'[18] often elide the question of precisely what kind of 'masculinity' early Soviet discourse assumed

---

13   See, for example, the photo-reportage 'Dvor stal pionerskim', *PP*, 81 (1933), pp. 4–5.

14   A. Babina, *Kak organizovat' dosug detei* (Moscow: Rabotnik prosveshcheniya, 1929), p. 7.

15   For the first, see A. Mitina, *Poleznye I vrednye igrushki* (Moscow: Okhrana materinstva i mladenchestva, 1927); for the second, *Metodicheskie pis'ma po doshkol'nomu vospitaniyu*, 14 (Moscow, 1927), 24. Permitted, though, were role-playing dolls such as Petrushka puppets and dolls in national dress, or figures with which socially-oriented games such as 'Central Food Market' could be played (see ibid., p. 25, and N. Bartram, *Muzei igrushki* (Leningrad: Academia, 1928), p. 34).

16   For examples of the latter, see V. A. Sukhomlinsky, *Pis'ma k synu* (Moscow: Prosveshchenie, 1979); *Rozhdenie grazhdanina*, 3rd edn (Moscow: Molodaya gvardiya, 1979); *Kniga o lyubvi* (Moscow: Molodaya gvardiya, 1983). For the conceptual background to such work, see Lynne Attwood, *The New Soviet Man and Woman: Sex-Role Socialization in the USSR* (Basingstoke: Macmillan, 1990).

17   See the late writings collected in L. S. Vygotsky, *Sobranie sochinenii*, 6 vols (Moscow: Pedagogika, 1982–84), IV, esp. pp. 340–67 ('Rannee detstvo', 1933–34), pp. 368–75 ('Krizis trekh let', 1933–34), and pp. 244–68 ('Problema vozrasta', 1932–34). For the comments on the instability of biological signifiers, see pp. 244–46 ('Problema vozrasta').

18   As, for example, in Elizabeth Waters, 'The Female Form in Soviet Political Iconography, 1917–32', in *Russia's Women: Accommodation, Resistance, Transformation*, ed. by Barbara Evans Clements, Barbara Alpen Engel, and Christine D. Worobec (Berkeley: University of California Press, 1991), pp. 225–42 (esp. pp. 227–82, 232–35); or Diane P. Koenker, 'Men Against Women on the Shop Floor in Early Soviet Russia: Gender and Class in the Socialist Workplace', *American Historical Review*, 100 (1995), 1438–64. For a discussion of some famous films of the early Soviet period, see Lynne Attwood, 'The 1920s', in *Red Women on the Silver Screen: Soviet Women and Cinema from the Beginning to the End of the Communist Era*, ed. by Lynne Attwood (London: Pandora, 1993), pp. 29–50.

to be 'universal'.¹⁹ An important source for the understanding of this is advice literature, such as A. K. Toporkov's *How to be Cultured* (1929), which presented a highly rationalistic and emotionally restrictive picture of manhood. The governing concept was *zakal*, 'self-tempering', an extremely rigorous and demanding code of physical and mental self-discipline, requiring exercise, hydrotherapeutic procedures such as the use of alternating douches of hot and cold water, efficiency at work, and whole-hearted application to the good of the collective at large.²⁰ Unlike the 'Soviet Don Juan'-style fantasies propounded by some early Soviet sensational belles-lettres (for example, Panteleimon Romanov's *No Cherry Blossom* (*Bez cheremukhi*), of 1927), machismo in the sense of erotic self-expression was taboo.²¹

The Soviet behaviour ideal propounded by normative guides was in no sense one that posited absolute licence for historical subjects: rather, it was one in which an individual's self-control replicated the control exercised by the 'benevolent despotism' of the regime itself (and its microcosm, the collective) over these subjects.²² Children were in no sense exempted from the obligation to impose discipline upon themselves and to be obedient to social discipline. Assertiveness on their part was tolerated only in so far as it did not threaten to disrupt the governance of right-thinking adults. Pioneers were encouraged to challenge backward members of society, and journals and newspapers reported exultantly on confrontations in which they had, say, harangued benighted old women about the evils of the Christmas tree, or exposed their parents to public ridicule for having attempted to subvert the ban on this seasonal decoration by adorning a pot-plant rather than a fir.²³ However, the Pioneer movement was, from its inception, subordinate to the governance of the Komsomol, and the leadership made efforts to ensure that those holding local positions of responsibility, such as troop leaders (*vozhatye*), were drawn from the Komsomol, rather than the Pioneer movement itself.²⁴ Even in the late 1920s and early 1930s, when the cult of child activism reached its height, Pioneer newspapers and journals carried articles on the need for discipline in schools, and key representations of children underlined that some categories of adult must be treated respectfully. As reported by *Pioneer Pravda* in October 1932, Pavlik

---

19 For a pioneering discussion of this topic, see Eliot Borenstein, *Men without Women: Masculinity and Revolution in Russian Fiction* (Durham, NC: Duke University Press, 2000).
20 See A. Toporkov, *Kak stat' kul'turnym* (Moscow: Rabotnik prosveshcheniya, 1929). On *zakal*, see Chapter 3 above.
21 On early Soviet eroticism, see especially Eric Naiman, *Sex in Public: The Incarnation of Early Soviet Ideology* (Princeton, NJ: Princeton University Press, 1997). The literal translation of Romanov's title is 'No Bird Cherry Blossom' (*cheremukha*, Prunus padus), but this tree does not have the same resonance in Anglophone folklore.
22 For a thought-provoking study of this side of Soviet culture, see Oleg Khakhordin, *The Collective and the Individual in Soviet Culture: A Study of Practices* (Berkeley: University of California Press, 2000).
23 T. Karpinskaya, 'Kak oboshli' bez elki', *Drug detei*, 2 (1930), 18.
24 See, for example, a document prepared by the Central Committee of the Komsomol, 'Sostav i podgotovka vozhatykh pionerotryada' (20 December 1927), which expresses concern about the youth and lack of training of many *vozhatye*. Central Repository of Documents of Youth Organisations (TsKhDMO), now Russian State Archive of Socio-Political History Youth Section (RGASPI-M), f. 1 op. 23 d. 788, ll. 13–20.

Morozov's denunciation of his father invited official sanction of his behaviour. Pavlik angled for the judge's collusion with the childish address *dyaden'ka* ('Uncle judge, I am acting not as a son, but as a Young Pioneer!'), assigning himself to an alternative kind of patriarchal family, one cemented by political conviction.[25] The hygienic ideals propounded for children likewise had a flavour of external control (the disciplining of adults by children) as well as (or indeed rather than) internal control (the child's regulation of his or her own body).[26]

On the one hand, children were supposed to exercise agency over their bodies, learning by heart and putting into practice sets of cleanliness rules such as were also found in manuals for adults: wash your hands before meals and your body daily, clean your teeth once a day, change your underwear and visit the banya once a week, get plenty of fresh air.[27] On the other, however, they were seen as morally fragile subjects who could not be expected to regulate themselves reliably: advice was therefore supplemented by control. This was especially the case in matters concerning child sexuality. A brochure published in 1929, for example, contained designs that were streamlined and ergonomic, but also coercive. Nightshirts were to be ankle length 'in order to stop children from becoming cold and indulging in the bad habit of touching their genitals, which provokes masturbation, a practice that it is very difficult to cure'. For the same reason, they were to have long sleeves so that children learned to keep their hands above the sheets.[28] Here, the child's ability to sleep comfortably came some way below propriety in the order of priorities.

It might seem attractive to see such instructions as evidence of 'Soviet puritanism', or perhaps of a more broadly Russian asceticism, with its roots in Orthodox culture.[29] But in fact, the obsession with policing children's sexuality has a quite specific history, and is of relatively recent origin, both in Russia and in the West.[30] And there were international parallels for other aspects of the early Soviet myth of

---

25   *PP*, 115 (1932), p. 4.
26   Since this essay was first published, I have written more extensively about this in 'Educating the Future Race: Children and Everyday Life in Early Soviet Russia', in *Everyday Life in Early Soviet Russia*, ed. by Kiaer and Naiman, pp. 256–81. See also Alla Sal'nikova, *Rossiiskoe detstvo v dvadtsatom veke: istoriya, teoriya i praktika issledovaniya* (Kazan': Kazanskii gosudarstvennyi universitet, 2007).
27   *Pionery — boitsy kul'tpokhoda*, ed. by L. Shelomov, M. Likhobabin, and V. Vel'tman [V. Panova] (Rostov-on-Don: Partizdat, 1933), p. 56.
28   *Odezhda rebenka-doshkol'nika*, p. 19.
29   On the latter, see for example Eve Levin, *Sex and Society in the World of the Orthodox Slavs* (Ithaca, NY: Cornell University Press, 1989), and Jane Costlow, Stephanie Sandler, and Judith Vowles, 'Introduction', in *Sexuality and the Body in Russian Culture*, ed. by Jane Costlow, Stephanie Sandler, and Judith Vowles (Stanford, CA: Stanford University Press, 1993), pp. 1–40.
30   The earliest guide that I have come across relating to this subject in Russia is A. Nikitin, *O vrednykh posledstviyakh rukobludiya, ili Gigienicheskie zamechaniya o neschastnykh tainykh privychkakh detei, v nazidanie roditelyam i nastavnikam* (St Petersburg: tipografiya Imperatorskoi Akademii Nauk, 1844); on later materials, see the discussion by Laura Engelstein in *The Keys to Happiness: Sex and the Search for Modernity in Fin de Siècle Russia* (Ithaca, NY: Cornell University Press, 1992), pp. 232–36, 284–86, 291–92. On the West, see for example the comments of Dr Henry Roberts in *The Mother's Advice Book* (London: 1911), p. 192, recommending pyjamas rather than a nightdress, as the latter was apt to ride up and leave the child 'naked and exposed'. On the history of such materials, see Alex Comfort, *The Anxiety Makers: Some Curious Preoccupations of the Medical Profession* (London: Nelson, 1967).

ideal childhood too. The emphasis on the ideal child as politically active simply took to extremes a concern to involve children in democratic institutions that had been widespread among Russian and Western liberals before 1917.[31] During the 1920s, precedents and parallels from beyond the Soviet Union were widely recognised: one of many significant cases is a highly laudatory article about Bedales, a co-educational, progressive school in the south of England, published in a Soviet educational journal in 1926.[32]

Equally, the playing-down of gender differences between children — or more accurately, the attempt to encourage girls to assimilate to a narrowly-defined, ascetic code of masculinity — had parallels and precedents elsewhere. It is interesting to record in this regard that the 'sexless' appearance of children does not seem to have attracted the ridicule that was expended on the 'boyish' appearance of Soviet women (evident, say, in the writings of E. M. Delafield, or in Ernst Lubitsch's 1939 Hollywood film *Ninotchka*, starring Greta Garbo in the role of a 'Bolshevik Cinderella', an unsmiling commissar in military dress who is transformed by her contact with Western men, fashion, and grooming).[33]

Early Soviet child-care struck contemporary Western observers as 'sensible' largely because it was so similar to the practices then considered 'modern' in the West. By the end of the nineteenth century, 'rational upbringing' — particularly as this was understood in Britain and in America — went with an emphasis upon streamlined clothing, grooming, and all other aspects of child management. 'Nursery furniture should be as scanty as is compatible with comfort [...]. Cold bathing is of the utmost value to children', argued Dr Henry Roberts in a manual for mothers published in 1911. He also observed, 'The ridiculous way in which young children are dressed is almost past arguing about', and advocated that children should be dressed in practical, warm fabrics such as wool and cellular cotton. The six absolute rules for children's dress were that it should be a bad conductor of heat, absorbent, porous, light, loose, and non-flammable.[34] Dress-making manuals, in similar vein, advocated simple shapes — round-necked shirts and shorts for boys, shift or smock dresses, or indeed blouses and culottes (alternatively known as 'divided skirts') for girls.[35] Girls were expected to dress in gym-slips (loose, short-skirted garments

---

31 For instance, S. T. Shatsky's 'Settlement', based in the Moscow area, was modelled on the 'Settlement' initiatives begun in America during the late nineteenth century. See S. T. Shatsky, 'Moi pedagogicheskii put'' in *S. T. Shatsky v ego pedagogicheskikh vyskazyvaniyakh*, ed. by M. N. Skatkin and L. N. Skatkin (Moscow: Uchpedgiz, 1958), pp. 9–28 (see also W. Partlett, 'Breaching Cultural Worlds with the Village School: Educational Visions, Local Initiative, and Rural Experience at S. T. Shatskii's Kaluga School System, 1919–1932', *Slavonic and East European Review*, 82.4 (2004), 847–85).
32 M. Shteingauz, 'Bidel'skaya shkola', *Prosveshchenie na transporte*, 3 (1926), 85–91; 4 (1926), 93–102.
33 E. M. Delafield, *I Visit the Soviets: The Provincial Lady Looks at Russia* (New York & London: Harper, 1937).
34 Roberts, *The Mothers' Advice Book*, pp. 41, 43, 190–91.
35 See, for example, the illustrations in Jane A. Fleming, *Garment Making: The Cutting-Out and Making-Up of Common-Sense Comfortable Clothing for Children* (Leeds: E. J. Arnold, 1912). A pioneering effort of this kind was launched by the Rational Dress Society in the late 1880s: see the masthead of *The Rational Dress Society's Gazette*, 1 (1888), 1, proclaiming the promotion of 'a style of dress based upon considerations of health, comfort, and beauty'. For a general discussion of children's clothes at this period, see Elizabeth Ewing, *History of Children's Costume* (London: Batsford, 1977), pp. 87–90,

with box pleats to allow for ease of movement), and to have their hair short or at the very least simply styled; the dress required for energetic games such as cricket, hockey, and lacrosse set the tone for clothing in a broad sense. 'Girly' decorations such as ribbons, frills, and lace were considered antiquated and inappropriate.

With hygiene in a physical sense went emotional hygiene. By the 1880s, 'orphanage discipline' had become the model for advanced parenting; feeding times were supposed to be ordered by the clock, rather than infant need; and practices such as kissing children and rocking them were severely discouraged.[36] Perhaps the most influential proponent of 'rational upbringing' for the new century was F. Truby King, a New Zealand medical practitioner who had derived his ideas about child-care from experience as an intensive stock-breeder. This left him with not only a pioneering formula for successful artificial infant feeding, but also with dogmatic ideas about the importance of strict regime and absence of fuss. As his daughter proclaimed in 1934:

> A Truby King baby has as much fresh air and sunlight as possible, and his right amount of sleep. His education begins right from the very first week, good habits being established which remain throughout his life [...]. Not treated as a plaything [...] he is the happiest thing alive.[37]

What this euphemistic description concealed was extreme rigidity in the treatment of infants, who were supposed to be given no more than five feeds over twenty-four hours, spaced at regular intervals during the day (night feeding was considered improper). Apart from over-feeding or irregular feeding, prohibitions included rocking baby to sleep, placing it in the parental bed, letting it have a dummy or suck its thumb, and failing to ensure that it defecated regularly first thing in the morning. Truby King's books contained photographs showing the super-babies that could be produced by his patent methods: two squat toddlers in summer dresses, for example, were captioned 'Healthy, happy little girls, ages two and nearly four years old. Good jaws and sound teeth. Nursed four-hourly from birth — never more than five times in twenty-four hours; plenty of fresh air and exercise — never any coddling'.[38] 'Coddling' was encouraged still less in the case of older children. 'Self-reliance' and 'backbone' became the watchwords, for girls as well as for boys.[39]

All of this, of course, had roots in the post-Enlightenment tradition of 'rational child management' going back to the work of thinkers such as John Locke (*Some Thoughts Concerning Education*, 1690) and Rousseau (*Émile*, 1762).[40] Theories of this kind developed along with the expansion of the category of 'child' to include

---

104–09.
36 See, for example, Eric Pritchard, *Infant Education* (London: Kimpton, 1907). There is a useful general discussion of this text and many similar ones in Christina Hardyment, *Perfect Parents: Baby-Care Advice Past and Present* (Oxford: Oxford University Press, 1995), esp. pp. 125–40.
37 Mary Truby King, *Mothercraft* (London: Simpkin Marshall, 1934), p. 4. On Truby King's biography, see ibid., pp. 1–4, and Hardyment, *Perfect Parents*, pp. 178–81.
38 F. Truby King, *The Expectant Mother and Baby's First Month* (London: Macmillan, 1924), pp. 117–18, 35.
39 See Hardyment, *Perfect Parents*, pp. 150–51 (on the 1910s), 173–81 (on the 1920s).
40 See Chapter 1 above.

individuals up to and sometimes into adolescence.[41] The medieval and early modern tradition of regarding small children (those under seven, the beginning of the 'age of reason' in Christian theology) as sexless was modified. 'The age of reason' expanded backwards, and 'the age of innocence' forwards, so that children were understood as both reasonable *and* innocent beings.[42] At any given time, reason or innocence might be accorded a greater weight; gender associations also fluctuated. The ideal of childhood was unisex, in that it was imposed upon both boys and girls, yet at any one time it tended to be coloured by the stereotypical traits of one or other gender (by no means always the male one).

In the early nineteenth century, the most prevalent type of ideal child in elite and commercial art was vaguely 'feminine' in coloration. In John Everett Millais's famous portrait *Bubbles* (1886), a small boy is shown with curls and a blue suit, looking with a sweetly unfocused expression to one side.[43] Frances Hodgson Burnett's *Little Lord Fauntleroy* (also dating from 1886) was a literary variant on the same theme, and Faunteroy's lace-collared velvet suit with knickerbockers, and long golden ringlets, were widely copied by late nineteenth-century mothers all over Europe and America.[44]

But the tradition that was more dominant among pedagogical writers (though not necessarily among mothers) tended to imagine an ideal child who was male, at any rate by default. Equally, the standard assumption was that the carer (at least during a child's first years) would be female. This led to the modulation of a traditional power asymmetry related to age (where the senior individual was assumed to be dominant) by factors of gender (according to Enlightenment perception, males were more assertive and more energetic, and also potentially more reasonable, than females). As Valerie Walkerdine points out, progressive educational theory had since the eighteenth century not only substituted 'covert watching' for 'overt

---

41 On the development of the theory of 'extended childhood', see for example Colin Heywood, *Childhood in Nineteenth-Century France: Work, Health and Education Among the classes populaires* (Cambridge: Cambridge University Press, 1988), pp. 3–4.
42 Locke regards children as reasonable beings from an early age: 'It seems plain to me, that the principle of all virtues and excellency lies in a power of denying ourselves the satisfaction of our own desires, where reason does not authorise them. This power is to be got and improved by custom, made easy and familiar by an early practice. If therefore I might be heard, I would advise that, contrary to the ordinary way, children should be used to submit their desires, and go without their longings, from their very cradles' (*Some Thoughts Concerning Education*, section 38: in *The Works of John Locke*, 10 vols (London: for J. Johnson, 1801), IX, 32). Rousseau's *Émile*, while acknowledging the child's need of support (control, help, and the exercise of judgement are provided by others), also insists on its autonomy from interference: 'Avant la vocation des parens la nature l'appelle à la vie humaine' (*Émile*, Book 1, Chapter 1: in *Œuvres complètes*, 5 vols, Bibliothèque de la Pléiade (Paris: Gallimard, 1959–95), IV, 247, 252).
43 This image, used to advertise Pears Soap in the late nineteenth and early twentieth century, and later in the possession of Gibbs Elida, the cosmetics company that bought up the Pears brand name in the 1980s, is widely reproduced in books on Millais and websites.
44 Frances Hodgson Burnett, *Little Lord Fauntleroy* (London: Frederick Warne, 1886). The book had gone into eight editions by 1888. See also Anne Higonnet, *Pictures of Innocence: The History and Crisis of Ideal Childhood* (London: Thames & Hudson, 1998); Hugh Cunningham, *Children and Childhood in Western Society since 1500* (London: Longman, 1995), p. 75.

disciplining', but also accorded the child 'a fantasy of omnipotent control over the Other — the teacher', making the latter 'the servant of the omnipotent child'.[45]

'Rational upbringing' in any form was relatively late to make an impact upon Russian society (as is evidenced, for example, by the late arrival of Locke's ideas, by the rather restricted circulation of Rousseau's educational theories until the mid-nineteenth century, or by the smallness of the readership for Pestalozzi).[46] However, by the 1850s, Tolstoy's writings were beginning to popularise Rousseau far more widely than before; Froebel's essays started to attract serious interest during the 1870s, a couple of decades after they first appeared in the West; by the early twentieth century, Montessori's writings were being translated immediately after they were published.[47] Given the Anglomania that gripped the Russian cultural elite in the early twentieth century, it was inevitable that 'rational upbringing' should also have had a strong influence at the level of everyday life. Russian childcare manuals, like foreign ones, emphasised the need to arrange light, airy, dust-free, and uncluttered quarters for children, and to dress them appropriately. Swaddling (*svivanie*) of infants was regarded critically, and a popular form of older children's attire for both sexes was the sailor suit, an English fashion perceived to be both egalitarian and unisex.[48]

At the same time, streamlining and 'emotional hygiene' were not universal. Indeed, the Romantic idealisation of childhood experience, and concomitant tendency to feminise children, was on the whole more dominant than in Western Europe, or certainly than in Britain or America. In the 1900s, high-status Russian parents still routinely dressed small boys well past the cradle stage in girls' clothing.[49]

---

45 Valerie Walkderine, *Schoolgirl Fictions* (London: Verso, 1990), pp. 22–24.
46 Locke's *Some Thoughts on Education* was first translated by Nikolai Popovsky as *O vospitanii detei gospodina Lokka*, 2 vols (Moscow: pechatano pri Imperatorskom Moskovskom universitete, 1759; reissued in 1760 and 1788). For the history of *Émile* in Russia, see Chapter 1 above.
47 On Tolstoy's educational theory and its Western roots, see for example Daniel Murphy, *Tolstoy and Education* (Blackrock: Irish Academic Press, 1992). Although translations of Froebel's texts first began appearing only in the 1910s (see, for example, *Pedagogicheskie sochineniya*, 2 vols (Moscow: K. I. Tikhomirov, 1913), the first kindergarten on Froebelian lines was opened in St Petersburg in 1871. The first Russian translation of Montessori's *Il metodo della pedagogia scientifica applicato all'educazione infantile nelle case dei bambini* (Rome: E. Loescher, 1913) came out in 1914 (as *Metod nauchnoi pedagogiki, primenyaemoi v domakh rebenka*, trans. by I. M. Solov'ev), and in 1915 Elizaveta Tikheeva produced a detailed (though also quite critical) account of a fact-finding mission to Montessori's own school in Rome (*Dom rebenka Montessori v Rime: ikh teoriya i praktika. Po lichnym vpechatleniyam* (Petrograd: tipografiya L. Ya. Ginzburga, 1915).
48 On rational nurseries, see for example A. P. Popova, 'Ukhod za novorozhdennym', in *Pervyi zhenskii kalendar'*, 8 (1906), 261–62 (cots were supposed to be steel and have no curtains, for instance); for an attack on swaddling, see ibid., p. 268: 'The swaddling of children has now fallen out of use [the author means in educated circles, obviously] because it only causes torment and harm to children'. The sailor suit was not worn by peasant- or working-class Russian children, but a very wide spectrum of children from the upper strata of Russian society, from Tsesarevich Aleksei through Vladimir Nabokov to middle-class Moscow children snapped by a passing photographer in 1910, wore the garment.
49 In England, on the other hand, a late-nineteenth century magazine, *Baby*, advised that 'boys should be breeched [put into trousers] as soon as they begin to run about easily' (quoted in Ewing, *A History of Children's Costume*, p. 105: exact reference not given).

As late as 1918, Vadim Shefner remembered being subjected to merciless teasing on his first day at a kindergarten because he was the only boy not in shorts and a shirt. The other boys shouted, 'A woman's dress! a woman's dress! the new boy's got a woman's dress!', while the girls greeted him with an insulting ditty usually used for inappropriately dressed girls:

> Как тебе не стыдно,
> Панталоны видно,
> Юбочка коротка,
> Ты моя сиротка!⁵⁰

[Look at you! | Knickers on view! | Skirt short and sweet | Like an orphan off the street.]

By the 1900s, even the 'intermediately masculine' 'Little Lord Fauntleroy' look was a little passé in the Anglophone world. In Russia, though, feminine clothes for small boys continued to be in use (just as Hodgson Burnett's book continued to be advertised by the catalogues of prestigious suppliers of children's goods, such as *Detskoe vospitanie* of Leont'evskii pereulok, Moscow).⁵¹

While the very fact that boys were starting to resent being dressed as girls indicates that the ethos of 'rational dress' had begun to make its mark on them, the cult of the tomboy seems to have made less impact on Russian girlhood than upon the comparable age-group in England or America. A catalogue produced by a prestigious shop in St Petersburg represents a large number of stiff and frilly outfits for girls. Every top is decorated with lace, embroidery, and often braiding as well.⁵²

Photographs of girls from well-off families reproduced in memoirs and family albums, and fashionable portraits, also illustrate quite elaborate costumes. A photograph of St Petersburg timber merchant's daughter Tamara Abel'son shows a stiffly starched white dress decorated with lace and buttoned to the neck; Tamara is also wearing a floppy white bow in her ringletted hair. While this image presents the child dressed for 'best', another, more informal family photograph of Tamara's cousins shows the girl, again, in a white dress, with only the boys in sailor suits.⁵³ The torment of uncomfortable curling-rags to produce the ringlets was familiar to many early twentieth-century girls.⁵⁴ More informal dress seems to have been reserved for girls from unconventional, even Bohemian, families, as in Mikhail

---

50 Vadim Shefner, *Imya dlya ptitsy, ili Chaepitie na zheltoi verande*, in his *Lachuga dolzhnika* (St Petersburg: Khudozhestvennaya literatura, 1995), p. 351.
51 See *Izdaniya A. I. Mamontova i magazina "Detskoe vospitanie"* (Moscow: A. I. Mamontov, 1900), p. 6, which lists *Malen'kii lord Fauntleroi* at a cost of 50 kopecks. The term 'intermediate masculinity' goes back to Edward Carpenter's 1911 essay, 'The Intermediate Sex', and became widespread in gender analysis of the 1990s: see for example James S. Campbell, '"For You May Touch Them Not": Misogyny, Homosexuality, and the Ethics of Passivity in First World War Poetry', *English Literary History*, 64.3 (1997), 827–28; Higonnet, *Pictures of Innocence*.
52 See *Preis-kurant bel'ya: Torgovyi dom "Paul' Karlson" (S.-Peterburg, Morskaya no. 18)* (St Petersburg: Torgovyi dom 'Paul Karlson', [c. 1900]), pp. 51–53.
53 See Rice, *Tamara*, plates opposite p. 146. On the Abel'son family, see also Chapter 9 above.
54 For example, Elizabeth (or Elizaveta) Hill, b. 1900, and brought up in an Anglo-Russian family in St Petersburg: see *In the Mind's Eye: The Memoirs of Dame Elizabeth Hill*, ed. by J. Stafford-Smith (Lewes: The Book Guild, 1999), p. 49.

Fig. 10.1. A page of clothing for small girls from the catalogue of Paul Karlson, Chemisier, St Petersburg, 1900. Author's collection.

Soviet practices were far more radical in terms of the recent history of Russia itself, though, than they were in terms of the international context. In British children's culture during the 1920s, 'rational dress' such as gymslips continued in force, short hair became much more widespread than it had been during the 1910s, and the heroines of girls' books went on being called boyish names, getting into various sorts of dangerous adventure, using lurid kinds of slang, and feeling contempt for tears and sentimentality.[65] This background was, as mentioned earlier, reflected in the attitudes of Western commentators to Soviet society. Whatever their unease about the 'indoctrination' of children they felt to be practised there, visiting journalists and educational and medical professionals were on the whole warmly approving of the Soviet state's efforts to transform traditional child-rearing.[66] It was the incomplete realisation of the hygienic ideal in practice, rather than its intrinsic nature, that came in for criticism. Ethel Mannin, generally well-disposed towards Soviet endeavours, found herself deeply disappointed when she asked to see a nursery. The supposedly exemplary establishment proved decidedly imperfect:

> I was shocked by the pallor of the children, by the fact that there wasn't a single window open in the place, by the lack of heating — it not being yet the fifteenth of October when — and not till then — heating is turned on; by the sight of babies sleeping indoors in sealed rooms instead of outside in the air, and by a plate of bread with flies wandering over it, by the condition of the infants' eyes and noses.[67]

In Soviet Russia itself, on the other hand, there were some signs of a more guarded attitude to the hygienic ethos on principle (and not just because its basic tenets were unfamiliar, as one must assume was the case of the staff in the model nursery that Mannin visited). For instance, Soviet baby books were if anything less rigid in terms of their prescription of regime than the advice literature of, say, F. Truby King.[68] For their part, many mothers ignored stern instructions never to rock or to kiss their babies: an American visitor noted that 'the Russians [were] always kissing their children', even when standing in clinic waiting-rooms whose walls were lined with posters condemning the practice.[69] And the emphasis on 'boyish' dress and manners for girls which trickled down into children's culture through the influence of schools and of the Pioneer movement attracted some ambivalent or even hostile

---

65 See, for example, Elinor M. Brent-Dyer, *The School at the Chalet* (London & Edinburgh: Chambers, 1925), whose heroine, Jo, feels deeply uncomfortable at the sentimental passion nurtured for her by a French coeval, Simone, who wants to be her *amie intime* and keeps bursting into tears.
66 On Western unease about indoctrination see, for example, the comments of Susan Lawrence, Under-Secretary of Health in the Labour Government of 1929–31, after visiting Soviet Russia: 'As is always the case with dogmatic education, there can be no free play of thought' (quoted in F. A. Mackenzie, *The Russian Crucifixion: The Full Story of the Persecution of Religion Under Bolshevism* (London: Jarrolds, [c. 1930]), p. 38). A more sympathetic account of Soviet 1920s education, but still with some significant reservations about regimentation, is Beatrice King, *Changing Man: The Education System of the USSR* (London: V. Golancz, 1936).
67 Mannin, 'Playtime of the Child in Modern Russia', pp. 171–72.
68 See, for example, G. N. Speransky, *Ukhod za rebenkom rannego vozrasta*, 4th edn (Moscow: Gosudarstvennoe meditsinskoe izdatel'stvo, 1929).
69 A. W. Field, *Protection of Women and Children in Soviet Russia* (New York: Dutton, 1932), p. 225.

comments from members of the intelligentsia. Vera Inber's story 'My Daughter' (1938) centred on a hair-raising caricature of a girl raised under 1920s egalitarian ideals. The story suggests that a typical girl at an 'advanced' school during the first days of Soviet power preferred acrobatics to reading, argued rudely with her parents about correct spelling, reacted with crude contempt to the idea of children's classics (branding, say, Aleksei Tolstoy's *Nikita's Childhood* as 'tripe', *buzovaya kniga*), and was more likely to spend the evening giggling with a schoolmate over an obscene drawing than to engage in civilised conversation with her mother.

> The minute she gets home, my daughter flings her books down on the sofa.
> 'Gimme some grub!' she yells.
> 'Marina, wash your hands first, please!'
> 'Why?'[70]

While this version of circumstances was created after the official move away from 'free education' during the early to mid-1930s, and hence is in a sense historically suspect, the work for children that Inber produced during the 1920s, such as *The Little Centipedes* (*Kroshki-sorokonozhki*, 1925), with its representation of an invertebrate family where mother washed clothes and looked after the children while father was at the office, indicates a lack of sympathy for the contemporary campaign to transform gender relations even while it was happening.[71] Propaganda of the 1920s might uniformly represent girls as miniature versions of the bobbed, serge-jacketed female comrade, but a marginal trend of representation continued to assimilate boys to girls, suggesting that children were cuddly, fragile, plump-cheeked, and curly-haired. Alexander Rodchenko's posters were counteracted by Natalia Dan'ko's porcelain statues of winsome tots.[72] Certainly, there were parents who thoroughly internalised new ideas about upbringing: earnest efforts to apply hygienic theories are depicted, for instance, in the genre of 'mothers' diaries' made popular by the pedological movement. Here mothers watched carefully over every detail of the child's development, and prided themselves on taking a more rational and up-to-date attitude to this, and especially to such matters as sex education and gender socialising, than the average parent.[73]

---

70 Vera Inber, 'O moei docheri', in *Sobranie sochinenii*, 4 vols (Moscow: Khudozhestvennaya literatura, 1965), II, 312–13.
71 Vera Inber, *Kroshki-sorokonozhki* (Leningrad & Moscow: Raduga 1925). The poem was reprinted later in the Soviet era without changes: see for example *Priklyucheniya sosul'ki* (Moscow: Detgiz, 1955), p. 21.
72 See N. Lobanov-Rostovsky, *Revolutionary Ceramics: Soviet Porcelain 1917–1927* (London; Studio Vista, 1990), plates 90 and 97. Cf. a 1929 sculpture by Innokenty Zhukov making a group of Young Octobrists into little fat cherubs: *PP*, 103 (1929).
73 See, for example, V. A. Rybnikova-Shilova, *Moi dnevnik: Zapiski o razvitii rebenka ot rozhdeniya do 3 1/2 let* (Orel: Gosudarstvennoe izdatel'stvo, 1923), which is typical in its obsession with norms of size, weight, physical and mental development, and in its concern with hygiene (manifested, for instance, in the avoidance of kissing and cuddling, and the regular administration of enemas); or A. L. Pavlova, *Dnevnik materi: Zapiski o razvitii rebenka ot rozhdeniya do $6^{1}/_{2}$ let* (Moscow: Gosudarstvennoe izdatel'stvo, 1924). Appropriate gender socialisation for such mothers signified androgynous rearing with a bias towards rational masculinity. Rybnikova-Shilova took pride in her son's early interest in tools and in toy cars (p. 64), and Pavlova expressed contempt for another mother who encouraged

Among girls themselves, attitudes to 'free education' and to 'rational dress' seem to have been broadly positive: the products of Soviet schools in the 1920s were tough-minded and self-confident. One memoirist brought up according to a relatively strict version of 1920s 'rational upbringing' — her parents allowed almost nothing in the bedrooms but metal bedsteads, reasoned with the children rather than punishing them, and strongly discouraged the use of demonstrative behaviour and pet names ('there was almost no sign in the family of "slobbering over people" and affectionate diminutives') — recalled herself as a boisterous and assertive young girl, who founded a secret society, complete with red-covered membership cards, aged twelve. Only slightly older, she persuaded a friend to take a short cut across the iced-up Neva in order to reach their drama classes — an episode that nearly ended in catastrophe.[74] By and large, new educational ideas provoked dissatisfaction only when they were held to license aggression on the part of boys.[75] As Zinaida Zhemchuzhnaya's tolerantly amused account of her daughter's education during this era makes clear, girls might have dressed like boys, and engaged in more assertive behaviour in the classroom, but they often chose not to mix with boys outside it:

> Lena zealously mugged up politics and knew exactly when and where the three Communist Internationals had been created, decorated the Lenin corner in the school with ribbons, wrote essays on heavyweight topics with dreadful spelling and grammar mistakes in them; she studied no history and geography because there weren't any textbooks, but all in all she led a normal school life with lots of friends of her own sex and her interests were those suitable to a child her age.[76]

Of course, where parents had fiercer objections to the new educational patterns than Zhemchuzhnaya had, or more traditional ideas, inter-generational conflict was likely to ensue. The writer Yuliya Drunina, born in 1925, remembered a tussle with her parents when the latter attempted to force her into wearing a hair-ribbon, which she and her schoolmates considered the epitome of 'bourgeois taste'. When Drunina failed to get her way by argument, she simply cut the ribbon off and discarded it, complete with the lock of hair that it was attached to.[77]

In Drunina's case, the result of this tussle seems to have been triumph on the part of the child, who achieved her object of shedding the hated decoration. Much though city-dwelling, educated parents were inclined to resent the 'anarchy' (as they saw it) of the educational process in the 1920s, and to contrast this unfavourably

---

her daughter in precocious 'feminine' caprice, appealing to her mother when asked to help Pavlova's son on with his coat: 'I'm ashamed to, mummy, I'm a girl and he's a boy' (p. 107).

74   I. F. Petrovskaya, *V kontse puti* (St Petersburg: [n pub.], 1999), pp. 8–9, 17.
75   On bullying in the playground and girls' resentment of it, see for example the memoirs of Ol'ga Nikolaevna (no surname given), published in Clementine G. K. Creuziger, *Childhood in Russia: Representation and Reality* (Langham, MD: University Press of America, 1996), pp. 5–65; and the recollections of a pupil at a former school for upper-class girls (*pansion*) after working-class boys appeared at the school in 1918: 'Things got very bad, there were almost no rules, and the boys were bullying [*obizhali*] the girls, and it was no use if you complained' (*DRE*, p. 49).
76   Zinaida Zhemchuzhnaya, *Put' izgnaniya: Ural, Kuban', Moskva, Kharbin, Tyan'tszin: Vospominaniya* (Tenafly, NJ: Ermitazh, 1987), p. 155.
77   *Sovetskie pisateli: avtobiografii*, ed. by Brainina and Nikitina, v, 174.

with the school education they had themselves received (academic in bent, single-sex, and devoting much attention to morality, decorum, and other aspects of moral education) with the 'educational anarchy' of the post-revolutionary era, they had usually absorbed enough of contemporary ideas on upbringing to be aware that bringing children to heel by force (through corporal punishment, for instance) was not an acceptable procedure.[78] On the face of it, full-scale conflict would have been much more likely to occur over gender egalitarianism in peasant families. The empowerment of children advocated by Soviet ideology generally went down badly in villages during the 1920s, where adults were likely to manifest their contempt for hectoring child activists in the most direct possible way. Mikhail Alekseev, brought up in a remote village during the 1930s,.remembered how the leader of his Pioneer 'agitational brigade', delegated to beard an aggressive adult villager, got a punch on the head that knocked him right out.[79] Gender egalitarianism flew in the face of the traditional practices observed in Russian peasant households, where a rigid division between work tasks and behaviour patterns along gender lines was inculcated from the moment that children began to be expected to contribute to the household economy (at around six or seven). Boys were sent off to herd large animals and help with work in the fields; girls were expected to co-operate in doing housework (laundry etc.), to give aid with the small animals, and to perform certain outdoor work that was female by custom (for example, raking hay and piling it in stacks). As they went about these quasi-adult tasks, peasant children wore cut-down versions of adult dress, a practice that persisted well into the second half of the twentieth century.[80] This was not simply because of the non-availability of purpose-made clothing: children who were old enough to move about autonomously were already considered in some respects miniature adults. As in peasant cultures all over Europe, the 'segregation of childhood' relative to adulthood was something alien.[81]

---

78 Child-care experts and Party officials in early Soviet Russia were uniformly hostile to the use of corporal punishment. See for example A. Epshtein, 'Ne bit', a razumno vospitvyvat'', *Drug detei*, 2 (1930), 2–5. This view persisted even after the restoration of discipline as a central value in upbringing during the mid-1930s. See for example A. A. Makarenko, *Kniga dlya roditelei* (Moscow: Krasnaya nov', 1937), pp. 194, 201–02, though Makarenko's *Pedagogicheskaya poema*, set in an orphanage, famously included a scene where the author described hitting out at one of the inmates and successfully calling him to order.
79 M. Alekseev, *Karyukha. Drachuny: Dilogiya* (Moscow: Sovetskii pisatel', 1988), p. 187.
80 For an extended analysis of gender divisions in the Russian countryside before 1917, see particularly Barbara Alpern Engel, *Between the Fields and the City: Women, Work and Family in Russia, 1861–1914* (Cambridge: Cambridge University Press, 1994). This topic has also received treatment in recent ethnographical studies such as B. A. Uspensky, *Filologicheskie razyskaniya v oblasti slavyanskykh drevnostei: relikty yazychestva v vostochnoslavyanskom kul'te Nikolaya Mirlikiiskogo* (Moscow: Izdatel'stvo Moskovskogo universiteta, 1982); A. K. Baiburin and I. Kon, *Etnicheskie stereotipy muzhskogo i zhenskogo povedeniya* (St Petersburg: Nauka, 1991). For the development of child-rearing practices in the twentieth century (and especially the persistence of many traditions into the late 1950s or longer), see David Ransel, *Village Mothers: Three Generations of Change in Russia and Tataria* (Bloomington: Indiana University Press, 2000).
81 On this, see M. J. Maynes, 'The Contours of Childhood', in *The European Experience of Declining Fertility, 1850–1970: The Quiet Revolution*, ed. by D. Levine and L. A Tilly (Oxford: Blackwell, 1982), pp. 104–05.

For many peasant communities, it remained so long after the Revolution as well.[82]

But if the official doctrine of appropriate childhood — meaning that children should not be required to undertake heavy work, should have ample leisure time which they spent under benign adult supervision, should be well-provided with material goods, and should be socialised in a way that played down relationships between the genders — cut directly across the rigid concepts of gender roles and high expectations of children's participation in the struggle for economic survival in the countryside, the danger of full-scale social upheaval at this level remained, for the first decades of Soviet power, largely unrealised. The limited development of the school network, even at primary level, and the erratic provision of education even in villages where schools notionally existed, muted any possible clash between propaganda images and established expectations. The main problem that vexed the authorities in the 1920s and early 1930s was getting girls in the schoolroom at all; there was a resigned acceptance of the fact that they were unlikely to take a leading part in the Pioneer movement. The model female activists celebrated in *Pioneer Pravda* almost all came from the city, and fiction aimed at peasant children concentrated on male characters not only during the 1920s, but throughout the 1930s as well.[83]

In any case, the potentially inflammatory nature of gender egalitarianism at the level of popular culture was soon curbed by a volte-face on the part of the Soviet regime itself. The representation of children is one of the areas of Soviet life where Nicholas Timasheff's famous hypothesis of a 'Great Retreat' in top-level ideology is most persuasive.[84] However, the shift away from the 1920s emphasis on the child as a social activist in miniature had a number of distinct phases. The first, beginning in 1932, brought a declaration that the Pioneer movement's primary mandate was support of the educational and disciplinary mission of schools.[85] The second, from 1934–35, celebrated the peace and prosperity enjoyed by Soviet children, and launched the notorious propaganda cult of 'happy childhood', which reached its apogee in late 1935 and early 1936.[86]

---

82 As recollected, say, in Alekseev's *Karyukha. Drachuny*.
83 See, for example, 'Rastet novyi chelovek', *PP*, 127 (1932), p. 1, showing a 'shock pupil' ('udarnitsa ucheby') from School no. 7 in Krasnopresnenskii District, Moscow, and cf. an item from *Izvestiya*, 19 October 1932, p. 4, showing Pionerka Slutskaya, also from Moscow, addressing a 'children's international congress' organised by *Pravda*. Male-centred fiction predominated, for example, in the peasant-targetted journal *Druzhnye rebyata* (later renamed as *Kolkhoznye rebyata*).
84 See Nicholas Timasheff, *The Great Retreat: The Growth and Decline of Communism in Russia* (New York: Dutton, 1946; repr. New York: Arno Press, 1972).
85 See the Party decree of 21 April 1932, 'O rabote pionerskoi organizatsii', *Partiinoe stroitel'stvo*, 11–12 (1932), 52–53.
86 In 1933, the Pioneer press began to make its contribution to the new propaganda myth of 'a prosperous life' proclaimed by Stalin in that year (see, for example, 'Zazhitochnaya zhizn'' — zhizn' kul'turnaya', *PP*, 123 (1933), pp. 4–5). By 1934, this was shifting to an emphasis on the particular prosperity enjoyed by children, with a proliferation of items on hobbies and toys (see for example *Pioner*, 1 (1934), 14, or 19 (1934), 23). The apogee was reached with the New Year issue of *PP*, which emblazoned its front page with a spread under the title 'Mechty schastlivykh', in which children set out their dreams: to learn to skate, to see the opera *The Snow Maiden*, to play the violin, as well as, of course, to see Stalin face to face.

Both of these phases were explicitly modelled on the larger changes occurring in Soviet society during the Second Five-Year Plan. New kinds of model children acted as miniature versions of the exemplary figures in the adult world. In 1932, the 'school shock worker' (*udarnik shkoly*) became the counterpart of the 'shock worker' (*udarnik*), while in 1935 huge publicity began to be given to the child prodigy, reviled in the 1920s as a loathsome phenomenon characteristic of bourgeois societies, where the genius innate to all children was suppressed in order that a few children might be turned into tiny stars. Like 'school shock workers', child prodigies were replications in miniature of the heroes currently dominating the adult world, in this case, Stakhanovites. *Notables of the Country of Soviets*, a panel painting displayed in the Soviet pavilion at the New York World's Fair in 1939, made the analogy crystal clear: at the forefront of the gathering, with the Stakhanovites, prize-winning scientists, shock pilots, and other famous adults standing behind them, was represented a group of five *Wunderkinder*.[87]

The shift between the 1920s ideal of child activism and the ideal that predominated in the late 1930s is well illustrated by a comparison of Arkady Gaidar's first novel, *School* (1930), about a child participant in the Civil War, and his last novel, *Timur and His Team* (1940), which showed a boy engaging in philanthropic activities with the full knowledge and approval of his father, a highly-placed military official. Remarkable too was the 'feminisation' of Pavlik Morozov evident in later versions of the legend. For example, Pavlik's denunciation of his father began to be executed in a greater and greater spirit of reluctance, until finally, in Vitaly Gubarev's version of 1947, it happened in private rather than in public, accompanied by copious tears:

> And Pavel collapses on the broad chest of this man whom he hardly knows, but who is as near and dear to him as family, and trembles from the sobs that have at last overtaken him.
> 'Uncle Dymov... Uncle Dymov...' he whispers, fighting for breath. 'My father is a traitor...'
> Dymov hurriedly strokes his head and his damp back and says dully:
> 'Don't, Pasha... don't, little boy...' and feels a warm tear rolling down his own cheek. 'Don't, Pasha! You're... you're a real Pioneer!'![88]

The shift in representation from a confident and vengeful Pavlik (who revelled in denouncing his father), to a tearful one, constituted an accommodation with changed gender ideals not only because of the stereotypical association of femininity and emotional softness, but because there already existed a female exemplum of the reluctant denouncer: Natasha, the ten-year-old heroine of Aleksandr Afinogenov's play, *Fear* (1931). Natasha discovers that her father has been lying to colleagues at his scientific institute about his social origins, and feels that she has to confide this information in a responsible adult. She duly breaks down and blurts out the truth to Bobrov, head of one of the laboratories:

---

87   For the 'shock pupil' scheme, see for example *PP*, 88 (1932), p. 3; *Notables of the Country of Soviets* is reproduced in *Stalinism as a Way of Life: A Narrative in Documents*, ed. by Lewis Siegelbaum and Andrei Sokolov (New Haven, CT: Yale University Press, 2000), plate 12.

88   Vitaly Gubarev, *Pavlik Morozov* [1947] (Simferopol': Krymizdat, 1949), pp. 38–39.

NATASHA   But why do I want to cry so much? Pioneers don't cry, Pioneers are always jolly. [*Bursts into tears and covers her face with a cushion.*]

Enter Bobrov.

BOBROV   Natasha, little girl, look at you here all alone... [*Takes her hand.*]

NATASHA   I can't cope any more... I... I wanted to tell auntie Klara. I'm so sorry for Papa, and I'm not saying anything. The silence is weighing me down.

BOBROV   Did Papa do something nasty to you?

NATASHA   It's not me he did something nasty to. He's deceived everyone. Oh, Uncle Kolya, why do I want to cry so much? Can I tell you all about papa's mother? We're friends, you and me, aren't we?

BOBROV   Of course, friends understand everything.[89]

If Gubarev's story 'feminised' Pavlik, by implication at least, it also introduced another semi-androgynous type with the fusion carried out from the other direction, as it were: Pavlik's cousin Motya, a person absent from all previous versions of the tale, who was a rampant idealist, like Pavlik, and who in some ways seemed more 'masculine' than he did. Take the following scene, where the children are exchanging visions of the future, Pavel's abstract and idealised, and Motya's down to earth and concrete: ' "We'll swap the horse plough for a tractor one, Uncle Vasil" [said Pavlik]. "And I'll be the tractor driver!" said Motya, then added sadly, "But I've never seen a tractor" '.[90] Yet at the same time, of course, Motya's vision was juxtaposed by doubts about whether it was realisable in her own case. So Sats's hostility to male Pioneers in skirts was also the signal for new doubts about the appropriateness of 'masculine' aspirations for girls. And just as in the 1920s, many areas of girlhood experience — the fantastical play, teasing, and squabbling attested as a central part of childhood experience in memoirs[91] — remained beyond the purview of a 'normal' childhood — not now because children were striving to be 'adult' as quickly as they could, but because 'normality' represented a return to traditional and rigid gender roles.[92]

* * * * *

89   A. Afinogenov, *Strakh, Izbrannoe*, 2 vols (Moscow: Iskusstvo, 1977), I, 226–27.

90   Gubarev, *Pavlik Morozov*, p. 31. For more on Motya, see Chapter 11 below. Motya's words rather comically reflect the real-life situation with women tractor-drivers in the Stalin era: even at the time when Pasha Angelina, the poster girl for this occupation, was at the zenith of her fame, it was hard for such women to find employment after training, and in the 1940s the number of female tractor drivers steeply declined. See Melanie Ilic, 'Traktoristka: Representations and Realities', in *Women in the Stalin Era*, ed. by M. Ilic (Basingstoke: Palgrave, 2001), pp. 110–31.

91   See, for example, the memoirs of Inna Shikheeva-Gaister, *Semeinaya khronika vremen kul'ta lichnosti* (Moscow: Nyudamed-IO, 1998). For an approach to girls' play that could productively be employed in the Russian context too, see M. Formanek-Brunell, 'Sugar and Spite: The Politics of Doll Play in Nineteenth-Century America', in *Small Worlds*, ed. by West and Petrik, pp. 107–24, which points out, for example, that girls did not always play families with their dolls, but used them for less conventional games, such as dolls' funerals, and that girls were prepared to do battle on behalf of their dolls.

92   For a discussion of childhood experience in the Stalin era, see my *Children's World*, Chapters 3, 10, and 11.

The first three decades of the twentieth century saw the appearance in Russia, under the direct influence of Western theories and practices, of a hygienic ethos of child-rearing (strict cleanliness accompanied by emotional restraint and the scrupulous, one could even say relentless, monitoring of the child's physical and mental existence). As in the West, the appearance of this ethos was accompanied by the development of a new version of the ideal child as assertive and emotionally independent, which in turn gave greater prominence to male children (provided they behaved in a properly disciplined manner) than to female ones. The handling of both boys and girls was supposed to orient itself towards a new cult of manliness as physical fitness, decisiveness, and industry — the qualities that were known in England as 'backbone' and in Russia as *zakal*. Before the Revolution, the new style of child-rearing had relatively limited impact, affecting, in the main, metropolitan intellectuals associated with the 'free education' movement, and other members of the educated elite. After the Revolution, however, what were seen as 'modern' practices in child-rearing received the official endorsement of the state, and 'boyish' behaviour and attitudes in children were disseminated in institutionalised child-care of all kinds, from kindergartens to orphanages to schools. From the mid-1930s, however, the rise of the myth of 'happy childhood' brought with it a quite different view of the ideal child, who was now supposed to be a docile and grateful subject of Soviet power. The emphasis on passive obedience in children in turn made the female child, especially in the age range six to ten, the preferred subject of propaganda, whether she was shown presenting a bouquet to a political leader, performing at a concert, or leading a delegation of top pupils from Moscow schools.

Some evidence suggests that the different trends in gender socialisation, and especially the growing emphasis on 'manly' behaviour as desirable even in quite small children, had at least limited effects on childhood experience. By the early twentieth century, small boys were becoming self-conscious when dressed as girls; the memoirs of girls who grew up during the 1920s and early 1930s record rather more episodes of risk-taking than those of girls who grew up during the late 1930s and early 1940s.[93] Yet at the same time, the considerable conservatism of children's behaviour should also be given due credit. Zhemchuzhnaya's reference to her daughter's 'normal school life with lots of friends of her own sex' was not just an indication of this observer's own views of what was 'normal'. Memoirs and direct observations record that children themselves fervently policed gender distinctions (though the precise nature of these distinctions might shift from generation to generation), and that even when being educated in co-educational schools, they selected friends of their own sex and banded together on gender lines.[94]

The 'androgynous' ethos of the 1920s did not necessarily achieve its aims of reducing differences between boys and girls, and by extension adult men and women.[95] But this limited success means that one should treat with scepticism the

---

93 On the latter, see, for example, Anna Mass's fictionalised memoirs, *Raznotsvetnye cherepki* (Moscow: Molodaya gvardiya, 1970), or Larisa Miller, *Dim and Distant Days* (Moscow: Glas, 2000).
94 This issue is explored, for instance, in M. V. Osorina, *Sekretnyi mir detei: v prostranstve mira vzroslykh* (St Petersburg: Piter, 1999).
95 It is notoriously difficult to draw a more than approximate correlation between upbringing

charges that it distorted childhood experience. In turn, the introduction of single-sex education in 1943, which also saw the introduction of syllabuses differentiated for boys and for girls according to particularly narrow-minded views of appropriate socialisation (so that, in one outpost of Soviet power, it was decreed that girls should read only the 'peace' chapters of Tolstoy's *War and Peace*),[96] not only failed to achieve its objective of enhancing social cohesion, but also failed to solve the problems of indiscipline and lack of application in the schools that had been a secondary goal of institutional change.[97] And so far as children's own breadth of experience went, it is possible to say that, on balance, the 'free education' of the 1910s, 1920s, and early 1930s, despite its blinkered association of 'backwardness' and femininity, and despite its much-publicised failures in an academic sense, offered some girls (and children generally) richer possibilities than the system that succeeded it, with its rigid emphasis on marks and on good conduct — an insight recognised in the re-adoption, in diluted form, of liberal methodology and gender egalitarianism in the Khrushchev era.[98]

My thanks to Natalia Pushkareva, Maria Osorina, and the late Vitaly Bezrogov for help with locating sources. This chapter was first published as 'Khochu byt' traktoristkoi!', *Sotsial'naya istorija: Ezhegodnik 2003* (2005), 385–410.

and adult personality, and this applies to gender socialisation as well. Suffice it to contrast the cases of Akhmatova, something of a 'tomboy' according to her own account in later life, yet decidedly cloistered and immobile as an adult, and Tsvetaeva, far more conventionally reared, but also a much less conventional adult in her attitude to what constituted appropriate feminine behaviour. All the same, there does seem to be some continuity between the egalitarian gender socialisation of the 1920s and, say, the participation of women in active combat during the Second World War, on which see Anna Krylova, *Soviet Women in Combat: A History of Violence on the Eastern Front* (Cambridge: Cambridge University Press, 2011).
96 See John Dunstan, *Soviet Schooling in the Second World War* (Basingstoke: Macmillan, 1997), p. 178. This particular decree was issued in the Udmurt Republic, but at this period the syllabus everywhere was segregated so girls only did pedagogy, domestic science, needlework, physical hygiene, and childcare, and boys only map-reading and orienteering (ibid., pp. 171–72).
97 This was one reason why the policy was reversed in 1955.
98 There were, of course, also numerous children who preferred the rigidity — which they saw as security and predictability — of the post-1932 Soviet school. Yakov Avidon, for example, remembered loving the daily ritual of register-taking, and even recitation of rote-learned homework struck him as an inviting task, which inspired in him a deep sense of responsibility. See Leonard J. Kent, *A Survivor of A Labor Camp Remembers: Expendable Children of Mother Russia* (Lewiston, NY: Mellen, 1997), pp. 185–87.

CHAPTER 11

'Comrade is a Sacred Word': Children and Soviet Friendship

[2009]

During the Soviet period, the proper management of the emotions became a state-sponsored ideology, accompanied by a network of techniques for 'work on the self' (*rabota nad soboi*), such as *zakal* (self-tempering).[1] One might call this, tongue in cheek, 'the Stalinist plan for the transformation of human nature', though *zakal* in fact did not receive endorsement from the leader or at the highest level. Rather, it was a 'middle-level' phenomenon in Soviet ideology, promoted by health experts such as hygienists and psychologists, and aimed at the Soviet masses in the broad sense (intelligentsia as well as workers and peasantry). The cultivation of stern virtues such as self-restraint, command of the will, bravery, and endurance of temperature extremes was supposed to be inculcated from childhood — from infancy, indeed, according to the number one early Soviet child-care guru, Speransky.[2] And the model child was one whose impulses were kept under control from very early, as in the case of the future war heroine Zoya Kosmodem'yanskaya and her brother Shura, a war hero in his own right.[3] In the biography of her children that she published in

---

1   On *zakal*, see Chapter 3 above. The topic of Soviet subjectivity has been extensively explored in the last decades. See, for example, the studies by Thomas Lahusen, *How Life Writes the Book: Real Socialism and Socialist Realism in Stalin's Russia* (Ithaca, NY: Cornell University Press, 1997); Halfin, *From Darkness to Light*; Jochen Hellbeck, *Revolution on My Mind: Writing a Diary under Stalin* (Cambridge, MA: Harvard University Press, 2006); Irina Paperno, *Stories of the Soviet Experience: Memoirs, Diaries, Dreams* (Ithaca, NY: Cornell University Press, 2009). Among important recent contributions to the history of the emotions in Russia and the Soviet Union, see Yan [=Jan] Plamper, Schamma Schahadat, and Marc Elie, *Rossiiskaya imperiya chuvstv* (Moscow: Novoe literaturnoe obozrenie, 2010); *Interpreting Emotions in Russia and Eastern Europe*, ed. by Mark D. Steinberg and Valeria Sobol (DeKalb: Northern Illinois University Press, 2011).
2   G. N. Speransky, *Ukhod za rebenkom rannego vozrasta*, 4th edn (Moscow: Gosudarstvennoe meditsinskoe izdatel'stvo, 1929), p. 129.
3   Zoya Kosmodem'yanskaya is renowned as the real-life person behind 'Partisan Girl Tanya', executed by the Nazis on 29 November 1941 (the 1944 film, *Zoya*, directed by Leo Arnshtam played a large part in her fame: for a historical study of the cult published since this essay reached print, see Dzhonatan Platt [=Jonathan Platt], 'Zoya Kosmodem'yanskaya mezdhu istrebleniem i zhertvoprinosheniem', *Novoe literaturnoe obozrenie*, 6 (2013) <https://magazines.gorky.media/nlo/2013/6/zoya-kosmodemyanskaya-mezhdu-istrebleniem-i-zhertvoprinosheniem.html> [accessed 29 September 2022]). Shura, after valiant service in a tank battalion (he had volunteered immediately after his sister's death, though aged only sixteen at the time) was killed on active service on 13 April 1945, a few months before his twentieth birthday. He was posthumously awarded the title of Hero of the Soviet Union.

collaboration with the pedagogical expert Frida Vigdorova, their mother, Lyubov', wrote:

> Both Zoya and Shura used to show their feelings in an extremely reserved, even cautious, way. As they grew up, this trait became more and more evident in them. They feared fine words like the plague. They rarely directly expressed love, tenderness, or excitement, anger or dislike. I would be able to tell their feelings, what they were going through emotionally, mainly by what I saw in their eyes, by their silence, by the way that Zoya walked from corner to corner of the room when she felt sad or anxious.[4]

In this perspective, losing hold became not only a path to vice, but also a vice in itself: externally-imposed 'control' and 'self-control' reinforced each other.[5] This scale of values was also widespread in late Soviet culture, with a 1967 encyclopaedia for parents seeing self-control as the natural result of maturation:

> The child gets older and gains more experience; he learns more and more about life, and much of what could formerly surprise him and make him anxious becomes everyday and routine. Alongside this, new, more elevated and complex feelings appear. Taking part in the life of the collective, in socially useful work, he more and more fully feels himself a citizen. He angrily condemns injustice and evil, warmly approves positive deeds on the part of his comrades and those surrounding him.[6]

At the same time, the point was not to curb your emotions completely. Here, the maturing child is still allowed to show anger, when rebuking his or her comrades. In line with this, some normative sources emphasised that repression was not a good idea. A 1929 childcare manual argued that quiet, obedient, silent children should be taken to the doctor and cured of this morbid condition.[7] Even in the Stalin era, when 'discipline' was definitely expected of older children, shows of feeling were more likely to be tolerated in younger ones. In particular, happiness — *vesel'e, radost', schast'e* — was supposed to be children's prerogative, and happiness retained an element of spontaneity: it was seen as a gift, an exceptional state, even a miracle. Obviously, this was true for adults as well, but once 'a happy childhood' had become a state-sponsored slogan in 1936, and had become associated especially with the authority of Stalin, there started to be an equivalence between young years and the state of happiness that Stalin's 1935 slogan, 'Life has become jollier!' had anticipated for all Soviet citizens. Children were supremely happy; childhood was the supremely happy phase of Soviet citizens' existence.[8] This association to some extent curbed or off-set the emphasis on self-control.

---

4   L. Kosmodem'yanskaya (with F. Vigdorova), *Povest' o Zoe i Shure* (Leningrad: Lenizdat, 1951), pp. 113–14.
5   A point made more generally in Oleg Kharkhordin, *The Collective and the Individual in Soviet Society: A Study of Practices* (Berkeley: University of California Press, 1999).
6   *Semeinoe vospitanie: slovar' dlya roditelei*, ed. by M. I. Kondakov and others (Moscow: Prosveshchenie 1967), p. 321.
7   A. Babina, *Kak organizovat' dosug detei* (Moscow: Rabotnik prosveshcheniya, 1929), p. 7.
8   Catriona Kelly, 'A Joyful Soviet Childhood: Licensed Happiness for Little Ones', in *Petrified Utopia: Happiness Soviet Style*, ed. by Marina Balina and Evgeny Dobrenko (London: Anthem Press, 2009), pp. 3–18.

The emphasis on age thresholds was ubiquitous in Soviet child-rearing guidance. Pedagogical literature and manuals for parents distinguished between different phases in a manner directly linked to the divisions of educational institutions: 'nursery' (*yasel'nyi*) age, 'pre-school' (*doshkol'nyi*), 'younger school pupils' (*mladshie shkol'niki*), and 'older school pupils' (*starshie shkol'niki*). In the Russian historical context, this banding by age was new. Orthodox theology did not formalise developmental phases, though such phases were sometimes alluded to in a pragmatic context. For instance, in 1908, the Senate proposed to allow children below the age of fourteen to convert from Orthodoxy to Lutheranism, if their parents were changing their faith.[9] And in popular Orthodoxy, it was generally accepted that a child could not sin before it could speak (and laugh).[10] In post-Counter-Reformational Catholic theology, on the other hand, seven was standardised as the beginning of reasonable understanding (and hence became the usual age for the ritual of First Holy Communion), and a rather less sharply defined age on the boundaries of puberty (somewhere between twelve and fourteen) was understood as the time at which mortal sin became possible, and hence the age at which a child could be confirmed (in the Catholic sense, i.e. anointed with chrism, tested on the catechism, etc.).[11] In Soviet teaching practice and parlance about children generally, the terms 'pre-school', 'younger school years' (from eight, and later seven), and 'older school years' (from about twelve) replicated the Catholic pattern closely, as did the break between the Pioneers and the Komsomol (somewhere between twelve and fourteen, depending on the era).

In turn, the sense that happiness (signalled by spontaneity and warmth) was an entitlement for children had significant effects upon the representation of, and normative prescriptions for, affective relationships such as friendship — the subject with which this chapter is mainly concerned. The dominant theme of friendship as an instrument of regulation in the collective (as in the description from the 1967 encyclopaedia quoted above, 'warmly approves positive deeds on the part of his comrades and those surrounding him') did not preclude other, and at times conflicting, interpretations. Both theoretical discussions and practical guidance, such as was offered by teachers, sought not only to correct and regulate children's behaviour, but also to reflect and to collude with this — something that reflected how Soviet ideologies and practices of child-rearing, particularly in the post-war years, were underlain by a tension between post-Romantic ideas about 'natural' childhood, and less permissive ideologies about preparing children for citizenship.[12]

9   Simon Dixon, 'Sergii (Stragorodskii) in the Russian Orthodox Diocese of Finland: Apostasy and Mixed Marriages, 1905–1917', *Slavonic and East European Review*, 82.1 (January 2004), 50–73 (p. 62). The proposal was in fact contested by the consistory authorities as 'harmful to Orthodoxy in Finland', and later, attempted prosecutions of Lutheran clergymen in the Grand Duchy were to collapse because of uncertainty about age thresholds for children. (See ibid., pp. 62, 63).
10   A. K. Baiburin, 'Etnograficheskie zametki o yazyke i slove v russkoi traditsii', *Antropologicheskii forum*, 3 (2005), 381–97 (pp. 386, 389).
11   The discussion of all this is one of the more interesting (though generally ignored) sections of Philippe Ariès, *L'Enfant et la vie familiale sous l'Ancien Régime* (Paris: Plon, 1960).
12   I have discussed this in more detail in *Children's World*.

The Boundaries of Intimate Relations

Soviet sources drew rigid distinctions between friendship in the sense of 'comradeliness', or the capacity to associate on a neutral, disinterested basis with the various members of the *kollektiv*, and a more dangerous kind of friendship, sometimes named as *druzhba*, sometimes by other words, based on exclusivity and self-interest, and threatening social atomisation.[13] It followed that sexual love, which (in conventional perceptions, such as those entertained by Bolshevik theorists) is unavoidably dualistic, was still less positively understood.[14] A normative definition from Ushakov's defining dictionary of 1940 gave thoroughly 'social' definitions of friendship, alongside a hierarchised definition of 'love' where sexual love was seen as inferior to other kinds. 'Comradeliness' and 'friendship' were defined with close similarity, both being related to the neutral terms *blizost'* [closeness] and *privyazannost'* [affection].[15] The entry on *Lyubov'* was considerably more detailed, giving primacy to non-sexual, abstract emanations of the emotion:

> A sense of attraction founded on shared interests and ideals, on the preparedness to devote your powers to a common cause. *Love for the motherland*. The same feeling founded on mutual inclination, sympathy, closeness. *Fraternal love*. Love for people. The same feeling, founded on instinct. *Maternal love*.

Only as a secondary meaning was sexual love mentioned, and with an ordering of linguistic usages that emphasised the danger of this variety of the emotion: 'The same feeling founded on sexual attraction; the relations of two people bound together by such love. *Unhappy love*'. Admittedly, the second linguistic usage given was 'happy love', but 'unrequited love' and 'platonic love' came next. The editors' didactic meaning was clear.

In some marginal respects, the Ushakov dictionary was quite 'physiological' and close to the spirit of the 1920s. For instance, the terms *lyubovnik* and *lyubovnitsa* [lover/mistress] were labelled 'obsolete and derog[atory]' ('ustarev.-neodobrit.'). This classification was to disappear from later dictionaries. But the distinction of *druzhba* from *tovarishchestvo* (and of *tovarishcheskie otnosheniya* from *priyatel'skie otnosheniya*), on the one hand, and of *druzhba* from *lyubov'*, on the other, was typical of the 1930s and 1940s. The rehabilitation of personal relationships in the late 1930s did nothing to reclaim or make respectable erotic love outside the family, a type of relationship that was so impermissible as to be effectively unmentionable (having

---

13   Oleg Kharkhordin, 'Druzhba: klassicheskie teorii i sovremennye zaboty' <http://eupress.ru/uploads/files/S-092_pages.pdf> [accessed 29 September 2022]; *Druzhba: ocherki po teorii praktik: sbornik statei*, ed. by Oleg Kharkhordin (St Petersburg: izdatel'stvo Evropeiskogo universiteta v Sankt-Peterburge, 2009).
14   An additional danger of *lyubov'*, in the euphemistic sense of 'making love' was its association with physiological damage. There is a large literature from the 1920s on sexual acts as will-sapping, etc.: see, for example, the works of the prolific A. L. Mendel'son on the 'struggle with masturbation', such as *Onanizm i bor'ba s nim*, 8th edn (Leningrad: Leningradskaya pravda, 1930).
15   The second meaning for *tovarishchestvo* (after 'collaboration', labelled as 'obs.'), was 'an intimacy founded on comradely relations'; *druzhba* was defined as 'close friendly relations, close acquaintance as the result of attraction and inclination' (D. N. Ushakov, G. O. Vinokur, *Tolkovyi slovar' russkogo yazyka*, 4 vols (Moscow, 1936–40), IV & I.

a mistress in Soviet films of this period was a diagnostic trait of foreign wreckers and spies).

The shift to the centre of *druzhba* as the primary category of affective relationship was indicated by the second edition of the *Great Soviet Encyclopaedia*. In the first edition, none of the terms *druzhba*, *lyubov'*, or *tovarishchestvo* had been the subject of an article. In the second, *druzhba* was the only one accorded space. By now, it had become an ornament and defining feature of Soviet society:

> In the exploitative class-antagonistic society, private property, competition, the drive for repression give birth among the governing classes to vulpine morals, hatred, and treachery. Relations of genuine, selfless F[riendship] are only found among the exploited majority, in the sphere of advanced people, in the course of the struggle for a more advanced society. In socialist society, where the exploiting classes have been liquidated, new social relations have formed — relations of friendly co-operation and mutual aid. In the Soviet collective, united as it is by the goal of building Communism, true friendship develops.[16]

A very particular kind of friendship was seen as central to Soviet society, one arising from 'the struggle to benefit the common good' ('bor'ba za obshchee delo'). Its foundation was 'high ideological commitment' ('vysokaya ideinost'). The perfect embodiment of such friendship, the article continued, was the relationship between Marx and Engels, or between Lenin and Stalin. Yet it should be clearly understood that social and political commitment was more important even than this valuable and intensely Soviet emotion:

> Communist morality rejects unprincipled F[riendship], such as attempts to justify, in the name of preserving 'friendly' relations, anti-patriotic acts, the breach of civic duty and of the rules of socialist communality. Genuine F[riendship] requires straightforward relations, the objective assessment of friends' acts, principled criticism and self-criticism. The Soviet person is obliged to be honest and direct in the exposure of his friends' mistakes, to help them correct these and prevent them in the future.[17]

In other words, the definition of *druzhba* was apophatic (by means of negation): *druzhba* should *not* be a bond between two or more people that threatened the larger values of Soviet society.[18] During the war years, this view of disinterested friendship reached its apogee: the friendship cultivated here was one contributing to victory in the struggle with fascism, the harmonious collaboration of comrades-in-arms.

---

16 *Bol'shaya sovetskaya entsiklopediya*, 2nd edn, 53 vols (Moscow: Sovetskaya entsiklopediya, 1949–65), XV, 238. Julian Graffy has helpfully pointed out to me that the titles of the Soviet film repertoire as listed in Segida and Zemlyanukhin's *Domashnyaya sinemateka: otechestvennaia kino, 1918–1996* (Moscow: Dubl'-D, 1996) are also a good indication of priorities: while *lyubov'* [love] outstrips *drug* [friend] at 221 titles versus 34, this is still a high number overall (cf. *schast'e* [happiness] at 61), and significantly higher than *tovarishch* [comrade] with just 8.
17 *Bol'shaya sovetskaya entsiklopediya*, XV, 238.
18 Contrary to what is asserted in Kharkhordin, 'Druzhba', p. 13, that Soviet 'official sources never praised friendship; *Pravda* never dedicated a single editorial to the subject', there actually was a substantial Soviet official literature on friendship as a form of self-criticism, a 'prophylactic' method of regulating the collective; however, an alternative understanding of *druzhba* as a protective and sheltering relationship was actively attacked. See further below.

Models of such friendship included Aleksandr Matrosov (who blocked a gun-barrel with his own body to protect his comrades) and the group of young partisans in Fadeev's novel *The Young Guard*, as well as Sergei Gerasimov's hugely successful film adaptation.[19]

Such representations of *druzhba* drew on a traditional understanding of the word as harmony, absence of conflict. There was an intimate tensile link, a similarity in difference, between *druzhba* and its opposite, *vrazhda*, or enmity. If one plays the popular letter-changing game generating one word from another, *drug* and *vrag* are only two steps away (much closer than 'enemy' and 'friend').[20]

Yet on balance, the Soviet understanding of virtuous and dangerous affective relationships was — like official culture's emotional map more generally — universalist and internationalist, rather than rooted in folk culture. The good versus bad friendship discussion is traceable to, at the latest, Aristotle, whose enigmatic lament 'O friends, there is no friend!' was later adopted in a famous essay of Montaigne's dealing with self-interested versus disinterested friendship. Here, the ideal friend is one who makes an astonishing gesture of self-sacrifice — remembering in his will someone he has not met, as in the case of Étienne de la Boétie, who left Montaigne his library.[21] Conduct books enshrined this division, while sometimes partially undermining it by suggesting that rational, disinterested friendship was the best way of getting ahead (which is to say, there were good selfish reasons for espousing this type of relationship as well). Baltasar Gracián y Morales, author of *El oráculo manual y arte de prudencia* (1647), translated into Russian in 1742, instructed readers in his Rule no. 31 to pick their friends on the basis of fortune, or as the Russian had it, 'ot shchastlivykh pol'sovatsa, a ot bezshchastnykh ubegat'' [make use of the fortunate, and from the unfortunate keep well away]. For its part, Gracián's Rule no. 40 counselled general popularity rather than the pursuit of exclusive relationships: 'U vsekh lyubov' poluchit'' [obtain love from all].[22]

If the 'pure/impure friendship' distinction had a long history, the friendship/love dichotomy, on the other hand, was of rather more recent origin (unless one chooses to see the kind of asexual love propounded by Pythagoras and Diotima to Socrates in *The Symposium* as a harbinger of the 'friendship' side of the dichotomy).[23] It

---

19 For a good discussion of this film, as well as real-life friendship groups (*kompanii*), see Juliane Fürst, *Stalin's Last Generation: Soviet Post-War Youth and the Emergence of Mature Socialism* (Oxford: Oxford University Press, 2010).

20 The Latinate terms 'enmity' and 'amity' capture this tensile link better than 'friend' and 'enemy', etymologically and morphologically distant terms, though the recent slang word 'frenemy' (a friend towards whom one feels hostility) also nicely bridges the gap.

21 Michel de Montaigne, 'De l'amitié', in *Essais*, ed. A. by Micha (Paris: Garnier-Flammarion, 1969), pp. 231–42, Chapter 23. Kenneth Dover, *Greek Popular Morality* (Oxford: Blackwell, 1974), pp. 201–05, argues that everyday Greek notions of friendship dwelt on the phenomenon in a positive sense: friendship was understood as a combination of compassion, honesty, self-sacrifice, capacity to forgive, and the avoidance of cruelty and of the giving of pain. The 'good friendship/ bad friendship' dichotomy does not seem to have been so relevant.

22 Baltasar Gracián y Morales, *Pridovrnoi chelovek s frantsuzskogo na rossiiskoi yazyk pereveden Kantselyarii Akademii Nauk Sekretarem Sergeem Volchkovym* (St Petersburg: pri Imperatorskoi Akademii Nauk, 1742), rules 31, 40.

23 As in the traditional understanding of the term, 'platonic love'. This term is known in English

became a widely developed theme in Enlightenment behaviour literature. For example, in her *Traité de l'amitié* (1736), Madame de Lambert suggested that that 'femmes d'un caractère raisonnable' [rational women] would cultivate platonic love rather than sensuality or flirtation.[24] Such attitudes were propounded in books for men as well. Joseph Grabiensky's *Conseils d'un ami à un jeune homme qui entre dans le monde* (Berlin, 1760), translated into Russian in 1765, recognised (conventionally for the time) the advantage to a young man's polish of spending time in female company:

> The association with the fair sex can have both a good and a bad effect. But should one recommend it to a young person? It will be said that an association of this kind makes our sex polite, lends it a certain tenderness of spirit and taste, which, as many assert, is the gift primarily of woman. This may perhaps be true, if the association is with a woman of good breeding [*khoroshee vospitanie*], in possession of reason, wisdom, and virtue.[25]

But this cautious recommendation of polite intercourse with women came alongside a stern warning against the pursuit of love: '*Love is an idol that demands nothing other than disorder and sin in sacrifice*'.[26]

At the same time, while recognising the unoriginality of the Soviet belief system in its descent from Enlightenment ideas, one should not exaggerate the significance of historical antecedents. Soviet propaganda itself tended precisely *not* to stress the long heritage of the ideas propounded. Rather, the assumption was that the new country's ideology drew exclusively on such pre-1917 authors as could be considered 'progressive' and 'radical', which would certainly not have included Lambert, Fénelon, or the many anonymous authors of Enlightenment conduct literature. And in propaganda for children, where even quotations from the Marxist-Leninist classics were made fairly sparingly, the explicit citation of other authorities was exceedingly rare. What children ingested, therefore, was something held to be unique; the exceptionality of Soviet morality was supposed to be (and often was) a source of patriotism in itself.

There were in any case certain very precisely 'Soviet' nuances of 'friendship', one of them being 'friendship of peoples', *druzhba narodov*. The article devoted to this in the second edition of the Great Soviet Encyclopaedia was more than three times the length of the piece on 'friendship' of the ordinary kind, and was accompanied by a substantial bibliography. It traced the term back to a speech given by Stalin to the collective farm workers of Tadzhikistan and Turkmenistan on 4 December 1935, and more broadly, the politics of tolerance, equality, and paternalism (with

since at least the early seventeenth century, according to *OED*; the earliest references in Russian date from the late eighteenth century, according to the 'Natsional'nyi korpus russkogo yazyka' <www.ruscorpora.ru> [accessed 29 September 2022].
24   A.-T. de Lambert, *Traité de l'amitié*, in *Recueil de divers écrits, sur l'amour et l'amitie, la politesse, la volupte, les sentimens agréables, l'esprit et le cœur* (Paris: Veuve Pissot, 1736); *Razsuzhdenie o druzhestve gospozhi de Lambert*, trans. by S. Smirnov (St Petersburg: pri Imperatorskoi Akademii Nauk, 1777).
25   Joseph Grabiensky, *Druzheskie sovety molodomu cheloveku, nachinayushchemu zhit' v svete*, 2nd edn (Moscow: pechatano pri Imperatorskom Moskovskom universitete, 1765), pp. 34–35.
26   Ibid.

the Russian nation's 'selfless aid' to the other nations forming the cement that kept 'the friendship of nations' together).[27] The new slogan was quoted in the 1943 national anthem, which apostrophised the USSR as 'friendship of peoples' trusty stronghold'. The allegory of 'friendship of peoples' remained in force after the war as well, with Stalin returning, in a speech made in April 1948, to the two principles of equality and difference that underlay *druzhba*. Difference was seen as the guarantor of equality:

> Soviet people consider that every nation, whether big or small, has its own qualities and characteristics, its specific features, which belong only to that nation and which other nations lack. [...] In this sense all nations — both small and large — are in the same position, and every nation is equal to any other nation.[28]

In other words, 'friendship' in this official sense rested above all upon the preservation of autonomy at one level, and of hierarchical values at another: all nations were equal, yet largeness or smallness also mattered. This kind of 'friendship' resembled what in other ideological systems would have been called a 'brotherhood' of nations; the point was that by employing the term 'friendship', the notion of ethnic difference (and cultural difference on the basis of ethnic difference) could be retained, thus introducing the idea of primordial nationality by the back door.[29] At the same time, 'friendship of nations' also propounded a particular notion of friendship: as an officially sanctioned, public link, rather than the expression of inner feeling, and as a connection based upon the demands of the commonweal generally, rather than upon considerations of self-interest.

'That's the sort of friendship we need!': Friendship and Comradeliness in Didactic Texts for Children

Soviet propaganda for children was by intention entirely parasitic upon adult models. This applied also to material dealing with emotions and affective relationships. At the same time, though the standard evaluative contours for affective relationships were adopted, these were sometimes also adjusted in significant ways.

Just as in propaganda for adults, the 'good friendship/ bad friendship' polarisation was pervasive, first making a significant impact in the second half of the 1930s (around the time when the ideology of 'friendship of peoples' was starting to be disseminated). At this point, items about *druzhba* proliferated in children's magazines. For example, a story by Elena Il'ina published in the Leningrad magazine *Koster*

---

27   *Bol'shaya sovetskaya entsiklopediya*, xv, 238–39.
28   'Rech' tovarishcha I. V. Stalina na obede v chest' Finlyandskoi Pravitel'stvennoi Delegatsii, 7 April 1948', *Pravda*, 13 April 1948, p. 1.
29   On which phenomenon more generally see Terry Martin, 'Modernization or Neo-Traditionalism? Ascribed Nationality and Soviet Primordialism', in *Stalinism: New Directions*, ed. by Sheila Fitzpatrick (London: Routledge, 2000), pp. 348–67; Albert Baiburin, '"The Wrong Nationality": Ascribed Identity in the Soviet Union', in *Russian Cultural Anthropology after the Collapse of Communism*, ed. by Albert Baiburin, Catriona Kelly, and Nikolai Vakhtin (London: Routledge, 2012), pp. 59–76.

(*The Bonfire*) during 1936 had at its centre a triangular relationship between three girls, Natasha, Tanya, and Marina. The tension caused by Natasha's jealousy of Tanya's admiration for her new friend Marina eventually led to the break-up of their relationship, to Natasha's particular distress (as she herself regretfully acknowledged, 'How sad it is to lose a friend').[30]

The emphasis on the dangers of excessive intimacy was typical of the time; a number of different items on the subject of friendship published in 1938 also took the same line. For instance, an article in *Koster* laboriously argued for the usefulness of friendship as an emotional link, but only provided that it was steered in a certain direction:

> Friendship is also good when those who are friendly rise to a higher level of development, become better, forge in themselves the traits of character that are proper to people in the new Communist society: that is, they should be honourable, brave, love their motherland and be armed with knowledge.
>
> And so if friendship facilitates all this, then it justifies itself. That sort of friendship is to be welcomed.[31]

While regarding friendship instrumentally, this understanding also conceptualised it supra-individually: as a means to the end of building the new society. Other items running in *Koster* during the year completed the picture of what was seen as 'necessary' and 'unnecessary' friendship. Friendship was pernicious when it disrupted the moral regulation of the broader collective (a case in point being the fellow pupils who banded together to ostracise a girl who reported disruptive behaviour by some boys to the class teacher).[32] However, it was to be viewed positively in several other contexts. One of these, strikingly enough, was relationships between children of opposite sexes.

Lida, the heroine of a school story that appeared in *Koster* in 1938, was teased by her school-fellows for becoming friendly with Yura, a boy of the same age (according to the general view, 'a girl and a boy can't be real friends'). Yet she interpreted this as a challenge, rather than as a deterrent, encouraged by a boy who insisted mixed-gender friendships were possible if one regarded girls as 'comrades of a different order' ('raznye tovarishchi'). At first this meant that Lida and Yura negotiated gender difference by essentially ignoring this. In a gesture that would hardly have reassured any boy readers worried that friendship with girls might be 'sissy', Lida was shown referring affectionately to her friend as 'Matil'da'. Later, though, Lida became trapped in the stereotypicality of her own expectations: when Yura refused to respond to provocation and to become involved in a fight, she rejected him as 'a coward'. In the end, though, all was resolved joyfully when Yura rescued her after a skiing accident, at the risk of frostbite to himself: after receiving a devoted letter from him as her 'faithful friend', she decided that she was the happiest girl in the world.[33]

30 E. Il'ina, 'Perepiska trekh shkol'nits', *Koster*, 4 (1936), 98–102.
31 M. Balan, 'Takaya nuzhna druzhba!', *Koster*, 10 (1938), 73.
32 'Razve v etom druzhba?', *Koster*, 10 (1938), 72.
33 D. Brodskaya, 'Dnevnik Lidy Karasevoi', *Koster*, 6 (1938), 33–44 (part 1); 7 (1938), 38–48 (part 2).

The relationship between a girl and a boy that bordered on, but did not quite spill over into, 'love', was seen as a specially elevated form of permissible friendship, one requiring suspension of prejudice in favour of higher ideals on both sides. Boys had to discard their view that 'all lasses have on their mind is clothes and girls' talk', while girls had to accommodate themselves to (and encourage) a type of masculine behaviour that did not include such 'backward' activities as fighting.[34]

As with material for adults, the 'disinterested friendship' model reached its quintessence during the war years.[35] For example, Pavel Zhurba, best-known for his hagiography of the war hero Alexander Matrosov, in 1942 published in blockade-stricken Leningrad *The Friends* (*Druz'ya*), a pamphlet presenting to a child audience the story of partisan warriors Ivan Kramchuk and Iosif Gofman, living embodiments of 'friendship of peoples' as well as martial valour.[36] Selected from many eager candidates to take part on a particularly dangerous reconnaissance expedition, the two men made their way through bog and moss, only to part without regret when duty demanded: 'Soaked with sweat and bog water, the friends embraced and, without looking round, went their separate ways'. The story ended in tragedy after Iosif was hacked slowly to pieces by the Germans; when Ivan discovered this, he made a solemn pledge of revenge: '"The swine!" Ivan yelled in a frenzy, "You will have no mercy! I shall gnaw your throats for the ruination of my country, for my black sorrow, for my friend!"'[37] Typical here was the taking-for-granted of friendship as an emotion: as with an arranged marriage, the partners in this dualistic relationship happily accepted the companionship of those they had not chosen. The notion of friendships as the expression of personal ties and interests had vanished — even as the negative counterpart to the ideal image of what friendship *should* be.

In the late 1940s, though, the theme of friendship made a significant return to journals for children; pedagogical literature also began to devote a significant amount of space to normative discussions of this relationship. The trigger for the discussion seems to have been Kalinin's speeches on 'communist education', collected as a volume in 1947, which contained various admonitions on the importance of disinterested *druzhba*.[38] As with other shifts in ideological perceptions, the official lives of Pavlik Morozov, which were updated at regular intervals to make the child seem relevant to new generations of Pioneers, paid tribute to this trend. The 1947 edition of Vitaly Gubarev's life of Pavlik introduced a friendship of which there had been no hint in earlier versions of the story. This was the relationship between Pavlik and his girl cousin Motya, who in Gubarev's story emerged as one of the few people in his village to share Pavlik's determination to strive for the future and his commitment to the cause. In a scene typical for children's literature at the time, the

---

34 Ibid., part 1, p. 41.
35 Stories about Aleksandr Matrosov and the novel *Molodaya gvardiya* were in any case popular — perhaps, indeed, primarily so — with older schoolchildren. For oral-historical sources on this, see, for example, CKQ-Oxf-03 PF8B, pp. 15–16; Oxf/Lev M-03 PF4A, p. 6.
36 To the Russian reader, 'Kramchuk' is just as explicitly Ukrainian as 'Gofman' is Jewish.
37 Pavel Zhurba, *Druz'ya* (Leningrad: [n. pub.], 1942), p. 8. The story was published by Voenizdat, the military publishing house, an indication of its perceived patriotic importance.
38 M. Kalinin, *O kommunisticheskom vospitanii* (Moscow: Molodaya gvardiya, 1947).

two had to brave small-minded teasing over their relationship ('Bridegroom and bride!'), but still remained firm friends.[39]

The positive model of friendship propounded was one of co-operation, but never collusion, preferably as expressed in some well-supervised context such as the school-room, a park of culture and rest, or a sporting venue. For example, N. Naidenova and S. Bulatov's hypnotically repetitive Young Pioneer song, 'Friendship', dwelled on the intellectual and moral benefits of having a friend whom one cultivated in this way:

> Если есть товарищ,
> Веселей учиться,
> Веселее вместе
> По лесу гулять,
> Книжкой интересной
> Можно поделиться,
> Вместе посмеяться,
> Вместе почитать.
> (Припев):
> Слава дружбе нашей пионерской,
> Помогает нам она во всем,
> Слава дружбе радостной и светлой,
> О которой песню мы поем!

[If you have a comrade, | Studying is more fun, | It's more fun both together | Walking in the woods. | You can share together | Some interesting reading, | You can laugh together, | Smiling as you read. | (Chorus): | Glory to our Pioneer friendship, | It helps us in all things, | Glory to joyful, radiant friendship, | The subject of our song!]

Having listed various sanctioned arenas for friendly relations (swimming, football, the House of Young Pioneers, the park, the ice-rink...), the song stressed that friends would always help 'in sadness and disaster'. It ended with a peroration to the place of sincerity in friendship:

> Будь правдив и честен,
> Не криви душою,
> Другу даже в шутку
> Никогда не лги,
> Дорожи сильнее
> Дружбою большою,
> Дружбу золотую
> Крепко береги.

---

39 Gubarev, *Pavlik Morozov*, p. 51. Though some newspaper stories of the mid-1930s mention 'Motya Potupchik' as one of Pavlik's school-friends, this character's name and her family relationship with the hero, if not her role in the plot, appear to play on Kataev's 1936 classic *Beleet parus odinokii*, in which the two boy heroes play a game of hide-and-seek with Garik's cousin Motya (in the edition of *Beleet parus* published in Moscow and Leningrad, 1951, this episode occurs on p. 172). On Motya and Pavlik, see also Chapter 10 above.

[Be true and honest | always be sincere | even as a joke | never lie to your friend. | As it sonorously rounds-off: | 'Keep your golden friendship | For many a long year'.][40]

The unspoken antagonist of the song was, of course, the kind of 'dark', base-metal friendship that permitted or encouraged lying, character weakness, and furtive behaviour of all kinds, and which — by implication — had as its arena the kinds of social spaces not mentioned in the poem, in particular the street and the *dvor*, or courtyard, seen since the early 1920s (and also before the Revolution) as the haunt of 'unsupervised' (*beznadzornye*) throngs of children, and of their unacceptable collective activities such as smoking, drinking, and fighting.[41]

The correlative of such official representations of appropriate friendship was, as with adults, the representation of official relationships as ideal forms of friendship. For example, children were supposed to consider their teachers, as well as their fellow pupils, their best friends.[42] And groups of children were supposed to engage in 'friendship' with other comparable groups: so, 'friendship of nations' got passed down to miniature level through the 'friendship' of classes from different Soviet republics (typically, a Moscow school, representing the centre, alongside one from the national and geographical 'periphery').[43] Children were encouraged to be 'friends' also with different members of the forces of law and order, as in the group of 'Young Friends of Soviet Border-Guards', set up in the 1930s. Popular also was the representation of another kind of strictly hierarchised, emotionally controlled, form of friendship: that between humans and animals. The perfect kind of friendship, then, would have been the friendship of a Soviet border-guard with his dog, or of a Pioneer group with the border-guard, or indeed of a Pioneer group with the border-guard's dog.

Yet there were also richer depictions of friendship in children's literature than this, and indeed, more sophisticated depictions than one would find in some Socialist Realist texts for adults. Two of the children's classics of the mid-1930s, *A White Sail Gleamed* (*Beleet parus odinokii*) and *The Little Golden Key* (*Zolotoi klyuchik*), are centred on friendships of quite a complex kind — seldom tested by real differences of opinion, let alone by quarrels, it is true, but tested by *shared* adversity (unlike the ordeals endured separately in war stories). Arkady Gaidar's 1940 classic *Timur and His Team* (immediately adapted for the big screen by Aleksandr Razumny) also places at its centre friendship, of a generalising, group-oriented kind. In documentary prose, there was also a wider comprehension of the institution than emerged in the usual good friendship/ bad friendship model from didactic texts. For instance, an article

---

40 N. Naidenova, S. Bulatov, 'Pesnya o druzhbe', *Vozhatyi*, 6 (1947), inside cover.
41 For a 1940s source with such a negative image of the *dvor*, see N. Sych, 'Vo dvore nashego doma', *Vozhatyi*, 5 (1948), 10, which reports the wails of a cat being tormented, and children playing war games (the boys in a *shtab*, or army headquarters, the girls in a 'field hospital'), and other such 'tedious' pursuits, until an active Pioneer takes things in hand and starts organising excursions to the Tauride Gardens etc.
42 See for example E. V. Aleksandrova, 'V druzhbe s uchitelyami', *Vozhatyi*, 10 (1950), 10–11. \
43 See for example L. Nikol'sky, 'Druzhba', *Vozhatyi*, 10 (1947), 11 (about the 'friendship' of schools in Moscow and Nal'chik).

in a collection directed at orphanage supervisors presented several different images of friendship at the same time: 'Normal friendship on the basis of doing homework and reading together is often deepened by children's feelings of mutual attraction'.[44] The text juxtaposes two fundamentally distinct views of friendship: mutual aid, on the one hand, and on the other, emotional affinity. Friendship, then, is perceived as not just a socially universal institution, but also an emotionally satisfactory one. The possible threat of undue individualism in this vision was averted by an emphasis, later in this discussion, that friendship was emotionally satisfactory also when observed from the outside: so, relationships between older and younger inmates in the orphanage were said to be 'touching'.[45] Nonetheless, however, a perception that friendship was not just about abstract 'comradeliness' had crept in, and during the late 1940s, in particular, more sophisticated representations of the emotional and moral desiderata and pitfalls of friendship started to be produced. Lev Kassil's novel, *My Dear Boys* (*Dorogie moi mal'chiki*), for instance, focuses on a group of boys in a provincial town who even manage — with the retrospective sanction of the local Party authorities — to run their own secret society.[46] Still more interesting was Valentina Oseeva's hugely popular novel of 1947, *Vasyok Trubachov and His Comrades* (*Vasyok Trubachov i ego tovarishchi*), where the boundaries between licit and illicit friendship were both underlined and called into question.

The plot of *Vasyok Trubachov* hinges on what a walking cliché of a character, the boys' stern but humane new teacher, Sergei Nikolaevich (in a twist of the usual terminology), describes as 'false comradeliness'.[47] As he proclaims, 'There is open, honest, Pioneer comradeliness and there is the petty, cowardly, lying effort to get people out of fixes'.[48] The most obviously culpable boys in the story, Mazin and Rusakov, have a relationship that is founded, from the beginning, on 'getting people out of fixes': early in the novel, Mazin saves Rusakov from a thrashing by his strict father by taking the blame for a broken window on himself. Thereafter, the usual collaborative classroom sin of *podskazka* (prompting other pupils during oral testing) is regularly committed.[49] And then eventually a more serious violation of propriety occurs: Mazin removes a piece of chalk from the classroom to create a diversion during a test, hoping to save his buddy from a public humiliation and poor marks when his turn comes to regurgitate the tasks learned for homework.

---

44 I. Geller, 'Uchebno-vospitatel'naya rabota 1-go Smolenskogo detskogo doma', *Uchebno-vospitatel'naya rabota v detskikh domakh. Byulleten'*, 1 (1941), 66.
45 Ibid.
46 Lev Kassil', *Dorogie moi mal'chishki* (Moscow: Detgiz, 1944).
47 See for example S. Kosov, 'Vasily Andreevich', in *Mitina pyaterka* (Moscow & Leningrad: Detgiz, 1952), pp. 3–10. The background to the representation of male teachers as ideal patriarchs in Soviet post-war children's literature (and also in adult literature, official art, and so on) was, of course, the deficit of male authority figures in real-life families and schools, a point of anxiety for successive generations of writers (see, for instance, I. Grekova's story, *A Ship of Widows* (1981), in which the young men raised by a collective of widows end up not amounting to much).
48 Valentina A. Oseeva, *Vasyok Trubachov i ego tovarishchi*, 2 vols (Leningrad: Detgiz, 1978), 1, 200.
49 On the traditions of *podskazka* and its role in allowing both pupils and teachers to cope with the over-demanding centralised programme, see Kelly, '"The School Waltz"'.

But this plainly illicit kind of bond is not the only kind to come in for criticism in the story. The friendship between Trubachov himself and his two closest companions, Bulgakov and Odintsov, is also represented as potentially subversive to good order. The three are too pent-up in each other, too exclusive, too eager to allow private feeling into the public domain. They even have the temerity to ask their teacher whether they may sit next to each other during classes:

> 'A threesome?' the teacher repeated. 'Is your class really divided into troikas of friends? So no-one else counts?'
> 'Weeeell, no, we're just friends... old mates, you know...' Odintsov explained.
> 'All right, let's accept that: you're old mates. That's all well and good, but sharing a desk with your old mates is completely unnecessary. And I'm not having it!' said Sergei Nikolaevich in a tone that brooked no argument.[50]

Friendship in the exclusive sense is perceived as incompatible with harmonious existence in the larger social unit. The term 'old mates' (*zakadychnye druz'ya*) is first used in the novel to apply to the bond between Mazin and Rusakov, which has clear negative associations. The bond that Trubachov and his friends have named using the same term also turns out to be fallible, though in quite a different way from the bond between Mazin and Rusakov. And indeed Trubachov's relationship with his closest friends has to be 'purged' before it can be allowed to continue.

When a plot by Mazin and Rusakov to disrupt a test gets Trubachov into trouble, Trubachov immediately turns on, and taunts, his fellow class monitor, and becomes — for a while — an embittered outsider. Odintsov then denounces Trubachov's behaviour in the wall newspaper, leading to shocked feelings about the betrayal of 'comradeship' in some of his classmates. Odintsov's own response is to ask them whether loyalty should be considered an absolute value: 'So if my comrade killed someone, I'm still supposed to keep mum?' (p. 157). Odintsov's action is, in the end, endorsed by Sergei Nikolaevich, and Vasyok Trubachov is brought to understand that goodwill cannot be stored up for those one is close to — it must be distributed round the wider community. To borrow the term used in 'Song of Friendship', amity is a kind of 'gold standard' that must not be squandered, but must also not be hoarded. Vasyok finishes by apologising even to his bossy and pedantic elderly aunt: 'And I've hurt your feelings too' (p. 202).

According to the categorisations of enlightened Soviet pedagogy, as expounded by Sergei Nikolaevich, 'friendship' or 'comradeliness' applied to a general and inclusive social harmony, a mechanism of good order that constrained tensions and precluded undesirable activities such as teasing or physical violence. It was this spirit that was reflected in a little sermon about relations between boys and girls published by a girl pupil in Vasyok's class, 'Link Leader Zorina', in the school's wall newspaper. At the moment, the author complained, boys and girls generally shunned each other, coming together only for spiteful trading of insults and low-level assaults:

> Many boys say: 'We always get on well — if someone's a pain, we thump him. But just try pulling a girl's hair — she'll go all huffy. So with girls, discipline

---

50 Oseeva, *Vasyok Trubachov i ego tovarishchi*, p. 98.

> goes out the window.' I don't agree: you don't have to thump anyone, but you do have to talk to girls in a friendly way and not jeer at them. And girls shouldn't sneer at boys and tease them either. Some of them are so spiteful, and that's not good. We've grown up together, been together since the first year, so let's be friends. I believe in friendship between boys and girls. You mustn't hurt anyone's feelings or jeer at them. (*Vasyok Trubachov i ego tovarishchi*, p. 97)

Zorina's position as 'link leader' (a subdivision of the overall Pioneer troop comprised by the class as a whole) gave her automatic authority. The well-policed kind of friendship sketched out here was also reflected in the musings of Mitya, Class 4 B's Pioneer leader:

> He regretted not having had a comradely chat with Trubachov. When you have a friendly chat one-to-one, such simple and much-needed words always come to mind. Your voice sounds different and you look into each other's eyes: you can't hide, and you can't hide anything either. (p. 187)

The idea of friendship as an instrument of self-criticism was, in terms of 1940s literature for children, utterly orthodox: one might compare Liya Geraskina's 1948 play, *Matriculation Exam* (*Attestat zrelosti*), where clever but conceited Valentin Listovsky has to be brought in hand, and his friend Zhenya is criticised at a Komsomol meeting for not having been the first to do it.[51]

At this level, it is not surprising that a contemporary reviewer saw Oseeva's novel as a positive textbook for the times. 'The central question is one seldom illuminated in children's literature', she (rather misleadingly) claimed:

> Therefore, the virtue of Oseeva's book is that she gives voice to good thoughts, ones with great significance for moral education. The author tries to make clear that the life of the school collective can only be based on friendship.[52]

While criticising some of the characterisation, the reviewer remained solidly behind what she saw as the moral import of the novel.

Yet in fact *Vasyok Trubachov* was more complicated in its message than this. Both 'virtuous' and 'vicious' child characters were shown as being caught up in a *shared* idea of how to be friends that was perceived as unacceptable only by outsiders — adults. The book hence acknowledged, albeit only by implication, the 'us and them' character of enforced socialisation. The idea of virtuous friendship that *Vasyok Trubachov* propounded was also rather contradictory. On the one hand, intimate friendship was seen as opaque in rational terms, as a place where refuge was taken from the demands of the wider society, and hence dangerous. Not for nothing was Mazin and Rusakov's preferred haunt an earth dug-out which they had constructed in a thicket, marked with monograms of their initials that gave the place the flavour of a bandit den. On the other hand, though, friendship was seen, within the novel, as useful precisely because it *did* lie beyond the wider world, because sincerity could be more easily expressed there, and because exchange of

---

[51] L. Geraskina, *Attestat zrelosti* (1948), *P'esy* (Moscow: Sovetskii pisatel', 1962). The play was reprinted several times and widely staged, and was adapted as a film (Tat'yana Lukashevich, Mosfil'm, 1954).
[52] O. Levina, 'Vasek Trubachev i ego tovarishchi', *Vozhatyi*, 3 (1948), 14.

affect could be less constrained. In other words, even while asserting the virtues of non-exclusive, community-wide friendship, Soviet writers were leaving space for reserve and intimacy, and sentimentally asserting the absolute moral value of this (as in the idyllic reference, in Mitya's musings, to 'somewhere where it is impossible to hide oneself'). Concealment was uniformly perceived as bad, and individual relationships were seen to verge on the furtive; yet, at the same time, candour was understood to be *primarily* possible in intimate contexts.[53]

Historically speaking, this perception fused together the attitudes of the early Enlightenment (as, for example, in Lambert) and of pre-Romanticism (as exemplified in Schiller's *Die Brüder* or Goethe's *Die Leiden des jungen Werthers*). In similar vein, an article published in *Koster* during 1946, and meant to prompt discussions at Pioneer meetings, cited a bewildering variety of different exemplary friendships. These included not only Lenin and Stalin (the acme of friendship), Marx and Engels, and Sergei Kirov and Iosif Kononov, killed by police during a Tomsk workers' demonstration in 1905 (Kirov was alleged to have visited Kononov after his death, kissed him and taken a scrap of bloodied flag from its hiding place in his dead friend's bosom), but also Orestes and Pylades.[54] While asserting that '[Communist] party friendship' ('partiinaya druzhba') was the highest form of the relationship, the article also emphasised the dependence of the relationship generally on shared intellectual interests: 'Friendship is a big, complicated feeling. Only people with many ideas, aims, and fateful desires in common can be friends'.[55]

In other words, while the view of friendship propounded to children was superficially one where detached comradeliness became the route to a virtuous attachment, friendship was also seen as a complex feeling that linked individuals together on the basis of personal interests and attitudes. And it was not only a peculiarly Soviet emotion (as *The Great Soviet Encyclopaedia* had claimed) but also a universal one. Similarly contradictory — though for rather different reasons — was the attitude to friendship's antipode, love.

Growing Towards the Family: The Place of Love in Propaganda for Children

While representations of friendship among adults and among children were strikingly similar in many respects, the central concept of 'comradeliness', when applied to children, often carried a freight of affect that was not present in adult exempla. Conversely, love in the sense of a romantic attachment between two individuals (always assumed in Soviet official discourse to be of opposite genders)

---

53   The ambivalence of *Vasyok Trubachov i ego tovarishchi* relative to the friendship vs comradeliness divide may help explain why the novel was not adapted for cinema till the Thaw era (Ilya Frez, 1955 and 1957). My thanks to Julian Graffy for this point.
54   Probably Kononov's role as the flag-carrier was crucial in elevating an otherwise fairly obscure figure to the friendship canon (on the post-war cult of the Soviet banner, see Jeremy Hicks, *The Victory Banner over the Reichstag: Film, Document, and Ritual in Russia's Contested Memory of World War II* (Pittsburgh, PA: University of Pittsburgh Press, 2020).
55   'Rasskazhite na pionerskom sbore. O druzhbe', *Koster*, 1 (1946), 10–11.

constituted a special case, where texts for children were concerned, because of the additional layer of sexual puritanism that overlay representations directed at those who were regarded not only as young, but also as innocent. From the early 1930s, child sexuality — anyway the subject of unease and embarrassment in Russian intellectual culture in previous decades — stopped being mentionable at all.[56] The result was that children were frequently warned of the dangers of love in much the same words that had been used by behaviour counsellors of the eighteenth century. In the words of Liya Geraskina's *Matriculation Exam*, 'Real friendship is more selfless and noble than love; it is less egotistical'.[57] Significantly, these words of warning were uttered during a conversation between a boy and a girl at a dance. Thus an age-old sexual ritual was defused by becoming the occasion for sententiae about the superiority of non-sexual relationships.

But there was a twist to the story: the boy and girl concerned eventually *did* end up in love and with plans to marry. Eager to prevent unseemly behaviour by young people though it might be, the Soviet moral establishment was equally committed to preparing them for 'normal' family relations, which were — from the mid-1930s, once more — understood to be ideally based on close emotional ties between man and woman, aimed at the conception, gestation, and upbringing of further generations. In other words, sexual activity was as essential to the Soviet ideal of marriage as to the Christian ideal from which it derived. The need to produce individuals suited for a life of progenitive monogamy was a major spur to educational policy as well as to ideological utterances throughout the Stalin era. The move to single-sex education was accompanied by a good deal of anxiety that single-sex schools should not produce characters whose relationship with the opposite sex was uneasy. As a contributor to *Izvestiya* wrote in 1943:

> The point is not at all to build some kind of a 'Great Wall of China' between boys and girls, and not that they should walk on different sides of the street We are only talking about separate education for girls and boys. That is the main thing. It is impossible to imagine that when single-sex education is introduced, boys and girls will not socialise together. They will be together in Houses of Young Pioneers, in institutions operating outside the walls of the school, in theatres, at social evenings in schools, and so on.[58]

Again one notes the allusion to safe, well-regulated spaces where contact between children might take place under the supervision of adults. Still, compared with the practices at pre-revolutionary secondary schools, the possibilities of association for children of the opposite sex were still quite significant.[59] An elite Moscow

---

56   On the pre-1917 period, see Laura Engelstein, *The Keys to Happiness: Sex and the Search for Modernity in fin-de-siècle Russia* (Ithaca, NY: Cornell University Press, 1992). During the 1920s, there was some relatively frank writing about child sexuality (see for example F. Orlov-Skomorovsky, *Golgofa rebenka* (Moscow: [n. pub.], 1921), but this constituted a marginal trend, and even progressive schools, it would seem, did not include sex education on the syllabus.
57   Geraskina, *P'esy*, p. 43.
58   A. Orlov, 'O razdel'nom obuchenii v shkolakh', *Izvestiya*, 10 August 1943, p. 4.
59   In pre-revolutionary secondary schools, attempts to police pupils' leisure took the form of draconian prohibitions on attending various forms of 'illicit' entertainment, etc.; not until the

girls' school where boys were not allowed in the building, ever, at any time, was very much an exception; on the whole, contact between the opposite sexes was encouraged at least on certain ritual occasions, such as the 'school-leavers' ball', an institution that became widespread at this period.[60]

In literature and cinema for children also, a friendship that became a love relationship and culminated in marriage, was widespread, being represented, for instance, in Veniamin Kaverin's hugely popular novel *Two Captains* (*Dva kapitana*) (awarded a Stalin Prize in 1946, and filmed by Vladimir Vengerov in 1956), as well as Fadeev's *The Young Guard* (*Molodaya gvardiya*).[61] In youth theatre, too, such 'sliding' relationships were a feature of the time. One might mention, alongside *Matriculation Certificate*, for example, Dmitry Shcheglov's piece, *Where the Pines Rustle* (*Gde sosny shumyat*), licensed for performance in the Leningrad Youth Theatre (TYuZ) in 1951, which hinged round a conflict in an Estonian lumber camp inhabited by a mixed population of Russians and Estonians. Two of the young lumber workers, Anti Vaklou and Andrei Bezborodov are both in love with Anna Sauko, a young Komsomol girl, and are also rivals at work. Gradually they learn to respect each other, while Andrei develops the courage to make his feelings clear to Anna. The play ends with a wedding between Andrei and Anna, accompanied by toasts to 'the innovators of the forest', and the development of a tendresse between Anti and Katerina Varnu.[62] Alongside an obvious point, that sentimental love was tolerable where it led to marriage, went the intertwining of love and 'friendship of nations' — the central relationship cemented the alliance of the Estonian and Russian peoples. A supremely *official* kind of affective relationship was allegorically linked to a personal relationship, and one also sanctioned by its role as a social institution.

In these respects, love could in fact seem (despite the moral threat that it presented if unsuitably indulged) more permissible, more to be encouraged, than friendship.[63] Soviet writing for children, for instance, provided no negative models of love, though there was some intolerance of 'lovey-dovey behaviour' (*lyubovnichan'e*), as manifested, for instance, in campaigns against the albums of sentimental poems that some older schoolchildren liked to collect. Instead, there was a single form of teleologically-directed close relationship, very much of the externalised kind

Ignat'ev reforms of 1915 was a concerted effort made to provide forms of 'rational leisure' through the school network, and then primarily for boys (by means of scouting, for example). See Kelly, *Children's World*, Chapter 12. The attitudes in Soviet schools of the 1940s were more like those in my London girls' school of the 1970s than like those in pre-1917 schools.

60   The school concerned was no. 175. See CKQ-Oxf-03 PF1A-B (woman, b. 1936) for a description of the curriculum and atmosphere.

61   It is notable also that there were two remakes of the key 'Soviet buddy' movies for children and adolescents in later decades: Evgeny Karelov's *Two Captains* (1976) and Aleksandr Blank and Sergei Linkov's *Timur and His Team* (released in the same year). Gerasimov's *The Young Guard* was re-released in 1964 after cuts to celebratory references to Stalin and reduction of footage relating to a traitor in the group after new historical research had revealed that the real culprit was someone else.

62   V. Shcheglov, *Gde sosny shumyat* (play, 1951). Typescript in Theatre Library, St Petersburg: C1 5-4-302.

63   For a further discussion, see *SSSR: territoriya lyubvi*, ed. by K. Bogdanov, N. Borisova, and Yu. Mur (Moscow: Novoe izdatel'stvo, 2008).

to be found in traditional fairy tales, and usually — as there — enduring entirely external obstacles, often, in addition, of an insubstantial or chimerical kind, before reaching the inevitable end of matrimony. The result could be that, paradoxically, given the governing view of childhood's sacrosanct character, Soviet children were sometimes exposed to material that might, in British or American culture, have been considered too 'adult' for their years.[64]

Beyond the Boundaries: Children's Lived Experiences of Friendship

> Int. What was interesting about school?
> Inf. Friendship.[65]

Tracing the norms of friendship set out in officially-sanctioned discourses is relatively straightforward. How the behaviour stereotypes set out in propaganda related to affective relationships as they were understood and practised by children is a more difficult question. Oral history provides some answers — though with the usual caveat about remembered experience and the possibility it has been retrospectively 'edited'. Be that as it may, friendships and personal relationships are one of the areas that informants are most eager to talk about (as opposed to ideology, say). As one might expect, much of the evidence suggests a palpable gap between ideal friendships as presented in propaganda and real friendships. Indeed, the endless warnings against 'bad friendship' point, as advice literature's negative prescriptions often do, to the pervasiveness of the behaviour that is criticised. Many — though by no means all — classes were split up into small interest groups (*razbity na kompanii*), and both within and between such groups, children often interpreted 'friendly' behaviour as signifying the sort of willingness to lend aid in a crisis, or 'getting out of fixes', so starkly criticised by the teacher in *Vasyok Trubachov*.[66] Semi-subversive mutual aid practices such as *podskazka* were pervasive, and friendship could be born not of mutual esteem and a rational sense of mutual interest, but out of much more raw kinds of attraction.[67] For instance, fighting was sometimes

---

64 My main example of this comes from the 1960s: V. Mukhina, Dnevnik materi (Moscow: Znanie, 1977), p. 341), records quaint remarks made by one of her twins, then aged just under six (this being in late 1966 or early 1967), after the two boys had watched a love film on television. But examples from the 1930s and 1940s could be found as well, for instance, the setting of literary works such as Evgeny Onegin on the school syllabus. It should be remarked that differences in drawing boundaries applied not just to sex. In Vasyok Trubachov, for example, there is an absolutely matter-of-fact reference to Sasha Bulgakov's father getting drunk (I, 14): after Sasha's mother tells her son how his father has been expressing wonder and pride in his family's achievement, the twelve-year old son replies 'patronisingly', 'He's always like that when he's had a few'. The scene is unthinkable in a British or American children's book of the same era, though a frightening drunk encountered on the street might have been allowable.
65 Oxf/Lev SPb-02 PF 7A, interview by Alexandra Piir, p. 56 (woman, b. Leningrad, 1931).
66 The question, 'Was your class friendly, or was it split up into kompanii?' was added to the questionnaire by my Russian collaborators. There is an extensive discussion of the role of the kompaniya in Fürst, Stalin's Last Generation.
67 Our respondents (of widely differing generations and social backgrounds) uniformly emphasised that yes, podskazka and the use of shpargalki did go on in their class (this information was often given with a collusive giggle).

not just a source of conflict among boys, but also a route to male bonding. In an interview conducted in late 2002, for instance, a man born in Leningrad in 1931, but of Bashkir descent, remembered starting a fight with a classmate in 1945 when the latter bent the corner of his jacket into the shape of a pig's ear in order to be offensive (oddly enough, the tormenter was himself Jewish). At this, the Bashkir boy duly bloodied his antagonist's nose. This incident led not to enmity, but to a firm friendship between the two.[68]

At the same time, some aspects of friendship among children did accord with official stereotypes of appropriate relations. For example, at least among girls, there was often co-operation over homework, as recalled by a Leningrad woman born in 1931:

> Back in my schooldays, in the post-war years, starting then, I was friends with Nina, Svetlana, Tanya, Sarochka, though she was a bit younger. Yes. And our families were friendly too. We used to go and visit, and Svetlana and Tanya and I were all in the same class, and they lived on Moskovsky prospect [...] and we on the factory territory opposite [...] we were a triangle. And we'd run over to see each other. Sometimes we did our homework in one place, sometimes in another, or a third again.[69]

Comparable 'mutual aid' (this time on a more general basis) was recorded by another working-class Leningrader who grew up in the 1930s:

> If you missed a day or two of school back then, they'd check up immediately. The class elder would say: 'Hey girls, who can go and visit? Someone had better go over.' Usually it was someone living nearby. We were all in one district, you didn't have to drag over the entire city. 'Go and see why so-and-so's not here.' And we'd take the homework over. That's what it was like. Not one pupil neglected. It was such a friendly, pleasant class cell [*yacheika*], like. We were all friendly, so we'd say: someone's being standoffish, someone couldn't care less. And if needed, the whole class would go over.[70]

Striking is the informant's use of *yacheika*, applied also to the primary organisation of the Communist Party in the workplace, for her peer group, and her interpretation of the class's surveillance as positive, with only negative terms for those who shunned collective practices.

Friendships between children were also susceptible to moulding through adult intervention of a more direct kind. For example, it was customary for Soviet teachers (as in *Vasyok Trubachov*) to separate established friends in the classroom layout, seating them at different desks, and to try and generate comradeliness by placing less obvious soulmates at the same desk. 'Class supervisors' might also use general meetings or class assemblies, or Pioneer meetings, in order to talk generally about friendship, or to single out particular individuals for commendation or

---

68   Oxf/Lev/SPb-O2, PF 8B, interview by Alexandra Piir, p. 20 (man, *b*. Leningrad, 1931).
69   Oxf/Lev/SPb-O2, PF 6B, interview by Alexandra Piir, p. 32 (woman, *b*. Leningrad, 1931). Similar memories are recorded in different generations also: see e.g. Oxf/Lev SPb-03, PF 15A, interview Alexandra Piir, p. 42 (woman, *b*. Leningrad,1969); CKQ Oxf-03 PF 10B, p. 10 (woman, *b*. Gelendzhik, 1975).
70   Oxf/Lev/SPb-O2, PF 3A, interview Alexandra Piir, p. 66 (woman, *b*. Leningrad, 1931).

correction.⁷¹ More elaborate types of management were sometimes engaged in too. For instance, in the mid-1950s a drama teacher at Moscow school no. 204 employed the subject matter of the *skazka* playlets that she was rehearsing with class 3 (made up of ten-year-olds) in order to thrust home didactic points about the need for friendship, aiming her sallies in particular at Rita and Volodya, who spent most of their time during rehearsals squabbling. In the diary she kept of the process, she recalled:

> I talk about his quarrels with Rita in passing, as it were, without pointing a moral, but making clear I don't approve.
> I ask, 'So you've quarrelled with Rita again?' He says, 'We've almost made up, only sometimes we do have a quarrel.'
> 'Don't you ever get bored?'
> 'No, we can't seem to manage any other way.'⁷²

This unsatisfactory response generated a lengthy correspondence in which the teacher relentlessly exploited the events in the play in order to provide Volodya with a commentary on his relationship with Rita:

> Dear Volodya,
> I can understand why you don't like playing the cockerel, but I absolutely can't understand why you keep quarrelling with Rita. Please write to me about it. Looking forward to hearing from you.
>   V. Shiryaeva.
>
> Dear Vera Grigor'evna,
> Me and Rita Davydenko quarrel because Rita Davydenko is so bossy and I really don't like it. That's why we don't get on. Goodbye. Looking forward to hearing from you.
>
> Dear Volodya, you're quite right. When a comrade starts ordering you around, it's not at all nice. But in that case you have to convince the comrade that he's not behaving in the right way, and not squabble and fight. What do you think? Goodbye. Looking forward to hearing from you.⁷³

After a lengthy correspondence, Volodya refused to back down. The teacher's solution was to give the bossy Rita the role of the narrator in the drama, so that she had to learn to speak slowly and clearly, rather than just loudly and with authority. What effect this actually had on the children concerned was not recorded.⁷⁴

Teachers did their best to manage boy-girl relationships too. Once co-education returned in 1955, this was followed by full institutionalisation of 23 February and 8 March as male versus female school festivals (with presents from either side).⁷⁵ But even in the late 1940s and early 1950s, many single-sex schools made efforts to organise contacts between boys and girls, and teachers and pedagogues expressed

---

71 In the 1940s, for example, a good deal of time was spent on maunderings about 'maidenly honour'. See, for example, CKQ-Oxf-03 PF1A, p. 3 (woman, *b.* Moscow, 1936).
72 V. Shiryaeva, 'Otchet o provedenii obsledovatel'skoi raboty v 204-i shkole v Moskve (1954–55 gg.)', RAO NA, f. 32, op. 1, d. 539, l. 229.
73 Ibid., l. 230.
74 Ibid.
75 See, for example, CKQ-Oxf-03 PF8B, pp. 14–15.

disquiet when these did not generate an immediate romantic spark. According to a critical report by inspectors from the Academy of Pedagogical Sciences who visited various Moscow schools in 1948:

> In School no. 19, they decided to hold joint evenings with the boys' school next door. The plan worked rather badly: the boys could only dance the foxtrot and were too shy to ask the girls to dance. One group of boys scribbled indecent graffiti on the walls of the girls' school. Then the girls sent a letter of protest to the boys' school via the District Committee of the Komsomol and demanded an apology from the boys, or otherwise the school doors would be closed to them. A federation of twelve boys duly arrived at the girls' school to apologise for the unworthy behaviour of their comrades.[76]

Interestingly, the response to this debacle on the part of the school director was not, as one might have supposed, to ban all further boy/girl meetings, but to argue that there was a need for *greater* contact (primarily of an intellectual kind) between the two sexes.[77] Comparably, a woman born in Sverdlovsk in 1931 who was an extremely enthusiastic attender at Pioneer camps throughout the 1940s, first as a Pioneer and then as a Pioneer assistant leader, recalled that, when one of the male assistant leaders started paying court to her, the general attitude was that she should take pity on him. The idea that he should have left her alone occurred to nobody, including, it should be said, the recipient of the unwanted attention herself.[78] Conversely, official puritanism could filter down to pupils as well: a particularly piquant example involves a class at Moscow School no. 175, where pupils in class 5 who were regularly subjected to lectures on 'maidenly honour' created an uproar when they discovered that the class teacher had a male admirer: 'The lessons we'd learned at school, in the history class and so on, we applied them right away to our own lives'.[79]

Yet at the same time, romantic relationships were constructed not only (or indeed mainly) on the basis of advice from teachers or other 'responsible adults'. According to recollections from informants, Russian literature (particularly nineteenth-century Russian literature) and information from classmates — as well as direct observation of adult behaviour — were fundamental in constructing ideas about such relationships. And first contacts with the opposite sex, at least in the 1940s, often had a clandestine flavour: for example, an informant born in Leningrad in 1931 remembered that the main place for meeting boys was ballroom-dancing classes, at which it was forbidden to speak, but where participants spent most of their time exchanging love-letters: 'And the most crazy romances used to start right away'.[80]

In the end, then, the stereotypes of lived friendships and romantic relationships did bear some resemblance to those set out in propaganda. Adult ambitions to mould affective relationships did have a direct impact, particularly through the

---

76 'Vneklassnaya rabota v shkole', RAO NA, f. 32, op. 1, d. 160, l. 41.
77 Ibid.
78 CKQ-E-03 PF3A, p. 4 (interview in Ekaterinburg by Catriona Kelly).
79 CKQ-Oxf-03 PF1A, pp. 3–4.
80 CKQ-Oxf-03 PF5B, p. 9.

influence of teachers, who might encourage or discourage actual relationships in a concrete sense, or particular types of relationship in the abstract, and whose own perceptions of appropriate behaviour were likely to be based, directly or indirectly, on didactic texts. This connection — of a muted, ramified kind — between propaganda and real behaviour bridges the divide between ideology and everyday life that commentators on the 1930s, and particularly the 1940s, have sometimes held to exist.[81] Propaganda itself, particularly from the late 1940s, became more complex, recognising the possibility of relationships with a higher degree of emotional warmth than had been allowed for in the early Soviet era. It is therefore misleading to see real friendships as touching on the official codes of behaviour only where they acted as the instrument of surveillance.[82] At the same time, children themselves often saw their friendships and romances — or aspects of these — as clandestine, a perception encouraged by didactic texts, which emphasised that all licit relationships should be under adult surveillance, a surveillance that (especially in the case of romantic friendships) fictional and real children often sought to evade. In the end, then, a somewhat paradoxical situation emerges: of private relationships that in signal respects resembled the patterns set up in official literature and didactic communication more generally, but which were also held to represent a refuge from official culture, an alternative way of life.

The idea for this essay goes back to a panel on friendship in Russia at the ASEEES Congress, USA, in 2009, organised by Oleg Kharkhordin. I am grateful to him for the initiative, and also to Svetlana Maslinskaya and other members of the editorial board of *Detskie chteniya*, where it was originally published.

81   See for example E. Zubkova, *Sovetskaya zhizn', 1945–1953* (Moscow: ROSSPEN, 2003); V. Shlapentokh, *Strakh i druzhba v nashem totalitarnom proshlom* (St Petersburg: Zvezda, 2003). In *Everyday Stalinism: Ordinary Life in Extraordinary Times: Soviet Russia in the 1930s* (New York: Oxford University Press, 1999), Sheila Fitzpatrick concentrates on 'everyday interactions that in some way involved the state', which she considers 'largely excludes topics like friendship, love, and some aspects of leisure and private sociability' (p. 3). Obviously, one has to distinguish between direct and indirect involvement — friendships and love affairs, unlike marriages or relationships with children, did not have to be registered with the state, and hence had no legal status and were less likely to be the subject of intervention at a formal level. But the efforts, using propaganda and agitation, to cajole and persuade individuals to conduct such relationships in certain ways represented an important *secondary* level of state intervention.
82   Here I take issue with Kharkhordin's interpretation in 'Druzhba'.

CHAPTER 12

Essential Luxuries: Goods for Children in the Last Decades of Soviet Power

[2007]

Roberto Benigni's sentimental, but also memorable film, *Life is Beautiful* (*La vita è bella*, 1997), culminates with scenes showing a father trying desperately to stop his son from realising that the family has been incarcerated in a concentration camp. Concealment from the guards is turned into hide-and-seek, and the drills and rollcalls are likewise presented as games. The father's 'magic' is even able to produce a happy ending, when the liberating American tanks — to the child's delighted eyes, all part of the game — arrive to put an end to the threat from which the father's subterfuge has symbolically (and in 'virtual reality', actually) protected the son.

The film raises a crucial issue: what, precisely, might be described as a *luxury* in conditions of shortage and deprivation? A means of shutting out reality? An item that is not generally available? Something you can do without? As Nabokov's 1936 story 'The Circle' suggested, the biggest luxury for émigrés of the 'first wave' was not to have a child who spoke French or German perfectly, but one who spoke his or her parents' language like a native. In recent years, the word 'luxury' in British English has changed from signifying something exotic to meaning a commodity at the top end of the mass market ('luxury bungalow', 'luxury Christmas pudding').[1] 'Luxury' does not mean 'superfluous', and the Christian condemnation of sensual delight in the term *luxuria* gets forgotten. A 'luxury' now means a small pleasure everyone is entitled to, rather than some commodity or activity that is the exclusive preserve of the rich.

---

1   Though sometimes a more exclusive meaning is retained. An article in the British Sunday newspaper *The Observer* on 2 December 2007 (Johnny Davis, 'Would Madam Care to Taste the Cloud Juice?' <http://observer.guardian.co.uk/magazine/story/0,,2218842,00.html> [accessed 30 September 2022]) reported that, where the average cost of bottled mineral water was then about £1 a litre, some customers in expensive restaurants were prepared to pay up to £30 a litre for 'glacial water', water shipped from Fiji and New Zealand or produced from a single spring in England, and so on. Renaud Gregoire, 'food and beverage director' of Claridges Hotel, London (one of the British capital's most expensive hotels), was quoted as saying, 'What is luxury if it's not about getting things not everyone can get?'

The phrase 'socialist luxury', recently used to capture the 1970s and 1980s culture that included the Polish hotel-building programme in a style that has been delightfully named the 'Communist grotesque', East German girlie magazines, or Yugoslav car marketing, raises issues of its own.[2] In early Soviet Russia, the whole phrase 'socialist luxury' would have seemed ridiculous.[3] Bolshevism drew on the double inheritance of Christian and intellectual asceticism: acquisition for its own sake was considered a moral and political fault. The architects of the new regime not only espoused the traditions of the radical intelligentsia back to the 1860s, but set their face against the spending patterns of the last years of Tsarist Russia.

By the late nineteenth century, an extremely prosperous urban elite (in many respects analogous to the 'new Russians' of the 1990s and 2000s) was spending large sums on clothes, food, and entertainments for its children.[4] A sense of the range of items considered acceptable, or indeed necessary, is given by shop catalogues of the day. Children's World, a specialist store in St Petersburg, offered a vast range of books and goods, and with a mail-order service.[5] An equally impressive selection of items could be purchased at Child-Reading in Moscow. The 1899 catalogue has pages of perambulators, cradles, baby changing tables, layettes, dolls, and games, with long dresses in white piqué for small babies costing six to eight roubles 'and upwards'.[6] The Paul Karlson department store in central St Petersburg also offered a vast range of items for children, including 'complete layettes from 30 roubles 50 kopecks up to 300 roubles' (at this period ten roubles a month was a standard sum for a maidservant's monthly wages). The catalogues were illustrated with engravings of extremely elaborate broderie anglaise and lace outfits with embroidery, pintucks, and ruffles.[7]

2   All of these subjects were addressed in excellent papers at the 'Socialist Luxury' conference. For the equally varied but slightly different published selection, see *Pleasures in Socialism: Leisure and Luxury in the Eastern Bloc*, ed. by David Crowley and Susan E. Reid (Evanston, IL: Northwestern University Press, 2010).
3   While less commonly used than in Anglophone culture, the phrase does have some resonance in post-Soviet Russia, though often of an ironic kind: see, for example, Kasya Popova's strictures on the Kamernyi teatr in Ekaterinburg: 'Teatr kak zerkalo zhizni', *Ural*, 8 (2007) <http://magazines.russ.ru/ural/2007/8/p16.html> [accessed 30 September 2022], where the author observes that the 'excessive and now out-of-date decor [of the Chamber Theatre, built in the 1980s] oppresses the spectator'. When I was having my late 1980s flat in St Petersburg redecorated, the building contractor, a former journalist, hearing that I had just given a paper at the 'Socialist Luxury' conference, laughed and said: 'You know, your own block is a case of "socialist luxury", back then the entire city wanted to live here' (the building in question is a Brezhnev-era block opposite the former Hotel Leningrad, itself a striking example of the 'Communist grotesque').
4   See Svetlana Boym, *Common Places: Mythologies of Everyday Life in Russia* (Cambridge, MA: Harvard University Press, 1994); my *Refining Russia*, Chapter 3.
5   See *Katalog magazina "Detskii mir"* (St Petersburg: Detskii mir, 1886). The shop was at no. 33 Liteinyi Prospekt. S. F. Svetlov, *Peterburgskaya zhizn' v kontse XIX stoletiya (v 1892 godu)*, ed. by A. M. Konechnyi (St Petersburg: Giperion, 1998), p. 55, lists three toyshops, Chernokhvostov's and Doinikov's in the Gostinyi dvor, and The Troitskaya Studio of Textbooks and Games (selling educational toys and games) at Troitskaya ulitsa, no. 9, but not this one.
6   *Katalog magazina "Detskoe vospitanie"* (Moscow: magazin 'Detskoe vospitanie', 1899), p. 7.
7   *Preis Kurant bel'ya. Postavshchik Dvora Ego Imperatorskogo Velichestva. Torgovyi dom "Paul Karlson". S-Peterburg. Morskaya, No. 18* (St Petersburg: Torgovyi dom 'Paul Karlson' [*c.* 1900]). See Chapter 10 for an illustration from this catalogue.

Memoirs by those who grew up in moneyed families at this period recollect conditions of extraordinary comfort. Tamara Abel'son, brought up in the family of a St Petersburg timber magnate in the 1900s, recalled that her mother used to organise, two or three times a year:

> A luncheon party from which all adults were excluded. Some forty of my friends were invited. We sat on small chairs around small tables. Our plates and cutlery were also small versions of the dining-room ones. Our meal was served by our servants' older children. Ivan took as much trouble in producing small spun-sugar centrepieces for my tables as he did over the larger ones required for my parents' banquets.

It is a relief to learn that 'unlike our elders, without hesitation we devoured [the centre-pieces] at the end of the meal'.[8]

Even Svetlana Stalina never enjoyed indulgence on this scale. Yet she did have — according to a 1939 brochure on the Stalin cult for children — toys that were beyond the reach of most Soviet children, including a doll whose eyes actually shut.[9] This was not considered problematic because there was nothing morally questionable about children's toys in themselves: every Pioneer Palace and Pioneer House was supposed to have its 'games cabinet'. The myth of 'happy childhood' provided a way of masking the incongruity of a situation where children of the elite had very different lives from those who came from ordinary families. Stalin would scarcely have shown off his collection of limousines to a delegation of factory workers; Svetlana's toys, no closer to the grasp of the average inhabitant of the USSR, could safely be put on view.

Economic centralisation (an ideal before 1928, a reality thereafter) made state-run organisations and enterprises responsible for the design, manufacture, and supply of consumer goods. From late 1935 onwards, consumer goods for children were given a central billing in *Pravda*.[10] In effect, purchasing any state goods for children, at least in reasonable quantities, was vigorously encouraged by advice literature (manuals of house management and women's magazines, for example). As a result of children's place in the political order, their status as manifestations of the Soviet state and Communist Party's care for Soviet subjects, consumer goods for children radiated a particular legitimacy. In theory, anything produced by the state and purchased in ordinary state shops (as opposed to 'acquired' on the black market, clandestinely

---

8   Rice, *Tamara*, pp. 18–19.
9   *Deti o Staline* (Moscow & Leningrad: Detizdat, 1939), p. 10.
10 *Pravda*, 3 February 1936, p. 4 (toys for youngest children, lack of toy cars and metro trains, lack of Meccano, toy censorship by Narkompros); 22 February 1936, p. 4 (shortages of teddy bears, celluloid dolls, cookers, and harmonicas); 25 March 1936 (toy telephone); 5 April 1936, p. 4 (shoddy dolls and bears); 22 September 1936, p. 4 (lack of toys in the newly-opened Leningrad Detskii mir, including dolls' china and children's furniture). An article in the edition of 25 April 1936, p. 6, reported a session of 'self-criticism' from manufacturers in Zagorsk (formerly Sergiev-Posad), but noted that production plans had still not been drawn up. Just before his death in June 1936, Maxim Gorky (a trusty barometer of government priorities) was working on a piece about toys and books for children, all of a strongly didactic kind (even the tinies were to have games such as a geography-quiz globe and a model block of flats): 'Zametki o detskikh knigakh i igrakh', in *Sobranie sochinenii*, XXVII, 518–20).

imported, or inherited) could be considered a legitimate and sanctioned possession. At the same time, not everything produced by state enterprises was functional in the narrow sense. In terms of mere survival, much was, strictly speaking, 'luxurious', or in the more customary term, 'superfluous' (*izlishnee*).

Soviet consumers, like any others, had to make decisions about priorities, which in their particular case were less to do with 'value for money' (the driving force in capitalist economies) than which scarce goods should be sought out. One answer to the question of what is 'luxurious' so far as children are concerned might be toys, at any rate in circumstances where the family can barely scrape enough to eat. At the same time, for many twentieth-century writers on childcare, toys were a developmental essential, as important to children as kasha or bread and milk. Even the simplest child-care manuals aimed at peasant and working-class mothers included material about toys, though such manuals insisted above all that toys should be hygienic, safe, and educational.[11]

In the early days of Soviet power, there was emphasis on improvisation and simplicity:

> A word on toys. Parents make many mistakes in this area. They think that only what you buy in a toyshop, purpose-made for children, can be called a toy. That is wrong. Domestic goods of various kinds are fine for young children. Often, little ones take a much bigger interest than they do in bought toys. In any case, it is hard to buy suitable toys for little children. Parents only waste their hard-earned cash — the child spurns the bought objects. You can give a child a doll from 10 months or so, but not one like those in many shops. Try a stick wrapped in a rag, or use the rag itself to make a kind of doll.[12]

However, once the New Economic Policy ended in 1928, the prejudice against shop-bought items ended also. The assumption was that things purchased in Soviet stores were appropriate for children. If they were not, then it was the fault of manufacturers, not of parents themselves.

Thus, the Stalin era saw a tension between a continuing undercurrent of asceticism, and the gradual expansion of the category of 'essentials' to include phenomena and objects that earlier generations would have considered 'luxuries'. In the late 1930s, the boundaries of permissible acquisition were drawn fairly tightly. Two narratives in *A Book for Parents* (1937) by the era's number one childcare guru, Anton Makarenko, exposed the terrible consequences of over-indulgence. In one, a librarian who ran her life round her son and daughter ended up with adolescents who never helped round the house and spent their time complaining that they wanted even more in the way of material goods than they already had. In another, two parents ensured that their little Viktor grew up with every possible educational advantage (lessons in German from early childhood, Schiller in the original from twelve), and tiptoed round the home while he did his schoolwork, but found themselves with an adult son who would not even agree to call in at a pharmacy on

---

11   See, for example, G. Speransky, *Sovety materyam* (Moscow: Institut sanitarnogo prosveshcheniya, 1952).
12   E, G. Bibanova, *Kak gotovit' iz rebenka v vozraste do 3-kh let budushchego stroitelya novoi zhizni* (Moscow & Leningrad: Moskovskii rabochii, 1927), p. 21.

his way out for the evening to fetch medicine for his sick father.[13] A lack of sufficient strictness, according to Makarenko, could only end by producing cuckoos in the nest: his model families were ones in which parents exercised exacting attitudes to their children, demanding that they help with household tasks and behave with due respectfulness towards their elders.

Makarenko's attitude to 'spoiling' was typical of the Stalin era, as expressed also in the caricatures of over-indulgent parents and their uppity children carried by the humorous magazine *Krokodil*.[14] Hard and fast judgements were made about the causes of this undesirable social phenomenon. One was prosperity: invariably, the spoiling parents were shown as members of the new Soviet middle class, such as 'responsible officials', engineers, factory managers, or top-ranked skilled workers (the father of Makarenko's priggish little Viktor was a high-level official in a central department of the Commissariat for Agriculture). They were not necessarily *meshchane*, materially-obsessed members of the petite bourgeoisie, the hate figures of Soviet propaganda: Viktor's parents had a clean, if threadbare, rug on the floor and a bust of Beethoven on the upright piano, as well as a collection of books that had obviously been well read (i.e. were not simply there for show).[15] The point was that, while living with due modesty themselves, and acquiring only goods with an obvious resonance of 'culturedness', they were bringing their children up otherwise.

How many children like 'Viktor' in fact existed might well inspire doubt. Oral history work relating to the 1930s and 1940s suggests that few resources for spoiling cascaded down to most families. The 'Children's World' interview project of 2002–05, involving over one hundred informants, turned up only one person who remembers being fed special food in the years before the Second World War:

> My nanny would stand over me by the hour with this huge plate of semolina kasha. She'd call out, 'Prince Ivan is coming! Prince Ivan is coming! Open the gates! Open the gates!' I would open my mouth and let the spoon slide in, but without swallowing, and then I'd go 'pppppppp!' [*imitates spitting the kasha out*]. And she'd start 'Prince Ivan is coming!' again.[16]

Waste on this level would have been quite out of the question in most families, even in the mid-1930s, when food shortages were not at their height. During and after the war, the situation became still more stringent. According to recollections

---

13 See Makarenko, *Kniga dlya roditelei*, pp. 244–84, pp. 90–96.
14 For post-war examples, see, for example, Yu. Uzvyakov, 'O malen'kikh dlya bol'shikh', *Krokodil*, 20 (1952), 4, which shows, for instance, desperate parents weaning a fat six-year-old off cigarettes by stuffing him on chocolate, and a beribboned small girl demanding to know why her father's official car has failed to turn up and made her late for school (p. 5); L. Soifertis, 'Vospitanie ottsov', *Krokodil*, 1 (1948), 11; E. Shcheglov, 'Plody vospitaniya', *Krokodil*, 6 (1948), 14. In *Deti Kremlya* (Moscow: Nazran'/AST, 1996), pp. 308–20, Larisa Vasil'eva reprints two denunciations of spoilt children from 1950 issues of *Komsomol'skaya pravda*: 'Diamara' (from a pretentious first name based on an acronym for 'Dialectical materialism'); and 'Plesen'' (Mould), and recalls the electric effects of these items on the 'outer circle elite' that she came from (the anti-heroine of the first sketch was an acquaintance of hers).
15 Makarenko, *Kniga dlya roditelei*, p. 89.
16 CKQ-Ox-03 PF5B, p. 6 (woman, *b.* 1931, Leningrad, father a 'Red Commander', mother did not work).

of those who grew up in the late 1940s, white bread seemed a nearly unheard-of treat, as even children from elite families (such as the daughter of two high-ranking officials in the Ministry of Trade) remember.[17] But children from a Leningrad working-class family were glad enough to eat bread of any colour, since that was often all they got.[18] For some informants at the bottom end of the social scale, hunger is the most penetrating memory of childhood. As late as the early 1960s, a girl from a poor family in Leningrad could write in a school essay 'My dream is having enough to eat' and be rewarded by an official reprimand for her 'petit-bourgeois' attitudes.[19]

Consumer goods were in still shorter supply. In the vast majority of cases, children, whatever social background they came from, wore made-over adult clothes and cast-offs. Against this general background of asceticism, however, some status differentials were evident. The children of professionals, such as engineers and doctors, were more likely to have their clothes made over from good-quality fabrics (if they came from a family of 'former people', the pre-revolutionary social elite, these might include heirlooms). By the late 1930s, some new items also found their way into the wardrobes of children from the Soviet intelligentsia and the families of party officials. Elena Bonner, for example, remembered owning a fashionable pair of sneakers with a blue band round them and rubber soles, a popular accoutrement among well-off girls at the time.[20] What working-class Soviet children had to wear, on the other hand, were worn-out rubber boots, rubber slip-ons or canvas sandals with rubber soles, or for that matter, traditional clogs; their coats were made over from 'old rags'. A straightforward item such as a warm cotton sweater seemed a real luxury.[21] Village children almost all still wore traditional homespun clothes.[22]

So far as other consumer goods are concerned, specially-designed furniture, for instance, was more or less unheard of. The repertoire of toys was likewise limited, with items such as doll's tea sets owned by children growing up in exceptional circumstances (small, well-off families). In villages, toys, and even bicycles, were still often home-made; most working-class children in cities could also expect rag dolls. The well-stocked 'children's world' of the 1900s had vanished completely.[23]

Much more began to be done for children in the post-Stalin era, partly because of a 'privatisation' of social life generally. Certainly, things did not change immediately, as one man remembered childhood in the 1960s:

---

17 Dreams of white bread: CKQ-Ox-03 PF 1A, p. 3 (woman, b. 1936, Moscow, daughter of Ministry of Trade officials).
18 Oxf/Lev SPb-02, PF9A, interview by Alexandra Piir, p. 51 (man, b. 1933, Leningrad, parents manual workers).
19 CKQ-Ox-03 PF5B, p. 6.
20 Elena Bonner, *Dochki-materi* (Moscow: Litera, 1994), p. 151.
21 See S. N. Tsendrovskaya, 'Krestovskii ostrov ot nepa [sic] do snyatiya blokady', *Nevskii arkhiv*, 2 (1995), 80–94 (p. 87). On worn-out rubber boots (*oporki*) and clogs, see Afanasy Salynsky in *Sovetskie pisateli*, ed. by Brainina and Nikitina, v, 397.
22 For example, all the informants in my own interviews in the village of Gerasimovka, on the Urals-Siberian borders, in 2003 recalled these.
23 See my *Children's World*, Chapters 10 and 11.

> We got our clothes from my elder brother, all the more since we were less than a year apart, so we shared what he passed on, and by then my brother was wearing what my father had finished with, and so on.[24]

But the expansion of single-family accommodation went with an increasing emphasis on the family as the primary centre of ethics and emotional involvement. As an informant born in 1969 remembered, in response to a question about the most important values in her early life:

> Family values mattered a lot. My parents operated a politics that was tightly focused on the family, the inner sense that we were all happy together. That was all very important. In the material sense? Probably not. They didn't reject it outright, but they always underlined that it wasn't the main thing. Later on, too, they went through hard times, money was always short, so they tried particularly hard not to fixate on that.[25]

The use of the term 'politics', which suggests precisely the construction of a conscious alternative to the official order. And here one gets precisely the kind of 'blocking out' strategy — we had no money, so we tried to think about something else — that was raised by the Benigni film.

The term 'politics' should not, however, be seen as necessarily subversive. Official norms were also altering, to emphasise precisely the need to provide for children as generously as possible. The second half of the twentieth century saw a modest shift towards 'enlightened' parenting, or — as working-class and peasant grandparents began to treat children less strictly — away from the sort of discipline and high expectations that they had sought to instil in their own children.[26] But this was not uniform. Our informants from working-class households almost always remembered being 'thrashed' for bad behaviour or bad marks at school, even if they grew up in the 1960s or the 1970s.[27] What did change much more markedly at this point was the *material* side of upbringing, a change pre-figured in normative literature. Official advice on baby management was very simple — unlike their

---

24 Oxf/Lev T-05 PF17A, p. 1 (man, b. 1950, Taganrog, mother and father metalworkers (mother also worked as dressmaker on the side).
25 RAO NN-01 PF11B, p. 25 (informant b. 1969, Gorky). This interview, by E. D. Petrova, was carried out in Sarov, Nizhny Novgorod province, in 2001, as part of a project organised by the Russian Academy of Education. My thanks to Vitaly Bezrogov for making the material available to me.
26 Cf. the complaints of an informant from Moscow province, b. 1922, recorded in the late 1990s: 'We reared the children in work. [...] But nowadays upbringing scarcely occurs' (David Ransel, *Village Mothers: Three Generations of Change in Russia and Tataria* (Bloomington: Indiana University Press, 2000), p. 152: cf. similar observations from other sources, p. 213). I myself heard this kind of view widely expressed when doing interviews in Gerasimovka. See CKQ-Gerasimovka-03, PF1A-1B, PF2A-2B.
27 There is nothing exceptional about this, internationally speaking: corporal punishment was widely practised in similar social circles in Britain, for instance — and not just in these circles, but in many families from the social elite too. The peculiarity of Russia, rather, lies in the commitment of well-educated parents to non-corporal methods of chastisement. The roots of this, I have argued in *Children's World*, probably lie in the rights of the *dvoryanstvo* (Russian gentry and nobility) not to endure corporal punishment, which were then logically extended to children as the ethos of 'free education' started to take hold.

pre-revolutionary predecessors, Soviet child-care gurus did not tell readers that they were supposed to have special changing mats, baby baths, layettes, and so on. But they did provide advice on diet. 'Every day children should get bread, butter, sugar, raw and cooked vegetables. Vegetables, berries, and fruits contain essential minerals', advised *House Management* (*Domovodstvo*), a compendium of domestic life published in 1965.[28]

The expanding sense that it was necessary to provide generously for children did not stop at food. So far as older children were concerned, consumer goods were also mentioned. For instance, *House Management* told parents that toddlers should have toys such as balls, skipping-ropes, sledges, and hoops.[29] *Izvestiya*'s weekend supplement, *Nedelya*, carried extensive coverage of items for children, including exotica such as an umbrella with a handle shaped like a flower, designed by a team of psychologists, sociologists, artists, and engineers, and imported Italian furniture.[30]

The potential social tensions likely to be caused by encouraging children to expect material things were occasionally recognised in the Soviet press, particularly when the desirable items were of 'foreign' origin. A disapproving article of 1984, for example, scathingly portrayed a youth craze for a new style of trousers called 'bananas'.[31] And a new problem had appeared in advice literature: what to do with the quantities of things that the 'normal' child was now assumed to have. The solution offered to families where the child did not have his or her own bedroom was a separate 'children's corner' which contained shelving for the offspring's various objects and possessions as well as a desk for school work.[32]

Official magazines sometimes poked fun at the idea of the child consumer, with *Nedelya* running a cartoon of a baby in its pram scanning a fashion magazine.[33] But the balance was none the less towards encouraging consumption. Parents who indulged their children excessively might be ridiculed, but parents who did not pay due attention to their children's needs in terms of acquiring material things were the subject of harsher criticism.[34]

28   *Domovodstvo* (Moscow: Kolos, 1965), p. 41.
29   Ibid., p. 45.
30   *Nedelya*, 29 (1980), p. 9; 5 (1977), p. 16. For more detail, see my *Children's World*, Chapter 12.
31   *Nedelya*, 3 (1984), p. 19. An item suggesting 'excess' of a different kind is an article that appeared in *Leningradskii rabochii* on 21 April 1973, p. 11, and which described how a boy had been given a puppy as a present: he had been obsessed with it for a month and had then lost interest. The unfortunate dog had disappeared. The item was strikingly similar to campaigns run regularly in Britain during the late twentieth century: 'A dog is for life, not just for Christmas'.
32   See, for example, *Nedelya*, 4 (1972), p. 10, which shows an attractively-presented 'children's corner' in the living room, with shelving space for toys and games.
33   *Nedelya*, 6 (1979), p. 6.
34   On criticism of parents for not doing enough for children, see for example the satirical story 'Detskii mir', *Nedelya*, 21 (1971), p. 20, where some parents spend the family money on clothes for themselves rather than a birthday present for their son. Parents were also starting to be expected to provide for their children in other esoteric ways: for example, on 19 January 1980 (p. 14), *Leningradskii rabochii* ran an article about the advantages of taking out insurance policies so that you could pay for a child's wedding, medical treatment should he or she be ill, or get a lump sum for some other contingency. This was not represented as an idiocy from the capitalist West, but as a perfectly sensible economic strategy.

Interest in the production of consumer goods for children did not stop at magazine articles. Records of production targets in Leningrad for 1965–67 reveal significant planned increases in the output of children's clothes for these years. Output of 'woollen trousers, preschool and school age' was supposed to rise by 52 per cent in the course of 1965, cotton trousers by 70 per cent, and various clothes of other kinds by 350 per cent.[35]

Statistics of this kind were primarily a statement of good intentions. Even so, back in the 1930s, good intentions on the part of the state had been represented by statistics about the expansion of crèches and clinics. Now the numbers of coats and trousers offered paramount evidence of concern for children's wellbeing.[36] In 1979, celebration of the International Year of the Child included 'increase in production levels and quality of children's goods, improvement of trade [...] further improvement of consumer services'.[37]

As part of the process, items that would, in earlier decades of Soviet power, have been seen as marginal or indeed superfluous, began to be presented as simple necessities, despite the fact that their real existence was often rather elusive. Like the designer clothes in British fashion magazines that are described as 'made to order' (for which read, samples not available to the general public), the prime goods in Soviet magazines were beyond the reach of ordinary mortals.[38] This was sometimes acknowledged openly: a 1962 article on shopping facilities published in *Leningrad Pravda* reported that many newly built areas of the Soviet Union's 'second capital' still lacked outlets for children's clothes.[39] Yet all the same, reporting of this kind in turn increased parents' sense of entitlement to goods that were *potentially* available. An article published in *Pravda* in 1966 generated a stream of letters, particularly from the provinces, confirming that the quantity and quality of children's clothes available was indeed wholly inadequate. The following complaints, sent from Nikolaevka, a village in Chelyabinsk province, Apsheronsk in Krasnodar Region, and Barnaul, were typical of the dozens sent in:

> You say, 'Only the best for children' [...] but whether things will ever get better in the provinces, I have no idea. Things are awful with children's clothes. You write that along with other things, what we find is ugly, out-of-date, fuzzy knit suits. So why can't we find suits of any kind out in the villages? We'd love to buy the stuff you don't want. We don't have a single suit or coat for children on sale. We wouldn't care how old-fashioned the clothes were provided we could buy them.

In Apsheronsk [Krasnodar Region], it's hard to buy trousers for boys aged 10–14, you can't always get white shirts either. We once had to go to Sochi [213 km away]

---

35 'Spravki vneshtatnykh instruktorov otdela, obsledovatel'skoi komissii, obkoma, profsoyuza, partkoma fabrik "Krasnoe znamya" i "Bolshevichka", upravlenii legkoi shveinoi promyshlennosti [...]', 20 August 1965–10 January 1966, TsGAIPD, f. 24, op. 127, d. 117, l. 41.
36 See for example the propaganda volume *Sovetskie deti* (Moscow & Leningrad: Iskusstvo, 1940).
37 'O provedenii goda rebenka v Leningrade', *Byulleten' Ispolnitel'nogo komiteta Leningradskogo gorodskogo soveta*, 8 (1979), 3–4.
38 These days, 'POA' (price on application).
39 A. Abaturov, 'Novosel i magaziny', *Leningradskaya pravda*, 22 February 1962, p. 2.

to get clothes for our son. And then it turned out that the Boys' Clothes shop only had girls' dresses, no boys' shirts at all. So we had to go to Golovinka [40 km further]. Useless. So we headed for Lazarevskaya [another 25 km], then Tuapse [50 km]. We didn't manage to buy anything. The sales staff just stared at us and shrugged. So we drove back to Apsheronsk [making a day's drive of c. 400 km].

In Barnaul you can hardly ever buy coats and suits for teenage boys. Even ordinary trousers are difficult these days.[40]

The letters from rank-and-file parents were accompanied by embarrassed missives from the factory blaming the problems on poor-quality raw materials. Two women workers from 'Kommunar' sewing factory in Khar'kov wrote: 'We can't make children's clothes to an adequate standard, but it's not our fault. There are problems all along the line. We depend on the textile factories, and they often send us substandard goods'.[41] Parents were encouraged to believe that children's needs were a legitimate goal, and that mere functionality was not enough — clothes should also be of reasonable quality and even attractive.[42] Hence, government and Party administrators found themselves locked in a contradictory position: the propaganda that they licensed created expectations which state production constantly failed to fulfil, as was recognised even in official Soviet sources.[43]

If even the heavily censored Soviet press could paint such a bleak picture of the mismatch between propaganda declarations and real achievements, it follows that actually accommodating expanded expectations of what a child needed placed almost intolerable stresses on parents. While the post-Stalin era did not see a repetition of the famine conditions of 1932–33 or 1946–47, there were periods of sharp supply crisis (for example, the late 1970s-1980s). At all times, providing children with the recommended amounts of nourishing foods, particularly milk, fresh vegetables, and fruit, demanded much time spent queuing, and often also large amounts of luck, or more likely, connections with shop staff or with well-placed friends. Food purchases could be made at the semi-private collective farm markets, but here prices were high. Even in the 1990s imported fruit was considered an

---

40 'Svodka pisem-otklikov na otchet, opublikovannyi v *Pravde* 11 noyabrya [1966] s soveshchaniya za stolom delovykh vstrech "Detyam — luchshee"', Russian State Archive of Recent History (RGANI), f. 5, op. 58, d. 104, ll. 122–32. Quotations ll. 124–25, 126–27.
41 Ibid., l. 127.
42 This is not to say that all letters dealt with attractive inessentials: in Leningrad in the late 1970s, one of the main issues preoccupying parents, newspaper editors, and Party leaders was tights for small children, a significant shortage in such a cold country. As one parent wrote in December 1976: 'I have a little daughter of four and a half. And not once in her lifetime have I been able to find any children's shop that has children's tights in a full range of sizes.' Central State Archive of Historico-Political Documents (TsGAIPD-SPb), f. 24, op. 165, d. 62, l. 5); cf. ibid., l. 2 (from a reader's letter to *Leningradskaya Pravda*). These letters were selected for inclusion in the report sent by *Leningradskaya pravda* and *Vechernii Leningrad*'s reader correspondence sections to the Leningrad Regional Committee of the CPSU, and were among the points marked in red by him. But parents were also complaining about less fundamental issues: cf. the following letter to *LP* (ibid., l. 1): 'I teach children bookbinding, but now our work is at a standstill. Where can we buy book-cloth and coloured paper for the bindings, material for headbands, gauze, and so on?'.
43 G. Oshurok, 'Pokupatel' i my: problemy torgovli', *Leningradskaya Pravda*, 15 April 1971, p. 3.

embarrassingly generous gift.⁴⁴ In the 1970s and 1980s, oranges and lemons were only regularly available in collective farm markets, where they cost a rouble each (then at least one per cent of a monthly wage for many Soviet citizens). Expensive in cities, they were not for sale at all in the Russian countryside, where the imperative to provide fruit and vegetables could only be satisfied by recourse to home-bottled produce.⁴⁵ Children's clothes were also scarce, as were toys, games, and various types of sporting equipment; purchasing such items on the black market was prohibitive. And there was no official state allocation for parents here, as there was with baby clothes.

Yet adults did what they could. If oral history is anything to go by, an ethos of 'everything for the children' was extremely widespread in the post-Stalin era. A woman whose children were born in the early 1980s recalled how her husband filled her younger daughter's pram with rattles:

> Where did he find those? It was very hard to buy them. And there was a whole pile of snow-white nappies. I'll remember it all my life. We always tried to buy books and educational games, paints and pencils and plasticine, we had all that in unlimited quantities. And I tried to make the most beautiful clothes I could. My daughter always wore white tights and light dresses. We tried to take them everywhere [...] to the park, the circus, the cinema. We bought everything that was necessary for childhood, we tried to do everything. I don't think there were any gaps. But we did instil spiritual and moral education into the children.⁴⁶

White and pale clothes were almost impossible to keep looking fresh in cities that were dusty or muddy depending on the season, and where water supplies were erratic and often tainted by rust or other stain-inducing substances.⁴⁷ Where children were concerned, it would seem, no 'luxury' was classed as such. For this informant, the supply of consumer goods was part of a continuum of appropriate upbringing, not distinct in its meaning from the 'spiritual and moral education' of which she spoke later.

The children of these generations also remember far more toys than those who grew up in earlier decades of Soviet power:

> I had this heap of soldiers — plastic ones, metal ones. Soviet, of course. In my early childhood, I had soft toys. I played with dolls a lot, teddy bears. And toy cars. I had loads of plastic toys, rubber ones. [...] Used to take baths with them sometimes.⁴⁸

---

44 Sigrid Rausing, *History, Memory, and Identity in Post-Soviet Estonia* (Oxford: Oxford University Press, 2004), p. 73.
45 Personal observation.
46 Oxf/Lev P-05 PF8B, p. 20 (woman, b. 1959).
47 I well remember taking a friend (from quite a privileged social background) shopping on one of her first visits to the West at the end of the 1980s, and discovering that she rejected anything in white or a pale colour. When I eventually asked her why, she replied, 'No-one wears white. Or maybe, prostitutes...'. For adult women, 'white' was not only impractical, but something that was associated with transgressive ostentation, which makes this informant's insistence on clothing her daughter in it a striking illustration of the different moral status of consumption on behalf of children.
48 Oxf/Lev P-07 PF38A, p. 2 (man, b. 1970, Perm', mother teacher, father engineer).

Many informants particularly treasured toys from Eastern Europe: 'A German doll that was bought for me on the day I was born, or that's what they said — that she was the same age as me. A beauty, she was, very big too. And soft toys'.[49] The numbers of toys that some children had by the early 1960s were quite large even by international standards. For example, as toddlers, the twin sons of the pedagogical writer Valeriya Mukhina, born in 1961, had around a dozen small animals (including a bear made of hygienic plastic and various denizens of the farmyard, a badger, a puss-in boots, and a wooden zebra). Alongside 'educational' items, such as building bricks, there were purely recreational toys, such as a red plastic car; later, they were given a tricycle and a rocking-horse.[50]

While by no means every child had a children's corner (their possessions might be in a box, a sideboard, or wall unit, or simply the bottom of a cupboard), some now did, and in any case, many separate family flats included designated space for the children.[51] In the words of a man born in 1970, the flat included 'the room for me and my sister, where we used to fight to the death as kids. A [children's] corner? Hm, just space divided off with a wardrobe. But when we played, we used the whole territory'.[52] The word 'corner' obviously evoked unheard-of privilege for this man, but what he was describing offered far more comfortable circumstances than those offered by the 'children's corner' of the 1920s, which was conceived as a small sliver of space shared with adults.

That the circumstances in which people lived were becoming more comfortable is suggested also by the fact that the early and/or central memories of informants from the late Soviet generations often hinge on material things.[53] For example, a lorry-driver's daughter from Leningrad born in 1969 warmly remembered, when interviewed, trips with her father to 'Children's World', one of the chain of state-run toyshops whose flagship store was on Lubyanka Square, next door to the headquarters of the Soviet secret police:[54]

49 Oxf/Lev P-07 PF41A, p. 2 (woman, *b.* 1971, Perm', mother cashier, father manual worker). Cf. CKQ Ox-03 PF10B, p. 7 (woman, *b.* 1975, Siberia, family moved to southern resort town in 1985, father pilot, mother pharmacist), here the informant describes a favourite German doll. On a toy elephant from East Germany see CKQ Ox-03 PF 2A, p. 4 (woman, *b.* 1957, Kirovograd province, brought up Odessa, father engineer, mother shop assistant).
50 See Mukhina's account of her twins' early development, based on a diary that she kept at the time: *Bliznetsy* (Moscow: Znanie, 1977); cf. my *Children's World*, Chapter 11.
51 A standard design of the Brezhnev era for a two-room flat to be used by a married couple with one or two children included one larger room (around seventeen square metres) used as a parental bedroom and living room, and one smaller room (around eleven square metres) primarily intended for children, since there was barely space in it for a full-size adult bed or divan.
52 Oxf/Lev P-07 PF38A, p. 2.
53 Our questionnaire began with a very general and open question, 'What are your most vivid memories of childhood?', or alternatively, 'What are your earliest memories of childhood?', to which some informants responded by denying they had enjoyed a 'childhood' of any kind at all (this was a standard response in villages), some by reminiscing about the war or about the arrest of a parent, some by talking about home life generally, some by mentioning an accident, some a treat or pleasant experience, etc. Pleasant experiences were definitely much commoner among those born from the late 1950s onwards.
54 This strange conjunction, as though to suggest the entire range of punishments and rewards

'The most vivid memory I have is of Dad taking me to "Children's World". He was very generous, and he always... you know... I'd arrive at the shop, and he'd buy everything I pointed at, I'd just say, "I want that." Although I wasn't spoilt, I was brought up knowing the value of money. But if I really wanted something, they'd try to go along with it.'

'So what did you usually get there? What did you point at?'

'I don't know... somehow I remember this doll I got given, a big, big one, that walked all by itself and said "Ma-ma".'[55]

For another informant, the gifts offered were of an edible kind, but just as vividly remembered: 'I remember when I was four, probably, and the neighbour's boy, well his dad, or his mum, more like, brought some dark chocolate [...] I'll remember it all my life'.[56] Other kinds of first memory include time in the country, which for this generation almost always meant a dacha, rather than a trip to some village where their grandparents or other relations were permanently domiciled.[57]

A dacha is a particularly interesting example of the 'luxury-necessity' dilemma: the idea was that spending time out of doors was essential to a child's health; yet investment in the property required quite a considerable financial outlay, especially if it were only accessible by car, which tended to be the case with the less prestigious (more affordable) 'garden house' settlements that were built in large numbers during the 1970s and 1980s.

Of course, one could argue that 'first memories' are made up of such experiences because they were relatively rare. And certainly people are eager to emphasise their straitened circumstances. A man born in Leningrad in 1972 remembered how he and the neighbours' boy, to his annoyance, had to make do with identical toys:

> When they were selling some nice children's toys, my mother would get a call, or my mother would ring them, and they'd buy the same things together... two sets of the same toys at once, for the two boys at the same time. Right. And so for some reason or other my mother would always make a mark on my toys with nail-varnish, so they didn't get mixed up.[58]

Here, the informant emphasises the simplicity of what was available, its standardisation. In comparable vein, a woman brought up in Taganrog in the 1970s and 1980s remembered that birthday presents had to last all year:

> Well... Given that money was scarce, I don't really... If I got a big doll once, then that was it. There weren't heaps of all kinds of... [...]. Back then some did have

---

available to the Soviet population, was actually highlighted in Sergei Mikhalkov's sequel to his popular *Dyadya Stepa* rhyming story, *Dyadya Stepa — militsioner*, in *Sobranie sochenii*, 4 vols (Moscow: Detizdat, 1963), 1, 83–93). Here the gentle giant policeman enacted the officially sanctioned policy of punishment for *bad* children by pursuing and bringing to justice a hooligan who had been damaging goods in — where else, but Detskii mir.

55 Oxf/Lev SPb-04 PF 14A, p. 1 (woman, b. 1969, Leningrad, parents manual workers).
56 Oxf/Lev P-07 PF42A, p. 1 (woman, b. 1961, Perm', mother primary school teacher, father engineer).
57 See, for example, Oxf/Lev WQ1 KM, p. 1 (written questionnaire based on the interview questionnaire, completed by a woman, b. 1979, Gorky, daughter of two engineers), and CKQ-Ox-03 PF12A, p. 1 (woman, b. 1958, Leningrad, parents from the creative intelligentsia).
58 Oxf/Lev SPb-03 PF 28A, p. 3 (man, b. 1972, Leningrad, single mother factory worker).

those things, but to be honest, they didn't spoil us with all that.[59]

The word 'spoil' — here used in the negative, to evoke a behaviour ethos that has 'nothing to do with how *we* lived' — constructs a borderline: yes, we were given things, but no, not to excess.

Another common narrative line in people's recollections is 'making do' without items that might be considered normal: 'There was a metal baby bath over the bathtub. And they would always say: look, when we brought you back from the maternity home, we didn't have a cot, of course, so that's where you slept'.[60] Thus an everyday object became a trigger of family mythology, a marker of times in the past when, 'of course', there was no cot.

Yet, despite this tendency to self-glorification through vignettes of self-denial (which itself is a widespread marker of 'Soviet' identity, irrespective of generation), informants brought up in the late 1950s to the 1980s do remember significantly more concrete items than most informants brought up in the three previous decades.[61] A crucial link is also created between consumption and the expression of identity. For example, the informant who remembers being given identical toys also remembers that anything *non*-standard now became a sign of individuality. It was better to have something damaged and different than something perfect and the same:

> They gave us two identical tanks that steered in the same way. Right. And we'd play with them... we were only nine or so, we had no idea the remote would do both tanks at once [...]. The neighbour didn't switch off his tank, and he left it in the kitchen. So when I started playing with my tank, his tank fell off the shelf and got broken. They glued it together, but I felt happy inside: finally, my tank looked different from his.[62]

Consumer goods had both the capacity to constrain the expression of selfhood and the capacity to enhance this: whichever way, they had now become crucial to ways of seeing oneself and the world.

It is interesting that the story about the toy tanks comes from somebody who grew up in a working-class family, a social background traditionally associated with collective values. In fact, generally, and for the first time in Soviet history, memories of consumption recorded by those born between the mid-1950s and mid-1970s differ little depending on social status. As the examples quoted above

---

59 Oxf/Lev T-04 PF 19B, p. 19 (woman, b. 1968, Taganrog, father driver, mother cashier).
60 Oxf/Lev P-05 PF21A, p. 2 (woman, b. 1958, Perm', brought up there and in Krasnokamsk, parents doctors).
61 Perhaps accidentally, simply because deprivation lasted longer in the Soviet Union than it did in Western Europe and affected a larger number of social strata. Stories about not having much as children are common among people who grew up in working-class families before the mid-1950s as well, but the picture was very different in prosperous middle-class and upper-class families, and in some cases toys were handed down between generations, completing the picture (for instance, my mother had kept a large wool-covered black lamb called Monica, a diabolo (cotton-reel-shaped toy meant for spinning on a string), and a large number of children's books from her own childhood in the 1920s, which my sister and I also used when growing up in the 1960s. None of my father's toys had survived, though his adopted sister had carefully shelved his books in her front parlour).
62 Oxf/Lev SPb-03 PF 28A, p. 3 (man, b. 1972, Leningrad, single mother factory worker).

indicate, children from working-class homes now recall being given toys in quite large quantities, and remember having purpose-made clothes, rather than outfits cut down from adult clothes, which might include, say, a sheepskin coat, a tracksuit, and zipped boots for winter days.[63] If particular goods were short, people might resort to DIY, as described by a man whose schooldays fell in the late 1950s and early 1960s:

> There are things you have to get for children, sports clothes, say, and there would be problems, there was nothing in the shops, and the school rules were tight, so I'd need, say, trunks, or a singlet — I'd just sit down and make it myself.[64]

But a shortage of sports clothes is not the same as a shortage of warm clothes or shoes, which this informant did not remember.

An important aspect of consumer culture for children, as for adults, in the last decades of Soviet power was the prestige of non-Soviet produced goods — whether from Eastern Europe, or the West. For one woman born in Leningrad in 1950, acquisition of such goods was a major event:

> When my nan gave me a present, my nan, God rest her, bought these Czech shoes, what they call ballet pumps these days, she paid 30 roubles — it was a fortune! And the whole school was in a faint. Because no-one else had those shoes, and it was really — oh my!!![65]

If ready-made goods could not be purchased, material might be available (for instance 'viscose from the GDR, very good it was').[66]

Close behind Eastern European goods followed 'model' products from leading Soviet factories — in this case the 'Sunrise' shoe factory in Leningrad: 'They sometimes sold English shoes, but you could never get hold of them [...] so Dad gave me some 'Sunrise' shoes for my birthday. They were *normal'nye*, good quality ballerina pumps'.[67]

The emphasis on how select, in market terms, treasured items were represents an important difference from the memories of earlier generations. Equally, the frequently-used word *normal'nyi* suggests both that access to such goods in reasonable quantities was to be expected, and that they would be of adequate quality ('OK, nice, good').[68]

The contrast with earlier decades is brought out vividly by descriptions of two

---

63   Oxf/Lev SPb-03 PF 28A, p. 6 (man, *b*. 1972, Leningrad, single mother factory worker).
64   Oxf/Lev T-05 PF17B, p. 12 (man, *b*. 1950, Taganrog, parents workers, worked as engineer and later as teacher). The only unusual element in this story is that it is a case of the man doing the sewing — as the informant explained shortly afterwards (p. 13), his mother worked part-time as a seamstress at home to earn money, and he had learned to sew from her, although at first was strongly discouraged.
65   Oxf/AHRC SPb-07 PF13A SA, p. 20 (woman, *b*. 1950, Leningrad, father in the armed forces, mother factory worker).
66   Ibid., p. 22.
67   Ibid., PF13B, p. 24
68   Cf. Krisztina Fehervary, 'American Kitchens, Luxury Bathrooms, and the Search for a "Normal" Life in Postsocialist Hungary', *Ethnos*, 67.3 (2002), 369–400.

different first days at school, in 1948 and in 1977:

> I well remember my first day at school. I was late, I had no shoes, so I went barefoot, it was September and very cold. And I arrived in a school in a dress my nan had made from a sack, she'd dyed it with onion skins and made me a dress. There I was in that dress, and grandad had made me a bag, put potatoes in the corners and sewed on two straps, for my back. That was what I wore and to this day I remember teacher, her eyes, her hair, her dress — she was so beautiful, my first teacher.[69]

> Yes, I remember my first day at school really well. I remember how my neighbour arrived, my mum's friend's son, and gave me some *Tea Rose* perfume. And my mum had a rose growing on the windowsill, and it had flowered that same day, 1 September 1978. And I put some of that *Tea Rose* on, it covered the scent of the real rose, and remember taking that perfume to school on 1 September.[70]

On the one hand, even essentials elude the child — shoes, a proper dress; on the other comes an ineffably useless gift, which, in a nice gesture of childish literalism, the recipient uses to improve on nature. Even if, as always with this type of autobiographical recollection, one needs to allow for self-mythologisation, the self-mythologisation in each case is of a very different order.

The First of September, the start date of the Soviet school, was a public ritual occasion. Families would dress the new entrant as well as they were able, press flowers of some kind into his or her small hand, and go off with him or her to the gathering outside the school to take photographs. A child who had been dressed less well than others, or who had a less nice gift for the teacher, would remember the event resentfully for decades, perhaps a lifetime. 'You were supposed to go with flowers', a woman born in Moscow province in 1972 remembered:

> And we didn't have any cellophane or foil, so mum wrapped them in newspaper. And I said, 'Mum, I can't, I can't go with newspaper, I'm not going,' and started crying. And she goes [...] 'We've not got foil, you're taking paper.' [...] Mum treated it like... I was off to the war, not my first day at school.[71]

---

69   Oxf/Lev T-04 PF21A, interview conducted in Taganrog by Lyubov' Terekhova, p. 12 (woman, b. 1941, worker settlement, Bryansk province, brought up by grandmother, who was a factory worker).

70   Oxf/Lev T-04 PF 7A, interview conducted in Taganrog by Lyubov' Terekhova, p. 12 (woman, b. 1970, Penza, mother house painter, father mechanic). Compare the following recollection of school days in the late Soviet era, which is equally strongly focused on material objects (Oxf/Lev P-07 PF40A, interview conducted in Perm' by Svetlana Sirotinina, p. 9 (woman, b. 1972, Perm', mother had a chemistry qualification (but worked in a manual job), father mechanic): 'The First of September, my first day at school. I couldn't get to sleep the night before — I was worried I wouldn't be able to open my pencil case. I had this plastic one, all in pink. Getting it open was tricky, but inside it was just amazing! A little clock, and abacus beads on little wires. I was really worried for some reason — it didn't open too well. Then when I actually got to school, it opened without any trouble. And I was soooo glad'.

71   CKQ-M-03 PF1B, interview conducted in Moscow by Yuliya Rybina, p. 4 (woman, b. 1972, Central Asia, moved to settlement near Moscow aged six; father served in the Interior Ministry forces, mother housewife).

There were other new festivals that emerged in the last decades of Soviet power. One of these was the birthday party. Only a few extremely privileged individuals recall such occasions being celebrated before the Second World War. By the late 1950s, birthdays had turned into big events, even in quite ordinary families.[72] A Leningrad man born in 1972, for instance, recalled the opulent boxes that used to be sent by family members living down south:

> We'd get a nice big, strong box or even two, and drag them back home. Yes. And they smelled so nice: a train smell and the first fruits, and there was lots of fresh greenery too, and presents, chocolates, jam.[73]

Efforts were not necessarily limited just to presents: in one Leningrad intelligentsia family, the adults would put on charades for the children and on one occasion even fixed up a kind of miniature circus act, with white mice from a scientist grandmother's laboratory running an obstacle course of wheels and hoops.[74]

By the 1970s, placing children at the centre of things was standard for many adults. Hedrick Smith, for instance, recalls how:

> One family we knew, very well off because of the father's high position in a ministry, allotted black caviar to the six-year-old boy almost daily. Typically for a small boy he balked at the taste, while adults in the household salivated enviously.[75]

Mothers I knew in the 1980s went to any amount of trouble to get tomatoes for their children during the winter months. Yet by no measure are food items of these kinds 'essential' for children — the vitamins contained in caviar and tomatoes can be supplied in other humbler substances, such as oily fish, apples, cucumber, cabbage, etc., or indeed the fish oil and dried rosehip supplements on sale in the USSR. In a literalisation of the phrase 'All the Best for Children', parents bought anything rare — bananas, lemons, tomatoes — convinced that because goods were scarce and expensive they were also 'best'.[76] In the words of the writer Zinovy Zinik,

---

[72] See, for example, Catriona Kelly, '"Den' rozhdeniya, prazdnik detstva": Celebrating Children's Birthdays in Twentieth-Century Russia', in *AB*60: Sbornik statei k 60-letiyu Al'berta Kashfullovicha Baiburina*, ed. by N. B. Vakhtin and G. A. Levinton (St Petersburg: izdatel'stvo Evropeiskogo universiteta v Sankt-Peterburge, 2007), pp. 264–77.

[73] Oxf/Lev SPb-03 PF28B, interview Alexandra Piir, p. 18 (man, b. 1972, Leningrad, single mother factory worker).

[74] CKQ-Ox-03 PF12B, interview Alexandra Piir, p. 5 (woman, b. 1958, Leningrad, parents both prominent members of the creative intelligentsia). Cf. Oxf/AHRC PF14A SA, p. 14 (woman, b. 1977, Leningrad, parents worked in scientific institute).

[75] Hedrick Smith, *The Russians* (New York: Ballantine Books, 1976), p. 192.

[76] A rather tragic case of the entrapment of parents between high-minded recommendations and economic deficit is described by Lidiya Chukovskaya in her memoir of Frida Vigdorova, where she recalls Vigdorova visiting buffets all over Moscow in order to buy oranges on behalf of the mother of a sick child: 'The boy was only allowed to have orange juice, and there was no fruit of any kind in Leningrad at the time' (L. Chukovskaya, 'Pamyati Fridy', in *Protsess isklyucheniya* (Moscow: Eksmo, 2007), p. 249). Rather than recommending the best solution easily available to parents, doctors had recommended 'the best' in an absolute sense, as they saw it (though from the point of view of modern paediatric practice, it is hard to imagine a condition in which orange juice, both high in acid and high in sugar, might be the *only* substance a sick child could digest).

'Children were never left in peace. They weren't dressed — they were wrapped up like parcels. They were stuffed to the gills, not fed'.[77] Parents, grandparents, and other relations unconsciously espoused a tradition of 'conspicuous consumption' that had been the target of irony since the late eighteenth century.[78] Yet they also gave consumption a new moral intonation, since no item, no matter how expensive or hard to find it might be, was regarded as 'luxurious' when it came to providing for one's children.

* * * * *

The history of provision for children in the post-Stalin era indicates just how problematic is the concept of 'socialist luxury'. Classically, luxury is associated with excess. In the USSR at this time, totally mundane objects came to seem 'luxuries' because they were constantly subject to shortage, while at the same time parents regarded such items — however scarce, hard to find, and in a strictly utilitarian sense unnecessary — as essential parts of the child's early experience. Any object or foodstuff manufactured for children (from romper suits to milk powder, from East German dolls to bicycles) could be understood as a vital element in proper childhood experience. Where, in the past, parents had been lectured about 'spoiling', they now were the targets of propaganda suggesting that whatever they could do for their children, at the cost of vast effort, might still not be enough.

Memories rarely include children purchasing goods with money they had earned themselves. Consumption in this era meant adults buying things for children. The anxiety-ridden struggle ensuing probably stemmed as much from parents' own social disempowerment and need for control over some domain of their existence as it did from a concern for children as such.[79] Providing for children was a way of ignoring one's own needs. But the selflessness had high costs: the expectation that parents should support their sons and daughters to a late stage of childhood (at least till children left school, and if they went into higher education, right up till they married).[80]

The results of the ethos of 'everything for the children' were not always beneficial to children either. Certainly, the efforts to provide for children were often appreciated (at least retrospectively). Those who grew up in the 1960s and

---

77 Zinovy Zinik, *U sebya za granitsei* (Moscow: Tri kvadrata, 2007), p. 252.

78 On moral condemnation of luxury goods, especially where produced outside Russia, see my *Refining Russia*, Chapter 2. On the history of exoticism, see K. Bogdanov, *O krokodilakh v Rossii: Ocherki iz istorii zaimstvovanii i ekzotizmov* (Moscow: Novoe literaturnoe obozrenie, 2006).

79 I would not wish to be misunderstood: clearly, all responsible adults in all societies want to provide properly for children. But the assumption that parents were doing their best for their children because they were crippling themselves to provide things that it was almost impossible to get was a more unusual trait in late Soviet culture.

80 Some of this can be sensed already in surveys of the early 1960s, as collected in B. A. Grushin, *Chetyre zhizni Rossii v zerkale oprosov obshchestvennogo mneniya: Ocherki massovogo soznaniya rossiyan vremen Khrushcheva, Brezhneva, Gorbacheva i Yel'tsina v 4-kh knigakh*, 4 vols (Moscow: Progress-Traditsiya, 2001), I, 298–99, table 3. This records that around twenty-five per cent of families were feeling emotional strain because of the need to provide material things.

1970s usually recall feeling an overwhelming feeling of security and wellbeing. But the drawbacks for children could include a very high burden of expectation. How could you let parents down who had provided for you like that? In some cases, too, the sense of being the only person in the family whom everybody really loved, and hence the target of competing 'charm offensives' from parents who did not themselves get on very well, could mean developing, at a very early stage, a capacity for diplomatic negotiation that would have done credit to the delegate of a non-aligned state at the UN.[81] Also, there were some areas of childhood experience that even dedicated parents could do little to change: the deficit of space for active games indoors; the polluted atmosphere of cities; and the shortage of playgrounds, particularly for older children.

In an overall sense, the state's encouragement to consume, which reached unprecedented heights from 1957 onwards, was a contribution to social differentiation. Once the official early Soviet ethos of 'willed poverty' and self-denial had dispersed, not having enough started to seem a sign of socio-economic failure, rather than of spiritual superiority. The presentation of attractive clothes, fridges, cars, or elegant furniture as not only permissible objects to own, but also essential objects, indicates the contradictory nature of the post-Stalinist consumer drive. Propaganda was now promising to all, objects that were in practice available only to the luckier members of society. One might compare the sour comments of a Western observer on another institution enshrining consumption, yet at the same time seen as virtuous and necessary, the Soviet palace of marriages: 'Although [the Palace] functioned in a proletarian state it was used exclusively by an elite with bourgeois pretensions'.[82]

However, the birthday party and the First of September festival were not the exclusive prerogative of 'an elite with bourgeois pretensions'. Where spending patterns were concerned, large numbers of working-class parents now conformed to the official norms of appropriate consumption for children. Thus, the last decades of Soviet power saw an ethos of 'extended childhood' (where children were deemed to be non-productive and to require, to cite the Soviet cliché, constant 'care and attention') spread to the majority of the Russian population.

Eventually, the result of the quixotic combination of encouragement to consume and failure to provide was frustration with Soviet power itself. By the end of the 1980s, sociological surveys were indicating a striking similarity between the proportion of the population that felt spending time with children was the main

---

81 See for example CKQ-Ox-03 PF12B, where the parents used their daughter to communicate with each other. Sometimes, too, parents' failure to measure up to the prevailing norms of generosity is remembered as causing resentment (as in the case of CKQ-M-03 PF1A, B). And, human nature being what it is, parents' efforts were not necessarily valued by children at the time when they were expended: by the late 1970s and early 1980s, the 'bratty' behaviour of some under-tens was widely observed by Russians and by foreign visitors. As an acquaintance of Hedrick Smith's summed up: 'You let your children *do* as they please and we *give* them what they please, and our children grow up selfish' (Smith, *The Russians*, p. 192).
82 Mervyn Matthews, *Mila and Mervusya: A Russian Wedding* (Bridgend: Seren, 1999), p. 196.

joy in life (52.7 per cent) and those who felt in one way or another dissatisfied with the state (53.2 per cent).[83] But in the post-Soviet era, the beneficiaries of the new slogan 'Everything for the children' (*Vse dlya detei*), the members of the 'last Soviet generations' began to express a particularly pure nostalgia for the Soviet past, and precisely at the level of consumption. Internet chat-rooms and forums abounded with recollections of the objects and foods that were once available. As participants in a discussion of 2005 wrote, overtly wallowing in nostalgia:

> I remember *bubliki* [boiled dough rings] for 6 kopecks, or 5 without the poppy seeds... three kings of chewing gum: orange, mint, and strawberry, and pastry slices and *korzhiki* [plain sweet biscuits] [...]
> Hey folks, remember those pastry slices, can't get them now!!
> [...] even any old bread was nice, with a crunchy crust, and warm, on the way home I'd eat half a loaf of black or white
> yum-yum-yum...[84]

The universal insight that things tasted nicer when you were a child was sharpened by the association of such foodstuffs with a vanished era. Now receded permanently into the past, these once familiar items had become 'luxuries' because they were no longer available: 'When you could get *rogaliki* [croissant-style pastries], I didn't like them. And now I want them, probably because they aren't there'.[85] Such nostalgia did not necessarily translate directly into a pro-Soviet political standpoint, since for many commentators, childhood was firmly denominated as an era in life that carries little meaning for the later adult, except perhaps when he or she was making decisions about how to raise his or her own children.[86] But the highly emotional recollections of once mundane objects pointed to a further stage in the evolution of 'socialist luxury': now, even what was once *freely* available and not even desired during the stereotypical 'happy childhood' came, once it was unavailable, to symbolise pleasures just out of reach. And so once more is demonstrated the 'late socialist double vision', whereby an object or phenomenon could be at one and the same time understood as being impossible, or nearly so, to obtain, yet also as something everyone was entitled to have, and where things everyone was entitled to have were at the same time 'luxuries', because there was always the possibility

---

83   A. A. Golov and Yu. A. Levada, *Sovetskii prostoi chelovek. Opyt sotsial'nogo portreta na rubezhe 60-kh*. (Moscow: Mirovoi okean, 1993), p. 279.
84   <http://76–82.ru/forum/viewtopic.php?t=96> [accessed 13 May 2021].
85   'Bulochnye' (2005), <http://76–82.ru/forum/viewtopic.php?t=96> [accessed 30 September 2022] (participant Petrovna, 22 October 2005).
86   Notable, for instance, is the absence of nostalgia for centrist authoritarianism in the political discussion posted on the same site as the bread and cakes discussion: <http://76–82.ru/forum/viewtopic.php?t=3167&postdays=0&postorder=asc&start=15> [accessed 30 September 2022]. Here my views differ somewhat from those expressed in L. Goralik, '"Rosagroeksporta syrka": Simvolika i simvoly sovetskoi epokhi v segodnyashnem rossiiskom brendinge', *Teoriya mody*, 3 (2007), 13–30, which sees people from the 'last Soviet generations' as precisely the main well-spring of nostalgia, since they can only remember what was good about the system. In practice, many do distinguish between childhood experience and adult experience at the era, or recognise that, enjoyable as childhood was back then, children live better now. See, for example, Oxf/Lev SPb-03 PF16B. P. 86 (woman. *b*. 1969, Leningrad, working-class parents).

they, like the feasts provided by magic in traditional folk tales, would suddenly and unpredictably vanish.[87]

This article was originally presented as a paper at the 'Socialist Luxury' conference held at the Victoria and Albert Museum, London, in January 2006. My thanks to the organisers, Susan Reid and David Crowley, and to the participants for their helpful comments

---

[87] The 2000s seem to have been the high point for this 'familiarity turned necessity' dynamic, certainly among young people: by 2010, discussion had moved on, probably because 'twenty-somethings' no longer had any conscious memory of the Soviet period. Debates about the quality or otherwise of Soviet produce are now the domain of the middle-aged.

PART V

On the Soviet Periphery

CHAPTER 13

❖

The Many Lives of Konon Molodyi ('Gordon Lonsdale'): Espionage, Disinformation, and the Moral Universe of the Late Cold War

[2021]

The figure of the *rezident*, a citizen living legally or illegally in a foreign country while also carrying out espionage on behalf of his homeland, has a rich and seductive history in Soviet and post-Soviet Russian popular culture.[1] One set of 'spymania' texts portrays the foreign subversive, working to corrupt foolish citizens of the USSR into surrendering confidential information or participating in acts of sabotage (*diversiya*).[2] Another dwells on the heroic bravery of the Soviet *rezident*, who, despite the threat of fierce reprisals, transmits vital messages over short-wave radio and provides his home intelligence agencies with essential briefings.

The most famous fictional example of the Soviet *rezident*, Vsevolod Vladimirov, also known as Maksim Isaev, and invented by writer Yulian Semyonov, was posted to Europe in 1927. He spent much of the next two decades living in the Third Reich under the guise of Max Otto von Stirlitz, a Prussian nobleman who had supposedly turned to the Soviet consulate for help after being robbed during a trip

---

1 In the KGB's top-secret *Dictionary of Counter-Intelligence*, the *rezident* was defined as 1) the manager of an agent network (someone drawn from the Communist Party or Komsomol, or a retired KGB operative, and 2) 'an officer of the intelligence services or secret agent directing the work of agents on one or other territory of the state under investigation. A R[*ezident*] may be a diplomat or some other representative of a foreign state (or agency etc.) with official accreditation in the state under investigation, or a non-citizen and permanent resident, or a citizen of that country, and also a person living there illegally' (*Kontrarazvedyvatel'nyi slovar'* (Moscow: Vysshaya krasnoznamennaya shkola Komitet gosudarstvennoi bezopasnosti pri Sovete ministrov SSSR, 1972), pp. 279–80). Numbered example 10064 downloadable from the Latvian State Archive on <https://kgb.arhivi.lv/dokumenti/vdk/pretizlukosanas-vardnica> [accessed 2 October 2022]. The second sense would be conveyed by the English term 'illegal', but I have avoided that here because legal settlers (such as diplomats) carrying out the collection of intelligence are also named *rezident*.
2 A famous example of the foreign *rezident* in the USSR was Mikhail Tul'ev, protagonist of *The Illegal's Mistake* (*Oshibka rezidenta*, 1968) and three later films made by Veniamin Dorman for the Gorky Studios. The key factor here was that Tul'ev changed allegiance in the course of his long history.

to Sydney. Originally the protagonist of novels written by Semyonov between 1963 and 1990, Stirlitz began his film career with an appearance in Boris Grigor'ev's *No Password Needed* (*Parol' ne nuzhen*, Gorky Studios, 1963). He was indelibly etched on national consciousness by Tatiana Lioznova's later, made-for-television film, *Seventeen Moments of Spring* (Mosfil'm), one of the biggest ever hits of the Soviet small screen when it was broadcast in 1973.

Stirlitz's ability to pose unchallenged as a Nazi officer, while still under the surface a staunch patriot of his Soviet homeland, created a character that reminded linguistics professor Revekka Frumkina, a shrewd and acerbic film viewer, of 'reading some old children's story'.[3] But millions were won over. Handsome, charming Stirlitz, played by heart-throb actor Vyacheslav Tikhonov, was not just a resonant figure of the time. He was a worthy successor to Heinrich Ekkert (real name Aleksei Fedotov, acted by Pavel Kadochnikov) in Boris Barnet's *The Secret Agent's Heroic Feat* (Mosfil'm, 1947), the *rezident* who captures not just the secret correspondence of a Nazi general, but the general himself, all evoked in sumptuous black-and-white.

Between Barnet and Lioznova came Savva Kulish (1936–2001), with *The Dead Season* (Lenfil'm, 1968), a film warmly praised by Lioznova when it was discussed at the Filmmakers' Union in Moscow immediately after its release.[4] Seductively shot, in the manner of Barnet's film, Kulish's work added a dash of humour to the presentation of Ladeinikov, the thoughtful and intelligent *rezident* at the centre (played by Donatas Banionis), pairing him with lightly-built, nervy Savushkin (Rolan Bykov), newly recruited as an agent and something of a liability. While Ladeinikov was effortlessly at home, Savushkin seemed perpetually on the verge of discovery (especially when having to swill down beer in order to seem 'English'). In due course he proved to be the weak link for the Soviet operation's devious enemies, war criminal Hass (Vladimir Erenberg) and West German secret agent Greban (Mauri Raus). Yet comic moments (as later with Stirlitz) never called into question the essential nobility of the *rezident*'s role.

Literary and cinema evocations likewise never allowed their heroic visions to be undermined by the requirement that the *rezident* achieve his patriotic duty by espousing untruths, 'living a lie' in the most literal sense. Spies are classic examples of boundary-crossers and impostors, using false documents, disguise, and invented biography to pass without trace (so they and their employers hope) into countries that are not their own. Their status depends on the exploitation of trust. They not only engage in activities that would be classed as 'treason' in their own country, but often in crimes of a lesser order too — personation, document fraud, embezzlement, bigamy. Some of this fraudulency belongs to the staple repertoire of the classic spy film: the doctored passport, the altered name, the disguise, the false friendship, and the deceiving love relationship. Yet the moral status of pretence never arises: the

---

3   R. Frumkina, 'The Naïve Viewer', *Russian Social Science Review*, 49.1 (2008), 24–37 (p. 25).
4   RGALI, f. 2936, op. 4, d. 533, ll. 28–29 ('I've never seen a better film in this genre [...] This is simply a film about human life, about an astonishing profession, about life generally [...] This film makes us look more closely at our own line of work').

basic presupposition is that inwardly, the spy remains exactly the same. Spies' ever-changing roles are mere performances; their proteanism is forced upon them, while their integrity is enduring.

In the official documentation of the intelligence agencies, too, moral ambiguity is seldom addressed directly. The top-secret *Dictionary of Counterintelligence*, published by the Scientific-Scholarly and Publishing Department of the KGB's Red Banner School in 1972, included no entry on, say, 'deception'. Instead, there was a long entry on 'the legend', 'the superficially plausible information prepared by the intelligence or counterintelligence agencies in order to lead the enemy to the wrong conclusion'.[5] As well as his 'cover story' (*legenda prikrytiya*), relating to the date and manner in which he had arrived in the country and the purposes of his work there, it was typical for the *rezident* to have a 'backup story' (*zashchitnaya/ zapasnaya legenda*), a 'legend within a legend' (*legenda v legende*), which he 'uses in cases where his basic story has been exposed'.[6]

The *legenda* or story was supposed to be a complex interplay of the genuine and the fake, including both 'true information' and 'specially organised exercises in disinformation'. 'In order to make the L[egend] less vulnerable, it is so far as possible packed with facts that are difficult or impossible to verify'. In other words, there was a tight connection between the *rezident*'s professional biography, his story or 'legend', and 'disinformation' in a broader sense, 'information specially prepared and used to generate in the enemy false perceptions of reality'.[7] The tradecraft of spies thus required from state agents the capacity for fraud and trickery that is more often associated, both in the Soviet Union and in other modern societies, with individuals at or beyond the fringes of legitimacy.[8] if James Bond was, in the famous phrase, 'licensed to kill', real life secret agents were, no less threateningly for the principles of rational governance, 'licensed to deceive'.

The intricate process by which such a 'story' or 'legend' was constructed, and the extent to which this pushed the boundaries of 'fake' and 'authentic' to their very limits, was everywhere on view in the life of Konon Trofimovich Molodyi (1922–1970), the secret agent who served as the model for Ladeinikov.

From 1954 to 1960, Molodyi was able to live more or less without suspicion as an illegal resident in the United Kingdom, under the guise of a Canadian citizen,

---

5   Here and below, *Kontrarazvedyvatel'nyi slovar'*, pp. 152–53.
6   Soviet secret service operatives of Cold War days (as opposed to clerical workers and informers) were always assumed in the normative literature to be male (though in real life this was by no means always the case — alongside Helen Kroger (Lona Cohen), appearing later in this essay, one could cite Melita Stedman Norwood, née Sirnis, 1912–2005, 'the Spy from Sainsburys', the British civil servant recruited by the NKVD in 1937, and exposed only at the end of her long life).
7   *Kontrarazvedyvatel'nyi slovar'*, p. 79.
8   There is a substantial literature on trickery in the Soviet system, including Golfo Alexopoulos's treatment of deception as a survival strategy in her *Stalin's Outcasts: Aliens, Citizens, and the Soviet State, 1926–1936* (Ithaca, NY: Cornell University Press, 2003), Fitzpatrick's *Tear Off the Masks*, and parts of Al'bert Baiburin, *Sovetskii pasport: istoriya, kul'tura, praktiki* (St Petersburg: izdatel'stvo Evropeiskogo universiteta v Sankt-Peterburge, 2017). Imaginary tricksters (though not Stirlitz and other secret agents) are discussed in Mark Lipovetsky, *Charms of the Cynical Reason: Tricksters in Soviet and Post-Soviet Culture* (Boston, MA: Academic Studies Press, 2011).

Gordon Lonsdale. The façade of 'Lonsdale's' biography was sustained by an elaborate bulwark of subterfuge. As a detailed report by MI5 officer Charles Elwell dated 18 October 1960, and held in the National Archives in London, recorded, the person known as 'Gordon Lonsdale' had acquired a driving licence in Vancouver in November 1954, and then a Canadian passport on 21 January 1955, with his occupation given as 'mechanic', and 'purpose of travel' specified as intention to undertake study in the United Kingdom.[9]

On 22 February 1955, immediately before his departure to Britain, he joined the Royal Overseas League, a club for the inhabitants of current and former British imperial territories, with headquarters in Green Park, central London. The League was where Lonsdale lived when he first arrived in London, and he was soon using its facilities for networking also. As Elwell noted, 'When first negotiating for a flat at the White House [a large and prestigious block in London's Regent's Park area] he gave as a reference Philip CRAWSHAW, Secretary of the Overseas League, which did much to launch him on his stay in the Mother Country by providing tickets for the House of Commons, the Garter Ceremony at Windsor Castle etc.'.[10]

Lonsdale was soon showing a capacity for easy friendship: on a bus trip round Europe, Elwell wrote, he had made connections with Isabel Jones, a nineteen-year-old Canadian student; Virginia Wright Laneford, from Richmond, Virginia; Peggy and Sammy Sellers, Edinburgh; Amy and John Cox, 'an elderly Australian couple from Perth, Australia'; John R. Schrader, the tour courier; Captain Raymond Keith Straw of the US Air Force and Mrs Mary Straw; Vivienne Day, 'a South African girl'; and 'Margaret McNab and Jane Dingle, both Canadians'. After he began studying at the School of Oriental and African Studies, University of London, he made numerous other friends, and was able to display proficiency in his formal studies too: 'At the end of the first course he was given a certificate by the professor of Chinese certifying that had he submitted for an examination at the end of the 1955–56 course, he would have achieved at least eighty percent'.[11]

---

9   C. J. L. Elwell, untitled biographical note on Gordon Arnold Lonsdale, National Archives of the United Kingdom (NA UK) KV-2/4383, f. 98. For a biography of Charles Elwell, see the *Daily Telegraph*, 22 January 2008 <https://www.telegraph.co.uk/news/obituaries/1576192/Charles-Elwell.html> [accessed 2 October 2022]. These biographical details were collected before the British security services were aware of 'Lonsdale's' espionage activities, so one can safely assume that they were not concocted in order to incriminate him. Much of the information was immaterial to the trial on charges of conspiracy to breach the Official Secrets Act, and hence does not appear in the later short biography used as evidence there (see NA UK CRIM 1/3604, File 1, ff. 183–84). Even after Lonsdale's conviction, Elwell was in many ways more sympathetic to him, as a professional in the same field, than to the British and other English-speaking contacts of Lonsdale under suspicion as individuals who might have been 'turned' by the Soviet spy, or who were simply furthering their own ends. See the many-volume case record related to Lonsdale, NA UK KV-2/4430–4466, for example NA UK KV-2/4449, ff. 12–13 (report on interview with Ralph Paton, a business associate of Lonsdale's, July 1961). A recent popular book on the Portland spy ring by Trevor Barnes, *Dead Doubles: The Extraordinary Worldwide Hunt for One of the Cold War's Most Notorious Spy Rings* (London: Weidenfeld & Nicolson, 2020), is partly based on a selective reading of Lonsdale's case files, but contains only a minimal outline of his biography.
10   Elwell, untitled biographical note on Gordon Arnold Lonsdale, NA UK KV-2/4383, f. 100.
11   Ibid.

His course in Oriental Studies completed, Lonsdale began looking for a job, and after considering the travel industry, opted for a completely different profession — working as a salesman specialising in automatic vending machines:

> In October 1956, he ordered from the AUTOMATIC MERCHANDISING COMPANY (AMCO) of 10 Oscar Road, Broadstairs, two Minstrel Juke Boxes for which he paid £500. AMCO was a firm founded by an engineer named Leonard Peter AYRES for the purpose of selling the juke boxes and vending machines he manufactured.[12]

He soon had juke boxes in various sites, including Peckham and Brixton (then two largely working-class areas of south-east London), but continued enjoying a lively social life, in the company, for instance, of Carla Panizzi, an Italian with whom he attended a British Council Master Vacation Course in December 1957.

By the start of 1959, Lonsdale was in trouble financially, and looking to sell his machines. He considered moving into medical equipment, but instead formed an alliance with a company selling a security locking device for car drivers branded as the 'Allo Switch'. The device was exhibited at the Ninth Brussels Annual Exhibition for inventors in 1960. In the autumn of the same year, he made another extended foreign trip. As Elwell wrote, 'There is some reason to think that his business associates have been embarrassed by his prolonged absence'. However, not all felt the same way: one contact, Caroline Mary (Mollie) Mieville Baker 'has given evidence of her faith in him by discharging one of his financial liabilities that had become due'.[13]

As cover for his espionage, Lonsdale's activities — attending lectures and classes at SOAS, selling vending machines, promoting inventions — were, for several years, successful. His chosen forms of employment made it easy to justify moving around different parts of London, and indeed beyond London. They provided an indeterminate source of income that could be used to conceal the retainer paid to him by the KGB. When Lonsdale first came on the radar of the British security services in the summer of 1960, they had no idea who he was and at first assumed he was Michał Kowalski, an official of the Polish Embassy; they only worked out the truth through a number-plate search.[14] But once the investigation had started, it revealed Lonsdale's lived reality to be quite unlike the austere patriotic commitment to duty espoused by Boris Barnet's wartime spy, Aleksei Fedotov.

To begin with, Lonsdale/Molodyi's contacts in the automatic machine world were murky. As Elwell noted, Lonsdale's close associate Michael Houlbrooke Bowers stood accused by Leonard Ayres, automatic machines manufacturer and AMCO's proprietor, of 'selling machines for other automatic machine companies for his personal gain instead of putting all his efforts into working for AMCO'.[15]

12   Ibid., f. 99. In testimony to Charles Elwell of MI5 on 14 July 1961, Ayres remembered that Lonsdale had also run two other vending machine companies, Peckham Automatics and Nero Vending Co.: NA UK KV-2/4450, ff. 78–79.
13   Ibid.
14   See W. J. Skardon (Special Branch), report dated 1 November 1960, NA UK KV-2/4381, f. 110.
15   C. J. L. Elwell, 'Brief Lives of Some of Lonsdale's Most Important Current Contacts', NA UK KV-2/4383, f. 104.

Indeed, Houlbrooke Bowers had a long-standing association with a competitor company, the Master Vending Machines Company, owned by one Sidney Levine, another employee of which, R. W. Jerram, had introduced Lonsdale to Ayres in the first place.[16]

In May 1959, just as AMCO was experiencing financial difficulties, the Master Vending Machines Company was enduring its own travails, with Frederick Young, a salesman for the company, on trial for forging a hire purchase agreement to the value of £810 (then a substantial sum).[17] In his defence, Young claimed that Sidney Levine, who had disappeared after the company's liquidation, had managed to spirit away half a million pounds when he vanished.[18] These were not the only dubious characters in Lonsdale's orbit. His friend, Mollie Baker, with her then husband, Howard Baker, had been charged in 1953 with obtaining credit by fraud. Michael Houlbrooke Bowers had attracted the attention of police in Amsterdam while he was working for the Master Vending Machines Company.[19] If there was money to be made in slot machines, it was not by honest means.

At least some of Lonsdale's business activities inhabited the fringes of the seedy underworld evoked in Graham Greene's *Brighton Rock*, where the line between business and criminal activity was fluid to non-existent. In this respect, the choice of lifestyle seems, for a *rezident*, rather harder to explain: at any moment, police interest in fake hire purchase agreements or vanishing investments might have thrown the entire operation under suspicion.

The reports that Lonsdale/Molodyi filed to his employers in the KGB cast his work with automatic machines in a very different light, remarking merely that the character of the business was convenient as a cloak for undercover work:

> In January 1957, the agent wrote to Moscow Centre: 'As agreed, while in London I ordered two juke boxes, for which I paid a fairly small deposit. The rest is to be paid off over the next two years. These machines provide useful business opportunities. If you spend 5000 dollars, in the course of six months to a year you can set up a business that requires no further investment, and after you have paid off what you owe, you can make up to 200 dollars a month. A

---

16   Ibid., ff. 101, 99.
17   In 1961, my parents purchased a four-bedroom house in a fairly prosperous area of London for £6500, so even allowing for increases in property prices running at several times the overall level of price inflation, £810 could taken as the equivalent of perhaps £10,000 today.
18   'Bubble-Gum King took £500,000, Says Salesman', *The Daily Mail*, 26 May 1959, p. 5. Like Lonsdale, Levine was not just of Russian extraction, but had Canadian connections (see NA UK KV-2/4383, f. 100). The only newspaper report on the Allo Switch that I have been able to find was published in Quebec: 'British Combination Switch "Shocks" Would-Be Thieves', *Quebec Telegraph*, 11 February 1956, p. 4. This may be coincidental, but it is clear that Canada was considered a safe haven for Soviet agents, a point noted with alarm in Elwell's report on Lonsdale.
19   NA UK KV-2/4383, ff. 98–107. The information relating to Lonsdale's business activities that I have been able to check appears to be accurate. The more questionable material in Elwell's report relates to guilt by association, such as the fact that Colonel Czeslaw Dega, allegedly head of the Polish Military Intelligence in London, used the same garage in London as Lonsdale, and that he and his car had been seen there at various times during August and September 1960 (ibid., l. 105). Elwell was to pursue this principle of 'guilt by association' in his later investigation of Lonsdale's contacts: see, for example, NA UK K-2/4449, K-2/4450, K-2/4451.

business of this kind allows you, firstly, to justify your residence in the country, and secondly, to visit other countries as and when required for periods of a month or couple of months.' He continued: 'In a year or so, I think I will expand to 10 machines or so. Once the debts are paid off, the machines will provide a very solid profit, and allow me to finance running a car, should this turn out to be necessary'.[20]

Alongside such displays of fiscal prudence, though, Lonsdale/Molodyi seems to have led a modest life from the point of view of espionage too. Most of the time, he ran just two agents: Harry Houghton, an employee at the Admiralty Underwater Weapons Establishment in Portland, a harbour town in Dorset, southwest England, and Houghton's mistress Ethel Gee, who had a clerical position in the same facility.[21] What is more, Lonsdale had 'inherited' Houghton, who had been recruited while working at the British Embassy in Warsaw. In any case, as an intelligence source, Houghton had notable minuses. Drunken and boastful, he had come under suspicion from his British Government employers and been removed from contact with secret documents. The intelligence of value in the case flowed from Ethel Gee, whom Houghton had persuaded to copy documents that she encountered in her office role.[22]

Another oddity of Lonsdale/Molodyi's activities was the extent of his contact with his radio operators, Peter and Helen Kroger (real names Morris and Lona Cohen), two experienced Soviet agents (Morris Cohen had begun working for the USSR as long ago as 1938). Lonsdale/Molodyi's repeated visits to Ruislip, a classic commuter-belt suburb of London, put the British security services on alert, and after a surveillance operation involving the neighbours, the Krogers' house emerged as his destination.[23] Among documents to surface in a search of Lonsdale's apartment was his correspondence with his wife Galina in microdot form. The letters revealed how emotionally important the Krogers had been:

> I spent New Year with my close friends [*krestnye*]. At exactly midnight Moscow time, we drank a toast in Stolichnaya [vodka] to all our friends in the Soviet Union. We drank a separate toast to you and the children. I personally felt very sad. It was my eighth New Year (starting in 1954) that I'd celebrated without you. A wise man said long ago — such is life. And I know that expression in so many languages that it's quite unpleasant.[24]

---

20   *Ocherki istorii rossiiskoi vneshnei razvedki*, ed. by E. M. Primakov and S. M. Lebedev, 6 vols (Moscow: Mezhudnarodnye otnosheniya, 2014), v, 115.
21   According to Christopher Andrew and Vasily Mitrokhin, *The Mitrokhin Archive*, 2 vols (London: Penguin, 1999–2005), I, 535, Molodyi's only other agent, and that for a very short time, was Melita Norwood (see above n. 7), a hard-working and efficient agent with deep Communist convictions who led a studiedly low-key life. It is difficult to imagine that they would have got on. MI5 also assumed that Lonsdale was running just two agents: NA UK KV-2/4377 (case file of Ethel Gee), f. 40.
22   See NA UK KV-2/4377 (case file of Ethel Gee), e.g. ff. 151–52.
23   Report by C. J. L. Elwell, 16 November 1960, NA UK KV-2-4383, f. 22.
24   Exhibit 78 at the trial of Gordon Lonsdale, 'Regina v. Lonsdale and Others', NA UK CRIM 1/3604, File 1, f. 44.

This soulful version of Molodyi contrasts sharply with the persona that he adopted during his period of illegal residence in London. A fellow-student at SOAS (and later leading sinologist) recalled him in retrospect as a 'drinking man'.[25] Lonsdale's way of life was extensively reported by the British press during the trial of the 'Portland spy ring' in March 1961, and mass-market newspapers such as the *Daily Mail* offered much sensationalist detail of his playboy pleasures and string of attractive girlfriends. Molodyi's KGB employers cannot have been delighted to read criticism of his unprofessional conduct as a spy (for, say, exposing the Krogers to surveillance), or, indeed, articles about the 'honey trap' used by the British security services as part of their investigation of Lonsdale.[26]

Whatever the truth of the playboy image, Lonsdale/Molodyi himself at least partially endorsed it. During March and April 1965, the popular London Sunday newspaper, *The People*, ran an exclusive 'world scoop': the memoirs of Gordon Lonsdale. The journalist responsible for co-ordinating the publication, Ken Gardner, had, according to his own account, already raised the possible publication of Lonsdale's 'story' when the latter was on trial. He had sent him books and newspapers while he was in prison, and after Lonsdale was released, Gardner had gone to a meeting with him in a hotel near Friedrichstrasse in East Berlin. At this meeting, Gardner alleged, Molodyi 'told me he needed money — and was prepared to sell his life story to get it'.[27] Over a series of interviews in the next week, Gardner collected 38,000 words of testimony from Lonsdale, before adapting this as a memoir. The style adopted was classic British popular journalism, heavy on racy anecdote. As Lonsdale, ventriloquised by Gardner, boasted:

> There was Daisy Wong, a Chinese nurse who worked in Leicester and spent her weekends in London, Ulla Nillson, a beautiful blonde from Sweden, Annemarie Schilling from Germany, Carla Panizzi from Italy — my address books were full of girls' names and addresses.[28]

According to Gardner, Lonsdale had tried to present him with a ready-made text, but he had rejected this out of hand:

> He had already prepared a manuscript, but I regarded it as useless. It contained very little new information.
> I said this would not do and that he would receive no money unless he revealed the full facts.
> He was most reluctant, but in the end greed won the day.[29]

---

25 Cited in 'Professor Göran Malmqvist' (anonymous profile of a SOAS alumnus) <https://www.soas.ac.uk/centenary/alumni-profiles/1950s/professor-gran-malmqvist.html> [accessed 2 October 2022].

26 See 'The Spymasters Made One Slip', *Daily Mail*, 24 March 1961, p. 9, and Hugh Saker, 'The Master Spy: A Pretty English Girl Trapped the Red Casanova', *The Daily Mirror*, 23 March 1961, p. 5, which gave a breathless account of how a red-haired female MI5 agent had been a central part of the surveillance.

27 Ken Gardner, 'Lonsdale the Liar: Ken Gardner Answers the Kremlin's Hokum', *The People*, 10 October 1965, p. 7.

28 Gordon Lonsdale, 'How I Stole Atom Secrets', *The People*, 28 March 1965, p. 2.

29 Gardner, 'Lonsdale the Liar', p. 7.

As Lonsdale/Molodyi corrected Gardner's text, he seemed very anxious about the prudence of exercising initiative ('he was so nervous he could not eat'). A few weeks later, he contacted Gardner again requesting an urgent meeting in Moscow:

> Now, Lonsdale told me he was in serious trouble for telling me too much — and actually accused me of placing unfair pressure on him when I interviewed him.
>
> He implored me to delete extensive passages. The effect of this would have been to reduce the manuscript to a sham, and I refused.

After many hours of argument, a compromise was reached in the form of a list of amendments 'which would not detract from the manuscript but which might help to save Lonsdale from the wrath of his accusers'.[30]

But Gardner double-crossed Lonsdale by implementing only some of the amendments. The text run by *The People* included passages that emphasised Lonsdale's lofty purpose ('It makes me happy to think that my colleagues and I, engaged in the invisible war for the preservation of peace, made our contribution towards progress'). It also claimed that Lonsdale had an interest in potential germ warfare at the UK biological research facility, Porton Down, thus making it sound as if he had his fingers in many espionage pies. (There is no evidence at all that Molodyi was concerned with the Porton Down research, which did not come to public attention until he was already in prison.)[31] However, Lonsdale's revelations to *The People* also included revealing accounts of his professional activities, such as the exact location of the dead letter boxes (*tainiki*) that he had used during his time as a spy.[32] Gardner's retelling of the story in terms of popular journalism, lending spice and local detail to what Lonsdale himself acknowledged were the dull duties of an illegal resident, must have made it seem dangerously loose-lipped so far as espionage professionals were concerned.

Six months later, another version of Lonsdale's memoirs was published in book form by a small London press.[33] This had significant differences of detail and tone — for instance, there was no longer any concrete information about dead letter boxes — and the book included a foreword by Lonsdale in which he specifically retracted the *People* publication as 'mutilated and distorted'.[34] Yet the girlfriends had not entirely disappeared. 'Raven-haired' Carla Panizzi, who had allegedly cooked

---

30 Ibid.
31 Only after the death of scientist Geoffrey Bacon from plague virus on 1 August 1962 did the existence of Porton Down become common knowledge in the UK. From then on, the potential threat to the public of the work done there was regularly the subject of disquiet. See the excellent discussion in Ulf Schmidt, *Secret Science: A Century of Poison Warfare and Human Experiments* (Oxford: Oxford University Press, 2015).
32 For instance, Lonsdale gave a lengthy description of how he eavesdropped in a pub near Vickers aeronautics factory after taking pictures of the plant and picked up gossip about double-time shifts, then parked in the vicinity of Wardour Street and went to the cinema in Leicester Square, where in the interval, he visited the loo, and put some queries about Vickers on a shelf below a concealed light fitting (Gordon Lonsdale, 'World Scoop', *The People*, 7 March 1965, p. 2). Cf. Lonsdale, 'How I Stole Atom Secrets' *The People* 28 March 1965, pp. 2–3.
33 *Spy: Twenty Years of Secret Service. Memoirs of Gordon Lonsdale* (London: Neville Spearman, 1965).
34 Ibid., p. 7.

omelettes and 'veal in 50 ways' for Lonsdale in his London accommodation, even appeared in a photograph published in the book version of the memoirs.[35]

For his part, Gardner attributed the discrepancy between book and newspaper to the fact that his informant had thought better of his own sincerity. But there is no reason to believe that what Lonsdale told him was necessarily more accurate than what appeared between hard covers six months later. More likely, the proliferation of contradictory and demonstrably misleading variants exemplified the genre of 'disinformation' that was starting to emerge as an important weapon in the Cold War.[36]

One might wonder whether that was all, however. The generation of alternative variants by Lonsdale and his associates had a defensive air too: the former agent seems to have had a history of speaking out of turn.[37] Interesting in this regard is the treatment of Molodyi's life history in *The Dead Season*. Molodyi, under the rather transparent alias of 'Colonel Panfilov' (Galina Molodaya's maiden name was Panfilova), was an official consultant on the movie, which was commissioned from Lenfil'm by the KGB through the government bureaucracy responsible for cinema management, Goskino.[38] The alias of Banionis's character, Ladeinikov, 'Lonsfield', was a patent echo of 'Lonsdale', while the germ warfare facility in 'Dorgate' echoed

---

35 Gordon Lonsdale, 'I Turned My Friends' Bungalow into a Radio Link with Moscow', *The People*, 4 April 1965, p. 2.

36 Both Lonsdale's memoirs also differ in significant ways from Elwell's report on Lonsdale's activities contained in the UK secret service files relating to the Portland case (see above), and from the material in his MI5 file. As I shall suggest below, Molodyi's Russian memoirs, on the other hand, in some ways correlate well with Elwell.

37 Cf. Valery Agranovsky, 'Professiya — inostranets', *Znamya*, 9 (1988), 152, on how Molodyi had originally worked, after his return, in the KGB's training institute but was then removed 'from any kind of business in our agency'. Retrospective accounts tend to exaggerate the extent of official disfavour for Molodyi (cf. the wholly laughable description of *The Dead Season*, watched by 69 million people, as 'a banned film': L. Kolosov and T. Molodyi, *Mertvyi sezon: konets legendy* (Moscow: 1998), p. 6). Nevertheless, the failure to assign the ex-*rezident* a position according to his talents is striking. Some of this sense of awkwardness has endured after Molodyi was posthumously turned into a hero. For instance, in the canonical series of popular biographies, 'The Lives of Remarkable People', the volume on Molodyi (V. Antonov, *Konon Molodyi* (Moscow: Molodaya gvardiya, 2018)), turns him into just one figure in a book that resembles less a biography than a tribute to the heroic work of the secret services generally, with substantial sections on Rudol'f Abel' and the Krogers, and an appendix with biographies of Molodyi's contacts in the KGB. There is, so far as I know, no parallel to this oblique approach elsewhere in the series.

38 On *The Dead Season*, see my *Soviet Art House: Lenfilm Studio under Brezhnev* (New York: Oxford University Press, 2021), Chapter 10. On the KGB's PR work in the late 1950s and early 1960, see Tomas Sniegon, 'Zheleznyi Feliks s zolotym serdtsem? Kul't Feliksa Dzerzhinskogo i "dobroi ChK" vo vremya bor'by s kul'tom lichnosti', in *Uroki Oktyabrya i praktiki sovetskoi sistemy, 1920-e-1950-e* (Moscow: ROSSPEN, 2018). See also the letter of 13 March 1965 from Chairman of the KGB USSR V. F. Nikitchenko to the TsK KPU, proposing to declassify materials relating to the 'heroic side of the activities of the organs of state security in the Ukraine' and 'invite representatives of writers' and artists' unions, newspaper and magazine editors, and directors of publishing houses to visit the KGB and inform them about materials that we could supply to them for use in their creative work' (Haluzevyy derzhavnyy arkhiv Sluzhby bezpeky Ukrainy [Central State Archive of the State Security Service, Ukraine], f. 16, op. 1, d. 949, ll. 425–27). Cf. the 6 January 1981 report on 'the preparation of works of literature and art dedicated to the activities of the organs of state security', ibid., f. 17, op. 1, d. 90, ll. 343–48.

Fig. 13.1. Donatas Banionis (right) as Ladeinikov in Kulish's *The Dead Season* (1968). Archive of Lenfil'm Studio.

the seaside town of Dorchester, not far from Porton Down. But it was one thing to allow these echoes (aimed at an export market — after all, the Soviet viewing public had no idea about the Portland spy ring trial), and another to give prominence to the actual Konon Molodyi. The sole correction that the management of the KGB requested when clearing *The Dead Season* was a change to agent Ladeinikov's first name 'from "Gordon" to something else'.[39]

In order to soften the possible association between Lonsfield and Lonsdale, scriptwriter Vladimir Vainshtok and his KGB contacts hit on the solution of linking *The Dead Season* with another and better-known Soviet agent. This was Rudol'f Abel' (real name William Fisher), born in 1903 in Newcastle upon Tyne, but the son of refugees from the Russian Empire. Like Lonsdale, Abel' had been the subject of a spy exchange. However, the reason for his arrest was information to the US authorities from his deputy, Reino Häyhänen, rather than a mistake on Abel''s own part.[40] In the USSR, Abel' was honoured as a 'master spy'. In the USA, he had been Molodyi's immediate superior. Providing a connection with him was a way of advantaging the Lonsdale story.

Accordingly, the finalised version of *The Dead Season*'s script echoed the famous exchange of Abel' for US pilot Francis Gary Powers on the Glienecke Bridge, 10

---

39 A. M. Malygin (then deputy chairman of the KGB) to chairman of Goskino A. V. Romanov, RGALI, f. 2944, op. 4, d. 1236, l. 50.

40 Molodyi was not solely to blame for his own arrest either, since triple Polish-Soviet-US agent Michał Goleniewski had alerted US intelligence to the presence of a spy in 'the British navy', leading to close surveillance on Molodyi's contact Houghton. But by being caught during an exchange in a public place, Molodyi had made himself vulnerable to possible accusations of carelessness. From 1962, the Soviet intelligence operation in the UK used an expanded force of legal residents at the embassy in London (Christopher Andrew, *The Sword and the Shield: The Mitrokhin Archive and the Secret History of the KGB* (New York, 1999), p. 538).

February 1962, rather than the exchange of Lonsdale for Wynne, which had taken place at Heerstrasse checkpoint in an obscure suburb of Berlin.[41] And the finished movie opened with a clip in which Rudolph Abel', lightly disguised in a toupee, underlined for viewers the deadly threat of germ warfare.

The association of Abel' and the hero of *The Dead Season* was notably successful, as Tat'yana Lioznova's reaction made clear:

> How surprised we are that the scriptwriter and director have allowed us to make the acquaintance of someone like Abel', the prototype of the hero of this movie. And what a great pleasure it was for me when I was able to look into the face of this person.[42]

An equally elaborate process of approach-avoidance went on after the former spy's death from heart failure during a mushroom-hunting expedition in 1970. An obituary in *Red Star* (*Krasnaya zvezda*), the only Soviet newspaper to mark his passing, referred exclusively to Molodyi's wartime activities as a surveillance officer.[43] Shortly afterwards, a version of his memoirs began being published in *Komsomol'skaya pravda* but in substantially edited form and recast in the third person.[44] It was not until 1988 that Molodyi had direct publicity, with his interview about the life of a spy run prominently in the journal *The Banner* (*Znamya*).[45] Two years later came a substantial memoir publication that, for the first time, confirmed officially that Lonsdale and Molodyi were the same person.[46] With the appearance, also in 1990, of his portrait on a Soviet stamp, 'Colonel Panfilov' finally stepped, for good and all, out of the shadows.[47]

The Molodyi revealed to the Soviet public was a very different figure from the protagonist of Lonsdale's English memoirs. Rather than make contact on arrival with the Royal Overseas League, the spy's alter ego Georgy Lonov, in *Komsomol'skaya pravda*'s 1970 publication, directed his steps first of all to London University, where

---

41 *The Times*, 22 April 1964, p. 14. The sequence was not actually filmed on the Glienecke Bridge, which is an imposing cantilevered structure many times longer than the one in the film. It was perhaps shot elsewhere on the crew's trip to East Germany in April 1968. The figures of the actors may well have been added in post-production.

42 RGALI, f. 2936, op. 4, d. 533, l. 29.

43 'Molodyi K. T.', *Krasnaya zvezda*, 15 October 1970, p. 1.

44 T. Podolin, 'Spetskomandirovka', *Komsomol'skaya pravda*, 20 November 1970, p. 4 (part 1); 21 November 1970, p. 4 (part 2); 22 November 1970, p. 4 (part 3); 23 November 1970, p. 4 (part 4); 24 November 1970, p. 4 (part 5); 25 November 1970, p. 4 (part 6); 26 November 1970, p. 4 (part 7); 27 November 1970, p. 4 (part 8); 28 November 1970, p. 4 (part 9); 2 December 1970, p. 4 (part 10); 3 December 1970, p. 4 (part 11); 4 December 1970, p. 4 (part 12); 8 December 1970, p. 4 (part 13); 9 December 1970, p. 4 (part 14); 10 December 1970, p. 4 (part 15); 11 December 1970, p. 4 (part 16).

45 Agranovsky, 'Professiya — inostranets'.

46 G. Lonsdale, *Moya professiya razvedchik: Vospominaniya ofitsera KGB*, ed. by N. V. Gubernatorov and others (Moscow: Orbita, 1990).

47 According to Andrew, *The Sword and the Shield*, p. 26, the background to this was a decision by V. A. Kryuchkov, deputy chairman of the KGB from 1974 and chairman from 1 October 1988, that there should be 'wider use of archive material' to 'publicize a "positive" image of the KGB and "its more celebrated cases"'.

Fig. 13.2. Konon Molodyi on a postage stamp <https://commons.wikimedia.org/wiki/File:The_Soviet_Union_1990_CPA_6268_stamp_(Soviet_Intelligence_Agents._Konon_Molody).jpg>.

he obediently listened to sage advice from the Professor of Chinese.[48] Gone were the pub visits, let alone the girlfriends: instead, this Lonsdale haunted bookshops. Rather than taking his contacts to night-clubs, he conducted them to concerts in the Royal Albert Hall. His main life, outside his studies, consisted in underground surveillance, including (as in *The Dead Season* and the English memoirs) not just the naval base at Portland, but also Porton Down. Ladeinikov had limited himself to an understanding of who worked at the sinister research establishment and their Nazi connections. Lonov, helped by his trusty assistant, 'Vil'son', had higher ambitions:

> Wilson carried out his task brilliantly. We will pass over the question of how, but Lonov soon had samples in his hands of the different types of bacteria. It was an odd feeling to hold in his hands the container, resembling as it did a thermos flask of small size. Wilson had conscientiously ensured that the temperature in the flask was kept stable and that the bacteria were provided with the proper nutritional medium.

48 The name of this person is wrongly given as 'Саймонс' (i.e. 'Simons'; he was in fact Walter Simon (1893–1981), a Jewish refugee from Nazi Germany), but the details of Molodyi's time at SOAS in Lonsdale, *Moya professiya razvedchik*, seem otherwise to be pretty accurate: cf. the information in K. Price, 'The SOAS Language Student Who Was a Soviet Spy' <https://blogs.soas.ac.uk/centenarytimeline/2015/12/10/the-soas-language-student-who-was-a-soviet-spy> [accessed 25 April 2022].

'We'll send it to Moscow Centre today', Lonov resolved. The question of how the precious cargo was to reach Moscow (by carrier pigeon, perhaps?) was left to the imagination of *Komsomol'skaya pravda*'s readers.[49]

Lonov was in all things obedient to his superiors, according to the rules set out by a senior intelligence official based in Paris, 'Jean', who was keen to ensure that Lonov 'paid special attention to setting up proper channels of communication with Moscow Centre'.[50] His recorded thoughts usually took the form of sententiae about the importance of hard work and prudence:

> Georgy had occasion to observe once more how important it is to be steeped in the customs and habits of the country where you intend to work. Without this, an agent cannot take a single step. This might all seem like obvious truths, as recorded in the memoirs of any competent agent. But in order really to know everything about a country, its everyday life, social life, the psychology of the different social strata, you need years of hard, attentive, analytical work.[51]

Impeccably committed to duty and hopelessly dull, Georgy Lonov totally lacked the charm that everyone recalled Molodyi as exuding. That this masterpiece of tedious rectitude became politically unacceptable almost before it was complete represents a comical hiccup of realpolitik.[52]

The next publication about the life of Molodyi saw the light of day nearly twenty years later, in 1988. It had a very different character. Rather than a linear history, the account of Molodyi by journalist Valery Agranovsky was presented as fragmentary remarks imparted in the course of face-to-face meetings with the man Agranovsky had known under yet another pseudonym, 'Konstantin Trofimovich Perfil'ev'. This version of Molodyi was considerably less *bien pensant* and docile than his 1970 alter ego. While emphasising his patriotism and taking care to cite Dzerzhinsky on frequent occasions, Agranovsky's interlocutor also underlined his competence in manipulating agents — you had to pick an unsuccessful and discontented person ripe for revenge against his employers. The spy's business career got much more attention than in 1970. Now, Lonsdale/Molodyi's activities with juke boxes and slot machines figured not just as expedient cover, but as a success story in its own right. He had made real money ('I got rich'), and he had lived a life of startling luxury: 'I had eight motor cars of different marques, and I used 100-octane petrol at five shillings a gallon; I had a villa outside London and a whole string of rooms in London's best hotels, rented by the month'.[53] As though 100-octane

---

49 Podolin, 'Spetskomandirovka', part 8.
50 Ibid., part 5.
51 Ibid., part 4.
52 A planned book version of the tale attributed to Podolin (in fact, the material was concocted by the committee of authors who compiled Lonsdale, *Moya professiya razvedchik*, making use of Molodyi's own writings, on which see the prefatory material, ibid.) never materialised, since by the early 1970s, Soviet foreign policy had shifted towards the encouragement of détente. On this shift, see Susanne Schattenberg, *Leonid Breschnew: Staatsman und Schauspieler im Schatten Stalins* (Cologne, Weimar, & Vienna: Böhlau, 2017).
53 Agranovsky, 'Professiya — inostranets', pp. 167, 146. According to secret service records, in 1960, Lonsdale was running a Studebaker (probably the Lark, a compact sedan manufactured in 1959–61); he had obtained it by trading in his previous vehicle, a Standard Companion, along with some bedroom furniture (not needed when he moved back to the White House) with an Irish garage

petrol were not fantastical enough, Molodyi boasted: 'Since I was a millionaire, I could afford to head off every now and then on my own yacht, *The Albatross*, with a professional captain'.[54] Molodyi, however, was represented not as an empty fantasist, but as a pioneer of the Kosygin economic reforms of 1965: 'My companies were well-regarded and they brought in real money — and this, by the way, long before the government passed the law making it requisite for Soviet enterprises to turn a profit'.[55] As a 1988 Soviet reader would have understood, Molodyi had also pioneered perestroika-era experiments with market capitalism.

The republication in 1990 of the memoirs originally issued by *Komsomol'skaya pravda* was also a contribution to the new values, rather than a tacit or explicit reversion to those of the Brezhnev era. The emergence of the book was openly linked by its authors or editors with the new political mood of glasnost' ('At present, the work of the KGB is regularly discussed at the Supreme Soviet of the USSR — and all of this is conveyed to the public in live broadcasts').[56] Not everything about the book had changed. The preposterous story about transferral of a container of deadly bacteria appeared in unchanged form. So did stories about Lonsdale's pining for his family and motherland: on significant Soviet holidays, 'I would lock the door, lay the table and serve a celebratory dinner for one, switch on my wireless and listen (through headphones of course) to Radio Moscow'.[57] But more notable overall than the features resembling those in *Komsomol'skaya pravda*'s text were the novelties in the 1990 version.

To begin with, Lonsdale was telling his story in the first person. There was also far more local detail, from the trip to remote regions of the Canadian north on the verge of winter, through remote wooden towns against the huge panorama of the sky, to the grim hotel by Waterloo Station, complete with coin-operated gas meter, where Lonsdale spent his first night in London. Most of the material about central control and morality included in *Komsomol'skaya pravda*'s version had now disappeared. And Lonsdale's business activities had a still larger place than in 1988. For instance, Lonsdale recounted meeting travel agent Hans Koch on the boat over from the USA, and getting an expert overview of Western business practices:

> 'I work in a travel company in New York. We organise special trips to Europe, for teachers and university professors.'
> 'So, are trips for teachers so different from trips for everyone else?'
> 'Of course. As well as the usual excursions, we offer our clients lectures in the best universities in Europe. At the end of the trip they get a special certificate saying they've attended lectures in this, this, and this university.'
> 'But that certificate is completely meaningless!'
> 'Quite right,' Hans smiled, 'but luckily, a good many of them don't realise that. And in any case, that document makes them look good and helps with

owner, Edmund Christopher Nevin, of 127a Victor Road, London W10 (NA UK, file KV-2-4383, ff. 101–02). His previous car, a Ford van, had been even more modest (ibid., f. 100).
54 Agranovsky, 'Professiya — inostranets', p. 173.
55 Ibid., p. 161.
56 Lonsdale, *Moya professiya razvedchik*, p. 5.
57 Ibid., p. 54. This might sound like an echo of Stirlitz, but the passage appeared in almost identical form before the release of Lioznova's film: Podolin, 'Spetskomandirovka', part 6. In fact, Lioznova was influenced by Kulish, not vice versa (see above).

their career. Also, our certificates are printed on parchment and have wax seals with silk ribbons. They look great hung on the wall.'

'Right,' I laughed. 'So if I don't get anywhere with the University of London, I'll buy your parchment fake. OK?' [58]

Alongside information about market segmentation, Lonsdale was also getting an education in the creation of value — in this case, the manufacture of meaningless certificates as artefacts for decorative display. Later, he was to note that expensive London shops and doctors imposed a five per cent surcharge on clients by charging them in guineas, rather than in pounds, a useful introduction to the 'price point'.[59]

In the 1990 life of Lonsdale, the purchase of juke boxes and slot machines was presented as advantageous not just because it aided conspiracy, but because it had offered Lonsdale a business education. The techniques used by an automatic machines dealer called Jerome (keep customer details on file, hook them with promises of big profit) were a lesson in the hard sell. But Lonsdale had quickly realised that making money out of slot machines was not easy. Even juke boxes, it turned out, were hard work: a new supply of records was essential to keep up customer interest; London shopkeepers were shrewd and drove a hard bargain; rushing round to far-flung districts of a big city wore you out.

All the same, there were unexpected benefits to business life. After Lonsdale became a director of a company, Thanet Trading, licensed to sell Israeli-made O'Girl chewing gum, a spate of machine thefts allowed the machine owners to cash in on their insurance value. Later, Lonsdale made money on the stock exchange through tips passed on by the mistress of a prominent stockbroker. He also invested directly in the Master Switch Company, intended to market an anti-car-theft device designed by the father of Tommy Rourke, a salesman at AMC. This was to prove his first real success, securing, so Lonsdale/Molodyi claimed, 'a gold medal at the International Exhibition in Brussels', and substantially raising the value of the parent company.[60]

All in all, *The Dead Season* and the various purported (auto)biographies present a whole variety of different Konons: the brooding figure of Ladeinikov, reflective and philosophical, in the movie; the orthodox *rezident* in the *Komsomol'skaya pravda* version; and the sharp-witted businessmen in the texts published during the late 1980s and 1990s (and in many versions up to the present). Which is correct? Was Molodyi simply deceiving his associates in London (his business contacts, his many girlfriends, his teachers and friends at SOAS)? Certainly, he was good at this, persuading even the professional policemen and lawyers with whom he had to deal that he was a figure of integrity and charm. His interviews with Elwell show him engaging in elaborate coquetry, supplying some genuine information (for example, about family members in Moscow), while refusing to provide essential details such as names.[61] Whether the promised information would have emerged had he been

58 Lonsdale, *Moya professiya razvedchik*, pp. 34–35.
59 Ibid., pp. 60–65.
60 Ibid., p. 202.
61 See, for example, the summary of interviews on 31 May, 21 and 22 June by C. J. L. Elwell, NA UK KV-2/4450, ff. 125–28.

granted a sentence reduction of the kind he asked for (twenty-five years down to three) is impossible to say.

In the meantime, Molodyi took care to provide little information that was not purely personal. He refused point-blank to pass on the names of any Soviet agents. But had he perhaps been deceiving his KGB superiors as well, supplying them with easily obtained intelligence, while living a life of pleasure and dalliance and making money for himself on the side? Some of his later descriptions of his success recall the wild fantasies of Khlestakov, the innocently bogus government inspector of Gogol's play. Whichever it was, the way in which Molodyi exaggerated the glamour and prestige of his life in Britain shows that the daily life of the *rezident* had allure both for him and his listeners.

Life in Moscow must have been far duller. At any rate, eyewitnesses reported that Molodyi took to drink after his return (as did Galina). He had expressed concern in advance to Elwell that he would not be trusted when he got back to Moscow:

> Whether he reveals anything to us or not he says that he will still be treated with suspicion when he returns to Moscow. The chances of his being able to clear himself will depend largely on whether he is known personally to his superiors or is just a name on a file.[62]

Certainly, his intelligence and expertise were drastically under-used.

Molodyi's broader family circle cannot have helped relations with Moscow Centre. He told Charles Elwell during his MI5 interrogations that all his relations were scientists.[63] This, while true of his parents (his father was a chemist and academic administrator, his mother a doctor), was a distinctly partial record of the truth. In fact, the families of both Trofim Molodyi (his father) and Evdokiya Naumova (his mother) belonged to the mercantile bourgeoisie, whose ethos was considered inimical to Soviet values. Worse, members of both families, and the Piankovs, with whom the Naumovs intermarried, left the USSR in the early 1920s and settled in Harbin, and later in America. Molodyi's paternal uncle, Alexei, and his maternal aunts, Tatiana Piankova and Anastasia Naumova, with Tatiana's daughter Nina, Konon's cousin, all settled in the San Francisco area. So did Tatiana's former husband, Sergei Piankov, his brother Andrei, his sister Nadezhda Belousovich and her husband, and possibly another Piankov brother also.[64] So far from severing contact with these undesirable (from the Soviet point of view) associates, Trofim and Evdokiya remained in close touch with them.

Konon's first trip abroad, on 3 September 1932 was to yet more émigré relations, his aunt Serafima and her husband Nikolai Lenkin, based in Tartu, Estonia. Here Konon lived for over a year while arrangements were made to obtain a US visa

---

62   For the comment to Elwell, see NA UK KV-2/4451, f. 142. On the post-return side of Molodyi's life, see, for example, Andrew and Mitrokhin, *The Mitrokhin Archive*, I, 537.
63   NA UK KV-2/4450, f. 125.
64   See the references to M. Piankov or Piankoff below. The FBI and MI5 took a close interest in these relations, compiling many elaborate family trees, though mainly because Molodyi's grandmother's maiden surname was Scriabin (Skryabin), and they were excited by the possibility that he might be a family connection of Vyacheslav Molotov (whose real surname was Scriabin — in fact, as with the composer Alexander Scriabin, there was no blood relationship of any kind).

(the process was held up by the fact that Tatiana Piankova had claimed on the application form she was his natural mother).[65] In August 1933, after Tatiana's story was accepted, the visa was finally cleared, and on 14 November 1933 Konon arrived in New York and then travelled to stay with Tatiana in San Francisco.[66]

A few months later, Tatiana moved to 2632 College Avenue, Berkeley, taking Konon with her. He attended first Willard Junior High, a public (but prestigious) middle school, before moving at the age of fourteen to the A to Zed School, an expensive private prep school, where he spent about another year and a half.[67] In the spring of 1938, however, Molodyi terminated his studies at the A to Zed and departed with Anastasia Naumova for Europe, landing at Plymouth. Also in the party were his cousin, Anna Simpson, her husband, a British civil servant in Hong Kong, and their daughter, Margarita. In the passenger manifest for the President Harding on 24 March 1938, Molodyi gave the Simpson's home address in Plymouth as his place of residence in the UK.

Travelling from 1932 Moscow to independent Estonia already represented a dislocation; still more the move half-way across the world to West Coast USA. Yet Konon, at least at the superficial level, adjusted easily. Family photographs show him perched, beaming, on the runner of the car driven by his cousin, George (Yura) Jaure, eight years his senior, and resident in the USA from 1931 (before that, George had lived with his mother, Serafima Lenkina, in Tartu). In the family snaps, we see Molodyi smiling amid family parties, or outside in the yard of his aunt's house. School yearbooks show extra-curricular activities — he was a member of the Willard Junior High chess club, and also (ironically given what came later) its pupil-discipline body, the Court of Control.[68] As George Jaure remembered, Konon had a 'pleasant, friendly personality'. Yet at the same time, George recalled only one

---

65   The shipping records and the Piankov and Naumova relations' naturalisation applications are available on ancestry.com. Konon arrived in Estonia on 3 September 1932, travelling with Tatiana Piankova, and then settled down to await the visa clearance. The presence of the two is recorded in the residents' list (*elanikkude nimekiri*) for 20 Jaama tänav dated on 29 December 1932: see electronic documents on the site of the National Archive of Estonia <https://www.ra.ee> [accessed 2 October 2022]. On 14 November 1933 (see the shipping lists on ancestry.com), Konon arrived in New York, sailing on the SS Majestic from Cherbourg. None of his relatives accompanied him, but he may well have been chaperoned by the passenger listed immediately before him, Mrs Anna Greenwich, a Russian national who was travelling to join her husband in New York via Riga, and who could also have travelled with him from Riga to Paris on the Nord Express, then onwards to Cherbourg. For the issues over the visa, see NA UK KV-2/4450, ff. 42–47.

66   Officials at the US Immigration and Naturalization were suspicious that Tatiana had not mentioned Konon Molodyi as her son when she entered the USA in 1923 and in her naturalisation documents in the following years. After assurances from Nina Piankova that she remembered being introduced to her 'stepbrother' in Moscow, and a detailed narrative from Tatiana about how she had left the infant Konon with a nurse in Eastern Russia and collected him again in 1932 before bringing him to Moscow, having only just realised that he was in fact alive, the District Director of Naturalization Services in San Francisco recommended that the visa be granted and denaturalisation proceedings dropped. For the arrival of Konon Molodyi (as Conon Molody), see the passenger manifest of the Majestic, publicly available on ancestry.com.

67   Molodyi (as Conon Molody) appears in the 1936 yearbook of Willard Junior High, in the graduating class (see ancestry.com). See also Tatiana Piankova's testimony to the FBI.

68   See the 1936 yearbook on ancestry.com.

Fig. 13.3. Konon Molodyi clings to the running-boards of his cousin George Jaure's car, probably in Berkeley around 1934. (UK National Archives, KV2-4451)

close friend (Irina Semochenko, exactly his age, and also a migrant from the former Russian Empire — her parents were originally from Kharkov). The hobbies that Jaure remembered were also mainly solitary ones: language acquisition, taxidermy, toy trains.[69]

Konon's life after leaving the USA is an open question. The documentary trail disappears with his arrival at Plymouth, and resurfaces only with the Second World War, during which he was several times decorated for bravery.[70] His aunts gave conflicting testimony to the FBI about Konon's later fate. Anastasia recalled that she had last seen him in Paris, about to begin a hiking tour before he embarked

---

[69] NA UK KV-2/4451, f. 44. The fact that only Irina was mentioned was perhaps because George did not wish to provide the FBI with information that they did not already have. Certainly, the only surviving information held by the FBI (as per my FoI requests) is a heavily redacted collection of materials relating to a US schoolmate of Molodyi's, Quentin Griffiths (see two Airtels of 11 June 1961 copied to CK on 4 February 2021). Re. the destruction of other materials, see the FBI's response to my follow-up request of 9 February 2021.

[70] The records are available on the comprehensive database, Podvig Naroda, 1941–45 <http://podvignaroda.ru/> [accessed 2 October 2022]. On 15 December 1942, Sergeant Konon Molodyi was awarded the 'For Battle Service' (*Za boevye zaslugi*) medal (he was then a cypher clerk (*pisar'*) in the 829th Army Intelligence Artillery Division of the 13th Army). On 25 November 1943, Konon Molodyi, now promoted to sergeant major and section commander in the 829th, was awarded the Order of the Red Star. Awards of the Patriotic War medal Second Class (18 July 1944, Junior Lieutenant Konon Molodyi, deputy staff commander of the army intelligence artillery division) and First Class (16 February 1945, Senior Lieutenant Konon Molodyi, holding the same position), followed.

on university studies in France or England. Tatiana, though, remembered that Konon had returned in the course of 1938 to Tartu. His family in Moscow, on the third hand, claimed that Konon's entire purpose in returning to Europe had been to rejoin his mother in Moscow, and that he arrived there in August 1938, shortly before his mother and sister got back from their own summer holiday.[71]

Of the three versions, the least convincing on first principles is the one about a speedy return to Moscow. Konon, as is clear from passenger manifests, left the USA on an American passport. How did he obtain a Soviet one, or at the very least a Soviet visa? How did he escape repression in an era where even writing to relations abroad put people in serious danger? Many of Konon's relatives had departed the USSR through Harbin, a place with the justified reputation of a nest of spies. Most were in professions that were, from the Soviet intelligentsia's point of view, at best déclassé, and at worst parasitic: Tatiana ran a private ballet school, Alexei was a janitor, Anastasia was a masseuse, aunt Nadezhda Belousovich's husband a taxi-driver. All of them had started naturalisation proceedings soon after they arrived in the USA, gleefully abandoning their Soviet (and indeed Russian) identity.[72] Yet Molodyi allegedly had no problem in entering the penultimate grade of a Moscow school (despite having covered almost none of the syllabus). After call-up in 1940, he was supposedly posted to an area of extreme strategic sensitivity — the 'Special Western Region' covering the recently-annexed territory of Western Ukraine and Western Belorussia.[73]

It seems more likely that Tatiana's version may be correct, and that Molody returned from the USA to Estonia. This itinerary also figured in the testimony of Anna Simpson, the relation with whom Konon and Anastasia Naumova had sailed to Europe in 1938:

> They first stopped in London and Plymouth, England, where Mr. SIMPSON'S mother, ELLEN SIMPSON, joined the group. ELLEN SIMPSON is now deceased. They finally left the ship at Le Havre, France, and proceeded via NAUMOVA's car to Tartu, Estonia.
> At Tartu NAUMOVA and KONON stayed with NAUMOVA's sister, SERAPHINA LENKINA. The SIMPSON family stayed in a hotel for a day or two and then went on by train to Finland and Latvia. ANNA understood KONON was to stay in Estonia and attend a well-known university, Urive or Uribe (phonetic).[74]

---

71   Contrast Naumova in NA UK file KV-2/4451, f. 47; Piankova in NA UK file KV-2/4453, document 1160Z; ibid., document 1173B; for the Moscow family's version, Vadim Molodyi, 'Ser Konon Trofimovich' <http://www.promegalit.ru/publics.php?id=7736> [accessed 25 April 2022].

72   There was one exception: the arrival documentation for Anastasia, Tatiana, Tatiana's daughter Nina, and her husband Sergei when they reached the USA from Harbin in 1923 cited 'brother M. Pianov [sic], Russian Consulate San Francisco' as their nearest relation in the USA. No other documentation about this person has come to light.

73   See, for example, Antonov, *Konon Molodyi*.

74   KV2/4452, document 1116A (24 July 1961), p. 6. 'Le Havre' may be a tactical error: the final stop of President Harding was in fact Hamburg, nearly 1000 km closer to Tartu (see the passenger lists for 1937–38 on <https://www.gjenvick.com/Passengers/Ships/PresidentHarding-PassengerLists.html> [accessed 2 October 2022]). However, all Molodyi's relations seem to have been understandably concerned to avoid suggesting that Molodyi had ever been on German or occupied territory.

Urive was evidently the transcriber's garbling of the Russian name for the University of Tartu between 1893 and 1918, the Imperial Yur'evskii University. Molodyi's name does not appear in records of student enrolments for the University of Tartu.[75] However, he was not eighteen until 1940, so perhaps spent the two years after he arrived in the final years of school. Or if Anna Simpson was correct in recalling later in the interview that Konon's planned subject was 'mining engineering', his natural destination would not have been Tartu University, but Tallinn University of Technology, the only Estonian institution offering the subject at the time[76] According to Estonian records of residence, the Lenkins had left Tartu by 1942 and were 'in Russia'; they no doubt fled following the German invasion in 1941.[77] The point when the multilingual Konon Molodyi (as well as English, he already knew German well) came to the attention of the Soviet authorities would then have been the months following the USSR's invasion of Estonia in July 1940. In a position where the Red Army was the occupying force, there was far less squeamishness about people with dubious connections who were potentially useful to Soviet intelligence-gathering. Molodyi's relations remembered that he spoke good German, and it was precisely work in deciphering German that he carried out during his four years of service at the front.

Molodyi was certainly conscripted into the Red Army after he returned to Moscow, but that could fit with the story about his arrival back home in the summer, while his mother and sister were away — only in 1940, rather than 1938. Certainly, there is no foundation for Molodyi's information to Charles Elwell that he had been a Soviet intelligence operative from 1940 and had 'served with the Russian guerrilla bands' during the war before being briefly imprisoned in 1945.[78]

But we probably should not search for authenticity in the first place. As Molodyi reportedly told journalist Valery Agranovsky, 'We illegal agents live by two or more biographies: our official one, the "cover story", and the real one, and really I don't know which of them I'm living by now and what my future life will be'.[79] Sensing the slipperiness of the case he was dealing with, Victor Durand, defence counsel for Peter and Helen Kroger, was to warn the jury at the trial of the 'Portland spy ring' about the difficulty of pronouncing with certainty on any element in the evidence:

---

75 See *Album Academicum Universitatis Tartuensis 1918–1944*, <http://www.ra.ee/apps/andmed/index.php/site/aaut> [accessed 2 October 2022] (the site does, however, list Nikolai Lenkin, 1891–1955, as a student of chemistry).

76 For the comment, NA KV2/4452, document 1116A, pp. 6–7; on the institution, see Enna Reinsalu, 'The Seventieth Anniversary of Mining Engineering in Estonia', *Oil Shale* (January 2008), DOI: 10.3176/oil.2008.2S.01. Konon's likeliest place of prior study would then have been Tartu's most prestigious science-oriented secondary school, the Hugo Treffner Gymnasium, founded as a German-speaking school in 1883. After the Soviet invasion of Estonia, the school remained open, but was renamed Tartu School no. 4. <https://www.htg.tartu.ee/en19/?q=node/22> [accessed 13 October 2021].

77 Estonian residence records for 1942 held by the National Archive of Estonia (Elanikkude ja kinnisvara teateloht) (Population and Property Owner Notification Sheet) <https://www.ra.ee/>) indicate that the Lenkins had left Tartu and were 'in Russia'.

78 NA UK file KV-2/4452, f. 125.

79 Agranovsky, 'Professiya — inostranets', pp. 168–69.

> This is a case which, by its very nature, has been full of intrigue. You may say that it has the characteristics of what is called a 'thriller', and there is a great temptation for all of us to speculate about a number of things which are left untied, to turn ourselves into amateur detectives, to wonder about this or wonder about that. Members of the jury, do not do that. Keep your feet firmly on the ground. Consider only the evidence given before you and do not enter into the realm of speculation.[80]

Molodyi's many reclothings of himself were classic 'disinformation', leaving serious uncertainty about what the 'original' or 'authentic' self may have amounted to. Even members of his family seem to have been taken in by the layers of legend. His nephew Vadim Molodyi, for example, published a short biographical essay in 2014. Here, alongside some fairly accurate accounts of Konon's peregrinations, he repeated the claims that Molodyi was a hugely successful businessman knighted by the Queen, and that he had been a gold-medal winner in Brussels.[81]

If the boundaries of fact and fantasy for intelligence officers are porous, so too are the dividing lines of identity. In John Buchan's famous First World War adventure, *Greenmantle* (1916), the narrator's close friend, the dashing Sandy Arbuthnot, comes to the brink of complete mental collapse after posing for months as the prophet leader of an Islamic rebellion in Turkey. Lonsdale/Molodyi's effort to pass as an Anglophile Canadian might have been less psychologically perilous, but required a comparable level of masquerade.[82] A woman who ran a music shop next to the office of Lonsdale's company office in Peckham Rye recalled that Lonsdale would often drop in to buy a record for one of his jukeboxes: 'He was great fun, always joking. He watched Princess Margaret's wedding with us on TV. I remember him saying how proud he was to be British'.[83] Leonard Ayres remembered Lonsdale as 'a hard worker with a smooth sales manner and an extremely acute business sense'.[84]

In terms of his effort to blend in, Molodyi's finest hour was his insistence at his trial that he was solely to blame for the compromising items discovered at the Krogers. As the *Daily Mail* reported, 'A barrister unconnected with the case said, "It was the last polite gesture of a gentleman." [...] Security chiefs of the Admiralty, MI5, Scotland Yard's Special Branch, huddled together and agreed it was a "damn good show"'.[85] There is an echo here of the cry, 'A glorious bet!' that greets the protagonist's catastrophic final stake in Pushkin's *Queen of Spades* — the tribute to the outsider whose spectacular act of self-destruction at last makes him part of a circle that he formerly could not enter. In both cases, *not* being a fraud was possible only at the price of self-immolation. But one can also put it differently: the price

---

80   Transcript of Regina v. Lonsdale and Others, Central Criminal Court, London, 13–22 March 1961, NA UK CRIM 1/3604, File 5, 22 March 1961, f. 2.
81   Molodyi, 'Ser Konon Trofimovich'.
82   *Daily Mail* reporter Harry Longmuir ('My Dupes', 22 March 1961, p. 12) in fact noticed that Lonsdale was reading in the dock John Masters's *The Lotus and the Wind* (1953), a still popular spy novel about the 'Great Game' in which the hero's wife is the 'lotus', decorative but fixed, and he is the 'wind' that ever departs and returns.
83   'The Spy Master!', *Daily Express*, 23 March 1961, p. 8
84   Ibid.
85   Longmuir, 'My Dupes'.

of glory is pretence. Either of those contentions may be right, or neither. Who, in the end, can tell?

Yet if the facts of Molodyi's life are impossible to distinguish from fiction of different kinds, sliding as they did into adventure stories, and sometimes into the classics of Russian literature, this elusiveness and ambiguity itself sheds important light on the propaganda conflicts current in the Cold War world of the post-Stalin years. The ideological cleavage between 'Communism' and 'capitalism' (as perceived in the USSR), or between 'Communism' and 'the free world' (in the preferred Western perspective) implied not just a bipolar, but a Manichean worldview: truth on one side, deceit on the other. However, the years between 1953 and 1989 were also a period of growing contact, co-operation, and social, cultural, and even economic (if not political) convergence.[86]

Molodyi's capacity to live in Britain unsuspected was the product of relative freedom in transnational relations. As the Lord Chief Justice, summing up in the trial of the Portland spy ring, put it: 'Members of the jury, do not be misled by the use of the word "enemy". We are not at war and nobody is, in that sense, an enemy'.[87] One of Molodyi's contacts, Mrs Sybil Isabel Prince, a retired school teacher and widow from New Zealand ('the very model of colonial elegance', Elwell noted approvingly) was delighted and relieved to hear that he was actually Russian: her greatest fear was that he was really a Canadian traitor.[88] In this ambiguous territory, it was possible for Molodyi not just to foster the effective gathering of intelligence by posing as Lonsdale, but also to experience some of the impact of migration to a culture that started to be less alien as time went by. While living as a visitor from Canada who needed to pose as British, he underwent more than superficial adaptation. Both testimony at the time and his later recollections point to psychological change, to a shift of interiority quite unlike anything that standard spy stories represented.

There is no doubt that Molodyi was, already by the time the war began, a Soviet patriot. The records for his first decoration in 1942 indicate that he was by then (aged just twenty) a full member of the Communist Party, and the citations refer to behaviour that indicates not just competent execution of the work of an artillery intelligence officer, but also physical bravery: several times, when the signals post in which he was working came under fire, Molodyi stayed put and used the information about the line of attack to pass on intelligence about the location of the enemy guns.[89] At the same time, it is clear that Molodyi, in his later years, was

---

86 Recent literature on contact and convergence includes Alexei Yurchak, *Everything Was Forever Until It Was No More: The 'Last' Soviet Generation* (Princeton, NJ: Princeton University Press, 2006); Paulina Bren, *The Greengrocer and His TV: The Culture of Communism after the 1968 Prague Spring* (Ithaca NY: Cornell University Press, 2010); Anne Gorsuch, *All This is Your World: Soviet Tourism At Home and Abroad after Stalin* (Oxford: Oxford University Press, 2011); Sergei Alymov, '"Activating the Human Factor?" The Late-Soviet Roots of Neoliberal Subjectivity', *Forum for Anthropology and Culture*, 14 (2018), 137–68.
87 Transcript of Regina v. Lonsdale and Others, Central Criminal Court, London, 13–22 March 1961, NA UK CRIM 1/3604, File 5, 22 March 1961, f. 17.
88 NA UK KV-2/4451, ff. 18–20.
89 See, for example, the citation for the award of the Red Star.

also a critical patriot who did not assume the superiority of Soviet culture to each and every other.

In this respect, *The Dead Season* was an accurate portrayal of Molodyi, enjoying popularity with thoughtful members of the intelligentsia who were curious about the West and suspicious of Manichean propaganda narratives.[90] Seen from the prospect of the early twenty-first century, too, Molodyi represents a transitional figure. More complex than Stirlitz on one side of the 'iron curtain', and James Bond on the other, he was also more straightforward and upright than the self-serving hero of Hossein Amini and James Watkin's 2018 television series, *McMafia*, or the protagonist of Vladimir Bortko's *The Soul of a Spy* (*Dusha shpiona*, 2015).

Molodyi's published memoirs, whatever their differences, portrayed a figure who was capable of friendship and, at some level, conviction, and hence a figure of divided loyalty, rather than no loyalty. Savva Kulish's *The Dead Season* was a significant achievement above all because it eschewed stereotypes of heroism.[91] Its secret agents were courageous rather than fearless (indeed, fear verging on paranoia was the besetting atmosphere of the movie) and vulnerable as well as stoical. Above all, they were peripheral to society. Ladeinikov's return to Moscow appeared to be a triumph, with cheering crowds waving flowers and brass bands. But then, the multitudes surged away in the wake of a sports team, leaving the freed agent to descend to the airport tarmac completely alone.

For some viewers, the 'radiant forests' of Russia brought patriotic uplift.[92] Yet Kulish ended with a much more emotionally ambiguous shot. Ladeinikov studies the Moscow architecture with a half-smile, oblivious to the chatter of the KGB general beside him. Suggesting the vexed nature of the agent's life, dangerous yet unrecognised, valorous but lonely, and emphasising shared humanity across ideological divides, *The Dead Season* was a thriller in the traditions of international late modernism, expounding the philosophy of a sorely tried patriotism based on universal values. It recognised Cold War conflict, yet also ethical universality. Between the manner in which Kulish and his artistic collaborators ennobled the

---

90 For example, the distinguished literary historian Irina Paperno, now a specialist in the history of subjectivity, who moved in a self-consciously anti-Soviet circle before her emigration from Leningrad in 1980, emphasised to me just how impressive she had found the film when she watched it shortly after its release.

91 In the post-Soviet period, the unconventionality of *The Dead Season* provoked the assumption that the film was somehow consciously subversive. For instance, there were claims that higher authority had refused to approve the choice of Banionis as Ladeinikov, and that the candidature of Vyacheslav Tikhonov was preferred. But Tikhonov did not even audition for *The Dead Season* (TsGALI-SPb., f. 257, op. 18, d. 1735, ll. 28–58, Second Creative Unit's discussion of the screen tests, 24 June 1968), and in any case, he would only have seemed a 'natural' choice to play a secret agent after the release of *Seventeen Moments of Spring* five years later. For his part, Banionis worked from 1970 as an agent for the Lithuanian KGB (see the list of live agents in the State Archive of Lithuania, 'Inventarnyi zhurnal No. 35 registratsii lichnykh del agentury' <http://www.kgbveikla.lt/uploads/kita/20180108_zurnalaso1.pdf> [accessed 2 October 2022], and LYA, f. K-18, ap. 1, b. 607, l. 4 <http://www.kgbveikla.lt/uploads/agentai/1601_1700/1665_banionis_bronius_02.pdf> [accessed 2 October 2022]), indicating that his association with the film was positively viewed by the security services.

92 For instance, Gleb Panfilov, TsGALI-SPb., f. 257, op. 18, d. 2015, l. 149.

story of Molodyi's years in England, and the adventures of 'Sir Lonsdale' twenty and more years later, lies a gulf of moral ambition as well as time.[93]

My gratitude to my fellow participants in a section on Russian tricksters at the ASEEES Congress, November 2019, Ilya Vinnitsky, Ekaterina Pravilova, and Ivan Fedyukin, and to the audience, for their comments on an earlier version of this text. I would also like to thank Joshua Sanborn, Joachim von Puttkamer and other participants in the Eastern Europe Today conference at the Imre Kertész Kolleg, University of Jena, June 2022.

[93] In Bortko's *Soul of a Spy*, the finale, in which Alex makes his way up a misty jetty to the bulk of the Russian mother ship, comes across as a clunky restoration of order rather than an ambiguous termination of a harrowing yet necessary mission.

CHAPTER 14

The Black-and-White Poppies of Russian Arthouse: Central Asian Directors at Lenfil'm

[2018]

If one were trying to sum up what 'Central Asian film' meant to the average Soviet viewer back in the Brezhnev era, Bolotbek Shamshiev's film *The Scarlet Poppies of Issyk-Kul*, released in 1972 by Kirgyzfil'm Studio, would be a tempting choice. Shot amid the striking and exotic scenery of the republic's premier tourist destination, the film was a so-called 'Eastern', or Western-style film set in Soviet Asia. The forces locked in Manichean conflict were not cowboys and Indians, but the supporters of the Bolshevik new order and the old guard of opium magnates. In the pre-credit sequence, the eponymous flowers dominated, creating an image at once lush, primitive, and with an exotic whiff of the forbidden. There were dashing horsemen, elderly men in traditional clothing, and, of course, veiled women.

FIG. 14.1. Image of a veiled woman, from Shamshiev's *The Scarlet Poppies of Issyk-Kul* (Kirgyzfilm Studio, 2971) <https://www.kino-teatr.ru/kino/movie/sov/197/foto/12/158665/>.

Films of this kind — tales of valour set in mountainous, rugged terrain, and portraying a mythical past lent legitimacy by its revolutionary associations — were typical of the output of Central Asian studios in the late Soviet period. As early as 1966, Goskino, the state bureaucracy that controlled the funding to studios across the USSR, and vetted their output, expressed polite impatience with the idea of yet another film on 'the institution of Soviet power in Bukhara'. It was to be hoped, Goskino's officials observed, that *The Arrow of Vengeance* (*Strela vozmediya*) turned out to be a major film, 'something new in the historical-revolutionary genre', since 'the film-makers of Central Asia, Tadzhikstan included, have turned to this theme on more than one occasion'.[1] But the mild disdain of cinema managers was no deterrent, and films of this kind continued rolling off the production line into the 1980s.[2] In turn, their colourful costumes and dramatic highland scenery shaped the perceptions among both Russians and Central Asians of the region itself. To this day, people from Central Asia living in Russian cities are likely to find that locals assume they come from 'the mountains', a perception that they may in turn self-ironise when talking about attitudes to migrants in Russian cities.[3]

In retrospective academic discussion, Central Asian movies tend to be lumped together with other types of 'Eastern' — for instance, those filmed in Siberia, southern Russia, or the Caucasus by Russian directors — or indeed the 'Red Westerns' popular right across the socialist bloc.[4] But there is an important difference. 'Red Westerns', such as those of the DDR, turned 'Red Indians' (Native

1   Letter from central Goskino to the chairman of Goskino in the Tadzhik SSR, 11 February 1966, RGALI, f. 2944, op. 5, d. 143, l. 26. Cf. ibid., ll. 34–35, rebuking Goskino in the Uzbek SSR for including two 'institution of Soviet power films' in the five planned for 1966.
2   For instance, Ali Khamraev and Akmal' Akbarkhodzhaev, *Red Sands* (*Krasnye peski*, Uzbekfil'm, 1968), Subkhat Khadimov, *Meeting at the Old Mosque* (*Vstrecha u staroi mecheti*, Tadzhikfil'm, 1969), Shaken Aitmatov, *Death of an Ataman* (*Konets atamana*, Kazakhfil'm, 1970), Ali Khamraev, *The Seventh Bullet* (*Sed'maya pulya*, Uzbekfil'm, 1972), Subkhat Khamidov, *The Mystery of the Forgotten Crossing* (*Taina zabytoi perepravy*, Tadzhikfil'm, 1974), Ali Khamraev, *The Bodyguard* (*Telokhranitel'*, Tadzhikfil'm, 1979), Yunus Yuzupchik, *The Hostage* (*Zalozhnik*, Tadzhikfil'm, 1983), and Mukhtar Aga-Mirzaev, *Never Shoot in Hot Blood* (*Strelyat' sgoryacha ne stoit*, Uzbekfil'm, 1983).
3   'INTERVIEWER: So can you tell me a bit about yourself, where you… INFORMANT: In the mountains (laughs ironically). INT: where you grew up. INF: In the mountains. INT: So whereabouts exactly? INF: (ironically) Aaaah, once the vodka ran out, in the mountains, and they packed me off into town for the vodka [laughs]' (interview by Irina Nazarova, 2008, Oxf/AHRC SPb-08 PF52 IN, p. 2; the informant actually hailed from Samarkand). For stereotyping by Russians, see for example, the following comment (7 November 2007) from a discussion of racism on 'Neva Forum', a St Petersburg online group: 'One of my friends won't ride in minibus taxis any more after this driver (and they're all immigrants from the mountains) asked her when she last had her period. How much do you not have to respect girls to do something like that?!… It's just so unpleasant…' (Neva Forum rasizm <http://nevaforum.ru/index.php?showtopic=2822&st=0> [accessed 20 April 2022]). Another reason for stereotyping, as here, is that Russians often confuse 'people of Caucasian nationality' and Central Asians, but the popular films have certainly added to this confusion, if not necessarily created it to start with.
4   An exception is Alexander Morrison, 'Settler Bolsheviks in the Soviet "Eastern"', in *Cinematic Settlers: The Settler Colonial World in Film*, ed. by J. Lahti and R. Weaver-Hightower (Abingdon: Routledge, 2020), pp. 88–103. See also the introductory remarks in Kirill Nourzhanov, 'Bandits, Warlords, National Heroes: Interpretations of the Basmachi Movement in Tajikistan', *Central Asian Survey*, 34.2 (2015), 177–78.

Americans) rather than 'Cowboys' into heroes. However, where 'natives' were concerned, they also reproduced the 'othering' and exoticisation characteristic of the Hollywood parent genre.[5] They did this without the participation of Native Americans, even as actors, let alone as scriptwriters or directors. The intriguing, or uncomfortable, point about Central Asian 'Easterns', on the other hand, is that locals — for example, film directors such as Shamshiev, Shaken Aimanov, and Sukhbat Khamidov, and administrators of film studios, not to speak of the officers of Goskino in the republics — acted as the moving forces behind their production. Large numbers of the actors were also Central Asians, or at the very least, people of (in Soviet and post-Soviet parlance) 'Asiatic appearance', such as Tatars: there was no 'blacking up'. What we have here is not just a case of stereotyping, but of auto-stereotyping. To use a more specific term, this was self-orientalisation, or the representation of non-Western culture according to conventions internalised from Western practice, as in the case of the Western-trained Ottoman artist, Osman Hamdi Bey, whose lush paintings of harem scenes confirmed extant Western beliefs about the culture of the Near East, but also seemed 'authentic' because of his origins in the culture that he portrayed.[6] Films such as *The Scarlet Poppies of Isyk-Kul* exercised comparable double claims to authority, showing audiences what they expected of 'the East', but providing the reassurance that this was not simply how outsiders saw the culture.

'Easterns' were thus not aimed purely or even mainly at outsiders; they were popular among Central Asian audiences. And their representational canons had elements of ambiguity. While 'Easterns' always represented Bolshevism as liberationist and morally superior, and traditional culture as corrupt and repressive, they also gave substantial space to the 'traditional culture' that was starting to be celebrated in the post-Stalin era as a positive force, provided it was recreated in sanitised form, purged of oppressive elements such as the subjugation of women.[7] In this perspective, a veiled woman represented both what Soviet Uzbek, Tadzhik, Kazakh, Turkmen, or Kirghiz identity defined itself by rejecting, and the type of nostalgic reconstruction that was proper to that identity in its latest incarnation.

5   See the extensive scholarly discussion of these films, for example Gerd Gemünden, 'Between Karl May and Karl Marx: The DEFA Indianerfilme (1965–1983)', *New German Critique*, 82 (2001), 25–38; Jon Raundalen, 'A Communist Takeover in the Dream Factory: Appropriation of Popular Genres by the East German Film Industry', *Slavonica*, 11.1 (2005), 69–86.
6   As Edhem Eldem has put it, Osman Hamdi Bey's Orientalist works 'are aesthetic constructions designed to attract the attention of a Western public by intelligently combining clichés with the privilege of being an "insider within the outside"' ('Making Sense of Osman Hamdi Bey and His Paintings', *Muqarnas*, 29.1 (2012), 339–83 (p. 374)). Eldem also emphasises the artist's enjoyment of dressing up in 'Oriental' clothing, in which he also appears in published photographs.
7   On the ambiguities with which 'traditional' culture was perceived, see, for example, Sergei Alymov, 'Na puti k "drevnei istorii narodov SSSR": maloizvestnye stranitsy nauchnoi biografii S. P. Tolstova', *Etnograficheskoe obozrenie*, 5 (2007), 125–44; Catriona Kelly, '"The Traditions of Our History": "Tradition" as Framework for National Identity in Post-Stalinist and Post-Soviet Russia', in *Loyalties, Solidarities, and Identities in Russian Culture*, ed. by Philip Ross Bullock and others (London : School of Slavonic and East European Studies, UCL, 2013), pp. 141–60. On the overall shift to instrumentalisation of nationality in the USSR's last years, see Ronald Suny, *The Revenge of the Past: Nationalism, Revolution, and the Collapse of the Soviet Union* (Stanford, CA: Stanford University Press, 1993).

(The veils shown were usually of the kind covering just the hair, rather than all or part of the face, so that they could seem a decorative element of costume rather than the sartorial equivalent of shackles.)[8] As Alexander Morrison has observed, *Scarlet Poppies* can be interpreted as 'a film infused with Kyrgyz ethnic sensibilities, which in many ways subverts the colonial text on which it is based'; moreover, these films, for the politicians in the republics who sponsored them, represented 'a small but important facet of the Soviet nation-building project'.[9]

My aim here is not a detailed analysis of the history and resonance of the 'Eastern' genre as practised in Central Asia, worthwhile though such an aim would be. Rather, I plan to trace, against this background of stereotypical perceptions and 'othering', the careers of three Central Asian directors who spent their lives, from student years onwards, resident in the Russian territories of the Soviet Union. These are Iskander Abdurakhmanovich Khamraev (1934–2009), an Uzbek from Tashkent, Dinara Kuldashovna Asanova (1942–1984), a Kirgiz from Frunze (now Dushanbe), and Roza Aizhanovna Orynbasarova (b. 1957), a Kazakh from Kentau.

All three directors trained at Moscow's All-Soviet State Institute of Cinema (VGIK), the Soviet Union's premier film school, and went on to work at Lenfil'm, the USSR's second-biggest studio after Mosfil'm. Officially, Lenfil'm was second only to Mosfil'm in terms of prestige (indeed, some would have argued that it was in first place relative to its artistic merits). Khamraev, Asanova, and Orynbasarova were the only Central Asian directors at the studio at any point of its history, and the latter two were doubly unusual figures in an industry where the vast majority of directors were men.[10] All of them shared the experience of moving to a hegemonic city, 'capital' (*stolitsa*), from a region that was considered marginal, part of the 'periphery' (*periferiya*).[11] In Leningrad, attitudes to this 'periphery' were

---

8   Eldem, 'Making Sense of Osman Hamdi Bey', p. 348, likewise emphasises the importance of ethnographical detail and visual pleasure: 'The assumption that every, or most of, Osman Hamdi Bey's paintings had some sort of message for the viewer makes us overlook the possibility that he might have been first and foremost a genre painter, whose main aim was to recreate plausible and aesthetically pleasant scenes, sometimes to the point of practicing collage-like variations by transferring characters or objects from one painting to another'.
9   Morrison, 'Settler Bolsheviks in the Soviet "Eastern"', pp. 99–100. For other discussions of Central Asian film in the late Soviet era, see *Cinema in Central Asia: Rewriting Cultural Histories*, ed. by Michael Rouland, Gulnara Abikeyeva and Birgit Beumers (London: I. B. Tauris, 2013), Part 1; Rico Isaacs, *Film and Identity in Kazakhstan: Soviet and Post-Soviet Identity in Central Asia* (London: I. B. Tauris, 2018), Chapters 2–3.
10   The LF studio re-organisation of 1961 left just one woman film director (*rezhisser-postanovshchik*) in place, as opposed to assistant directors and various other kinds of amanuenses: Nadezhda Kosheverova (1902–1989), a specialist in fairy-tale subjects and other material for a juvenile audience. It took nearly fifteen years before Dinara Asanova joined her. The third woman director of prominence in the 1970s, Kira Muratova, was a temporary 'blow-in' from the Odessa Film Studios and disappeared after making one film. The Ukrainian director Natalia Troshchenko, who began working at Lenfil'm in 1956, was mainly active as a second director [first AD] till the 1970s, and later mainly as a co-director.
11   The word *stolitsa* derives from *prestol* [throne] and is the term used for the national capital (in the Soviet case, Moscow). However, it can also be used regionally (thus, Sverdlovsk/Ekaterinburg has the honorific title, *stolitsa Urala*, 'capital of the Urals'), and in the post-Stalin era it was increasingly common for Leningrad to be described as the country's *kul'turnaya stolitsa*, 'capital of culture', or the country's 'northern capital', etc. As for *periferiya*, this term was first applied in the early Soviet period

particularly condescending, as one of Isaiah Berlin's informants (probably the poet Anna Akhmatova) told him when he visited the city as a young diplomat in 1946:

> The [official] 'line' at present was to devote attention to the lesser-known parts of the Soviet Union, such as Siberia or Tadzhikstan [...] a mass of pseudo-archaic lyrics and bogus ballads and epics and official poetry generally [...] were driving out whatever originality there was among these primitive or semi-medieval peoples. They asserted with much pride that the Leningrad literary papers were commendably free from this incubus, which cluttered up the pages of the Moscow literary weekly, although they made an exception in favour of Georgian and Armenian literature, which contained works of true genius. For their own part they are not ashamed of the tradition of Pushkin and Blok, Baudelaire and Verhaeren, and would not exchange them for all the poetical treasures of Uzbekistan or Azerbaijan, whatever might be the fashion 'in Moscow'; and more on the same lines.[12]

This type of prejudice persisted in later decades also. In 1963, a joint discussion of the Leningrad Section of the Union of Architects and the Lenproekt Institute of City Planning attributed the slow progress that was being made in the production of modern, stylish wallpaper designs to the fact that most of what was made ended up going to 'the periphery'. In the words of one of the architects involved, the most popular designs were 'Chinese Vase' and 'Tobacco Leaves', and other abominations, too, had to be confected with this audience in mind: 'The trading organisations base themselves on the demands from the periphery, and what is supposedly needed there, in line with national [i.e. ethnic] tastes, is wallpaper imitating carpets, tapestries, and so on, with low-quality designs'.[13]

Against this background, creative artists who moved to the metropolis were likely to experience not just the 'spatial dislocation' plus 'continuity of aspiration' that Jeff Sahadeo noted in his oral history of Central Asians in Moscow and Leningrad at this period, but also an acute version of the 'fear of being singled out as naïve or uncouth incomers' to which he also drew attention.[14] One result was a high degree of assimilation to the surrounding Russian culture. The only director in whose work Central Asian motifs were explicitly present was Khamraev. This came at a quite specific point of his career, and, as I shall show, for reasons that made the invocation of Central Asian connections a prudent defensive move. In the cases of Asanova and Orynbasarova, we have instances of at most displaced and oblique

---

as a preferable alternative to *provintsiya*, or 'province', which was held to be condescending. However, it rapidly itself acquired denigratory overtones, as the passage quoted below indicates. The fact that Central Asia was considered part of the *periferiya* trumped the fact that Tashkent and Dushanbe were capital cities of Soviet republics.

12   Isaiah Berlin. *Flourishing: Letters 1928–1946*, ed. by Henry Hardy (London: Pimlico, 2005), pp. 608–09. Presumably by 'the Moscow literary weekly' he meant the *Literaturnaia gazeta*.
13   'Stenograficheskii otchet Leningradskogo Otdela Soyuza Arkhitektorov SSSR. Zasedane Arkhitekturno-tekhnicheskogo soveta sovmestno s Pravleniem LO Soyuza Arkhitektorov SSSR', 8 February 1963. TsGANTD [Tsentral'nyi gosudarstvennyi arkhiv nauchno-tekhnicheskoi dokumentatsii], f. 386, op. 1–6, d. 196, l. 6, l. 9.
14   Jeff Sahadeo, 'Soviet "Blacks" and Place Making in Leningrad and Moscow', *Slavic Review*, 71.2 (2012), 331–58 (pp. 333, 340).

invocation of Central Asian experience in what was primarily self-presentation as a Russian intellectual.

This situation was fundamentally different to the contemporary case of Chingiz Aitmatov (1928–2008), a Central Asian writer who was able to invoke regional subjects (as in *Farewell, Gulsary*, 1966) without risk to his status as a major writer. (One could compare the Abhazian writer Fazil Iskander or the Chuvash poet Gennady Aigi.) What explained the distinction were perceptions among filmmakers that the region's cinema was an unsophisticated product of the periphery. By and large, 'Easterns' set in Central Asia were a speciality of film studios based in the region. (A rule-proving exception was Vladimir Motyl's *White Sun of the Desert* (Experimental Film Studio, 1970), co-produced by Mosfil'm and Lenfil'm, which was distinct from Uzbekfil'm or Tadzhikfil'm products because of a markedly ironic or parodic, even grotesque, edge, and also because Russian actors playing Russians occupied the centre of the action.)

The view that 'Easterns' were a crude form of cinematic production that was distant from true 'cine-art' seems to have been particularly prevalent at Lenfil'm, a studio characterised by disdain for crowd-pleasing blockbusters. As the studio's general director, Ilya Kiselev, lamented in 1968, 'Our movies have the stamp of gloom on them, the stamp of damnation and despair, and viewers make their feelings pretty clear'. There was a snobbish attitude to more upbeat topics, he moaned, and yet the Civil War comedy-operetta *Wedding at Malinovka* had attracted over a million viewers just in Khar'kov during the year of its release.[15] *Wedding at Malinovka* was very like an 'Eastern', with beautiful bosomy young women in embroidered dresses and stern bearded Bolsheviks on curvetting stallions. Studio discussion at Lenfil'm did not presume to notice Central Asian Civil War movies, but it is fair to assume response to them would have been just as chilly.

This 'snobbery', as Kiselev called it, was a persistent part of Lenfil'm's corporate identity, and so was the penchant for aesthetically challenging films that avoided soothing visual cliché. Audiences themselves were sensitive to this too, and of course, still more, incoming directors. Contrary to the customary academic discussion of cinema, which tends to focus on famous auteurs, audience perception of film was driven less by loyalty to particular directors (people were often only dimly aware of who had made which film) than by subject-matter, genre, actors, and, indeed, the studio responsible for the production. All of these were heightened in newspaper and street advertising for the latest releases. The audience appeal of actors was clear also from the popular film magazine, *Soviet Screen*, which almost always carried a photographic portrait, often of a pretty starlet, on its rear cover.

The draw of film personalities has, not surprisingly, begun to attract attention from historians over the last decade or so. Late Soviet genre film (the 'Eastern', however, not included) has been the subject of a substantial study by Alexander Prokhorov and Elena Prokhorova.[16] But what Soviet parlance termed the

---

15 TsGAIPD-SPb., f. 1369, op. 5, d. 89, l. 7.
16 On film personalities, see Kristin Roth-Ey, *Moscow Prime Time: How the Soviet Union Built the Media Empire that Lost the Cold War* (Ithaca, NY: Cornell University Press, 2011), and Christine Evans,

'handwriting' (*pocherk*) of studios, or more broadly, their 'brand' (*marka*), has figured little.[17] Yet one effect of the boosting of the regions under Khrushchev and Brezhnev was to give film studios a greater degree of diversity than they had under the Moscow-centred homogenisation of the Stalin era. And alongside their familiarity with famous actors, late Soviet audiences also recognised a studio's marque and its associations — indeed, were more likely to have views on this than on the characteristics of particular film directors.

I remember myself being told by a friend, as we decided whether or not to watch what turned out to be an entertaining if vacuous picture about an overworked mother of ten children, 'You know what they say: there are good films. There are mediocre films. There are bad films. And then there's Dovzhenko...' (referring to the studio housed in Kiev).[18] In 2015, as I presented a paper at a film seminar in University College London, I was told by a self-nominated informant that when he, as a young teenager in the 1970s, helped unload film canisters for the club in his small Central Asian village, 'if I saw "Lenfil'm" written on those canisters, I just decided I wouldn't bother turning up for the movie. Now Mosfil'm, Kazakhfil'm — that would be something exciting'.

Soviet film sociology of the 1970s — then being rapidly developed in pursuit of the drive to make the industry more attractive to audiences, and thus give a better return for state investment — confirms this picture of specific public expectations attached to particular studios. Indeed, a 1976 Leningrad study established that ordinary viewers, film-makers, and officials responsible for film distribution all had slightly different rankings. Ordinary members of the public (this from a socially diverse sample in Leningrad) put France, Mosfil'm, and the USA (in that order) at the top, with Lenfil'm fifth (above England [*sic*] but below Italy). The next highest-ranking Soviet studio, Dovzhenko, stood more than forty points below Lenfil'm (17.7 per cent of respondents ranked it as 'good' versus 61 per cent for Lenfil'm). Much further down the scale were the film studios of the Caucasus (3.3 per cent ranked them as 'good', 18.3 per cent as 'middling', and 46 per cent as 'bad'). Right at the bottom was Central Asia, with 2.2 per cent 'good', 13.6 per cent 'middling', and 54.7 per cent 'bad'. Among professional film-makers, on the other hand, Italy, the USA, and France (in that order) all outranked Mosfil'm, while Lenfil'm and most of the Soviet studios, including 'Kazakhstan and Central Asia', came at the bottom of the table. Among distributors, the list ran from France, USA, and Italy at the top, Mosfil'm just below, and Dovzhenko and Moldovafil'm at the bottom (with Central

---

Between 'Truth' and 'Time': A History of Soviet Central Television (New Haven, CT: Yale University Press, 2016). Alexander Prokhorov and Elena Prokhorova, *Film and Television Genres of the Late Soviet Era* (London: Routledge, 2016).

17 For studies of 'handwriting', see, for example, Jamie Miller, 'Soviet Politics and the Mezhrabpom Studio in the Soviet Union during the 1920s and 1930s', *Historical Journal of Film, Radio and Television*, 32.4 (2012), 521–35, DOI: 10.1080/01439685.2012.727340; Alexander Graham, 'Aesthetic Innovation and the Politics of Film Production at Lenfil'm, 1968–1991' (unpublished Ph.D Thesis, University of London, 2020), as well as my *Soviet Art House*. Aleksei Fedorchenko's documentary film, *Cinema of the Era of Change* (2019) is an affectionate portrait of Sverdlovsk Film Studio in its last two decades of existence.

18 Voronezh, 1981.

Asia doing a little better than these last, just below Lenfil'm).[19]

The extent to which these figures reflected actual popularity is open to dispute. As V. P. Ostashevskaya, former head of the studio Informburo, reported to Lenfil'm's Party organisation of creative workers in 1977, even information about number of copies of a given film in circulation was hard to obtain, since a title would be printed in several different factories, so that only the State Film Distribution Board (Goskinoprokat) knew the overall total, 'and they don't give out that figure'. In any case, it was common for numerous copies to lie around unused.[20] Figures for ticket sales were not necessarily more revealing, since there was no way of disaggregating repeat visits by the same person. However, there was at the very least an increasing concern, as economies of scale became more important, and Soviet cultural managers specifically promoted the genre of *kassovyi fil'm* (box-office hit or blockbuster), that viewing statistics should offer useful information. Older types of market research, such as *Soviet Screen's* surveys of reader favourites, were no longer given much credence. And according to the new viewer sociology, even the most widely-watched Central Asian films — say, *Death of an Ataman* with 30 million viewers — ranked significantly below such pan-Soviet hits as Mosfil'm's *Shield and Sword* (*Shchit i mech*, Vladimir Basov, 1969), with 227 million viewers, Bollywood's *Sangam* (Raj Kapoor, 1964), with 115 million, or indeed *Anna Karenina* (Aleksandr Zarkhi, Mosfil'm, 81 million).[21] The status of studios could go up or down in critical esteem depending on a particular season: in 1970 or 1977, Lenfil'm would likely have been higher up the list, because particular films released in the previous two years had a significant impact.[22] However, Central Asian studios seem consistently to have trailed in the rankings.[23]

I don't at all intend to belittle the impact of Central Asian cinema in its place of origin, the recognised quality of some films made by its studios (such as Tolomush Okeev's *The Wild One* (*Lyutyi*), 1983), or the strength of, say, Kazakh film since 1991.[24] Rather, I mean to suggest that the reach of Central Asian cinema into the

---

19 *Otchet o nauchno-issledovatel'skoi rabote po teme "kino i zritel'"* (Leningrad: NII kompleksnykh sotsiologicheskikh issledovanii pri LGU im. A. A. Zhdanova. Laboratoriya sotsiologicheskikh issledovanii, 1976). The publication is marked 'For internal use only' ('dlya sluzhebnogo pol'zovaniya').
20 TsGAIPD-SPb., f. 1369, op. 5, d. 191, l. 57.
21 Ibid., ll. 59–60.
22 For instance, Ilya Averbakh's *Degree of Risk* (*Stepen' riska*) and Savva Kulish's *The Dead Season* (*Mertvyi sezon*) in 1968, and Sergei Mikaelyan's *The Bonus* (*Premiya*, 1975) which was awarded a State Prize in 1976.
23 When in Voronezh as a student, I remember seeing Georgian, Ukrainian, and Moldavian films, as well as Russian-made ones, including both art films and popular hits such as Emil Loteanu's *Gypsies are Found Near Heaven* (*Tabor ukhodit v nebo*, Mosfil'm, 1976) or Samvel Gasparov's *Bread, Gold, and Revolvers* (*Khleb, zoloto i nagan*, Gorky Studio, 1980), not to speak of Indian films, but I do not remember a single Central Asian title in either category.
24 Among more senior directors who have made a name is Rustam Khamdamov (see above). Younger directors with a high reputation include Yusup Razykov, Gul'shad Omarova, Zhanna Issabayeva, Sergey Dvortsevoy, Djakhongir Kasimov, and many others. See the special issue of *Studies in Russian and Soviet Cinema*, 4 (2010), 187–240; Rouland, Abikeyeva and Beumers, *Cinema in Central Asia*, Part 3; Isaacs, *Film and Identity in Kazakhstan*, Chapters 3–7.

Russian-speaking parts of the USSR during the late Soviet period was limited. Notable from the point of view of film-making professionals was that Central Asian films lacked the artistic aura of, say, Georgian ones (which were 'very unpopular' with the ordinary Russian viewer, but the subject of adulation among film professionals and some members of the intelligentsia).[25] They did not even have the cachet of art films from the Baltic states.[26] Though Central Asia had been the wartime home of Mosfil'm and Lenfil'm after these were evacuated in 1941 from the beleaguered capitals, laying the foundation of post-war cinema in the region, the interchange was more or less a one-way street. So far as I know, not one Central Asian director made a career in either of the two capitals in the Stalin years (unlike Georgian Mikeil Chiaureli at Mosfil'm, the winner of five Stalin prizes). Indeed, in the post-Stalin years, Mosfil'm at least continued to be more or less a closed shop for 'Asiatic' directors, as opposed to Georgians (Georgy Danelia, Eldar Shengelaia, Mikhail Kalatozov), Moldavian Emil Loteanu, and so on.[27]

The situation at Lenfil'm, however, was different, certainly after 1961, when the studio underwent a major restructuring accompanied by a drive to recruit and promote young directors and film-makers. The effort to get rid of 'ballast' and encourage new talent led to the employment of a significant cohort of directors who did not have a standard Russian ethnic profile, including not just Georgian Rezo Esadze, but Yuly Fait (of ethnic German descent), Sergei Mikaelyan (Armenian), Augustas Baltrušaitis (Lithuanian), alongside the Russian Jews who had always had a significant presence at the studio (including Grigory Kozintsev, Joseph Heifitz, Vladimir Vengerov, and in the younger generation, Naum Birman and Solomon Shuster), and Siberians such as Viktor Tregubovich and Vitaly Mel'nikov.[28] It was probably harder to get a job at Lenfil'm if you were from some unromantic part of

---

25 For the unpopularity of Georgian films with mainstream audiences, see TsGAIPD-SPb, f. 1369, op. 5, d. 249, l. 36 (Lenfil'm creative workers' Party organisation meeting, 1981); for references to their popularity with professionals, see ibid. ('as we all understand, they are on a high level in terms of their artistry'). Ramaz Sharabidze's 1977 film *The Return* (*dabreneba;Vozvrashchenie*) had barely reached 1.5 million viewers, not much over a tenth of Lenfil'm's average figures at the time (ibid., ll. 36, 33).
26 For example, Vytautas Žalakevičius' 1965 war film, *No-one Wanted to Die* (*Niekas nenorėjo mirti*; *Nikto ne khotel umirat'*) was awarded a State Prize in 1965. Baltic actors were highly favoured in the Russian metropolis also, with Donatas Banionis starring in many famous art films, from Grigory Kozintsev's *King Lear* (*Korol' Lir*, 1971) to Andrei Tarkovsky's *Solaris* (*Solyaris*, 1972) (in both cases, the dialogue was dubbed as he was felt to have a 'foreign accent').
27 The rule-proving exception was Rustam Khamdamov (b. 1944, Tashkent); however, the only films that he was able to direct, *In the Mountains Is My Heart* (*V gorakh moe serdtse*, 1967) and *Unexpected Joys* (*Nechayannye radosti*, 1974) ended up suppressed. Khamdamov mainly worked as a costume designer thereafter, and returned to directing only in the 1990s. Ali Khamraev, also from Uzbekistan, who achieved international recognition for some of his films and has lived in Italy during recent decades, made just one movie at Mosfil'm, *The Garden of Desires* (*Sad zhelanii*), and even that only after the complete restructuring of the studio following the Fifth Congress of the Union of Soviet Film-Makers in 1986 (see <). The film racked up only 800,000 viewers (ibid.), putting an end to Khamraev's chances in a new commercial world.
28 Cf. one of Jeff Sahadeo's informants: 'In a unique position as an Uzbek figure skater, Shuhrat Kazbekov reported that "people loved me"; good relations with Russians continued during his career as a stuntman at Leningrad Film Studios' ('Soviet "Blacks"', pp. 353–54).

the Russian provinces than it was if you happened to be from a national minority.

Yet prejudices against Central Asia persisted. Lenfil'm's flamboyant general director, Ilya Kiselev, himself reportedly of Roma origin, and, according to his official biography, born and brought up in southern Ukraine, ruminated during a 1962 discussion of directors who were supposedly surplus to requirements that two of them, Nikolai Rozantsev and Adol'f Bergunker, could maybe be sent off to Kirgizfil'm for a while (as an alternative to a future of working as assistant directors or toiling in the film-dubbing or restoration departments).[29] This view that Central Asia was for 'deadbeats' helps explain why, in the post-1961 period, just three incomers from the region managed to make a career as lead director (*rezhisser-postanovshchik*), and that at the price of more or less complete Russification not just in terms of language use, but also of artistic choices.

The first of the three to arrive at Lenfil'm, Iskander Khamraev, was an immediate beneficiary of the expansion of studio staffs in the Khrushchev era. After studying language and literature (*filologiya*) at Tashkent University, he had moved to VGIK in 1954, and had arrived at Lenfil'm immediately after graduating. His first film, *The Old-Timer* (*Starozhil*), about two boys living in the Soviet new town of Volzhsky, one of whom has to recover from a seriously swelled head after a street is named in his honour, was completed in 1961. The orthodox nature of Khamraev's choice of script presaged a future as director with a penchant for work in politically reliable ('ideologically sound', *ideologicheski vyderzhannye*) genres, for instance, the war film *Hospital Train* (*Poezd miloserdiya*, 1964), the production movie *An Ordinary Month* (*Obychnyi mesyats*, 1976), and the post-war kolkhoz drama *Salt of the Earth* (*Sol' zemli*, 1978). Later photographs show him as dapper and self-confident, parading the expensive wardrobe of an elite Soviet (and post-Soviet) official artist.[30]

But if he followed his mentor, Friedrich Ermler, in this mixture of political orthodoxy and worldliness, Khamraev also employed a diluted version of Ermler's adventurous visual style, using overhead and tracking shots, and playing off different actors' physiques one against another. This was already evident in *The Old-Timer*, supervised by Ermler, which attracted enough approval in Lenfil'm to allow Khamraev the post of staff director in the Third Creative Unit.[31] The assignation to him of *The Hospital Train* was also a mark of favour, since Vera Panova, the scriptwriter (the story was taken from her 1946 novel *The Travelling Companions*, *Sputniki*), was Lenfil'm's biggest star at the time, and was insistent that her work was filmed either by 'old masters' or 'young talents'. In 1963, the studio's Party organisation approvingly recorded that, while some youngsters were turning in half-baked shooting scripts, Khamraev was one of a number who had reached

29 TsGAIPD-SPb., f. 1369, op. 5, d. 44, ll. 159–67.
30 See, for example, <https://www.ruspeach.com/news/14343/> [accessed 20 April 2022].
31 At a meeting of the Party Committee on 17 October 1961, held immediately after the creative units were set up upon an order from the Ministry of Culture, it was decided that Khamraev would be assigned to a unit 'if his next picture turns out well'. Evidently, it was considered that it had. TsGAIPD-SPb., f. 1369, op. 5, d. 35, l. 132. 'Creative units' were mini-studios within Lenfil'm that oversaw production at the initial stages, clearing the film before it was signed off by the studio-wide artistic council.

a good standard.³² Despite problems with casting, and conflicts on set, the film successfully reached completion in 1964, and avoided the rumpus with the cinema regulatory bodies provoked by some other work in the Third Unit, particularly Viktor Sokolov's generation-conflict drama, *When the Bridges Go Up*.³³ Neatly constructed, effectively introducing a cast of varied characters, and retaining a sense of martial sweep despite (or because of) the confined space in which it was filmed (mostly inside a train, or rather, the mock-up of one in the studio) and the limited time-lapse (just under ninety minutes), *The Hospital Train* was, all in all, a success.

With *The Hospital Train*, Khamraev successfully assimilated to the 'quality film' standards of Lenfil'm, and should have had an easy path to his next project. In fact, five years of what was known as 'creative shutdown' (*tvorcheskii prostoi*) followed. Nothing in the making of *The Hospital Train* presaged this gap in commissions. Certainly, the Party Committee had grumbled about footage filmed over and above what was agreed in the shooting script, but this was a frequent issue with young directors and seems to have been put down to inexperience.³⁴ On 9 February 1965, Khamraev figured on a list of promising youngsters presented to a Party meeting.³⁵

The trouble began just one day later, when Khamraev's application for candidate membership came up before the Bureau of the Creative Workers' Communist Party organisation. As one of very few younger directors, and film-makers generally, who was prepared even to consider membership, he could have expected that acceptance would be a formality, and the Bureau would duly pass his application to the studio's Party Committee, and thence to the District Committee. But the announcement of his candidature posted in the studio on 22 January 1965 had stirred up a full-scale scandal. M. E. Gil'bo, a Party member, had come forward with an accusation of 'immoral behaviour', and on 10 February, the Bureau of the Creative Workers' Party organisation reviewed in detail the substance of the case.³⁶

Allegedly, Khamraev had coerced a drama student of about twenty who was up for a part in *The Hospital Train*, to visit him at home for 'a rehearsal', despite her repeated attempts to suggest that she did not think this was a good idea.³⁷ After she arrived, it was reported, Khamraev had plied her with alcohol before turning out the lights and starting to sexually harass her (*pristavat'*). When she begged him to leave her alone, since she was sexually inexperienced, he punched her in the

---

32   TsGAIPD-SPb., f. 1369, op. 5, d. 60, l. 63.
33   On the casting problems, see 'Prosmotr materiala i obsuzhdenie sostoyaniya raboty na kartine "Poezd miloserdiya"', 26 March 1964, TsGAIPD-SPb., f. 1369, op. 5, d. 64, ll. 42–50. One issue was the trouble in finding anyone to play Lena, the young rural ingénue (the director eventually settled on one of the most noteworthy actresses of the day, young Ukrainian Zhanna Prokhorenko), and another the behaviour of the male lead, Valentin Zubkov, talented, photogenic, and with a good screen presence, but with the widespread fault of a fondness for the vodka bottle. On the conflicts on set, see TsGAIPD-SPb., f. 1369, op. 5, d. 72, l. 131.
34   TsGAIPD-SPb., f. 1369, op. 5, d. 64, l. 49. It was noted that Khamraev should 'take heed of the criticism and advice offered' by the Party Committee.
35   TsGAIPD-SPb., f. 1369, op. 5, d. 69, l. 9.
36   Here and below, references to TsGAIPD-SPb., f. 1369, op. 5, d. 72, ll. 109–11.
37   The victim's full name is given in the source, but as she is still alive and active in the film world, I have edited it out here.

mouth, and she tried to run from the room only to find the door locked. After she threatened to scream, Khamraev let her out and she took refuge in the bathroom, only to have him burst in waving a knife. He eventually let her go, giving her five roubles for a taxi. Since she could not go back to her lodgings (where she was sharing a room with several others), his victim went to her teacher at drama school and immediately reported the incident to him. However, it was not this teacher who had raised the alarm, but the husband of a friend of the victim, a naval captain, who had first threatened Khamraev and then, when this had no effect, reported the incident to Gil'bo.[38]

On top of these charges, the Bureau's review of the case had noted that this was the third such accusation to be made against Khamraev. In 1961, a complaint about harassment of a teenage girl appearing in *The Old-Timer* had been sent to the Party Committee, and in 1964, an actress playing one of the nurses in *The Hospital Train* had allegedly been attacked in a hotel in Novgorod and rescued by a stranger in the hotel who had heard her screaming.

When the Bureau confronted Khamraev with the new accusations, he denied all knowledge of the incident, insisting he had never had any meetings with the actress, or seen her at his home. But at the same time, he retracted his application to join the Party. This was seen in the Bureau as an oblique admission of guilt: 'I don't think that is an acceptable position, whether for a Party member or for someone who is not. If Khamraev thinks he is innocent, he should rehabilitate himself', observed Irina Tarsanova, a well-respected senior editor at Lenfil'm. Camera operator Moisei Magid called it 'an attempt to wriggle out of the situation'. This expressed the mood of the meeting, and the Bureau withdrew its recommendation of Khamraev's candidacy and referred 'the facts at our disposal relating to various immoral acts on the part of film director Khamraev' to the general director of Lenfil'm.[39]

Whether or not the accusations against Khamraev were accurate is impossible to establish at this distance. The point is that they were taken at the time to be well-founded. By all accounts, sexual harassment was far from unknown at Lenfil'm.[40] So far as I can tell, however, this was the only case that reached full discussion in the Party administration throughout the entire post-Stalin period.[41] Perhaps it was

---

38 I have not been able to track down information about Gil'bo, but I assume that she worked in the studio administration.
39 TsGAIPD-SPb., f. 1369, op. 5, d. 72, l. 111.
40 There are comparable alleged cases from other film studios also. For instance, in *Cinema of the Era of Change*, Aleksei Fedorchenko recalled that when he was auditioning, aged about twelve, for the part of the young Mikhail Lomonsov in Yaroslav Lapshin's *The Smoke of the Fatherland* (*Dym otechestva*, 1980), a Sverdlovsk Studio biopic of the famous eighteenth-century writer and scientist, Lapshin called him over, alone, to his apartment for a casting session and asked Fedorchenko to remove his trousers, on the grounds that there would be a scene in the film where Lomonosov was subjected to a flogging. Fedorchenko refused and quickly left. He did not get the part.
41 I have to date read most of the run of Party Committee materials between 1961 and 1985, and have not come across a comparable case. Admittedly, some sensitive personal material is inaccessible (it is closed off when the files are issued), but references in passing from elsewhere in the files make it clear that much of the prohibited material relates to financial transgressions (and occasional examples to the fall-out from divorce cases).

the youth and inexperience of Khamraev's alleged targets that was the problem, or the violence involved, or the number of accusations, or all three factors at the same time. But it is also possible that Khamraev's status as a Central Asian and the perception that sexual and other abuse of women was rife in this particular periphery had something to do with the readiness to believe the accusations raised against the director. At any rate, the accusation stood, and Khamraev's association with Lenfil'm was now at serious risk.

Yet Khamraev was not in fact dismissed from Lenfil'm, which raises questions about how he managed to survive. One answer lay in problems that beset several of the other young directors in the Third Creative Unit at much the same time, and collectively precipitated a staffing crisis. In particular, Yuly Fait's film based on another script by Vera Panova, *A Boy and a Girl*, ran into significant problems in 1965 because of the perception that it was indecent. It was formally banned in the autumn of 1966, immediately before its Moscow premiere. A public indictment on grounds of immorality was considerably more embarrassing to Lenfil'm's management than a private accusation of attempted rape. Fait's film inspired letters from outraged generals claiming that their favourite holiday resort on the Black Sea had been besmirched, not to speak of reprisals against Lenfil'm from the Party hierarchy; Khamraev's case remained a murky affair of manageable proportions.

But another factor in Khamraev's survival was that he was able to call on his local connections. Previously, he had shown no interest at all in filming Central Asian topics. But for his next project, *Her Name is Spring* (*Ee imya vesna*, 1969), released a full five years after *The Hospital Train*, he chose *The Mighty Wave* (*Moguchaya volna*, 1964), a novel about life behind the front lines during the Second World War by Shafar Rashidov. No mere scribbler, the author was the First Secretary of the Central Committee of the Communist Party of Uzbekistan, who presided over a tight network of clientelist relations during his two decades' tenure of the most powerful political position in the republic.[42] The only previous film version of work by Rashidov had been significantly less prestigious: a cartoon film of his tale in the folk style, *Nargis*, directed by Vladimir Polkovnikov for the state animation studio, Soyuzmul'tfil'm, in 1965. The release of this film may have suggested to Khamraev that a film based on Rashidov's work would accord him the sort of high-level protection that was needed at Lenfil'm, and provide him with the rehabilitation that his denial of the sexual harassment revelations had not secured.[43]

---

42 See, for example, Alisher Ilkhamov, 'Neopatrimonialism, Interest Groups, and Patronage Networks: The Impasses of the Governance System in Uzbekistan', *Central Asian Survey*, 26.1 (2007), 65–84. For another, not necessarily contradictory, view of Rashidov as a successful exponent of late socialist internationalism, see Ricardo Mario Cucciolla, 'Sharaf Rashidov and the International Dimensions of Soviet Uzbekistan', *Central Asian Survey*, 39.2 (2020), 185–201.

43 Certainly, Khamraev retained some pull with Ilya Kiselev, general director of Lenfil'm: on 5 March 1966, just over a year after the scandal erupted, the latter wrote on Khamraev's behalf to the head of the Leningrad City Telephone Network to request the installation of a line in Khamraev's apartment (this normally required years of waiting). 'It is often necessary to decide urgently various questions to do with the production of movies', Kiselev wrote (TsGALI-SPb., f. 257, op. 18, d. 1458, l. 45. Khamraev continued to attend meetings of the Third Creative Unit's Artistic Council through the spring and summer of 1966 as well (TsGALI-SPb., f. 257, op. 18, d. 1480, l. 1–37, ll. 233–57).

Be that as it may, Khamraev made *Her Name is Spring* into a touching if sentimental story about a school romance between two young people that turned into real love, despite obstacles along the way: Pulat, played by handsome Talgat Nigmatulin, is rejected from the army on health grounds, which damages his self-esteem. Khamraev's first film in colour, it had plenty of audience-friendly material: handsome young people, surges of yearning, and exotic street scenes (with even the odd disused mosque in view, not to speak of fields of poppies).[44] At times it was endearingly goofy, as in a sequence at the end of the film when Pulat and Bakhor (Larisa Zubkovich), enjoying a last moment together after Pulat managed to argue his way into the army, frolicked in the spray from a street hose. Overall, *Her Name is Spring* was considered a successful movie. Opinions at Lenfil'm, on the other hand, were much less flattering: Khamraev's movie was bluntly described as 'awful'.[45] Most ambitious directors at Lenfil'm still firmly preferred black-and-white to colour; with those splashes of scarlet, Khamraev had undermined his pretensions to arthouse status.[46]

Illustrating the paradoxes of the late Soviet cinema, which was a valuable gravy train for figures from the so-called 'second culture', or artistic underground, Khamraev chose to collaborate on the script of *Her Name is Spring* with Vladimir Maramzin (1934–2021), officially an engineer and children's writer, but also author of celebrated *samizdat* work such as *Pushmepullyou* (*Tyanitolkai*, 1966), about a writer's conversation with an urbane and bonhomous officer of the KGB. Maramzin asked for his name to be removed from the finished film, no doubt sensing that the project was hardly consonant with his reputation in the alternative arts world.[47] However, Maramzin and Khamraev went on to collaborate again, this time on a proposal for a film called *The Son* (*Syn*), about a market trader who heads for Tashkent after the terrible earthquake of 1966 in order to try and help with the recovery. Welcomed at Lenfil'm (the script was praised by well-known author Vera Panova), the project was, however, received with derision at Goskino: 'Should an event such as the Tashkent earthquake really be evoked by showing on the screen and parading before readers such primitive characters as this?'[48]

---

44 The entire studio was switching from black-and-white at this point, under pressure from administrators, who believed that colour had more public appeal. See, for example, the comment by Lenfil'm's chief engineer, I. P. Aleksander: 'The [Soviet] resident wants to see colour films. I would like our directors to make them' (TsGAIPD-SPb., f. 1369, op. 5, d. 43).
45 TsGAIPD-SPb., f. 1359, op. 5, d. 97, l. 76; ibid. d. 104, l. 19 ('the picture's awful, but outside the studio it's been well-received').
46 Among directors still filming in black-and-white during the late 1960s were, for example, Gleb Panfilov, Ilya Averbakh, and Savva Kulish. Vitaly Mel'nikov was made to shoot *Mother's Got Married* (1969) in colour, to fierce resistance from the production group, and the final version of the film retained black-and-white segments.
47 TsGALI, f. 257, op. 18, d. 2302, l. 42. In 1975, Maramzin's work as editor on a five-volume *samizdat* edition of Joseph Brodsky, exiled in 1972 from the USSR, led to his arrest and arraignment on charges of anti-Soviet activity. On the trial, see *A Chronicle of Current Events*, 31 March 1975 <https://chronicle-of-current-events.com/2020/08/21/the-trial-of-vladimir-maramzin-19-21-february-1975-35-4/>. After acknowledging his faults and making a plea for clemency, Maramzin was given a five-year suspended sentence and followed Brodsky into exile. He continues to reside in Paris today.
48 Letter from V. Sytin and A. Balikhin, 28 November 1969, TsGALI-SPb., f. 257, op. 21, d. 171, ll. 32–33.

FIG. 14.2. Publicity still from Khamraev's *The Black Sands*. Archive of Lenfil'm Studio.

Khamraev was luckier with his next project, begun in the summer of 1970, and a collaboration with a much safer scriptwriter than Maramzin, Sergei Potepalov (b. 1937), whose first film, *The Book of Moabit* (*Moabitskaya tetrad'*, Lenfil'm, 1968), about the Tatar poet and war hero Musa Jalil, had been very well received. *In the Black Sands*, based on a novel by Kazakh writer Moris Simashko, was a classic 'Eastern', depicting as it did a young, handsome shepherd, Chary Esenov, and his search for revenge after his family is slaughtered at the hands of a local class oppressor (*bai*).

This was a propitious time to embark on an excursion into genre film-making for a whole variety of reasons. The Czechoslovak crisis of 1968 had raised suspicions of popular Western films as the likely instruments of anti-Soviet slander, accompanied by a determination to expand the production of reliable home-created substitutes.[49] Added to this, Motyl''s *White Sun of the Desert* (*Beloe solntse pustyni*) had shown that 'Easterns' could combine political acceptability with high viewing figures (around 35 million).[50] Cinema planners no doubt envisaged that a comparable film made by an actual Central Asian would do even better, consolidating the 'peripheral' audience and hitting figures more like 50 million.

In the Black Sands actually turned out to be an also-ran in terms of ticket sales.[51] But it hit the spot ideologically (celebrating 'the friendship and mutual aid of the brother republics, born in bloody battle with the enemy', as Lenfil'm's Party

---

49   See, for example, the discussion at Goskino on 28 June 1968, at which anxiety was expressed about the numbers of copies of Western films in circulation and about 'the principles of selection': RGALI, f. 2944, op. 1, d. 497, ll. 3–82.
50   The film was mentioned with approbation among a list of high-grossing examples of the genre at a Central Committee discussion of adventure films on 6 March 1976, RGANI, f. 5, op. 68, d. 630, ll. 2–3. For the viewing figures, see, for example, Oksana Barinova, 'Yarkii svet "Beloi pustyni"', 30 March 2020, Istoriya.RF <https://histrf.ru/read/articles/iarkii-sviet-bielogho-solntsa-pustyni-lieghiendarnomu-filmu-polvieka> [accessed 21 July 2021].
51   I have not been able to find precise data, but it was certainly not one of the big hits recorded in surveys of 1976 and 1977.

secretary Ida Rumyantseva put it at a meeting in 1972).[52] And it was also, within its lights, a well-made film. Camera operator Aleksandr Chechulin (1932–1991) had done outstanding work in such famous films as Gennady Poloka's *The Republic of SHKID* (1966) and Savva Kulish's *The Dead Season* (1968), and — of geological if not geographical relevance — Viktor Sadovsky's documentary *The Gold of the High Tatra Mountains* (*Zoloto vysokikh Tatr*, 1970). His footage for *In the Black Sands*, his first feature film to be shot in colour, was equally seductive. And the narrative of the film resembled the best Westerns in its juxtaposition of claustrophobic, menacing interiors (as in the deserted house that Chary, the male lead, explores at the beginning) and huge, subtly orchestrated panoramas. As though further to expiate the 1965 scandal, Khamraev introduced a sub-plot about a young girl whose betrothal was rapidly followed by her rape at the hands of the marauding associates of Shamurad, the film's villain, followed by her dramatic self-immolation outside the devastated settlement.

In the Black Sands was not quite Khamraev's last venture into Central Asian subject matter. His next film was *The Most Important Day* (*Samyi vazhnyi den'*, 1974), a co-production with Uzbekfil'm, with a cast mainly of Uzbek actors. The movie returned to the 1920s, though without the 'Eastern' genre requirements: instead, it was a pure 'friendship of nations' story about the collective farmers of Fergana dispatching in gratitude a trainload of fruit to the munition workers of the Putilov Factory.[53] By the sound of it, the result was even more 'awful' than *Her Name is Spring*, and certainly, the film seems to have sunk without trace in the studio, let alone beyond. Whichever way, *The Most Important Day* marked Khamraev's last tribute to Central Asian material. By now he had, evidently, managed to rehabilitate himself with Lenfil'm and pay his dues to his network of compatriots. His later films returned entirely to standard Russian Soviet topics (notably, the historical trilogy based on Georgy Markov's *The Strogov Family* (*Strogovy*), of which he made the second two instalments, released in 1978 and 1985, and a film about life in a Soviet office, *The Red Arrow* (*Krasnaya Strela*, co-directed with Igor Sheshukov, 1986).

Before smartly positioning himself, in the post-Soviet era, as a genre film expert of a different kind (like Sergei Potepalov, he collaborated on the wildly popular and lucrative crime series *The Road of Smashed Streetlights* (*Ulitsa razbitykh fonarei*), 1998), Khamraev made just one more film with an orientalist theme, though this time set in the Russian Federation: *When the Echo Responds* (*Kogda otzovetsya ekho*, 1988). Co-directed with Chechen director Iles Tataev and made by the local television studio in Groznyi, it focused on the life of a demobbed sergeant who, in 1945, arrives home with a chest full of bravery medals to find his village destroyed, and is then discovered there by the local military commandant, who has him deported to Kazakhstan. The film, however, soon skipped away from this politically sensitive

---

52   TsGAIPD-SPb., f. 1359, op. 5, d. 118, l. 215.
53   Or so one is informed by the kino-teatr.ru website <http://www.kino-teatr.ru/kino/movie/sov/11646/annot/> [accessed 3 October 2022]. The film is not available on the internet and has only one online comment by someone who claims actually to have seen it.

topic to portray a conflict in modern Chechnya after the hero's return, culminating in the murder of his daughter and his revenge on her killer. No significant footage of Kazakhstan was included. So far as Khamraev was concerned, involvement was probably a tribute to the fashionable trend for de-Stalinising movies (begun by Tengiz Abuladze's much superior *Repentance* (*monanieba; Pokayanie*), 1986), and it certainly had no echo in his later work.

If Khamraev largely provides an example of a career built on political expediency (*kon"yunktura*), Dinara Asanova was at the other end of a Soviet film artist's spectrum of possible self-definition. Even before studying at VGIK, she had established close connections with the alternative intelligentsia. In 1963, while working as a director's assistant at Kirgizfil'm, she joined the production group for *Heat* (*Znoi*), the diploma feature of Larisa Shepit'ko (1938–1979), later to be one of the most important directors of the late 1960s. Once Asanova reached Moscow a couple of years later, she continued to display notable independence of mind: 'She was alone right from the beginning', director Sergei Solov'ev remembered. 'And not just because the other, more changeable ones, were all men. Overall, Dinara was — not solitary exactly, but just always separate.'[54] Her close friends outside the institute included Vladimir Rossel's (1914–2000), a translator from Ukrainian and Polish, and his wife Elena, at whose Krasnaya Pakhra dacha she met such luminaries of the late 1960s alternative culture as the guitar poets Vladimir Vysotsky and Bulat Okudzhava, as well as official Soviet writers of an adventurous kind (Yury Tendryakov, Bella Akhmadulina, Novella Matveeva).[55] Her interest in Russian culture was intense: as Elena Rossel's remembered, 'Dinara, with her Kirgiz father and Tatar mother, sang Russian folk songs in the most astonishing way, as they are sung only deep in the Russian countryside'.[56]

Yet while noting Asanova's command of Russian culture, her contacts could not help noticing her alien traits as well. Sergei Solovyov and his circle gave her the nickname 'Dika', from the Russian word *dikii* or 'wild, savage'.[57] Bulat Okudzhava, who recognised her talent from the start ('from day one I saw a master artist of a highly unusual kind'), recalled her back then as 'a very young woman, almost a girl, frail, slender, both ugly and beautiful at the same time. If you looked at her face, you saw the Orient, Asia. When she talked, she was a Russian intellectual'.[58] This sense of ambiguity persisted. Viktor Aristov, who joined Lenfil'm around the same time as Asanova, and who was also from Kirgizia, later recalled the hand-to-mouth existence the two led as young incomers:

> Degrading, insulting poverty — we spent our lives moving around, renting a room there, a flat here, for us and our families. We had no place to call our

---

54 See the compendious collection of writings by and memoirs about Dinara Asanova, compiled by her former editor at Lenfil'm, Frizheta Gukasyan, *U menya net vremeni govorit' nepravdu: dnevnikovye zapisi, rezhisserskie zametki, stat'i, interv'yu Dinary Asanovoi, vospominaniya o nei* (Leningrad: Iskusstvo, 1989), p. 246 (hereafter referenced as *UMNVGP*).
55 Elena Rossel's in *UMNVGP*, pp. 259–69.
56 *UMNVGP*, p. 261.
57 Ibid., p. 246. *Blagorodnyi dikar'*, for instance, is 'noble savage'.
58 *UMNVGP*, p. 376.

own and zero chance to get one; she was considered not to have a future and no-one gave me a moment's serious thought.

Dinara, he concluded, was 'provocatively foreign in this northern city'. Her first film, *Rudolfio* (1969), a twenty-five-minute short made as her final-year project at VGIK, 'did not even have a precarious perch on the banks of the mainstream'.[59]

And indeed, Asanova's debut, taken from a story that Valentin Rasputin (1937–2015) had written at the start of his literary career, was predicated on oddity.[60] Its protagonist, Io, an ordinary schoolgirl in an unremarkable apartment block, develops a powerful crush on Rudolf, a married man about two decades her senior who happens to be one of her neighbours. Over the four years that had elapsed since the story was first published in 1965, the subject matter had become, in official Soviet terms, not so much thought-provoking as risky.

Despite Asanova's tactful adaptation (the action was transferred to somewhere in the Baltic countries, which had a reputation for Western-style laissez-faire when it came to morals), the film proved scandalous ('an extremely dubious moral effect is generated', complained Irina Kokoreva, a senior official at Goskino). Asanova was granted her degree from VGIK only after support from the eminent director Mark Donskoi.[61] Goskino demanded a wide-ranging recut, to include a scene where Rudolf treated Io to a sermon about forward behaviour unbecoming to young girls in the manner of Pushkin's Evgeny Onegin. Through all this, the management of the Third Creative Unit backed Asanova, but at the end of 1969 the unit was closed down and she lost her studio patrons. Like Khamraev — though for very different reasons — she took an extended career break, partly spent on maternity leave. Only in the autumn of 1973 did Goskino allow her another chance.

Goskino's suspicion of Asanova was in some respects justified. While not a dissident in the sense of member of the political opposition, she was close to the developing underground scene (what was known as *dissidentstvuyushchii*, or 'dissidentish'). Her husband, Nikolai Yudin, was a painter specialising in religious, occult, and esoteric subjects, and she had friends in the world of underground photography, such as Sergei Mikhailov, who shot a remarkable portrait of her not long after *Rudolfio* was released.[62]

None of Asanova's later films was set outside Russia, indeed, most of them were filmed in Leningrad and its environs. But her capacity to fit into the life even of one of the USSR's more permissive studios was at best limited. Her films espoused a 'new wave' ethos of exploratory film-making, with heavy use of improvisation, that were closer to Czech or Polish film of the 1960s than to Soviet film even in its more adventurous manifestations. *Woodpeckers Don't Get Headaches* (*Ne bolit golova u dyatla*), released — after many arguments with Goskino — in 1974, focused on a teenager, Mukha, whose talent as a jazz percussionist puts him at odds with his

---

59   Ibid., pp. 352–53.
60   For a detailed discussion of Asanova's films and their production history, see my *Soviet Art House*, Chapter 12.
61   UMNVGP, p. 265 (Elena Rossel's).
62   <https://www.pinterest.ca/pin/473792823269600349/> [accessed 3 October 2022].

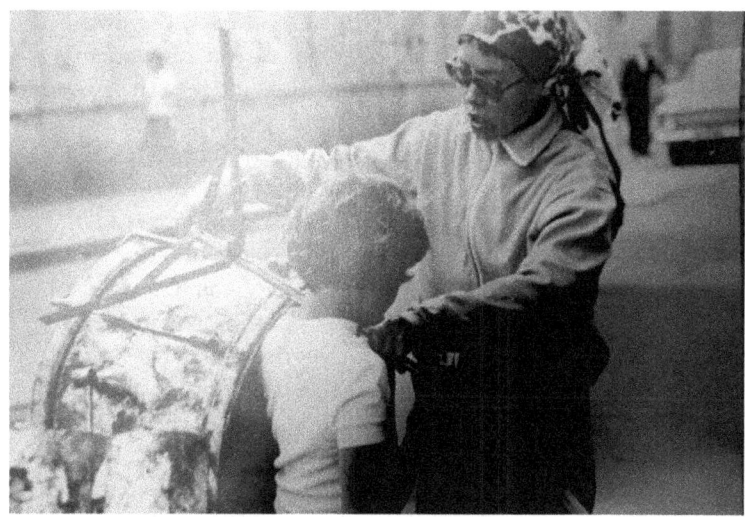

Fig. 14.3. Dinara Asanova on the set of her *Woodpeckers Don't Get Headaches*. 1974. Archive of Lenfil'm Studio.

working-class parents (his brother was a star in the much safer world of Soviet sport).

The film was officially rated 'poor', despite esteem for Asanova's work among other young film directors. Later, the cinema establishment reached a partial accommodation with Asanova — her second full-length feature, *Key for Personal Use Only* (*Klyuch bez prava peredachi*, 1976), won Best Director and Best Actor prizes at the All-Soviet Film Festival in Riga (1977) — but her work continued to provoke criticism on aesthetic as well as ideological grounds. The fact that she was able to make films at all was because she addressed subjects that the government and Party bureaucracies had identified as priorities for the film industry (disaffected young people, alcoholism, family breakdown).

Asanova's pace of film-making was by any standards Stakhanovite. Between 1975 and 1984, she made seven full-length features and two films for television, and this in the context of a film industry where one film every two or three years was the norm. Her record testified not just to her talent and energy (each film was extensively researched, as her surviving notes indicate), but also to the anxieties of a 'peripheral' outsider who could not expect to be taken seriously unless she over-achieved. Her early death in 1985, aged just forty-two, while on a location shoot for yet another film, was testament to the stress that this struggle for recognition had provoked, as well as to the hard drinking that Asanova had used to wind down from the tensions of such a merciless schedule of creative work.

The distinctions between Khamraev and Asanova can be attributed to many factors: personality, taste, milieu, and not least gender. But they were also the product of generation. A '1970-er', Asanova developed as an artist at a point when a serious alternative culture had come into being, and when, moreover, the political opposition in the Russian capitals (and across the country) increasingly had an anti-Communist, Russocentric flavour.[63] In this context, the non-Russian origins of someone who identified with the non-official arts movement were likely to impact on their work only in an oblique and abstract way. It is certainly possible to see in the lead characters in Asanova's films some measure of her own social and artistic precarity. They included, alongside the boy who does not fit in because of his musical talent, an out-of-control drunk (*The Pity of It* (*Beda*), 1979), the girl nobody likes (*Worthless* (*Nikudyshnaya*), 1980), young offenders (*The Lads* (*Patsany*), 1983), the embarrassingly garrulous woman who has no-one but her driver to talk to and impulsively abducts a baby (*My Sweet, Dear, Only Love* (*Milyi, dorogoi, lyubimyi, edinstvennyi*), 1984). But the viewer was not invited to identify protagonists and director, nor did Asanova invite the comparison in what she wrote about her films or told journalists about them in interviews. Equally, she never mentioned, let alone explained, her long-distance attitude to her ethnic (in Soviet terms, 'national') origins, which surfaced mainly in her treatment of her son Vladimir, known by his mother in private by the Koranic Arabic name Anvar (*Anwar*, 'light'), and dispatched at intervals to stay with his grandmother in Frunze.[64]

Asanova was, for all her breadth of reading and capacity for intelligent contemplation, primarily an emotional and intuitive film artist. The possibility of intellectual engagement with Central Asian origins was to be realised only later, by Roza Orynbasarova, a director from what has been referred to as 'the last Soviet generation'.[65] Originally trained as a documentary maker, she arrived at Lenfil'm in very different circumstances from either of her two predecessors. In the late 1980s, Lenfil'm went through another period of restructuring, not, this time, as the result of a transformation planned by Goskino, but in the wake of the collapse of the central management of the Soviet film industry. After the Fifth Congress of the Union of Film-Makers, convened on 13 May 1986, had thrown out the entire board of management and elected Elem Klimov, an admired artist who had no history as an apparatchik, the long-standing push by film professionals to exercise more influence on editorial and administrative policy gained traction. Perestroika-era policies of budget devolution (*khozraschet*) put the finishing touches to the de-centralisation of film production. The old creative units, with no control over budgets and distribution, were replaced by new entities that, although still called 'units', were financially and artistically autonomous companies, using Lenfil'm as a facility for their own productions.

63 For a good discussion of the 1970s, see Josephine von Zitzewitz, *Poetry and the Leningrad Religious-Philosophical Seminar, 1974–1980: Music for a Deaf Age* (Oxford: Legenda, 2016).
64 It is not clear whether Anwar Sadat, President of Egypt, was the inspiration for the name; Asanova's interest may simply have stemmed from the mystical associations of light. On the boy's stays in Frunze, see the memoir of film critic Lyudmila Donets, 'Na zare tumannoi yunosti', in *U menya net vremeni govorit' nepravdu*, ed. by Gukasyan, pp. 250–59 (p. 256). As the actor Mikhail Gluzsky recalled, Volodya/Anvar found his work as a child actor traumatic (Gukasyan, *U menya net vremeni govorit' nepravdu,*, p. 310), and after his mother's death, the boy led a troubled life as a homeless drug addict and alcoholic, estranged from his father and stepmother and refusing to contact any of Asanova's associates.
65 See Alexei Yurchak, *The Last Soviet Generation* (Princeton, NJ: Princeton University Press, 2006).

One of these entities, 'The Unit of First and Experimental Films', was headed by film director Aleksei German, who had made his name as an extraordinary talent with *My Friend Ivan Lapshin* (*Moi drug Ivan Lapshin*, released in 1984 after lengthy delays). As the name suggests, it was a hatchery for work by young directors that was meant to be unconventional and challenging. In the past, such novice artists had arrived at Lenfil'm through the state system of assignation (*raspredelenie*) operating in all Soviet institutions of higher education, which matched professional vacancies and suitable trainees. Whether the trainee in question was considered 'suitable' for Lenfil'm (or, on the other hand, dispatched to languish in the 'periphery') was closely related to perceived talent. In Asanova's case, the fact that she was a pupil of Mikhail Romm — a venerated figure at Lenfil'm as well as a famous director — smoothed the path to 'assignation'. But in the new era, German himself visited VGIK to scout for talent.

Disappointed with the graduates from the feature films course, German decided to review work by the documentalists as well. Roza Orynbasarova's diploma short, *Achisai*, a remarkable poetic evocation of an unmodernised village not far from Kentau, shot in grainy black-and-white, caught the master director's eye. Before long, Orynbasarova found herself with an offer to join 'First and Experimental Films'. As she remembered nearly twenty years later, Orybasarova was astonished by the offer. German was a cult figure with her generation:

> In the mid-1980s, we students, of course, had heard all about the banning of German's films and then how they were allowed, about how they'd been shelved,[66] about the bits cut out, the wiped negatives. We worshipped him and dreamt of working at Lenfilm.[67]

Toiling under German's direction proved to be tough, however. He was a most exacting mentor, partly because he believed that deprivation and suffering were the roots of serious art. His attitude varied from passive aggressive ('Don't worry: if you screw up the worst that can happen is that you'll be out on your ear') to unqualified aggressive. The editors dried Orynbasarova's tears and told him that she had to stand up to German and ignore his jibes. The artistic council's review of her shooting script (which she was not allowed to attend, contrary to Lenfil'm's practice in the past) was lengthy, and, Orsynbasarova could hear from outside the door, controversial. German, when she was finally admitted, told her, as though underlining her gender, that his wife Svetlana Karmalita had succeeded in convincing him to give the project a go. He could not resist another dig: 'A film director I admire announced it was impossible to allow a Kazakh woman to film our Russian classics. So I told him he wasn't Russian either. That's how it goes: toughen up'.[68]

66   *Postavit' na polku* is professional slang for the fate of a film not approved for general release, whether because it was stopped in production or not cleared for release by Goskino, formally rejected by the Film Distribution Board, or withdrawn from circulation after release. The sealed canisters of film were removed from the director and the studio and shelved (hence the name) in a classified section of the State Film Archive (Gosfil'mofond), where they might remain for years or decades.
67   Quoted from Aleksandr Pozdnyakov's interview with Roza Orynbasarova in his *Bol'shoi German* (St Petersburg: KinoMel'nitsa, 2016), p. 157.
68   Ibid., p. 159. Evidently, the person whose comment German reported, embellished, or invented

The irony was that the 'Russian classic' which German had assigned to Orynbasarova was Mikhail Kuprin's masterpiece of xenophobic Orientalism, *Staff Captain Rybnikov* (*Shtabs-kapitan Rybnikov*), written during the jingoistic frenzy that accompanied the Russo-Japanese War of 1904–05. The central figure of the story was a Japanese agent posing as the officer in question, 'little, swarthy, lame, strangely talkative, untidy-looking and not especially sober'.

Rybnikov (whose very name, derived from 'fish', already suggests impertinent dietary othering) is accepted as a harmless bore and nonentity in Petersburg society. But an investigative journalist, Vladimir Shchavinsky, is professionally equipped with a higher level of percipience, and he soon spots something odd in Rybnikov's appearance:

> From the side, it was an ordinary Russian, slightly Kalmyk-looking face: a small round forehead topped by a domed cranium, a Russian potato nose, a sparse coarse-textured black moustache and beard, a close-shaved head with a large patch of grey, a face of weatherbeaten yellow... But as Rybnikov turned to face Shchavinsky, he immediately reminded the latter of someone he knew. There was something completely familiar, but undefinable, in those narrow, glittering, coffee-coloured little eyes set aslant, in the anxious slope of the black brows starting up from the bridge of the nose, in the energetic dryness of the skin, and in the general expression of that face — malevolent, mocking, clever, even arrogant, but something not so much human as animal, or to be more accurate — belonging to a creature from another planet.

It takes only another couple of pages for Shchavinsky to get to the point: 'a Japanese, that's what he looks like!' From then on it is simple to note other defects in Rybnikov's camouflage: his over-careful recitation of the Lord's Prayer, and indeed, his generally hyper-correct Russian, not to speak of the fact that, while always acting as though he were slightly drunk, he's never to be seen with a glass in his hands.

Equally quick to smell a rat is a prostitute, while Rybnikov is enjoying her services in an expensive brothel. She begins calling him 'my little Japanese' long before he, in the ultimate moment of passion, cries out something in a language she does not know. It is in turn the prostitute, privileged witness to this moment of cultural striptease, who denounces Rybnikov to the police, precipitating a grotesque attempt at suicide that places Rybnikov, severely injured but still alive, at the mercy of his Russian pursuers. In the ultimate inversion of the Japanese code of honour, suicide becomes as a bungled act of cowardice rather than a ritualised act of triumph over the self.

The assumption that Orynbasarova was intrinsically qualified by ethnic origins to adapt this racist tosh for screen bespeaks the gross insensitivity of her mentors. (Though hardly more intelligent was the idea that she was somehow *dis*qualified to adapt one of the 'Russian classics'.) German's commission, and the debate over

---

was Joseph Heifitz, Lenfil'm's most stellar director of literary adaptations, and, from a Russian nationalist point of view, 'not really Russian' (in the official Soviet understanding, 'Jewish' was an ethnic identifier, not a religious denomination). German's riposte, while rhetorically effective, was scandalous in terms of prevailing intelligentsia attitudes to courtesy.

Orynbasarova's competence to take it on, marked the transition from the sentimental 'friendship of peoples' back in the 1970s to a specifically post-Soviet understanding of the appropriate attitudes on the part of Russians to minority nationalities. Now, self-assertive insolence (what in Russian is known as *khamstvo*) was quite in order.

It testifies to Orynbasarova's talent and determination that, on the basis of a propaganda text about 'unmasking' racial intruders, she produced a film, *Sacrifice for the Emperor* (1991), which was a subtle and sophisticated study of ambiguous identity. The customary locution of approximate relation to the original, 'based on motifs from', was an accurate description of her intelligent literary adaptation. Wholly altering the end and many other key scenes, and providing a refined, rather Japanese-flavoured, *mise en scène* to make up for Kuprin's careless uninterest in his characters' surroundings, Orynbasarova also declined to act on German's suggestion that she cast an actual 'Asiatic' in the title role, searching instead for a Russian who could 'convey the elusive Japanese soul'.[69]

As the phrasing suggests, Orynbasarova substituted for Kuprin's obsession with outward appearance, where Rybnikov's expression of emotion had purely physiological promptings, an emphasis on the staff captain's interior world. His role as a 'spy' became purely incidental: rather, he was an intelligent and inquisitive observer of a world that seemed as much historically as geographically unfamiliar. Perhaps Orynbasarova used him, as Asanova did Mukha, as a kind of autobiographical mask, but he also stood for the film's spectator in a different time and place. As he stared at the congregation and serving priests at a Russian Orthodox mass, he spoke for a society in which religious practice was centrally present for the first time since 1918.

Aleksei German, an artist whose emotional register was primarily *nadryv*, or the identity-dissolving outburst, had probably expected some completely different resolution, much more faithful to Kuprin's original. But Orynbasarova had contrived to exceed his expectations, or to outwit them. Her 'sacrifice for the Emperor' was not an abdication of personal or creative responsibility. She survived her ordeal with German to win a debut film award in Moscow, and went on to make several other well-regarded films, most of them also addressing the theme of the cultural outsider.[70] With the work of this director, inspired by Vasily Shukshin and Andrei Tarkovsky as well as Bergman, Fellini, Visconti, Bertolucci, Vigo, Reggio, and not least Kurosawa, Russian-made Central Asian film entered a new phase of post-colonial reflective synthesis — a very long way away from the superficial charm of the 'Eastern'.[71]

---

69 Pozdnyakov, *Bol'shoi German*, p. 158.
70 For instance, *The Waiting Room* (1993) dealt with the new rich and their antagonistic relations with traditional Petersburgers, the documentary *Farukh and Diana* (2000) with the Uzbek and Jewish stars of the Mariinsky, Farukh Ruzimatov and Diana Vishneva, and as of latest reports, Orynbasarova was trying to secure funding for a Russian-Kazakh co-production of a historical film about a Kazakh khan's experiences in St Petersburg against the background of the Decembrist uprising in 1825.
71 For the influences, see Pozdnyakov, *Bol'shoi German*, p. 157.

332   THE BLACK-AND-WHITE POPPIES OF RUSSIAN ARTHOUSE

FIG. 14.4. Image from Orynbasarova's *A Sacrifice for the Emperor* <https://www.kino-teatr.ru/kino/movie/sov/2219/foto/718884/> [accessed 24 October 2022].

★ ★ ★ ★ ★

Iskander Khamraev, Dinara Asanova and Roza Oynbasarova represented three very different models of artistic self-assertion by Central Asian film directors working in the Russian metropolis. As I have argued, Central Asian directors, unlike some others from ethnic minorities (particularly Georgians), were not automatically credited with the signs of likely artistic promise. Caucasian film auteurs (from Abuladze to Paradzhanov) were some of the most admired figures of the post-Stalin era; Central Asian film, on the other hand, tended to be associated with mass-market 'Easterns' of the sort that competed with foreign-produced Westerns or Bollywood. Iskander Khamraev, the oldest director, was also the only one of the three directly to employ Central Asian material, though mainly, it would seem, in order to rescue himself from career disaster. One of his four such film projects, *In the Black Sands*, was a well-made and watchable film, if not a major hit, that confirmed Khamraev as a skilled exponent of genre cinema.

More complicated were the careers of the other two, younger, directors placed in a city that was, on the one hand, cosmopolitan, but on the other, traditionally understood by its denizens as a stronghold of 'European' values. By personality, education, and aesthetic preference a Russian intellectual, Dinara Asanova was, at the same time, in close contact with circles in the 'alternative art' movement that were strongly coloured by a rising preoccupation with national origins. She had to struggle to be taken seriously not just in the studio, but beyond, though at the same time, her unusual talents were quickly recognised, and the very marginality of her work gave this a kind of counter-cultural lustre. Yet the 'alternative' flavour of her cinema, with its emphasis on improvisation, was closer to, say, the work of Agnès Varda than to the 'Asiatic' character that careless observers often noted in her appearance. Any resemblance to her protagonists was of an abstract kind (as awkward, socially peripheral figures that lack self-confidence and obvious authority).

Arriving in the film-making world considerably later, when the Soviet world of Lenfil'm had to all intents and purposes disintegrated, Rosa Orynbasarova confronted stereotyping that was equally persistent and in significant respects more assertive and crude, indeed crass. But the very obviousness of the expectations that greeted her provoked a more obvious level of engagement with prevailing perceptions of the 'Asiatic'. Rather than turning supposedly universal ('Russian') experience into a hidden narrative of the Central Asian artist's difference, as Asanova had, she turned the experience of the 'Oriental', whose approximation to the receiving culture is always somehow 'wrong', into a figure for the dislocations of the post-Soviet era itself.

To what extent one can generalise from these cases to conclusions about the Central Asian presence in Soviet Russian culture of the post-Stalin era remains an open question. In many respects, Asanova and Orynbasarova had less in common with establishment-oriented Khamraev than with another wayward, non-conformist woman artist, Kira Muratova — though Muratova was more confrontational than they, no doubt helped by the fact that she retained the Romanian passport to which she was entitled by birth throughout her decades of life in the Soviet Union.[72] There is no evidence that either Asanova or Orynbasarova felt a sense of regional affinity (*zemlyachestvo*) with Khamraev, and Asanova, for one, was far closer to the ethnically Russian (though Kirgizia-born) Aristov. While Khamraev and Asanova started out in the same creative unit (the Third), they were to make their later careers in two other units, the First (for Asanova), which was more strongly associated with art films, and the Second (for Khamraev), known in studio parlance as the 'official unit'. Yet the perception that Central Asian origins were somehow relevant to the definition of character and artistic purpose persisted among the Russians they worked with, even if they were of little conscious interest to the Central Asian directors themselves, and this in turn meant that self-definition by explicit rejection of such associations, if nothing else, was bound to play a central, if hidden, role as they shaped their lives in cinema.

I am grateful to the AHRC for sponsoring my work on the history of Lenfil'm (see also my *Soviet Art House*), and to Alexander Morrison, organiser of the 'Central Asia in Russian Language and Culture' conference, New College, Oxford, March 2018, and the participants in the event, for their helpful comments. This essay acts as a kind of prequel to my current project, 'Making History: Films about the Past between Stalin and Gorbachev', which includes films by directors from the Caucasus, Central Asia, the Baltic, Ukraine, Moldova and Belarus as well as Russian directors.

---

72 As is clear from the studio contract for the movie she made at Lenfil'm, *Getting to Know the World*. See Chapter 15 of my *Soviet Art House*.

INDEX

In both the index and the main text, the transliteration is a modified form of British Standard: spelling of first names and place names is simplified (Olga not Ol'ga, Izrail not Izrail', Tatiana, Natalia, Yaroslavl, etc.), omitting the soft sign ('); however, the soft sign is included in transliterations of surnames, since it affects library cataloguing and so on.

Abel', Rudolf (William Fisher) 293–94
Abel'son, Tamara 193, 221
 see also Talbot Rice, Tamara
Aberconway, Christabel 143
Abuladze, Tengiz:
 Repentance (*monanieba*; *Pokayanie*) 325
Adams, Helen McClelland (author's grandmother) 3–4
Adams, John Robinson (author's great-grandfather) 3–4
Afinogenov, Aleksandr 230
Agranovsky, Valery, journalist 296–97
Aigi, Gennady, poet 314
Aitmatov, Chingiz, writer 314
Akhmadulina, Bella, poet 325
Akhmatova, Anna, poet 10, 137–53, 233 n. 95, 313
 'Lot's Wife' 176
 Poem Without a Hero 153
Akkerman (Bilhorod-Dnistrovs'kyi) 204
Aksakov, Ivan 42, 47, 58
alcohol, consumption of 72, 96, 100, 115, 246, 253 n. 64, 289, 290, 328, 339
Alekseev, Mikhail, writer 228
Alexander I, emperor, 15, 30, 53
Alexander II, emperor, 43
Alexandra Feodorovna, empress 30, 31, 52, 54, 58
Alexandra Iosifovna, grand duchess 49
Alexis Mikhailovich, tsar 43
d'Allonville, Armand-François, army officer and memoirist 21
'Allo switch', car security device 287, 298
alternative culture:
 in the late Soviet period, 326, 327–28
Al'tman, Natan, artist 137
Amini, Hossein, scriptwriter:
 McMafia 304
androgyny 213, 217
animals 81–103, 124–25, 165–67
 and slavery 85–103
 and work 87–103
 control over humans 81–82
 cruelty to 4, 84, 90–91, 95–96
 experiments on 81–82, 84
 rights of 84–87

Anne, saint 16, 148–50
Anne of Orange, princess 54
Annensky, Innokenty, poet 74, 77
Anrep, Boris, mosaic artist 10, 137–53
Anrep, Helen (Maitland) 139
Anrep, Yuliya (Khitrovo) 141
An-sky, Semyon (Rapoport, Shloime) 194, 196
'anti-salon' 42
 see also Russian radicals
anti-Semitism 200–06
Aphrodite 35
Apollo 35
Aquinas, Thomas 86, 91
Arctic, explorers of 62
aristocracy 19, 39, 42–59
Aristov, Viktor 325
Aristotle 102, 240
Asanova, Dinara 312, 325–28, 329
 portrait of, by Sergei Mikhailov 326
 Key for Personal Use Only 327
 The Pity of It (*Beda*) 328
 Rudolfio 326
 Woodpeckers Don't Get Headaches (*Ne bolit golova u dyatla*) 326
 Worthless (*Nikudyshnaya*) 328
autobiography 33–34, 43–47, 58, 63, 176–77
 children's 181–90
 fragmentation in 44
 mother-child relationship in 44
 readership in 43
Automatic Merchandising Company (AMCO) 287–88
Avvakum, archpriest and Old Believer leader 43
Ayres, Leonard 287–88, 304

Bage, Robert 64
Baker, Howard 288
Baker, Mollie (Caroline Mary) 287, 288
Ba---lina, Klavdiya, child patient 114–15
Banionis, Donatas, actor 284, 292, 306 n. 91, 317 n. 26
Bank of England building 140
Baratynsky, Evgeny, poet 25
Barnet, Boris, film director:
 The Secret Agent's Heroic Feat (*Podvig rezidenta*) 284, 287

Poulain de la Barre, François 18
Barto, Agniya, children's writer 162, 208
bears 124, 167, 261 n. 10, 269
Belorussia 112, 131, 196, 302
Belyi, Andrei, poet 73 n. 48
Benenson family 198
Benenson, Manya 201
Benigni, Roberto, actor and director:
   La Vita è bella 259
Bentham, Jeremy 85–86, 91
Berggol'ts Olga 143
Bergman, Ingmar 331
Berkeley, California 300
Berkov, Pavel 204
Bertolucci, Bernardo 331
Leprince de Beaumont, Jeanne-Marie 28–29
Bill'-Belotserkovsky, Vladimir, writer 195
Blok, Aleksandr, poet 153, 166, 325
   Little Puppet Booth 166
Bluebeard 22, 25
Boétie, Étienne de 240
Bollywood 332
The Bonfire (*Koster*), children's magazine 243
border-guards, cult of 246
Bowen, Elizabeth 224 n. 61
Bowers, Toni 17
Brazil, Angela 223
Britten, Benjamin:
   The Turn of the Screw 158
   War Requiem 157
Bruce, Praskovya 45
Brunswick, Ruth Mack, psychoanalyst 126, 130, 132
Bryullov, Karl 20, 33
Buchan, John:
   Greenmantle 304
Bukhara 191
Bulatov, Sergei (composer) 245
Burnett, Frances Hodgson:
   Little Lord Fauntleroy 219, 221
butterflies 108
Bykov, Rollan, actor 284
Byzantine art 145, 148
Byzantium 21

capitalism 297, 305
Catherine II, empress 10, 15, 18, 28, 30, 31, 45
Catholicism 3, 52, 146–53, 237
cemetery architecture 15, 62
Central Asia 307–10
   cinema of 307–12, 315–16
   prejudice against 313–14, 317–18
   see also Orientalism
Chagall, Marc 201
Chaliapin, Fedor 7
Charskaya, Lidiya, children's writer 223–24
Chekhov, Anton:
   Three Sisters 72

Chenil Gallery 140
Cherkassov, Aleksandr 45
Chernigov Province 204
Chernyshevsky, Nikolai, writer 62, 64
Trotti de la Chétardie, Jacques-Joachim 17
children and childhood 4, 5, 6, 10, 61, 62, 74, 76, 88,
   91 n. 31, 94 n. 41, 105–35, 139, 141, 155–279
   in the late eighteenth and early nineteenth century
     16, 20, 26, 27, 28, 29, 33–34
   in the mid nineteenth century 42, 45, 48, 52, 57
   in the late nineteenth and early twentieth century
     105–35, 175–208
   in the Soviet period 155–71, 211–279
   age thresholds of childhood 237
   consumer goods for children 261–62, 264, 267–70,
     276
   shortages of 268–69
   corporal punishment of children 265
   'extended' childhood 277
   children in Jewish culture 191–209
   'spoiling' of children 263
   see also autobiography, children's; clothes; education;
     games; toys
Children's Theatre (from 1936, Central Children's
   Theatre), Moscow 159–63
Children's World department store, Moscow 270
Chotzinoff, Samuel, memoirist 204
Chukovsky, Kornei, children's writer and critic 160,
   162, 169
Churchill, Winston, 142
clothes 23–24, 116, 127, 128, 129, 212–13, 216, 217–18,
   220–22, 260, 264–66, 273
Cocteau, Jean 139 n. 10
Coetzee J. M. 86–87
Coker, Margot (author's first cousin once removed) 7
Communism 135, 164, 239, 305
comradeliness 238–39, 247, 254
'conservative Romanticism' 42
conservatism 42–59
Constantine, grand duke 49
Cooper, Diana 143
Cormack, John 9
'corporeal economy' 67
Cossacks 205
Costello, Elizabeth, fictional character 86–87, 99
Coué, Émile 66
courage 74
court, Russian royal 53–59
'cover story' (*legenda*), in spying 285
cowardice 74, 243, 247, 330
Czechoslovakia 323
   cinema of 326

dachas 271
D'Alton, John, bishop 146
Danilov, V. P. 183
Dan'ko, Natalia, sculptor-ceramicist 226

Dante 33, 146
Dashkova, Ekaterina 44 n. 11, 54
defecation 109, 115, 127
Delafield, E. M. 217
Deleuze, Gilles 107
Derzhavin, Gavrila, poet 15, 21 n. 19
Derzhavina, Ekaterina 15
Descartes, René 86
Dictionary of Counterintelligence (*Kontrrazvedyvatel'nyi slovar'*) 285
Diderot, Denis 29
Diotima 240
disinformation (*dezinformatsiya*), in spying 285, 292, 304
Disney, Walt 167
diversiya (sabotage) 283
Dolgorukova, Aleksandra, mistress of Alexander II 55
domesticity 5, 59
Domostroi, household manual 17, 20, 65 n. 15
Donald Duck 167
Dorigné, Michel 156
Dorré, Gina M. 101
Douglass, Frederick 99
dreams 105–06, 126–27, 130
Drunina, Yuliya 227
Dublin 8
duelling 26, 68–72, 111
Dunaevsky, Isaak, composer 158
Durova, Natalia, woman soldier and memoirist 223
Dymshits, Valery 199 n. 33, 206, 207
Dzhavakha, Nina, fictional character 223

'Eastern', film genre 309–11
Edinburgh 2, 4, 140, 286
education 16–18, 57, 181–82, 186, 195, 229, 237–52
Edwards, Joe 64
egalitarianism 42, 67, 69, 161
  see also gender egalitarianism
Église de Notre Dame de France, Leicester Square 139 n. 9
Eisenstein, Sergei 158, 169
Ekaterinoslav Province 203
Ekkert, Heinrich 284
Elena Pavlovna, grand duchess 51, 54 n. 31
Eliot, T. S. 143
Elizabeth, empress 53, 58
Elwell, Charles, officer of MI5 286, 299
emigration 120, 180–81, 197, 283–307, 313–33
Émile 31–32
'emotional management' 235–36
Enlightenment ideas, as influence in the Soviet period 241, 249
d'Épinay, Louise 29, 32
Ermler, Friedrich, film director 318
Esenin, Sergei, poet 75
Estonia 302–03
  see also Tartu
ethnography 118–19, 194–95, 198

etiquette 49–52, 55
Etkind, Alexander 113

Fadeev, Aleksandr, writer:
  The Young Guard [*Molodaya Gvardiya*], novel 240
fascism 239
  anti-fascism 263
FBI 299 n. 64, 301
fear 120–27, 130–34
Fielding, Henry 6
Fellini, Federico 331
femininity 15–59, 64–65, 113, 213–14, 211–33, 243–44
Fénelon, François 17–19
'file selves' 178
Finnian, saint 150
First Congress of Soviet Writers 160, 211
First Congress of Children's Writers 162
First of September (start of school year festival) 274
The First Tractor (*Pervyi traktor*), photograph 212
First World War 143, 202–03
Fletcher, F. Morley 140
folk songs 325
folk tales 108–09
Fonteyn, Margot 142
Food 260, 261, 262, 263, 266, 268–69, 275
forgetting 176, 178
Forsh, Olga, writer 120–21
Figner, Vera, political activist 57
Frederiks, Mariya, lady-in-waiting 49, 52
'free world' 305
Freud, Sigmund 10, 105–20, 170, 179, 180, 184
Friendly Kids (*Druzhnye rebyata*), children's magazine 164
friendship 24, 52, 54, 57–58, 102–03, 139–40, 201, 235–55, 284, 305–06
  between boys 247–50, 254
  between boys and girls 242–43
  between girls 243, 254
  between men 240–41
  between men and women 24, 241
  between women 52, 54, 57–58
  impact of Russian literature on 256
  'friendship of peoples' 241–42, 244, 246, 252, 304, 323–25, 331
Fry, Roger 139, 140
future, orientation towards in early Soviet period 178, 212, 231, 244

Gaidar, Arkady, children's writer:
  School (*Shkola*) 230
  Timur and His Team (*Timur i ego komanda*) 63, 230, 246, 252
Galiani, Ferdinando 27, 32–33
Galich, Aleksandr, poet 157
games 9, 53, 214, 218, 223 n. 57, 231 n. 91, 246 n. 41, 259, 260, 261, 266 n. 32, 269, 277
Garbo, Greta 143, 217

Gardner, Ken, journalist 291
Gastev, Aleksei, utopian theorist 62
   'the Gastev system' 62
Gee, Ethel, spy 289
gender egalitarianism 64, 228–29, 233
   opposition to, in peasant society 228–29
Genlis, Stéphanie de 29–30, 52, 57
Georgia, cinema in 315, 316, 317
   see also Abuladze, Tengiz
Gerasimov, Sergei, film director:
   The Young Guard [*Molodaya Gvardiya*] 240, 252 n. 61
Geraskina, Liya, children's writer:
   The Matriculation Exam [*Attestat zrelosti*] 249, 251, 252
germ warfare 291–92, 296
   see also Porton Down
German, Aleksei 329, 330–31
   My Friend Ivan Lapshin 329
Ghosh, Nalini 5
gifts 5, 22, 107–08, 130, 139, 183, 193, 194, 255, 271, 275
   as form of commemoration (*suveniry*) 176
Ginger, fictional character 98
Ginzburg, Carlo 118
Ginzburg, Lidiya 200
Giotto 150 n. 35
Goethe, Johann Wolfgang von:
   Die Leiden des Jungen Werthers 250
Gogol, Nikolai, writer 131 n. 71
   The Government Inspector (*Revizor*) 299
   Memoirs of a Madman (*Zapiski sumasshedshego*) 120
Gompertz, Lewis, campaigner against cruelty to animals 92–93
Goncharov, Ivan, writer 72
Goncharova, Natalia, *see* Pushkina, Natalia
Gorky, Maxim 160, 177, 208 n. 74, 261 n. 10
Goskino 326
Gournay, Marie Le Jars de 18
Grabiensky, Joseph 67 n. 25, 241
Gracián y Morales, Baltasar 240
Gray, Gordon, archbishop, later cardinal 3
The Great Soviet Encyclopedia (*Bol'shaya sovetskaya entsiklopediya*) 239, 241
Greek Orthodox Cathedral of the Divine Wisdom, London 140
Greene, Graham:
   Brighton Rock 288
Grinshtein, Chaim and Revekka 191–92
Guattari, Félix 107
Gubarev, Vitaly, children's writer 244
Gumilev, Nikolai, poet 71, 137

'happy childhood', cult of 229, 236–37, 278
Harbin 299, 302
Hermaphroditos 35
History of Works and Factories (*Istoriya fabrik i zavodov*) 177

History, writing of 1–2
Hoffmann, E. T. A. 22
Holmgren, Beth 46
Hone, Evie, painter and stained-glass designer 146
Hoogenboom, Hilde 47
Houghton, Harry, spy 289
House of Commons, London 286
hygiene 61–62, 65, 212, 217–18, 225, 226 n. 73, 233 n. 96
   'emotional hygiene' 218, 220
   'hygiene of mental labour' 62
hygienists 235

Ignatovich, Boris, photographer 212
Il'ina, Elena, children's writer 242
illness 54, 61, 66, 95–96, 105–20, 127, 194, 263, 275 n. 76
   as characteristic of the female sex 32–33
Imperial Russian Army 68–71, 141, 182, 204
Inber, Vera, poet 198, 226
inorodtsy 193
International Children's Day 157
International Year of the Child 267
intimacy 39, 45, 46, 50–51, 52, 118, 238–42, 243, 249, 250
Ioganson, Natalia, schoolgirl autobiographer 124 n. 51, 182, 188–89
Ireland 4, 5, 6 n. 6, 8–9, 90–91, 118, 138, 146–53, 196 n. 18
Iskander, Fazil, writer 314

Jaffé, Daniel 156
Joachim, saint 148
Jaure, George (Yuri), cousin of Konon Molodyi 301
Jewish communities 191–98
   assimilation in 193–94, 196
   changes in at the end of the nineteenth century 191–93
   family life in 191–94
   infant and childcare in 198, 204
   naming patterns in 197
   nursery education and 199
   and orphans 206–07
   and pogroms 201–02, 205–06
Jewish Pale of Settlement 191–92
John, Augustus 140, 143
John of Kronstadt, priest and saint 189
Jowitt, William 143

Kalinin, Mikhail 244
Kapnist, Ekaterina (Catherine d'Allonville) 21–25
Kapnist, Nikolai, historian and writer 34, 58
Kapnist, Vasily 21
Kapnist Sofiya, *see* Kapnist-Skalon, Sofiya
Karamzin, Nikolai, writer and historian 29 n. 25, 34–35, 53, 58
Karavaeva, Anna, writer 75

Karmalita, Svetlana, writer 329
Kassil', Lev, children's writer:
   My Dear Boys (*Dorogie moi mal'chiki*) 247
Kataev, Valentin, writer:
   A White Sail Gleamed (*Beleet parus odinokii*) 246
Kaverin, Veniamin, writer:
   The Two Captains (*Dva kapitana*) 252
Kelly, Alexander (Alec or Alex) (author's father) 3, 5, 7
Kelly, James (author's adopted grandfather) 3
Kelly, Mary (author's adopted grandmother) 3
Kelly, Mary (author's adopted aunt) 3
KGB 285, 287, 288, 290, 294, 297, 299, 306, 322
Khamraev, Iskander, film director 312, 318–25
   Her Name is Spring (*Ee imya vesna*) 321
   The Hospital Train (*Poezd miloserdiya*) 318–19
   In the Black Sands (*V chernykh peskakh*), 323–24
   The Most Important Day (*Samyi vazhnyi den'*) 324
   The Old-Timer (*Starozhil*) 318, 320
   The Road of Smashed Streetlights (*Ulitsa razbitykh fonarei*) 324
   The Son (*Syn*) 322
   The Strogov Family (*Strogovy*) 324
   When the Echo Responds (*Kogda otzovetsya echo*) 324
Kharkov 140, 212 n. 3, 268, 301, 314
Khrushchev, Andrei, official in the Russian Admiralty 17
Khrushchev, Nikita 10, 159, 233, 315, 318
King, F. Truby 218, 225
Kipling, Rudyard:
   'If' 65 n. 14
Kirgizia 325
Kirov, Sergei, Communist Party leader 250
Kiselev, Ilya 314
Klein, Melanie 124
Klimov, Elem, film director 328
Kneller, Godfrey 6
Knoepflmacher, U. C. 169
Kokoreva, Irina, Goskino official 326
Kolliander, Tito, memoirist 203
Komsomol 161, 162, 178, 215, 237, 252, 256, 283 n. 1
Kosmodem'yanskaya, Lyubov', mother of Shura and Zoya 236
Kosmodem'yanskaya, Shura, war hero 235–36
Kosmodem'yanskaya, Zoya, war heroine 235–36
Kozlov, Spiridon, juvenile autobiographer 184, 200
Kozlova, Natalia 177
Kramorov, Grigory, pupil at the Vvedenskaya Classical High School, St Petersburg 202
Kroger, Helen (Lona Cohen) 289, 303
Kroger Peter (Morris Cohen) 289, 303
Kulish, Savva, film director:
   The Dead Season 284, 306–07, 324
Kuprin, Aleksandr, writer:
   The Duel (*Duel'*) 71
   Staff Captain Rybnikov (*Shtabs-kapitan Rybnikov*) 330–31
Kurosawa, Akira 331

Kuznetsov, Dimitry, juvenile autobiographer 185–88
Kyne, John, bishop 147

ladies-in-waiting, role of 43, 45, 48–57, 59 n. 41
Lamb, Henry 140
Lambert, Anne-Thérèse de 17–19, 28–29, 241, 250
Larina, Tatiana, fictional character 25, 37–39
Lauens, J.-P. 140
Lazarevskaya, Yulianiya, Orthodox saint 16
Lazarevskoe Cemetery 14–16
Lazeev, Petr, juvenile memoirist 183, 184
Lenfil'm studio 313–33
Lenin, Vladimir 1, 62, 239, 250
'Lenin corner' in schools 227
Leningrad 1, 121, 177, 207, 242, 252, 254, 256, 264, 267, 270, 271, 273, 275, 306 n. 90
   cinema of, *see* Lenfil'm
   snobbery towards 'periphery' in 313
Leningrad blockade 143, 244
Leningrad province 128 n. 48
Leningrad Youth Theatre (TYuZ) 252
Lenkin, Nikolai, Konon Molodyi's uncle 299, 303 n. 75, n. 77
Lenkina Serafima, Konon Molodyi's aunt 299, 300, 302–03, 303 n. 77
Lermontov, Mikhail, poet 71, 110, 112, 119
Lieven, Charlotte, royal governess 54
Lioznova, Tatiana, film director 284, 294
Lissitsky, El, artist 208
'Little Red Riding Hood' 108, 130, 135 n. 78, 162
Locke, John 218, 225
London 5, 138, 286–93, 296–99, 302, 315
Lonsdale, Gordon, *see* Molodyi, Konon
Lotman, Yu. M. 38, 41, 47, 71 n. 40
love 18, 21–25, 63, 102, 141–42, 238, 250–53
Lugton, Annie (author's grandmother) 3
Luknitsky, Pavel, writer 141
Lutheranism 208 n. 34, 237
   see also pietism
luxury as concept 259–60, 262

McClelland, Helen (author's great-grandmother) 3–4
Makarenko, Anton 178, 213, 262
Malinovsky, Ienya (Malinsky, Iona), Jewish orphan 206
Mandelstam, Nadezhda, memoirist 45–46
Manford, Simon 3
Mannin, Ethel 225
Mansergh, Jessie 223, 224
Maramzin, Vladimir, writer 322
Margaret, princess 304
marginality 3 n. 3, 8–9, 12, 44, 75 n. 51, 77, 176, 197, 226, 238, 267, 312, 332
Maria Aleksandrovna, grand duchess, daughter of Alexander II 43
Maria Feodorovna, empress 31, 54
Maria Nikolaevna, empress, wife of Alexander II 43, 51, 58

marriage 15–39, 53–54
　dynastic 19
　as goal for Soviet children 251
Martin, Louis-Aimé 36
Mary, mother of God 16, 149–50
Marx, Karl 239, 250
Marshak, Samuil, children's writer and translator 65 n. 14, 155, 160, 162, 163, 167, 200
　note 39, 208 n. 74, 211 n. 3
masculinity 61–77
Mathew, Gervase, Catholic priest 147, 150
Matrosov, Aleksandr, war hero 244
Matveeva, Novella, poet 325
Mayakovsky, Vladimir, poet 75, 94 n. 44
Stirling-Maxwell, John, of Keir House 140
Meade, L. T. 223
Amishal-Meisels, Ziva 201
Mekhil'chinkov, Trofim, juvenile memoirist 188
memory 175–81, 275
　children and 178–81
Mendel'son, Mira (Mariya Tsetsiliya), writer 170
mesmerism 23
MI5 286, 289 n. 21, 299 n. 64, 304
　see also Elwell, Charles
Midgley, Mary 88
militarism 63, 67–68, 69, 75–76
Millais, John Everett:
　Bubbles 219
Millett, Paul 89
Milyutin, Dmitry, Minister of War of the Russian Empire, 69
Mirrlees, Hope, writer (author's first cousin once removed) 7
Mirsky, D. S., literary critic 7
Mitchell, Sally 224
Modigliani, Amedeo 137
Molodaya, Galina (née Panfilova), wife of Konon Molodyi 289, 292
Molodyi, Konon, spy 285–307
　autobiographies of, in English 291–92
　autobiographies of, in Russian 295–99
　death of 294
　fondness for drink 290, 299
　inclination to indiscretion 291–92
　money-making schemes of 297
　playboy image of 290–91
　on postage stamp 297
Moncrieff, Alexander (author's grandfather) 2–3
Moncrieff, Margaret (author's mother) 2–5
Montaigne, Michel de 240
Moor, Dmitry, artist 178
mosaic as art form 139–48
Morhange, Angelica 146
Morozov, Pavel (Pavlik), boy hero 162 n. 24, 164–65, 167, 178, 212, 216, 230–31, 244–45
mother-and-child relations 44

motherhood, cult of 16–21
　elective 20
　pedagogical 16–21, 42
'The Mother of God's Descent into Hell' 145
'Mother Russia' 76
motoring 66
Motyl', Vladimir, film director:
　White Sun of the Desert (*Beloe solntse pustyni*) 323
Müller, Jorgen Peter 64
Mullingar 138
　Cathedral of Christ the King 138–39, 146–53
Muratova, Kira, film director 333
Muzgiz 155

Nabokov, Vladimir D., lawyer 70 n. 34
Nabokov, Vladimir, writer 10, 75–76, 193, 204, 220 n. 48, 224 n. 62, 259
Naidenova, Natalia, poet 245
National Gallery, London 138
　vestibule mosaics in 142–46, 151
Naumova, Anastasia, aunt of Konon Molodyi 299–300
Nedobrovo, Nikolai, writer 137, 142, 151
Nest'ev, Izrail 155–56
New Year celebrations, Soviet, 289
Nicholas I, emperor 10, 30, 49–50, 53
Nicholas II, emperor 187
Nietzsche, Friedrich 64
Nikon, patriarch 43
Ninotchka (film directed by Ernst Lubitsch) 217
Nordman, Natalia 44
nostalgia 131, 141, 179 n. 18, 278
　see also memory
Nye, Robert A. 67–68

Obholzer, Karin 119
Oblomov, Ilya, fictional character 72, 133
Odessa 117, 191
Okudzhava, Bulat, writer 325
Onegin, Evgeny, fictional character, 37–39, 326
oral history 253
Orestes 250
Orientalism, 310–30
Orynbasarova, Roza 312, 328–32
　Sacrifice for the Emperor (*Zhertva dlya imperatora*) 331–32
Oseeva, Valentina, children's writer:
　Vasyok Trubachov and his Comrades (*Vasyok Trubachov i ego tovarishchi*) 247–50
Oswald, John 91
othering 311–12, 330
　see also anti-Semitism, Orientalism
Ovid 35
Ovsyanniko-Kulikovsky, D. A., professor 72–73

Pandora, character in myth 22
'Panfilov, Colonel', see Molodyi, Konon
Panizzi, Carla 287, 291, 292

Pankeev, Sergei ('the Wolfman') 105–35
Panova, Vera, writer 44, 318, 321
Paperno, Irina 47
Pares, Bernard 73
Paris 10–12
paternalism 88
Patrick, saint 147
Pattison, John (author's great-great-great grandfather) 2
Paul I, emperor 15, 30, 31, 53
Pavlishcheva, Olga, sister of Aleksandr Pushkin 36
Pavlov, Ivan, biologist 81–82
Payot, Jules 64–65, 66, 67–68
The People 291–92
Pennington, Sarah 17
Pestalozzi, Johann Heinrich 220
Peterson, Eleonore, mother of Anna Tyutcheva 42
Petrushka (fairground puppet hero) 167, 214 n. 15
Petrushka the Foreigner (*Petrushka-inostranets*) 167
Piankova, Tatiana, Konon Molodyi's aunt 299, 300, 302
pietism 52
piety 16, 20, 21 n. 18, 52, 163, 186
'piety of the stomach' (*Fressfrommigkeit*) 186
pilots 62
Pioneer (*Pioner*), magazine 164
Pioneer Pravda (*Pionerskaya pravda*), newspaper 164, 213, 228
Pioneer movement 124 n. 50, n. 52, 157, 161, 164, 165, 211, 212, 213, 215–16, 225, 228–29, 230
  concept of friendship in 245–47, 249, 250, 254, 256, 261
Plato:
  The Symposium 240
play 98, 125, 162 n. 24, 165, 223 n. 57, 231, 272
  see also toys
Polish film 326
Polomoshnov, Petr 183
Polyakov, Petr 182
Portland 289
Portland spy ring 289–90, 305
Porton Down 292, 293
Potemkin, Leonid, diarist 63
Poulenc, Francis 10
Powell, Enoch 6
power 41, 54, 102
pregnancy 19, 32, 54
Primatt, Humphrey 91
primordialism 5, 242
Prince Ivan and the Grey Wolf 166
Prokofiev, Oleg, younger son of Sergei Prokofiev 169–70
Prokofiev, Sergei 155–71
  On Guard for Peace (*Na strazhe mira*) 156–58
  Peter and the Wolf (*Petya i volk*) 156, 158–71
  Winter Bonfire (*Zimnii koster*) 155–56, 166
Prokofieva, Lina, wife of Sergei Prokofiev 155–71
Prokhorov, Alexander 314
Prokhorova, Elena 314

Protestant Action Society 9
Protestants 9, 196 n. 18, 198
  see also Lutheranism
Psyche, character in myth 22
psychoanalysis 105–35
  see also Freud, Sigmund
Pushkin, Aleksandr, poet 10, 15, 21, 26–28, 32–39, 161
  'At the beginning of life I remember a school' ('V nachale zhizni shkolu pomnyu ya'), 34–35
  Evgeny Onegin 25, 37–39, 167–68, 253 n. 64, 326
  letters to Natalia Pushkina 26–28, 36–37
  library of 28
  The Queen of Spades (*Pikovaya dama*) 304
  Ruslan and Lyudmila (*Ruslan i Lyudmila*) 35–36
Pushkina, Natalia, wife of Aleksandr Pushkin 26–28
Pygmalion, character in myth 22
Pythagoras 240

Rashidov, Shafar, Uzbek Communist Party leader and writer 321
'rational upbringing' 217, 224, 227
Red Army 157 n. 10, 177, 178, 301, 303, 322
Regan, Tom 84
Reggio, Godfrey 331
Baines Reid, Talbot 224
Mayne Reid, Thomas 155
Repin, Ilya, painter 42
Reyfman, Irina 68
rezident 283–85, 288, 299
Talbot Rice, Tamara 208
  see also Abel'son, Tamara
Rieber, Alfred 56
Roberts, Henry, physician 217
Robinson, Harlow 156, 164
Rodchenko, Alexander 212, 226
Rogozhina, Nina 155
Romanov, Panteleimon 215
Romm, Mikhail, film director 329
Rossel's, Elena, translator 325
Rossel's Vladimir, translator 325
Rosslyn, Wendy 138
Rossolimo, G. I., neurologist 134 n. 78, 179–80
Rostova, Natasha, fictional character 27
Rousseau, Jean-Jacques 29, 31–32, 42 n. 3, 118, 218, 220
Royal Albert Hall, London 295
Royal Overseas League, London 286, 295
Russell, Bertrand 143
Russell, Maud 143
Russian Orthodoxy 48, 50, 52, 55, 150, 193–94, 237
Russian radicals 42, 58, 260
  autobiographies of 47–48
  family relations among 179
Russian State Historical Archive 181
Rutherford, Ernest 143
Rybnikov, Nikolai, pedagogue 176, 179–80, 200

Saksonskaya (Grushman), Nina, writer 208
Samoilova, Yuliya, countess 20
Sats, Natalia, theatre director 159–63, 170–71, 208, 211
Schiller, Friedrich:
   Die Brüder 250
Schopenhauer, Arthur 64
School of Oriental and African Studies, University of London (SOAS) 286, 287, 295, 298
Second Five-Year Plan 230
Second World War 1, 9, 143, 235–36, 239, 244
self-control 236
self-denial 272
self-orientalisation 311
Semyonov, Yulian, writer 283
Sentimentalism 33, 42
Senyavsky, G., pogrom witness and participant 205
Serov, Valentin, painter 42
Serova Valentina, composer and music critic 42
Sewell, Anna 10
   Black Beauty 94–102
sex 19, 26, 54, 55, 107–09, 112, 131
   children and 105–20, 216, 219, 251
Shamshiev, Bolotbek, film director:
   The Scarlet Poppies of Issyk-Kul (*Ysyk-Keldun kyzgadaktary*) 309
Sharp, Evelyn 223
Shcheglov, Dmitry, playwright:
   Where the Pines Rustle (*Gde sosny shumyat*) 252
Shcherbatov M. M., historian 28
Shefner, Vadim, writer 221
shell shock 76
Shepit'ko, Larisa, film director:
   Heat (*Znoi*) 325
Shishkov, Aleksandr, admiral and writer 48
Shkol'nik, Mariya, memoirist 195
Shostakovich, Dmitry, composer 156
Simonovich (Efimova), Nina, art puppeteer 208
Singer, Peter 84–85
Kapnist-Skalon, Sofiya, memoirist 21–26
skazka (folk tale, fairy tale) 162–63, 253
   see also 'Little Red Riding Hood'; 'The Wolf and the Seven Kids'
Slane, hill of 147
slavery 85, 83–103
Slavophile movement, 42, 47–48, 59
Slobodskaya, Oda, singer 7
Slutsky, Boris, poet 157
Smith, Hedrick 275
Smolensk province 127–28
Social Darwinism 66
social hierarchies 67, 86, 187
social mobility 3–4, 67–69
   in Jewish families 200, 207–08
Socrates 240
Sokolov, Viktor, film director 319
sonambulism 23, 114

Spalding, Frances 139
Speransky, Georgy, paediatrician 235
spiritualism 55
spying 283–333
   and fraud 284–85, 288
   imposture in 284–85
   techniques of 292
Stakhanovites 62, 230
Stalin, Joseph 10, 160 n. 17, 235, 242, 250, 261
Stalina, Svetlana, daughter of Joseph Stalin 261
'Stepford Wives' 22
stereotyping, ethnic 115–16
Stirlitz, Max Otto von, fictional character 283–84, 306
Stites, Richard 47
Stolitsa, Zinaida, writer 72
Stone, Lawrence 39
Beecher Stowe, Harriet 97
   Uncle Tom's Cabin 97, 99
Strachey, Lytton 140
Struve, Gleb, poet and literary historian 142
subjectivity 2, 43, 46–47
Suvorin, Aleksei 69
Synod, Most Holy, school system of 181

'Table of Ranks' 67
Tartu 299, 300
Tashkent 322
Tate Gallery 140
teachers 61, 182–86, 187, 189, 202, 237, 247–48, 254–56, 298, 299
Tendryakov, Yury, writer 325
Tikhonov, Vyacheslav, actor 284
Timur and His Team (*Timur i ego komanda*) film by Aleksandr Razymnyi) 252
Tolstoy, Aleksei N.:
   The Little Golden Key (*Zolotoi klyuchik*) 166, 169, 246
Tolstoy, Leo 1, 7, 10, 27, 42, 44, 124
   followers of 189
   Childhood (*Detstvo*) 179
   Kholstomer 94–102
tomboys 223
   see also androgyny
Toporkov, A. K., anthropologist 215
Tovrov, Jessica 39
toys 164, 183, 214, 229 n. 86, 260 n. 5, 260, 261, 262, 264, 266, 269–73
tradition, rebellion against by children 185–86, 226–27, 249
traditionalism 311
treachery 305
trees 105–06, 130
Trubachov, Vasyok, fictional character 248
   see also Oseeva, Valentina
Tukhachevsky, Mikhail, marshal of the Red Army 160
Turgenev, Ivan, writer 111
Tyutchev, Fedor, poet 42

Tyutcheva, Anna, 42–59

Ukraine 9, 21 n. 19, 108, 117, 204, 302, 314
Union of Filmmakers 328
Ushakov's Dictionary (*Tolkovyi slovar' russkogo yazyka*) 238

Vagankovo Cemetery 62
Varda, Agnès 332
Vasilieva, Elizaveta, poet 163
Vasilievka 111, 118 n. 32
vegetarianism 91–92, 100
Veitser, Izrail, People's Commissar for Trade 159
vending machines 287, 298
Vengerov, Vladimir, film director:
    Two Captains (*Dva kapitana*) 252
    see also Kataev, Valentin
Verevkin, N. N. ('Rakhmannyi'), writer 33
Verne, Jules 195, 224
Victoria, queen 41
Vienna 8, 131–32
Vigdorova, Frida, teacher and pedagogical writer 236
Vigée Le Brun, Elisabeth 17
Vigo, Jean 331
Vilenkin family 193, 197
Boudier de Villemert, Pierre-Joseph 17
Visconti, Luchino 331
Vitebsk 204
Vladimir Province 122
Vladimirov, Vsevolod ('Maksim Isaev'), fictional character, see Stirlitz, Max Otto von
vodka 289
Volga-Volga (film) 166
Volkonskaya, Mariya, princess 25
Volkova, Mariya, lover of Boris Anrep 143
Volkova, Olga, first wife of Gleb Anrep 143
Voloshin, Maksimilian, poet 71
Volunteer Army 205 n. 66
vospitannitsa, see ward
Voysey, Frances (author's great-aunt) 4
Vygotsky, Lev, psychologist 214
Vysotsky, Vladimir, actor and guitar poet 325

ward (*vospitannitsa*) as social institution 20
Walicki, Andrzej 42
Walkerdine, Valerie 219
Warner, Marina 41, 126
Watkins, James:
    McMafia 304
Wedding at Malinovka (*Svad'ba v Malinovke*), film by Andrei Tutyshkin 314
Werewolves 126
West, the 1–2, 47
Sackville-West, Edward 143
Westminster Cathedral, London 140
Williams, Howard 100
willpower 62–67, 73–77, 235
Windsor Castle 286
'The Wolf and Seven Kids' (folktale) 107
The Wolf and Seven Kids (animation film) 166
Wolfman, see Pankeev, Sergei
wolves 105–08, 110, 112–13, 120–31
    as sources of moral judgement 112–13
Wood, Elizabeth 213
Wynne, Greville 293

Yakovleva, Mar'ya, honorand of tomb in the Lazar'evskoe Cemetery 16
Yaroslavl 205
Yudovin, Solomon, photographer 194

Zak, Sofiya, writer 208
zakal [backbone] 61–67, 73–77
zakalivanie [regime for developing backbone] 61–63, 65–66
Zakrevskaya, Agrafenya, society beauty 25
Zelenin, Dmitry, ethnographer 127
Zhemchuzhnaya, Zinaida, memoirist 227
Zhukovsky, Vasily, poet 30
Zhukova, Mariya, writer 33
Zhurba, Pavel, writer 244
Zinik, Zinovy, writer 275–76
Zolotarev, I. A. 72
Zoshchenko, Mikhail, writer 133

www.ingramcontent.com/pod-product-compliance
Lightning Source LLC
Chambersburg PA
CBHW080322170426
43193CB00017B/2870